Sec'n a (level (yr1)
(CPA)

skip 4?

chp. 1 McFall '91 + history chp.
        +Professor? 4 in Canada book
2 CPA ethics code   Linden et al. (05) 4
        + CAP code   Snyder & Elliott (05)   Canadian
                                             Canadian ↗
3 DSM-V paper? stigma? Wakefield. Keyes.
4 casestudy paper?
5 - assessment validity meta-analysis?
                                Meyer
   - empirically-based assessments to
        e.g. Joiner: evidence-based assess.
6 SCID , MINI   of depression
   MSE videotape
   Cukrowitz article re: suicide

7

8 chp. 3 Pseudoscience book
   CES-D online see "favorites" in Internet
                                      explorer
9

10 Weisz et al. (05) Amer. 4.
    Stice et al. 07 Annual Review] Clin. 4
    mindfulness + prevent relapse in dep.?
11 Barlow (04) Psychological Treatments
    APA Evidence-based practice paper
12 Hunsley & Lee (07)
13 efficacy of psychotherapy Bratton meta-analysis

INTRODUCTION TO
Clinical Psychology
An Evidence-Based Approach

INTRODUCTION TO
Clinical Psychology

An Evidence-Based Approach

JOHN HUNSLEY | CATHERINE M. LEE

JOHN WILEY & SONS CANADA, LTD.

Library and Archives Canada Cataloguing in Publication

Hunsley, John, 1959-
  Introduction to clinical psychology / John Hunsley, Catherine M. Lee.

Includes bibliographical references and index.
ISBN-13: 978-0-470-83580-7
ISBN-10: 0-470-83580-X

  1. Clinical psychology--Textbooks. I. Lee, Catherine M.
(Catherine Mary), 1955- II. Title.

RC467.H85 2005   616.89   C2005-905602-9

Production Credits

Acquisitions Editor: Michael Valerio
Editorial Manager: Karen Staudinger
Publishing Services Director: Karen Bryan
Marketing Manager: Isabelle Moreau
Developmental Editor: Amanjeet Chauhan
Editorial Assistant: Sara Vanderwillik
New Media Editor: Elsa Passera
Design: Interrobang Graphic Design, Inc.
Cover Design: Swap Advertising + Design
Cover Images: Michael Lee; Getty Images
Printing & Binding: Tri-Graphic Printing Limited

Printed and bound in Canada
10 9 8 7 6 5 4 3 2 1

John Wiley & Sons Canada, Ltd.
6045 Freemont Blvd.
Mississauga, Ontario L5R 4J3
WILEY   Visit our website at: www.wiley.ca

DEDICATION

To our family,
near and far.

Preface

Between us, we have almost half a century of experience in clinical psychology. We share a passion for a profession that has the potential to make an important contribution to the understanding of human nature and to the alleviation of human suffering. We have written this book to introduce to students the theories and practices of clinical psychology and convey the important work that clinical psychologists do. The book is designed to be helpful not only to those who will go on to careers in clinical psychology, but also to those who will choose other career paths.

KEY FEATURES

Clinical psychology has evolved greatly since its initial development. In order to convey the nature of contemporary practice of clinical psychology, we have incorporated three distinct features through all of the chapters.

Evidence-Based Approach

Concerns about healthcare costs, together with growing demands from well-informed healthcare consumers, have highlighted the need for clinical psychology to adopt evidence-based assessment and interventions. Many popular theories that have guided clinical practice for decades do not have supporting evidence. Throughout the text, we present theories and practices in terms of their empirical support. If a technique or strategy is used frequently in practice, but has not been supported empirically, we say so. We believe that our approach reflects the new realities in clinical psychology and the ongoing commitment of psychologists to deliver services that are the best science has to offer.

Diversity

Diversity is a concept that must be understood as encompassing numerous human characteristics. We highlight the need for sensitivity to issues that include culture, ethnicity, sexual orientation, socioeconomic status, family type, and geographic location. Throughout the text we include relevant assessment and treatment examples to illustrate the importance and the challenges of professional sensitivity to diversity issues in research and practice.

Lifespan Perspective

A lifespan perspective has been adopted throughout the text. Examples illustrate issues with respect to children, adolescents, adults, and older adults. As many undergraduate students taking an introductory course in clinical psychology are unlikely to have decided on the age of clients with which they eventually wish to work, it will be appealing to learn about clinical psychology across the lifespan. It is important for the student to appreciate that assessment and treatment plans can vary depending upon age of the individual.

TEXT ORGANIZATION

The text can be roughly divided into three sections. The first section sets the stage for the second section on assessment, which in turn is the foundation for the third section in intervention in clinical psychology. In Chapter 1 we provide a definition of clinical psychology, describing its history and explaining similarities and differences between clinical psychology and other mental health professions. Chapter 2 addresses the diverse roles of clinical psychologists, all of which are based on the pillars of science and ethics. The importance of attention to ethical issues is highlighted not just in this chapter but throughout the text. An appendix to this chapter on *Applications to Graduate School* is designed to help students in decision-making as well as planning an application. The third chapter is an overview of issues related to classification and diagnosis. In this chapter, we introduce two individuals, an adult (Teresa) and an adolescent (Carl), whose psychological services we describe in subsequent chapters. Chapter 4 presents key issues on research methods, underlining the ways they are employed to address clinically meaningful questions.

In the second section, Chapters 5-9 address assessment issues in clinical psychology, highlighting ethical issues that must guide psychological practice. Chapter 5 provides an overview of the purposes of psychological assessment, a review of key concepts in psychological testing, and an examination of the distinction between testing and assessment. Chapter 6 presents information on clinical interviews and clinical observation, emphasizing developmental considerations relevant to these commonly used assessment methods. Intellectual and cognitive assessment are discussed in Chapter 7. Chapter 8 covers self-report and projective assessment, with in-depth examination of the usefulness of different assessment strategies. The challenges of integrating assessment data and making clinical decisions are illustrated in Chapter 9, with reference to services for Teresa (who was introduced in Chapter 3).

The third section on intervention covers both prevention and treatment. Chapter 10 highlights issues in prevention, describing programs designed for at-risk youth. In Chapter 11 we provide a brief overview of approaches to psychological intervention, describing the theoretical foundations of current evidence-based approaches and presenting data on the nature and course of psychotherapy. Chapters 12 and 13 present an overview of current evidence-based treatments for adults (Chapter 12) and for children and adolescents (Chapter 13). The case of Carl (who was introduced in Chapter 2) is used to illustrate issues in developing treatment plans. Chapter 14 provides information on evidence-based treatment elements derived from therapy process and therapy process-outcome research. Finally, in Chapter 15, we examine issues in the practice of clinical psychology in the areas of health psychology, clinical neuropsychology, and forensic psychology.

FEATURES OF INTEREST TO THE STUDENT

Within each chapter certain features have been incorporated to aid student learning. This text is designed to introduce clinical psychology in a reader-friendly and accessible manner, highlighting the varied and dynamic areas of the discipline.

Chapter Outline

Each chapter begins with an outline that prepares the student for the material to be covered.

Case Studies

In courses in clinical psychology, case examples are the tool through which abstract material is brought to life. In addition to the extended case presentations in Chapters 3, 9, and 13, case material is embedded throughout the text to illustrate issues in different developmental periods and with a diverse clientele. Reflecting the terminology in current practice, we alternate our use of the terms "patient" and "client." All the case examples we describe are based on our clinical experience. We have blended details about different people into composites to illustrate clinical issues. The case examples do not, therefore, represent specific individuals and all the names are fictitious.

Viewpoint Boxes

In each chapter controversial issues and new directions in the field are highlighted in Viewpoint boxes. In addition to addressing historically important themes, such as *IQ and its Correlates*, Viewpoint boxes explore new directions in clinical psychology, such as *Positive Psychology*, the controversies over *Prescription Privileges, Psychological Testing on the Internet*, and *Genetics and Psychopathology*. The inclusion of Viewpoint boxes on *Developmental Considerations in ADHD* and *Assessing Cognitive Functioning in Older Adults* reflect a lifespan perspective. Debates around evidence-based assessment are discussed in viewpoint boxes examining *Child Custody Evaluation, Risk Assessment*, and *Are Projective Drawings Welcome in the Courtroom?* The expansion of the practice of clinical psychology to health is illustrated in Viewpoint boxes *Health Promotion and Prevention in Older Adults* and *Insomnia: No Need to Lose Sleep Over It!* Current issues in treatment research are explored in Viewpoint boxes including *The EMDR Controversy* and *Sudden Gains in Therapy*.

Profile Boxes

In order to bring to life the reality of being a clinical psychologist, we have used Profile boxes to introduce clinical psychologists. We invited Canadian clinical psychologists to answer questions about their careers. Furthermore, to give students a sense of the varied activities in which psychologists engage, we asked six psychologists who work in different types of settings to describe a typical work week. We also profiled two organizations that offer training in the provision of psychological services to groups who often have limited access to services. We invited colleagues whom we consider fine examples of clinical psychologists, and we chose people whom we hope you will find inspiring. As you read the profile boxes we know that you will be struck by the wide range of activities in which clinical psychologists engage, the range of challenges they address in their work, and the creativity with which psychological principles are applied to reduce human suffering and improve psychosocial functioning.

Summary and Conclusions

At the end of each chapter, a section draws together the material discussed in the chapter.

Critical Thinking Questions

To help in identifying themes for discussion, key questions have been designed to provoke debate on both traditional and emerging issues in clinical psychology.

Key Terms and Key Names

Throughout each chapter important terms and names are highlighted in bold. These are an important study aid to highlight the most salient points of each chapter.

Additional Resources

To help provide some guidance for students who wish to explore an issue in greater depth, additional resources have been cited for various journals, books, and websites.

ACKNOWLEDGEMENTS

We have appreciated the support and guidance of many people during the preparation of this book. Thanks are due to Michael Valerio, the Acquisitions Editor who promoted the idea of a text on contemporary clinical psychology. His enthusiasm for the project and persistent optimism were contagious. Developmental Editor Amanjeet Chauhan coordinated the phases of production with dedication and an openness to input. Many colleagues provided encouragement throughout the preparation of the book. We are particularly grateful for the wisdom of those with extensive experience in writing books, including Eric Mash and Vicky Phares. We consulted numerous people on diverse topics and benefited from their input. Karen Cohen (Registrar of the Canadian Psychological Association) and Catherine Yarrow (Registrar of the College of Psychologists of Ontario) were generous in providing invaluable consultation on professional issues. Mireille Côté and Krista Luedeman offered useful comments on the Appendix on *Applications to Graduate School*. Jean Grenier made insightful comments on insomnia. The book is enriched by the contributions of the psychologists who agreed to be profiled. We appreciate their cooperation and willingness to talk about their careers, and special thanks go to them. They are: Drs. Martin Antony, Linda Baker, Stéphane Bouchard, Keith Dobson, David Dozois, Heather Hadjistavropoulos, Paul Hewitt, Adam Horvath, Sue Johnson, Charlotte Johnston, Sally Kuehn, Maggie Mamen, Eric Mash, Patrick McGrath, Bob McIlwraith, Kerry Mothersill, Don Saklofske, Michael Vallis, Dan Waschbusch, and Stephen Wormith.

Thoughtful and informative reviews helped us to clarify the text. Thanks are due to:

Alan Carr	University College Dublin
Catherine Costigan	University of Victoria
Bruno Deswaene	Université de Reims
Deborah Dobson	University of Calgary
David J.A. Dozois	University of Western Ontario

Douglas French   Université de Moncton
Philippe Joly   Université Reims Champagne Ardenne
Mark Lau   University of Toronto
Fabien Legrand   Université Reims Champagne Ardenne
Jeannette McGlone   Dalhousie University
Norm O'Rourke   Simon Fraser University
Christine Purdon   University of Waterloo
Jacques F. Richard   Université de Moncton
Doug Symons   Acadia University
Michael T. Vallis   Dalhousie University
David Vollick   University of Western Ontario

Last, but not least, we are grateful for the ongoing support of friends and family. Their questions, words of encouragement, and willingness to provide their views on diverse aspects of textbook production were greatly appreciated. Our sons Robbie and Nicholas sustained remarkable patience, allowing us the opportunity to focus on the book for well over a year. Thank you both for your tolerance and your interest in our work.

About the Authors

John Hunsley received a PhD from the University of Waterloo in 1985. He is a professor in the clinical psychology program at the University of Ottawa and was the director of the university's Centre for Psychological Services from 1997 to 2005. He teaches graduate courses in Cognitive-Behavioural Therapy, Clinical Decision-Making, and Clinical Research Methods and supervises the clinical training of graduate students in the APA/CPA accredited clinical program and internship at the University of Ottawa.

Dr. Hunsley's research interests focus on the delivery of psychological services and the scientific basis of psychological assessment and treatment. He has authored over 70 articles and chapters focused on psychological adjustment, assessment, intervention, and professional issues. Dr. Hunsley is a Fellow of the Canadian Psychological Association (CPA) and a Fellow of the CPA's Clinical Psychology Section. He was Chair of the Clinical Psychology Section task force on Empirically Supported Treatments and is a former Chair of CPA Family Psychology Section. He was a member of the Council of the College of Psychologists of Ontario and is a former Chair of the Client Relations Committee of the College. Currently he is a member of the Association of State and Provincial Psychology Board's Examination Committee, serves on the editorial boards of *Journal of Personality Assessment* and *Scientific Review of Mental Health Practice*, and from 2007-2010 will be the editor of *Canadian Psychology*. He maintains a private practice in the treatment of mood and anxiety disorders.

Catherine M. Lee earned a PhD from the University of Western Ontario in 1988. She is Vice Dean and Secretary of the Faculty of Social Sciences and Professor of Psychology at the University of Ottawa. She served as Director of the clinical psychology program from 1998-2002. Dr. Lee teaches graduate courses in Psychology of the Family, Evidence-Based Services for Children and Families, and Psychological Assessment. In addition, she supervises the clinical training of practicum students and interns at the Centre for Psychological Services. Her research interests focus on family functioning, the involvement of fathers in the family, and co-parenting. She has authored over 50 articles and chapters focused on family adjustment to diverse stressors and to the delivery of psychological services. Her research has been supported by grants from the National Health Research and Development Program, the Social Sciences and Humanities Research Council of Canada, and the Ontario Mental Health Foundation. Dr. Lee is an *ad hoc* reviewer for many granting agencies and scholarly journals and she serves on the editorial board of *Cognitive and Behavioral Practice*. Dr. Lee is a Fellow of the Canadian Psychological Association (CPA). She was the founding Chair of the Family Section of CPA, and is the current Chair of the Clinical Section of the CPA. Dr. Lee is a site visitor for the Accreditation Panel of the Canadian Psychological Association. She maintains a private practice working with children and families.

Brief Table of Contents

Table of Contents

CHAPTER 1

The Evolution of Clinical Psychology

INTRODUCTION

As we enter the twenty-first century the potential for clinical psychology to make important contributions to the health of individuals, families, and society is abundantly clear. Throughout this text we will illustrate with compelling evidence that clinical psychologists have developed treatments that are effective in reducing the severity of an impressive range of health problems and disorders and, in some cases, eliminating these conditions entirely. To fully appreciate the importance of such health services it is necessary to understand the scope of the public health problem facing health care systems in North America and other parts of the world. A national survey of the mental health and well-being of Canadians aged 15 years and older found that as many people suffered from clinical depression as from common chronic health conditions such as heart disease and diabetes (Statistics Canada, 2003a). Furthermore, 1 out of every 10 Canadian adolescents and adults reported symptoms consistent with a diagnosis of a mental disorder such as alcohol or illicit drug dependence, a mood disorder (i.e., major depressive disorder or bipolar disorder), or a serious anxiety disorder (i.e., social phobia, panic disorder, or panic disorder with agoraphobia). Perhaps due to the stressfulness of living and/or working conditions, the rate of mental health problems is even higher among certain groups than in the general population. For example, a health survey of members of Canada's military forces found that 1 in 6 of the regular military personnel reported symptoms indicative of major depressive disorder, social phobia, post-traumatic stress disorder, panic disorder, generalized anxiety disorder, or alcohol dependence (Statistics Canada, 2003b).

Other countries also report extensive mental health problems. In 1999 the Surgeon General of the United States released a report on the mental health of Americans (U.S. Department of Health and Human Services, 1999). Using data from national epidemiological studies he estimated that over a one-year period 21% of Americans suffered from anxiety disorders, mood disorders, schizophrenia and other psychotic conditions, antisocial personality disorder, anorexia nervosa, or severe cognitive impairments. The estimate that 1 in 5 people suffers from a mental disorder applied to all age groups, including children, adolescents, adults, and older adults. The report also presented data showing that in countries with established market economies (such as Canada, the United States, the United Kingdom, Australia, and New Zealand), the economic burden of mental disorders, mental illness, and suicide in terms of health care costs and lost productivity is second only to that of cardiovascular conditions.

Data from the World Health Organization (presented in **Table 1.1**) illustrate the scope of mental health problems in different countries. Worldwide there are hundreds of millions of people suffering from mental disorders. However, most mental disorders are overlooked or misdiagnosed and only a small percentage of those who suffer from a mental disorder ever receive treatment. Even if these people receive treatment for other health concerns, in most cases—regardless of the wealth or level of development of the country in which they live—mental health problems are neglected. This is particularly troubling because there are relatively inexpensive treatments (psychological and/or pharmacological) that are effective for most of these conditions.

TABLE 1.1   World Health Organization Mental Health: The Bare Facts

❑ At any given time there are 450 million people worldwide suffering from mental, neurological, and behavioural problems.

❑ It is predicted that the number of people suffering from these problems will increase in the future.

❑ Mental health problems are found in all countries.

❑ Mental health problems cause suffering, social exclusion, disability, and poor quality of life.

❑ Mental health problems increase mortality.

❑ Mental health problems have staggering economic costs.

❑ One in every four people seeking other health services has a diagnosable mental, neurological, or behavioural problem that is unlikely to be diagnosed or treated.

❑ Mental health problems are associated with poor compliance with medical regimens for other disorders.

❑ Cost-effective treatments exist for most disorders; if they were applied properly, people could function better in their communities.

❑ There is greater stigma associated with mental health problems than with physical health problems.

❑ Most countries do not allocate sufficient funds to address mental, neurological, and behavioural problems.

Adapted from World Health Organization (2004a)

In addition to the pressing problems posed by mental disorders, there is mounting evidence that lifestyle and psychosocial factors are related to many of the causes of death in Western countries. As you will learn in Chapters 10 and 15 there is evidence that psychological services can dramatically reduce the negative health impact of these lifestyle and psychosocial risk factors. A large-scale study of the causes of mortality in the United States reached startling conclusions (Mokdad, Marks, Stroup, & Gerberding, 2004). Although dramatic causes such as motor vehicle accidents accounted for 2% of deaths, and shooting fatalities accounted for 1% of deaths, the leading causes of death were related to tobacco smoking (18.1%), poor diet and physical inactivity (16.6%), and alcohol consumption (3.5%). Adding the numbers together, these data demonstrate that at least 40% of fatalities were attributable to entirely preventable—or treatable—factors.

A DEFINITION OF CLINICAL PSYCHOLOGY

As we consider the pain and suffering experienced by people with mental and physical health problems, the interpersonal effects of their distress on their family, friends, and coworkers, and the tragedy of untimely death, the need for effective services to identify and address these problems is evident. It is inevitable that at many points in our lives each of us will be affected, either directly or indirectly, by the emotional distress of psychological disorders. The first experience may be helping a friend through confusion and anger stemming from a loved one's suicide. As a university student you may be faced with the challenges of helping a roommate with an eating disorder who binges and purges. Young parents may provide support to another young parent who is desperate to find appropriate services for a child with autistic disorder. In mid-life, you may be faced with the burden of caring for an elderly parent suffering from dementia, or may be attempting to support a partner who is chronically anxious and who avoids social gatherings. Clinical psychology is the branch of psychology that focuses on developing assessment strategies and interventions to deal with these painful experiences that touch everyone's life.

Let's consider definitions of clinical psychology. **Table 1.2** provides some examples of definitions and descriptions of clinical psychology from different countries. Despite some differences in emphasis, a common theme running through these definitions from the United States, Britain, and New Zealand is that clinical psychology is based firmly on scientifically supported psychological theories and principles. Clinical psychology is a science-based profession. Furthermore, the development of effective prevention and intervention services relies on basic research into the nature of emotional distress and well-being. The practice of clinical psychology uses scientifically based methods to reliably and validly assess both normal and abnormal human functioning. Clinical psychology involves gathering evidence regarding optimal strategies for delivering health care services.

TABLE 1.2   Definitions of Clinical Psychology

American Psychological Association, Society of Clinical Psychology
"The field of Clinical Psychology integrates science, theory, and practice to understand, predict, and alleviate maladjustment, disability, and discomfort as well as to promote human adaptation, adjustment, and personal development. Clinical Psychology focuses on the intellectual, emotional, biological, psychological, social, and behavioral aspects of human functioning across the life span, in varying cultures, and at all socioeconomic levels."

British Psychological Society, Division of Clinical Psychology
"Clinical psychology aims to reduce psychological distress and to enhance and promote psychological well-being by the systematic application of knowledge derived from psychological theory and data."

New Zealand College of Clinical Psychologists
"Psychology is the science of behaviour. Psychologists seek to understand emotion, thinking, personality, skill, learning, motivation, perception, and sensation through the study of individuals, families, groups and culture. Clinical Psychology seeks to apply psychological understandings with individuals and families who may wish to change or develop, often for the alleviation of suffering and the achievement of their personal goals."

Over the decades the nature and definition of clinical psychology has shifted, expanded, and evolved. From an initial primary focus on assessment, evaluation, and diagnosis, the scope of clinical psychology has grown. Clinical psychology now also includes numerous approaches to intervention and prevention services that are provided to individuals, couples, and families. The practice of clinical psychology also covers indirect services that do not involve contact with those suffering from a mental disorder, such as consultation activities, research, program development, program evaluation, supervision of other mental health professionals, and administration of health care services. Given the ever-changing nature of the field, the only certainty about clinical psychology is that it will continue to evolve. Only time will tell whether this evolution ultimately leads to a decreasing focus on traditional activities of assessment and treatment (as predicted by some experts), to an increasing focus on the use of psychopharmacological agents to treat mental illness and mental health problems (as promoted by some psychologists and some psychological associations), or to some other form of preferred practice. The changing nature of clinical psychology does, however, require that any definition of the field be treated as temporary, to be maintained for as long as it accurately reflects the field. The definition of clinical psychology must be altered and updated as innovations and new directions emerge.

The Canadian Psychological Association's Section on Clinical Psychology developed an excellent document that defines the current nature of clinical psychology, provides general principles intended to apply whatever the future changes in the field, and firmly grounds the practice of clinical psychology in the context of professional ethics and responsibility. An excerpt of this definition is presented in **Table 1.3**. In developing this definition the Section on Clinical Psychology sought input from numerous sources, including the members of the section, the executive committees of other sections within the Canadian Psychological Association, and the executive committees of several national organizations in Canada for which the definition might be relevant, such as the Canadian Council of Clinical Psychology Programs, the Council of Provincial Associations of Psychology, and the Canadian Register of Health Service Providers in Psychology (Vallis & Howes, 1996). Throughout the book you may notice other examples that illustrate the importance of conducting wide-ranging consultation in order to achieve consensus on important issues in the profession. Consultation is a hallmark of successful initiatives in clinical psychology.

TABLE 1.3   Definition of Clinical Psychology

Approved by the Clinical Section and the Board of Directors of the Canadian Psychological Association, May 1993

Clinical psychology is a broad field of practice and research within the discipline of psychology, which applies psychological principles to the assessment, prevention, amelioration, and rehabilitation of psychological distress, disability, dysfunctional behaviour, and health-risk behaviour, and to the enhancement of psychological and physical well-being.

Clinical psychology includes both scientific research focusing on the search for general principles, and clinical service, focusing on the study and care of clients, and information gathered from each of these activities influences practice and research.

Clinical psychology is a broad approach to human problems (both individual and interpersonal) consisting of assessment, diagnosis, consultation, treatment, program development, administration, and research with regard to numerous populations, including children, adolescents, adults, the elderly, families, groups, and disadvantaged persons. There is overlap between some areas of clinical psychology and other professional fields of psychology such as counselling psychology and clinical neuropsychology, as well as some professional fields outside of psychology, such as psychiatry and social work.

Clinical psychology is devoted to the principles of human welfare and professional conduct as outlined in the Canadian Psychological Association's Canadian Code of Ethics for Psychologists. According to this code the activities of clinical psychologists are directed toward: respect for the dignity of persons; responsible caring; integrity in relationships; and responsibility to society.

Reprinted with permission from the Canadian Psychological Association

Despite the apparent overlap in the various definitions of clinical psychology that we presented in **Table 1.2**, there is still very active debate about the extent to which clinical psychology can or should be based solely on the science of psychology. Some psychologists doubt that clinical psychology can ever be effectively guided by scientific knowledge. Critics of a science-based approach to clinical psychology express concerns that:

a. group-based data cannot be used in working with an individual; they argue that because a great deal of psychological research is based on research designs that involve the study of groups of individuals it is difficult to determine the relevance of research results to any specific individual;

b. clients have problems now and we cannot afford to wait for the research; developing, conducting, and replicating research findings takes substantial time and thus the information provided by researchers inevitably lags behind the needs of clinicians to provide services to people in distress;

c. each individual's unique constellation of life experience, culture, and societal context makes it unlikely that general psychological principles can ever provide much useful guidance in alleviating emotional distress or interpersonal conflict; and

d. there is simply no research evidence on how to understand or treat many of the human problems confronted by clinical psychologists on a daily basis.

Although these kinds of concerns sound reasonable enough, they lead to the suggestion of basing clinical practice on the individual psychologist's gut feelings, intuition, or experience. The idea that clinical psychology is primarily a healing art, rather than primarily a science-based practice, is extremely problematic. As we discuss in subsequent chapters, there is ample evidence that people are prone to a host of decision-making errors and biases. Because clinicians are not immune from these errors and biases they risk making serious mistakes in evaluating and treating clients. Thus, over-reliance on the clinician's professional experience and general orientation to understanding human functioning can be risky if it is not balanced with the application of scientifically based knowledge.

At the other end of the spectrum there are clinical psychologists for whom the current definitions of clinical psychology do not go far enough in ensuring that science is at the heart of all clinical services offered to the public. A passionate proponent of this position is Richard McFall, who in his 1991 presidential address to the Society for a Science of Clinical Psychology (a section of the American Psychological Association's Society of Clinical Psychology), challenged the field to provide only psychological services that had been established through research to be effective and safe (McFall, 1991). The key elements of his *Manifesto for a Science of Clinical Psychology* are presented in **Table 1.4**.

McFall's manifesto adopted a position on the role of science in clinical psychology that many clinical psychologists initially found too extreme. McFall's demand that only scientifically supported treatments should be offered to the public met with strong opposition from many clinical psychologists. The manifesto sparked a lively debate about the appropriateness and the ethics of routinely offering a psychological service (or any health service for that matter) that does not have document-ed, scientifically sound evidence demonstrating its effectiveness. There is no doubt that the vast majority of people who seek psychological services are in significant distress and are hoping to receive treatments that will reduce their distress and improve their overall functioning. Do you think it is responsible to offer services that have no evidence of effectiveness? When effective treatments exist, is it reasonable to continue to offer services of undocumented effectiveness? As we discuss in the next chapter, it is fascinating to note that the movement for evidence-based practice in health care servic-es places demands on all health services that are remarkably similar to those expressed by McFall's first corollary. In less than two decades a position that was originally considered extreme has become main-stream in many health care systems and a goal espoused by several health care professions.

TABLE 1.4   McFall's Manifesto for a Science of Clinical Psychology

Cardinal Principle
Scientific clinical psychology is the only legitimate and acceptable form of clinical psychology.

First Corollary
Psychological services should not be administered to the public (except under strict experimental conditions) until they have met the following four minimal criteria:

Criterion 1 The exact nature of the service must be described clearly.

Criterion 2 The claimed benefits of the service must be stated explicitly.

Criterion 3 These claimed benefits must be validated scientifically.

Criterion 4 Possible negative side effects that might outweigh any benefits must be ruled out empirically.

Second Corollary
The primary and overriding objective of doctoral programs in clinical psychology must be to produce the most competent clinical scientists possible.

Adapted from McFall (1991)

MENTAL HEALTH PROFESSIONS

The definitions of clinical psychology provide an important perspective on the nature and function of modern clinical psychology. However, to clearly establish what clinical psychology is and is not, it is necessary to draw comparisons with other domains within psychology and with other health care professions whose services and client populations overlap those of clinical psychology. Within the field of psychology, what is unique about clinical psychology? The definitions we presented emphasized that clinical psychology is primarily concerned with the *application* of psychological knowledge in assessment, prevention, and/or intervention in problems in thoughts, behaviours, and feelings. Of course, in addition to providing psychological services many clinical psychologists also conduct psychological research and contribute important information to the science of psychology. Nevertheless, the objective of research in clinical psychology is to produce knowledge that can be used to guide the development and *application* of psychological services. Clinical psychology shares many of the research methods, approaches to statistical analysis, and measurement strategies found in other areas of psychology. Many areas of psychology, such as cognitive, developmental, learning, personality, physiological, and social, generate research that has direct or indirect applicability to clinical psychology activities. However, the key purpose of research in these other areas of psychology is to generate basic knowledge about human functioning and to enhance, in general terms, our understanding of people. The fact that some of this knowledge can be used to assess and treat dysfunction and thereby improve human functioning is of secondary importance.

Counselling Psychology

Two branches of applied psychology—counselling psychology and clinical psychology—have comparable aims. Historically, the distinction between clinical and counselling psychology was in terms of the severity of problems treated. Traditionally the focus of clinical psychology was on the assessment and treatment of psychopathology: that is, manifestations of anxiety, depression, and other symptoms that were of sufficient severity to warrant a clinical diagnosis. On the other hand, counselling psychologists provided services to individuals who were dealing with normal challenges in life—those predictable developmental transitions such as leaving home to work or to attend university or college, changes in work or interpersonal roles, and handling the stress associated with academic or work demands. Simply put, counselling psychologists dealt with people who were, by and large, well-adjusted, whereas clinical psychologists dealt with people who were experiencing significant problems in their lives and who were unable to manage the resulting emotional and behavioural symptoms. Another distinction was the type of setting in which the practitioners worked. Counselling psychologists were most commonly employed in educational settings (such as college or university counselling clinics) or general community clinics in which various social and psychological services are available. Clinical psychologists, in contrast, were most likely to be employed in hospital settings—both in general hospitals and in psychiatric facilities.

These traditional distinctions between clinical and counselling psychologists are fading due to changes within both professions. Nowadays, counselling psychologists provide services to individuals who are having difficulty functioning: for example, treatments for university students suffering from disorders such as major depressive disorder, panic disorder, social phobia, or eating disorders. Recent data from an American university counselling centre provide compelling evidence for the increased levels of maladjustment among those seeking services from counselling psychologists. Benton, Robertson, Tseng, Newton, and Benton (2003) reported data from more than 13,000 clients seen at the Kansas State University counselling centre from 1988 to 2001.

Until 1994, relationship problems were the most frequently reported problem for which students sought services at the centre (reported by approximately half of students), but subsequently stress and anxiety problems became the more frequently reported problem area (reported by approximately two-thirds of students). During the 13-year period of the study, a number of presenting problems were increasingly reported, including academic problems, depressive symptoms, and grief. The frequency of other commonly seen problems at university counselling centres, such as uncertainties around educational and vocational choices, waxed and waned over time: 25% of student clients sought help for these problems in 1988, compared with 12% in 1994, and 25% in 2001. Benton and colleagues concluded that, compared with the late 1980s, students

Recent research has shown that students seen at a university counselling centre had problems such as relationship issues, suicidal ideation, sexual assault, and personality disorders.

seen at the centre in the more recent period presented with more complex problems; in addition to common student problems such as family and relationship issues they also presented with more severe problems such as anxiety, depression, suicidal ideation, sexual assault, and personality disorders.

Over time clinical psychologists have expanded their practice to address human problems outside the usual realm of mental health services by providing services such as couple therapy, consultation, and treatment for people dealing with chronic illness and stress-related disorders. Thus clinical psychologists developed services for individuals who would not meet criteria for any psychopathological condition. Of course, at one level, it is a rather tenuous decision to mark professional boundaries between counselling and clinical psychology on the basis of the possible differences between what constitutes "normal" range distress and abnormal levels of distress. Depending on the point in time in which someone seeks help, the same person might present with symptoms severe enough to meet diagnostic criteria for a mental disorder or with less severe, subclinical symptoms. A fascinating example of this point comes from the Collaborative Longitudinal Personality Disorders Study (Gunderson et al., 2003). Researchers found that 14% of the people diagnosed with borderline personality disorder at the outset of the study no longer evidenced symptoms consistent with diagnostic criteria six months later. Initial errors in diagnosis could not explain these results, especially as a diagnosis of a personality disorder requires evidence of a lifelong pattern of problems beginning in late adolescence or early adulthood. Instead it appeared that the temporary abatement of symptoms could be traced to the resolution of significant stressors in people's lives. These data indicate that both counselling and clinical psychologists need to be able to understand, assess, and treat symptoms that may fall on either side of a diagnostic boundary.

In many countries there is no distinction between clinical and counselling psychology; in others the distinction is becoming less and less meaningful for any practical purpose. In Canada, for example, in the province of Ontario, the regulatory body for the profession of psychology (the College of Psychologists of Ontario) requires that both counselling and clinical psychologists have the training and expertise to diagnose mental disorders. Just like clinical psychology, counselling psychology promotes the use of scientifically based interventions. This drive to provide evidence-based services is likely to have substantial implications for both training and practice in counselling psychology (Waehler, Kalodner, Wampold, & Lichtenberg, 2000). The source of the distinction between the two psychology professions in some countries is that clinical and counselling psychologists are usually trained in different academic settings and in different academic traditions. Counselling psychology programs are found, for the most part, in faculties of education and/or departments of educational psychology. Clinical psychology programs, on the other hand, are based in psychology departments. Data from a survey by Norcross, Sayette, Mayne, Karg, and Turkson (1998) indicate that clinical programs attract far more applicants than do counselling programs and that counselling programs have a greater representation of ethnic minority students. Research on clinical disorders is more commonly conducted in clinical programs and research on minority adjustment and academic/vocational issues is more frequently conducted in counselling programs.

School Psychology

School psychologists have specialized training in both psychology and in education. In the United States school psychologists are employed in diverse organizations such as schools, clinics, and hospitals, and in private practice. In Canada, most school psychologists are employed by school boards. Given the focus on children's functioning, there is a natural overlap between school psychology and child clinical psychology. Historically, school psychology emphasized services related specifically to the learning of children and adolescents, including the assessment of intellectual functioning, the evaluation of learning difficulties, and consultation to teachers, students, and parents about strategies for optimizing students' learning potential. Clinical child psychology focused on the treatment of diagnosable mental disorder. Over time, the scope of school psychology has expanded in response to the demands of parents, school systems, and governments. Because of growing awareness of the deleterious effects on learning of child and adolescent psychopathology, parental psychopathology, and stressful family circumstances, the work of school psychologists now addresses students' mental health and life circumstances more broadly. The role of school psychologists now includes attention to social, emotional, and medical factors in a context of learning and development. These changes, combined with legal obligations that schools provide the most appropriate education for all children, have resulted in school psychologists diagnosing a range of disorders of childhood and adolescence as well as developing school and/or family-based programs to assist students to learn to the best of their abilities. School psychologists have also taken a leadership role in the development of school-based prevention programs designed to promote social skills, to reduce bullying, to facilitate conflict resolution, and to prevent violence. These are described in detail in Chapter 10.

Despite the increasingly close connections between school and child clinical psychology it is likely that the two disciplines will remain distinct, at least in the near future. A survey of American school and child clinical psychologists clearly illustrates this point. Tryon (2000) found that, in a sample of 363 psychologists, whereas three-quarters of school psychologists endorsed the position that training programs in school and clinical psychology should merge in order to provide improved services for school-based and school-linked mental health services, fewer than half of the child clinical psychologists endorsed a merger. It therefore appears likely that distinctions in training will continue, with child clinical psychology programs requiring relatively more training in intervention and, overall, more supervised experience than programs in school psychology (Minke & Brown, 1996).

Psychiatry

Psychiatrists are physicians who specialize in the diagnosis, treatment, and prevention of mental illnesses. Like all physicians, in medical school they learn about the functioning of the human body and the health services that physicians provide. As with other medical specialties, training as a psychiatrist requires three to five years of residency training after the successful completion of basic medical training. A range of residency options are possible, including both broad training in psychiatric services as well as specific training in subspecialties such as child psychiatry or geropsychiatry. Once they have completed specialization in psychiatry, psychiatrists rarely examine or treat the basic health problems that were covered in their medical training.

Psychiatric training differs in important ways from applied psychology training. First, psychiatric training deals extensively with physiological and biochemical systems and emphasizes biological functioning and abnormalities. Psychiatrists are well-qualified to determine whether mental disorders are the result of medical problems and to unravel the possible interactions between physical illnesses and emotional disturbances. Psychiatric training provides the skills to evaluate the extent to which psychological symptoms result from or are exacerbated by medications used to treat physical ailments and chronic illnesses. On the other hand, compared with psychologists, psychiatrists receive relatively little training in human psychological development, cognition, learning, or psychological functioning in general. Standard psychiatric training provides only limited training in research skills such as research design and statistical analysis. Many psychiatrists have become active researchers and have contributed in important ways to the knowledge base of the neurosciences and human sciences. Nevertheless, the average psychiatry resident receives far less training in research than does the average graduate student in clinical psychology. An expert panel in the United States warned that unless research training in psychiatric residency programs was dramatically strengthened, research by American psychiatrists risked dwindling to the point of "extinction" (McLellan, 2003).

Another fundamental difference between training in clinical psychology and psychiatry is that psychiatric training generally emphasizes psychopharmacological treatment over psychological treatment. Accordingly, compared with psychologists, psychiatrists tend to receive very little training in the use of scientifically based psychological assessment and psychotherapy. Historically psychiatrists were trained in forms of psychoanalytic and psychodynamic treatments such as those developed by Sigmund Freud, Carl Jung, and Alfred Adler. Due in part to the proliferation of effective psychopharmacological treatments in recent decades and the growing emphasis on evidence-based practice in psychiatry, there has been a waning of emphasis on training in psychoanalytic and long-term psychodynamic psychotherapy. There is growing attention paid to training psychiatrists in evidence-based treatments, which may include cognitive-behavioural and interpersonal therapies (cf. Hoge, Tondora, & Stuart, 2003; Martin, Saperson, & Maddigan, 2003). Despite the tendency for psychiatrists to favour psychopharmacological approaches to treatment, psychiatrists were among the pioneers in the development of evidence-based psychological treatments: Aaron Beck was the primary developer of cognitive therapy for depression (and subsequently other disorders), Gerald Weissman was the primary developer of the interpersonal treatment of depression, and Isaac Marks has played a prominent role in the development of cognitive-behavioural treatments for anxiety disorders. Thus, although the relative emphasis of psychotherapy within the profession differs from that in clinical psychology, the provision of psychotherapeutic services remains, for many psychiatrists, a central aspect of psychiatric services. Attesting to this, the Canadian Psychiatric Association issued a position statement characterizing the provision of psychotherapy as an integral component of psychiatric care (Chaimowitz, 2004). Similarly, in 1998, the American Academy of Child and Adolescent Psychiatry took the position that psychotherapy must remain a core skill in the practice of child and adolescent psychiatry.

Until recently an important distinction between clinical psychologists and psychiatrists was that only psychiatrists could prescribe medication. However, in some American jurisdictions, this is no longer the case. Programs through the federal Department of Defence and the Indian Health Service as well as some state legislatures have made provisions for psychologists to receive training to prescribe psychoactive medication. Canadian psychologists do not currently have prescription privileges.

The profession of psychiatry is facing a worldwide problem in recruiting new professionals. In many countries, even those as socially and economically different as Britain and India, the number of graduating medical students who wish to specialize in psychiatry has been insufficient to meet the demand for psychiatrists (Brockington & Mumford, 2002; Tharyan, John, Tharyan, & Braganza, 2001). In the United States, the number of medical students seeking psychiatric residencies has fallen by over 40% since the 1980s—only 3% of American medical students now seek psychiatric training (Tamaskar & McGinnis, 2002). Several surveys of medical students have found that psychiatry is considered less professionally satisfying than other medical specialities. Feifel, Moutier, and Swerdlow (1999), for example, found that internal medicine, pediatrics, and surgery were all seen as more desirable career choices than psychiatry.

Dr. Aaron Beck, the primary developer of cognitive therapy for depression, pictured here with Dr. Albert Ellis, who developed Rational Emotive Therapy (discussed later in this text).

Clinical Social Work

Social workers focus on ways to improve the health and well-being of individuals, families, groups, and communities. Social work practice includes activities such as policy development, program planning, program management, research consultation, case management, discharge planning, counselling, therapy, and advocacy (Canadian Institute for Health Information, 2004). Social workers are employed in diverse settings including hospitals, community mental health centres, mental health clinics, schools, advocacy organizations, government departments, social service agencies, child welfare settings, family service agencies, correctional facilities, social housing organizations, family courts, employee assistance programs, school boards, and private counselling and consultation agencies (Canadian Institute for Health Information, 2004). In 7 of 10 Canadian provinces, the title Social Worker and Registered Social Worker are protected in legislation and can only be used by those who meet the regulations and standards of their provincial regulatory bodies. In 2002 there were 76.8 licensed social workers per 100,000 people in Canada; the ratio across provinces varied widely from a high of 183.6 per 100,000 in Newfoundland and Labrador, to a low of 33.3 per 100,000 in British Columbia (Canadian Institute for Health Information, 2004).

Many social workers function as part of a mental health team in the role of caseworker who, in collaboration with the patient, coordinates services with a range of social and community agencies, medical services, and other services (such as vocational or sheltered employment activities). In their role as case managers, social workers assist patients to navigate what is often experienced as a maze of service providers and a series of conflicting demands presented by various agencies. Case management is especially important in assisting people who suffer from severe and debilitating mental disorders such as schizophrenia and bipolar disorder.

Across jurisdictions there is variability in the education required to practise social work. For example, the Alberta College of Social Workers requires a two-year diploma, whereas other Canadian provinces require an undergraduate or a master's degree in social work. Social work training programs emphasize the social determinants and consequences of mental health and illness. As is the case in applied psychology and psychiatry, clinical social work faces increasing demands to provide evidence-based services (e.g., Myers & Thyer, 1997). Given the move across so many mental health professions toward evidence-based services, evidence-based therapy, such as interpersonal therapy or cognitive therapy for the treatment of adult depression, could be provided by psychologists, psychiatrists, or clinical social workers.

Other Mental Health Professions

Psychiatric nurses are professionals who offer services to individuals whose primary care needs relate to mental and developmental health (Canadian Institute for Health Information, 2004). Psychiatric nurses are responsible for managing administrative matters in inpatient settings, providing psychoeducation and counselling, and supervising ancillary services provided by others (such as nurses' aides and volunteers). In the four western Canadian provinces, where registered psychiatric nurses are regulated as a distinct profession, there were 54.4 per 100,000 people in 2002. Psychiatric nurses are employed in diverse settings including acute psychiatry, long-term geriatric care and home care, residential and community programs for the developmentally handicapped, forensic psychiatry, institutional and community-based corrections facilities, community mental health programs, special education programs for children, employee assistance programs, child guidance and family therapy clinics, chemical dependency programs, hospitals and special care homes, women's shelters and clinics, residential and community programs for adolescents, psychiatric nursing education, sheltered workshops, rehabilitation programs, vocational programs, self-help groups, as well as private practice (Canadian Institute for Health Information, 2004). In all these settings, psychiatric nurses are on the front lines providing direct services, as well as training and consultation. Practitioners of this speciality typically receive their training as part of a two- or three-year diploma program or during a baccalaureate degree. In addition to the regular training in general nursing, psychiatric nurses receive training in the management and treatment of those with mental disorders warranting admission to a hospital or other similar institution.

In the residential care of children and adolescents with emotional and behavioural problems, frontline services may also be offered by child and youth care workers. Child and youth care workers usually have two-year college training in child development and behaviour management. In an attempt to meet the demand for mental health services while minimizing costs of services, outpatient services are often provided by mental health counsellors. In most cases these counsellors have a college diploma or certificate based on a structured program of training (often less than two years in duration) focused on the assessment and treatment of specific mental health problems such as addictions or trauma. There is also a growing number of counsellors trained in applied behavioural analysis, a systematic form of assessment and intervention that is the treatment of choice for pervasive developmental disorders such as autistic disorder. Of all the professionals presented in this chapter, child and youth care workers and counsellors have the least training and are the least likely to be members of a regulated profession.

AVAILABILITY OF MENTAL HEALTH SERVICE PROVIDERS

There is wide variability in access to major mental health professions in different countries. Data from the World Health Organization indicate that the mental health needs of approximately half the world's nations are woefully underserved by trained professionals, with fewer than 1 psychologist, psychiatrist, or social worker for each 100,000 people (World Health Organization, 2004a). If we recall the data on the prevalence of mental health problems, even conservative estimates indicate that 1 in 10 people suffer from a mental disorder. Thus, in half the world, there is only one mental health professional for each 10,000 people who suffer from a mental disorder.

Canadian data indicate that in 2002 there were 43.2 licensed psychologists for every 100,000 people (Canadian Institute for Health Information, 2004). **Table 1.5** provides details on the relative numbers of psychologists and psychiatrists in different countries. In Canada, the United States, and New Zealand, there are substantially more psychologists providing mental health services than there are psychiatrists. This pattern does not apply in all countries, however, as evidenced by the data from United Kingdom, where there are comparable numbers of psychologists and psychiatrists, and Australia, where there are substantially more psychiatrists than psychologists. Although the sheer numbers of professionals providing mental health services in a country provides some indication of the adequacy of the health care system, it can mask regional disparities that affect the population. Key among such regional disparities is the difference between services available in urban and rural areas. By and large those living in rural areas have fewer mental health professionals than do those living in urban areas. Although in Canada the ratio of psychologists to psychiatrists is approximately 3 to 1, in rural areas of Alberta, Newfoundland and Labrador, and Quebec the ratio of psychologists to psychiatrists is estimated to be 15 to 1 (Canadian Psychological Association, 1999). In Chapter 11 you will learn about an innovative training program to prepare psychologists for rural practice.

TABLE 1.5   World Health Organization Data on Psychologists and Psychiatrists in Selected Countries

	Psychologists (per 100,000 people)	Psychiatrists (per 100,000 people)
Canada	35.0	12.0
United States	26.4	10.5
United Kingdom	9.0	11.0
Ireland	9.7	5.2
Australia	5.0	14.0
New Zealand	27.0	6.6
France	not reported	20.0
Germany	not reported	7.3

Adapted from World Health Organization (2004b).

A BRIEF HISTORY OF CLINICAL PSYCHOLOGY

In considering the history of clinical psychology, it is useful to think in terms of interwoven threads that include the history of assessment and treatment within clinical psychology, the history of clinical psychology becoming a profession, the history of the treatment of mental illness, and the history of psychology itself. In the remainder of the chapter we will provide an overview of key aspects of clinical psychology's history. Because clinical psychology has developed in differing ways and rates in various countries, we cannot do justice to the multitude of important events that have shaped, and continue to shape, the discipline worldwide. In this section we highlight events that have contributed significantly to the current form of clinical psychology evident in most English-speaking countries. Due to space constraints, we have not included all critical occurrences that were instrumental in the development and application of clinical psychology in non-English speaking countries. Nevertheless, in reading the following pages you should get a general sense of the influences that contributed to the growth of clinical psychology in North America and elsewhere. Given the key role of American clinical psychology in shaping the face of clinical psychology worldwide, much of what follows highlights key events within the United States. You will notice that not all the key figures who were influential in the development of clinical psychology were psychologists, but also include philosophers and psychiatrists and members of related professions.

The Roots of Clinical Psychology

Numerous scholarly texts on the history of psychopathology and its treatment describe early proponents of the view that mental disturbances were caused by natural causes, rather than by demonic possession. Among the early Greek scholars in the period of 500–300 B.C., Hippocrates (often called the father of medicine) emphasized what is now known as a **biopsychosocial approach** to understanding both physical and psychological disorders (i.e., biological, psychological, and social influences on health and illness must be considered). In textbooks of abnormal psychology and personality you will have learned about Hippocrates' "bodily fluid" theory that imbalances in the levels of blood, black bile, yellow bile, and phlegm are responsible for emotional disturbance. The philosophers Plato and Aristotle are both credited with promoting some of Hippocrates' ideas, even though they did so in different ways. Plato emphasized the role of societal forces and psychological needs in the development and alleviation of mental disorders, whereas Aristotle emphasized the biological determinants of mental disorders.

In the late 1500s, St. Vincent de Paul proposed that mental and physical illnesses were caused by natural forces and that the extreme manifestations of mental disturbances such as psychotic behaviour were not caused by witchcraft or by satanic possession. Unfortunately, the dominant approach to the treatment of mental illness in Europe and North America in the subsequent centuries was anything but humane. Those suffering from severe mental illness were isolated in asylums, most of which were far from conducive to the promotion of mental health. Numerous accounts of these institutions paint a picture of pain, despair, and desolation. Living conditions were often squalid and the more aggressive patients were chained to walls. Treatments consisted of *time honoured* approaches to calming extreme behaviour such as bleeding with knives or leeches (this was believed to reduce excitation due to an excess of blood) or immersion in frigid water.

During the period of the Enlightenment in Europe and North America that began in the latter half of the 1700s, a new worldview emerged in which problems could be analysed, understood, and solved and that the methods of science could be applied to all natural phenomena, including the human experience. The impact of this philosophical movement on the treatment of the mentally ill was astounding. Reformer Philippe Pinel, the director of a major asylum in Paris in the late 1700s, ordered that the chains be removed from all mental patients and that patients be treated humanely. Around the same time in England, William Tuke advocated for the development of hospitals based on modern ideas of appropriate care and established a country retreat in which patients lived and worked. In the United States, Benjamin Rush promoted the use of moral therapy with the mentally ill (a treatment philosophy that encouraged the use of compassion and patience rather than physical punishment or restraints).

About this time, within European medicine the speciality of neurology was growing rapidly. The increased attention to mental disorders led to the recognition that a number of conditions, such as hysteria (i.e., extreme, dramatic, and often odd behaviour including limb paralysis), could not easily be accounted for with purely biological explanations. Jean Martin Charcot, in France, is credited with being the primary developer of clinical neurology. As his fame grew, so did his emphasis on the role of psychological factors in hysteria. Charcot's use of suggestion and hypnosis to treat this condition initially attracted the attention of many physicians and medical students. Notable members of this group include Pierre Janet and Sigmund Freud, who initially embraced Charcot's theories and his use of hypnosis but later went on to develop their own theories to account for hysteria.

The History of Assessment in Clinical Psychology

The early history of clinical psychology is largely the history of clinical assessment, as clinical psychology developed from psychology's focus on measuring, describing, and understanding human behaviour. Indeed, with some exceptions we discuss in the next section, clinical psychology was almost entirely an assessment-based discipline until the middle part of the twentieth century. Milestones in the history of assessment in clinical psychology are noted in **Table 1.6**.

The German Wilhelm Wundt advocated psychology as the study of human experience, establishing the first psychology laboratory.

By the latter part of the 1800s, the influence of the Enlightenment worldview was also evident in the burgeoning application of scientific principles to understanding both normal and abnormal human behaviour. In England, Francis Galton studied individual differences among people, especially differences in motor skills and reaction times, which he believed were related to differences in intelligence. In Germany, Wilhelm Wundt, who studied sensation and perception, established the first psychology laboratory and was a central figure in advocating for psychology as the study of human experience. The American James McKeen Cattell, who at one time worked with Wundt, focused scientific attention on the connection between reaction time and intelligence. He is credited with coining the term *mental tests* to describe the battery of tests and tasks he developed to evaluate people's cognitive functioning.

TABLE 1.6   Timeline for History of Assessment in Clinical Psychology

1879	Germany: *Measurement*. Wundt opens first psychology laboratory measuring sensory processes.
1899	Germany: *Diagnosis*. Kraepelin develops first diagnostic system.
1905	France: *Intelligence testing*. Binet and Simon develop test to assess intellectual abilities in schoolchildren.
1917	U.S.: *Intelligence testing*. Army Alpha and Army Beta tests developed to select soldiers.
1920s	Switzerland: *Projective testing of personality*. Rorschach publishes book on interpretation of inkblots.
1939	U.S.: *Intelligence testing*. Wechsler develops the Wechsler-Bellevue test of adult intelligence.
1940s	U.S.: *Projective testing of personality*. Murray and Morgan publish Thematic Apperception Test. Canada: *Intelligence testing*. Revised Examination M used for selection and assignment in the military.
1943	U.S.: *Actuarial assessment of personality*. Hathaway publishes Minnesota Multiphasic Personality Inventory.
1952	U.S.: *Diagnosis*. American Psychiatric Association publishes *Diagnostic and Statistical Manual of Mental Disorders*.
1954	U.S.: *Challenge to clinical decision-making*. Meehl distinguishes between statistical and clinical decision-making.
1968	U.S.: *Challenge to personality assessment*. Mischel proposes an alternative behavioural approach to assessment. U.S.: *Diagnosis*. American Psychiatric Association publishes second edition of *Diagnostic and Statistical Manual of Mental Disorders*.
1970s	U.S.: *Dimensional approach to child problems*. Quay, Achenbach, and Conners publish empirically based rating scales of child problems.
1980	U.S.: *Diagnosis*. American Psychiatric Association publishes third edition of *Diagnostic and Statistical Manual of Mental Disorders*.
1994	U.S.: *Diagnosis*. American Psychiatric Association publishes fourth edition of *Diagnostic and Statistical Manual of Mental Disorders*.

Without a doubt the pre-eminent individuals who influenced the early work on assessment in clinical psychology are the German psychiatrist Emil Kraepelin and the French psychologist Alfred Binet. Kraepelin was convinced that all mental disorders were due to biological factors and that the biological causes of the disorders could not be effectively treated by the rather primitive methods available in the late 1800s and early 1900s. Accordingly, he devoted his career to the study and classification of mental disorders in the hope that his work would result in a scientifically based classification system that would have treatment implications. Consistent with scientific approaches of the time, a key component of Kraepelin's approach to classification was to examine the way in which various symptoms covaried. Kraepelin assumed that by examining the symptomatic behaviour of a large number of patients it would be possible to discern the kinds of disturbances of affect, thought, and behaviour that typically co-occurred. In Kraepelin's view this would provide insights into the nature of mental disorders. Kraepelin called these groups of symptoms that frequently co-occurred **syndromes** and his classification system was built around identifying the ways in which these syndromes related to and differed from each other. Thus, the presence of a single symptom was considered of little value in determining the nature of the disorder suffered by the patient. However, Kraepelin assumed that by considering the entire range of symptoms exhibited by the patient it should be possible to identify the precise disorder from which he or she was suffering. As his study of symptoms and syndromes deepened, he realized that there were consistent differences between disorders in terms of when the symptoms first occurred (i.e., onset of the disorder) and the manner in which the disorder progressed subsequently (i.e., the course of the disorder). Kraepelin's classification system was unparalleled and his classification of what is now known as schizophrenia was one of his major accomplishments. Even though some clinical psychologists have reservations about the value or validity of psychiatric diagnosis, Kraepelin's influence on modern psychiatry and clinical psychology is substantial. The nature and structure of current mental disorder classification systems, such as the American Psychiatric Association's *Diagnostic and Statistical Manual* and the World Health Organization's *International Classification of Diseases* (which are discussed in Chapter 3), have their origins in Kraepelin's work. Reference to these classification systems is an integral part of routine professional activities ranging from conducting psychopathology research to billing for psychological services.

Alfred Binet's contribution to clinical psychology is quite different although no less substantial. In the early years of the twentieth century, the French government wanted all children to receive schooling to maximize their potential to learn and develop. In particular there was concern to provide an education to those children with limited cognitive abilities who were unlikely to benefit from typical teaching methods. Before any special educational programs could be implemented it was necessary to reliably identify children in need of such programs. Binet and his colleague Theodore Simon were invited to develop a strategy to measure mental skills that could yield information relevant to the identification of children with limited intelligence. By 1908 the two colleagues had developed the Binet-Simon scale of intelligence that consisted of more than 50 tests of mental skills that could be administered to children between the ages of 3 and 13 years. Binet and Simon gathered extensive data on a large number of children: that is, they established norms. As we describe in more detail in Chapter 5, norms allow for the comparison of test scores obtained by an individual to the range of scores within the general population or within specific subgroups of the general population. Thus, by comparing the intelligence test score obtained by a particular child with norms for children of the same age, the child's level of intelligence could be determined. In 1916 Lewis Terman published a modification of this scale for use in the United States, the Stanford-Binet Intelligence Test, that was the first widely available, scientifically based test of human intelligence. Binet's work established the importance of standardization in the development of psychological tests and the importance of references to normative data in interpreting test results.

Building on Binet's pioneering work and Terman's adaptation of the Binet-Simon test, the field of psychological assessment grew rapidly. With the entry of the United States into the First World War, the American government needed procedures to quickly determine the fitness of many thousands of recruits to serve in the military. Physicians were employed to evaluate the physical fitness of the recruits for various military activities. In addition, it was necessary to find a way to evaluate mental fitness and mental abilities. Therefore, a committee of the relatively newly established American Psychological Association (APA, established in 1892) was struck to develop a system for classifying the men in terms of their mental functioning. This committee was chaired by Robert Yerkes, APA president. Within a short time the committee developed a measure of verbal mental abilities, called the Army Alpha test, that could be administered in a group format (thus minimizing the cost and time of administration). They also developed a test of nonverbal mental abilities, the Army Beta test, for assessing recruits who were unable to read or who had limited English language skills. This involvement of psychologists in a key American government initiative set the stage for psychologists to be recognized in North America for their expertise in test construction and in the measurement of individual differences. A second legacy of this process was the establishment of the first standards for the development of scientifically sound psychological tests. A third legacy was that, as a result of the value placed on these testing-related skills, the discipline of clinical psychology was officially recognized within the APA by the creation of the Section on Clinical Psychology in 1919.

During the next two decades, several approaches to clinical assessment flourished. Measurement of abilities continued to be a central focus for clinical psychologists. A milestone in the development of intelligence tests for adults was reached in 1939 with the release of the Wechsler-Bellevue test. Its developer, David Wechsler, subsequently developed intelligence tests for the entire age range (Wechsler Preschool and Primary Scale of Intelligence, Wechsler Intelligence Scale for Children, Wechsler Adult Intelligence Scale) and the most commonly used general measure of memory (Wechsler Memory Scale). Although other intelligence scales have since been developed for children and adults, the Wechsler scales are considered the *gold standard* in the assessment of intellectual abilities. The Wechsler scales will be discussed at length in Chapter 7. This period also saw the development of interest tests, with measures such as the Strong Vocational Interest Blank and the Kuder Preference Record, that were developed for training and personnel hiring purposes. Early self-report measures of temperament and personality became available with the release of Woodworth's Personal Data Sheet and the Allport-Vernon Study of Values.

Psychological tests were used to assess the mental fitness and mental abilities of American army recruits during World War I.

The 1930s also witnessed the emergence of projective tests to evaluate personality and psychological functioning. Whereas intelligence tests measure performance on a task, and paper and pencil personality tests are based on self-description, projective tests are predicated on the notion that an individual's interpretation of a situation is determined by their personality characteristics. Thus a person's response to an ambiguous stimulus is presumed to tell us something about the person's mental functioning. One of the most influential and widely used projective tests, the Rorschach inkblot test, was published by Swiss psychiatrist Hermann Rorschach in 1921. Although the test received a decidedly cool reception among psychiatric and psychological circles in Europe, it received a new lease on life when German psychologist Bruno Klopfer, who emigrated to the United States in 1934, began instructing psychology students at Columbia University in the use of the inkblots. The Rorschach inkblot test was also used in assessing children. Another projective technique that was considered suitable for both adults and children was the House-Tree-Person test that involved interpretation of the psychological meaning of qualities of the person's drawing. Around the same time, American psychologists Henry Murray and Christina Morgan working at the Harvard Psychological Clinic published the Thematic Apperception Test (TAT) that was comprised of 20 pictures. Strongly opposed to the growing tendency to study psychological phenomena with experimental methods, Murray distanced himself from the mainstream of academic psychology but was greatly influenced in his thinking by the psychoanalytic writings of Sigmund Freud and Carl Jung. The development of projective tests proceeded without attention to the basic test construction objectives of standardization, reliability, validity, and norms, which has led to long-standing concerns about the quality and utility of many projective tests. These issues will be discussed at greater length in Chapter 8.

With the advent of the Second World War, psychologists once again became actively involved in the development and use of selection tests for the armed forces. In Canada the Test Construction Committee of the Canadian Psychological Association was responsible for the development of the Revised Examination M test that consisted of both verbal and nonverbal ability tests used in the selection and assignment of military personnel. However, the assessment milestone of the 1940s was unquestionably the publication of the Minnesota Multiphasic Personality Inventory (MMPI) by psychologist Starke Hathaway in 1943. The MMPI was, for many years to come, the epitome of the criterion-oriented approach to psychological test construction. The goal of the MMPI was to provide an easily administered test that could effectively screen for psychological disturbances among adults. To this end, Hathaway generated hundreds of test items that were administered to psychiatric patients; items that were strongly associated with specific diagnoses were retained and then combined to make scales within the test. The ability of these scales to distinguish between those with and without psychiatric diagnoses was examined and modifications to the scales were made based on these data. Evidence for the final scales' reliability and validity was gathered and normative data (although rather poor) were obtained. Thus, in contrast to the projective tests, the development and interpretation MMPI relied extensively on attention to statistical procedures and test development criteria. Research on the MMPI is discussed in Chapter 8.

The fundamental differences between projective tests that rely heavily on clinical judgement and the MMPI that relies on statistical analysis set the stage for a critical evaluation of the value and accuracy of assessment in clinical psychology in the 1950s and 1960s. Paul Meehl's (1954) review of the relative strengths of clinically and statistically based assessment highlighted a number of problems that plagued the assessment enterprise in clinical psychology. In essence, Meehl's review of the literature found that a purely clinical approach to assessment was typically inferior to a more statistically oriented approach to accurately describing or diagnosing adults. By clinical, Meehl referred to the typical collection of interview and other information that was then used, sometimes with standardized test data, to generate descriptions and predictions of behaviour. The statistical approach, in contrast, involved the use of basic demographic information (such as age, gender, and health information) and data from standardized tests that were entered into statistical equations to yield descriptions and/or predictions. This latter approach was similar to risk estimates calculated by insurance companies to assign differential insurance policy costs based on estimated risk. A point often lost in the ensuing debate about the value of clinical judgement was that Meehl advocated strongly for the use of clinical experience in generating hypotheses about human functioning or about particular client characteristics. He maintained, however, that once these hypotheses were formulated, whether for research or clinical purposes, scientific methods (including, whenever possible, standardized psychological measures) must be used to test the viability of the hypotheses.

The publication in 1968, a little over a decade after Meehl's critique of clinical assessment practices, of Walter Mischel's compelling analysis of the shortcomings of personality traits for understanding human behaviour further eroded many clinical psychologists' confidence in the validity of their assessment work. Up to then, much of the research on personality had focused on the measurement and study of traits—that is, co-occurring characteristics that not only defined the personality of an individual but also were the primary influences in determining how an individual would react in a given situation. Mischel's work illustrated that these personality traits had more to do with how a person was viewed by others than with what a person actually did. Moreover, research on the predictive validity of personality traits typically yielded results of only moderate strength—in other words, knowing someone's personality traits provided very little useful information if you wished to know what someone would actually feel, think, or do in a particular situation. Much more accurate predictions of psychological experience could be obtained by considering both the person's past experiences in similar situations and the environmental influences on the person's behaviour in the situation.

Although many personality researchers and clinical psychologists believed that Mischel had underestimated the influence of personality factors and overestimated the power of social situations in determining behaviour, Mischel's analysis bolstered the rising influence of behavioural assessment approaches on clinical assessment. Initial behavioural approaches to assessment involved the identification of specific behaviours deemed to be central to the person's distress, either by virtue of being a key symptom that should be changed in therapy or by being a central factor responsible for causing and/or maintaining the person's distress. Based on learning principles encompassed under operant, classical, and observational learning paradigms, behavioural assessment focused on easily defined and observable events, current behaviours, and situational/environment determinants of behaviour. For much of the 1960s and 1970s, behavioural assessment largely involved obtaining frequency, rate, and duration measures describing the behaviours of interest. Compared with the self-report and projective personality assessment approaches, behavioural assessment was much more focused on the gathering of clinical data that had immediate and obvious value in the planning and evaluation of treatment strategies. As behavioural strategies often require observation by a third party, they were most commonly applied in treating problems of children and of patients in hospitals or residential institutions. Observation strategies are described in Chapter 6.

Although sound tools for the assessment of children's intellectual functioning were developed early in the twentieth century, empirically based assessment of children's emotional and behavioural problems did not begin in earnest until the 1970s with the publication of the first rating scales of children's behaviour. Different scales pioneered by Thomas Achenbach, Herbert Quay, and Keith Conners shared the same reliance on description of behaviours and on empirically derived scales to assess children's functioning. These scales required parents to rate the extent to which a particular behaviour was typical of their child. Like the MMPI, the items on these scales were subjected to factor analysis, so that scale scores were derived empirically. Such rating scales provide information on children's functioning on a number of dimensions rather than yielding a categorical diagnosis.

In the 1980s, the publication of the third edition of the American Psychiatric Association's *Diagnostic and Statistical Manual of Mental Disorders (DSM)* led to increased attention on the value of structured interview approaches to gathering diagnostic information. For many years research had consistently demonstrated that clinicians (including clinical psychologists and psychiatrists) were very inconsistent in how they interviewed patients; such inconsistencies were evident both from clinician to clinician and even within the same clinician over time. The result of these inconsistencies often led to the same individual being assigned very different diagnoses from clinicians. Such diagnostic inconsistency has the potential to dramatically affect the types of treatments recommended to the patient. The DSM-III was an explicit attempt to improve the reliability of psychiatric diagnoses by providing as much clear guidance as possible on specific criteria that must be met to render a diagnosis. Based on the common measurement strategy in psychopathology research of using a standardized, structured interview to generate diagnostic information, clinicians were strongly encouraged to either use scientifically established structured interviews to diagnose DSM-III disorders or, at a minimum, to ensure that the necessary diagnostic criteria were met before a diagnosis was assigned. In the development of structured diagnostic interviews for children, there has been particular attention to ensure that questions are formulated in a manner that is developmentally appropriate. So for example, it is not suitable to ask complex questions about the duration of a problem to a child who has not yet developed a concept of time. Issues related to interviewing are addressed in Chapter 6.

Finally, the most striking change in psychological assessment over the past two decades has been the increased attention to the relevance of assessment data for treatment planning and treatment evaluation. Decades of research amply demonstrate that psychologists can create assessment tools for myriad constructs. Many thousands of studies have been published on the reliability and validity of a huge range of psychological measures. However, it has become increasingly clear that to justify the time and expense involved in clinical assessment this vast knowledge must be applied in ways that are directly pertinent to improving the lives of people suffering psychological distress. Combined with concerns about costs and accountability of health care systems worldwide, this has highlighted two issues that clinical psychologists involved in assessment are beginning to address. The first issue is one of **clinical utility**: that is, does having assessment data on a patient actually provide information that leads to a clinical outcome that is better (or faster, or less expensive) than would be the case if the psychologist did not have the assessment data? This issue reflects the problem that all too often research on clinical psychology is disconnected from research on interventions in clinical psychology and vice versa. As concerns about health care costs mount, clinical psychologists must justify to those who pay for their services the relevance of their assessment activities. The second, and related, current issue is one of **service evaluation**. Put bluntly, individual clinical psychologists are under increasing pressure to demonstrate that their services work. This has resulted in renewed attention to the role of clinical assessment in documenting progress and outcome in treatment. However, this need to demonstrate treatment effectiveness leads to a different type of clinical assessment than has often been used in the past. Whereas many clinical psychology measures were developed to give a broadly based psychological picture of the whole person, current assessment practices require that measures focus on specific problems (or strengths), that they are brief, and that they are amenable to repeated use. The measurement tools that are useful for generating an individual's psychological profile are not necessarily the ones that are relevant to the repeated assessment of someone receiving treatment. Accordingly, a minor revolution in the nature of clinical assessment is currently underway, with some traditional measures falling from favour and some longstanding, but underused assessment strategies coming to the fore. These issues are discussed in greater detail in Chapters 6, 7, and 8.

The History of Intervention in Clinical Psychology

Milestones in the evolution of intervention in clinical psychology are noted in **Table 1.7**. The modern history of psychotherapy is typically seen as beginning with the work of Sigmund Freud and the development of psychoanalysis. As indicated earlier in this chapter, a number of European psychiatrists such as Charcot and Janet were actively involved in using verbal rather than physical approaches to the treatment of mental disorders in the late 1800s. Freud is credited with developing the first elaborated approach to the psychotherapeutic treatment of common psychological difficulties, even though subsequent historical analysis of his work suggests that it may not have been as original or revolutionary as he often suggested (Ellenberger, 1970). The 1900 publication of his book *The Interpretation of Dreams* marked an important milestone for the psychoanalytic movement and attracted both supporters and detractors. In subsequent years psychiatrists such as Carl Jung and Alfred Adler joined Freud to develop and promote a psychoanalytic approach to the understanding and treatment of mental disorders. Ultimately, they and other followers split from Freud to develop their own theories and interventions.

The early decades of the 1900s were marked by the growth of numerous psychodynamic treatment approaches in Europe, which then spread to North America. These approaches differed widely in their core principles and techniques, but all were based on the assumption that most psychopathology stemmed from unconscious processes. For Freud, the unconscious was the source of all psychic energy as well as the repository of all our disappointments, hurts, and unfulfilled sexual and aggressive desires. He hypothesized that to protect ourselves from the pain of continually re-experiencing these negative emotions and memories we use a number of strategies called defence mechanisms such as denial, repression, and intellectualization. The goal of treatment is for the patient to gain insight into the origin of his or her problems (i.e., the painful contents of the unconscious) and the ways in which the defence mechanisms inadvertently block the person's full psychological development. Jung's model involved an aspect of the unconscious similar to Freud's (called the personal unconscious) but also included a much more positive form

TABLE 1.7   Timeline for History of Intervention in Clinical Psychology

1896	U.S.: Witmer opens first psychology clinic.
1900–1930s	Europe, U.S., U.K.: Development of psychoanalytic approaches.
1920s	U.S.: First behavioural treatment of anxiety by Cover Jones.
1940s	U.S. and Europe: Increased demand for services to deal with war-related distress.
1942	U.S.: Rogers publishes *Counseling and Psychotherapy*, introducing a client-centred approach.
1952	England: Eysenck publishes review questioning the usefulness of psychotherapy with adults.
1957	U.S.: Levitt publishes review questioning usefulness of psychotherapy with children.
1958	South Africa: Wolpe publishes article on behavioural treatment of phobias.
1977	Canada: Meichenbaum publishes *Cognitive-Behavior Modification: An Integrative Approach*
1979	U.S.: Beck, Rush, Shaw, and Emery publish *Cognitive Therapy for Depression*.
1980	U.S.: Smith, Glass, and Miller publish *Effects of Psychotherapy* providing results of meta-analytic review of treatment for adults.
1987	U.S.: Weisz, Weiss, Alicke, and Klotz publish meta-analytic review of treatment for children and adolescents.
1995	American Psychological Association, Division of Clinical Psychology defines criteria to evaluate degree of empirical support for treatments.

(called the collective unconscious) that could promote the individual's psychological growth. Jungian treatment emphasized, therefore, not only the importance of developing an awareness of the personal unconscious but also an appreciation and harnessing of the power of the collective unconscious.

Later psychodynamic models tended to de-emphasize the importance of unconscious determinants of behaviour. Alfred Adler's approach, for example, focused on the role of societal forces and socialization pressures in the development of personality and the treatment of disorders. His theory emphasized the impact of birth order on personality and the impact of social comparison processes in which we may underestimate or overestimate our personal strengths and weaknesses. Anna Freud, a daughter of Sigmund Freud, who had received analysis from her father when she was a child, developed ego psychology that encourages the person to develop skills that can help address current problems. Although her approach still considered the unconscious a force to be reckoned with, she highlighted the role of conscious efforts to adjust to past difficulties and current life obstacles. Anna Freud took a leading role in modifying psychoanalytic approaches in treatment with children.

Even though they were undoubtedly influential in the development of clinical psychology treatments, these psychodynamic approaches were not the only contributors to our current forms of psychotherapy. Two other distinct approaches to the treatment of psychological distress emerged during the first decades of the twentieth century. Lightner Witmer, an American student of Wundt's credited with being the first to use the term "clinical psychology," developed a clinic offering psychological services in 1896 and university training in clinical psychology in 1904. Witmer was a university professor whose interests lay primarily in the application of research on learning and memory processes. He consulted with teachers and others in school settings to apply the new science of psychology to the assessment and remediation of learning difficulties, intellectual and developmental delays, and, to some extent, behaviour problems. In retrospect it is ironic that the psychologist often described as the father of clinical psychology was really setting the stage for what would now be seen as school psychology. A second example of the application of scientific psychology to the understanding and treatment of psychological disorders can be found in conditioning research in the 1920s. John Watson demonstrated that it was possible to use conditioning principles to explain the development of phobias with his famous experiment with little Albert and furry white animals and objects. The next important step that had important implications for treatment purposes was when Mary Cover Jones showed that the principles of conditioning could be used to extinguish a phobic reaction in a child. This initial work utilizing animal and human learning concepts and procedures set the stage for what would later become behaviour therapy.

In the 1940s and 1950s the demand for psychotherapy grew dramatically, due largely to the need to provide mental health services for both members of the military and to members of the public who were affected by the horror and losses of the war. In the United States, for example, the need for mental health professionals to provide counselling and therapy to returning soldiers could not be met by the relatively small number of psychiatrists practising in the country. As a result, the Veterans' Administration agency turned to the profession of clinical psychology, hiring many psychologists and providing a substantial infusion of funds to aid in the formation of new training programs in clinical psychology. This led to an enormous increase in the number of clinical psychologists in the United States and to the eventual establishment in later decades of clinical psychologists' reputation as among the best trained practitioners of psychotherapy.

The 1940s and 1950s also saw a proliferation in the forms of psychotherapy available to the public. A major new movement in psychotherapy was initiated with the publication in 1942 of Carl Rogers' book *Counseling and Psychotherapy*. In contrast to the then dominant psychoanalytic approach, Rogers' approach was rooted in an assumption that people were inherently capable of developing in a positive, healthy manner. The primary goal of therapy, therefore, was to provide a supportive environment in which clients could reconnect with their emotions, their losses, and their aspirations and thereby discover their true potential for growth. Rogers' work was crucial in the development of humanistic approaches to the understanding and treatment of human problems, an approach that has been termed the third force in psychotherapy (with psychodynamic and behavioural approaches being the first two). Of equal, if not greater importance, Rogers was an early and firm advocate of the need to conduct systematic research on the process and outcome of psychotherapy. His position was markedly different from that typical of the time, as what frequently passed as psychotherapy research was little more than case studies. You will learn more about the limitations of the case study approach to the study of human functioning in Chapter 4. Changes were occurring in the psychodynamic approach to treatment as well, with Alexander and French publishing their book *Psychoanalytic Therapy* in 1946 in which they made a compelling case for briefer forms of psychoanalytic treatment. In the mid 1950s Harry Stack Sullivan provided details on interpersonally focused strategies for intervening with patients. Outside the psychodynamic realm, new approaches within a humanistic/existential/experiential tradition were introduced, including Fritz Perls' concepts and procedures of gestalt therapy and Viktor Frankl's logotherapy. Finally, Joseph Wolpe published his work on systematic desensitization in 1958, thus setting the stage for the dramatic growth of the behavioural (and cognitive) therapies.

Hans Eysenck's (1952) critique of the effectiveness of psychotherapy was a turning point for psychotherapy research and training. Eysenck argued that the rates of improvement among clients receiving either psychodynamic or eclectic (i.e., an unspecified mix of theories and techniques) therapy were comparable to rates of remission of symptoms among clients receiving no therapy at all. He contended, therefore, that there was no evidence that the most commonly used forms of psychotherapy had any demonstrable effect. Although later proponents of these treatments pointed out substantial flaws in his arguments, Eysenck's review had two dramatic effects on the field. First, it crystallized dissatisfaction among many psychologists who did not agree with a psychodynamic approach to treatment and led to efforts to establish treatments that were directly connected to psychology's empirically derived knowledge. Second, it resulted in a flurry of research activity in the coming decades focused on evaluating both new and traditional forms of psychotherapy. As we will see throughout this book, advances in psychological services for children and families often follow the same trends as are seen in services for adults; however, there is usually a time lag of a few years. Reviews of the child

Dr. Hans Eysenck, shown here circa 1968.

psychotherapy research (Levitt, 1957) reached similar conclusions to Eysenck with respect to adult psychotherapy.

The 1960s and 1970s, consequently, were decades marked by an increase in both the numbers of psychotherapies available to the public and in the amount of research devoted to understanding whether psychotherapy was effective (and, if it was, what made it effective). In the early 1960s Albert Ellis developed Rational Emotive Therapy and Eric Berne introduced Transactional Analysis (an early forerunner of therapies aimed at enhancing personal growth and development as much as treating psychopathology). Using learning principles such as contingencies, shaping, and reinforcement, behaviour modification and behaviour therapy became widely used during this time to address problems as diverse as self-injurious behaviour, phobic avoidance, hyperactive behaviour, and sexual dysfunction. In tune with the growing attention to cognitive phenomena in psychology in general, behaviour therapy began to address cognitive elements in treatment. The publication in the late 1970s of two influential books laid the foundation of what is now known as cognitive-behaviour therapy. These now classic texts were Don Meichenbaum's *Cognitive-Behavior Modification: An Integrated Approach*, which was published in 1977, and the first comprehensive treatment manual *Cognitive Therapy of Depression: A Treatment Manual* by Aaron Beck and his colleagues John Rush, Brian Shaw, and Gary Emery, which appeared in 1979. Cognitive-behavioural approaches are equally applicable to address adults' and children's problems and gained popularity in the 1970s.

Another milestone was reached in 1980 when Smith, Glass, and Miller used a statistical technique called **meta-analysis** to review 475 controlled studies of psychotherapy. This technique (described in detail in Chapter 4) provides a means by which groups of studies can be statistically combined and compared. Their primary finding was that psychotherapy, in general, was clearly very effective, with the average person receiving therapy being better off after therapy than 80% of people with similar problems who did not receive therapy. The researchers also examined the effectiveness of various types of treatment. Using different analytic techniques, they found that although there was general equivalence across divergent forms of psychotherapy, there were some therapies that were superior to others for specific disorders and clinical problems. As we will see in Chapters 12 and 14, these results fuelled debates about the relative merits of psychotherapies that persist to the present. Seven years later, a meta-analysis reported similar results for psychotherapy for children and adolescents, with 79% of treated children being better off after treatment than children and adolescents with similar problems who did not receive psychotherapy (Weisz, Weiss, Alicke & Klotz, 1987). The impact of research such as this is addressed in Chapter 13.

The 1980s and 1990s saw several key developments in the history of psychotherapy. There was a dramatic increase in the amount of research on psychotherapy. Furthermore, there was a profound improvement in the methodological sophistication of those studies, with an increasing use of treatment manuals to guide interventions and standardized diagnostic criteria for assessing those receiving treatment. Numerous societal and health care pressures fuelled the demand for the development and dissemination of effective short-term treatments (i.e., fewer than 20 to 25 sessions). This demand for short-term treatments was welcomed by proponents of disorder-specific cognitive-behavioural treatments. In addition, psychodynamic and humanistic/existential/experiential approaches were adapted to provide services over a shorter period of time. Numerous forms of inter-personally focused psychodynamic treatments emerged in Britain, Canada, and the United States, including Time-Limited Dynamic Psychotherapy developed by Hans Strupp and his colleagues. Within the experiential orientation the emphasis was on more structured and directive interventions that melded traditional principles and values with contemporary knowledge of emotional functioning. Key among the proponents of this process-experiential treatment approach were Les Greenberg in Canada and Robert Elliott in the United States.

It should be clear from this overview that the practice of clinical psychology has been influenced by research on the impact of psychotherapy. Another landmark event occurred in 1995 with the release of the report by the American Psychological Association Division of Clinical Psychology's *Task Force on Promotion and Dissemination of Psychological Procedures*. The impetus for this task force came from increasing pressure in the United States for health care practices to be both demonstrably effective and cost-effective. Legislation and state case law were being used to shape the nature of both federal and state health care policy, and there appeared to be a very real danger that access to mental health and behavioural health care services might be diminished because of perceptions that such services were both expensive and relatively ineffective. Clearly a response from organized psychology was needed to underscore the effectiveness of psychological interventions for certain disorders and conditions. The task force developed empirical criteria to aid in the determination of whether an intervention was efficacious in the treatment of a given disorder or clinical problem. Using these criteria, the task force then produced an initial list of efficacious treatments. The term **efficacy** is used to denote evidence that a treatment was shown to work under research conditions that emphasized internal validity, with the term **effectiveness** being reserved to describe evidence that the treatment was shown to work in real world conditions. Predictably, this initiative was embraced by some clinical psychologists and treated with scorn by others. Regardless of the strengths or limitations of this and related initiatives (which we discuss in Chapters 12 and 13), it has forever changed how clinical psychologists view the connection between empirical evidence and their therapeutic services.

The History of Prevention in Clinical Psychology

Unfortunately the history of prevention efforts in clinical psychology is much shorter than the history of assessment or intervention. This is because, as outlined above, the profession of clinical psychology started with an assessment focus and then added the dimension of intervention. As clinical psychologists were incorporated into national health care systems, in both public and private sectors, they adopted the priorities of these systems, which, until very recently, did not include much in the way of prevention efforts. Due to growing concerns about the dire health consequences of smoking and the need to promote safer sex practices to reduce the incidence of AIDS and sexually transmitted diseases, clinical psychologists now frequently play an important role in public health initiatives to change lifestyle-related illnesses. Concerns about the apparent increase in depression in the United States have led a number of clinical psychologists to develop prevention programs aimed at educating adolescents and young adults about depression and the types of psychological coping skills that can be used to maintain good mental health. Another societal problem, violence in intimate relationships, is also the focus of preventive efforts headed by clinical psychologists. In Canada, for example, psychologists David Wolfe and Peter Jaffe have developed school-based programs designed to reduce violence in dating relationships as well as in families. In Chapter 10 we describe the current status of prevention programs in clinical psychology.

THE FUTURE

Predicting future events is always an uncertain business. Nevertheless, some brave psychologists have ventured to give their prognostications for future developments in clinical psychology. Groth-Marnat (2000), an authority on psychological assessment issues, recently offered some predictions about what is likely to transpire in the realm of clinical assessment in the next 50 years. Some of his predictions are almost sure-bets, such as revisions to the DSM, the Wechsler intelligence tests, and the MMPI. For others, he went out on a limb, predicting that advances in virtual reality technology will allow ability testing based on the simulation of life and work situations by 2020. The most dramatic prediction was that by 2035 measures based on the results of human genome research will be incorporated into clinical assessments.

In predicting the future of psychotherapy, Norcross, Hedges, and Prochaska (2002) took a different approach to Groth-Marnat. They surveyed prominent psychotherapy researchers regarding the predictions for psychotherapy trends. Experts agreed that by 2010 it is likely that evidence-based psychotherapies will be required by health care systems and that psychotherapy research will provide clear evidence for the treatments of choice for certain disorders and patients. They also predicted that the level of involvement of psychologists in providing psychotherapy will remain the same as today, but that the involvement of psychiatrists will drop and the involvement of master's-level counsellors, clinical social workers, and psychiatric nurses will increase. Theoretical orientations were also expected to change, with increases likely in those espousing cognitive and behavioural approaches, interpersonal approaches, and culturally sensitive approaches; psychoanalytic and a number of humanistic/experiential approaches were expected to decline in the coming years.

Of course only time will tell which, if any, of these predictions will come to pass. Given the history of clinical psychology, perhaps the only certainty for the future is that exciting changes are in store for the profession and for those whose practise it.

SUMMARY AND CONCLUSIONS

Worldwide, mental health problems have staggering emotional and financial costs. Compared with physical health problems, mental health problems are woefully underserved. There is a trend across all mental health professions to develop and disseminate evidence-based services so that these serious problems can be effectively and economically addressed.

Clinical psychology shares with other mental health professions a concern to assess and intervene in the prevention and treatment of emotional, behavioural, and neurological problems. In contrast to psychiatry and psychiatric nursing that have their roots in the treatment of pathology, psychology is grounded in the science of human behaviour. Among the mental health professions, psychology is unique in its long-standing research tradition. From the beginning of their academic training, students in psychology learn to understand, interpret, and conduct methodologically sound research.

In tracing the history of psychological assessment, intervention, and prevention, it is clear that systematic observation and evaluation is a hallmark of clinical psychology. Drawing on a wealth of knowledge about human functioning and development, clinical psychologists have earned recognition of their expertise in assessment, treatment, and prevention of serious problems. The field of clinical psychology is in a process of constant evolution.

Critical Thinking Questions

Are mental health problems as serious as physical health problems?

In what ways is clinical psychology similar to other mental health professions?

In what ways is clinical psychology distinct from other mental health professions?

In what ways has scientific thinking shaped the evolution of clinical psychology?

Key Terms

biopsychosocial approach	meta-analysis
clinical utility	service evaluation
effectiveness	syndrome
efficacy	

Key Names

Alfred Binet	Richard McFall
Hans Eysenck	Paul Meehl
Emil Kraepelin	Carl Rogers

ADDITIONAL RESOURCES
Journal

Professional Psychology: Research and Practice.

Books

Dobson, K., & Dobson, D. (Eds.). (1993). *Professional psychology in Canada.* Toronto, ON: Hogrefe & Huber Publishers.

Routh, D. K. (1994). *Clinical psychology since 1917: Science, practice, and organization.* New York: Plenum Press.

Websites

Canadian Psychological Association, Clinical Psychology Section: <http://www.cpa.ca/clinical.html>

Website of the American Psychological Association, Division 12, Society for Clinical Psychology: <http://www.cpa.ca/clinical.html>

American Psychological Association, Division 53, Society for Child and Adolescent Clinical Psychology: <http://www.apa.org/about/division/div53.html>

CHAPTER 2

Contemporary Clinical Psychology

INTRODUCTION

Clinical psychology is a fascinating profession. Few university graduate programs prepare students for such varied and challenging careers. Depending on personal preferences and job requirements, a clinical psychologist may devote professional time to (a) providing psychological services, (b) conducting research and providing clinical training, (c) consulting with other professionals and agencies, or (d) all of the above. Moreover, it is common for the relative balance of activities to shift over the span of a career, so that a psychologist may have phases when she or he devotes the greatest emphasis to research and other times that are mainly devoted to administration or teaching. In this way, the psychologist has a multitude of different interests within a single career in psychology. Clinical psychologists work with individuals (at any stage in the lifespan), couples, families, groups, and organizations. Many clinical psychologists work in the domain of mental health (e.g., treating anxiety disorders, disruptive behaviour disorders, mood disorders, schizophrenia, or substance abuse disorders). A large number of clinical psychologists conduct research and provide health services outside this traditional domain (e.g., stress, coping with pain, promoting adherence to medical treatment regimens) and/or provide services related to relationship functioning (e.g., couples therapy, parent training, family therapy).

In 2004 *Psychology Today* and *PacifiCare Behavioral Health* commissioned a survey of American adults' experience with and attitudes to mental health treatment entitled *Therapy in America 2004*. Five hundred adults took part in telephone interviews and 1,730 adults completed the survey on-line. One question asked "which mental health profession is most helpful in resolving personal, emotional, or mental health problems?" Of those who had an opinion on this, psychologists were seen as the most helpful by 29% of respondents whereas psychiatrists were seen as the most helpful by 19%. It is heartening to know that the public views psychologists as helpful mental health care providers. However, as you can see in **Figure 2.1** there are enormous international disparities in the extent to which people have access to mental heath services from psychologists. The Scandinavian countries, along with New Zealand, Canada, and the United States are, relatively speaking, well-served by psychologists. Unfortunately, the same cannot be said of many other countries, especially those in Africa and Asia.

In this chapter we will describe the range of activities in which clinical psychologists engage and some of the settings in which they work. To bring these activities to life, we have asked three Canadian clinical psychologists who work in different settings to describe their usual professional activities over the course of a week. In reading these descriptions of professional activities in the three profile boxes you will probably be struck by the busy and varied nature of their professional time. You may recall that in Chapter 1 we talked about what we consider a touchstone of

Figure 2.1   WHO distribution of psychologists in mental health services/100,000 population

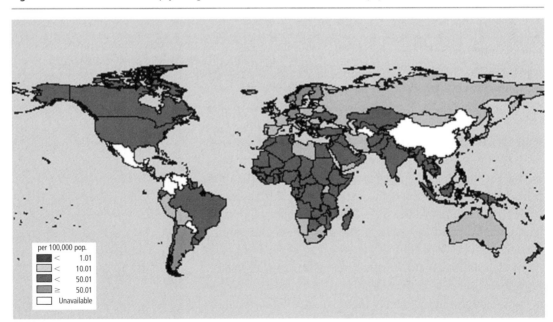

per 100,000 pop.
- < 1.01
- < 10.01
- < 50.01
- ≥ 50.01
- Unavailable

Reproduced with permission from the World Health Organization.

clinical psychology: science-based practice. In this chapter, we introduce a second touchstone of clinical psychology: professional ethics. Because clinical psychologists, as health care providers, must meet training and licensing requirements in order to practise, we provide a perspective on licensing requirements. In the final sections of the chapter we will present the nature of clinical psychology and the nature of training in clinical psychology in Canada.

ACTIVITIES OF CLINICAL PSYCHOLOGISTS

Over the years, a number of surveys have documented the nature of the activities undertaken by clinical psychologists. Some activities, such as assessment and research, have stayed relatively constant in terms of the numbers of psychologists who frequently engage in them. As we explained in Chapter 1, following the Second World War there was a steady rise in the numbers of clinical psychologists providing psychotherapy. Using the most current data available (Hunsley & Lefebvre, 1990; Norcross, Karg, & Prochaska, 1997), **Table 2.1** shows the percentages of clinical psychologists who engage in different professional activities. In interpreting these data, two things should be kept in mind. First, the data from both surveys are several years old and so probably do not fully capture practice patterns in the new millennium. Second, survey information can provide a useful overview of general trends among clinical psychologists, but does not indicate the variability in professional activities among individual clinical psychologists.

TABLE 2.1   Professional Activities of Clinical Psychologists in Canada and the USA

Activity	Percentage of Psychologists Who Engage in Each Activity	
	Canada[a]	USA[b]
Assessment	76	74
Psychotherapy	98	84
Consultation	68	54
Research	32	47
Teaching	44	50
Supervision	61	62
Administration	56	52

[a] Hunsley & Lefebvre (1990); [b] Norcross, Karg, & Prochaska (1997)

Profile Boxes 2.1, **2.2**, and **2.3** introduce three Canadian clinical psychologists. Dr. Kerry Mothersill is employed in a hospital in Alberta (Box 2.1), Dr. Heather Hadjistavropoulos is the director of the clinical psychology program at the University of Regina (Box 2.2), and Dr. Maggie Mamen is a psychologist in private practice in Ontario (Box 2.3). Across these three settings, all three psychologists have full and varied schedules.

PROFILE BOX 2.1

DR. KERRY MOTHERSILL

I received my Ph.D. in Clinical Psychology from the University of Western Ontario in 1980 and then completed advanced training at the Center for Cognitive Therapy, University of Pennsylvania. I am a Founding Member of The Academy of Cognitive Therapy. I have held executive positions in a number of psychology organizations including President of the Psychologists' Association of Alberta (PAA), President of the Canadian Council of Professional Psychology Programs (CCPPP), and Chair of the Clinical Section of the Canadian Psychological Association (CPA). Recent conference presentations focused on internship training and on psychological factors in health care interventions. I am a Site Visitor for the Accreditation Panel of CPA and an Oral Examiner for the College of Alberta Psychologists.

Dr. Kerry Mothersill

I am the coordinator of Cognitive Behavioural Therapy and Program Facilitator of the Outpatient Mental Health Program as well as a Co-Director of the Pre-doctoral Internship Training Program in Clinical Psychology at the Calgary Health Region. I am an Adjunct Associate Professor in the Department of Psychology at the University of Calgary. In addition, I have a private practice specializing in cognitive therapy and personal injury assessments.

A TYPICAL WEEK

On Monday morning I provided cognitive behavioural therapy (CBT) to a lawyer with a major depressive disorder. As usual, I completed progress notes immediately after the 50-minute session. Then I met with a research assistant to go over brief reviews of outcome research that she prepared on the effectiveness of CBT in the treatment of several diagnostic problems. These summary paragraphs will be included in initial therapy reports prepared by the CBT therapists for referring physicians. During the afternoon, I dictated an intake report and a discharge summary. Then I attended a meeting of the region-wide Quality Improvement Committee. A session with a client with generalized anxiety disorder closed out the day.

On Tuesday morning I took part in the triage committee that reviews referrals for therapy. Next I attended a multidisciplinary meeting in which we deliberated over options for dealing with our lengthy waiting list. In the afternoon, I participated in an interview of a psychologist who had applied for a position on the team. Following a therapy session with a client suffering from obsessive compulsive disorder, I reviewed the results of psychological testing administered by an intern and reviewed her initial draft of the assessment report.

On Wednesday morning I conducted an assessment interview with a client with attentional problems. An intern and a practicum student observed the session. Following a brief review of the initial findings, the intern administered a number of psychometric measures. I then chaired the weekly meeting of the CBT therapists and trainees. An intern presented her work with a client diagnosed with social phobia and presented the recent empirically supported treatments for the problem. After lunch with the CBT group, I observed an intern's therapy session with a panic disordered client and provided feedback. I then provided therapy to a client in her late 50s who is adjusting to the recent loss of her husband. During the remainder of the day, I organized and updated a binder of readings on ethics and updated our Internship Training Manual.

On Thursday morning I conducted therapy sessions with two clients: one with complicated grief reaction and another suffering from post-traumatic stress disorder. Next, I met with another psychologist who wanted to consult around possible treatment strategies for a client who presented with depression as well as strong avoidant personality patterns. I then assisted colleagues who were having difficulty with our new on-line professional service data collection system. In the afternoon, I prepared summaries of material on cost-effectiveness of psychological services that would be sent to insurance companies to encourage them to consider referring clients for psychological services. Prior to a termination session with a client who had been successful in decreasing his post-marital separation depression, I provided supervision to a psychiatric resident.

On Friday, I provided therapy to a client who had suffered several depressive episodes. Next I participated in a teleconference with the executive committee of the CPA Clinical Section to plan the upcoming conference and to review advocacy initiatives. Then I reviewed therapy tapes of sessions conducted by a practicum student and made notes for supervision. Following a session of CBT and pain management counselling for a recently injured client with depression, I entered my statistics for the week's activities, finalized the outline for the course I will teach at the University of Calgary next term, and reviewed the client reports prepared by several of the CBT staff. Reading and replying to emails as well as making phone calls usually takes upwards of 45 minutes a day.

PROFILE BOX 2.2

DR. HEATHER HADJISTAVROPOULOS

Dr. Heather
Hadjistavropoulos

I obtained my Ph.D. in Clinical Psychology at the University of British Columbia in 1995. Since 1996 I have been a registered psychologist in the province of Saskatchewan assessing and treating clients with a wide variety of psychological problems. I am a Full Professor at the University of Regina and Director of the Clinical Psychology Program that is accredited by the Canadian Psychological Association. In addition, I run the Psychology Training Clinic that provides services to clients in the community while offering students valuable training experiences.

My research is concentrated in two main areas. My first passion is the study of how psychological factors influence health. A second area of research about which I am very enthusiastic is the study of health care quality and ways to improve it. My research has been funded by the Canadian Health Services Research Foundation and the Canadian Institute of Health Research. I have published 45 articles and chapters and given 35 conference presentations.

A TYPICAL WEEK

On Monday morning I began writing a paper on the health care experiences and psychological and physical functioning of patients with congestive heart failure. This included interview and questionnaire data from 68 patients that were collected six months after discharge from hospital. In the afternoon, during my office hours several graduate and undergraduate students stopped by to discuss upcoming assignments. I also met with a student interested in pursuing graduate studies and advised her on strategies to improve her chances of admission to graduate school. I spent the rest of the afternoon teaching a graduate course in psychological assessment.

On Tuesday a doctoral student and I conducted an intake assessment at the Psychology Training Clinic on a client who is suffering from depression. This involved conducting a 90-minute interview and having the client complete several questionnaires. Then I conducted clinical supervision by watching a videotape of a student conducting therapy with a client who is suffering from generalized anxiety disorder and discussing the strengths of the session and directions for future sessions. I then drove to a nearby pool to watch my son and his 2nd grade class swim. Later in the afternoon, I gave a lecture on eating disorders to an undergraduate class in abnormal psychology. After this, I spent several hours marking exams.

On Wednesday morning I saw a client whose primary problem is chronic pain that has lead to depression as well as marital problems. After the interview, I drafted a report for the Workers' Compensation Board recommending that he receive psychological services to address the depression and marital problems that are now interfering with his ability to focus on his recovery from the injury and return to work. In the afternoon I chaired a clinical committee meeting to review student progress through the program. I also had a conference call with colleagues in Saskatoon to talk about the training of psychologists in Saskatchewan.

On Thursday I revised a clinical program policy manual and brochure for graduate students. I also contacted community psychologists to discuss future practicum placements. In the afternoon, I updated and then gave a lecture on personality disorders to my class on abnormal psychology. After this I reviewed a manuscript for a scholarly journal.

On Friday morning I ran a group for older adults in which I demonstrated various relaxation strategies to cope with pain. This is part of a research project in which my colleagues and I are exploring the effectiveness of pain management groups for helping older adults cope with chronic pain. In the afternoon, I met with my graduate students to talk about their research projects. I also spent several hours designing a new study that I hope to carry out on how to help people who are extremely worried about their health. Later in the afternoon, I met with several health care professionals and decision-makers in Regina to talk about the results of a study examining the psychological, physical, and social needs of 234 older adults receiving home care. Finally, I spent several hours completing a financial statement showing how I have spent funding that has been provided to me to conduct my research.

PROFILE BOX 2.3

DR. MAGGIE MAMEN

Dr. Maggie Mamen

I trained as a secretary before beginning studies in psychology at Carleton University. Studying psychology at the same time as having children (one per degree), I learned how to draft papers and research proposals in my head while caring for my family, doing laundry, and preparing meals. I completed a full-year pre-doctoral internship at the Children's Hospital of Eastern Ontario and was employed there after my graduation. I subsequently worked at the former Carleton Board of Education for several years before establishing a multidisciplinary private practice with colleagues from psychology, education, speech-language pathology, social work, and psychiatry. I was appointed to the Ontario Board of Examiners in Psychology in 1990, and was the first elected President of the College of Psychologists of Ontario in 1993–94. My current clinical work is primarily with families, children with learning, emotional, or behaviour problems, and adolescents, while my passions are writing and making presentations to a wide variety of audiences.

A TYPICAL WEEK

Three days each week are full clinical days, including intakes, assessments, feedback sessions, and therapy. Once a month, my colleagues and I have a brown-bag, professional development lunch so that we can stay abreast of the latest developments in research, assessment materials, and areas of general interest, as well as sharing challenging cases for collegial advice and support. The remaining two weekdays are spent on paperwork, handling requests for presentations, consulting with other professionals, scoring assessment protocols, meeting with schools or attending case conferences, catching up with a week's worth of phone messages, mail, bills, administrative issues, and generally emerging from under a pile of files, with always some time set aside for exercise and walking the dogs. Weekends and evenings are for catching up with e-mail, writing reports, or more creative projects such as articles for magazines, or working on a new book, along with frequent presentations, seminars, and workshops for professionals and/or parents. I love these opportunities to advocate for the profession, and to reach a wide audience, as well as to indulge my extraverted need to perform.

In order to stay in touch with, and give back to, the profession, twice a year I chair oral examination teams for the College of Psychologists of Ontario. I find this so educational that I include it as part of my ongoing Quality Assurance program. In addition, I chair Pre-Hearing Conferences for the Discipline Committee of the College as part of the alternate dispute resolution process dealing with the small number of individuals who violate our professional standards of practice. This is again educational, albeit in a different way, and has made me acutely aware of our collective responsibility for ensuring that our colleagues practise legally, ethically, and morally so that the public is protected. Supervision of psychologists or psychological associates preparing for registration is a wonderful opportunity to work with some of the finest young practitioners in town, and constantly restores my faith in the ongoing viability of our profession.

The joys of private practice are endless. Quite apart from the ability to work my own hours with a wonderful group of colleagues and motivated clients, there is the opportunity to practise without being inhibited by "institutional correctness." There is something incredibly humbling about collecting fees directly from the individuals we serve. It makes me extraordinarily aware of and sensitive to the need to collaborate closely with clients to ensure that appropriate goals are set and that whatever is invested in the therapeutic process is wisely spent. Having been trained in the scientist-practitioner model, I am constantly plagued by unanswered research questions. There is, unfortunately, little opportunity for research in my private practice. Over the years, I have learned three important lessons from my clients: that the more I know, the more I know what I don't know; that human beings are capable of extraordinary fortitude and resilience; and that I need to remind myself that I am simply "hired help."

Assessment and Diagnosis

It is virtually impossible to be a clinical psychologist and not do some form of psychological assessment. As you can see in the profile boxes, all three psychologists spend part of their time conducting psychological assessments and diagnoses. Most commonly assessment activities involve evaluating the psychological functioning of an individual or a relationship (such as a couple, a parent-child relationship, or a family). Some assessments focus on the way a social unit functions (such as interactions within and between departments of an agency, or between an agency and the recipients of the agency's services). The precise nature of the assessment activities depends, to a large part, on the purpose of the assessment. Let's take an example of a psychologist who wants to be able to judge with confidence whether seven-year-old Joshua has behaviour problems that are serious enough to justify placement in a special service. The psychologist may focus on whether Joshua's behaviour meets criteria for a diagnosis of oppositional defiant disorder. If, however, the psychologist is conducting an assessment prior to beginning parent training, the focus of the assessment will be to gain a precise understanding of the behaviours that the parents wish to change (such as the intensity, frequency, and duration of defiant behaviour) and contextual variables that affect Joshua's behaviour (such as parental consistency, marital conflict, or the presence of a replacement teacher in the classroom). Thus, if the goal of the assessment is to determine eligibility for a service, assessment may be the sole function of the psychologist's service. On the other hand, even when the primary service is psychotherapy, assessment plays an important role in the planning, monitoring, and evaluation of the intervention.

In the later chapters on assessment you will see the ingenuity with which psychologists have developed scientifically sound assessment tools to assess a host of psychological phenomena in infants, children, adults, and the elderly. Generally speaking these tools fall into one of several categories that will be discussed in Chapters 6, 7, and 8: interviews, observational systems, intellectual and cognitive measures, self-report measures, and projective measures. Moreover, in reaching a clinical formulation most clinical psychologists combine data obtained from a number of assessment methods such as interviewing, self-report measures, observations, performance (or skill) tasks, and reports from informants other than the patient (see Chapter 9).

As you will see in Chapter 5, regardless of the precise form and purpose of the assessment activity, all assessments share a primary goal of aiding the understanding of the person's current level of psychosocial functioning. Without a sense of how the person is doing now, in terms of such important human variables as emotions, behaviours, symptoms, and relationships, it is simply not possible to provide meaningful psychological services. However, as you will learn in Chapter 9, psychological assessment is much more than just testing: it involves the collection of multiple types of data that are then integrated into a coherent formulation of the problem experienced by the person or groups being assessed.

In many instances, formulating a diagnosis is part of the assessment process. As we describe in more detail in Chapter 3, diagnoses provide a concise statement about the nature of a person's disorder or dysfunction. Having established a diagnosis, the psychologist can efficiently search the scientific literature to update his or her knowledge of the disorder's etiology, course, prognosis, and beneficial treatments. In Canada and the United States the dominant diagnostic system used by clinical psychologists is the *Diagnostic and Statistical Manual of Mental Disorders* (DSM) published by the American Psychiatric Association, of which the most recent version is the DSM-IV-TR. Other countries have adopted the World Health Organization's (WHO) *International Classification of Diseases* (ICD) and the *Clinical Modification* of the system (which includes codes for specific diseases and disorders). The ICD is now in its tenth edition (ICD-10), but the Clinical Modification (i.e., ICD-10-CM) was under development and had not yet been released for clinical use at the time of the writing of this text.

Intervention

Survey data from Hunsley and Lefebvre (1990) and Norcross and colleagues (1997) indicate that the average clinical psychologist devoted over a third of his or her professional time to providing psychotherapy. Canadian clinical psychologists most frequently provided individual therapy (with 86% of psychologists offering these services to adults and 59% of psychologists offering services to children and adolescents). Marital/couples therapy and family therapy were also provided by a large number of Canadian psychologists (60% and 47%, respectively), with group therapy less frequently offered (22% of psychologists offered group therapy for adults, 10% offered group therapy for children or adolescents). As we describe in Chapters 12 and 13, there is a wealth of evidence to suggest that psychotherapy can be effective in treating a wide range of health problems. As you will see in the profile boxes, the proportion of time devoted to psychotherapy varies across the different employment settings. However, as we discussed in Chapter 1, psychologists are not the only health care professionals who offer psychotherapeutic services. Survey data from the Canadian province of Ontario indicated that of those people aged 15 to 64 years who sought health care services for mental health reasons only 10% were seen by psychologists (Lin, Goering, Offord, Campbell, & Boyle, 1996). Many of the services provided by medical practitioners involved the provision of psychoactive medications, a form of treatment that cannot be provided by most psychologists (see **Viewpoint Box 2.1** for more details).

VIEWPOINT BOX 2.1

SHOULD PSYCHOLOGISTS SEEK PRESCRIPTION PRIVILEGES?

In the United States some states and federal government departments allow psychologists to prescribe psychoactive medication. The American debate around prescription privileges has been intense. Advocates of prescription privileges for psychologists argue that there is strong evidence of brain-behaviour links, so that a biological approach to the treatment of psychological disorders is not incompatible with psychological training; second, they note psychologists can be at least as competent as other health care professionals in prescribing medication for psychological disorders. They highlight the fact that most psychoactive medications are prescribed by general practitioners whose training in mental health issues is limited to a few weeks of placement with a psychiatrist. They suggest that underserved segments of the population such as those in rural areas and the elderly could benefit from the extension of prescription privileges to psychologists.

Physicians have strongly opposed the extension of prescription privileges to psychologists, citing the importance of full medical training to prepare the practitioner to understand the impact of psychoactive medication on other physical systems. Within psychology critics argue that psychologists' distinctive expertise is in the development and application of empirically based assessment and psychological interventions. They express concern that the inclusion of adequate training in psychopharmacology would inevitably come at the expense of training in psychological issues.

To date, the Canadian Psychological Association has not taken a position on this issue. Within Canada, the strongest support for prescription privileges comes from the Canadian Psychological Association Section on Psychopharmacology. Canadian critics of prescription privileges such as psychologists David Dozois and Keith Dobson have highlighted that the Canadian Code of Ethics encourages psychologists to work in a collaborative fashion with other health care professionals rather than attempting to duplicate their services. Fundamental differences between the American and Canadian health care systems also play a role in the debate. Under Canada's publicly funded health care system, it is likely that the federal government would have concerns that additional numbers of practitioners eligible to prescribe expensive psychopharmacological treatments would contribute to mushrooming health care costs (Romanow & Marchildon, 2003).

In popular movies or television series, psychotherapy is often presented as a life-long commitment to frequent treatment sessions with a psychologist or psychiatrist. In reality the majority of people who receive psychotherapy attend fewer than 10 sessions. A large minority of clients come for only one or two sessions, and the median number of therapy sessions is in the range of 5 to 13. This is true internationally, across clients presenting dramatically different problems. Furthermore these basic data about psychotherapy have stayed remarkably stable over several decades (Phillips, 1991).

As the expression "talk therapy" implies, psychotherapy uses verbal means for the therapist to promote change. But what actually happens in psychotherapy? An innovative survey examined this question. In a web-based questionnaire the Practice Directorate of the American

Actors Billy Crystal as psychotherapist Dr. Ben Sobel, and Robert De Niro as his client Paul Vitti, in *Analyze That*.

Psychological Association (APA, 2003) asked 241 clinical psychologists questions just after they completed a psychotherapy session. Virtually all psychologists reported discussing current stressors related to the client's problems and interpersonal relationships or relationship patterns. The most commonly reported techniques (reported by more than 75% of respondents) were to identify or challenge thoughts, relate thoughts to feelings, focus on affect by validating or labelling emotions, gather information, and guide or direct the client.

As we indicated in Chapter 1, different theoretical approaches to psychotherapy emphasize different aspects of human experience in understanding and treating psychological distress and disorder. The dominant approaches include psychodynamic, cognitive-behavioural, experiential, and interpersonal (which, in some instances, is closely related to psychodynamic). Additionally a number of clinicians describe their orientation as eclectic or integrative, meaning that they blend concepts and strategies from two or more approaches. **Table 2.2** presents details on the theoretical orientation of clinical psychologists in North America. The general picture suggests that a cognitive-behavioural approach is the most popular single orientation, although substantial numbers of clinical psychologists describe their practice as eclectic. This conclusion is consistent with results from a survey of psychological treatment services offered in hospitals in Canada (Humble et al.,

2004). Respondents to the survey were asked to rank order the theoretical orientations of psychologists working in hospital settings. Across the country, cognitive-behavioural treatments were the most popular, with 46% of hospitals offering such therapies as the main therapeutic approach. A significant minority of hospitals (16%) offered treatment described as eclectic. Relatively few hospitals reported that the treatment approach was predominantly psychodynamic (6.5%) or experiential (6.5%).

TABLE 2.2   Theoretical Orientations

Orientation	Canada		United States	
	Hunsley & Lefebvre (1990)	Warner (1991)	Norcross et al. (1997)	APA (2003)
Cognitive-Behavioural	46%	37%	37%	28%
Psychodynamic	19%	11%	18%	17%
Experiential	15%	11%	4%	<5%
Interpersonal	—	—	4%	<5%
Eclectic	48%	33%	27%	45%

Note: In some cases the total reported exceeds 100% because psychologists were permitted to indicate more than one orientation in the survey.

Does the theoretical orientation actually make a difference in what therapists do in sessions? Although the evidence from the APA (2003) on-line survey revealed a number of commonalities in therapy sessions across clinical psychologists, clear orientation-related differences were also apparent. For example, compared with psychodynamic clinicians, cognitive-behavioural clinicians were significantly more likely to spend time providing psychoeducation by informing the client about the nature of the presenting problem; they were also more likely to encourage the client to ask questions, to collaboratively set an agenda for the session with the client, to encourage the client to engage in specific activities (including homework assignments to be done between therapy sessions), and to teach coping skills. In contrast, compared with cognitive-behavioural clinicians, those espousing a psychodynamic approach were significantly more likely to explore the client's childhood experiences, to relate the client's reactions to the therapist to patterns in the client's family of origin, and to explore dysfunctional patterns of behaviour and relationship expectations.

Prevention

You may remember from Chapter 1 that prevention activities are a relatively new addition to the skill set of clinical psychologists. Accordingly, only a small percentage of clinical psychologists devote professional time to this activity. Prevention services are categorized according to the stage in the course of a disorder at which they are introduced. Primary prevention involves the prevention of a disease or disorder before it actually occurs. Secondary prevention is designed to reduce the recurrence of a disease or disorder that has already developed and been diagnosed. Tertiary prevention refers to efforts to reduce the overall disability that results from the disease or disorder.

You will learn more about prevention in Chapter 10. Generally speaking, prevention activities tend to focus on either reducing risk factors or enhancing protective factors. Risk factors are characteristics of an individual or of an individual's life circumstances that increase the likelihood of the development of a disorder. For example, smoking, being overweight, having high cholesterol levels, and having a family history of heart disease are all risk factors for the development of heart disease. Protective factors, on the other hand, are individual or environmental characteristics that lessen the likelihood of eventually developing a disease or disorder. Regular exercise and a diet low in saturated fats are considered protective factors that reduce the risk of developing heart disease.

Prevention efforts are usually based in community settings, as opposed to institutional settings such as hospitals or private clinical psychology practices. Prevention programs can be offered to large groups of people at a time, such as educating parents about issues around bullying in the schoolyard, or educating parents of at-risk children in effective behaviour management strategies. Alternatively, prevention programs may be offered in a one-on-one format, as is often done in teaching life skills to individuals already diagnosed with severe mental illness. Most commonly the role of the clinical psychologist is to develop, implement, and evaluate the prevention programs. The prevention program is often delivered by mental health professionals such as nurses, counsellors, or social workers.

Consultation

Clinical psychologists often act in the role of consultant. Providing information, advice, and recommendations about how best to assess, understand, or treat a client is called **clinical consultation**. Both Dr. Mamen and Dr. Mothersill devote considerable time to this activity. When the focus of the consultation is related to developing a prevention or intervention program, evaluating how well an organization is doing in providing a health care or related service, or providing an opinion on policies on health care services set by an organization, the terms **organizational consultation** or "community consultation" are typically used.

Throughout the history of the profession, clinical psychologists have offered clinical consultation. As a member of a multidisciplinary team, a clinical psychologist receives requests to provide guidance about a patient who is under the care of another professional. For example, one of us was asked to suggest how hospital staff could best handle an elderly, dementing patient's confusion and growing anger over his inability to understand what was being served to him in his meals. Another request came from a child daycare centre that wanted help in dealing with a disruptive two-year-old. It is a common (and highly ethical) practice for clinical psychologists to

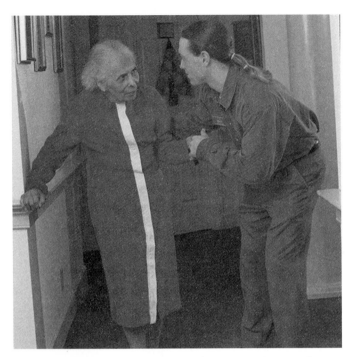

Clinical psychologists may be asked to provide guidance about a patient who is under the care of another professional.

request an opinion from a fellow clinical psychologist on how to handle a particularly difficult or challenging assessment or treatment issue that has arisen.

Consultation to agencies often falls into one of several categories: needs assessment, program development, program evaluation, and policy consultation. Needs assessments are required to determine the extent of an unmet health care need in an identified population. A clinical psychologist might be asked, for example, to conduct a needs assessment to determine whether there are mechanisms to ensure that new immigrants are aware of health care services available in their community. Once a needs assessment has established the scope of the need, a psychologist might be hired to develop a program to educate the target population about the available services. The final step involves determining whether or not the program was successful in achieving its goal, by conducting a program evaluation. The program evaluation assesses the extent to which the program was carried out as intended and the extent to which the program objectives were met. Another type of consultation, policy consultation, focuses on determining whether an agency's policy is congruent with its mission or is consistent with professional standards or scientific evidence. For example, a clinical psychologist might be engaged to provide an opinion on the suitability of a health care company's policy regarding reimbursement of psychotherapy services to health care providers.

Research

All clinical psychologists are trained to conduct and evaluate research. University coursework provides initial training in research methods that is put into practice by conducting a doctoral dissertation. Moreover, the profession's ethical codes require clinical psychologists to continue to attend to practice-relevant research throughout their professional careers. Whereas all clinical psychologists should be informed research consumers, only a minority of clinical psychologists regularly engage in producing research. Drs. Mamen and Mothersill both devote time to keeping up with the latest research and in disseminating this knowledge to other professionals and to the public. In the past, much of the research in clinical psychology came from university settings and was conducted or supervised by clinical psychology faculty members in departments of psychology or in medical schools. Faculty members in university are typically expected to devote their professional time to research and teaching. With the growing recognition of the need for science-based health care in many parts of the world, it is now increasingly common for clinical psychologists in publicly funded institutions such as hospitals to devote part of their workload to research. In Chapter 15 you will read about Dr. Michael Vallis, a hospital-based clinical health psychologist whose workload includes research as well as the provision of psychological services. Because of psychologists' extensive training in research methodology and statistics, in some instances hospital-based clinical psychologists are employed primarily as researchers, with psychological service delivery as a secondary component of their work. Such psychologists may actually have a greater proportion of their workload devoted to research than most academics do. A survey of clinical psychology faculty members in American universities (Himelein & Putnam, 2001) found that conducting and supervising research accounted for only 17% of professors' work time. Dr. Hadjistavropoulos, who is a prolific researcher, describes devoting almost a third of her time to research. Because of the central role that empirical evidence plays in guiding the provision of psychological services, some private practitioners have made it a priority to be regularly involved in research activities.

Clinical psychologists conduct research on an impressive range of topics including normal human functioning, psychopathology, assessment, intervention, and/or prevention. Let's consider examples of the types of research conducted by clinical psychologists. In studying normal human functioning, clinical psychologists conduct research on personality, memory processes, intimate relationships, parenting, child development, and aging. Clinical psychologists carry out research aimed at improving our understanding of the nature and causes of conditions as varied as sexual pain disorders, depression in the elderly, disruptive behaviour disorders, pathological gambling, and insomnia. Measures of perfectionism, anxiety sensitivity, infant pain, trauma, and scores of other phenomena have been developed in recent years. With respect to prevention and intervention, clinical psychologists study resilience in the face of adversity, treatments for marital conflict, early intervention strategies for childhood anxiety disorders, factors that predict premature termination from therapy, and patterns of mental health service use in various countries. To help you locate clinical psychology research, **Appendix 1** provides an overview of the major journals in the field.

Teaching and Supervision

Full-time professors in clinical psychology engage in different types of teaching activities. They typically teach both undergraduate and graduate courses in psychology, and in some programs they also supervise graduate students in the provision of psychological services. Himelein and Putnam (2001) found that these different teaching activities accounted for 26%, 11%, and 4%, respectively, of the average American clinical psychology professor's work time.

COURSES

The type of courses taught depends on the professor's areas of specialization and expertise. Undergraduate courses commonly taught by clinical psychology professors include psycho-pathology, personality theories, human adjustment, interpersonal processes, psychology of women, family psychology, geropsychology, and, of course, introduction to clinical psychology. In addition, these professors teach advanced courses to small groups of graduate students on top-ics such as professional ethics and issues, psychological assessment, psychotherapy, multicultural counselling, psychopathology, clinical research methods, program evaluation, and health psych-ology. Dr. Hadjistavropoulos devotes a significant part of her workload to undergraduate and graduate teaching.

University courses are taught by both full-time and part-time professors. In most univer-sities some clinical psychologists who work in the community are employed as part-time instructors and teach one or two undergraduate courses each year. Dr. Mothersill is a great exam-ple of a community psychologist who makes a substantial contribution to teaching. Clinical psychology programs also hire these professionals to teach specialized graduate courses in areas not covered by full-time faculty (e.g., neuropsychology, rehabilitation psychology). Psychologists employed in hospital settings often contribute to the training of both psychology and medical students by offering seminars or workshops on select aspects of clinical psychology.

CINICAL SUPERVISION

A central part of the training of clinical psychologists involves conducting psychological assess-ment and intervention. After taking advanced courses in these topics, graduate students provide services to the public under the close supervision of licensed clinical psychologists. Clinical supervision is offered in either a group or individual format. This first clinical experience under the supervision of a licensed psychologist is called a **practicum**. Some clinical psychology pro-grams operate an in-house psychology training clinic in which faculty members supervise students in the provision of services such as intellectual assessment, diagnostic evaluation, indi-vidual therapy, group therapy, and family therapy. Dr. Hadjistavropoulos has recently established a state-of-the-art training clinic at the University of Regina. All training programs, including those that offer in-house training, rely on the active participation of clinical psychologists in the com-munity in providing training opportunities for graduate students. Within the clinical psychology community, there are strong links between university-based training programs and community-based training in diverse settings. Dr. Hadjistavropoulos' duties include establishing these links so that students can benefit from the wealth of training opportunities in the community. Thus clinical psychologists in general medical hospitals, residential treatment settings for adolescents, rehabilitation centres, and psychiatric hospitals may all contribute to the supervision and training of future clinical psychologists. As an example Dr. Mothersill is actively engaged in the supervision of both practicum students and interns.

In most Canadian clinical psychology programs graduate students obtain between 1,200 and 3,000 hours of practicum training during their graduate training. Following the completion of all other aspects of their training (with the possible exception of the defence of a doctoral thesis), students then complete a full-time, year-long **internship** in which they are supervised in the provision of psychological services in settings such hospitals, workers' compensation boards, or community agencies. In their survey of clinical supervision in Canadian academic and community service settings (mainly hospitals), Johnston and Stewart (2000) found that practicum students were supervised primarily by academic clinical psychologists whereas interns were more likely to be supervised by clinical psychologists in service settings.

RESEARCH SUPERVISION

The guidance provided by the research supervisor (who may be a psychologist working outside the university) is evident at many stages of the student's program. Initially supervision involves assisting graduate students in understanding the research literature in a chosen area and then conceptualizing the research that the student will conduct as part of his or her degree. Before the research is conducted, the supervisor ensures that it will be done in an ethical manner and is approved by an institutional research ethics board. The supervisor typically provides input on study design, sampling considerations, measurement selection, statistical analysis, and, finally, the interpretation and presentation of the research. Dr. Hadjistavropoulos devotes many hours a week to research supervision.

Dr. Hadjistavropoulos in the state-of-the-art psychology training clinic at the University of Regina.

Administration

Of necessity, most clinical psychologists are involved in administrative activities. In a solo private practice this includes the activities necessary to maintain an efficient and professional business, such as bookkeeping and supervision of personnel. Dr. Mamen notes that many hours are devoted to these responsibilities. In institutional settings such as hospitals and universities, psychologists are expected to contribute to the overall running of the institution by involvement in committees and by assuming management positions. For example, clinical psychologists often serve on the research ethics boards of institutions. In hospital settings they may sit on committees dealing with research, quality assurance, and community relations. Dr. Mothersill is engaged in various multidisciplinary committees within the hospital and at a regional level. Within universities, clinical psychologists often serve on committees for the hiring of new professors, the running of the undergraduate psychology program, and the selection of new graduate students. Management positions in universities are likely to include director of the clinical psychology program (as described by Dr. Hadjistravropoulos), director of the training clinic, chair of the psychology department, and possibly dean of the faculty. Clinical psychologists in hospital or related medical settings may be found in a range of management positions including discipline leader within a mental health team, chief psychologist in a department of psychology, or director of an entire service (e.g., rehabilitation services, child mental health services).

Clinical psychologists often spend considerable time participating in committees dealing with research, quality assurance, community relations, or the overall running of an institution.

EMPLOYMENT SETTINGS

So far, we have mentioned a range of work settings in which clinical psychologists might be employed. To concretely illustrate this, **Table 2.3** summarizes the results of surveys examining the employment settings of Canadian and American clinical psychologists. In both countries the number of clinical psychologists like Dr. Mamen working in independent practice has grown considerably the past three decades. Moreover, even those psychologists employed in an institutional setting like Dr. Mothersill frequently have part-time private practices: Hunsley and Lefebvre (1990) found that 40% of Canadian clinical psychologists listed private practice as a secondary work setting.

TABLE 2.3   Employment Settings for Clinical Psychologists

Setting	Canada[a]	USA[b]
Private Practice	33	40
General Hospital	12	4
Psychiatric Hospital	10	5
Outpatient Clinic	19	4
University Psychology Dept.	8	15

[a] Hunsley & Lefebvre (1990); [b] Norcross, Karg, & Prochaska (1997)

In Canada, a large number of clinical psychologists are employed in hospitals or outpatient clinics. Historically these settings were linked to departments of psychiatry, rehabilitation services for war veterans, or pediatric services (Hearn & Evans, 1993). Currently within hospitals, traditional organizational structures based on departments have been replaced by program models in which health professionals, including psychologists, are appointed to a specific program or service and by matrix models in which psychologists have responsibility to both a specific program and to general psychological services. A survey by Humble and colleagues (2004) found that, currently, only a fifth of Canadian hospitals have an identified department of psychology. These researchers also found that, although the ratio of full-time psychologists to hospital beds had improved from 1:131 in 1992 to 1:53 in 1999, one-third of hospitals did not employ a full-time clinical psychologist.

The survey data we have presented do not include information on a number of alternative employment opportunities for clinical psychologists. For example, clinical psychologists are often employed in residential treatment clinics, correctional and forensic settings, government agencies focused on personnel selection and training, and private research and consulting firms. Some clinical psychologists with expertise in public policy are employed in government ministries and departments, public health organizations, or research granting agencies.

THE TWO PILLARS OF CLINICAL PSYCHOLOGY: SCIENCE AND ETHICS

As we emphasized in Chapter 1, the profession of clinical psychology is founded on the application of the results of empirical research to address emotional, behavioural, and neurological problems. In all their activities, whether providing psychological services to the public, planning new research endeavours, teaching undergraduate courses, or providing input on health care policy matters, it is crucial that clinical psychologists maintain their knowledge of research relevant to their activities. As you will learn in this section, ethical codes of conduct require that clinical psychologists maintain their knowledge of the scientific foundation of their professional activities. All three psychologists profiled in this chapter devote regular time to keeping up to date with research in their field. Ethical principles set out fundamental guidelines for the way that psychologists work professionally. They include: respect for people, the responsible provision of services, the maintenance of integrity in professional relationships, and professional responsibilities to society. In all their professional activities clinical psychologists must always remain aware of the importance of questioning one's services. Questions such as "What is the evidence for what I am planning to do?" and "What are the relative risks and benefits to my patients (or students, or research participants) of the course of action I am considering?" must always be foremost in the mind of a clinical psychologist.

Most clinical psychologists agree that professional services should be informed by research evidence. Disagreement starts to creep in when the discussion turns to just "how" the research should inform (or determine) practice and just "what" constitutes research evidence. You may recall that in Chapter 1 we described McFall's manifesto for a science of clinical psychology, which urged that no service should be provided unless there is empirical evidence that it is valid and effective. At the other extreme, some psychologists take a position that they should simply be mindful of general, basic research findings on human functioning. The "what" issue ranges from the position that all personal and clinical experience should be considered research evidence to the position that only the results of experimental studies should constitute the knowledge base of clinical psychology. Of course, very few psychologists hold opinions represented by these extremes; nevertheless, there is considerable variability in how the role of science is interpreted. For example, Peterson (2004) suggested that we should accept that some of the problems facing clinicians cannot be studied by scientific methods. Accordingly, he argued that we must rely on intuition and experience in such cases. In response to this, Nathan (2004) suggested that one must be aware of the potential harm that may occur to patients when there is no science to guide practice. Rather than relying on intuition in such situations, he countered that the best practice in such a scenario would be to offer no service rather than risk providing the wrong or harmful treatment.

Despite the large body of evidence available to clinical psychologists, science cannot provide a research-based solution for each situation confronted by a clinician. From our perspective, an evidence-based approach to clinical services involves the use of the evidence whenever it is available—however, when no evidence is available to guide services, the clinical psychologist can optimize services by maintaining a scientific frame of mind. This involves a systematic, questioning, and self-critical approach to determining the relevance of a service and then monitoring its effects to determine whether the outcome is primarily beneficial or harmful. Lilienfeld, Lynn, and Lohr (2003) suggested this requires the clinician to strike a balance between excessive open-mindedness (i.e., "anything goes") and excessive scepticism (i.e., "only proven services are acceptable"). Science is an evolving compilation of ideas, theories, and facts. Science is also a method of formulating and testing hypotheses. As you will see in Chapter 4, the same type of scientific thinking that influences methodological designs behind multi-million dollar treatment studies can also guide the clinical activities of each individual psychologist.

So what, exactly, is the problem with the call from Peterson (and many other clinical psychologists) for clinicians to use their intuition and experience to guide their work? Intuition is often described as a felt-sense about something that cannot be entirely described, put into words, or accounted for. From a scientific perspective, the problem with using intuition to guide service delivery is that, by definition, a systematic, questioning, and self-critical approach is the polar opposite of intuition. From a health care system perspective, there is another issue: how would you feel about a dentist, surgeon, or gynaecologist using intuition in providing services to you or to someone you care about? Imagine your reaction to a dentist who told you that she *felt* that fluoride treatments were not useful, a surgeon who said he had a *sense* of the tissue that needed to be

removed and so did not rely on laboratory analysis, or a gynaecologist who said she knew that some women find PAP tests difficult and *guessed* you looked healthy enough so would not bother with the test? Similarly, how would you feel on learning that a psychologist failed to provide a treatment that was known to be effective for a problem such as agoraphobia, explaining that he had a strong intuition that you would be better served by another approach? So what about relying on clinical experience? After all, it only seems reasonable to assume that experienced clinicians are better than novice clinicians, doesn't it? Unfortunately, this assumption is contradicted by most research on clinical psychologists and other health service providers. Numerous studies have shown that when given identical information, experienced clinicians are no better than clinicians-in-training at making accurate,

It is not acceptable for a clinical psychologist to rely on intuition, rather than empirical evidence, in treating a problem such as arachnophobia.

valid decisions (Garb, 1998). The main reason that experience does not necessarily guarantee quality service is that it is exceedingly difficult to learn from clinical experience. Clinical psychologists must frequently deal with complex and ambiguous situations in which they must make decisions and, in almost all instances, they receive no feedback about the accuracy of these decisions (Garb & Boyle, 2003). Without the possibility of corrective feedback, it is extremely unlikely those poor practices can be detected and stopped or that good practices can be identified and enhanced. Therefore, a scientifically oriented clinical psychologist must be constantly aware of the need to check his or her assumptions and activities.

We often rely on the basic assumptions of a theoretical orientation to guide our clinical practice. That is, of course, the whole point of a theoretical orientation: it directs the clinician's attention to phenomena and to possible explanations that are deemed most relevant and it diverts attention from aspects of the client's experience that are deemed irrelevant. It must be remembered, however, that theories of human functioning are essentially maps and that, to truly know if the map is accurate, it must be put to the test. Sometimes, theories are wrong, and the failure to test a theory can have serious consequences. You may recall from previous psychology courses how Freud became puzzled at the number of young female patients who reported sexual abuse. It seemed inconceivable to him that so many women had been abused as children, so he developed an alternative explanation or theory that these women were expressing sexual fantasies. Freud's theories carried great conviction and were accepted as correct without scientific testing. Surveys conducted many years later revealed that alarming numbers of children of both genders are, indeed, sexually abused.

Fortunately, other theorists have permitted their theories to be scientifically tested. The best illustration of this is the work of Carl Rogers. As you learned in Chapter 1, Carl Rogers proposed that therapy must provide a supportive environment in which clients reconnect with aspects of themselves and thereby discover their potential for growth. Rogers balanced his own strong convictions with powerful advocacy of the need for research into psychotherapy. He masked the identity of his clients, then provided researchers with transcripts of his therapy sessions. Truax (1966) analysed sessions of a successful long-term therapy case to determine whether client-centred therapy's key therapeutic condition of *unconditional positive regard* occurred and, if it did, whether it was linked to positive client outcomes. Contradicting Rogers' own model, Truax found that Rogers did not provide positive regard unconditionally. Instead, (consciously or unconsciously) he employed empathy, acceptance, and directiveness as reinforcers of selective client behaviour. In other words, consistent with basic learning models, Rogers *shaped* client behaviour over the course of the therapy and used the reinforcers of empathy and acceptance to bring about client change. So, for example, he paid more attention when the client talked about emotions than he did when the client talked about other issues. This is, of course, important information about how a therapist can help a client change, but it also illustrates that the client-centred condition of *unconditional* positive regard is not likely to be a key aspect of successful treatment. We owe a debt of gratitude to Carl Rogers for being more concerned to learn about the process of change than he was about promoting his own views. Adopting a scientific position involves putting our ideas to the test and risking the discovery that some ideas that make a lot of sense to us, may, in fact, be wrong. The best scientists are driven by curiosity that is twinned with openness to input and a willingness to be proved wrong.

Basing clinical psychology services on research is crucially important, but so is the need to provide services ethically. According to Sinclair (1993), the modern interest in developing ethical codes for research and professional services can be traced to the Nuremberg war crime trials that occurred after the Second World War. After the horrific discovery of atrocities conducted by the Nazis under the guise of medical science, a code of ethics in medical research was developed. This code was the first to incorporate the idea that the person who is being experimented on must understand what is being done and must agree to participate. This concept of **informed consent** now applies both to patients and to research participants and is the cornerstone of professional and research ethical codes. The American Psychological Association developed a code of ethics for psychologists shortly after the Second World War and has revised it several times, most recently in 2002. Within Canada, there was agreement to adopt the early versions of the APA code of ethics and it was not until the 1980s that a uniquely Canadian code of ethics for psychologists was developed. The Canadian code was designed to reflect Canadian legal traditions, apply to all areas of psychology, and serve as a teaching tool.

The *Canadian Code of Ethics for Psychologists* (Canadian Psychological Association, 2000) is now in its third edition and is intended to provide guidance to all members of the CPA in all of the capacities in which a psychologist might function, including research, clinical service, teaching, consultation, administration, and social policy activities. The same ethical standards are expected of psychologists in all their roles. There are four ethical principles in the *Code*: Respect for the Dignity of Persons, Responsible Caring, Integrity in Relationships, and Responsibility to Society. A definition is provided for each principle and a list of specific ethical standards illustrate the application of the principle. These standards include minimal expectations about the attitudes and behaviours of Canadian psychologists performing their work as psychologists. Two examples illustrate the nature of these standards. Under the principle of Respect for the Dignity of Persons, there is a standard regarding non-discrimination. According to this standard, psychologists should not practise, condone, facilitate, or collaborate with any form of unjust discrimination. Under the principle of Responsible Caring, there is a standard regarding the maximizing of benefits: psychologists should select interventions that are relevant to the needs and characteristics of the client and that are likely to be efficacious based on established theory or empirical evidence. Psychologists also have an ethical obligation to ensure that their services are not affected by their own distress, an issue discussed in **Viewpoint Box 2.2**.

VIEWPOINT BOX 2.2

DISTRESS IN CLINICAL PSYCHOLOGISTS AND HOW THEY DEAL WITH IT

Ethical codes require psychologists to be self-aware and to ensure that they do not offer psychological services when their functioning is impaired. Just as any health professional should not offer services when laid low with incapacitating allergies or a vicious flu virus, psychologists should not offer psychological services when their own emotional health gets in the way of them doing their job effectively.

Are psychologists psychologically healthy?

Psychologists are not immune from the life events that affect everyone. Like everyone else, psychologists experience painful events such as the death of a loved one, serious illness, or accident. Psychologists are human—they sometimes doubt their professional competence, they have children who get into trouble, they argue with their partners, worry about their elderly parents, and feel lonely when they are away from their friends and loved ones for an extended time. Not surprisingly, in a survey of 522 practising psychologists, Sherman and Thelen (1998) found that the more life events psychologists experienced, the more impairment in professional roles they reported.

What kinds of work stress do psychologists face?

Like many health care professionals, psychologists face challenges in effectively managing their time, making sure that they find a balance between offering services, writing notes and reports, answering phone calls, supervising training activities, providing service to the profession, and engaging in continuing education to keep up to date with research advances in the field. Furthermore, the nature of their work may expose psychologists to particular stressors. People often wonder how psychologists cope with a professional life spent working with troubled clients who have experienced trauma or abuse, who are angry, sad, afraid, confused, or difficult to get along with. Sherman and Thelen reported that almost three-quarters of the psychologists who responded to their survey worked with difficult clients who had serious emotional problems or who were suicidal.

Are psychologists traumatized by their work?

It has been suggested that working with people who have experienced trauma can cause psychologists to experience symptoms such as intrusive thoughts, extreme distress, and changes in beliefs and attitudes. This phenomenon has been referred to as vicarious traumatization, burnout, compassion fatigue, and secondary traumatic stress. Although there has been a great deal of clinical attention to this phenomenon, there has been relatively little systematic research on the topic. A recent review by Sabin-Farrell and Turpin (2003) found evidence that mental health professionals have emotional responses to hearing traumatic material, but noted that these responses are a natural and short-term reaction. Some studies have found more intense psychological distress to be associated with the percentage of trauma survivors in the caseload and to being newer to that type of work. Research has not demonstrated evidence that working with trauma survivors is associated with changes in beliefs and attitudes.

How do psychologists cope?

Research has found that psychologists engage in a number of health-promoting activities. Work-related strategies include taking breaks during the workday, consulting with colleagues on difficult issues, practising good time management including scheduling time for paperwork and phone calls, and limiting the caseload in terms of both volume and in the types of clients seen. Other health-promoting activities included devoting time to hobbies, taking vacations, engaging in regular exercise, and taking part in church and spiritual activities. In dealing with personal and professional challenges, psychologists engage in constructive problem-solving. Psychologists also seek psychological services to address serious difficulties. So, just as a dentist needs to practise oral hygiene and have regular checkups, psychologists need to adopt healthy lifestyles and seek professional help when they encounter difficulties.

Several features of the *Code* set it apart from other codes of ethics for psychologists (Sinclair, 1998). First, all versions of the *Code* were developed from an analysis of the international and interdisciplinary literature on codes of ethics. Second, empirical methods were used to incorporate the knowledge of Canadian psychologists into the *Code*. Third, an explicit model of ethical decision-making is embedded in the *Code*, in contrast to other codes that rely primarily on absolute and prescriptive standards. So, instead of listing what psychologists should and should not do, the decision-making model promotes a way of thinking and a way to resolve apparent dilemmas or situations in which two principles seem to conflict. There is evidence that the model works well, as both psychologists and nonpsychologists are able to use the principles to achieve acceptable solutions to ethical dilemmas (Seitz & O'Neill, 1996). Fourth, there is differential weighting of the four ethical principles so that it is clear that Respect for the Dignity of Persons should usually be given greater weight in decision-making than the principle of Responsibility to

Society. Overall, there is evidence that, compared with other codes, the Canadian *Code* meets the goal of enhanced educational value and provides a clear rationale for decision-making (Malloy, Hadjistavropoulos, Douaud, & Smythe, 2002).

TRAINING IN CLINICAL PSYCHOLOGY

Psychology programs are extremely popular in all universities and colleges. The Canadian Association of University Teachers' data convincingly demonstrate that psychology is very attractive to students (CAUT, 2005). In 2001–2002, more than 26,000 students were enrolled in undergraduate psychology programs in Canada. The only fields of study attracting a greater number of students were business/commerce (with more than 36,000 students) and liberal arts and sciences/general studies/humanities (with more than 45,000 students). With 338 doctorates awarded in psychology in 2001, psychology was second only to engineering (480 doctorates) in terms of the number of doctorates awarded within a discipline (CAUT, 2005). The majority of students enrolled in psychology programs were women (79.3% in undergraduate programs and 73.5% in doctoral programs).

For many years clinical psychology has been the most popular field within graduate programs in psychology. Clinical psychology programs attract far more applications than do other graduate programs in psychology and they also graduate more students than do other psychology programs. The 2002 data for American universities show that 38% of Ph.D.s in psychology were in clinical psychology. In comparison, 15% of Ph.D.s awarded that year were in counselling psychology and 6% were in social psychology. Consistent with these percentages, 48% of those receiving a psychology Ph.D. in 2002 were employed in providing professional services, with 22% in research and development and another 22% in teaching (National Opinion Research Center, 2004).

Models of Training in Clinical Psychology

Three models guide the training of clinical psychologists: the scientist-practitioner model, the clinical scientist model, and the practitioner-scholar model. Doctoral programs awarding the Ph.D. in clinical psychology follow the scientist-practitioner model. This training model was first endorsed by the APA at a training conference held in Boulder, Colorado (Raimy, 1950) and is known as the *Boulder Model*. In the **scientist-practitioner model** graduate students must develop and demonstrate competencies in research and psychological service provision. As in any other Ph.D. program, students undertake original research and defend this research at a dissertation defence to demonstrate competency in research. Clinical skills, such as interviewing, test administration, assessment report writing, psychotherapy, and clinical consultation are learned in practicum training throughout the program. These skills are enhanced and refined during the internship year, a period in which the student is employed full-time to deliver psychological services under the supervision of licensed psychologists in an organized health care setting. The guiding philosophy underlying the scientist-practitioner model is that clinical psychologists should be capable of producing research and utilizing empirical evidence to guide their clinical services. There is substantial variability among scientist-practitioner oriented programs regarding the relative balance of science and practice in training and, more importantly, regarding the manner in which students are trained in the integration of science and practice. Some programs that strongly promote the development of research skills now identify themselves as espousing a **clinical scientist model**.

In the 1950s and 1960s most graduates from Boulder model programs were employed in practice settings with primary responsibility for clinical service. These psychologists very rarely conducted any research after completing the doctoral dissertation. At a training conference in Vail, Colorado participants expressed their dissatisfaction with the manner in which the scientist-practitioner model was applied in many training programs and developed a new model, the **practitioner-scholar model**, which was refined at subsequent conferences (Peterson et al., 1991). The practitioner-scholar model was designed to emphasize training in the clinical skills that most clinical psychologists would need in a service setting and to place less emphasis on research skills taught in Ph.D. programs. Programs training students in the practitioner-scholar model offered a different degree, the Psy.D. Over the years, many Psy.D. programs have developed research requirements that include considerable research training and the completion of a research project. Compared with PhD. Programs, Psy.D. programs place less emphasis on experimental designs and large sample analyses and greater emphasis on naturalistic designs and the evaluation of individual cases or service-oriented programs. Psy.D. programs are designed to train research consumers who are informed by science in their service activities but who do not need the skills to conduct research.

Ph.D. programs are offered by universities, whereas Psy.D. programs are found both at universities and, in the United States, in free-standing professional schools. Many in the profession have expressed concerns about the proliferation of the free-standing schools. Critics note factors that negatively affect the quality of students' training, including larger class sizes, lower financial support, and an overreliance on part-time instructors with little experience in research or teaching.

The main distinction between Ph.D. and Psy.D. models of training is the weight given to science and practice. Using survey data from APA accredited scientist-practitioner and practitioner-scholar programs, Cherry, Messenger, and Jacoby (2000) found distinct profiles consistent with the nature of each model. Students in both types of program had comparable amounts of clinical service delivery during their training, but students in scientist-practitioner programs were more involved in research than were students in practitioner-scholar programs. Similarly, graduates of both programs spent the majority of their professional time providing clinical services (around 60%), whereas graduates from scientist-practitioner programs spent more time than did graduates from practitioner-scholar programs in research activities (10% versus 2%). There are other important factors to consider, however, in selecting a training program. Norcross et al. (1998) compared the characteristics of clinical psychology programs offering Ph.D. and Psy.D. degrees. They found that Ph.D. programs accepted, on average, 6% of applicants, whereas Psy.D. programs accepted an average of 17% of applicants. Sixty-five percent of Ph.D. programs offered tuition fee waivers and assistantships (such as teaching or research assistantships); only 22% of Psy.D. programs did so. In terms of theoretical orientation, there are clear differences as well, with the dominant orientation in Ph.D. programs being cognitive-behavioural (48%) and the dominant orientation in Psy.D. programs being psychodynamic (36%).

Accreditation of Clinical Psychology Programs

The American Psychological Association (APA) was the first to develop an **accreditation** process designed to ensure that training programs maintain standards that meet the profession's expectations for the education of clinical psychologists. In 1969 the Ontario Psychological Association (OPA) developed accreditation guidelines for university programs and hospital internships in the province. By 1980, there were four Canadian university training programs accredited by APA and six Ontario university training programs accredited by OPA (Doyle, Edwards, & Robinson, 1993). In response to the growth of clinical psychology training throughout Canada, accreditation standards and processes were established by the CPA in 1984. A few years later, in recognition of CPA accreditation, OPA ceased its accreditation activities.

Until 1998, CPA had consistently reaffirmed the scientist-practitioner model of training as the only acceptable form of training in accredited clinical psychology programs. A change of policy occurred in 1998 with the approval by CPA of the accreditation of Canadian Psy.D. programs. The CPA accreditation requirements for such programs are very similar to those used for accrediting Ph.D. programs and stipulate that, to be eligible for accreditation, a Psy.D. program must be university based. Therefore both APA and CPA have accreditation criteria for evaluating the quality of clinical psychology training in both clinical training models. A program that receives accreditation from one or both associations has met, therefore, the high standards of training set by the profession and graduates from the program are likely to receive some of the best training available in clinical psychology. Students are strongly advised, therefore, to seek training in an accredited clinical psychology program. **Table 2.4** lists the clinical psychology programs in Canada that are accredited by CPA and/or APA. All these programs are Ph.D. programs. Although some Psy.D. programs have recently been developed in Quebec, none have been in operation for a sufficient period of time that would allow them to seek accreditation.

TABLE 2.4   Accredited Clinical Psychology Programs in Canada

University	Province	Accreditation
Concordia University	Quebec	APA & CPA
Dalhouse University	Nova Scotia	APA & CPA
McGill University (also has a CPA accredited Counselling Psychology program)	Quebec	APA & CPA
Queen's University	Ontario	APA & CPA
Simon Fraser University	British Columbia	APA & CPA
Université de Montréal (also has a CPA Accredited Clinical Neuropsychology program)	Quebec	CPA
Université Laval	Quebec	CPA
University of British Columbia (also has a CPA accredited Counselling Psychology program)	British Columbia	APA & CPA
University of Calgary	Alberta	CPA
University of Manitoba	Manitoba	APA & CPA
University of Ottawa	Ontario	APA & CPA
University of New Brunswick	New Brunswick	APA & CPA
University of Regina	Saskatchewan	CPA
University of Saskatchewan	Saskatchewan	APA & CPA
University of Toronto/ Ontario Institute for Studies in Education (this is a combined program in clinical and school psychology)	Ontario	APA
University of Victoria	British Columbia	APA & CPA
University of Waterloo	Ontario	APA & CPA
University of Western Ontario	Ontario	APA & CPA
University of Windsor	Ontario	APA & CPA
York University (there are two accredited programs, one in Clinical Developmental and one in Adult Clinical)	Ontario	APA & CPA

A major challenge facing all training programs is to ensure that students are prepared to provide psychological services to an increasingly diverse population. Statistics Canada predicts that by 2017, 1 out of every 5 people in Canada could be a member of a visible minority (Statistics Canada, 2005). Because the issue of diversity is influenced by geographical, historical, and sociological factors, there is no single way for clinical psychology training to address diversity training. As an example, think of the challenges for a training program in developing a curriculum and a set of training experiences to educate students in working with indigenous peoples. Such programs in Canada, the United States, and New Zealand would look very different for several reasons. One reason for these differences would be the degree of cultural heterogeneity within the indigenous population (greater in North America than in New Zealand). Another reason for the differences would stem from the history of relations of the indigenous communities with the dominant culture in each country. The history of open conflict and of treaty agreements is starkly different when comparing the First Nations and Inuit in Canada, the Native Americans in the United States, and the Maori in New Zealand.

Even neighbouring countries such as Canada and the United States differ dramatically with respect to population characteristics such as age and income. Bowman (2000) noted major differences in the cultural composition of the two countries. She also noted that visible minorities constitute a smaller proportion of the Canadian than the U.S. population. The most common cultural origins of Canadian visible minorities are (in descending order of frequency) Asian, First Nations, and African; for the American population the most common visible minorities have (in descending order of frequency) African, Latin American, Asian, and Native American origins. Differences in linguistic diversity are also important to consider. A larger proportion of Americans than Canadians speak English at home. Furthermore Canada has twice as many new immigrants per capita as does the United States.

Diversity is more, however, than culture and language. Clinical psychologists must be aware that diversity encompasses age, income, sexual orientation, disability, family structure, and geographical location. Those wishing to provide services in a rural setting, for example, need to be aware of the distinct nature of stressors people face in rural areas (e.g., higher levels of unemployment and accidents) and of the fact that rural areas tend to have higher levels of indigenous people and a lower overall level of education compared with urban settings (Barbopoulos & Clark, 2003). In Chapter 11 we describe an innovative program to offer services to people living in remote areas, as well as a program to train psychologists for rural practice. Because of the myriad ways in which diversity is expressed in a country, it is highly unlikely that all clinical psychologists could develop special knowledge of all the types of diversity they may encounter. What is more important (and more respectful of the ways in which diversity might be expressed among a psychologist's clients), therefore, is for a psychologist to (a) be aware of diversity issues, (b) be open to discussing these issues with clients (when appropriate), (c) have the interpersonal skills to effectively communicate about these issues, and (d) have the research skills to interpret and design research that is sensitive to diversity factors (cf. Hertzsprung & Dobson, 2000). Attention to diversity issues requires a balancing act in which universal human norms, specific group norms, and individual characteristics are considered in tandem with the continuum of normal-abnormal behaviour.

LICENSURE IN CLINICAL PSYCHOLOGY

Health care professionals are licensed to provide their services in the jurisdiction in which they practise. Licensed health care professionals, such as clinical psychologists, must meet minimal requirements for their academic and clinical training and are required by law to provide ethical and competent services. They are also regulated by a professional organization (e.g., College of Psychologists) that holds them accountable for their professional activities. Without some form of licensing there is no regulatory body to ensure that the public is protected when receiving health care services.

Licensure requirements in clinical psychology vary from country to country. In some countries, such as the United States, to become a clinical psychologist requires training at the doctoral level. In most European countries a master's degrees is required, whereas in other countries, such as Canada, Australia, New Zealand, and Britain, doctoral level training is preferred, although it may be possible for someone with master's level training to become licensed as a clinical psychologist. In some countries, such as New Zealand, registration is compulsory for psychologists working in the public sector, but is optional (although strongly recommended) for psychologists in private practice.

Table 2.5 provides information on the level of graduate training required for licensure in Canada. In some jurisdictions those with master's degrees can be registered as psychologists; in others the title "psychologist" is reserved for those with doctorates and the title "psychological associate" is used for those with a master's degree. As we mentioned in Chapter 1, in 2002 there were well over 13,000 licensed psychologists and psychological associates in Canada (Canadian Institute for Health Information, 2004). In British Columbia and Ontario the scope of practice of the two titles is identical (i.e., those holding either title can provide all forms of psychological service), whereas in Manitoba a psychological associate can only practise under the auspices of a supervising psychologist. In all jurisdictions except Quebec, the registration process involves a period of supervision by licensed psychologists (or psychological associates) before a person is able to practise autonomously. In most provinces the length of this supervised period is longer for those with a master's degree, in recognition that doctoral applicants receive far more supervised training during their graduate degree.

The final requirement for registration in most jurisdictions involves examinations of knowledge of psychological and professional issues. Typically this includes a written examination of knowledge of basic and applied psychology (the *Examination for Professional Practice in Psychology*, a standard exam used across North America that is set by the Association of State and Provincial Psychology Boards) and an oral examination that assesses knowledge of professional practice, professional ethics, and jurisprudence relevant to the practice of psychology. Dr. Mamen regularly devotes time to participating in licensure exams. British Columbia and Ontario also require that psychological associates and psychologists pass a written examination that covers jurisprudence and ethical issues. As is readily evident from the table, even after completing a graduate degree in psychology it takes at least another year before a person has the right to use the title "psychologist" and to autonomously offer psychological services to the public.

TABLE 2.5   Licensure Requirements for Psychologists in Canada

Province/Territory	Degree	Supervision	Examinations
Alberta	Master's	1 year	EPPP Oral
British Columbia	Doctorate (Psychologist) Master's (P. Associate)	1 year 3 years	EPPP Jurisprudence Oral
Manitoba	Doctorate (Psychologist) Master's (P. Associate)	1 year 2 years	EPPP Oral
New Brunswick	Master's	1 year (Doctorate) 4 years (Master's)	EPPP Oral
Newfoundland & Labrador	Master's	1 year (Doctorate) 2 years (Master's)	EPPP
Northwest Territories	Master's	1 year	Exam may be required
Nova Scotia	Master's	1 year (Doctorate) 6 years (Master's)	EPPP Oral
Nunavut	No legislation governing licensure of psychologists		
Ontario	Doctorate (Psychologist) Master's (P. Associate)	1 year 5 years	EPPP Jurisprudence Oral
Prince Edward Island	Master's	1 year (Doctorate) 2 years (Master's)	EPPP Oral
Quebec	Master's (move to Doctorate planned)	None	None
Saskatchewan	Master's	1 year	EPPP Oral
Yukon	No legislation governing licensure of psychologists		

Note: P. Associate = Psychological Associate, EPPP = *Examination for Professional Practice in Psychology*

As Table 2.5 demonstrates, there is considerable variability in licensure requirements across Canada, including variability in educational requirements, supervision requirements, and examination requirements. Because of these differing requirements, there has been, until recently, no assurance that psychologists licensed in different provinces have comparable levels of competence in providing services to the public. Moreover, a psychologist wishing to move from one jurisdiction to another might have to meet additional requirements to be registered in the new jurisdiction. To address these concerns, representatives of the regulatory bodies responsible for the licensing of psychologists and psychological associates in Canada signed a *Mutual Recognition Agreement* (MRA) in 2001. The MRA specifies that, to be licensed as a psychologist or psychological associate in Canada, an individual must have been evaluated as possessing core competencies in interpersonal relationships, assessment and evaluation, intervention and consultation, research, and ethics and standards. Although several years have passed since the signing of this agreement, most regulatory bodies are not yet fully compliant with the agreement but should be so by 2010. Delays in full implementation of the agreement are due in part to the need for changes in provincial legislation that govern the practice of psychology.

A fundamental goal of the MRA was to establish the conditions under which a licensed psychologist could have his or her qualifications recognized in another Canadian jurisdiction. The MRA should also prove to be a significant benefit for the public. Currently it is possible to become registered as a psychologist without having completed a training program in clinical psychology (accredited or unaccredited). In Canada, all that is required in any jurisdiction is a graduate degree in psychology. This made sense at a time when there were few accredited clinical psychology programs. We recognize that many competent clinical psychologists who have made important contributions to the field obtained their training outside of accredited programs. In our opinion, however, the profession of clinical psychology has developed to the point where the completion of a clinical training program (preferably one that is accredited) should be the academic requirement for licensing and the ability to autonomously provide clinical services to the public. In some American states, training in an accredited program (or training comparable to that received in an accredited program) is required for licensure. Despite the fact that the number of accredited clinical training programs in Canada has grown in recent years, the MRA does not require that someone applying for licensure be a graduate of a clinical program. The MRA does provide a set of very clear training requirements that must be met by all people applying for licensure. Therefore, individuals with graduate degrees in experimental psychology who wish to become licensed will require additional training in professional service provision to be eligible for licensure. Although this falls short of the ideal of requiring accredited clinical training for licensing, we see this as a significant step forward in the profession of clinical psychology.

To assist students who may be considering a career in clinical psychology, **Appendix 2** describes procedures for applying to graduate school in clinical psychology. The appendix begins with the important question of how to decide whether pursuing training in clinical psychology is the right choice for you. Subsequent sections address whether you would be eligible for admission to a doctoral program in clinical psychology, the application process itself, and finally, strategies to strengthen your application.

SUMMARY AND CONCLUSIONS

Clinical psychologists engage in diverse activities and are employed in many different settings. There is debate within the field about the relative weight that should be given to research in both training and the practice of clinical psychology. Canada has been a world leader in the development of a Code of Ethics that guides decision-making that is respectful of individuals and that promotes well-being. Graduate training in clinical psychology involves coursework, supervised practicum training, a doctoral dissertation, and a full-time internship. Across different countries and within countries there are different requirements to become licensed as a clinical psychologist. In North America, there is an increasing number of accredited programs that have well-developed training models.

Critical Thinking Questions

What role should intuition play in the practice of clinical psychology?

What is the usefulness of theories in the practice of clinical psychology?

How can a psychologist prepare for all the diversity he or she will encounter in a professional career?

How does training in the different models of clinical psychology (scientist-practitioner, practitioner-scholar, and clinical scientist) prepare students for different types of positions in clinical psychology?

What are the advantages and disadvantages of psychologists having the privilege of prescribing psychoactive medication?

Key Terms

accreditation	licensure
clinical consultation	organizational consultation
clinical scientist model	practicum
informed consent	practitioner-scholar model
internship	scientist-practitioner model

ADDITIONAL RESOURCES
Books

Bellack, A. S. & Hersen, M. (Eds.). (1998). *Comprehensive clinical psychology, Volume 2: Professional issues*. New York: Pergamon.

Dobson, K. S. & Dobson, D. G. (Eds.). (1993). *Professional psychology in Canada* (pp. 248–284). Toronto, ON: Hogrefe & Huber.

Evans, D. R. (Ed.). (2004). *The law, standard, and ethics in the practice of psychology, 2nd ed.* Toronto, ON: Emond Montgomery Publications.

Truscott, D., & Crook, K. H. (2004). *Ethics and the practice of psychology in Canada*. Edmonton, AB: University of Alberta Press.

Websites

American Psychological Association <http://www.apa.org> provides information on accreditation as well as listing accredited programs. Provides links to licensing organizations in the United States.

Association of State and Provincial Psychology Boards <http://www.asppb.org> is the association of Canadian and U.S. licensing boards in psychology.

Australian Psychological Society <http://www.psychologicalsociety.com.au> provides information on licensure in Australia, including an assessment of psychology qualifications for candidates from overseas who wish to be registered as a psychologist in Australia.

British Psychological Society <http://www.bps.org.uk> includes an excellent publication *So you want to be a psychologist* that is packed with information about training and careers in psychology in the United Kingdom.

Canadian Psychological Association <http://www.cpa.ca> provides information on accreditation as well as listing accredited programs. Provides links to licensing organizations in Canada.

New Zealand Psychological Society <http://www.psychology.org.nz> provides links to the regulatory body, the New Zealand Psychologists Board

CHAPTER 3

Classification and Diagnosis

INTRODUCTION

Every person is unique: each of us has his or her own aspirations, goals, challenges, vulnerabilities, and problems. Everyone is influenced by genetics, physiology, and life experiences. Yet as we all know from daily experience, in order to describe, understand, and predict the responses of others, we must search for common elements of human behaviour in this ocean of uniqueness. To manage the complexities of life we tend to categorize, classify, and search for patterns. Without a way to conceptualize and categorize the reactions of friends, family members, and co-workers, it would be impossible for us to navigate through life.

Classification is also a central element of all branches of science and social science. A classification system allows scientists to organize, describe, and relate the subject matter of their discipline, be they subatomic particles, microscopic forms of life, social systems, or celestial bodies. A range of features can be used to classify objects or concepts, including form, function, and purpose. Moreover, any object can be classified in a number of ways: a stone can be classified based on its composition, its shape, its value, its site of origin, or the geological period in which it was formed. As we will see in this chapter, two key aspects of the adequacy of classification systems are validity and utility (Kendell & Jablensky, 2003). **Validity** refers to the extent to which the principles used in classifying an object are effective in capturing the nature of reality. **Utility** refers to the usefulness of the resulting classification scheme. Another critically important issue we will discuss in the chapter is the underlying structure of the classification system. Classification can be based on a **categorical approach** in which an object is determined to either be a member of a category or not. The assumption underlying categorical classification is that there is an important qualitative difference between objects that are members of a category and those that are not. An extreme example of a categorical approach is to classify objects as either living or non-living. A categorical approach to psychopathology involves assigning a diagnosis such as major depressive disorder: the person is judged to have the disorder or not to have the disorder. In a categorical classification system categories may or may not be overlapping, but members of a category should be very similar to one another.

A **dimensional approach** to classification is based on the assumption that objects differ in the extent to which they possess certain characteristics or properties. This approach focuses on quantitative differences among objects and reflects the assumption that all objects can be arranged on a continuum to indicate the degree of membership in a category. Weight and height are prime examples of ways that dimensional approaches are used to classify objects or people. In a dimensional classification system different dimensions may or may not be related, but it is essential that the dimensions reflect significant higher order constructs rather than simple descriptive features (e.g., a construct such as neuroticism, rather than specific psychological phenomena such as sadness, nervousness, loneliness, poor self-esteem, or poor self-confidence). In the field of child psychopathology several researchers such as Thomas Achenbach, Keith Conners, and Herbert Quay have gathered information about children's difficulties from multiple informants and then used factor analysis to identify the symptoms that tend to co-occur. Achenbach's work has yielded two broad-band dimensions of problems: externalizing problems and internalizing problems. Externalizing problems are acting-out problems such as yelling, destroying things, stealing, and aggression. Internalizing problems refer to feelings of sadness, worry, and withdrawn behaviour. Using a dimensional approach, a child's functioning could be described according to the intensity of externalizing and internalizing problems. Later in the chapter we will examine the family of measures developed by Achenbach to gather data from multiple informants about child problems.

A **diagnostic system** is a classification based on rules used to organize and understand diseases and disorders. When these decision-making rules are applied to the symptoms of a specific individual, the classification system yields a **diagnosis** that concisely describes the person's condition. **Table 3.1** lists some of the purposes of diagnostic systems used by psychologists and psychiatrists. Most health care practitioners are generally in favour of using diagnostic systems, for all the reasons listed in the table. Despite the advantages of diagnosis, there are also possible drawbacks, such as stigmatization of the person receiving the diagnosis and the potential for an inaccurate diagnosis to result in harmful or inappropriate treatment. A reality faced by most health care providers (whether practising in an institutional setting such as a hospital or in a private practice), is that it is necessary to diagnose a patient to determine if the patient is eligible for certain services (e.g., extra academic support for students with learning disabilities). Furthermore, many insurance companies require a diagnosis before they will agree to reimburse the clinician for his or her services.

TABLE 3.1   The Uses of a Diagnostic System

- Provide a concise description of essential aspects of the patient's condition

- Reflect best current scientific knowledge of psychopathology

- Provide a common language for clinicians, researchers, and, increasingly, patients to use in discussing mental health conditions

- Indicate possible causes of the current condition (i.e., etiology)

- Indicate possible future developments in the condition (i.e., prognosis)

- Provide guidance on possible co-existing problems or conditions that should be evaluated

- Provide guidance on treatment options to be considered

- Provide a key term that can be used by clinicians to search the scientific literature for most current information on the condition

- Provide a framework for determining reimbursement of health services and eligibility for special programs or services

---

As we discussed in Chapter 1, modern attempts to classify and diagnose abnormal human behaviour can be traced to Emil Kraepelin, whose initial work on dementia praecox (now called schizophrenia) and manic-depressive insanity (now called bipolar mood disorder) set the stage for current psychiatric diagnostic systems. The so-called neo-Kraepelinian approach to classification has characteristics such as viewing each diagnosis as a medical disease, using specific criteria to define a category, and emphasizing the importance of diagnostic reliability (Blashfield, 1991). In the past few decades, this approach to psychiatric classification has been augmented with elements of a prototype model. The defining feature of the prototype model approach is that members of a diagnostic category may differ in the degree to which they represent the concepts underlying the category. As an example, dogs are more prototypic of the category "mammals" than are platypuses. Applying the prototype model to psychiatric diagnosis implies that not all people receiving the same diagnosis have exactly the same set of symptoms. Accordingly, in contrast to strict neo-Kraepelinian assumptions, two people with the same diagnosis may not have exactly the same disorder and therefore may require somewhat different treatment.

In this chapter we will present the classification and diagnostic systems most commonly used by clinical psychologists. The main example we will examine is the *Diagnostic and Statistical Manual of Mental Disorders* of the American Psychiatric Association. We will concentrate much of our discussion in this chapter on determining the validity and utility of a diagnostic system. We begin by examining what constitutes abnormal human behaviour and how scientists try to understand the ways such behaviours develop into full-blown clinical disorders.

DEFINING ABNORMAL BEHAVIOUR AND MENTAL DISORDERS

As we mentioned in Chapter 1, clinical psychologists now provide a range of psychological services to people with and without diagnosable conditions. Therefore you may wonder who cares about determining what constitutes abnormal behaviour. The quick answer is that most of us care about whether our experiences and behaviours are normal or abnormal. In fact, many people consult psychologists to find out whether the problems and symptoms they (or their loved ones) are experiencing are normal or abnormal. For example, Richard may be very concerned that he and his wife are having occasional disagreements, Rebecca may be concerned that she sometimes feels sad about the recent death of her father, Sue may be worried about her son Peter who counts backward from 100 and says a prayer every time he begins to feel nervous, and Courtenay may be worried by the frequent thoughts of hurting herself that seem to be put into her mind by other people. In all likelihood the first two clients are experiencing normal, predictable events that occur to almost everyone in a similar situation. A responsible psychologist should convey this information to the clients and determine whether any treatment is truly warranted. In some cases, brief psychoeducation and reassurance may be the only services that are required. In contrast, the child of the third client may be developing a clinical disorder (depending on how much the activities interfere with his daily functioning) and the fourth client is clearly having an experience that is abnormal. In these latter two cases the psychologist is likely to recommend further assessment and treatment.

Abnormal behaviour is not just rare, unusual, or bizarre behaviour, for the context in which the behaviour occurs is extremely important. Consider the following behaviours: Camille throws herself on the floor when asked to do anything such as take a bath, tidy up her things, or stop an enjoyable activity; Paul cannot be left alone with the family pets as he treats them roughly; Justin says he and his stuffed turtle are going on a magic adventure; Heather masturbates in public; Danielle cries uncontrollably for extended periods and is disinterested in food. Are these behaviours abnormal? Without more information, we cannot say. One important issue is the person's age. We will interpret Camille's temper tantrums and oppositional behaviour differently according to whether she is 2, 22, or 82. If she is two years old there is likely no cause for alarm. Although the behaviour would be grossly abnormal for both a 22- year-old and an 82-year old, it is likely that the underlying cause would be different at different ages. Similarly, rough treatment of animals is not unusual in a preschool age child, but is often associated with serious psychopathology when it occurs in older children. We cannot judge the behaviour of Justin or

Heather without knowing their ages: what would be age-appropriate in a very young child would be very troublesome in an adolescent or adult. Danielle's sad behaviour cannot be understood without knowing the context; if she has just learned of the death of a loved one, her behaviour is likely part of a normal reaction to grief. Her cultural heritage will also contribute to the way in which her grief is expressed: in some cultures she may appear outwardly unmoved by her loss, whereas in other cultures she may wail and rip her clothes. Diagnostic criteria for many childhood disorders specify that the symptom must be developmentally inappropriate. Therefore the clinician must have a good sense of the range of normal behaviour in a particular developmental period in order to be able to judge what is abnormal.

Without knowing the context of a person's behaviour, we cannot say whether that person's behaviour is abnormal.

Developmental Psychopathology

A **developmental psychopathology** approach examines problem behaviour in relation to the milestones that are specific to each stage of development. This approach underlines that biological and behavioural systems are constantly changing. It also emphasizes the importance of major developmental transitions (such as starting daycare, learning to speak, going to school, or puberty) as well as disruptions to normal patterns of development (such as loss of a parent, the effects of poverty, or exposure to trauma). Central to this approach is a reliance on empirical knowledge of normal development. So, for example, in understanding problems in very young children, it is essential to be informed by research on attachment and on sleep. Understanding difficulties that are evident in preschool age children requires knowledge of language development and of ways that adults promote children's self-esteem and self-control. Problems in school-age children can be considered in the context of what we know about academic functioning, peer relationships, and harmonious families.

The developmental psychopathology approach has been particularly useful in understanding problems of infancy and childhood, but it can also be applied to help us understand the challenges of later phases in development such as retirement and bereavement. A developmental psychopathology approach involves not only a snapshot of the client's current difficulties, but also consideration of the course of the problem if left untreated. The adoption of this approach has allowed clinical psychologists to draw on a vast literature about parenting, child neglect and abuse, and the effects of conflict on family members when considering diagnostic issues.

Diagnosis

No diagnosis is based on a single symptom. Diagnostic criteria include a cluster of symptoms that go together. Medical students often report that in learning about different disorders they recognize symptoms that they have experienced and worry that they may suffer from the serious disorder they are studying. Parents, too, hear about symptoms that are associated with childhood disorders and may be tempted to assign an amateur diagnosis of attention-deficit/hyperactivity disorder to the child at the next table in a restaurant who is whooping with delight and flicking food at a friend.

Much has been written about the degree to which personal, cultural, or professional values influence the determination of what is abnormal or disordered. In defining abnormality it is extremely important to rely on scientific evidence, not just value judgements. Sometimes a theoretical model blocks our awareness of a problem. One of the clearest examples is the diagnosis of depression. Although the problem of depression in adults has been recognized for centuries, it is only in the last 25 years that mental health professionals have turned their attention to childhood depression. The major reason for this stunning oversight is that according to the dominant theoretical model, childhood depression was impossible. According to psychoanalytic models, depression is a disorder of the superego. It is therefore impossible to develop depression until the stage of development at which the superego emerges. A child's psyche is not sufficiently developed to use the types of defences that result in the experience of depression. Simple application of behavioural models developed on adults also made it impossible to detect depression in children. A primary symptom of adult depression is sadness. However, children express both happiness and sadness in different ways from adults. A very young child may laugh aloud expressing spontaneous pleasure, she may sing, or skip exuberantly. Such overt expressions of pleasure are unusual in adults. Adults may express sadness verbally, whereas children are more likely to express disinterest or boredom. Another example of age-related similarities and differences in a diagnosis is discussed in **Viewpoint Box 3.1**.

VIEWPOINT BOX 3.1

DEVELOPMENTAL CONSIDERATIONS IN ATTENTION-DEFICIT/HYPERACTIVITY DISORDER

Attention-deficit/hyperactivity disorder (ADHD) is one of the most common disorders of childhood, affecting one or two children in every school classroom. Parents usually recall that the first signs of ADHD occurred when their children were toddlers. Diagnostic criteria require the appearance of problems before the age of seven. However, the most common time for a child to be diagnosed is in elementary school and some children who suffer from the disorder may never receive a formal diagnosis. The diagnosis of ADHD requires evidence of difficulties in multiple settings. Children with ADHD often suffer from other mental disorders, including disruptive behaviour disorders, mood disorders, and anxiety disorders.

Children diagnosed with ADHD show persistent and maladaptive symptoms of inattention and/or hyperactivity-impulsivity that are *inconsistent with developmental level*. This means that the child's behaviour must be outside the range of behaviour that is commonly seen in children of that age. This presents a diagnostic challenge as there is great variability in very young children's ability to sustain attention, to engage in quiet activities, and to think before acting. There is also considerable instability in children's behaviour, so that not all three-year-olds with extreme inattention, hyperactivity, or impulsiveness go on to develop ADHD.

When children begin school they face increased demands to sustain attention, to work quietly, and to control their impulses. This often sets the stage for teachers to identify those children whose behaviour is outside the range of normal behaviour. Although first-time parents may feel at a loss in determining whether their son's high-energy, demanding style is just part of being a boy, teachers have the advantage of being able to compare their son to the hundreds of other boys with whom they have worked.

Over the decades, various definitions of the disorder have emphasized different features. Each version of the DSM reflected contemporary efforts to make meaningful distinctions between different subtypes. An important shift occurred in DSM-III when the core difficulties of the disorder were seen as cognitive difficulties with attention rather than as a problem of overactivity. As we have noted before, the way we think about a disorder can lead clinicians to have some blind spots. Because the extremely disruptive physical signs of hyperactivity tend to decrease with age, it was originally thought that this was a chronic disorder of childhood that diminished during adolescence. It was only once the disorder was viewed as based on attention difficulties that it was possible to recognize continuity of symptoms into adulthood.

Adults with ADHD are at risk for disruptions in their work, education, and relation-ships. Researchers have recently recognized that it may be useful to address parental ADHD symptoms before attempting to train parents in techniques to help children manage their symptoms.

In the search to understand the etiology and course of ADHD, researchers rely on knowledge derived from developmental psychology, cognitive psychology, and psychology of the family. Even though this disorder is biologically based, psycholog-ical factors affect its course as well as the development of comorbid disorders often associated with ADHD.

Defining Disorder

The *Diagnostic and Statistical Manual of Mental Disorders*, fourth edition-text revision (DSM-IV-TR; American Psychiatric Association, 2000) defines a mental disorder in the following manner:

> "…each of the mental disorders is conceptualized as a clinically significant behavioural or psychological syndrome or pattern that occurs in an individual and that is associated with present distress (e.g., a painful symptom) or disability (i.e., impairment in one or more important areas of functioning) or with a significantly increased risk of suffering death, pain, disability, or an important loss of freedom. In addition, this syndrome or pattern must not be merely an expectable or culturally sanctioned response to a particular event, for example, the death of a loved one. Whatever its original cause, it must currently be consid-ered a manifestation of a behavioural, psychological, or biological dysfunction in the individual. Neither deviant behaviour (e.g., political, religious, or sexual) nor conflicts that are primarily between the individual and society are mental disorders unless the deviance or conflict is a symptom of a dysfunction in the individual, as described above." (American Psychiatric Association, 2000 p. xxxi)

This widely accepted definition is somewhat cumbersome. It would be valuable to have a clear, concise definition of mental disorder that could be applied to any behaviour or pattern of behaviours to determine whether a disorder is evident. Fortunately there is just such a definition. Wakefield (1992) proposed simply that mental disorder be defined as a **harmful dysfunction**. This widely endorsed definition implies that a classification of abnormality or disorder involves a value judgement. Thus diagnosis of a disorder does not just require the co-occurrence of a set of statistically rare symptoms or behaviours, but requires that there is something wrong or dys-functional and that this dysfunction causes harm to the individual or to those around him or her. In other words, some form of pathology is evident and this pathology causes impairment. The requirement that both conditions be satisfied is critical, as it is relatively common to have some form of pathology without it necessarily resulting in impairment. A biological example of this would be that a person who has hypertension might not be aware of any impairment in functioning. Terms such as "dysfunctional" and "harmful" are, of course, somewhat value-laden, but as we presented in the section on developmental psychopathology, research evidence can be used, at least partially, to operationalize these concepts. Widiger (Widiger, 2004; Widiger & Sankis, 2000) has suggested that a third concept—**dyscontrol**—be added to this definition of mental disorder. That is, the resulting impairment must be involuntary or, at least, not readily controlled. This addition is potentially important because it means that someone who intentionally and wilfully engages in unacceptable behaviour such as sexually abusing a child would not be considered to have a mental disorder. Dyscontrol, however, is also a value-laden term that is difficult to operationalize.

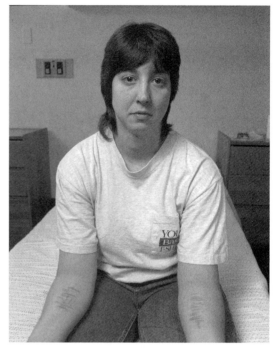

This woman shows clear evidence of having a harmful dysfunction that she has difficulty controlling.

PROFILE BOX 3.1

DR. CHARLOTTE JOHNSTON

After completing my B.A. and M.Sc. degrees in psychology from the University of Calgary I moved to the United States to complete my Ph.D. in clinical psychology at Florida State University, then returned to Canada for a psychology internship at the Child and Family Centre at McMaster University. I am currently a professor in the Clinical Psychology Program in the Department of Psychology at the University of British Columbia and a registered psychologist in British Columbia. I teach courses on clinical psychology at the undergraduate level and clinical child psychology at the graduate level. My

Dr. Charlotte Johnston

clinical activities and research focus primarily on families of children with disruptive disorders such as attention-deficit/hyperactivity disorder (ADHD). My research has investigated parent and child characteristics that are associated with parent-child conflict, and how parents' explanations of child behaviour are related to their responses to psychological and pharmacological treatments for ADHD. I also conduct workshops and public lectures on ADHD for professionals and families. I live in Vancouver with my husband, an emergency physician, and our two cats.

What made you choose to become a clinical psychologist?

When I first went to university, I knew I liked working with children. Psychology seemed to offer a chance to learn about a broad range of ways in which children develop and function, including how children fit within families. In psychology courses I got hooked on research and its application in understanding and improving the problems of childhood. In graduate school I wanted to be involved in both research and its application in the area of child disorders. Clinical psychology, with its focus on the integration of science and practice, was a perfect match for these interests and I haven't regretted the choice for a moment.

What is the most rewarding part of your job as a clinical psychologist?

The most rewarding aspect of this profession is the diversity of activities that I participate in. On any given day, I'm likely to do any or all of clinical practice, research, and teaching.

What is the greatest challenge facing you as a clinical psychologist?

Integrating science and practice. This integration is essential and is what makes clinical psychology strong. However, it also makes our job difficult. I struggle to apply research findings in clinical work and with how to ask research questions that have real clinical relevance. We are constantly challenged with educating others, including consumers of psychological services and policy makers, about this integration and about the importance of clinical psychology being evidence-based.

Some people suggest that ADHD is not a valid diagnosis or that the problem is overdiagnosed. As a psychologist who has researched ADHD what is your reaction to that perspective?

ADHD is in pretty good shape in terms of its validity compared with many other psychological disorders. We know quite a lot about the symptoms of the disorder and how they relate to other child characteristics, how they respond to treatment, and how to distinguish this cluster of symptoms from other disorders. In 2002 a group of experts in the area of ADHD research signed a joint consensus statement outlining the overwhelming evidence that supports the validity of this disorder (Barkley, et al. 2002).

In some studies it does appear that a small percentage of children being treated for the disorder do not meet criteria for diagnosis. However, there are also studies that show that there are children who meet criteria for the disorder, but who are not diagnosed or receiving services. Thus, there is evidence that, in some cases, ADHD is actually under-diagnosed rather than over-diagnosed. One of the most pressing goals of research and clinical practice in the area of ADHD must be to improve the validity of our assessment and diagnostic practices in order to minimize both over- and under-diagnosis of the disorder.

How do you integrate science and practice in your work?

The clinical work and research that I do are related and each helps me to understand the other. For example, when I work with a family this offers insight that I can use to design research studies to test the effectiveness of different parenting strategies, or how we can assess the barriers that prevent families from implementing these strat-egies. In my clinical work, I choose evidence-based assessments and interventions as much as possible. However I also need to consider how applicable the research evidence is to the particular child and family that I am seeing. If the evidence is based on families or circumstances that are quite different from my client and my circumstances (e.g., the studies were conducted with two-parent, middle-class families and my client is being raised by a single grandmother living in poverty), I may need to modify the treatment. However, I will do this knowing that I am venturing into relatively uncharted territory and that I must evaluate the effects of the modified treatment on an ongoing basis (e.g., using brief measures to track progress on a session by session basis).

What do you see as the most exciting changes in the profession of clinical psychology?

Dissemination of our services. We need to invest greater efforts in communicating that psychological treatments exist that have proven useful for many people and many types of psychological problems. And these treatments are often more cost-effective than no treatment or than other forms of treatment.

Once we have evidence that an assessment or intervention is useful, we must consider the level of training that is needed for its implementation. Should these assessments or treatments be restricted to clinical psychologists? Alternately, could individuals with less training deliver these services more efficiently and just as effectively? Although it is tempting to "protect the turf" of clinical psychology, these questions need empirical answers and it should be the evidence rather than professional protectionism that guides health service policies.

Prevalence of Mental Disorders

So just how common are mental disorders? Using the DSM-IV definition of mental disorder and its criteria for anxiety disorders, mood disorders, impulse control disorders (such as bulimia and attention-deficit/hyperactivity disorder), and substance abuse disorders, the World Health Organization Mental Health Survey Consortium (2004) carried out surveys of people 18 years of age and older in 14 countries: Colombia, Mexico, and the United States (the Americas); Belgium, France, Germany, Italy, the Netherlands, Spain, and Ukraine (Europe); Lebanon (the Middle East); Nigeria (Africa); and Japan and China (Asia). Sample sizes ranged from approximately 1,700 participants in Japan to almost 9,300 participants in the United States. Twelve-month prevalence data (i.e., the percentage of people meeting diagnostic criteria during the period of a year) from this massive survey are presented in Table 3.2.

TABLE 3.2　Prevalence of Selected Mental Disorders

Country	Anxiety	Mood	Impulse-Control	Substance Abuse	Any Disorder
Colombia	10.0%	6.8%	3.9%	2.8%	17.8%
Mexico	6.8%	4.8%	1.3%	2.5%	12.2%
United States	18.2%	9.6%	6.8%	3.8%	26.4%
Belgium	6.9%	6.2%	1.0%	1.2%	12.0%
France	12.0%	8.5%	1.4%	0.7%	18.4%
Germany	6.2%	3.6%	0.3%	1.1%	9.1%
Italy	5.8%	3.8%	0.3%	0.1%	8.2%
Netherlands	8.8%	6.9%	1.3%	3.0%	14.9%
Spain	5.9%	4.9%	0.5%	0.3%	9.2%
Ukraine	7.1%	9.1%	3.2%	6.4%	20.5%
Lebanon	11.2%	0.8%	1.7%	1.3%	16.9%
Nigeria	3.3%	0.8%	—	0.8%	4.7%
Japan	5.3%	3.1%	1.0%	1.7%	8.8%
China-Beijing	3.2%	2.5%	2.6%	2.6%	9.1%
China-Shanghai	2.4%	1.7%	0.7%	0.5%	4.3%

Adapted from World Health Organization Mental Health Survey Consortium (2004).

As you can see, overall prevalence rates varied greatly from country to country, ranging from 4.3% in Shanghai to 26.4% in the United States. In all but one country (Ukraine), anxiety disorders were the most common mental disorder, with mood disorders being the next most common set of mental disorders. It is interesting to note that the six countries included in the surveys that are classified by the World Bank as less developed (China, Colombia, Lebanon, Mexico, Nigeria, and Ukraine) had some of the lowest and highest total prevalence rates. The authors of the report recognized that the failure to include schizophrenia in the surveys was problematic. They argued, however, that previous research has shown that many people diagnosed with schizophrenia would also receive a diagnosis that was included in the surveys. Therefore, the authors believed that the overall picture of the worldwide prevalence of people meeting criteria for at least one mental disorder is accurate. Hearing that millions of people worldwide suffer from anxiety disorders is different from imagining the life of a person who suffers from an anxiety disorder. To provide you with a fuller appreciation of what mental disorders are like, we have included cases describing two people—Carl, an adolescent, and Teresa, an adult—who were referred to us for the treatment of an anxiety disorder. The cases we present in the book are based on our clinical practice. Whenever we present an example of a person suffering from a mental disorder, we have taken care to conceal the person's identity by changing some parts of the background information. You will learn more about Carl and Teresa in later chapters on assessment and intervention.

CASE EXAMPLE
C A R L

Carl is a 12-year-old boy who has lived in Canada since the age of 10. He was referred for psychological services to address symptoms of anxiety, hypervigilance, and sleep disturbance. According to his mother, Carl was a normal child whose birth and early childhood were unremarkable. However, when Carl was three years old, his country suffered extreme strife and conflict that culminated in ethnic cleansing. Carl, his mother, and twin sister were separated from his father and learned only months later that the father had been brutally killed. Following the loss of his father, repeated exposure to mob violence, and months of sheltering from continued threat of death, Carl displayed behaviour that is found in some very young children's response to trauma—he withdrew from the world and became mute. Although he has made remarkable progress and in many ways has a normal life, to this day, Carl continues to re-experience images of the scene in which the family was fleeing for their lives, the small children clinging to their parents. In addition, he re-experiences images of corpses, blood, and body parts, drawn not only from direct experience, but also from personal accounts he has heard and media images he has seen.

As his mother attempted to rebuild the family life following such horrific loss and exposure to violence, Carl sought reassurance by clinging to two attachment figures: his mother and his twin sister. The availability of these two people to provide comfort and reassurance enabled him to gradually venture into the world by attending school. During this time, as safety was slowly re-established, Carl was surrounded by evidence of the genocide. All the adults in his life had experienced terror and loss.

The fragile equilibrium that had been achieved by the time he was nine years old was shattered when the family was exposed to renewed threats of death unless they dropped charges against those accused of killing Carl's father. In contrast to the experience at the age of three, when he was too young to cognitively understand what was happening and could respond only on an emotional level, at the age of nine Carl was intellectually mature enough to understand that his family could be harmed. He was terrified at the possibility of unprovoked attacks and at the risk of dying or losing yet another family member.

Since his arrival in Canada, Carl has begun the process of rebuilding his life. He attends school and has friends with whom he enjoys spending time. He is a keen soccer player. Although he and his twin no longer cling to one another, they are very important to one another. Nevertheless, Carl continues to be haunted by his experiences. Images of the violence disturb his sleep. He is fearful at night, unwilling to sleep alone and troubled that noises are of intruders coming to murder the family. Battle scenes in movies evoke memories and a panic response. Carl is troubled by talk about the genocide experiences, covering his ears and yelling at his mother to stop talking about it. Carl experiences somatic symptoms of anxiety including pounding heart and dizziness. This symptom profile is consistent with a diagnosis of posttraumatic stress disorder. In addition to experiencing unusual symptoms, there is clear evidence of harmful dysfunction: the symptoms get in the way of Carl enjoying all the regular experiences of a teenager, they interfere with his sleep, and they are distressing to him. Despite his best efforts and that of his family, Carl is unable to control these symptoms.

Carl's current adjustment is a testament to his mother's resolute determination to create security for her children. He has benefited from the secure life he experienced prior to the genocide, by his mother's steadfast efforts to create a normal life, and by the availability of a twin sister. However, he was exposed, not to a single life-threatening experience, but to sustained life-threatening experiences over a prolonged period. Nothing will erase the memories and psychological scars of his early childhood trauma. Toward the end of the book we will discuss evidence-based psychological services that could reduce symptom severity, so that Carl will be able to function without daily, debilitating anxiety.

CASE EXAMPLE
TERESA

Teresa is a married 27-year-old mother with a six-month-old baby, Evan. Teresa was referred for psychological services by her family physician due to intrusive worries and repeated checking behaviours. Teresa had a regular childhood in a loving family. She describes herself as always having been a worried person, but as never previously having had to seek psychological services. Her husband Jeff is a successful executive in an information technology company. The couple lives in a pleasant suburb and enjoys an above-average income. They attend social activities associated with Jeff's work. In addition, Teresa attends a mother and baby group with other young mothers whom she met in pre-natal classes.

Teresa reports that over recent years she has been increasingly preoccupied with worries about making mistakes that might harm other people. She first became aware of these worries in her role as a nurse. Having been proud of her profession for several years, Teresa became preoccupied with worries that she might make an error in dispensing medication and that one of the people in her care would be harmed by her actions. As her worries increased, she became progressively more distressed at the potential harm she might cause and devoted more and more time to checking that she was not making errors. She finally dealt with her stress by quitting her job when she became pregnant with her first child.

Even though Teresa eliminated her work stress she continued to feel worried. She is particularly troubled by fears when driving that she has inadvertently knocked over a pedestrian or a cyclist. These thoughts are triggered whenever she hits a bump in the road or if she has momentarily lost concentration during her driving. When Teresa has such thoughts she imagines the victim lying injured in the road, so she circles back looking for him or her. She has a tendency to stop the car and examine the pavement for signs of blood. She may ask passers-by if they witnessed an accident or if they have seen an injured person limping away. Only when she has circled the area many times without discovering evidence of an accident is she able to continue. Episodes of checking delay most journeys including grocery shopping, trips out with the baby, and picking Jeff up from work. Even after she has searched for evidence, Teresa is vigilant in listening to the radio and watching television to check for reports of a hit and run accident. She also quizzes people she knows about whether they have heard about an accident.

Teresa also worries that she may accidentally harm her baby. Cleaning the house poses a special challenge as she becomes distressed at thoughts she may have spilled a household cleaning product near the baby. She responds to these worries by changing the baby's clothes and washing the area in which the baby is located. The cleaning routines required to reassure her that the baby has not been contaminated with a toxic product can take several hours.

Teresa recognizes that these worries are unusual. She believes her thoughts are excessive and that her checking is out of proportion to the likelihood she has actually caused any harm. She is embarrassed by her symptoms and worries that other people will think that she is crazy. She is grateful to Jeff for tolerating her extreme thoughts and behaviours. Teresa's symptom profile is consistent with a diagnosis of obsessive compulsive disorder.

Even though Teresa recognizes that these thoughts and behaviours are out of proportion to the likelihood that she has harmed anyone, she is unable to control them. Her husband's attempts at reassurance and reasoning have also met with failure. Despite his desire to be loyal and supportive, Jeff is frustrated at Teresa's odd behaviours. Her need for reassurance is draining and he is embarrassed to think his wife may be crazy. In the assessment chapters we will present tools that can be used to assess the extent of Teresa's problems and describe the process of assessing her difficulties.

Understanding the Development of Mental Disorders

Modern theories regarding the etiology of mental disorders are all based on variations of a biopsychosocial model. That is, the presence of a mental disorder is determined by a blend of biological, psychological, and social factors, although the precise contribution of each of the three factors varies from disorder to disorder. Additionally, etiological theories tend to favour certain factors within the general biopsychosocial model: a number of biological theories emphasize genetic elements, whereas most psychological theories tend to emphasize cognitive, developmental, and interpersonal elements. **Viewpoint Box 3.2** examines issues related to genetics and psychopathology.

VIEWPOINT BOX 3.2

GENETICS AND PSYCHOPATHOLOGY

At the beginning of the new millennium, scientists announced that they had developed a working draft of all three billion letters of DNA in the human genome. If, as geneticists predict, we will soon understand the basis for the influence of genetics on behaviour, does this mean that we should abandon research efforts to understand the contribution of the environment to the development of psychopathology? Will psychological assessment and intervention soon be replaced by genetic assessment and pharmacological interventions? What does it mean to know that a disorder has a genetic linkage? Will all future psychopathology research focus on analysis at the molecular level?

In a recent review of the status of research in psychopathology in the postgenomic era, Plomin and McGuffin (2003) highlighted that, when a disorder is described as heritable, this simply tells us that variations in the person's DNA affect the risk of that person developing a particular disorder. Efforts to identify genes responsible for different disorders have revealed that only very rare disorders such as Huntington's disease are linked to a single gene. In the case of these single gene disorders, the presence of the gene is necessary and sufficient for the emergence of the disorder. Most types of psychopathology appear to be related to multiple genes and their interaction with the environment. Each gene is therefore responsible for only a small part of the variance in the emergence of the disorder. If a disorder is associated with multiple genes, then it follows that the more of those genes a person carries, the more severe their symptoms would be. Thus a multi-gene effect is consistent with a dimensional view of psychopathology.

Plomin and McGuffin summarized the state of knowledge with respect to a number of disorders. Large-scale studies have not yet identified single genes involved in schizophrenia, although there is some promising evidence based on a meta-analysis of 3,000 people indicating a gene that is associated with a small but significant increase in risk of developing schizophrenia. Similarly, no single gene has been associated with mood disorders, but some genes appear to be associated with slightly higher risk of developing these disorders. Three genes have been found that are responsible for early onset dementia of the Alzheimer's type, thus explaining the emergence of only 2% of all Alzheimer's cases. Researchers are examining various possible linkages that could explain the emergence of autistic disorder. Many rare single gene disorders are associated with severe mental retardation. Evidence with respect to mild retardation suggests the cumulative influence of multiple genes. Researchers have also begun to identify genetic patterns that are associated with protection against the development of disorders. Intolerance to the effects of alcohol that is found among half of East Asian individuals is thought to deter excessive alcohol consumption and may be related to lower rates of alcoholism among Asian individuals than in Caucasian individuals.

Plomin and McGuffin make a compelling argument for research in *behavioural genomics*: the study of the links between psychological processes and genetic functioning. They note that although biological studies of mice can be very useful in generating testable hypotheses with respect to some disorders, such as anxiety disorders and dementia, they are not suitable for the study of disorders related to social interaction such as autism and communication disorders. The availability of painless and inexpensive strategies to obtain DNA will make it possible for behavioural researchers to incorporate into their research designs the effects of genetic variation. It would be a mistake, therefore, to see identification of genes that contribute to the emergence of psychopathology as replacing the need for psychological research. There may be many exciting ways that genetic information can be included in the design of psychological research in order to elucidate the important links between genetics and the environment.

In keeping with our emphasis on the need for empirical evidence, we move now to consider some of the recent research on the development of abnormal behaviour. This is a huge scientific literature and we have space to highlight only a few of the most exciting issues in the emergence of psychological disorders. One such issue is the role that the buildup of life stress plays in placing people at risk for developing a disorder. A good example of this line of research is a study by Turner and Lloyd (2004). These researchers interviewed more than 1,800 young American adults (aged 18–23 years). Researchers asked questions about a wide range of major stressful experiences, such as parental unemployment, being abandoned by one or both parents, life-threatening illness, forced sexual intercourse, being shot at with a gun, witnessing someone being seriously injured or killed, being in a serious car crash, and experiencing physical abuse from a dating partner. Some, but not all, of the experiences they asked about are potentially traumatic. In addition they asked questions about both current psychological symptoms and lifetime experience of diagnosable disorder. The researchers' goal was to examine the links between stress and first episodes (i.e., the first occurrence of a diagnosable condition) of anxiety and depressive disorders. Of the 33 stressors they examined, 26 were associated with significantly increased risk of subsequently developing an anxiety or mood disorder. Across gender and ethnicity (Hispanic American, African American, and non-Hispanic white American), the odds of developing a disorder increased with the number of stressors experienced. A second example, using an interpersonal stress model, comes from a study by Hammen, Shih, and Brennan (2004) that examined the complex intergenerational transmission of depression among approximately 800 Australian adolescents and their mothers. The researchers found that depression in maternal grandmothers predicted maternal depression and interpersonal stress. The maternal depression, in turn, influenced the mothers' interpersonal stress *and* the development of their children's social competence. The interpersonal stress experienced by the mothers also contributed to the children's interpersonal stress and to their children's depression. The final piece of the stress/disorder chain was that the poor social competence and high interpersonal stress in the children predicted their own development of depressive symptoms.

Although life stress is clearly implicated in the development of many disorders, not all people exposed to major stressors develop a disorder and, if disorders do develop, they do not do so at the same time or rate for all people. An emerging area of etiological research explores individual differences in the emergence of psychological disorders. This requires the longitudinal study of large numbers of people and the use of very sophisticated statistical analyses. A fascinating example of such research is a study by Cole et al. (2002) in which 12 waves of data were collected (Grades 4 to 11) from 1,570 American children/adolescents and their parents. The main goal of the study was to investigate normative developmental shifts in the rate at which depressive symptoms emerge. The researchers found that the rate at which depressive symptoms occurred in children and adolescents was not consistent over the course of their development. Data from parents and children both indicated that there was a significant increase in the rate of depressive symptoms between the sixth and seventh grade. The average rate of change before this period and after this period was relatively stable, suggesting that there are destabilizing factors influencing child development and the subsequent experience of depressive symptoms in late childhood/early adolescence. Also worth noting was that the symptoms of depression increased much more rapidly for girls than for boys, starting at the period between the fifth and seventh grades. Based on these data, researchers interested in examining the initial development and maintenance of depression can now focus on the critical time period identified by Cole and colleagues to more closely investigate factors implicated in the emergence (and non-emergence) of depression.

A final line of etiological research we'd like to illustrate deals with the importance of having solid normative data on what constitutes typical distress and problem behaviours. All children, adolescents, and adults have occasional psychological challenges and difficulties, but just how many of these problems is it

Normative data on what constitutes problem behaviours are valuable for clinical psychologists providing services to children and families.

normal to have? Bongers, Koot, van der Ende, and Verhulst (2003) examined this question using parent-reported data from the Child Behavior Checklist (a measure we discuss more in the final section of the chapter) for a representative sample of more than 2,000 Dutch children. The sample was recruited through municipal registers and data were collected over a 10-year period at two-year intervals. The researchers examined normal levels of such problems as anxiety, somatic complaints, aggressive behaviour, attention problems, and social problems. Results from this study provide clinicians with valuable normative data for each year between the ages of 4 and 18 (for girls and boys separately). For example, a clinical psychologist providing services to a family can determine whether the level of a child's aggressive behaviour reported by a parent is comparable to, or much greater than, what is normally expected for a child of that age and gender. This information, in turn, is likely to influence the nature of the information and services offered to the family.

THE DSM APPROACH TO DIAGNOSIS

In the following sections we describe the historical context for the development of the current diagnostic system used in much of the world: the DSM-IV and the DSM-IV-Text Revision (DSM-IV-TR). We then describe the main features of the DSM-IV before moving on to consider the shortcomings of the approach to diagnosis that underlies the DSM.

The Evolution of the DSM

Each edition of the DSM reflects the status of diagnosis at the time of its publication. The first edition of the DSM published by the American Psychiatric Association in 1952 was rather vague and heavily emphasized psychodynamic etiological factors for the majority of the disorders. According to Shea (1991), the limitations of the original DSM were relatively unimportant as diagnosis was not seen as an important or pressing issue and only one form of treatment—psychoanalysis—was available. At the time of the publication of the second edition in 1968 new treatment options were becoming available (including drug treatments) and psychiatric researchers were increasingly examining biological and neurological aspects of mental disorders. As a result, in the second edition the psychodynamic orientation was less prominent and there was greater precision in terminology (Shea, 1991).

The third edition of the DSM, published in 1980, marked a dramatic departure from the first two editions. In developing the manual, much effort was devoted to improving the organization and classification of mental disorders. This was evident in many different ways. First, the manual was explicitly atheoretical—this allowed for the possibility of greater acceptance within the mental health field and for the introduction of concrete behavioural descriptions of most disorders. Second, the diagnostic criteria were much more explicit than was the case previously, with lists of symptoms provided for each diagnosis. Third, as a significant part of the effort to improve upon the reliability of psychiatric diagnoses, thousands of patients and hundreds of clinicians were involved in field trials of the diagnostic system. Fourth, a multiaxial diagnostic system was introduced, which encouraged clinicians to consider more than just symptoms in diagnosing a person. These were ambitious changes that required much more attention to the scientific literature and to scientific classification principles than did the previous two editions. In order to reflect advances occurring in the burgeoning psychopathology literature, a revision of the DSM-III with updated information and some alterations in diagnostic criteria was published in 1987.

Given the widespread acceptance of DSM-III and DSM-III-R in the clinical and research communities, the use of the manuals by many different mental health professionals, and the use of the manual for teaching and reimbursement purposes, great efforts were made in the preparation of the DSM-IV. Work groups composed of research experts and clinicians in the field were established for each major class of mental disorders. Exhaustive literature reviews were written and proposals were developed for diagnostic criteria. Liaisons were established with scores of mental health and professional organizations, both within the United States and internationally. The resulting manual, although far from perfect as we will see in a subsequent section, was developed in a far more collaborative and scientifically informed manner than were any of the preceding editions of the DSM.

The DSM-IV was published in 1994. The DSM-IV-Text Revision, published in 2000, corrected errors identified in the DSM-IV text, updated the scientific information provided about disorders, and made some alterations to enhance the educational value of the DSM-IV. These changes in the text are particularly important as DSM-IV information was based on reviews of the scientific literature that were completed in 1992. As much has been learned since then, and the next new edition of the DSM is not likely to be published for several years, the text revision provides an important bridge between the DSM-IV and the future DSM-V. The text revision did not include changes in the criteria used to diagnose a disorder or changes in the listing of disorders. For ease of reading we will refer to the DSM-IV when discussing the structure and criteria, as these are identical in both fourth edition versions of the diagnostic system.

The DSM-IV

The DSM-IV is an example of a categorical approach to classification. As we described earlier in the chapter, this means that mental disorders are classified on the basis of specific defining criteria. In reviewing the organization of the DSM-IV, Clark, Watson, and Reynolds (1995) expressed concern about the lack of a unified scientific system underlying the structure of the classification system. As shown in **Table 3.3**, there are 17 diagnostic classes within the DSM-IV. Clark et al. pointed out that, although the majority of diagnostic classes are based on shared characteristics of their constituent symptoms such as anxiety disorders or sleep disorders, about a third of the classes are organized on what can only be described as rather eclectic and pragmatic grounds. For example, the only common feature among the disorders listed in the class "Disorders Usually First Diagnosed in Infancy, Childhood, or Adolescence" is the likely age at which the disorder is diagnosed. Moreover, many mood and anxiety disorders are first diagnosed in childhood and persist into adulthood, yet they are not included in this diagnostic class (Widiger & Sankis, 2000). As we will see when we later discuss limitations to the DSM-IV, this approach can be misleading and may have, at times, little clinical value (or utility).

TABLE 3.3   DSM-IV and DSM-IV-TR Diagnostic Classes

Disorders Usually First Diagnosed in Infancy, Childhood, or Adolescence

Examples: Mental Retardation, Pervasive Developmental Disorders, Attention-Deficit and Disruptive Behavior Disorders

Delirium, Dementia, and Amnestic and Other Cognitive Disorders

Examples: Substance Intoxication Delirium, Dementia of the Alzheimer's Type, Substance-Induced Persisting Amnestic Disorder

Mental Disorders Due to a General Medical Condition

Examples: Catatonic Disorder Due to (General Medical Condition), Personality Change Due to (General Medical Condition)

Substance-Related Disorders

Examples: Alcohol-Related Disorders, Inhalant-Related Disorders, Nicotine-Related Disorders

Schizophrenia and Other Psychotic Disorders

Examples: Schizophrenia, Schizoaffective Disorder, Delusional Disorder

Mood Disorders

Examples: Depressive Disorders, Bipolar Disorders

Anxiety Disorders

Examples: Social Phobia, Obsessive-Compulsive Disorder, Generalized Anxiety Disorder

Somatoform Disorders

Examples: Conversion Disorder, Pain Disorder, Body Dysmorphic Disorder

Factitious Disorders

Examples: Factitious Disorder With Predominantly Psychological Signs and Symptoms, Factitious Disorder With Predominantly Physical Signs and Symptoms

Dissociative Disorders

Examples: Dissociative Amnesia, Dissociative Fugue, Dissociative Identity Disorder

Sexual and Gender Identity Disorders

Examples: Sexual Dysfunctions, Paraphilias, Gender Identity Disorders

Eating Disorders

Examples: Anorexia Nervosa, Bulimia Nervosa

Sleep Disorders

Examples: Primary Sleep Disorders, Sleep Disorders Related to Another Mental Disorder, Other Sleep Disorders

Impulse-Control Disorders Not Elsewhere Classified

Examples: Kleptomania, Pyromania, Pathological Gambling

Adjustment Disorders

Examples: Adjustment Disorder with Depressed Mood, Adjustment Disorder With Disturbance of Conduct

Personality Disorders

Examples: Paranoid Personality Disorder, Borderline Personality Disorder, Avoidant Personality Disorder

Other Conditions That May Be a Focus of Clinical Attention

Examples: Medication-Induced Movement Disorders, Relational Problems, Problems Related to Abuse or Neglect

The DSM-IV also uses a multiaxial classification approach. Aspects of a person's symptoms and general functioning are rated on five different axes. As illustrated in **Table 3.4**, the first two axes provide specific details about the nature of the mental disorder(s) experienced by the person. The remaining three axes provide information on the medical and psychosocial context in which the symptoms and disorders are occurring.

TABLE 3.4   The Multiaxial Classification System of the DSM-IV

Axis I: Clinical Disorders and Other Conditions That May Be a Focus of Clinical Attention

This axis includes all the mental disorders in the DSM-IV except for Personality Disorders and Mental Retardation. If more than one Axis I disorder is present, all disorders are diagnosed and reported on this axis.

Axis II: Personality Disorder and Mental Retardation

This axis includes all diagnoses related to Personality Disorders and Mental Retardation. The listing of these disorders on a separate axis was done to ensure that these conditions are not overlooked when attention is directed to the Axis I disorders. This is important as it is often the Axis I disorders for which people seek treatment.

Axis III: General Medical Conditions

This axis is for providing information on the person's current medical conditions that is potentially relevant to the understanding and/or treatment of the person's Axis I and Axis II disorders.

Axis IV: Psychosocial and Environmental Problems

This axis is for reporting psychosocial and environmental information that may influence the diagnosis, treatment, and prognosis of the mental disorders diagnosed on Axis I and Axis II. The elements to be considered include the following:

- problems with primary support group

- problems related to the social environment

- educational problems

- occupational problems

- housing problems

- economic problems

- problems with access to health care services

- problems related to interaction with the legal system/crime

- other psychosocial and environmental problems

Axis V: Global Assessment of Functioning

On this axis the clinician provides an overall rating of the person's level of functioning. The Global Assessment of Functioning (GAF) Scale is included for this purpose. The GAF Scale ranges from 1 to 100 based on consideration of psychological, social, and occupational functioning. For example, someone who is rated in the 1–10 range is in persistent danger of hurting himself, herself, or others; someone who is rated in the 41–50 range has serious symptoms or has serious impairment in social, occupational, or school functioning; and someone who is rated in the 81–90 range has no or minimal symptoms, with good functioning in all areas of life.

Reprinted with permission from the *Diagnostic and Statistical Manual of Mental Disorders, Text Revision,* Copyright 2000. American Psychiatric Association.

For each mental disorder listed in the DSM-IV, a wealth of information is provided on diagnostic features, subtypes (if applicable), associated features and disorders, prevalence, course, familial pattern, differential diagnosis, and specific culture, age, and gender features. These details provide a context for a fuller appreciation of what is known about the mental disorder and alert the clinician to important aspects that should be considered during the evaluation of the person. Following this information the necessary diagnostic criteria are presented. For some disorders, such as bulimia nervosa, the same diagnostic criteria must be met by everyone who is assigned the diagnosis, although some variability in subtypes of the disorder is possible (see **Table 3.5**). However, for many disorders, such as posttraumatic stress disorder (PTSD), there is enormous variability permitted in the constellation of symptoms required for the diagnosis (see **Table 3.6**). Both elements of criterion A must be met, but criterion B can be met in 5 different ways, and criteria C (at least 3 of any of 7 symptoms) and D (at least 2 of any of 5 symptoms) can be met in dozens of different ways. Bulimia nervosa is an example of a diagnosis that is defined *monothetically* (i.e., all criteria are met in the same manner for people with the diagnosis), whereas PTSD is an example of a diagnosis that is defined *polythetically* (i.e., people diagnosed with this disorder may exhibit markedly different patterns of symptoms).

TABLE 3.5   DSM-IV Diagnostic Criteria for Bulimia Nervosa

A. Recurrent episodes of binge eating. An episode of binge eating is characterized by both of the following:

    (1) eating, in a discrete period of time (e.g., within any 2-hour period), an amount of food that is definitely larger than most people would eat during a similar period of time and under similar circumstances

    (2) a sense of lack of control over eating during the episode (e.g., a feeling that one cannot stop eating or control what or how much one is eating)

B. Recurrent inappropriate compensatory behaviour in order to prevent weight gain, such as self-induced vomiting; misuse of laxatives, diuretics, enemas, or other medications; fasting; or excessive exercise.

C. The binge eating and inappropriate compensatory behaviours both occur, on average, at least twice a week for 3 months.

D. Self-evaluation is unduly influenced by body shape and weight.

E. The disturbance does not occur exclusively during episodes of Anorexia Nervosa.

Specify type:

    Purging Type: during the current episode of Bulimia Nervosa, the person has regularly engaged in a self-induced vomiting or the misuse of laxatives, diuretics, or enemas

    Nonpurging Type: during the current episode of Bulimia Nervosa, the person has used other inappropriate compensatory behaviours, such as fasting or excessive exercise, but has not regularly engaged in self-induced vomiting or the misuse of laxatives, diuretics, or enemas

TABLE 3.6   DSM-IV Diagnostic Criteria for Posttraumatic Stress Disorder

A. The person has been exposed to a traumatic event in which both of the following were present:

    (1) the person experienced, witnessed, or was confronted with an event or events that involved actual or threatened death or serious injury, or a threat to the physical integrity of self or others

    (2) the person's response involved intense fear, helplessness, or horror. **Note:** In children, this may be expressed instead by disorganized or agitated behavior

B. The traumatic event is persistently re-experienced in one (or more) of the following ways:

    (1) recurrent and intrusive distressing recollections of the event, including images, thoughts, or perceptions. **Note:** In young children, repetitive play may occur in which themes or aspects of the trauma are expressed.

    (2) recurrent distressing dreams of the event. **Note:** In children, there may be frightening dreams without recognizable content.

    (3) acting or feeling as if the traumatic event were recurring (includes a sense of reliving the experience, illusions, hallucinations, and dissociative flashback episodes, including those that occur on awakening or when intoxicated). **Note:** In young children, trauma-specific re-enactment may occur.

    (4) intense psychological distress at exposure to internal or external cues that symbolize or resemble an aspect of the traumatic event

    (5) physiological reactivity on exposure to internal or external cues that symbolize or resemble an aspect of the traumatic event

C. Persistent avoidance of stimuli associated with the trauma and numbing of general responsiveness (not present before the trauma), as indicated by three (or more) of the following:

    (1) efforts to avoid thoughts, feelings, or conversations associated with the trauma

    (2) efforts to avoid activities, places, or people that arouse recollections of the trauma

    (3) inability to recall an important aspect of the trauma

    (4) markedly diminished interest or participation in significant activities

    (5) feeling of detachment or estrangement from others

    (6) restricted range of affect (e.g., unable to have loving feelings)

    (7) sense of a foreshortened future (e.g., does not expect to have a career, marriage, or children, or a normal life span)

D. Persistent symptoms of increased arousal (not present before the trauma), as indicated by two (or more) of the following:

    (1) difficulty falling or staying asleep

    (2) irritability or outbursts of anger

    (3) difficulty concentrating

    (4) hypervigilance

continued...

(5) exaggerated startle response

E. Duration of the disturbance (symptoms in Criteria B, C, and D) is more than 1 month.

F. The disturbance causes clinically significant distress or impairment in social, occupational, or other important areas of functioning.

Specify if:

Acute: if duration of symptoms is less than 3 months

Chronic: if duration of symptoms is 3 months or more

Specify if:

With Delayed Onset: if onset of symptoms is at least 6 months after the stressor

Reprinted with permission from the *Diagnostic and Statistical Manual of Mental Disorders, Text Revision,* Copyright 2000. American Psychiatric Association.

In the development of the DSM-IV attention was focused on ethnic and cultural considerations. This is extremely important for the system to be relevant and valid for international use (such as the World Health Organization Mental Health Survey described previously) and use in culturally diverse populations within a country. The DSM-IV and DSM-IV-TR include several types of information that enhance the cultural relevance of the diagnostic system. First, when the scientific evidence exists for cultural/ethnic variations in the clinical presentations of a mental disorder, this information is provided in the text accompanying the diagnostic criteria. Second, a number of culture-specific disorders (often called culture-bound syndromes) are described in an appendix. Examples include *boufée delirante* (a syndrome observed in West Africa and Haiti involving a sudden outburst of agitated and aggressive behaviour, along with considerable confusion and excitement), *mal de ojo* (a concept of the "evil eye" found in many Mediterranean cultures; children are at heightened risk for this syndrome, which may include symptoms of fitful sleep, crying with no apparent cause, vomiting, and fever), and *pibloktoq* (a syndrome found primarily in Inuit communities involving a dissociative episode accompanied by extreme excitement and followed by convulsive seizures and coma lasting up to 12 hours). Finally, information is provided to assist the clinician in making a culturally sensitive and appropriate diagnosis and overall clinical formulation. This includes directing attention to the cultural identity of the person being evaluated, cultural explanations for the individual's disorder, cultural factors related to the psychosocial environment and the person's functioning, and cultural aspects of the relationship between the person and the clinician.

Comorbidity occurs when a person receives diagnoses for two or more disorders at a specific point in time. Hierarchical exclusionary rules were used in DSM-III to deal with the challenge of people presenting with comorbid disorders. In essence these rules meant, for the majority of diagnoses, it was possible to meet criteria for only one diagnosis at a given point in time. If a person met criteria for two or more disorders, a diagnosis was given only for the disorder that was highest in the disorder hierarchy developed for DSM-III. For example, if a person met criteria for major depressive disorder and for an anxiety disorder, only the mood disorder diagnosis could be given. No theoretical rationale or empirical evidence was provided to support these rules. The decision to handle the challenge of comorbidity by defining it out of existence had little positive effect on research or practice. As a result of considerable professional protest, most of these rules were dropped for the DSM-III-R.

The extent of comorbidity in clinical populations is substantial. Brown, Campbell, Lehman, Grisham, and Mancill (2001) assessed the comorbidity of current and lifetime DSM-IV anxiety and mood disorders in more than 1,100 American adults seeking services for stress and anxiety disorders. Among individuals currently meeting diagnostic criteria for an anxiety or mood disorder, 57% also met criteria for another Axis I disorder. For example, among those diagnosed with panic disorder, 36% met criteria for another anxiety disorder and 17% met criteria for a mood disorder. Among those diagnosed with major depressive disorder, 64% met criteria for an anxiety disorder. When lifetime diagnoses were examined, the extent of comorbidity ballooned: 81% of those currently diagnosed with a mood disorder or anxiety disorder also met criteria for another Axis I disorder at some point in their lifetimes. These data show how arbitrary decision rules like those used in DSM-III can distort reality.

Overall, whether based on clinical samples (i.e., those seeking services) or on community samples, most epidemiological surveys find, in country after country, comorbidity rates that exceed 40% (Clark et al., 1995). When individuals with a single disorder are compared with those with comorbid disorders, a very clear pattern emerges: those with comorbid conditions are more severely impaired in daily life functioning, are more likely to have a chronic history of mental health problems, have more physical health problems, and use more health care services (Newman, Moffitt, Caspi, & Silva, 1998). These characteristics have clear consequences for both research and clinical services. On the research side, accurately representing the extent of comorbidity in research samples is necessary to accurately estimate the relation between a disorder and its correlates. On

Those with comorbid conditions are likely to be severely impaired in daily life functioning, have a chronic history of mental health problems, have more physical health problems, and use more health care services.

the clinical service side, people with comorbid disorders are likely to present with psychosocial characteristics that make the planning and delivery of services more complex (Newman et al., 1998). Moreover, if these services are based on treatment research that used patients without comorbid disorders or if these services are focused on only one of the disorders, the services may be suboptimal and may underestimate the scope or duration of treatment necessary for satisfactory outcomes. Because of these concerns, as we will see in the chapters on psychotherapy, psychotherapy researchers are increasingly attuned to the importance of not excluding individuals with coexisting disorders from their studies. Taking this a step further, anxiety disorder expert David Barlow has recently developed and tested a unified treatment for emotional disorders that incorporates aspects of efficacious treatments for mood and anxiety disorders (Barlow, Allen, & Choate, 2004).

There is no question that the later editions of the DSM have revolutionized psychiatric diagnosis. As a result of the improvements that started with the DSM-III, the system has become the gold standard for establishing diagnoses in most areas of psychopathology research. Kendell and Jablensky (2003) defined the utility of a diagnostic system as the extent to which the system provides nontrivial information about prognosis or treatment outcome and/or provides testable propositions about variables associated with the diagnosis. On the basis of this definition, they argued that the DSM-IV has utility, as it provides clinicians with information on likelihood of recovery, relapse, deterioration, and social functioning. The presentation of clear descriptive information has also facilitated the diagnostic training of mental health professionals. This clarity of presentation, combined with unprecedented access to information via the Internet, also allows the public to access comprehensible information on mental disorders that they can use in understanding their symptoms and in seeking mental health services. Indeed the concept of clinical utility is becoming so important in health care services that a number of prominent experts on psychiatric diagnosis have strongly argued for the consideration of utility to be explicitly considered in planning the next edition of the DSM (First et al., 2004).

Limitations of the DSM-IV

Early versions of the DSM have often been described as highly politicized, with science sometimes taking a backseat to prevailing professional views. The current process of requiring systematic research reviews for established diagnoses and for diagnoses proposed for inclusion in the manual has reduced, but not eliminated, such concerns (see our later discussion in this chapter of acute stress disorder). The DSM-IV is not, however, without problems. In this section we will highlight questions that have been raised about the system in the following realms: the definition of abnormality, diagnostic reliability, the heterogeneity of symptom profiles within a disorder, the validity of diagnoses, and the continuing use of a categorical approach to classification.

DEFINING ABNORMALITY (REVISITED)

Earlier in the chapter we presented the DSM-IV and DSM-IV-TR definition of mental disorder. Although this definition should apply to all conditions described in the diagnostic system, Wakefield (1997) has shown that this is not the case. One of the examples he provided was that a depressive reaction, if it is due to uncomplicated bereavement, is not seen as a mood disorder. This is presumably due to the assumption that depressive symptoms are a normal part of grieving. However, even though research has established that depressive symptoms are a common reaction to other significant life stressors, such as divorce or terminal illness, no such exclusions apply to these stressors. It is clear that the requirement that the disorder must not be "merely an expectable or culturally sanctioned response to a particular event" is not applied consistently. As researchers learn more about usual responses to stressful events, this raises the very significant question about the relevance of excluding "expectable" reactions from diagnostic consideration even if these reactions clearly meet the criteria of clinically significant distress or disability.

A second concern that has been raised repeatedly since the introduction of the DSM-III is that, in an effort to ensure coverage of all forms of clinical distress, the diagnostic system may over-diagnose mental disorders. The statistic we cited earlier in the chapter about one-quarter of all American adults having a mental disorder is not an isolated finding, with other estimates suggesting that at least 30% of American adults meet diagnostic criteria for a mental disorder (e.g., Regier et al., 1998). Such epidemiological data have led to calls for more stringent definitions of mental disorder, as many experts doubt that the prevalence of mental disorders can be this high. In response to these concerns, Kessler et al. (2003) used epidemiological data to examine the extent to which diagnostic data predicted psychosocial functioning a decade later. They began by categorizing the diagnostic data based on the severity of the condition: 3.2% of survey respondents met criteria for severe disorders, 3.2% met criteria for serious disorders, 8.7% were classified as having a moderate severity disorder, and 16.0% were classified as mild cases of disorders. Next, they related this classification information to data gathered for the decade following the diagnosis; these data included information on hospitalization for mental health problems, work disability due to a mental disorder, suicide attempts, and whether the survey participants met the criteria for serious (or severe) mental disorder. Kessler and colleagues found a linear relation between disorder severity and subsequent problems in psychosocial functioning. The elevated risk for subsequent psychosocial problems was evident even among those classified as having mild disorders. In fact, compared with people with no diagnosable condition, those suffering from a mild disorder were 2.4 times more likely to develop significant psychosocial problems. Accordingly, the researchers argued that, like physical disorders, mental disorders vary in severity, but even mild mental disorders are associated with substantial subsequent risk for impaired functioning and should be represented within a diagnostic system.

DIAGNOSTIC RELIABILITY

Since the third edition, the DSM has been designed to enhance the reliability of clinical judgement; that is, to enhance the extent to which professionals agree on the presence of a diagnosable condition and on the nature of the condition. Each new version of the system has undergone field testing to determine the extent to which the goal of improved reliability has been attained. Without question, in comparison to DSM-II, there have been substantial improvements in diagnostic reliability. However, evidence from these field trials and other research indicates that the level of inter-rater reliability on the assigning of diagnoses falls below ideal levels.

Kirk (2004) summarized reliability data for several child and adolescent disorders. In evaluating diagnostic reliability it is important to consider two types of reliability. First, reliability studies have examined the ability of independent evaluators to provide diagnoses that fall within the same general category (e.g., within the category of attention-deficit and disruptive behaviour disorders). Most studies examining this form of reliability have found that reliability values can sometimes, but not always, attain an acceptable level (i.e., a value of at least .70 on a measure of inter-rater reliability known as the kappa statistic). Second, reliability studies have also examined the extent to which independent evaluators agree on the same specific diagnosis (e.g., separation anxiety disorder, conduct disorder). Kirk reported that, in such studies, reliability levels often fail to attain an acceptable level. He also noted that there is often extreme variability in reliability values noted from different sites in DSM field trials, with reliability (kappa) values ranging from extremely low (e.g., .18) to extremely high (e.g., 1.0). Because the presence or absence of a diagnosis often determines whether a child is eligible for special health and/or educational services, much more needs to be done to improve the reliability of the DSM system.

HETEROGENEITY OF SYMPTOM PROFILES

One of the aspects of the DSM that could contribute to problems with reliability is the polythetic nature of most of the disorders. Although it would be unrealistic to have a rigid set of criteria that must be met by everyone who has the same disorder, the fact that such extensive symptom variability is permitted in the DSM-IV negatively affects inter-rater reliability. There may also be another critical drawback to the polythetic approach to diagnosis. Variability in response to treatment, whether psychological or pharmacological, could be related to variability in symptom profiles among treated patients. Yet, because the level of analysis is typically on the relation between diagnosis and outcome, the connection between different symptom profiles and treatment responsiveness could be overlooked.

Such limitations of a polythetic approach have been recognized for decades and attempts to address these limitations have often focused on establishing clinically relevant subtypes within a diagnosis. As Clark et al. (1995) noted, few of these efforts have been successful and many of the subtypes described in DSM-IV have only limited empirical support. The distinction between purging and nonpurging types of bulimia (see Table 3.5) is one of the few with a firm empirical basis: individuals who purge are likely to have more severe psychopathology than are those who don't. There are many disorders for which no viable or useful subtypes have been established. As Clark et al. (1995) pointed out, an incredible range of specifiers is available for major depressive disorder, including severity, chronicity, and the nature of some symptoms (e.g., catatonic or melancholic features). The resulting range of symptoms and features covered under this diagnosis is so diverse that it seems verging on impossible—or meaningless—for a single diagnosis to be applied to all the possible patient profiles.

DIAGNOSTIC VALIDITY

As we discussed earlier in the chapter, validity is a central criterion that must be considered in evaluating a classification system. Kendell and Jablensky (2003) defined diagnostic validity as an indication that a disorder is a discrete entity that has clear boundaries with other disorders. Kendell and Jablensky suggested that very few mental disorders have demonstrated diagnostic validity. It is noteworthy that all the examples of valid diagnoses that they listed were conditions with clear biological causes, including Down's syndrome and Huntington's disease.

A prime example of a diagnosis with questionable validity is acute stress disorder (ASD). This diagnosis involves the development of anxiety, dissociative features, and other symptoms within a month following exposure to a traumatic stressor. As Harvey and Bryant (2002) noted, ASD was introduced into DSM-IV to fill a vacuum that existed around the diagnosis of PTSD. A diagnosis of PTSD cannot be applied to such symptoms if they occur within a month of the traumatic event (see Table 3.6). ASD was defined, therefore, as a disorder in which PTSD-like disorders occurred shortly after the trauma. If symptoms of ASD persist for more than a month after the event, then a diagnosis of PTSD may be appropriate and the ASD diagnosis would be superseded. This opens the possibility that researchers might be able to establish the nature of connections between initial distress following trauma (i.e., ASD) and more chronic distress (i.e., PTSD).

There have been a number of criticisms raised about ASD, all of which raise major questions about its diagnostic validity. The criticisms, as summarized by Harvey and Bryant (2002), include: the requirement for dissociative symptoms is not consistent with research on trauma reactions, it is inappropriate to introduce a diagnosis into DSM-IV in order to predict another diagnosis, it is inappropriate to introduce a diagnosis that has almost no supporting empirical evidence, it is not justifiable to distinguish between two diagnoses with comparable symptoms simply on the basis of symptom duration, and there is a great likelihood that the diagnosis could pathologize transient stress reactions that do not require the attention of mental health professionals. The introduction of ASD has certainly served to promote research into acute stress reactions. Nevertheless, it seems clear that the questions raised by the inclusion of this diagnosis outweigh any value it has had in serving as an impetus for research.

CATEGORICAL VERSUS DIMENSIONAL CLASSIFICATION

Comorbidity is a clinical fact. When a categorical classification system is used, the presence of comorbidity contradicts the assumption that diagnostic categories are discrete and nonoverlapping. The DSM-IV explicitly acknowledges that each category of mental disorder need not be a discrete entity—yet doing so opens up the possibility that a dimensional system may better represent the nature of mental disorders. As noted in the DSM-IV, there are no commonly agreed upon dimensional systems that could replace the DSM-IV categorical approach. Later in the chapter we will describe some very promising research that may make a diagnostic system at least partially based on dimensional classification a reality in the future.

There has been a great deal of controversy in the area of depression research about whether depression is a discrete diagnostic category or whether it should be viewed as existing on a continuum that includes both clinical symptoms and subclinical distress. The most sophisticated research now suggests that depression may encompass both a specific condition and a continuum. Santor and Coyne (2001), for example, obtained clinician ratings of symptoms on samples of clinically depressed adults and nonclinically depressed—but distressed—adults. When depressed and nondepressed individuals with comparable levels of clinician-rated depressive symptoms were compared, group differences on specific symptoms were apparent. Depressed mood, anhedonia (lack of pleasure), and suicidality were more likely to be evident in the depressed group, whereas hypochondriasis and insomnia were more evident in the nondepressed group. Thus, although the severity of depressive symptoms can be expressed on a continuum, Santor and Coyne argued that the use of a continuum (or dimensional) model might mask important and diagnostically relevant group differences. Using self-report measures of depressive symptoms, research on both clinical (Ruscio & Ruscio, 2000) and nonclinical (Beach & Amir, 2003) samples have found evidence for both categorical and dimensional features. Specifically, analyses of self-report items expressing distress (e.g., discouragement, loss of interest in others) appear to yield a dimensional perspective on the continuum of subclinical to clinical depression. In contrast, analyses of self-report items of somatic symptoms (e.g., sleep disturbance, weight loss) appear to provide strong evidence that some depressive symptoms are best understood as constituting a discrete disorder.

In conducting research on the underlying structure of mental disorders we can also step back from examining a specific disorder and explore patterns that may exist across disorders. Based on epidemiological data, it is increasingly clear that comorbidity cannot be explained as being simply due to either symptom overlap among diagnostic categories or to methodological problems in research. Instead it seems that there are a number of core pathological processes that underlie the overt expression of a seemingly diverse range of symptoms (Widiger & Clark, 2000). Specifically, the internalizing and externalizing dimensions that were first identified with respect to children's problems also are helpful in understanding adult problems. For example, in a study of young New Zealand adults, Krueger, Caspi, Moffitt, and Silva (1998) found that a two-factor model accounted for the expression of psychological symptoms at ages 18 and 21 years. Anxiety disorder and mood disorders constituted an underlying internalizing factor and the conduct disorder and substance abuse disorders were indicators of an externalizing factor. A major cross-cultural study examining the structure of psychiatric comorbidity in 14 countries (Netherlands, Germany, United Kingdom, France, Italy, Greece, Turkey, Japan, China, India, Nigeria, Brazil, Chile, and the United States) tested for the presence of these factors. Krueger, Chentsova-Dutton, Markon, Goldberg, and Ormel (2003) found that depression, somatic disorders, and anxiety consistently formed a single factor, whereas symptoms of alcohol abuse consistently formed a second factor. The inclusion of data from a variety of Western and non-Western countries strengthens the conclusion that there may

Among adults, substance abuse disorders are typically seen as indicators of an externalizing form of psychopathhology.

be internalizing and externalizing psychopathological characteristics that underlie many mental disorders. We will return to this perspective in the final section of this chapter.

OTHER CLASSIFICATION SYSTEMS

The *International Statistical Classification of Diseases and Related Health Problems* (ICD-10) is the statistical classification of all health conditions developed by the World Health Organization and is now in its tenth edition (WHO, 1992). The way in which the ICD-10 is used varies from country to country. Most countries use it, at a minimum, to classify causes of death. In the United States and some other countries a clinical modification of the ICD has often been used to classify diagnoses for all conditions and reasons for visits for health care services. The clinical modification provides more precision about each diagnosis and the person's condition than does the comparable ICD; this is important because more detail is required if the information is to be used for service provision purposes than if it is to be used for statistical purposes (such as reporting population-based trends in illness).

At present, work on a draft of the clinical modification for ICD-10 (ICD-10-CM) has been completed, but it has not yet been implemented; as a result, health care practitioners in the United States and other countries continue to use the clinical modification of the ninth edition of the ICD (ICD-9-CM). The Mental and Behavioural Disorders section found in the ICD-10 and the draft ICD-10-CM is compatible with the DSM-IV, although there are some differences in the way in which diagnoses are described or conceptualized. For example, acute stress reaction is defined differently than is the DSM-IV acute stress disorder—it is not seen as a potential precursor to PTSD—and a broader, more diffuse set of anxiety and depressive symptoms is presented, with the timeframe for symptom expression being the first two days following a traumatic event (Harvey & Bryant, 2002).

The World Health Organization has also developed a companion classification system for the ICD that is called the *International Classification of Functioning, Disability and Health* (ICF). Moving beyond the classification of disease and illnesses, the ICF provides a system for describing health and health-related conditions. With respect to functioning and disability (i.e., impairments in functioning, activity limitations, or participation restrictions), information is coded for both the person's body (functions of body systems and body structures) and the person's societal involvement (activities and participation). It is also possible to use the ICF to code environmental factors that affect a person's health functioning. The focus on overall functioning and disability, as opposed to just a clinical diagnosis, is particularly important for psychologists working in rehabilitation and pain management services.

A fundamentally different approach to the classification of mental disorders is found in the *Achenbach System of Empirically Based Assessment* (ASEBA; Achenbach, 2002). ASEBA is a family of empirically derived assessment tools to measure competence and problems across the lifespan. Measures are available to be completed by parents of very young children (Child Behavior Checklist/1.5 to 5) and school-age children (CBCL/6-18). Parallel measures can be completed by adolescents (Youth Self Report: YSR) and by young adults (Young Adult Self-Report: YASR). In addition, measures have been developed for teachers and caregivers of very young children (Caregiver-Teacher Report Form/2-5) and for teachers of school-age children (Teacher Report Form, TRF 5-18). The ASEBA was designed to provide a standardized, normative framework for rating child competence and problems and for integrating information from different raters. As mentioned earlier in the chapter, behaviour problem scales were derived empirically through factor analysis. The scales yield broad band measures of internalizing (withdrawn, somatic complaints, and anxious/depressed) and externalizing problems (delinquent and aggressive), as well as measures of finer grained syndromes. Some syndromes are found only for certain age and sex groupings, and some are evident only on one measure. Clinical cut-off scores allow both a dimensional and categorical approach to be taken to child problems. In addition, some of the measures allow an assessment of DSM symptoms.

Hundreds of studies have demonstrated that these measures are both reliable and valid. As the measures have been validated in many languages, they have been used to assess child psychopathology in different countries. Research with the ASEBA has confirmed that it is common for there to be only modest correlations between different raters of a child's problems. One very help-ful feature of the ASEBA is a Cross-Informant Comparison that provides information on the correlation between different raters of the same problem, as well as a comparison to normative data. So, for example, 14-year-old Dylan's responses to the YSR might show that he sees himself as having only a few externalizing problems, whereas his mother sees him as having clinically significant exter-nalizing problems, but the degree of agreement between them is average for 14-year-olds and their mothers. The ASEBA is widely used in clinics and schools as well as in research contexts. The ASEBA has the distinction of being easy to administer (it requires only a fifth grade reading level and takes less than 20 minutes to complete), clinically useful (it distinguishes between clinically significant and normal levels of problems and is sensitive to change), and valuable for research (the broad band dimensions of internalizing and externalizing problems have been shown to be useful in understand-ing both child and adult problems). The recent development of scales for adults allows this system to be used to assess individuals across the lifespan.

SUMMARY AND CONCLUSIONS

Classification is a fundamental human activity. The classification of mental disorders draws on both a neo-Kraepelinian tradition as well as on a more recent developmental psychopathology approach that takes into account contextual variables such as developmental stage. The definition of a mental disorder requires not only that behaviours are abnormal, but also that they cause harm to the indi-vidual and that they are outside the individual's control. In North America, the most commonly used system is the *Diagnostic and Statistical Manual of Mental Disorders*. Over time this manual has moved toward placing a greater reliance on evidence-based diagnosis. In turn, the development of clear deci-sion-making rules has enabled advances to be made in the study of psychopathology. Cross-cultural studies using the DSM system have revealed great variability across countries in the incidence of dis-orders. The most common types of disorders found in all countries are anxiety disorders and mood disorders. An alternative approach to categorical diagnosis is to assess individuals on important dimensions of functioning. The dimensions of internalizing and externalizing problems that were originally identified from studies of child psychopathology are also proving to be useful in under-standing adult psychopathology.

Critical Thinking Questions

What are the benefits of classification?

Why should we care about whether a behaviour is abnormal or not?

How does culture influence definitions of normality and abnormality?

What is the role of basic research in psychology in informing the diagnosis of mental disorders?

How can we make sense out of differing prevalence rates of mental disorders across countries?

What are the advantages and disadvantages for a young person such as Carl of receiving a diagnosis of PTSD?

K e y   T e r m s

categorical approach	dimensional approach
comorbidity	dyscontrol
developmental psychopathology	harmful dysfunction
diagnosis	utility
diagnostic system	validity

K e y   N a m e s

Thomas Achenbach	Emil Kraepelin
Keith Conners	Herbert Quay

ADDITIONAL RESOURCES
Journals

Journal of Abnormal Psychology

Journal of Abnormal Child Psychology

Archives of General Psychiatry

American Journal of Psychiatry

Canadian Journal of Psychiatry

Book

First, M. B., & Tasman, A. (Eds.). (2004). *DSM-IV mental disorders: Diagnosis, etiology, & treatment.* Hoboken, NJ: John Wiley & Sons.

CHAPTER 4

Research Methods in Clinical Psychology

INTRODUCTION

"Will I get over my bulimia if I follow this therapy?"

"I have a bipolar disorder, so how likely is it that my children will have this disorder too?"

"Is there anything that can be done to help my son who has autism?"

"How much time is my mother likely to have before her dementia makes it impossible for her to safely live on her own?"

"What effect will my divorce have on my young daughter?"

Psychologists who provide services to the public face questions like these daily. Clinical psychologists are constantly confronted with questions that require answers based on solid research data. The people asking these and myriad similar questions deserve far more than a response based simply on a hunch—they deserve the best information that science can provide them.

According to our professional standards and our ethical codes, people have a right to expect psychological services that are firmly based on psychological science. This is known as **evidence-based practice**—basing clinical services and health care policy, whenever feasible, on replicated evidence gathered from scientific studies (Institute of Medicine, 2002; Sackett, Rosenberg, Gray, Haynes, & Richardson, 1996). Evidence-based practice requires psychologists to be not only sensitive and empathic, but also well-informed about current research relevant to the services they provide. The effective scientist-practitioner thinks in a scientific manner and applies knowledge derived from research with care and compassion. The antithesis of evidence-based practice is practice based on tradition and authority, what some have facetiously called *eminence-based practice*. The public should be sceptical about accepting opinions simply because they come from a supposed expert, such as Dr. Phil or Dr. Ruth. As Mullen and Streiner (2004) rightly stated, the opinions of even recognized experts are just that—opinions—unless their views are supported by the best available empirical evidence. Moreover, as illustrated in **Table 4.1**, we cannot simply rely on common sense as a guide to appropriate decision-making, as there are often logical inconsistencies in the way that people process information and make decisions. Although such inconsistencies may be of little consequence when facing a decision about what brand of breakfast cereal to buy, they can have enormous effects on decisions related to seeking and following through on health care services. **Viewpoint Box 4.1** on research examining the effectiveness of psychotherapy for children and adolescents provides a compelling illustration of the need for research even on questions to which we think we have clear answers.

TABLE 4.1   Some Common Errors in Thinking

Faulty Reasoning: A form of argument that is inaccurate or misleading in some way.
Example: "Psychologists have provided effective services for decades without having research available on what makes treatment effective. Therefore there is no reason for me to bother reading this research in order to be effective." One of the ways in which this is inaccurate is that the argument does not provide any proof that the services of these unspecified psychologists were effective.

False Dilemma: This fallacy takes the form of reducing the range of options available to just two (usually extreme) options.
Example: "Either I accept the treatment that the psychologist is suggesting or I just give up trying to change." Clearly other options are available, including asking the psychologist what treatment options might be available or consulting another psychologist (or other health care provider) to obtain a second opinion.

Golden Mean Fallacy: This logical error involves assuming that the most valid conclusion to reach is a compromise of two competing positions.
Example: "I have heard that both cognitive and psychodynamic treatments can be helpful for the type of problems I have, so I really should look for a treatment that combines both cognitive and psychodynamic elements." Assuming that the original statement about effective treatments is correct, there is no reason to assume that a synthesis of the two treatments would be more effective than either treatment on its own.

The Straw Person Argument: This involves mischaracterizing a position in order to make it look absurd or unpalatable.
Example: "Anyone who would prescribe a drug to treat my symptoms just wants to turn me into a mindless, soulless robot." It is highly unlikely that the health care professional recommending medication has this goal in mind, but it provides a simplistic rationale for rejecting the possibility of taking the medication.

continued...

Affirming the Consequent: This logical error takes the following form: first, assume that *x* is a cause of *y*, then, when *y* is observed, conclude that *x* must have caused it.

Example: "People who have schizophrenia always act in a bizarre manner. This person is acting bizarrely. So obviously, this person has schizophrenia." There are problems with this, including the fact that people with schizophrenia do not always act in a bizarre manner and that there can be many explanations for bizarre behaviour other than the presence of a psychotic disorder.

Appeal to Ignorance: This mistake takes the form of arguing that, because there is no evidence to prove a position is wrong, the position must be correct.

Example: "There is no scientific evidence that having my patients sing and dance while they remember the trauma that they experienced harms them or is ineffective. So, of course, this new form of therapy has to be helpful." The lack of evidence to demonstrate harm or ineffectiveness is not, of course, equivalent to the presence of evidence for the beneficial effects of the treatment.

Adapted from K. S. Pope, 2003

VIEWPOINT BOX 4.1

EFFECTIVENESS OF PSYCHOTHERAPY FOR CHILDREN AND ADOLESCENTS

Meta-analyses of treatments for children suggest that psychological interventions are efficacious in reducing behavioural and emotional problems. However, the treatments that have been studied differ in important ways from the most commonly offered treatments for children. The types of treatments that are represented in meta-analyses are mostly behavioural treatments that are time-limited, highly structured, and delivered in a consistent fashion. There has been relatively little evaluation of traditional child psychotherapy and the few studies that have been conducted yielded very discouraging results. So we know from meta-analysis that there are efficacious treatments for children, but there is little evidence that traditional therapy—the kind that is most readily available to children—actually works. Before we dismiss traditional therapy, it is important to make sure that it has been properly tested.

Weiss, Catron, Harris, and Phung (1999) screened children using teacher, peer, and self-report measures of psychopathology. Families of children with significant problems were then contacted and invited to take part in the study. Children with behavioural problems were then randomly assigned to receive either traditional psychotherapy (*n* = 76) or academic tutoring (*n* = 84). Children in the traditional psychotherapy group received child-oriented therapy from experienced clinicians with graduate training in a mental health profession. The therapists were free to use their judgement in providing whatever services they deemed necessary. They then responded to a scale describing the different therapeutic techniques they favoured.

Therapists in this study favoured cognitive and psychodynamic approaches over behavioural approaches. Children in the therapy group received an average of 60 sessions. To control for the extra adult attention received by children in the therapy group, children in the academic tutoring group received on average 53 tutoring sessions from teachers and graduate students in special education. Academic tutors were required to avoid therapeutic interactions. Audiotapes of tutoring sessions were reviewed to ensure that tutors adhered to the non-therapy rule.

Outcome assessments were based on data from multiple informants (parent, teacher, and self-report) and took place at six-month intervals, at the end of treatment, and at one-year follow-up. Analyses indicated that children in the two groups were similar for 16 of the 17 variables assessed. The only way in which they differed was that parents of children in the treatment group had slightly more education than did parents of children in the tutoring group. We can be confident therefore that the process of random assignment was successful in ensuring that the two groups were similar before the children started receiving services. At the end of the services, children in both groups had improved in terms of their psychopathology as rated by children, parents, and teachers. There were no differences in the rates of improvement between children in the therapy group and children in the tutoring group. The only difference between groups was in terms of parent satisfaction, with parents reporting higher levels of satisfaction with therapy than with tutoring.

To check whether child psychotherapy would show a *sleeper effect*, with positive effects taking a longer time to be evident, a follow-up was also conducted (Weiss, Catron, & Harris, 2000). Two-year follow-up data presented essentially the same picture: there was no compelling evidence that the provision of traditional child psychotherapy produced superior effects to those found with academic tutoring. The results of this carefully controlled study, although requiring replication, are powerful. They do not provide any data to justify the substantial costs associated with providing children with lengthy child psychotherapy. They raise ethical issues about whether one can justify continuing to offer traditional child psychotherapy when the most likely change is that parents are satisfied that their children are receiving services. If a friend were to ask you to recommend services for a child with emotional and behavioural problems, what would you suggest?

The evolution of the treatment of obsessive-compulsive disorder (OCD) is a good example of the way that research can inform practice (Thomas & Rosqvist, 2003). You may recall that in Chapter 3 we described Teresa, who suffered from OCD. Literature dating back centuries describes people who suffered from what we now call obsessions and compulsions. The clinical focus on OCD started in the 1800s when these obsessions and compulsions were seen as a mental problem. Until the 1960s, OCD was considered an untreatable disorder, so someone like Teresa might have received a diagnosis, but would not have received services that were likely to help. However, the prognosis for individuals with OCD changed dramatically with the development of behavioural treatments that included the key treatment components of exposure (i.e., generating anxiety for the individual by deliberate exposure to the anxiety-provoking thoughts or external stimuli) and response prevention (i.e., stopping the person from engaging in the rituals that are typically used to inappropriately manage the anxiety). At present, when this form of treatment is used, most people with OCD experience substantial improvements in functioning (Abramowitz, 1997). However, there were many dead ends and wrong turns along the road to the development of effective behavioural therapy for OCD. For example, it was common in the 1970s and 1980s for a thought-stopping component to be included in OCD treatments. This required the person to yell "Stop" or to make a loud noise whenever unwanted, intrusive thoughts occurred. This treatment was not very practical. Imagine the response you might get from others in the library or the bus if you were to yell "Stop" or make a loud noise every now and again. Even more problematic, later research showed that trying not to think about something often has a paradoxical effect: it results in the increased persistence of intrusive thoughts! If we ask you not to think of taking a break from studying and having a delicious snack, you may notice that images of appetizing snacks keep popping into your head.

In this chapter we provide a brief introduction to the kinds of issues that must be considered in designing and interpreting research in clinical psychology. The majority of issues that we touch on apply to research in other areas of psychology, but we will highlight their relevance to the practice of clinical psychology and discuss some challenges that only clinical researchers face in testing their research hypotheses. To give you a sense of the whole research endeavour, we begin by discussing the way research hypotheses are generated. Then we emphasize that the researcher must be sensitive to ethical issues in the planning, conduct, and reporting of research. Next, we describe a number of clinically relevant research designs, and highlight aspects of sampling, measurement, and statistical analyses. We conclude this chapter by attending to factors that influence the reporting and utilization of research results. Even though the focus of this chapter is on research design *per se*, it is important to be aware that the type of disciplined thinking required to design a good study is also necessary to design and evaluate appropriate psychological services for the public.

Imagine the response from these students if you were working at the next table and all of a sudden yelled "STOP" as part of your thought-stopping treatment.

GENERATING RESEARCH HYPOTHESES

How does a researcher get ideas of what to study? **Table 4.2** shows some of the many possible sources of research ideas, including personal experience, professional experience, and knowledge of the scientific literature. Whatever the source or inspiration for our research ideas, our thinking is always influenced by the type of theory we hold about human behaviour. In some instances the researcher uses a formal theory to generate a research idea; this is known as following a deductive process. In other instances the researcher follows an inductive process, for example, deriving an idea from repeated observations of everyday events. Even though the inductive process is not explicitly guided by theory, it is influenced by the researcher's informal theories, including his or her theoretical orientation and general worldview. Not only do theories influence the types of research ideas the researcher generates, they also influence the way the researcher interprets the data he or she obtains from the completed research study. In other words, researchers are not immune from the potential biasing effects of their own beliefs and values. Despite the potential for theories to mislead researchers in their interpretation of the results of research, science could not progress without theories, for theories serve to organize and give meaning to the results of research endeavours and to generate new ideas to be tested in future research.

TABLE 4.2   Possible Sources of Research Ideas

Everyday Experience and Observation
Example: Noticing that your children's friends are troubled by their parents' divorce.

Professional Experience and Observation
Example: Noticing a pattern among one's patients that seems to indicate a connection between feelings of social rejection and specific early childhood experiences.

Addressing Applied Problems and Needs
Example: Testing whether a successful psychoeducational treatment package for helping police officers better manage work stress can be adapted to alleviate the distress of victims of serious motor vehicle accidents.

Previous Research
Example: Attempting to reconcile contradictory findings in previous research by comparing the phenomenon in clinic and community samples, as variations in sampling may be responsible for these inconsistent findings.

Theory
Example: Directly comparing the ability of two different theories of motivation to predict which distressed couples will stay in couples' therapy and which couples will terminate services prematurely.

After developing a general research idea, scientists follow a number of steps to ensure that the idea is properly formulated and tested. First, the researcher consults the published research on the phenomenon of interest. Second, assuming that there is no research that has directly tested the idea, the researcher begins to formalize ideas so that they can be tested in a scientific manner. This requires translating abstract ideas into something that can be measured. For example, a researcher interested in violence may decide to measure the frequency and intensity of violent acts in the previous year. Part of this task of **operationalizing** an abstract concept requires that the researcher consider the precise nature of the relations among the concepts that form the research idea (see **Table 4.3**). A major challenge in operationalizing an idea is ensuring that the resulting operational definition fully captures the key aspects inherent in the original idea. Third, the researcher must carefully consider the extent to which the research idea may be based on cultural assumptions that may limit the applicability or relevance of the planned research (American Psychological Association, 2003). Ensuring the cultural relevance of the planned research and the use of appropriate samples of participants can do much to enhance the value of the research. Fourth, the researcher must begin to consider how to ensure the testing of the idea is done ethically. Based on ethical considerations, the researcher must recognize that some research design options are inappropriate for testing his or her idea (e.g., using random assignment in an experiment to determine who experiences violence). Finally, the researcher must draw together all the results of the previous steps to sketch out the study procedures. Along the way some aspects of the planned study may need to be dropped or modified due to practical constraints (e.g., insufficient funds available, lack of appropriate measures).

Choices about the ethical conduct, type of research design, sample of participants, and measures used all influence the research hypothesis that will be tested. For example, a simple statement such as "Increased anxiety is associated with more errors in social interactions" could be translated into a number of very different research hypotheses, each dependent on the specific choices made about methodological features of the study. To determine whether increased anxiety was associated with more errors in social interaction across people with different levels of trait anxiety, the design would include research participants of varying anxiety levels. If the researcher wished to determine whether the statement was true within individuals as they became more or less anxious, then the design would require that participants be tested repeatedly as they experienced different levels of anxiety. This might also involve the researcher attempting to manipulate the participants' anxiety levels, in which case the hypothesis would be recast as "An increase in anxiety causes more errors in social interactions." If the researcher wished to determine if the statement was true for all ages, this would require participants of different ages. The bottom line is that researchers must ensure that the research methods match the hypothesis to be tested.

TABLE 4.3 Conceptualizing the Relations Among Concepts/Variables

1. **What are the relations among the variables of interest?**

   Correlation: The variables are associated with each other.

   Example: Mothers' ratings of children's behaviour problems are correlated with fathers' scores of children's behaviour problems.

   Cause: One variable directly or indirectly influences the level of a second variable.

   Example: A child's hyperactive symptoms result in parental stress.

2. **What are the factors that influence the relations among variables?**

   Moderation: One variable influences the direction or size of the relation between two other variables.

   Example: The negative effects of marital conflict on children are lower in families with a strong parental alliance than they are in families with a poor parental alliance.

3. **How does one variable influence a second variable?**

   Mediation: The influence of one variable on a second variable is due, in whole or in part, to the influence of a third variable.

   Example: The link between maternal HIV status and children's depressive symptoms is partially explained by maternal depressive symptoms.

4. **Is it possible to alter an outcome of interest?**

   Prevention: An attempt to decrease the likelihood that an undesirable outcome occurs.

   Example: School-based programs to decrease bullying.

   Intervention: An attempt to decrease or eliminate an undesirable outcome that has already occurred.

   Example: Treatment to reduce bingeing and purging.

Adapted from Kazdin (1999)

ETHICS IN RESEARCH

An investigator must pay close attention to ethical factors in the design, conduct, and reporting of research. This is true for all science, but is especially important in clinical psychology research in which research participants are vulnerable due to their psychological distress and/or to the fact that they may be receiving treatment services as part of the research. The quest for knowledge must never compromise the welfare of research participants. *The Canadian Code of Ethics for Psychologists* (Canadian Psychological Association, 2000), described in Chapter 2, does not distinguish between research ethics and clinical practice ethics. Instead, the psychologist is expected to apply the general principles (Respect for the Dignity of Persons, Responsible Caring, Integrity in Relationships, and Responsibility to Society) in a research context just as he or she would in other parts of the professional role. Other psychological organizations, such as the American Psychological Association (APA), the Australian Psychological Society, and the British Psychological Society include in their ethical codes sections addressing the application of ethical principles in a research context (Rae & Sullivan, 2003).

Illustrating the range of ethical issues that must be considered throughout the research process, **Table 4.4** provides a summary of research-relevant ethical principles found in the APA code of conduct (2002). These principles underline that attention to the welfare of research participants (and animal subjects) and honesty in the presentation of research findings are overarching themes to which psychologists must attend. The issue of informed consent is particularly important, as this provides an assurance that a research participant is fully aware of the benefits or risks of research involvement. An example of a consent form for a clinical psychology research study is presented in **Table 4.5**.

TABLE 4.4   American Psychological Association Ethical Principles for Research and Publication

1. **Institutional Approval**

   When required, institutional approval for research must be obtained and the research must be conducted in accordance with the approved research protocol.

2. **Informed Consent for Research**

   When obtaining informed consent, potential participants must be informed of the purpose of the research, their rights to decline or withdraw participation, the possible consequences of declining or withdrawing, the possible consequences of being involved in the research, any benefits stemming from research involvement, limits of confidentiality, incentives for research participation, and whom to contact for questions about the research and participants' rights.

3. **Informed Consent for Recording**

   Informed consent for recording voices or images must be obtained prior to the recording unless the research consists solely of observations in public places or the research design involves some form of deception that requires that informed consent be sought after the recording has been completed.

4. **Client/Patient, Student, and Subordinate Research Participants**

   When research is conducted with clients/patients, students, or subordinates, steps must be taken to protect the potential participants from adverse consequences of declining or withdrawing participation.

5. **Dispensing With Informed Consent**

   It may be possible to dispense with informed consent only where the research would not be expected to cause harm or distress or where permitted by law or government regulation.

6. **Offering Inducements for Research Participation**

   Excessive or inappropriate monetary or other inducements for research are to be avoided if such inducements are likely to coerce participation in the research.

continued...

7. **Deception in Research**

Deception is not used in research unless it is justified by the study's likely value and the use of nondeceptive procedures is not feasible. Deception cannot be used if the research is likely to cause physical pain or severe emotional distress. When deception is used, participants must be informed about the nature of deception as early as is feasible.

8. **Debriefing**

Participants must have an opportunity to promptly obtain information about the nature, results, and conclusions of the research and steps must be taken to attempt to correct any misconceptions about the research.

9. **Humane Care and Use of Animals in Research**

Animals used in research must be acquired, cared for, used, and disposed of in compliance with laws, government regulations, and professional standards. All those involved in the use of animals in research must be instructed in the care, maintenance, and handling of the animals. Reasonable efforts are made to minimize the discomfort and pain of animal subjects and, if an animal's life is to be terminated, the act must proceed rapidly and with an effort to minimize pain.

10. **Reporting Research Results**

Fabrication of data is not permitted and reasonable steps must be taken to correct any significant errors found in published research reports.

11. **Plagiarism**

The work or data of others is not presented by a researcher as his/her own.

12. **Publication Credit**

Authorship of a publication must accurately reflect the contributions of the author(s); minor contributions to the research or the writing of the publication do not merit authorship.

13. **Duplicate Publication of Data**

Data that have been previously published are not published subsequently as original data.

14. **Sharing Research Data for Verification**

After results are published, researchers must ensure that their data are available for verification or re-analysis by other competent professionals.

15. **Obligations on Reviewers**

Those who review material submitted for publication or for grant support respect the confidentiality of the material.

Adapted from APA (2003).

TABLE 4.5 Sample Consent Form

Dr. Chris Brown
Department of Psychology, University of Canada
Telephone number: (123) 456-7890
Email address: chrisbrown@ucanada.ca

We are conducting a study to better understand the factors that are involved in decisions to seek and receive psychological services. This study is being conducted by Dr. Chris Brown, a professor at the Department of Psychology at the University of Canada. We would like to interview you about the factors that played a role in your decision to request psychological services at the Department of Psychology's Psychological Service Centre and about the expectations you have for therapy or counselling. The interview will take place either prior to or following an appointment you have at the Psychological Service Centre. Participation in the interview will take approximately 30 minutes. You will receive an honorarium of $15 for your participation in this study. This will be given to you following the completion of the interview.

I consent to participate in this study. I understand that I am agreeing to be interviewed and that the interview will involve approximately 30 minutes of my time. I understand that as the questions deal with personal decisions about seeking psychological treatment, I may experience some slight distress in answering the questions. I have received assurances from the researcher that every effort will be made to minimize the likelihood of any distress. Nevertheless, I have the right to refuse to answer any question. I also understand that I am free to withdraw from this study at any time. Any decision to withdraw from the study will not affect the status of the services I am receiving at the Psychological Service Centre.

I understand that all my answers will be kept strictly confidential; not even my therapist will have access to any information related to this study. My information will be kept in a locked filing cabinet, and only members of the research team will have access to the information.

I understand that my anonymity will be assured by never using my name or identifying information in the analysis and reporting of this study. Only a code number will be used to identify my information and all reports of this study will involve combined information from all participants.

I understand that if I have any questions or concerns about the study I can contact Dr. Brown at (123) 456-7890 or at chrisbrown@ucanada.ca. If I wish, I can also contact the university protocol officer for ethics in research at (123) 456-0000 or at protocolethics@ucanada.ca to obtain information or to make a complaint about the ethical conduct of this study.

Finally I understand that I can receive a summary of findings at the completion of the study.

There are two copies of this consent form, one of which I may keep.

Participant's Signature: _____

Date: _____

Researcher's Signature: _____

Date: _____

I wish to receive a summary of the findings of this study upon its completion.

     YES ❑   NO ❑

Prior to data collection the researcher must obtain approval for conducting the research from the institution in which he or she works. In Canadian institutions, research ethics boards (REBs) are charged with ensuring that the proposed research conforms to the policy statement on the ethical conduct of research formulated by the Canadian Institutes of Health Research, the Natural Sciences and Engineering Research Council of Canada, and the Social Sciences and Humanities Research Council of Canada. This means that the researcher must provide extensive details about the proposed study to the institution's REB. This involves providing both general information about the nature of the study and the procedures involved, as well as information specific to ethical considerations in the recruitment and research involvement of participants. **Table 4.6** lists the types of information that a researcher must provide when seeking REB approval to conduct a study.

TABLE 4.6   Sample Form for Requesting Ethics Evaluation of a Research Project

This application form must be completed and submitted by all researchers planning to use human participants in their research study. All questions must be answered fully.

1. **Type of Research**

   Example: Honours' student thesis project, doctoral dissertation, professor's research

2. **Researchers**

   Please provide names, addresses, and institutional affiliations.

3. **Research Project**

   Please provide title, anticipated starting and completion dates, and funding source. Please provide a summary (i.e., no more than 6 pages) of the proposed research that includes full details of the proposed methodology.

4. **Research Participants**

   Please provide details about the number of participants required and their ages and any special characteristics they must possess.

5. **Participant Recruitment**

   Please provide details on how and where participants will be recruited. If an organization has consented to provide support for participant recruitment, please provide evidence of this consent. Who will be responsible for contacting potential participants? Please provide copies of all forms or scripts used to recruit participants. If children are to be recruited, what steps have been taken to ensure that they and their legal guardians are provided with developmentally appropriate descriptions of the research and the nature of participation in the research?

6. **Screening of Participants**

   Will any steps be taken to select or exclude individuals from research participation? If yes, please include copies of the materials used for this screening.

7. **Research Participation**

   What, exactly, are the participants asked to do in the research? Please provide copies of all measures or interviews that will be completed and a full description of all tasks that participations will be asked to complete.

continued...

8. **Informed Consent**

   Please provide a copy of the consent to research form. What steps have been taken to ensure that there is no coercion to participate in the research? What steps have been taken to ensure that all requests for participants and descriptions of the research are done in a respectful and culturally appropriate manner?

9. **Potential Harms and Benefits**

   Please describe the potential harms to research participants, including physical harm, psychological harm, legal harms or inconveniences, or economic inconveniences. What steps are to been taken to minimize these harms? Please describe the potential benefits of the research and why the potential benefits of the study outweigh its potential harms.

10. **Anonymity**

    What steps will be taken to ensure the anonymity of participants during the research and in any presentation of the research results?

11. **Confidentiality**

    Please describe who will collect the data, who will have access to the data, and how the data will be stored. How long will the data be maintained?

RESEARCH DESIGNS

As we describe in the following sections, numerous research designs are used in clinical psychology research. These designs vary in the degree of experimental manipulation (from naturalistic observation of behaviour to true experimental designs) and in the number of participants involved (from single participant designs to epidemiological designs using tens of thousands of participants). Although it is tempting to view certain designs as better or stronger than others, such a view represents an oversimplification of research in a given domain. All designs have advantages and disadvantages. As we describe below, some designs are better than others in terms of controlling certain threats to research validity. We cannot determine the value of a design without knowing the state of knowledge in a research domain. For example, once a research area is well-developed, correlational designs are unlikely to add anything new to the scientific literature. On the other hand, in a relatively new research area, even a relatively simple case study may make a meaningful contribution to the literature.

No single study can answer all of the important questions in a research area. Often a good study generates far more questions than answers. Research must be seen as cumulative, with each study contributing to the knowledge base of an area. Clinical psychology, as broadly defined in Chapter 1, involves the application of scientific knowledge to the understanding and treatment of psychological disorders and distress. Many different research areas are relevant to the practice of clinical psychology. It is obvious that clinical practice should be informed by research on assessment, prevention, and intervention. In addition, clinical practice can be enriched by knowledge of research on psychopathology, stress and coping, normal development, normal family processes, and many other areas.

Students learning about research methods in psychology may find the rationale behind a number of basic research design features obscure or hard to comprehend. One way to think of these design features is as strategies that address potential shortcomings of psychological research. For example, some studies use control (or comparison) groups to examine similarities and differences between groups. This is done to address the criticism that a pattern seen in the research group of interest—such as the tendency for depressed individuals to expect to perform poorly in social interactions—may also be true for those who are not depressed. In experimental designs, participants are randomly assigned to the experimental groups. This strategy is used to increase the likelihood that all groups are comparable prior to an experimental manipulation occurring (such as receiving treatment or being on a waiting list for treatment). After all, if groups are not equivalent prior to the manipulation it is much more difficult to argue that any group difference evident after the manipulation is indeed due to the manipulation. Researchers usually remain cautious about study results until the study is replicated, preferably by a different group of researchers. No matter how important the results of a study appear to be, they are of little or no value unless similar results are independently obtained by others working in the field. Imagine that a car manufacturer advertises a new car with incredible fuel efficiency. These claims are not very convincing unless they are obtained by others who test drive the same model of car.

Over the years, psychologists have identified a relatively large number of design problems that can undermine the validity of a research study. Of course, if steps are taken to overcome these problems prior to conducting a study, the validity of a study is protected or strengthened. Therefore researchers have gone to great lengths to develop and promote the use of a classification system that covers the majority of potential problems. As originally conceptualized by Donald Campbell (e.g., Cook & Campbell, 1979), these potential design problems can be classified as representing threats to the **internal validity**, **external**

Dr. Donald Campbell encouraged researchers to pay more attention to potential design problems that can undermine a study's validity.

validity, or **statistical conclusion validity** of a study. We will deal with the first two categories of threats to validity now and will discuss threats to statistical conclusion validity later in the chapter.

Internal validity refers to the extent to which the interpretations drawn from the results of a study can be justified and alternative interpretations can be reasonably ruled out. **Table 4.7** describes the types of threats to internal validity that psychologists must attend to in designing their research. **External validity** refers to the extent to which the interpretations drawn from the results of a study can be generalized beyond the narrow boundaries of the specific study in question. **Table 4.8** describes the types of threats to external validity that psychologists must attend to in designing their research.

TABLE 4.7   Some Common Threats to the Internal Validity of a Study

History: This threat involves the influence of events that occur outside the context of the study that influence or account for the results of the study.

Maturation: Changes in the participants due to their psychological or physical development that cannot be disentangled from the experimental manipulation can pose a threat to internal validity.

Testing: Repeated testing may influence the results of a study due to the participants' familiarity with a test and memory of how they responded previously on a test or measure.

Instrumentation: In longitudinal studies, changes in the definition of constructs and in their measurement can make the interpretation of changes in participants' responses much more difficult, if not impossible.

Statistical Regression: Extreme scores on measures, both high and low, tend to be less extreme upon retesting. This may mean that changes in scores in a study may be due to regression, rather than an experimental manipulation.

Selection Biases: This threat involves the effect that systematic differences in recruiting participants or assigning participants to experimental conditions may have on the outcome of the study.

Attrition: The loss of participants in a study over time may bias the results if there are systematic differences between those who remain in the study and those who withdraw from the study.

Adapted from Cook and Campbell (1979)

A close reading of these two tables shows that there is no perfect study and researchers must balance internal and external validity. The more a researcher attempts to deal with threats to internal validity, the more he or she opens up the study to threats to external validity, and vice versa. By reducing threats to internal validity, the researcher opts to have as "clean" a study as possible. Typically, scientists give priority to concerns about internal validity as this allows a relatively straightforward interpretation of the study's findings. Once again, though, the need to give priority to addressing internal or external validity threats depends on the state of the research field. Take, for example, the field of psychotherapy research. Research from the 1970s to the 1990s emphasized the need to control threats to internal validity. Treatment manuals were used to operationalize the nature of treatments and numerous methodological and statistical strategies were developed to minimize effects due to selection biases and to attrition. Careful attention to threats to internal validity enabled scientists to gather relatively unambiguous evidence of clinical efficacy of many treatments. As you learned in Chapter 1, "efficacy" is the term used to describe treatment effects in tightly controlled experimental designs. Once psychotherapy researchers know these treatments are helpful under tightly controlled conditions, they can move on to loosen some experimental controls on internal validity in order to enhance the external validity of subsequent treatment studies. Thus, in the next stage of treatment research, participation selection criteria may be relaxed, close monitoring of therapist interventions may be eliminated, and timelines for the delivery of services may be made more flexible, permitting an assessment of clinical effectiveness. In Chapter 1 you learned that effectiveness refers to treatment effects in "real world" treatment settings and contexts, with typical patients and typical therapists.

TABLE 4.8   Some Common Threats to the External Validity of a Study

Sample Characteristics: External validity can be limited because of the degree to which the characteristics of the research participants, such as their sociodemographic and psychological characteristics, map on to other samples and populations of interest.

Stimulus Characteristics and Settings: Aside from the participants, features of the study such as the institutional setting and the characteristics of those involved in the conduct of the study (e.g., therapists in a treatment study) may constrain the generalizability of obtained results.

Reactivity of Research Arrangements: By virtue of being in a study, participants may respond differently than they would in other contexts. This can severely limit the extent to which the results of the study provide information about how people behave outside of the research context.

Reactivity of Assessment: Participants' awareness that their behaviours, moods, attitudes, etc. are being monitored may influence how they respond in the study and these alterations in response may not be consistent with their responses once the study is completed.

Timing of Measurement: The decision about when to measure variables may result in conclusions that are not true for all time points (e.g., observed effects that appear stable over time may in fact not be stable between measurement periods).

Adapted from Cook and Campbell (1979)

Case Studies

Like in medicine, case studies have a long and important history in clinical psychology. Descriptions of unusual presenting problems or of novel treatments have enriched the professional literature. A typical case study involves a detailed presentation of an individual patient, couple, or family illustrating some new or rare observation or treatment innovation. Case studies are a valuable format for making preliminary connections between events, behaviours, and symptoms that have not been addressed in extant research. Case studies can be a rich source of research hypotheses regarding the etiology or maintenance of disorders. They can also be the initial testing ground for innovative assessment or intervention strategies. Case studies have heuristic value—they draw the attention of other professionals to a phenomenon.

The scientific value of case studies is relatively low because they do not allow for the rigorous testing of hypotheses. The major weakness of the case study method is that most threats to internal validity cannot be adequately addressed (Kazdin, 1981). Take, for example, a case study on the treatment of Joe's temper tantrums around homework. Usually the author of the case study reports the client's symptoms or presenting problems prior to and following treatment (such as the number of tantrums and their intensity). Although the author would probably like to claim that any improvement was due to treatment effects, alternative explanations cannot be ruled out in this simple research design. The observed changes could be due to a number of other factors unrelated to therapy, including normal developmental changes (i.e., maturation—the simple effects of Joe growing older or having no homework in the holidays), the abating of symptoms that typically occurs over time (i.e., regression to the mean), or life events outside of therapy (i.e., history effects, such as getting a new teacher).

Joe's difficulties around homework decreased after he began working with a new teacher.

Single Case Designs

The limitations of the case study can be at least partially addressed in a number of ways, even when the focus of the study remains on an individual patient (or couple or family) or on a very small number of patients (Hayes, Barlow, & Nelson-Gray, 1999; Morgan & Morgan, 2001). Threats such as maturation and regression to the mean can be easily handled by the simple strategy of extending the period of time that the person is assessed and the frequency with which the assessments occurs. To address the threat of changing criteria or definitions of the problems/symptoms (i.e., instrumentation), the same measures can be used at each assessment point, rather than, for example, relying on one parent's ratings for pre-test and the other parent's ratings for post-test. Also the measures should be standardized and, if at all possible, well-established, rather than potentially unstable and biased clinician observations. The possibility that observed changes are due to extra-treatment events can be partially addressed by clearly defining the nature of the therapeutic intervention and precisely noting when it occurred. Thus, *if* the problems were relatively consistent and stable prior to the target intervention *and* the change occurs very shortly after the intervention, *then* a case can be made for the change being due to the intervention. **Figure 4.1** illustrates a number of these features in what is commonly known as an A-B single case design, with the A period representing the level of symptoms prior to the intervention (also known as the baseline) and the B period representing the level

Figure 4.1   A-B Design

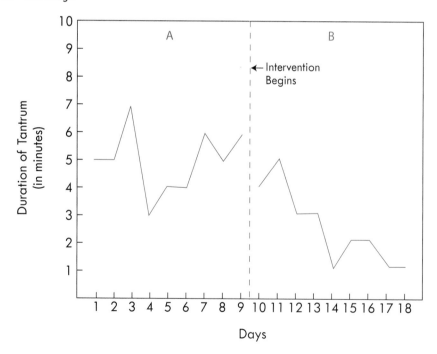

of symptoms following the intervention. Although intervention effects are typically determined by visual inspection of graphed data (such as represented in Figure 4.1), a number of statistical tests can be used to determine if statistically significant changes occurred (e.g., Morley & Adams, 1989). Such tests can be especially valuable if the baseline assessment of symptoms shows a very variable pattern.

Two design strategies improve on the straightforward A-B design by ruling out the threat of history to the validity of the study. The first option is to conduct a small series of A-B designs using the same intervention with a number of individuals presenting with similar problems. If the data for three or four cases are collected sequentially (i.e., the people receiving the intervention do not all receive the intervention at the same point in time) and the symptom levels consistently appear to change following the intervention, then the researcher's contention that the intervention was responsible for the change is very strong. A second option is to use what is known as an A-B-A single case design. This is similar to the A-B design except that the treatment is withdrawn after a few weeks and data continue to be collected for a second A period (i.e., a period in which no treatment occurs). For example, Joe's parents could be asked to ignore tantrums and reward homework completion during period B, and to return to their regular reaction of reminders, threats, and bribes during the second A period. If Joe's tantrums return to pre-treatment levels, then a strong case can be made for the effectiveness of the intervention. The major drawback to this design is that, for many types of therapeutic interventions, it may not be possible to have the person refrain from using the treatment strategies during the second A period, especially if the strategies have been effective in reducing symptom levels for a few weeks.

Correlational Designs

Correlational designs are probably the most commonly used research designs in clinical psychology. The focus of these designs, no matter how complex they are, is on the examination of association among variables. Although researchers may be tempted to make causal statements about associations in the data, they are inappropriate, as correlational designs can never determine causality. Even when one variable temporally precedes another variable, a causal connection cannot be established, as the apparent effect of the first variable on the second could be due to the influence of an unmeasured third variable. The hallmarks of the scientific study of causality in human functioning are the use of experimental manipulation and random assignment to conditions. Both of these design features are absent in correlational designs.

It is a mistake to equate correlational *analyses* with correlational *designs*. Correlational designs can be analysed with all types of statistics, including correlations, partial correlations, multiple regression, and t-tests, or analysis of variance (ANOVA). For example, many studies compare the performance on a laboratory task (e.g., a simulated social interaction) of people diagnosed with a DSM-IV disorder with that of people with no diagnosis. Even though there are discrete groups and an ANOVA is conducted to analyse group performance on the lab task, this is a correlational design.

No manipulation occurs (i.e., all participants experience the same conditions in the study) and participants are not randomly assigned to conditions. Sometimes researchers using a correlational design decide to artificially create groups from the data they collected by using median splits or some type of cut-off score to categorize participants as high or low on a dimension. Again, the use of group comparisons in the data analysis should not be confused with an experimental design. It is also worth noting that the common strategy of dichotomizing continuous variables is rarely appropriate and can frequently yield misleading results (MacCallum, Zhang, Preacher, & Rucker, 2002; Streiner, 2002). One of the main drawbacks of this strategy is that median splits are often used to form the two groups (i.e., half of the participants are assigned to each group). Whether a score is assigned to the "high" group or the "low" group depends on the median score for the set of participants. Therefore, as median scores are likely to differ across studies, the same participant score may be assigned to the "high" group in one study and the "low" group in another.

Correlational designs come in many forms. Some are purely descriptive in nature, such as the bulk of epidemiological research that is devoted to the study of the incidence (the rate of new cases of a disorder in a specific time period), prevalence (the overall rate of cases of a disorder in a specific time period) and distribution (rates of disorders across geographic areas and/or sociodemographic characteristics) of disorders in a population. A good example of this type of study is the World Health Organization World Mental Health Survey Consortium (2004) study described in Chapter 3. Epidemiological data are often used to describe people's use of health care services. Hunsley, Lee, and Aubry (1999), for example, used data from the Canadian government's National Population Health Survey to examine the sociodemographic characteristics of Canadian adults who consulted a psychologist for health or mental health reasons over the period of a year.

Correlational designs can be used to examine the underlying structure of a measure or a set of measures. This is known as **factor analysis**. Factor analysis is often used in the development of a measure to determine which items contribute meaningfully to the test, but can also be used to determine the conceptual dimensions that underlie a set of variables (e.g., in a study measures of psychological symptoms may form a single factor that is frequently labelled negative affectivity). Exploratory factor analysis is used when the researcher has no prior hypotheses about the structure of the data. In contrast, a more demanding form of factor analysis, known as confirmatory factor analysis, is used to test a specific hypothesis regarding the nature of the factor structure (Floyd & Widaman, 1995).

Most frequently, correlational designs are employed to examine the relations among discrete variables in an effort to develop or test a conceptual model. One such design involves the testing of a **moderator** variable (see Table 4.3). A moderator variable is one that influences the strength of the relation between a predictor variable and a criterion variable (Holmbeck, 1997). For example, the relation between the experience of stressful life events and psychological distress may be moderated by the type of coping strategies used. In general, moderator analyses are used to enhance the researcher's ability to predict as much variance as possible in a criterion variable. Another common design involves the testing of **mediator** variables. A mediator variable explains the mechanism by which a predictor variable influences a criterion variable (Holmbeck, 1997). For example, the relation between parental psychopathology and child adjustment may be due, partially or entirely, to the quality of the parenting relationship between parent and child. In general, mediator analyses are used to explicate the conceptual link among variables. As an aside, moderator and mediator analyses have also been proposed for use with experimental designs such as randomized clinical trials (Kraemer, Wilson, Fairburn, & Agras, 2002).

A final correlational design that is increasingly used in clinical psychology research is known as **structural equation modelling** (SEM; e.g., Hoyle & Smith, 1994). SEM is a comprehensive approach

The relation between parental psychopathology and child adjustment may be due, partially or entirely, to the quality of the parenting relationship between parent and child.

to testing an entire theoretical model. This design combines elements of confirmatory factor analysis and mediator analyses. First, the researcher lays out a structural model that shows how relevant variables are related to each other; this is akin to mediator analyses. Then the researcher considers the measurement model and selects multiple measures for each variable in the model; this is akin to confirmatory factor analysis. There are several strengths to this design. The analysis of the measurement model allows the researcher to obtain relatively pure measures of a construct that are derived from multiple measures used for each variable. These measures are then used to test a comprehensive structural model, rather than testing isolated aspects of the model one at a time as is typically done in mediator analyses. However, despite the complexity and strength of this design, SEM can only determine the extent to which a hypothesized causal model fits the study's data; it cannot unequivocally demonstrate that the hypothesized causal model is true. Nevertheless, it is possible to apply SEM to data gathered from experimental designs to make stronger statements about causal relations among some variables (MacCallum & Austin, 2000). One challenge in some areas of research is that SEM requires a relatively large sample (i.e., more than 200 participants).

Quasi-Experimental Designs

Quasi-experimental designs involve some form of manipulation by the researcher. Such a manipulation may take many forms, including variations in the nature of the information provided prior to undertaking some task, exposure to different levels of noise while completing a task, or different types of treatment conditions. Quasi-experimental designs do not, however, involve random assignment to experimental conditions. A weakness of this design is that, because participants are not randomly assigned to the different conditions or levels of the independent variable, the effect of the independent variable on the dependent variable may be confounded with extraneous influences. This, of course, raises the question of why anyone would fail to use an experimental design. The answer is very simple: in many situations it is simply not ethical or feasible to randomly assign participants to conditions.

A study of health care systems by Bickman (1996) illustrates the usefulness of quasi-experimental designs when experimental designs are not suitable. The central focus of the study was determining whether an enhanced set of mental health care services, when added to usual care, resulted in improvements in participants' psychological and social functioning. The enhanced care condition was extensive, with cost and training considerations limiting the availability of the condition to a single American site. Because all participants in the area knew that the enhanced care was available, it would have been impossible to randomly assign participants to enhanced and usual care conditions. Instead, the researchers selected a site elsewhere in the United States that was comparable in terms of the population of potential participants and in terms of the usual mental health services available. Data were collected from participants at both sites to determine the effect of the enhanced care intervention.

The most frequently used quasi-experimental designs involve the comparison of two previously established groups of participants. In the simplest design, one group receives the intervention, the other doesn't. Data are collected after the intervention and then analysed. Although this design may be cost-effective and relatively straightforward because only one wave of data collection is required, the obvious weakness of this design is that the two groups may differ substantially prior to the intervention, thereby confounding the results. A stronger design is one in which data are also collected prior to the intervention. Thus, if any pre-intervention differences exist, they can be controlled for statistically, although this is less desirable than using random assignment.

Experimental Designs

Experimental designs involve both random assignment to condition and experimental manipulation. These features allow the researcher to draw relatively unambiguous conclusions about the effects of the independent variable on the dependent variable. We say "relatively" unambiguous because results may be confounded by variability in the manner in which the manipulation occurred (e.g., therapists who are supposed to be providing the same treatment may differ in how closely they follow the treatment manual) or by the random assignment of participants failing to yield groups equivalent on all dimensions prior to the intervention (this is often due to using too small a sample).

Compared with all other research designs, experimental designs provide the best protection against threats to internal validity. As with quasi-experimental designs, the strongest design is one in which both pre-intervention and post-intervention data are collected. Sometimes, however, concerns about reactivity to testing may lead a researcher to dispense with obtaining pre-intervention data, which results in a weakening of the ability to determine if the groups were truly equivalent at the outset of the study. By skimming the pages of scientific journals in clinical psychology you will find many examples of experimental designs, often called true experiments. In the realm of psychotherapy research, these types of designs are typically known as randomized clinical trials or **randomized controlled trials**.

Meta-Analysis

Until the 1980s, reviews summarizing research findings in a specific research realm were based on qualitative (that is, non-numerical) methods. Somewhat like a sophisticated term paper, reviews provided a narrative account of the various studies, their strengths, weaknesses, and findings, and then drew conclusions about the state of knowledge. This traditional form of review is still used for summarizing conceptual and methodological approaches used in researching a topic. However, a quantitative form of research review known as **meta-analysis** is now the standard for making a general statement about the findings in a research field (Harris, 2003). Meta-analysis involves a complex set of statistical procedures to quantitatively review research in an area. An analogy to a typical research study may be helpful to explain what meta-analysis is. A typical study involves the collection of data from multiple research participants; the data are then summed and overall trends in the group of participants are examined using statistical procedures. The same general process occurs in meta-analysis, but the "participants" in a meta-analysis are research studies rather than individuals.

In a single research study, similar data are collected from all participants. Obviously this is not possible in a meta-analysis, for the original research studies are likely to have employed a range of measures for assessing outcome. Meta-analysis combines the results of prior research using a common metric called an **effect size** (Rosenthal & DiMatteo, 2001). An effect size is the difference between the means of the experimental (that is, the treatment) group and the control group, divided by the standard deviation of either the control group or the pooled sample of both groups. Effect sizes can also be calculated for data obtained from correlational studies.

Meta-analysis offers numerous advantages over traditional research reviews or single empirical studies. For example, statistical analyses, rather than the author's impressions, guide the conclusions drawn about a research topic. Moreover, by including data from many studies, the number of research participants on whom conclusions are based is dramatically increased. This greatly enhances the researcher's power to detect an effect and improves the generalizability of the conclusions drawn on the basis of the literature. Given its methodological and statistical strengths, meta-analysis is increasingly used to determine the current state of knowledge about many areas of research and to assist in the development of health care policies regarding the provision of medical and psychological services.

SELECTING RESEARCH PARTICIPANTS AND MEASURES

We cannot emphasize enough that no single study can answer all the questions in a research field. At best, a study adds a small amount of knowledge to a field. To be certain that this knowledge is meaningful researchers must be cognizant of the strengths and limitations of their studies and must strive to reduce threats to the validity of the research. As we described in Tables 4.7 and 4.8, many of the threats to the internal and external validity of a study can be addressed by considering a number of participant sample and measurement parameters. In the following sections we highlight some issues that researchers must consider in order to maximize the validity of a study.

Selecting the Sample, the Sample Size, and the Sampling Strategy

Biases in sample characteristics and selection can have an enormous impact on the researcher's ability to accurately interpret study results. For example, a study based on data obtained from Caucasian male university students is likely to have rather limited generalizability, and the researcher must ensure that his or her conclusions accurately reflect the fact that the findings may not apply across gender, ethnicity, educational level, and socioeconomic status. Likewise, a study of parenting values based on data from two biological-parent families residing in the same home may provide very valuable information, but the results may not generalize to other family constellations, such as step-families, single-parent families, or families with same-sex parents.

As a starting point, therefore, the researcher needs to consider how best to optimize the fit between (a) the characteristics of the population to which the results will be generalized and (b) the type of sample that should be recruited for the study. The next consideration is the number of participants required for the study. Without a sufficient number of participants, a study will not have the statistical power needed to detect the very effect it was designed to examine. Psychotherapy outcome research illustrates this challenge. Most experimental studies in which a treatment condition is compared with a no-treatment control condition have sufficient sample sizes and power to detect an effect due to treatment; however, a review of experiments in which two treatments were compared with each other found that only half of published studies had sufficient sample sizes and power to detect a difference between treatments (Kazdin & Bass, 1989). As we will discuss in Chapter 14, this means that the interpretation that all psychotherapies have comparable effects may be based, at least partially, on research design weaknesses. Based on the statistical work of **Jacob Cohen**, many tools are available to assist in determining the optimal number of participants to recruit for a study based on the phenomenon under investigation, the research design, and the type of planned data analysis (e.g., Cohen, 1992).

Decisions about the strategies used to recruit research participants can also affect the validity and generalizability of a study. Two examples illustrate the potential research limitations of sampling strategies. A number of studies have examined the extent to which victims of childhood sexual abuse exhibit psychological symp-

Researchers need to remain aware of the differences in sociodemographic, psychological, and personality variables when recruiting research participants.

toms and disorders as adults. Contradictory findings have been reported with respect to dissociative symptoms, with some studies finding little evidence of dissociative symptoms and others finding substantial evidence of the link between childhood victimization and later dissociative symptoms. Much of the apparent discrepancy between such findings appears to be due to variations in sampling strategies. The studies finding little or no connection tend to use community samples, whereas those reporting strong connections tend to use samples from psychological or psychiatric clinics. Thus evidence for dissociative symptoms depends on the extent to which participants are experiencing clinical distress and/or seeking services for their distress (Rumstein-McKean & Hunsley, 2001). A second example comes from research on marital functioning. Karney and colleagues (1995) conducted two studies: in the first, couples were recruited through newspaper advertisements and, in the second, research participants were solicited from public records of marriage licences. The two samples of participants differed on many sociodemographic, psychological, personality, and marital quality variables. Because of these differences, many of the significant associations found among these variables in one study were not found in the second. These two examples demonstrate the need for researchers to attend to sampling strategies, both in the design of a study and in interpretation of findings.

Measurement Options and the Importance of Psychometric Properties

A multitude of measurement options are available to clinical psychologists conducting research. No option is necessarily the best for all types of studies. Instead, as we have repeatedly emphasized, the strengths and limitations of a measurement option (or a research design or a sampling strategy) must be carefully considered, along with the degree to which the measurement option fits the research hypothesis and other aspects of the planned study. **Table 4.9** provides a summary of the range of general measurement modalities that may be appropriate for a study. In many studies, multiple measures of each variable are selected. This enhances the likelihood that the variable of interest has been fully or adequately measured in the study. However, as the time required for study participation increases, it may affect the type of person who is able and willing to take part, thereby affecting external validity.

TABLE 4.9   Measurement Options

Self-Report Measures: The research participant completes a questionnaire describing some aspect of himself or herself. This may range from global self-ratings, such as one's overall happiness or psychological adjustment, to very specific self-ratings, such as one's anxiety while completing a research task.

Informant-Report Measures: Information about a target research participant is gathered from other individuals. In clinical psychology research, this is typically someone who is well-acquainted with the participant, such as a marital partner, a parent, or a teacher. Data may also be obtained for individuals with only limited experience with the participants: in studies of social interaction, for example, informant-report measures may be gathered from all the participants who interacted with a given participant.

Rater Evaluations: Data may be obtained from someone knowledgeable about a participant's involvement in a study, such as a rater who viewed videotapes of the participant performing a task or a therapist who provided treatment to the participant. Such rating can range from evaluations of very specific to very global features.

Performance Measures: Participants may be asked to complete tasks in a study, such as a visuo-motor task, a response time task, an identification task, or a task related to specific intellectual or social skills. The quality of the participant's performance on the task is used as data in the study.

Projective Measures: A technique, such as a storytelling task, may be used to assess the underlying needs or motives of a research participant. The assumption in using such measures is that they provide data that are different from those obtained through self-report.

Observation of Behaviour: Coding systems or general ratings may be used to summarize elements of a participant's actual behaviour. This may occur in either naturalistic settings such as the family home, or in laboratory settings.

Psychophysiological Measures: A range of measurement options is available to evaluate a participant's biological characteristics. These include measures of autonomic arousal, cardiovascular activity, and neurological functioning.

Archival Data: Research data are often obtained from information sources that exist apart from the actual research study. This may include such sources as police records, health care utilization records, and academic records.

The psychometric properties of a measurement strategy have a dramatic effect on the outcome of a study. Reliability—the degree of consistency in the measurement—and validity—the degree to which the construct of interest is accurately measured—both affect the quality of a study and the likelihood that a hypothesis is tested appropriately. **Table 4.10** provides a summary of the psychometric properties that a researcher should consider in selecting a measurement tool. In a recent meta-analysis, Dr. Norm O'Rourke (**Profile Box 4.1**) drew attention to the need to consider whether measures are equally reliable across different samples (O'Rourke, 2004). Although there are literally thousands of established measures and assessment procedures available, in some instances researchers may choose to develop a measurement tool specifically for the study. In such cases the researcher must take particular care to be certain that the measure is both reliable and valid.

TABLE 4.10   Psychometric Properties of Measures

Reliability

Internal Consistency: The degree to which elements of the measure (such as items on a test) are homogeneous.

Test-Retest Reliability: The stability over time of scores on a measure.

Inter-Rater Reliability: The consistency of scores on a measure across different raters or observers.

Validity

Content Validity: The extent to which the measure fully and accurately represents all elements of the domain of the construct being assessed.

Face Validity: The extent to which the measure overtly appears to be measuring the construct of interest.

Criterion Validity: The association of a measure with some criterion of central relevance to the construct, such as differentiating between groups of research participants.

Concurrent Validity: The association of a measure with other relevant data measured at the same point in time.

Predictive Validity: The association of a measure with other relevant data measured at some future point in time.

Convergent Validity: The association between a measure and either other measures of the same construct or conceptually related constructs.

Discriminant Validity: The association between measures that, conceptually, should not be related.

Incremental Validity: The extent to which a measure adds to the prediction of a criterion beyond what can be predicted with other measurement data.

PROFILE BOX 4.1

DR. NORM O'ROURKE

Dr. Norm O'Rourke

I completed a degree in Business Administration and worked in the advertising industry for several years before returning to university. The decision to pursue a career in clinical psychology was precipitated by a need to find meaning and purpose in my work. Although my original goal was to become a practising psychotherapist, I soon realized that research was of equal if not greater interest to me. Over my career, I have found a synergy between these two pillars of the scientist-practitioner model. I am particularly interested in older adults and their families. I am an Assistant Professor at Simon Fraser University with appointments in the Departments of Gerontology and Psychology. I am a registered psychologist in the province of British Columbia. It is clear that clinical geropsychology is a field that will see continued growth in coming years as persons over 84 years of age constitute the fastest-growing proportion of populations in most Western nations. Although the current cohort of older adults may be reluctant to seek psychological services, we predict that aging baby boomers will seek services and will expect psychologists to be well-prepared to treat the concerns of later life.

What made you choose to become a clinical psychologist?

Clinical psychology affords me tremendous liberty as both a clinician and researcher. The range of work opportunities with a Ph.D. in clinical psychology is considerable. In addition to my university duties (e.g., teaching, administration), I choose which topics to study, which advocacy groups to assist, and the peers with whom I work. I expect change rather than consistency to define the profession in years to come; this presents both challenges and untold opportunities.

What is the most rewarding part of your job as a clinical psychologist?

The most rewarding part of my work is the ability to make a meaningful difference in people's lives. Helping patients achieve change, make important decisions, and overcome psychological distress is truly gratifying. Also I take tremendous satisfaction in adding to the body of knowledge in the relatively new field of clinical geropsychology.

What is the greatest challenge facing you as a clinical psychologist?

As one who works in the health care system, the challenges I face as a clinician are similar to those of other allied health professionals. In the last decade, we have seen the virtual elimination of hospital-funded research positions in Canada (i.e., those not funded with time-limited, soft money from external sources) as well as stand-alone psychology departments. Increasingly, hospital administrators are concerned solely with direct medical care to the exclusion of other treatments of importance to patient recovery and wellness. As a discipline, psychology must do a better job of educating policy-makers and administrators as to the cost effectiveness and efficacy of empirically supported interventions.

Tell us about the importance of appropriate measurement when investigating elder-ly samples and the work you have done in this area.

All too often I see that instruments first developed and validated for use with younger people are naïvely administered to older adults. This practice fails to recognize that the psychometric properties of measures derived from one population do not automatically translate to others. As an example, I recently conducted a meta-analysis that examined factors affecting the reliability of responses to a common depression screening measure, the Center for Epidemiological Studies-Depression Scale (CES-D). The results of this study suggest that reliability estimates even for commonly used measures such as the CES-D vary across populations. I hope that such research will encourage psychologists to be more attuned to between-group differences and to how these differences affect the utility of the instruments they commonly use.

How do you integrate science and practice in your work?

The scientist-practitioner model provides clinical psychologists with the skills to directly examine the effectiveness of treatments. Furthermore, clinical work provides opportunities to identify research questions. That's how my most widely cited study began. While working in the UBC Memory Disorders Clinic, I noticed that spouses of persons with dementia who appeared to cope most effectively in this role tended to selectively reconstruct their relationship histories (i.e., to negate negative memories and perceptions of their spouses). My subsequent research has supported the existence of this phenomenon and has led to an overall theory of well-being related to selective attention and retention of interpersonal information.

What do you see as the most exciting changes in the profession of clinical psychology?

The issue of prescription privileges for psychologists will be one that will force us to define the future of the profession. This is not a move that I support. Already, graduate education is extensive; the prospect of adding two years of training in psychopharmacology is daunting. More likely, psychopharmacology would replace research training. However, it is research training and expertise that distinguish clinical psychology as a discipline. Psychologists' ability to both practise and study psychotherapy has led to major advances in the development of empirically supported treatments. It would be very unfortunate if we abandoned the scientist-practitioner model to become yet another set of agents for the pharmaceutical industry.

ANALYSING THE DATA

Once data are collected, the researcher must conduct data analyses to determine the extent to which his or her research hypotheses have been supported. Because appropriate data analysis is an integral part of a valid study and there are a multitude of options for data analysis, the researcher should carefully consider analysis options when designing the study. Guidelines on statistical methods are available to assist a researcher in making these important decisions (Wilkinson & the Task Force on Statistical Inference, 1999). Just as there are a number of threats to the internal and external validity of a study, so too are there many threats to the **statistical conclusion validity** of a study. Statistical conclusion validity refers to aspects of the data analysis that influence the validity of the conclusions drawn about the results of the research study. Common threats to statistical conclusion validity are outlined in **Table 4.11**. As with other threats to validity, careful attention to these threats during the design of a study can increase the likelihood of accurately detecting an effect in the study.

TABLE 4.11   Some Common Threats to the Statistical Conclusion Validity of a Study

Low Statistical Power: Statistical power refers to the ability to detect group differences when such differences truly exist. If a study has low statistical power, often caused by the use of samples that are too small, the researcher may not be able to accurately conclude that group differences were found in the study.

Multiple Comparisons and Their Effects on Error Rates: Most studies involve the testing of multiple research hypotheses, with multiple measures used to operationalize key constructs. The researcher needs to consider how many analyses to conduct and the error rate to use for analyses in order to have a reasonable balance between the desire to avoid *Type I errors* (i.e., concluding there is an effect when no true effect exists) and *Type II errors* (i.e., concluding there is no effect when a true effect exists).

continued...

Procedural Variability: Even with clear instructions and procedures to follow, those conducting the research (such as interviewers, observational raters, and therapists) may differ in how they interpret or use the instructions and procedures. Increases in variability in a study decrease the ability to detect a phenomenon or experimental effect.

Participant Heterogeneity: Variability in participant characteristics may result in differential results within the sample. Again, by increasing variability within a study, it is more difficult to detect a true effect.

Measurement Unreliability: The less reliable a measure, the more that measurement error influences the data obtained from participants. This increases within-study variability and negatively affects the ability to detect an effect.

Statistical and Clinical Significance

Researchers in psychology commonly rely on statistical tests to determine the outcome of a study and the degree to which a research hypothesis was supported. However, in clinical psychology research, statistical significance is necessary but not sufficient to fully evaluate the results of a study. Because the field of clinical psychology focuses on the application of psychological know-ledge to improve human functioning, researchers must also address whether the results have any practical significance. In treatment research, this is known as **clinical significance**. Clinical significance has been defined in a number of ways, but all definitions share an emphasis on evaluating the degree to which the intervention has had a meaningful impact on the functioning of the treated participants. Just as there are different definitions, so too are there several distinct methods for calculating clinical significance, some of which use group data and others that focus on the data from individual participants in a treatment study (Kraemer et al., 2003; Wise, 2004). One commonly used approach is to evaluate, for each participant, whether the participant could be said to be functioning in the normal range. This may involve the use of norms, cut-off scores on scales, or pre-determined criteria (such as being employed or being able to function without assistance when performing self-care tasks) to operationalize normal range functioning. A second commonly used method developed by Neil Jacobson and colleagues, called the *reliable change index*, determines whether a participant's pre-treatment to post-treatment change on a scale is statistically greater than what would be expected due to measurement error. If it is, and if the score on the scale has moved to within two standard deviations of the mean score for a nondisordered sample, then a clinically significant change is said to have occurred (Jacobson & Truax, 1991). It is important to note that different methods for calculating clinical significance may yield different conclusions (Bauer, Lambert, & Nielsen, 2004) so, as with traditional data analyses, the researcher must make sure that appropriate clinical significance methods are used in a study.

TABLE 4.12   How to Critically Evaluate a Research Study

The fact that a study is published does not mean that it is perfect. In fact, there is no such thing as a perfect study. Instead, studies vary in the degree to which the researchers have successfully addressed important issues and have successfully dealt with threats to internal, external, and statistical conclusion validity. Below are some questions you should ask yourself when reading a published study in order to develop a critical eye for research.

Title: Does the title accurately reflect the content of the article?

Introduction: Is the background information on the research area presented clearly and logically? Is there unnecessary detail that is confusing or misleading? Is there a clear statement of the purpose of the study and/or of the research hypotheses?

Participants: Are the chosen participants appropriate for the study topic? To what extent can results be generalized from the study's sample to other populations of interest? Are recruitment methods described? Were any analyses conducted to determine if there were effects due to differing methods? Was there attrition in the study and, if so, how was it handled statistically and interpretatively? If control/comparison groups were used, were they appropriate for the hypotheses being tested? In an experiment, was assignment to condition truly random?

Measures: Are the psychometric properties (i.e., reliability and validity) reported and are they adequate? If interviewers or coders were used, are inter-rater reliability values reported? Are the chosen measures developmentally and culturally appropriate for the participants? How well do the measures evaluate the variables included in the research hypotheses?

Procedures: In general, are the procedures appropriate for testing the research hypotheses? For example, was the training of raters/interviewers/therapists reported and does it seem adequate? Overall, are the procedures described in sufficient detail that the study could be replicated?

Results: Are the statistical analyses appropriate for the research hypotheses and the research design? Are the assumptions for the analyses met or were they violated? Was there any attention to whether the sample size was sufficient to detect a true effect in the study? Was there an appropriate balance between avoiding Type I and Type II errors? Do the tables provide enough detail (or too much) to aid in understanding the obtained results? Were *post hoc* analyses conducted and, if they were, did the researchers exercise caution in interpreting the findings? If the study was a randomized clinical trial, were clinical significance methods used?

Discussion: Are the results fully discussed? Are there clear statements about the extent to which the research hypotheses were supported? Does the researcher inappropriately interpret nonsignificant results? Is there a reasonable discussion of the limitations of the study? How well does the researcher integrate his or her findings with previous work in the area? Are viable alternative explanations of the obtained results considered in a meaningful manner?

SUMMARY AND CONCLUSIONS

Throughout this book we emphasize the importance of a solid research foundation for the practice of clinical psychology. In this chapter we have given a brief overview of the research process, highlighting the decisions that the researcher must make at all stages of the process in order to conduct ethical research and to balance the needs of internal and external validity. Perhaps the most important message is that there is no perfect study and that the different methodological features all have advantages and disadvantages. Just as the researcher must weigh different choices carefully, so too must the informed research consumer be aware of the effects of different methodological features in interpreting results in a reasonable manner. **Table 4.12** summarizes a number of issues that, as novice research consumers, you should consider when reading the clinical psychology research literature.

Critical Thinking Questions

What are the differences between evidence-based practice and eminence-based practice?

How can science help if the treatment is unhelpful?

How is the science of clinical psychology different from the science of other types of psychology?

What ethical issues are particularly important in the science of clinical psychology?

How do theories affect the research process?

How can different research designs be suitable at different stages of the development of knowledge in a field?

How does a psychologist decide whether to maximize internal validity or external validity?

Should greater weight be given to the findings of experimental studies than to other types of designs?

If a psychologist wants to study people diagnosed with a specific disorder, why does it matter how they are recruited into the study?

Key Terms

clinical significance	meta-analysis
effect size	moderator
evidence-based practice	operationalizing

external validity

factor analysis

internal validity

mediator

randomized controlled trial

statistical conclusion validity

structural equation modelling

K e y   N a m e s

Donald Campbell   Jacob Cohen   Neil Jacobson

ADDITIONAL RESOURCES

Books

Hayes, S. C., Barlow, D. H., & Nelson-Gray, R. O. (1999). *The scientist practitioner: Research and accountability in the age of managed care* (2nd ed.). Needham Heights, MA: Allyn & Bacon.

Kazdin, A. E. (2003). *Research design in clinical psychology* (4th ed.). Needham Heights, MA: Allyn & Bacon.

Kazdin, A. E. (Ed.). (2003). *Methodological issues and strategies in clinical research* (3rd ed.). Washington, DC: American Psychological Association.

Kendall, P. C., Butcher, J. N., & Holmbeck, G. N. (1999). *Handbook of research methods in clinical psychology* (2nd ed.). New York: John Wiley & Sons, Inc.

Roberts, M. C., & Ilardi, S. S. (2003). *Handbook of research methods in clinical psychology.* Oxford: Blackwell Publishing Ltd.

Thomas, J. C., & Hersen, M. (Eds.). (2003). *Understanding research in clinical and counseling psychology.* Mahwah, NJ: Lawrence Erlbaum Associates.

CHAPTER 5

Assessment: Overview

INTRODUCTION

As we outlined in Chapter 3, the classification of phenomena is a central aspect of all sciences and social sciences. Classification is only possible, however, through the collection of data in a process known as assessment. Assessment and classification activities are not solely the domain of the sciences though. In our society people are routinely assessed and classified for a variety of purposes. In the educational system students are assessed virtually every day from the time they begin school at the age of 4 or 5 until they complete their education some 12 to 25 years later. Assessments of knowledge and skill through examinations, projects, homework assignments, and class presentations are used to assign grades. These assessments are essentially a form of classification. Based on these grades and other assessment data (such as personal interviews and entrance examinations) students gain admission to (or are rejected from) private schools, universities, or graduate programs. In the work realm most people undergo some form of assessment to determine whether they should be offered a job. In many cases such assessments are highly subjective and thus are potentially biased and unfair. Once hired, employees are subject to constant informal assessment by their supervisors to determine their abilities and job performance. Increasingly many employees receive formal evaluations of their functioning that may be tied to salary increases or advancement in the organization. Even when you apply for a credit card, loan, or mortgage you (or more precisely your credit history and credit risk) are assessed.

Psychological assessment strategies and tools are used increasingly for a number of educational and employment purposes. However, in this chapter and in the following four chapters we focus on the use of psychological assessment for clinical purposes. Along the way we introduce you to the domains and methods of assessment most commonly found in clinical psychology. In these chapters we will show you the potential value of clinical assessment and make you aware of the challenges that clinical psychologists face in gathering and integrating assessment information.

PSYCHOLOGICAL ASSESSMENT

As we just indicated, we are all assessed on a regular basis. Moreover, as human beings, we all constantly engage in informal assessment activities related to our day-to-day lives. We use information (i.e., assessment data) to help us make both small decisions (such as whether to tell a classmate that a clothing label is sticking out, to confide something in a friend, or to ask someone on a date) and more important decisions (such as whether to accept an offer for graduate school, to move in with an intimate partner, or to begin attempting to conceive a child with the partner). Data such as facial expressions, tone of voice, previous experiences with a person, and our own emotional reactions all influence our decisions. In most cases these assessment processes occur automatically, which has the potential to negatively influence the accuracy of decisions. These issues in clinical decision-making are explored in greater depth in Chapter 9.

So what makes psychological assessment, or more specifically clinical assessment, different from other types of assessment? Psychological assessment is an iterative decision-making process in which data are systematically collected on the person (or persons), the person's history, and the person's physical, social, and cultural environments. Based on an initial understanding of the problem to be assessed, preliminary information is gathered that, in most cases, leads to a refinement of our understanding of the problem and to an alteration in our assessment activities. This cycle then repeats itself until the psychologist decides enough information has been collected to provide an adequate response to the assessment question. Psychological assessment involves the gathering and integration of multiple types of data from multiple sources and perspectives; at a minimum this involves information provided by the client and information based on the psychologist's observation of the client during a clinical interview. Furthermore, all psychological assessments are undertaken with specific goals in mind, such as (a) determining the cognitive abilities of a child in order to facilitate the implementation of remedial educational strategies, (b) identifying the characteristics and behaviours associated with an adolescent's repeated social rejection, or (c) determining the nature of the emotional impairment experienced by an anxious adult.

The deliberate and conscious focus on assessment goals leads a psychologist to clearly and precisely formulate the questions to be addressed during the assessment. With these questions in mind, the psychologist then selects the most appropriate assessment methods and tools for answering the assessment questions. As the assessment data are collected, the psychologist begins to generate hypotheses about the client being assessed and, therefore, may alter or refine his or her assessment questions to examine these hypotheses. This typically leads to the use of additional assessment procedures and the review of other data. Once all the assessment data have been collected, the psychologist then must make sense of the information and meaningfully address the inevitable inconsistencies and contradictions that occur in all assessment situations. As part of this integration and interpretation process the psychologist generates more hypotheses and strives to evaluate the extent of the evidence for and against these hypotheses. In most instances, prior to generating a final set of conclusions designed to answer the assessment questions, the psychologist consults with the client (and possibly others) about the accuracy of these conclusions.

Although psychologists vary in their assessment practices due to differences in factors such as training and theoretical orientation, all clinical psychologists should be competent in conducting assessments. In 1999 a presidential task force of the American Psychological Association's Division 12 (Clinical Psychology) published recommendations for a model training curriculum in clinical assessment. As shown in **Table 5.1**, in developing psychological assessment competencies, graduate students must acquire knowledge and skills in a range of conceptual and applied topics. More recently, as part of a 2002 conference on defining and evaluating competencies in professional psychology, a psychological assessment working group identified the core competencies in psychological assessment. The results of these efforts were published by Krishnamurthy et al. (2004) and are presented in **Table 5.2**. As you can see from the table, achieving and maintaining competence in psychological assessment is no easy feat. Consistent with the recommendations for training in Table 5.1, competence in assessment requires both conceptual knowledge and practical assessment skills. Although not explicitly recognized in the competency listings, another significant challenge is that clinical psychologists must make sure that their knowledge and skills are up to date. As we will see in Chapters 7 and 8, new measures continue to be developed and many of the major psychological tests are regularly updated every few years.

TABLE 5.1   A Model Curriculum for Clinical Psychology Assessment: Recommendations from the American Psychological Association, Division 12 Presidential Task Force (1999)

Conceptual Areas
Normality, norms, and standardization
Reliability
Validity
Threats to validity (bias, deception, malingering)
Clinical decision-making (sources of error, optimal strategies)

Applied Topics
Intellectual assessment
Self-report personality assessment
Neuropsychological assessment
Diagnostic assessment (meaning of diagnoses, reliability, sources of data)
Structured interviews and behavioural observation with children and adolescents
Parent rating scales for child/adolescent assessment
Specific skills relevant to focus of graduate program (e.g., test construction, assessment of disabled individuals, risk assessments)
Assessment data integration and report writing
Ethics and legal issues in assessment

TABLE 5.2   Core Competencies in Psychological Assessment

• Knowledge of psychometric theory

• Knowledge of the scientific, theoretical, empirical, and contextual bases of psychological assessment

• Knowledge, skills, and techniques to assess cognitive, affective, behavioural, and personality dimensions of human experience

• Ability to assess intervention outcomes

• Ability to evaluate critically the multiple roles, contexts, and relationships in which clients and psychologists function and the reciprocal impact of these on the assessment activity

• Ability to establish, maintain, and understand the collaborative professional relationship involved in the assessment activity

• Understanding of the relation between assessment and intervention, assessment as an intervention, and intervention planning

• Technical assessment skills, including problem/goal identification and case conceptualization, understanding and selection of appropriate assessment methods, effective use of the assessment methods, systematic data gathering, integration and analysis of information, understandable, useful, and responsive communication of findings, and development of recommendations

Adapted from Krishnamurthy et al. (2004)

The Purposes of Psychological Assessment

As you may remember learning in Chapters 1 and 2, psychological assessment has always been an important professional activity for clinical psychologists. Even though the roles of clinical psychologists have expanded over the decades, assessment continues to be an extremely important task for clinical psychologists. Psychological assessments may be conducted for myriad reasons. The first important distinction is between situations in which psychological assessment is the main clinical service provided and situations in which the psychological assessment is part of a broader clinical service (Hunsley, Crabb, & Mash, 2004).

ASSESSMENT-FOCUSED SERVICES VERSUS INTERVENTION-FOCUSED SERVICES

Some psychological assessments are stand-alone services. Examples include child custody evaluation to determine the best parenting arrangements for children whose parents are separating or divorcing, psychoedu-

Psychological assessments may be initiated to diagnose learning disorders.

cational assessments to diagnose learning disorders and to identify cognitive strengths and weaknesses, neuropsychological assessments to evaluate the extent of cognitive and memory impairment following a serious concussion, and psychosocial functioning/diagnostic assessment to evaluate the psychological sequelae of a motor vehicle accident. In these cases an assessment is initiated to answer basic questions about the person's current functioning and to provide recommendations for remediation of problems, whether by a psychologist or by another health care or education specialist. In some instances the clinical psychologist may also be asked to provide an opinion on whether the person's current level of functioning is substantially different from a prior level of functioning (e.g., before a car accident or a work-related injury).

These **assessment-focused services** are conducted primarily to provide information that can be used to address a person's current or anticipated psychosocial deficits. Thus the conclusions and recommendations provided by the psychologist may have an enormous impact on the person's life circumstances, such as whether a parent will be awarded sole custody of a child or whether an injured worker will receive a disability pension. Psychologists therefore must be conscious of the potential influence of their services. They must ensure that they use empirically supported assessment tools and that they follow all ethical standards in providing these services (a point we address more fully later in the chapter). Some individuals themselves request a psychological assessment; at other times the request for an assessment is made by another person or an organization (e.g., a court-mandated child custody evaluation). In conducting the assessment the psychologist must be cognizant of these referral factors, for they may influence the extent to which the person being assessed is motivated to emphasize the psychological strengths or their psychological impairments (see Table 5.2 regarding the importance of awareness of the context of assessment). It is also important that psychologists have thorough knowledge of the legal context in which their assessments will be used. It is possible, for example, that their assessments may be challenged by the person being assessed or by an institution or agency that initially requested the assessment (e.g., an insurance company).

VIEWPOINT BOX 5.1

CHILD CUSTODY EVALUATIONS

The majority of divorcing parents reach an agreement about the arrangements for parenting their children on their own, or with the help of legal and mental health professionals. A small minority of parents who are unable to reach an agreement turn to the legal system to resolve the dilemma of parenting arrangements after divorce. Judges in turn seek advice from mental health professionals by ordering child custody evaluation by a mental health professional.

With training in child development and expertise in psychological assessment, clinical psychologists should be well-placed to offer informed opinions about optimal parenting plans for these conflicted families. However, the provision of child custody evaluations is a professional minefield, yielding large numbers of complaints about professional misconduct. In response to these problems, guidelines have been drawn up by various organizations including the American Psychological Association (APA, 1994) and the Association of Family and Conciliation Courts (AFCC, 1994). One of the most comprehensive sets of guidelines was prepared by the Ontario Psychological Association (OPA, 1998). The OPA guidelines lay out in detail the many types of assessment data that must be gathered to perform a competent assessment. It is easy to see how the process of conducting interviews with parents, children, and new partners, carrying out observations of various family members, administering psychological tests to adults and children, and synthesizing reports from collateral sources such as teachers and therapists is likely to be a lengthy and costly procedure. A survey of American psychologists indicated that the evaluation process took on average 21.1 hours (Ackerman & Ackerman, 1997). Given the hourly rates charged by psychologists, it is clear that the cost of the average child custody evaluation runs into thousands of dollars. Ackerman and Ackerman also presented some very troubling data on the tests most commonly used by psychologists in child custody evaluation. In assessing children, psychologists reported commonly using a range of projective tests such as the Children's Apperception Test, the Sentence Completion Test, the Rorschach test, and projective drawings. These projective tests fall far short of the scientific standards of demonstrating reliability and validity, and having norms (Hunsley, Lee, & Wood, 2003). In assessing adults, the most commonly used test was the MMPI-2, followed by the Rorschach. No validity studies have supported the usefulness of these tests in predicting the best parenting arrangement for divorced families. Of particular concern, there are several websites describing the subscales of the MMPI-2 and advising parents on the most appropriate responses to provide in order to appear well-functioning.

To more directly assess what it is evaluators do, Horvath, Logan, and Walker (2002) conducted content analyses of 135 reports included in official court documents. In contrast to the self-report methodology used by Ackerman and Ackerman (1997), this strategy allowed the investigators to directly examine what evaluators did, rather than what they said they do. Horvath and colleagues found great variability in the extent to which APA guidelines were followed. Interviews sometimes failed to address critical issues such as domestic violence and child abuse. Results of this study underline the need for practitioners to use multiple methods to evaluate family functioning and to rely only on well-validated assessment strategies in making recommendations that are of such importance to children and their families.

Although it is preferable for parents to reach their own agreement on postdivorce parenting arrangements, this is not always possible. Parents seeking a child custody evaluation should be informed of professional guidelines so that they can ensure that the professional who is offering to conduct a child custody evaluation will complete a comprehensive and valid assessment that will yield helpful recommendations.

As clinical psychologists have become more involved in providing intervention services to patients, there has also been a shift in the type of assessments they conduct. Most psychological assessments, for the majority of psychologists, are now provided in the context of intervention

Intervention-focused assessment includes an evaluation of life circumstances and psychosocial functioning.

services. In these **intervention-focused assessment services**, the psychological assessment is not a stand-alone service, but is conducted as a first step in providing an effective intervention. All intervention should involve some assessment. For example, an initial evaluation of the client's life circumstances and psychosocial functioning is necessary to determine whether psychological treatment is warranted or whether some other form of intervention should be recommended. Pretreatment assessment findings are used to determine appropriate psychological interventions. These data also provide a useful point of comparison for interpreting any subsequent assessment findings during or after treatment.

Thus far we have categorized assessment activities as roughly falling into one of two domains: stand-alone assessment in which the main intent is to present conclusions and recommendations about the person's functioning and assessments in which the main intent is to intervene to improve the person's functioning, with the assessment data being used in support of this service. Although this dichotomy is useful in thinking about psychological assessment, it is rather simplistic and does not fairly represent the variety of purposes for which assessment is conducted. Therefore, to deepen your knowledge of why psychologists conduct assessments, we will focus on the following range of inter-related assessment purposes: screening, diagnosis/case formulation, prognosis, treatment design and planning, treatment monitoring, and treatment evaluation (cf. Hunsley et al., 2004). We will return to several of these topics in Chapter 9 when we examine the decision-making processes associated with the clinical use of assessment data.

SCREENING

Given their expertise in measurement and psychometrics, psychologists are often called on to assist in the development or implementation of **screening** measures. Depending on the nature of the screening and the screening site, psychologists may or may not be directly involved in conducting screening assessments. The purpose of screening for a disorder, condition, or characteristic is to identify, as accurately as possible, individuals who may have problems of a clinical magnitude or who may be at risk for developing such problems. Individuals who are screened may not have sought out assessment services; rather, they are receiving the assessment as part of the routine operations of a clinic, school, hospital, or employment setting. For example, Weiss, Ernst, Cham, and Nick (2003) described the development of a five-item screening tool to identify ongoing intimate partner violence. The measure was designed to be administered in hospital emergency departments, a setting that provides a unique opportunity to identify victims of partner violence. These victims may come to emergency departments seeking medical services for violence-related injuries or they may be seeking services for other injuries or health problems. The accurate identification of victims of partner violence in a hospital offers an opportunity for medical and social service staff to contact victims about the legal, financial, and psychological options to consider for addressing the violence.

People may also actively seek out a screening assessment. In the United States there are national screening days for a number of psychological disorders, including the National Alcohol Screening Day, the National Depression Screening Day, and the National Anxiety Disorders Screening Day. These screening days have many sponsors, including the American Psychiatric Association, the American Psychological Association, and American Medical Association. The screening can be done on-line or in person at many community-based health care settings such as general hospitals, mental health clinics, and speciality health care providers' offices. Hundreds of thousands of Americans each year are screened for mental health problems in this manner.

DIAGNOSIS/CASE FORMULATION

In the context of psychological assessment, the term "diagnosis" is often used in two related but distinct ways. Diagnosis typically means the use of assessment data to formulate a clinical diagnosis such as those listed in the DSM-IV-TR (see Chapter 3 for details). In this case, interview data, psychological test data, and reports from significant others may be used to determine the nature and scope of the symptoms the person is experiencing. With this information in hand, diagnostic criteria are examined to determine whether the symptom profile matches criteria for Axis I or II diagnoses. As we described in Chapter 3, knowing the diagnosis for a person helps clinicians communicate with other health professionals and search the scientific literature for information on associated features such as etiology and prognosis. Diagnostic information can also provide key information on the types of treatment options that have been found to be effective in clinical trials (Nelson-Gray, 2003). Thus diagnosis can provide an initial framework for a treatment plan that can be modified in order to ensure that it fully addresses the client's concerns and takes into account their particular life circumstances.

Historically, the term "diagnosis" was used to describe the entire process of conducting a psychological assessment and formulating a clinical picture of the client. The origins of this use of the term stem from a time when diagnostic criteria for psychological and psychiatric disorders were ambiguous and relatively uninformative for clinical purposes (i.e., during the era of DSM-I and DSM-II). Thus, in the past, "diagnosis," or "psychodiagnosis," referred to the process in which the psychologist used interview and testing data to render a comprehensive representation of the patient's psychological makeup (cf. Rapaport, Gill, & Schafer, 1968). Although the term "psychodiagnosis" is still used by some clinicians (primarily those with a psychodynamic orientation), we will use **case formulation** to describe the use of assessment data to develop a comprehensive and clinically relevant conceptualization of a patient's psychological functioning. We see numerous advantages to this choice, as the use of the term "case formulation" is common now, does not have a connection with a specific theoretical orientation, and avoids any confusion with the term "diagnosis" (which we use in its limited sense to apply to the use of diagnostic criteria).

PROGNOSIS/PREDICTION

Whether stated explicitly or not at the completion of an assessment, psychological assessment always implies some form of prediction about the patient's future. For example, recommendations that the person seek psychotherapy to address bulimic symptoms or that special academic tutoring is needed to compensate for a learning disability imply that, without some form of intervention, the present problems will either continue or worsen. **Prognosis** refers to the use of assessment data, in combination with relevant empirical literature, to make predictions about the future course of a patient's psychological functioning. Although the psychopathology literature provides information for this task, it must always be remembered that these studies deal with future outcomes at the group level. The clinician's task is to use this probabilistic information (e.g., "60% of patients with this diagnosis experience a recurrence of their symptoms within 2 years") in a manner that takes into account the unique circumstances of the patient being assessed.

One of the biggest challenges clinicians face is attempting to make their predictions as accurate as possible. In any attempts to enhance the accuracy of predictions, a number of factors must be considered such as time and cost, the consequences of inaccurate decisions, and the base rate of the predicted outcome. Although it is always possible to collect more and more assessment data, this comes with certain consequences. Time spent on assessment may mean less time is available to provide an intervention for the patient. The cost of an assessment should not be underestimated: more time spent on assessment means that someone (e.g., the client) or some organization (e.g., the client's health insurance plan) must cover these costs. The clinician must therefore strike a balance between the desire to obtain more information and the need to be conscious of the very real constraints that influence the scope of the assessment.

Prediction errors are inevitable—no one can predict with 100% accuracy. However, not all errors have the same psychological or financial cost. A failure to detect attention-deficit/hyperactivity disorder may result in several years of frustration and academic and social failures for a child and his or her family, whereas a failure to detect a mild specific phobia is unlikely to have the same generalized impact. In older adults symptoms of impaired memory, difficulties in thinking, and problems in concentration may occur as features of both major depressive disorder and dementia. A misdiagnosis has the potential not only to result in ineffective treatment but also to add to the burden experienced by the individual. Errors can also occur in which a person is diagnosed when, in fact, no diagnosis is warranted. For example, if a person were diagnosed with major depressive disorder when they were simply showing signs of uncomplicated bereavement, it could lead to both unnecessary treatment and stigmatization. All of these types of errors are influenced by the **base rate** of a problem or diagnosis; that is, the frequency with which the problem/diagnosis occurs in the population. In a nutshell, the less frequently that a problem occurs, the more likely a prediction error will occur. As many of the predictions that clinical psychologists make are about rare conditions or *low base rate events*—such as the presence of an eating disorder, the likelihood that the person will be violent in the future, or the likelihood of a future suicide attempt—the consequences of error must be seriously considered.

Errors in clinical prediction can occur in many assessment activities, including screening efforts, diagnosis, and case formulation. To better understand how clinical psychologists attempt to address the issue of error, it is necessary to understand some of the basic concepts used in decision theory. There is, of course, the situation in which the prediction is accurate. As presented in **Table 5.3**, this can mean either that the prediction that an event will occur was accurate (*true positive*) or that the prediction of a non-event was accurate (e.g., that no diagnosis was warranted or that a specific event such as a suicide attempt would not occur—*true negative*). However, just as a prediction can be correct in two distinct ways, there are two types of incorrect predictions. A *false positive* occurs when the psychologist predicts that an event will occur but, in fact, it does not occur. Conversely, a *false negative* occurs when an event occurs that was not predicted by the psychologist.

TABLE 5.3   Accuracy and Errors in Clinical Prediction

Prediction	True Event	True Non-Event
Event	True Positives (A)	False Positives (B)
Non-Event	False Negatives (C)	True Negatives (D)

Sensitivity: A / (A + C)

Specificity: D / (D + B)

In referring to accuracy in clinical predictions, psychologists employ two additional concepts: sensitivity and specificity. **Sensitivity** refers to the number of times an event is predicted, across cases, compared with the total number of times that the event actually occurs. More simply, sensitivity (or selectivity; Hogan, 2003) is the proportion of true positives identified by the assessment (Groth-Marnat, 2003). Arithmetically it is determined by dividing the number of true positives by the sum of true positives and false negatives. In contrast, **specificity** deals with the prediction of non-events. It refers to the number of times a non-event is predicted across cases compared with the total number of times that no event occurred; alternatively it can be considered as the relative proportion of true negatives (Groth-Marnat, 2003). Arithmetically it is determined by dividing the number of true negatives by the sum of true negatives and the false positives. Let's assume that a psychologist conducted assessments on hospital inpatients in a psychiatric ward in order to predict who was at risk for future suicide attempts. In our example, sensitivity provides information on how well the assessment procedures were able to detect future suicide attempts and specificity provides information on how well the assessment procedures were able to identify individuals who would not attempt suicide. There are serious consequences associated with failing to detect a person who went on to make a suicide attempt, but there are also costs and consequences for each nonsuicidal person who is erroneously categorized as potentially suicidal—the person's freedom and privacy will have been restricted and considerable personnel resources will have been directed into monitoring. Of course it would be ideal if an assessment had both high sensitivity and high specificity but, in reality, this is rarely the case. Therefore a decision about which assessment procedures to select should be informed by a thorough consideration of the procedure's sensitivity and specificity and the psychological and financial costs stemming from inaccurate clinical predictions.

TREATMENT PLANNING

As we discussed earlier in the chapter, much of the assessment work conducted by psychologists is designed to inform treatment-related decisions. Once the psychologist and client have reached a decision that treatment is required, the obvious question then becomes what exactly the treatment should be. Treatment planning is the process by which information about the client (including sociodemographic and psychological characteristics, diagnoses, and life context) are used in combination with the scientific literature on psychotherapy to develop a proposed course of action that addresses the client's needs and circumstances. As described by Mariush (2002), treatment planning serves many purposes. First, it provides a clear focus for treatment and gives the client realistic expectations about the process and likely outcome of treatment. The plan also establishes a standard against which treatment progress can be measured. Within the context of health service provision, a treatment plan is a valuable tool that facilitates communication among professionals working with the client, provides a clear statement about the nature of the planned services to agencies that may need to authorize and/or pay for the services, and provides a document that can be reviewed as part of an agency's quality assurance activities to ensure that appropriate services are being provided. The collaborative effort between psychologist and client to develop and implement a treatment plan should also establish a good foundation for the subsequent challenges of psychotherapy. Rather than simply agreeing to a vague statement about therapy, a formal treatment plan ensures that a client can provide truly informed consent for the procedures he or she is about to undertake.

A starting point in developing a treatment plan is to determine whether there are treatment options with established effectiveness for the types of problems the client presents. Consideration must be given to the extent to which the characteristics of the client match those of research participants in relevant clinical trials. The better the fit, the greater the psychologist's confidence in choosing one form of treatment. However, even if the fit is relatively poor—as is often the case in dealing with clients with a minority ethnic/cultural background—treatment outcome studies can still provide useful starting points

It is always necessary to tailor the treatment to suit the client's unique circumstances.

for developing a treatment plan. Regardless of the fit, it is always necessary to tailor the treatment to suit the client's unique circumstances.

To be useful, a treatment plan must address three general areas: problem identification, treatment goals, and treatment strategies and tactics (Mariush, 2002). A clear statement of the problems to be addressed provides the necessary starting point for understanding the proposed treatment and for, eventually, determining the treatment's success. For treatment to be efficient and focused, goals must be specified. Goals can include both ultimate goals for treatment and intermediate goals that must be attained in order to reach the ultimate treatment goals. For example, in helping Morgan overcome bulimic symptoms, the ultimate treatment goal may be the development of appropriate body image and of effective emotion regulation skills. The short-term goal, on the other hand, may be the reduction of bingeing behaviour by establishing a routine of eating three healthy meals a day. For Cynthia, who has been cutting her arms, the short-term goal may be a reduction in self-harming behaviour, with a longer-term goal of establishing good study habits, enlarging her social network, and dealing with conflict in her family. Finally, a description of treatment strategies provides information on the general approach to addressing the clinical problems whereas a description of treatment tactics provides details of specific tasks, procedures, or techniques that will be used in treatment. To address Simon's symptoms of depression and relationship conflict, for example, the treatment strategy may be to use individual interpersonal therapy or to use emotionally focused couples therapy (EFT) with both Simon and his partner Chris. The treatment tactics, however, would deal with the specific elements of treatment, such as, within EFT, having the couple work on emotionally reconnecting with each other and developing renewed trust in each other's emotional availability. Only with a thorough and accurate assessment is it possible to specify the type of strategies and tactics that are best suited to deal with a client's presenting problems.

TREATMENT MONITORING

Once a clear treatment plan is in place, it then is necessary to closely monitor the impact of treatment. Treatment monitoring is a crucial element of effective treatment as it allows for changes in the treatment plan based upon the patient's response to treatment. Thus, if a patient is progressing extremely well, it may be possible to shorten treatment or to focus subsequent phases of treatment on other issues of concern to the patient. Alternatively, if the treatment is less than optimally effective, close monitoring of treatment progress provides an opportunity to alter the treatment. All clinicians have an implicit sense of how the patient is progressing, but we are referring to explicitly monitoring progress through the use of specific questions or psychological measures. By providing data on problems in the process of treatment (such as difficulties in the therapeutic relationship) and obstacles the patient is encountering in following through on therapeutic activities (such as not doing assigned tasks outside the therapy session), treatment monitoring can provide an opportunity to reorient treatment efforts to avoid potential treatment failure (Mash & Hunsley, 1993).

In order to repeatedly evaluate elements of the treatment process (such as the therapeutic relationship and compliance with tasks) and alterations in psychological functioning (including changes in symptom frequency, intensity, and duration), psychologists use interviews, brief psychological tests, and/or tests specifically tailored to the client's problems and goals (Kazdin, 1993). Research by psychologist Michael Lambert and his colleagues demonstrated compellingly that routine treatment monitoring has the potential to substantially affect treatment outcome. In a meta-analysis of three large-scale studies, Lambert et al. (2003) found that by using monitoring data to alert clinicians to treatment progress, the likelihood of client deterioration was reduced and the positive effects of psychotherapy were enhanced. In these studies, treatment monitoring data were routinely collected on more than 2,500 patients in a range of treatment settings such as university counselling centres and outpatient treatment clinics. These patients were being seen by qualified professionals who espoused the full range of theoretical orientations typically found in practice settings. The same very simple experimental manipulation was used in all studies: patient and clinician dyads were randomly assigned to a "no feedback condition" in which the treatment monitoring data were not provided to the clinician or to a "feedback condition" in which the clinician was given the data. Across studies in the "no feedback condition,"

Lambert and colleagues found that 21% of patients deteriorated and 21% experienced clinically important improvements in functioning. However, in the "feedback condition," the number of clients who experienced deterioration was reduced by a third (to 13%) and the proportion of successful treatment cases increased by two-thirds (to 35%). These results present a convincing argument that clinical psychologists have an ethical responsibility to routinely gather treatment monitoring data in order to enhance the likelihood of successful treatment outcome.

TREATMENT EVALUATION

In most clinical psychology settings, treatment outcome data have typically been collected to document the extent to which psychological services such as psychotherapy are effective in achieving stated goals. A comparison of outcome data with intake data provides an indication of how much change, if any, has occurred during treatment of a particular individual. There is also a growing trend to use outcome data as indicators of how well an entire system of care is functioning. Whereas data gathered for treatment monitoring can affect treatment services provided to an individual client, data gathered for treatment outcome purposes can yield information relevant to an entire psychological practice or service.

Ogles, Lambert, and Fields (2002) described a range of ways in which treatment outcome data can be used to bring about changes in service provision activities. At the level of individual psychologists working in an agency, aggregating data across patients can provide useful information about a psychologist's success in working with patients. When compared with data obtained from other psychologists in the agency, these data also have the potential to yield information about psychologists who are performing at above or below average levels. Those psychologists whose treatment services are less successful could receive feedback and given additional supervision or training to rectify the situation. On the other hand, a practice analysis of the relatively successful clinicians' activities could provide indications of certain clinical skills or knowledge that set these individuals apart from their colleagues. Training sessions for all clin-icians could then focus on the dissemination of these identified areas of strength in order to improve the overall effectiveness of those working in the service setting. Of course, whether providing feedback to an individual psychologist or making group comparisons among practitioners, it is essential to take into account the service context. For example, if one psychologist in an agency provides services to clients with chronic mental health problems and a history of unsuccessful treatment, it would be unfair to compare outcome data with those obtained by psychologists working with less distressed clients. Using outcome data to make comparisons across psychologists requires close attention to the actual caseload and mix of clients for each psychologist.

Treatment outcome data can also be used to document the typical range of outcomes clients experience and the nature and duration of treatment required to obtain successful outcomes. With these data in hand, clinicians can then provide accurate estimates to clients and any third party payers about the likely benefits, duration, and costs of treatment. Comparing these data across agencies providing similar services may reveal particular strengths and weaknesses in an agency. Consultation with other agencies could then yield avenues for improved outcomes through changes in administrative and/or clinical procedures (e.g., adopting more effective treatment strategies for dealing with clients diagnosed with cocaine dependence and cocaine abuse). Based on data available from published clinical trials of psychotherapy or from treatment centres acknowledged to be leaders in the field, individual practitioners and agencies can set benchmarks against which their own treatment outcome data can be compared. Such comparisons can lead to quality assurance strategies for improvements in areas of suboptimal service delivery.

Data on typical treatment responses can be used to enhance the outcome of a course of treatment for a client. Several groups of psychotherapy researchers have used large data sets based on repeated measures of client progress to establish profiles of symptom reduction and improvements in functioning over the course of treatment. When this information is used by clinicians in the context of treatment monitoring, it becomes possible to identify when the client's progress is less than what is typically found for those with similar problems. Ogles et al. (2002) described a data monitoring system in which a graph depicting typical client progress is used as a comparison against which the progress of a specific client can be charted. On a session by session basis, if the client's assessment score is found to be significantly less than that obtained by the typical client, the clinician is alerted to the fact that progress is suboptimal and that, eventually, treatment failure is a possibility. Based on this, the psychologist can then engage the client in discussions about problems in the process of treatment, thus potentially resulting in changes in the treatment plan (cf. the meta-analytic findings of Lambert et al., 2003).

PSYCHOLOGICAL TESTING

You will have learned in many of your psychology courses that psychologists have expertise in the development and use of tests in the study and treatment of human functioning. Although you may find magazines filled with quick tests of various concepts, developing a scientifically sound psychological test requires more than simply writing a few questions and finding a good name for the test. Psychologists are required to follow the *Standards for Educational and Psychological Testing* (American Educational Research Association, American Psychological Association, & National Council on Measurement in Education, 1999) in developing and using tests and assessment procedures. As we will see in the following sections, a number of criteria must be met if a psychological test is to have any value in research or clinical practice.

But first, let's consider what exactly a psychological test is. Although it might seem to be a relatively simple task to define a test, it turns out to be a rather difficult thing to do. In the *Standards* (AERA et al., 1999) a test is defined in the following manner: "An evaluative device or procedure in which a sample of an examinee's behavior in a specified domain is obtained and subsequently evaluated and scored using a standardized process" (p. 183). This definition, although general enough to encompass various methods of testing (including interviewing, observation, and self-report), is rather awkward and may not be immediately understood by nonpsychologists. Accordingly, Hogan (2003) suggested a more user-friendly definition that is consistent with the *Standards* and other prominent sources of information on psychological testing. His definition is: "A test is a standardized process or device that yields information about a sample of behavior or cognitive processes in a quantified manner" (p. 43). Hunsley et al ., (2003) defined a test according to its intended use. *If* (a) the clinician's intent is to collect a sample of behaviour that will be used to generate statements about a person, a person's experiences, or a person's psychological functioning *and* (b) a claim is made or implied by the clinician that the accuracy or validity of these statements come from the way in which the sample of behaviour was collected and interpreted, and not just from the clinician's expertise, authority, or special qualifications, *then* the process used to collect and interpret the behavioural sample is a psychological test and must meet the standards established for psychological tests. So, for example, although you may be able to quickly develop a questionnaire designed to measure some aspect of human functioning, it is not a test until it has been demonstrated to have met the standards of reliability, validity, and norms.

PROFILE BOX 5.1

DR. DAVID J. A. DOZOIS

Dr. David J. A. Dozois

I received my Ph.D. in Clinical Psychology from the University of Calgary in 1999. I am an Associate Professor in the Departments of Psychology and Psychiatry at the University of Western Ontario. I am registered as a psychologist in the province of Ontario and certified with the Academy of Cognitive Therapy. I have received early career awards from the Canadian Psychological Association, the National Alliance for Research on Schizophrenia and Depression, and the Ontario Mental Health Foundation. In 2005 I was elected Director: Science of the Canadian Psychological Association. In addition to my research and teaching, I also maintain a clinical practice.

My research examines cognitive factors related to depression. I investigate how people who are depressed, or prone to depression, think about themselves, exhibit attention or memory biases toward negative information, and organize self-relevant stimuli. I am also interested in how these cognitive mechanisms develop, how they contribute to depression and its relapse, and how they change with treatment (e.g., cognitive therapy). My colleagues and I are also studying new ways to enhance the delivery of cognitive therapy for anxiety disorders. Additional research interests include cognitive-behavioural theories and therapy and the assessment of psychopathology.

What made you choose to become a clinical psychologist?

I always knew that I wanted to be in a helping profession and I really enjoyed my psychology classes when I was an undergraduate student. When I entered graduate school, I was initially determined to be a clinician, but I became more and more passionate about research as time went on. Although I love clinical practice (and continue to do it), I believe that in my position as a university professor, I have the potential to make a broader contribution.

What is the most rewarding part of your job as a clinical psychologist?

What I find most gratifying about being a clinical psychologist is that there is considerable diversity in this career. A clinical psychologist wears a number of different "hats" (e.g., teacher, researcher, supervisor, clinician, consultant) and I find this stimulating. I count it a tremendous privilege to train future clinicians and researchers and to be involved in their career development. The opportunity to produce research that will change our understanding of depression and anxiety, and improve its treatment, is also very rewarding.

What is the greatest challenge facing you as a clinical psychologist?

Perhaps the greatest challenge that I face is finding (or mustering) the time to engage in all the exciting things that I would like to be involved with. There are a lot of pressures on your time in this career. Aside from teaching graduate and undergraduate courses and writing research articles and book chapters, a professor's duties also include evaluating grant applications, reviewing research articles, writing grant proposals, supervising graduate students, advising honours students, presenting data at conferences, serving on departmental and university committees, advancing the profession through external committee work, and the list goes on. Fortunately, I have been able to maintain a balanced life while juggling these various responsibilities, but this can be quite difficult at times.

Tell us about the importance of evidence-based assessment.

Evidence-based assessment—the evaluation of diagnostic criteria, symptom severity, and theory-specific mechanisms of change—serves a number of important functions.

I believe that by using multiple assessment strategies, I am better able to obtain accurate information about a patient's current level of functioning, develop solid case formulations, and introduce psychological interventions that meet the specific needs of my patients. In addition, evidence-based assessment enhances my ability to demonstrate clinical efficacy (i.e., showing that what I am doing in therapy works), provides valuable information with which to evaluate my hypotheses and impressions about patients, helps me make accurate diagnoses, affords me the opportunity to monitor the efficacy of treatment over time, and improves my ability to predict and prevent relapse. The distinction between assessment and therapy is, in many ways, blurry as there is a dynamic interplay between the two: assessment informs treatment and one needs to regularly reassess as treatment progresses.

How do you integrate science and practice in your work?

I believe that many great research questions stem from clinical practice. I am also convinced that clinical practice is greatly enhanced when it is informed by the empirical literature. I very much adhere to the scientist-practitioner model in my own work and try to bring both sides of it into my teaching. In addition to keeping up on the latest research literature that is pertinent to my clinical work, I routinely and systematically evaluate treatment outcome. At the beginning of treatment, I conduct a thorough intake assessment with my patients so that I can gain a clear sense of what their presenting problems are, what factors might be contributing to the onset or maintenance of their difficulties, and how I may best intervene. Each week, I also ask my patients to complete symptom-based questionnaires and other self-report instruments so that I can determine whether my interventions are successful or whether I need to reconceptualize the case or confront motivational issues. My research is also clinically applied and informed by clinical issues.

What do you see as the most exciting changes in the profession of clinical psychology?

There are many exciting trends in the profession of clinical psychology. One change that I find particularly exciting is the increased demand for empirically supported treatments and assessment strategies. I appreciate this age of increased accountability because I believe that it will enhance our profession and the care that we provide. We have been able to demonstrate not only that psychotherapy works, but also that it is cost-effective and prevents relapse. I am also excited about the fact that research continues to refine and advance our understanding of vulnerability to psychopathology and mechanisms of change. With such increased understanding, we will be better able to treat and prevent mental disorders and promote mental health and quality of life.

Assessment versus Testing

As is readily apparent in the Hunsley et al. (2003) definition, not all information gathered by a psychologist involves psychological testing. This underscores a more general point that psychological assessment and psychological testing are not synonymous. Consistent with the definitions of psychological tests, testing occurs when a particular device is used to gather a sample of behaviour from a client, a score is assigned to the resulting sample, and comparisons with the scores of other people are made in order to interpret the client's score. Assessment is more complex and multifaceted than testing and may or may not involve the use of psychological tests. Assessment requires the integration of life history information and clinical observation of the client with, in most cases, the results obtained from psychological tests and information provided on the client by significant others in the client's life (Hunsley, 2002). The result from a test is a score that can be interpreted based on comparisons with the scores of others; the result from an assessment is a coherent, unified description of the client or selected aspects of the client's experience.

VIEWPOINT BOX 5.2

PSYCHOLOGICAL TESTING ON THE INTERNET

As you surf the Internet you have probably come across sites that offer psychological testing. Some of these sites are offered as a public service by health organizations. Others are more like commercials for pharmaceutical companies—once you have agreed that you suffer from a number of symptoms of a disorder, you may receive a recommendation to talk to your physician about the usefulness of a particular medication in treating those symptoms. Some sites offer psychological testing as a form of entertainment and others are commercial enterprises requiring you to pay for psychological testing. It is important to know that these on-line services are psychological *testing* rather than psychological *assessment*. On-line testing is not the same as having a psychological assessment. On-line testing may be part of a psychological assessment, but it can never be considered a substitute for a psychological assessment (Buchanan, 2002).

According to Statistics Canada data, the majority of Canadian households in metropolitan areas have at least one regular Internet user. Although children living in single parent families are less likely to have Internet access at home, the widespread availability of computers in school increases access for all young people. Canada ranks among the top countries in the world in terms of the proportion of the population with access to the Internet (Statistics Canada, 2002). With the exponential growth in access to the Internet and its increasing use in diverse activities, it is inevitable that mounting numbers of people may use the Internet to find information about mental health issues. A US survey found that 23% of Internet users have searched for information about mental health issues on-line (Pew Internet, 2003).

Many paper and pencil psychological tests in questionnaire format can easily be adapted for on-line administration. Currently, many well-respected psychological tests may be completed on-line through secure sites. On-line completion of tests allows for accurate scoring and rapid feedback. Tests can be updated quickly and new versions introduced at very low cost. Test administration can be adapted to clients with special needs and versions can be made available in many different languages. The potential to offer psychological testing services cheaply to large numbers of people, some of whom may live in remote areas and who may have only limited access to face-to-face services with a mental health professional, is a very appealing one. However, before we accept unconditionally the potential benefits of psychological testing via the Internet, we must consider psychometric, ethical, legal, and practical issues (Naglieri et al., 2004).

The use of psychological tests on the Internet should be guided by the same principles that guide the use of any psychological tests. However, as you are aware, the Internet is unregulated. Ethical practices dictate that the test developer must demonstrate that the test is reliable, valid, and has norms. The issue of norms is particularly important as Internet access may make a test that was normed on a homogenous sample available to a much broader sample of the population. One of the most important professional issues is whether Internet testing is conducted as part of a psychological assessment in which the psychologist also gathers other data about the client and in which the client is provided face-to-face feedback about the assessment results.

Recent research shows that Internet samples are diverse and that results found through Internet responses are similar to those obtained by traditional methods (Gosling, Vazire, Srivastava, & John, 2004). This suggests that the use of the Internet for psychological research and testing can be done appropriately and, therefore, will likely increase in the coming years. If you are considering psychological testing on the Internet you need to be just as careful as if you were seeking psychological testing in a traditional format. You need to consider the credentials of the organization that is offering services and the scientific basis of the tools. No score should ever be interpreted in isolation. To be useful it must be considered part of the information gathered in the process of psychological assessment.

All mental health professionals conduct assessments, but psychologists receive far more training in issues related to testing and are far more likely to use tests than are other mental health professionals. The data in **Table 5.4** illustrate this point. Palmiter (2004) surveyed various professionals who provide mental health services to children and adolescents in the United States. As shown in the table, all professionals are likely to interview the child/adolescent and the family. However, compared to other mental health professionals, psychologists are much more likely to use tests to obtain information about their young clients. These differences were evident for all forms of tests, including measures completed by parents and teachers, measures completed by the child/adolescent, and measures of intelligence and academic achievement. The accurate assessment of children and youth poses a considerable challenge to clinical psychologists. Children and adolescents differ from adults, and are in a process of rapid cognitive, physical, and emotional development. Furthermore, children and adolescents rarely refer themselves for psychological services—they are referred by adults such as parents and teachers. The lives of children and adolescents are best understood with reference to the contexts in which they are embedded—in families, schools, and peer groups. Therefore, assessment of children and adolescents requires that a much larger number and variety of tests and measures be used than is typically the case for adults (Mash & Hunsley, in press). Adding to this challenge is that child and adolescent assessment, by its very nature, involves the integration of information obtained from multiple methods (e.g., interviews, ratings, direct observations), informants (e.g., child, parent, teacher), and settings (e.g., home, classroom).

TABLE 5.4   Assessing Children and Adolescents: What Do Clinicians Do?

Assessment Method	% Clinicians[a]	% Psychologists[b]
Family interview	89.1	90.9
Individual child/adolescent interview	83.0	83.3
Review previous treatment records	70.7	63.6
Review previous educational testing	50.9	62.1
Naturalistic observation	44.3	33.3
Review recent report cards	37.4	54.5*
Parent behaviour rating scales	34.8	60.6*
Teacher behaviour rating scales	33.5	50.0*
Child/adolescent self-report rating scales	25.7	40.9*
Intelligence testing	26.1	40.9*
Achievement testing	17.8	33.3*
Personality testing	16.5	33.3*

[a]Data are from a sample of 230 American clinicians (psychiatric social workers, psychiatric nurses, counsellors) who work with children and adolescents (Palmiter, 2004).

[b]Data are from a sample of 66 American doctoral-level psychologists who work with children and adolescents (Palmiter, 2004).

*Percentages using this method are significantly different at $p < .05$.

The collection of diverse forms of information and the subsequent integration of this information are defining aspects of psychological assessment. As previously outlined in Table 5.2, there are many distinct competencies that are required for psychologists to conduct meaningful assessments. Gary Groth-Marnat (2003) nicely captured what is required of a clinical psychologist when conducting an assessment:

> "The central role of the clinician performing psychological assessment is that of an expert in human behavior who must deal with complex processes and understand test scores in the context of a person's life. The clinician must have knowledge concerning problem areas and, on the basis of this knowledge, form a general idea regarding behaviors to observe and areas in which to collect relevant data. This involves an awareness and appreciation of multiple causation, interactional influences, and multiple relationships" (p. 4).

Psychometric Considerations

The entire range of issues involved in test construction and validation are covered in courses on test construction and psychometric theory. We will restrict our discussion here to reviewing the requirements for a test to be both scientifically sound and clinically useful. These psychometric elements, which hold for all types of psychological tests, are standardization (of stimuli, administration, and scoring), reliability, validity, and norms.

STANDARDIZATION

As indicated in the test definitions we presented, **standardization** is an essential aspect of a psychological test. Standardization implies consistency across clinicians and testing occasions in the procedure used to administer and score the test (Anastasi & Urbina, 1997). Without standardization it is virtually impossible for the clinician to replicate the information gathered in an assessment or for any other clinician to do so. Furthermore, without standardization, test results are likely to be highly specific to the unique aspects of the testing situation and are unlikely to provide data that can be generalized to testing by another psychologist, let alone to other situations in the person's life. Standardization is necessary to reduce variability in the testing situation. Consequently, test developers provide detailed instructions regarding the nature of the stimuli, administrative procedures, time limits, and the types of verbal probes and permissible responses to the client's questions. Instructions are provided for scoring the test. For many tests only simple addition of responses is required but for many tests there are complex scoring rules that may require extensive training to achieve proficiency. It is essential that psychologists are trained in scoring the test and that they adhere to established scoring criteria. Unfortunately it is relatively common for some psychologists to disregard the use of such scoring criteria in favour of nonstandardized, personally developed approaches to scoring. For example, in a survey of 293 American school psychologists, Kennedy, Faust, Willis, and Piotrowski (1994) found that approximately 50% of survey respondents used personalized scoring for projective tests and more than 10% used personalized scoring for self-report measures of depression.

RELIABILITY

We briefly touched on the psychometric properties of reliability and validity in Chapter 4 (see Table 4.10). Basically, reliability refers to the consistency of the test, including whether all aspects of the test contribute in a meaningful way to the data obtained (**internal consistency**), whether similar results would be obtained if the person was retested at some point after the initial test (**test-retest reliability**), and whether similar results would be obtained if the test was conducted and/or scored by another evaluator (**inter-rater** or **inter-scorer reliability**). Reliable results are necessary if we wish to generalize the test results and their psychological implications beyond the immediate assessment situation. Standardization of stimuli, administration, and scoring are preconditions for good reliability, but do not ensure adequate test reliability. A test may consist of too many components that are influenced by irrelevant client characteristics, the testing situation (such as the demand characteristics associated with the purpose of the testing), or the behaviour of the assessing psychologist. Or, to take another example, the scoring criteria for the test may be too complicated or lacking in detail to permit reliable scoring.

A question that typically arises in both clinical and research situations is just how reliable a test must be. As with many questions in psychology, the answer to this is not entirely straightforward. First, there are numerous psychological tests for which one would not expect internal consistency or test-retest reliability to be very high (Streiner, 2003). Take the example of a measure of stressful life events. You have probably seen such tests in other psychology courses or in popular magazines. They involve the listing of various possible life events that an individual may experience (e.g., death of a significant other, loss of employment, marriage, birth of a child) and usually ask the respondent to indicate which events occurred in the last year. Internal consistency of such tests is irrelevant, as the items are not necessarily related to each other. Likewise, if such a test was taken at the age of 18 and then again at the age of 25, one would not necessarily expect high test-retest reliability—such a test is not intended to measure a characteristic that is stable over time. On the other hand, inter-scorer reliability is very relevant to a stressful life event test, because the responses to the test and the total score obtained on the test should be unaffected by who administered and scored the test.

So, let's return to the question of how much reliability is necessary. As Hogan (2003) suggested, this is a similar question to how high a ladder should be—the answer in both cases is that it depends on the purpose you have in mind. Although there is a range of perspectives on the issue, there is a clear consensus that the level of acceptable reliability for tests used for clinical purposes must be greater than it is for tests used for research purposes. In considering internal consistency reliability, a number of authors have suggested that a value of .90 is the minimum required for a clinical test (e.g., Nunnally & Bernstein, 1994). For research purposes, values greater than .70 are typically seen as sufficient, with lower values being unacceptable (e.g.,

Kaplan & Saccuzzo, 2001). The main reason that high reliability is so important for clinical purposes is that reliability directly influences the standard error of measurement (SEM), an index that provides information on the accuracy of a test score. In concrete terms, the larger the SEM, the more error there is likely to be in a test score. This can be extremely important in clinical work where precise test cut-off scores are used, such as in determining whether a child's measured intelligence is high enough to warrant access to a gifted school program. The size of the SEM for the score directly affects the rates of false positives and false negatives for any clinical decision (i.e., the larger the SEM, the more error there is in the test scores, which cumulatively leads to more classification errors as gifted or not gifted).

VALIDITY

When we consider test validity we are evaluating the degree to which the test truly measures what it purports to measure. A standardized and reliable test does not necessarily yield valid data, for a test purporting to measure construct A may in fact measure construct B. Test validity is a matter of ensuring that the test actually samples the type of behaviour that is relevant to the underlying psychological construct (content validity), that it provides data consistent with theoretical postulates associated with the phenomenon being assessed (concurrent, predictive, and convergent validity), and that it provides a relatively pure measure of the construct that is minimally contaminated by other psychological constructs (discriminant validity). In applied contexts, such as in clinical assessment, an

In clinical assessment, "the more data the better" is not necessarily true. Too much data can lead to increased costs and the introduction of error into the assessment.

additional form of validity should be considered, namely incremental validity: the extent to which a measure adds to the prediction of a criterion above what can be predicted by other sources of data (Hunsley & Meyer, 2003; Sechrest, 1963). It is not necessarily a case of "the more data the better" in clinical assessment. As described previously, there are costs associated with the collection of assessment data. The collection of excessive amounts of data can lead to both unnecessary costs and the introduction of unnecessary error creeping into the assessment. Despite the clear importance of incremental validity in conducting clinical assessments, there is currently very little research available to guide clinical psychologists in their selection and use of tests (Hunsley, 2003).

Although it is common to talk about a test being either valid or invalid, validity is not a dichotomous variable. Many psychological tests consist of subscales designed to measure specific aspects of a more general construct. For such tests it is inappropriate to refer to the validity of the test *per se*, because the validity of each subscale must be established. Moreover, validity is always conditional and must be established within certain parameters. Simply because a test is valid for specific purposes within specific groups of people, it does not follow that it is valid for other purposes or groups. For example, knowing that an intelligence test is a valid predictor of academic functioning does not also automatically support its use as a test for determining child custody arrangements. Furthermore, test validity across characteristics such as gender, age, ethnicity, and socioeconomic status cannot simply be assumed based on validity data for any particular group of people—it must be empirically demonstrated.

NORMS

For a test to be clinically useful, it must meet the criteria of standardization, reliability, and validity. However, to meaningfully interpret the results obtained from a client, it is essential to use either norms or specific criterion-related cut-off scores (AERA et al., 1999). Without such reference information, it is impossible to determine the precise meaning of any test results. Knowing that a person scored low or high on a test (i.e., relative to the range of possible scores) provides no meaningful information; the results must be compared with some type of standard in order to have meaning. In psychological assessment, comparisons must be made to either criteria that have been set for the test (e.g., a certain degree of accuracy as demonstrated in the test is necessary for the satisfactory performance of a job) or to some form of norms.

For most purposes in clinical psychology, test developers focus on establishing norms for their tests. Selection of the target population(s) for establishing the norms and then developing the norms requires a series of decisions. Most importantly, decisions must be made about the populations to which the test is to be applied. It is possible to establish norms for comparing a specific score to those that might be obtained within the general population or within specific subgroups of the general population (e.g., gender-specific norms). It is also possible to establish norms for determining the likelihood of membership in specific theoretical or concrete categories (e.g., nondistressed versus psychologically disordered groups). As with validity considerations, it may be necessary to develop multiple norms for a test based on the group being assessed and the testing purpose. A critical aspect of test norms is the quality of the normative sample. It is very common to find tests that have norms based on samples of convenience—in other words, data were obtained from a group of research participants in a specific location and may not be representative of scores that would be obtained by others. Common convenience samples include undergraduate students, hospital inpatients, or patients in a single psychology clinic. Such norms should be treated very sceptically, as no effort was taken to ensure that the members of the normative group were comparable in age, gender, ethnicity, or educational level (for example) to those who are likely to take the test as part of a clinical assessment. There are some commonly used psychological tests, such as the Wechsler scales of intelligence (see Chapter 7), that have nationally representative norms. With these types of norms, great care has been taken to ensure that test scores were obtained from a group of research participants selected to be representative of the national population for whom the test will be used. Accordingly one can have much more confidence in the value and relevance of such norms.

There are three main categories of test norms: percentile ranks, standard scores, and developmental norms (Hogan, 2003). A *percentile rank* indicates the percentage of those in the normative group whose scores fell below a given test score. If a test score of 25 is associated with a percentile rank of 81 this indicates that 81% of those in the normative group scored at or below a test score of 25. As you may have seen in Appendix 2 , most students applying to graduate programs in clinical psychology are required to take the *Graduate Record Examination (GRE)*. Typically the results from this test are reported as percentile ranks. The use of *standard scores* is very common with psychological tests. To develop a standard score a *z*-score is calculated. As you will no doubt recall from other psychology courses, this involves subtracting the mean of the test scores from a specific test score and dividing the resulting number by the standard deviation of the test scores. Many psychological tests, such as the Minnesota Multiphasic Personality Inventory-2 (MMPI-2; described in detail in Chapter 8), convert a calculated *z*-score to a distribution in which the mean score is 50 and the standard deviation is 10 (i.e., a *T*-score). The GRE uses a different distribution in which the mean score is set at 500 and the standard deviation is 100. **Figure 5.1** presents the distribution of

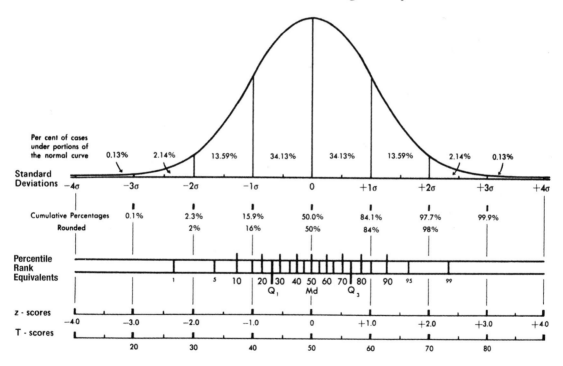

Figure 5.1   Equivalence of several types of norms in the normal curve. Reprinted with permission from Harcourt Assessment Inc.

scores under a normal curve and allows you to interpret the normative meaning of a percentile rank or a standard score. Using this figure you can see that a *T*-score of 71 on the MMPI-2 means that the score is greater than that obtained by more than 98% of the normative sample. Finally, *development norms* are used when the psychological construct being assessed develops systematically over time. The intelligence test developed by Alfred Binet used mental age equivalents to quantify the intellectual status of children (i.e., a child's score was comparable to the average child of a given age). The Woodcock-Johnson III Tests of Cognitive Abilities uses both age equivalents (i.e., the age level in the normative sample at which the mean score is the same as the test score under consideration) and grade equivalents (i.e., the grade level in the normative sample at which the mean score is the same as the test score under consideration) to quantify achievement performance.

Testing Practices in Clinical Psychology

In Chapter 2 we described testing and assessment as central activities for most clinical psychologists. In Chapters 7 and 8 we describe in detail a number of commonly used psychological tests, with a particular emphasis on those that have substantial evidence of reliability and validity. Our intent in this section is to briefly present to you the tests that clinical psychologists typically use. As you read the following paragraphs we'd like you to keep in mind the unfortunate fact that, as Groth-Marnat (2003) noted, many clinical psychologists fail to take into account the psychometric qualities of tests or the strength of the empirical literature regarding the tests. In other words, although some commonly used tests have outstanding psychometric properties, others fall woefully short of professional standards. We will have much more to say about this lamentable state of affairs in subsequent chapters.

There is a long history of surveys of clinical psychologists' practice activities and use of different types of tests. **Table 5.5** presents information from recent surveys of American clinical psychologists. Data from Cashel's (2002) survey of 162 clinical psychologists working with children and adolescents suggested that intelligence tests, behaviour rating scales completed by parents and teachers (and, in some cases, the youth themselves), and brief projective tests are commonly used. In their survey of 137 clinical psychologists, Piotrowski, Belter, and Keller (1998) asked respondents about the most important tests used in clinical practice. Although the specific tests differed from those reported in the Cashel (2002) study, a similar pattern emerged, with intelligence, self-report personality inventories, and projective measures seen as most important. Of concern in both these surveys is the frequent reliance on projective tests. Compared with intelligence tests, personality inventories, and behaviour rating scales, projective tests are far less likely to be standardized, to have norms, or to possess acceptable levels of reliability and validity (Hunsley et al , 2003). For example, although the Rorschach Inkblot Test can be administered, scored, and interpreted in a standardized manner, this is not the case for the clinical use of sentence completion tasks, the Draw-A-Person Test, or the Thematic Apperception Test.

TABLE 5.5   Test Usage Among American Clinical Psychologists

Five Tests Most Commonly Used in Child and Adolescent Assessment[a]

Wechsler Intelligence Scale for Children

Achenbach System of Empirically Based Assessment

Sentence Completion Tests

Conners' Parent and Teacher Rating Scales

Draw-A-Person Test

Five Tests Rated As Most Important in Assessment Practices[b]

Minnesota Multiphasic Personality Inventory (both adult and adolescent versions)

Wechsler Intelligence Scales (both adult and child versions)

Rorschach Inkblot Test

Millon Inventories

Thematic Apperception Test

[a]from Cashel (2002); [b] from Piotrowski, Belter, and Keller (1998)

There are two important systems-level factors in understanding the choice of commonly used tests among clinical psychologists: country of practice and nature of doctoral assessment training. In a survey of 158 British clinical psychologists, Bekhit, Thomas, Lalonde, and Jolley (2002) found that British psychologists were much less likely than American psychologists to use psychological tests. Clear differences in test usage also emerged in their survey. Among British clinical psychologists, the tests seen as most important for clinical practice were the Wechsler intelligence scales (adult and child versions), the Wechsler Memory Scale, the Beck Depression Inventory, the National Adult Reading Test, and the Millon Personality Inventories. In contrast to American data, extremely few respondents rated the Thematic Apperception Test and the Rorschach as important for clinical use (7.5% and 5%, respectively). With respect to training program influences, data from Childs and Eyde's (2002) survey of approximately half the APA-accredited clinical psychology programs in Canada and the United States are very informative. They found that more than two-thirds of surveyed programs taught doctoral students to use the Wechsler intelligence scales, the MMPI scales, the Rorschach Inkblot Test, and the Thematic Apperception Test. This definitely helps explain the Piotrowski et al. (1998) data: psychologists are simply using the tests that they were trained to use. If we consider the model curriculum recommendations found in Table 5.1, the Childs and Eyde (2002) data suggest that there are some very significant weaknesses in the way in which most programs approach assessment training. Although almost every surveyed program provided training in the interpretation and reporting of test results, less than two-thirds provided instruction on the topics of reliability and validity, and only 20% had a course that covered issues related to norms and norming. In light of the need for competencies in psychometric theory and the scientific, theoretical, empirical, and contextual bases of psychological assessment presented in Table 5.2, it is abundantly obvious that many training programs are not adequately addressing the need for training in psychological assessment.

VIEWPOINT BOX 5.3

POSITIVE PSYCHOLOGY: ASSESSMENT OF RESOURCES AND STRENGTHS

Many of the tools we will describe in the chapters on psychological assessment are designed to measure symptoms, problems, or difficulties. All training programs require students to complete a course in psychopathology. The field of psychopathology allows for the sophisticated assessment of countless ways that individuals can experience problems in their thoughts, feelings, and behaviours. Clinical psychologists are trained to distinguish between different types of difficulties and to make diagnoses of mental disorders. A relatively neglected part of the equation has been the measurement of clients' resources and strengths.

Some mental health professions have a tradition of considering client strengths. For example, school counsellors and social workers have a habit of considering the client's strengths and competence as well as weaknesses. Assessments conducted by these professionals rarely involve well-validated measures. In comparison to the wealth of psychological tools for assessing problems, very few validated assessment strategies focus on measurement of internal resources or personal strengths or external resources and supports. The Achenbach System of Empirically Based Assessment (ASEBA) is an important exception. The ASEBA includes not only scales addressing problematic behaviours, but social competence as well, with questions addressing the child's sports, activities, chores, relationships, and school performance. The newly developed scales for adults also include measurement of adaptive functioning.

It is easy to understand how strengths and resources can be overlooked. When a person seeks psychological services, it is usually because there is a problem: he or she is sad, can't concentrate, is having difficulties in relationships, or having trouble managing anger. In the psychologist's office the client may be asked to describe his or her difficulties. However, the person's strengths and resources may hold the key to the solution to the problem. For example, a child who is experiencing shyness may be a talented musician or artist, a parent who is struggling to communicate with his or her rebellious adolescent may be a calm and effective communicator at work, a depressed person who is worried about finding a job may derive some satisfaction from responsibilities as a volunteer. Similarly, there may be resources that could make a significant difference in the client's life. A child may respond well to a sensitive tutor, a teenage mother may get useful advice from another young parent, or an elderly person may be comforted by phone contact with a sibling who lives far away.

Research on the ways that people cope with life transitions and challenges can guide the choice of resources and strengths to examine. For example, the now famous Brown and Harris study (1978) revealed that young women were much more vulnerable to depression if they lacked a confiding relationship. An important dimension to assess is therefore the availability of a person in whom to confide. The work of Katz and Gottman (1993) showed that parents' style of dealing with emotions could provide an important buffer that protected children from the harmful effects of marital conflict. This suggests that it would be useful to assess the extent to which parents are able to help children understand, express, and manage strong feelings.

With the development of positive psychology (e.g., Aspinwall & Staudinger, 2003; Lopez & Snyder, 2003), greater attention is being devoted to the study of personal strengths. Psychologists are beginning to expand their vocabulary of those qualities that are helpful in dealing with life's challenges: courage, tenacity, loyalty, kindness, honesty, and integrity. As new measures are developed, psychologists may develop a more balanced approach to assessment, one that examines both the vulnerabilities and fragility that bring clients to seek psychological services and the strengths and resources that they need to discover and build on in order to benefit from services.

Psychological Testing and Assessment: Ethical Considerations

As we described in Chapter 2, the profession of clinical psychology has two main pillars: science and ethics. Thus far in the chapter we have focused almost exclusively on the scientific side of psychological assessment. It is now time to consider the main ethical issues psychologists encounter in conducting assessments.

In Chapter 2 we described the ethical principles, such as responsible caring, that are represented in the Canadian Code of Ethics (CPA, 2000). Obviously all those principles apply when assessments are conducted by Canadian psychologists. Depending on the jurisdiction in which a psychologist practises, there may be national and/or provincial/state codes of conduct that prescribe certain steps that must be taken when providing assessments. Both the American Psychological Association (APA, 2002) and the Association of State and Provincial Psychology Boards (ASPPB, 2005) have codes of conduct that contain elements specific to assessment activities. In order to avoid differences in codes and legal requirements across jurisdictions we focus our presentation of ethical issues on generic issues in assessment rather than on a specific code of conduct.

When considering ethical issues in assessment, the first and foremost issue is that of informed consent. People undergoing a psychological assessment must be provided with sufficient details about the assessment to be able to make an informed decision about participation. Information must be provided about the nature and purpose of the assessment, the fees, the involvement of other parties in the assessment, and any limits to confidentiality. Based on this information, the client must then agree to the assessment before any service can commence. In some instances it may not be possible to obtain freely given informed consent because the person is, in some fashion, being compelled to undergo the assessment. Common examples include situations in which a court has mandated an assessment or an assessment is being undertaken to determine an individual's competence or capacity to make decisions. For example, Wendy, a seriously depressed mother who is engaged in a battle for the custody of her child with her formerly abusive partner, may feel that she has little choice about whether to participate in a child custody evaluation if she wishes to retain her parenting arrangement with her child. Similarly, Trent, who was charged with manslaughter following a motor vehicle accident, may feel he has little choice about participating in a psychological assessment that will address whether symptoms of attention-deficit/hyperactivity disorder contributed to the accident. In these situations psychologists should still strive to provide as much information about the assessment as is appropriate in these cases. Most codes of conduct indicate that psychologists have a responsibility to adequately communicate the results of the assessment to the client. Not only must the psychologist provide the information, but he or she must take reasonable steps to ensure that the client understands the results.

Obtaining informed consent is the first task in psychological assessment.

All information collected as part of a psychological assessment must be treated as confidential. This means that no information gathered in the assessment can be released to others without the client's consent. Although this seems rather straightforward, there are exceptions to this. For example, if the psychologist learns that the client is intent on committing suicide, has a clear plan for this, and has the means to carry out the plan, the psychologist has an obligation to break confidentiality in order to secure the client's safety. When a child volunteers in the course of intelligence testing that he or she is upset because a parent punished him or her with a belt, then the psychologist has a legal obligation to inform the child protection authorities. Limits to confidentiality must thus be explained to the client as part of the informed consent procedures.

In many countries legislation allows people to access their health records. In other words, whatever is in a client file, with very few exceptions, can be seen by the client, and clients can authorize the release of file information to others such as teachers, lawyers, or other health care providers. This poses a potential challenge for psychologists, as they are also required to protect the security and copyrights of test materials. As a result it is becoming standard practice among psychologists to distinguish between test data and test material *per se*. Test data, like other parts of a client file, may be released to clients and appropriate others upon the request of the client (or the client's guardian or legal representative). Test material, including actual test questions and manuals, are not part of the file and must not be released. The distinction between test data and test material has caused publishers of psychological tests to alter the format of some tests. It was common practice for self-report measures, for example, to have both the test questions and a space for scoring the test on the same sheet. This made it impossible to physically separate the test data (i.e., the client's score or circled responses to questions) from the test itself. Accordingly the format of many of these tests has been altered to provide a separate sheet on which the client provides a response and the test is scored.

In conducting assessments psychologists have an ethical responsibility to be knowledgeable about test properties such as standardization, reliability, validity, and norms. They must also be familiar with the proper use and interpretation of the tests they use. It is particularly important that psychologists be aware of the tests' strengths and limitations with respect to psychological characteristics such as age, gender, and cultural background. When providing feedback about the assessment to the client or to others designated by the client, psychologists have a responsibility to clearly indicate the limits to the certainty of their findings. This pertains to all aspects of assessment results, including diagnoses, clinical judgements, and clinical predictions. They also have an obligation to indicate the basis for their results and must clearly indicate the sources of data used in an assessment. It is becoming increasingly common for psychologists to use computer-generated interpretive reports when using personality, intelligence, or achievement tests. Psychologists who use the interpretive statements contained in the computer-generated report should acknowledge the sources of the statements in the assessment report. This ensures that the basis for the conclusions obtained from the interpretive report is clearly presented.

SUMMARY AND CONCLUSIONS

In this chapter we have reviewed some of the many purposes of psychological assessment. We have highlighted that in addition to stand-alone assessment services, psychological assessment can be used in screening, diagnosis and case formulation, prediction, treatment planning, and monitoring the effectiveness of interventions. An important distinction was drawn between psychological assessment, which refers to an entire process of inquiry, and psychological testing, which may be used as part of that process. We have argued that psychologists have special expertise in the use of tests, and that for a tool to be considered a psychological test it must meet strict criteria in terms of standardization, reliability, validity, and norms. Survey data reveal that, unfortunately, many North American universities continue to offer training in assessment procedures that fall short of the definition of a psychological test and many psychologists routinely use tests that are inappropriate. We reviewed ethical issues related to consent to assessment services.

Critical Thinking Questions

How is psychological assessment different from other types of assessment?

Why do psychologists collect multiple types of information in their assessments?

What are the essential ingredients of a useful psychological test?

Is there a problem with basing decisions on unstandardized tests?

Key Terms

assessment-focused services

base rate

case formulation

internal consistency

inter-rater reliability

inter-scorer reliability

intervention-focused assessment services

prognosis

screening

sensitivity

specificity

standardization

test-retest reliability

Key Names

Gary Groth-Marnat   Michael Lambert

ADDITIONAL RESOURCES

Websites

Screening Mental Health, Inc., an American non-profit organization that offers and coordinates screening days for several mental health problems: http://mentalhealthscreening.org

Buros Center for Testing, which provides listings of tests and test reviews: http://www.unl.edu/buros

Books

Anastasi, A., & Urbina, S. (1997). *Psychological testing* (7th ed.). Upper Saddle River, NJ : Prentice-Hall, Inc.

Groth-Marnat, G. (2003). *Handbook of psychological assessment* (4th ed.). Hoboken, NJ: John Wiley & Sons.

Hersen, M. (Ed.). (2004). *The comprehensive handbook of psychological assessment* (Vols. 1–4). New York: Johns Wiley & Sons.

Hogan, T. P. (2003). *Psychological testing: A practical introduction*. Hoboken, NJ: John Wiley & Sons.

Journal Article

Wood, J. M., Garb, H. N., Lilienfeld, S. O., & Nezworski, M. T. (2002). Clinical assessment. *Annual Review of Psychology, 53,* 519–543.

CHAPTER 6

Assessment: Interviewing and Observation

INTRODUCTION

Among the wealth of strategies used in clinical assessments, interviews and observations are commonly used by almost every psychologist. Across diverse theoretical orientations, the tools clinical psychologists use to assess clients inevitably include talking to them and observing them. Interviews are used in overlapping ways for both clinical assessment and psychotherapy (see **Figure 6.1**). In Chapter 5 we raised the issue of informed consent to psychological services. Before embarking on any clinical assessment interview, the psychologist must explain to clients that the interview is confidential and must also carefully explain the limits to that confidentiality. Unlike lawyers, psychologists do not have client privilege. Psychologists are obliged to break confidentiality if a child or an adult is at risk of being seriously harmed.

One of the oldest types of interviews, the **mental status examination**, was developed by psychiatrist Adolf Meyer early in the 20th century. The mental status examination was designed to be used in much the same way as physical examinations were used by general practitioners. The mental status examination includes questions designed to assess the patient's thinking, perceptions, and mood, as well as to allow observation of appearance, speech, and interpersonal relations. In common practice, psychiatrists select questions from the mental status examination, but do not administer it in a standardized way. Although psychiatrists continue to use the mental status examination, it is not widely used by psychologists.

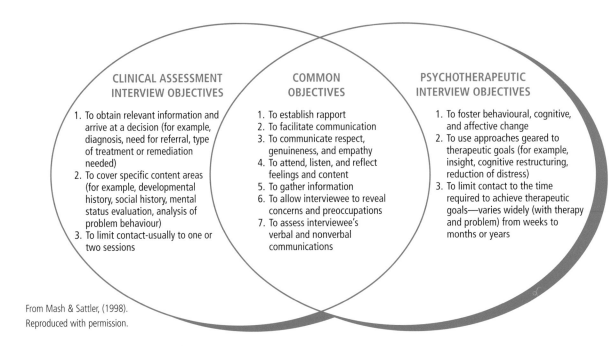

CLINICAL ASSESSMENT
INTERVIEW OBJECTIVES

1. To obtain relevant information and arrive at a decision (for example, diagnosis, need for referral, type of treatment or remediation needed)
2. To cover specific content areas (for example, developmental history, social history, mental status evaluation, analysis of problem behaviour)
3. To limit contact-usually to one or two sessions

COMMON
OBJECTIVES

1. To establish rapport
2. To facilitate communication
3. To communicate respect, genuineness, and empathy
4. To attend, listen, and reflect feelings and content
5. To gather information
6. To allow interviewee to reveal concerns and preoccupations
7. To assess interviewee's verbal and nonverbal communications

PSYCHOTHERAPEUTIC
INTERVIEW OBJECTIVES

1. To foster behavioural, cognitive, and affective change
2. To use approaches geared to therapeutic goals (for example, insight, cognitive restructuring, reduction of distress)
3. To limit contact to the time required to achieve therapeutic goals—varies widely (with therapy and problem) from weeks to months or years

From Mash & Sattler, (1998). Reproduced with permission.

Figure 6.1   Differences and similarities between clinical assessment interviews and psychotherapeutic interviews.

Psychologists use clinical interviews for diverse purposes. They are an integral component of both stand-alone assessments and assessments that are part of the delivery of psychological services. Interviews are the most common strategy to gather information necessary to make a diagnosis, but also serve many additional purposes. They are also used to obtain information for case formulation, problem definition, and goal-setting. Interview data include material that cannot be assessed in psychometric tests that is important in generating hypotheses and elaborating on themes that have been identified in other assessment strategies. The clinical interview is a valuable tool, not just as a source of information, but also for developing a collaborative relationship between client and psychologist.

Different types of interviews are used for different purposes. Clinical interviews vary in their degree of structure. In unstructured interviews, the psychologist decides what questions to ask and to follow up on as the interview unfolds. Semi-structured interviews allow the psychologist some flexibility in questioning and the order of questions. Highly structured interviews specify the precise ways that questions should be posed and queries made, as well as defining the types of responses necessary to score a particular symptom as present. You may recall that in Chapter 4 we discussed the need to balance threats to internal validity and external validity; similarly, in considering interview formats the psychologist must weigh the advantages of structure with the advantages of flexibility.

By far the vast majority of clinical assessment interviews are unstructured, following the format preferred by the individual psychologist. Even though unstructured clinical assessment interviews do not follow a set script, they are distinct from regular conversation in important ways. We will explain some of the differences between clinical assessment interviews and regular conversations. Psychologists are trained how to ask questions and how to listen. The way that questions are formulated can encourage clients to give a "yes-no" type answer, or to elaborate and explain in greater detail. Listening skills include verbal strategies to convey understanding and to clarify what the client has said, as well as nonverbal behaviours that convey that the psychologist is attentively tracking the conversation.

Although it is possible to make some general assumptions about the kinds of behaviour that enable psychologists to gather important information from clients, it is essential to be aware of ethnic and cultural considerations that must be taken into account in interviewing a diverse clientele. For example, orthodox Jews observing *shomer negiyah* are not permitted to touch a member of the opposite sex, so may refuse to shake hands with the psychologist. The psychologist must therefore be careful not to interpret as social withdrawal, lack of engagement, or surliness what is actually observance of a religious edict.

In this chapter we will illustrate some strategies that are used in assessment interviews designed to define the client's problems, formulate client goals, and obtain an accurate description of ways the client has attempted to solve these problems in the past. We will also present ways that the skills required in interviewing an individual must be adapted when the psychologist is interviewing a couple or a family. You can imagine that a clinical psychologist who focused attention entirely on the perspective of one person would quickly lose rapport with other family members. So, in working with more than one client, the psychologist must be adept at ensuring each person has an opportunity to talk.

For many decades children were considered to be unreliable informants, so all pertinent clinical information was gathered from the significant adults in their lives. There has been growing recognition that children can provide important information about their experiences, thoughts, and feelings. However, it is not sufficient to simply scale down an adult interview for use with children. Although face-to-face interviews are a common way for adults to gather information, this strategy poses special challenges with children. We will describe some of the developmental issues that must be taken into account when interviewing children, including their level of cognitive development, their emotional expression, and their suggestibility. Given the limitations of child interviews, diagnostic information is also obtained from adults who know the child well, such as parents, teachers, and caregivers.

Interviews offer rich opportunities for the psychologist to observe the client. The psychologist is attentive to the client's appearance, behaviour, affect, and responses to questions. Couple, parent-child, and family interviews also provide the opportunity to observe the ways that family members interact, the way they take turns, how they handle disagreement, etc. Psychologists

Clinical psychologists can gather important data from observations in naturalistic settings.

also find it useful to observe children and families in more naturalistic environments, such as in a playroom, at home, or at school. We will discuss the types of information that can be gathered from observations. In the final section of the chapter, we will discuss the usefulness of self-monitoring as a clinical assessment strategy, in which the client keeps track of and records the details of relevant thoughts, behaviours, or feelings.

ETHICAL ISSUES: LIMITS OF CONFIDENTIALITY

Ethical codes dictate that psychologists must provide confidential services. This means that the psychologist is bound to maintain secrecy with respect to the material that is revealed in the course of providing psychological services. Although it might be tempting to tell others of the interesting things that a client reported, the psychologist is bound to respect the client's privacy and must not discuss details with other people without the client's permission. However, there are limits to confidentiality. As we discussed in Chapter 5, in some cases, a third party such as a school board, an insurance company, or a family court judge has requested the assessment. In those circumstances, the client must give permission for the results of the assessment to be sent to the third party. There are also legal obligations to break confidentiality when a person's safety is at risk. Canadian provinces all have child protection laws that require professionals to inform the local child protection agency if there is a suspicion that a child may be in need of protection. Psychologists are required to take steps to ensure that clients are protected from self-harm and that others are protected if a client plans to harm someone else. Because the psychologist-client relationship is not a privileged one like the lawyer-client relationship, psychological reports and records can be subpoenaed by the court, and the psychologist can be required to testify with respect to the psychological services he or she has provided. Psychologists must ensure that clients understand these limits to confidentiality before they enter into an agreement to receive psychological services. **Table 6.1** provides an example of the way that a psychologist might introduce the **limits of**

confidentiality at the beginning of a first appointment. As you can imagine, a statement that sets out all kinds of unpleasant scenarios, such as child abuse, suicide, homicide, and court cases, is a very clear signal that the conversation that will follow is a professional one. By calmly explaining the limits of confidentiality the psychologist demonstrates that in the context of psychological services, the client's rights are protected, the person's safety is considered paramount, and that it is possible to talk about very difficult issues.

TABLE 6.1   Limits of Confidentiality: A Heavy Way to Start a Conversation, but a Professional Way to Start an Assessment Interview

"Everything that is said here is private. I will not tell other people what's talked about. There are some important exceptions to that rule. First, if you told me that a child was being hurt in some way, then by law I have to do something to protect the child, that is, I'd have to get in touch with the Children's Aid Society. Second, if I heard that you were finding things so tough that you felt life just wasn't worth living anymore, then I'd have to take steps to protect you. Basically, if I hear anyone is in danger of being hurt by someone else or by him or herself, then I can't keep things private, but must do something to protect the person. Third, if there was ever some kind of a court case, then a judge could ask me to give testimony, could ask me about these sessions, or ask to see my notes.

Do you understand? Do you have any questions? I know this is a heavy way to get started, but I believe it is important to say this to all clients, just so you know where you stand."

UNSTRUCTURED ASSESSMENT INTERVIEWS

In conducting clinical interviews, psychologists create a safe environment designed to make the client more at ease to talk about the issues that are troubling to him or her. The assessment interview is conducted free from disruptions; the psychologist does not answer the phone or respond to email messages during interviews. The psychologist's office usually includes comfortable seating, unobtrusive décor, and appropriate lighting. Many offices are soundproofed to limit distracting background noises. The psychologist adopts a calm and relaxed stance designed to put clients at ease. However, the clinical interview is not a social visit. It differs in important ways from the conversations a client may have with friends, with the hairdresser, or with a stranger on a long train journey. If you choose a career in clinical psychology because you have always liked talking to people and are considered by your friends and family to be a good listener, you may be surprised to discover that you will need to learn to interact in very different ways in your future role as a psychologist. Allowing a person to simply tell his or her story is not the same as conducting a clinical assessment interview. Empathic listening may be sufficient to provide temporary relief to a distressed friend, but it is not sufficient to enable the psychologist to formulate a diagnosis or to begin treatment planning. **Table 6.2** lists some of the ways that clinical interviews differ from regular conversations. Because an assessment interview is not a regular conversation, the client may feel more at ease in discussing painful or embarrassing issues than he or she would be willing to discuss in chats with friends.

TABLE 6.2   Differences between Clinical Interviews and Social Conversations

Social Conversation	Clinical Interview
Can take place anywhere	Usually in an office
May be overheard by others	Private
Variable duration	Usually an hour
Details may be repeated in other conversations: "I was chatting to Chris who was telling me about…"	Confidential, except to protect safety or with client's written permission
Purpose is relationship maintenance	Purpose is both information gathering and establishing a collaborative relationship
Free-flowing according to each person's interest	Goal-directed; keeps to an agenda; clear sequence; keeps to relevant themes
Reciprocal: "something similar happened to me…" "that reminds me of the time when I…."	Focused on the client
Each person waits for an opening to make a comment: "now you mention worries…"	Clinician interrupts and redirects conversation: "Do you ever worry…"
Maintenance of relationship usually takes precedence over gathering information	May require persistent questioning
Commonly avoids painful topics	Clinician raises painful topics such as abuse, violence, suicide
Participants rarely take notes	Psychologist may take notes
Not documented	Notes of session are kept by the psychologist
Not recorded	With client's permission may be audio or videorecorded

The psychologist is responsible for structuring the session to ensure that relevant topics are covered. The psychologist's theoretical orientation and training will determine the extent to which he or she directs the session, the questions that are asked, and the topics that are covered. Psychologists are trained to formulate questions in a manner that facilitates the client's engagement in the interview. One important distinction is between **open** and **closed questions**. Open questions allow the client to provide elaborate responses and cannot be answered with a simple "yes" or "no." Closed questions, on the other hand, can be answered with a single word. Each has advantages and disadvantages. Open questions allow the client to give a more complex answer and do not suggest a particular response is required. However, open questions may invite the client to launch into a rambling description that may be of limited relevance, in which case the psychologist must direct the client back to the topic at hand. Closed questions, on the other hand, yield brief, less ambiguous answers, allowing the rapid coverage of many topics. **Table 6.3** gives examples of open and closed questions. Many psychologists find it useful to begin discussion of a topic with an open-ended question and to follow up with closed questions that clarify details of the response.

TABLE 6.3   Open and Closed Questions

Open	Closed
Who lives in your house?	Does your Dad live with you?
What was your reaction when you found out you were pregnant?	Were you pleased when you found out you were pregnant?
How do you show affection?	Do you kiss your partner?
What do your parents do when you break curfew?	Do you get grounded when you break curfew?
What happens when you argue?	Do you hit her when you argue?
Tell me about the kinds of things that make you feel anxious.	Were you anxious when you gave a presentation to the class?
How did your reactions compare to what you usually feel?	Did you feel better after taking a deep breath?
How would your life be different if you make the changes you want in therapy?	Do you think you will be able to work again when you no longer feel depressed?

Because the phrasing of the question can influence the type of answer, psychologists are careful not to ask leading questions or to put words in the client's mouth. The client's initial response to a question may be noncommittal or vague, requiring the psychologist to encourage the client to elaborate or to explain: "tell me what you mean…tell me more about that." Contrary to the conventions of regular conversation, the psychologist gently persists with a line of questioning until the question has been answered. As clinical assessment interviews are not the same as regular conversation, the psychologist may ask difficult questions. Sometimes clients are at a loss how to answer and must reflect before answering. Psychologists use silence to allow the client time to reflect and do not feel obliged to fill in the gaps in conversation as they might in a social context.

Attending Skills

Clinical assessment requires skills not only in asking questions, but also in listening. **Table 6.4** lists a number of listening skills. In an assessment interview, the psychologist attends carefully to what is being said as well as to nonverbal behaviour. There may be important discrepancies between what a person is saying and how he or she is behaving (e.g., Nathan agitatedly rubs his hands together while simultaneously reporting that everything is fine in his relationship). The psychologist also uses nonverbal behaviour such as nods, eye contact, and vocalizations such as "Mmm…" and "Uh huh" to communicate that he or she is tracking the conversation without interrupting the flow of what is being said. Periodically, the psychologist summarizes and paraphrases the client's statement as a way of clarifying that he or she understands what is being said. Emotional reflections are statements related to the client's nonverbal behaviour and the content of the responses that focus attention on the client's affect: "it sounds as though that was very painful for you" or "you seem very angry about that."

TABLE 6.4 Listening Skills

Nondirective Listening Response	Description	Primary Intent/Effect
Attending behaviour	Eye contact, leaning forward, head nods, facial expressions, etc.	Facilitates or inhibits spontaneous client talk.
Silence	Absence of verbal activity.	Places pressure on clients to talk. Allows "cooling off" time. Allows interviewer to consider next response.
Clarification	Attempted restating of a client's message, preceded or followed by a closed question (e.g., "Do I have that right?").	Clarifies unclear client statements and verifies the accuracy of what the interviewer heard.
Paraphrase	Reflection of rephrasing of the content of what the client said.	Assures clients you hear them accurately and allows them to hear what they said.
Sensory-based paraphrase	Paraphrase that uses the client's clearly expressed sensory modalities.	Enhances rapport and empathy.
Nondirective reflection of feeling	Restatement or rephrasing of clearly stated emotion.	Enhances clients' experience of empathy and encourages their further emotional expression.
Summarization	Brief review of several topics covered during a session.	Enhances recall of session content and ties together or integrates themes covered in a session.

From Sommers-Flanagan & Sommers-Flanagan, 2003. Reprinted with permission.

A key difference between clinical assessment interviews and regular conversations is that they focus exclusively on the client. The psychologist does not take turns in describing similar experiences that he or she has had. In Chapter 14 you will learn that therapist self-disclosure can facilitate a positive therapeutic alliance, however, therapeutic self-disclosure is not the same as the reciprocal sharing of personal information that takes place in social relationships. In deciding whether or not to self-disclose, the therapist is guided by the client's interests, rather than by a personal need to vent or to gain approval from the client.

It is essential that the psychologist ask questions and listen to the client's answers in a manner that is respectful and non-judgemental. During the course of an assessment interview clients reveal, often for the first time, painful, embarrassing, or frightening experiences they have had. They may be concerned about how they will be judged by others and how the psychologist will react to the disclosure of this sensitive information. Whether the client is someone coming to terms with his sexual identity, seeking to reconcile mixed feelings toward a parent who abandoned her as a child, or hoping that fears about going crazy are unfounded, the client requires support from the psychologist when providing details about concerns. In situations in which the client describes a behaviour that the psychologist cannot condone or finds abhorrent, the psychologist must still maintain a non-blaming stance and seek to understand the client's perspective. The psychologist's goal is to gather information and convey understanding of what the client is communicating, even if the psychologist does not approve of the behaviour. **Table 6.5** gives an example of the ways a psychologist might use questions and listening skills in interviewing a man who has been referred for an assessment to determine his suitability for an anger management program.

TABLE 6.5   Sample Interview Illustrating Questions and Listening Skills

Psychologist:	What happens when you argue? (open question)
Client:	Well it sometimes gets out of hand.
Psychologist:	Tell me what you mean by that. (clarification)
Client:	Well I never mean to hurt her.
Psychologist:	What is it that you do? (open question)
Client:	I am not proud of this, I am not a bully.
Psychologist:	Sounds like you are ashamed of what happens. (emotional reflection)
Client:	Yeah, it just gets out of hand sometimes. I don't think I am a wife-beater.
Psychologist:	When the two of you argue, you do things that you are not comfortable about, that you don't like. (summarize)
Client:	Mmm, hmm.

continued…

Psychologist:	Tell me about the last time you argued and things got out of hand—what happened? (open question)
Client:	She was on my case, and I said let's just leave it, I didn't want a fight, but she kept on, then when I started to walk out, she stood in my way, so I pushed her out of the way.
Psychologist:	When you pushed her, did she fall? (closed question)
Client:	Yeah, she kind of stumbled against the fridge, I didn't mean to hurt her, I just wanted to get out.
Psychologist:	How often do your arguments end up in pushing and shoving? (open question)
Client:	Not too often.
Psychologist:	Every day? Every week? Every month or so? (closed question)
Client:	Probably most weeks, I guess.

VIEWPOINT BOX 6.1

SCREENING FOR EXPOSURE TO VIOLENCE

Carl, aged 12, presented at a local mental health centre with symptoms of fearfulness, physiological arousal, and difficulties sleeping. He was diagnosed with generalized anxiety disorder.

Melissa, aged 14, was assessed prior to sentencing for assault charges and diagnosed with conduct disorder.

Sheila, aged 35, presented to her family physician with loss of pleasure in usual activities, weight loss, and difficulties concentrating. She was diagnosed with major depressive disorder.

Carl (who was introduced in Chapter 2) was not asked and did not volunteer information about the bloody scenes he had witnessed as his father was murdered in a war-torn country. As a result, the PTSD diagnosis was overlooked and his anxiety symptoms were misinterpreted as generalized anxiety. Melissa was not asked and did not describe witnessing her father beating her mother. Similarly, she remained quiet about the violence in her current dating relationship. Sheila was not asked and was too ashamed to tell about the repeated violence she suffered from her husband.

Violence affected these three people profoundly. It caused pain, shame, self-doubt, fearfulness and anger. It altered the way they thought about relationships, the way they thought about themselves, and their views of the world. Exposure to violence can result in feelings of numbing and avoidance. The person who has been a victim or witness to violence may avoid thinking about it; he or she may respond in a dull way that masks the intensity of her feelings. Repeated exposure to violence can also lead to desensitization and minimization so that the person feels that abusive treatment is to be expected and should not be complained about. The victim or witness of violence may be afraid of the repercussions of talking about the violence—fear of retribution by the perpetrator, and fear of blame by others for remaining in the relationship or for having provoked the abuse in the first place.

Psychologists and other mental health professionals are troubled by violence. It is upsetting to discover that innocent people are harmed by strangers and also by those who are close to them. It is particularly troubling to know that nobody is immune from the threat of violence. Psychological assessment must include routine screening to determine whether the person has been a witness and/or a victim of violence. Questions must be phrased in a sensitive and open way that allows the client to acknowledge what he or she has experienced. A client who is asked directly if she has been abused may reply that she has not, if she considers that she deserved to be slapped and pushed around for having left the house in a mess. Sensitive questioning offers a number of possible responses. The psychologist may note:

> "Sometimes when couples argue, one person leaves the room; in other couples, one person may give the silent treatment; sometimes one person may say very hurtful things; in some couples one person may treat the other like a punching bag. What kinds of things does your partner do when he is angry?"

In addition to the types of questions that are asked, it is important to consider the context in which such screening is conducted. Asking a woman about partner abuse in the presence of her partner is likely to yield denial. She may simply not be safe to disclose what she has suffered.

Learning about Carl's witnessing of his father's murder leads the psychologist to understand his difficulties in a different way. If Carl is suffering from posttraumatic stress disorder, he may benefit from exposure-based treatment. Finding out that Melissa was a child witness to violence and is now the victim of partner abuse helps us understand her aggressive behaviour and underlines the necessity for her to learn ways to protect herself and ways to assert herself appropriately in relationships. Sheila's depression may be understood differently in the context of the abuse she has suffered. Issues around her current and future safety must take priority in treatment.

Contextual Information

The assessment interview is often used to gather contextual information. This may include demographic information about the client's current context (such as age, living arrangement, family composition, school, or employment), developmental history, previous psychological services, medical history, educational background, and exposure to stressful or traumatic life events. The type of background information considered essential to an assessment depends on the theoretical orientation of the psychologist as well as on the type of services offered. For example, psychodynamically oriented psychologists typically devote more time to discussing childhood events and concerns than do psychologists with a cognitive-behavioural orientation. Many hours could be devoted to gathering information about a person's life—the challenge for clinical psychologists is to selectively focus on aspects that are most relevant for understanding the client's problems and the personal resources that could be brought to bear on the problems.

Culturally Sensitive Interviewing

Canada is increasingly a multicultural society. As the population becomes more ethnically diverse, there is greater attention paid to the subtle and dramatic ways that different racial, ethnic, and linguistic groups think, act, and behave. Both the Canadian Psychological Association and the American Psychological Association have developed guidelines for ethical practice with diverse populations (American Psychological Association, 2002; Canadian Psychological Association, 2001). In interviewing clients the psychologist must be sensitive to ethnic, socioeconomic, regional, and spiritual variables that affect the client's experience (Takushi & Uomoto, 2001).

As no psychologist can expect to be familiar with all of the cultural diversity he or she will encounter in his or her professional life, it is necessary to be aware of any cultural blind spots. This means that the psychologist must not assume that communication patterns and styles are

Psychologists must be sensitive to the fact that communication styles may differ across ethnic groups.

universal. The same behaviour may have different significance in a different group. Eye contact is a good example. Whereas in the 1970s and 1980s most clinical psychology training programs taught students to maintain eye contact with clients, there is now greater sensitivity that in some cultures, too much eye contact may be perceived as intimidating. Similarly, it would be an error to interpret an averted gaze as evidence of avoidance, as it may simply represent a respectful stance toward an authority figure.

Cultures vary in the degree of importance that is paid to punctuality—arriving late to an interview may be a sign of disorganization and lack of motivation within some groups, but may simply reflect a more casual attitude toward time in others. A psychologist assessing a child who had recently arrived in Canada from Africa found that attendance at assessment appointments was sporadic, with the client and her mother often arriving late. On one occasion when the client and her mother did not show up for an appointment, the psychologist called the family to re-schedule and was surprised to hear that the outgoing message on the family's answering machine was for her, announcing that as it was a beautiful day, the family had decided to go to the beach instead of coming to the psychologist's office. The psychologist also noted that during the assess-ment the child performed poorly on timed tasks. In understanding the challenges the child faced in adjusting to the Canadian school system, it was very helpful to appreciate culturally based dif-ferences in the importance of time.

There is great variability across individuals with respect to their comfort with open-ended questions. A client who expected to be asked highly structured questions might appear disorgan-ized and confused when faced with a less structured interview. Psychologists must be aware of potential differences such as these and must be willing to ask clients to explain the ways that things work in their cultural group. As psychologists expand their services to a diverse clientele, they may face challenges in assessing clients who do not speak English or French. To address this, interpreters may be used. This presents new challenges in terms of confidentiality as well as in ensuring that the interpreter is competent in conveying the subtleties of what is said by both psychologist and client. The pitfalls of poor translation are numerous. One early version of the Wechsler Intelligence Scale for Children asked children "what is the thing to do if you cut your finger?" A poor French-Canadian translation that was in circulation in parts of Canada asked the child "what is the thing to do if you cut your finger off?" It is clear that a small error made a big difference in the type of question being asked. Children asked the poor translation were more likely to provide an answer such as "I would cry," for which they gained no points.

Defining Problems and Goals

Clients often arrive in psychologists' offices with vaguely defined complaints about themselves or other people. They make general statements about themselves such as "I can't get along with people" or describe their loved ones in unclear ways such as "he's irresponsible." The challenge with these labels is that they could mean anything, as we all have somewhat different standards for judging behaviours and reactions. Does the person who cannot get along with others have violent outbursts or simply wish he or she had a more active social life? Many words that are diagnostic labels are also used regularly in everyday conversation. You may hear a parent describe a child as hyperactive or anxious, a co-worker describe a person as paranoid, or a television news announcer wonder if someone is schizophrenic. In assessment interviews, the psychologist helps the client elaborate on the problem. Cognitive-behavioural psychologists, in particular, ask clients many questions designed to translate the complaint into a behavioural description of the problem. These details are essential for the psychologist to have a clear sense of the patterns within the problem area, as this information will form the basis of a treatment plan. **Table 6.6** shows questions that might be asked to help the client move from a vague description to one that clearly describes the problem, its frequency, intensity, and duration. For many clients, this is not an easy task and requires gentle persistence on the part of the clinical psychologist to obtain a clear definition of the problem, rather than a general and vague complaint.

Once the problem has been defined in behavioural terms, it is easier to determine whether the client meets criteria for diagnosis of a particular problem. In making these decisions, the psychologist must have a good understanding of normative behaviour. For example, in assessing a child who may suffer from attention/deficit-hyperactivity disorder the psychologist must decide whether the child's activity level, impulsivity, and attention span are within normal limits for a child that age, or whether they are unusual.

After clarifying the definition of the problem, a cognitive-behavioural psychologist then seeks a clear definition of the client's goals. Like problems, goals are often defined in vague terms: "I'd like to feel better;" "I wish my child would be more respectful;" "I wish my partner and I could get along better." Unless goals are formulated in more concrete terms, it is impossible to determine whether there is progress toward reaching them. So the formulation of concrete goals is an essential step in determining whether psychological services are helpful. **Table 6.7** gives examples of the types of questions psychologists ask to help clients more clearly identify their goals for treatment.

TABLE 6.6   Problem Definition Questions

Clients come to psychologists with vague complaints about themselves or other people:

- I'm a loser
- I'm depressed
- I can't get along with people
- I can't seem to get started
- s/he never listens; s/he's defiant
- s/he won't do anything; s/he's irresponsible/lazy
- s/he hurts people; s/he's aggressive
- s/he never thinks; s/he's impulsive
- s/he's so clingy; s/he's dependent
- s/he has trouble at school; s/he's dumb
- s/he has fits/tantrums

To translate the complaint into a behavioural description of the problem, psychologists ask:

Tell me what you mean by "depressed."

"Trouble" means different things to different people, what does it mean to you?

When you say s/he is aggressive, what is it that s/he does?

Give me an example of what you mean by "clingy."

I'm trying to get a picture in my head of what you mean by "defiant." Help me imagine what s/he is doing when s/he is defiant.

Questions about the frequency of the problem

How often does s/he...?

Does it happen every day?

Many times a day...?

Questions about the duration of the problem

When did this start?

Can you remember a time when this didn't happen?

Are there times when s/he does not....?

How long has s/he been.....?

Questions about the intensity of the problem

How long does it last?

What does s/he break?

How hard does s/he hit?

TABLE 6.7   Goal Definition Questions

At the end of our sessions, what would lead you to decide that it had been worthwhile?

How would you know you had not wasted your time?

If services here were to be helpful, what would be different?

- Goal must be important to the client

- Goal must be expressed in terms of the ways people behave

If you and Pat were to get along better what would you be doing then that you are not doing now?

How would Marcel show he was happier?

- Goals must be small, simple, and achievable

If there was a change in the right direction, what would it be?

Yes, it would be great to win the lottery, but let's suppose that doesn't happen—what would have to happen for your financial worries to decrease a bit?

I understand that what you most want is to finish high school. If we were to break that down into steps, what would be the first step?

- Goal must be in positive terms:

So, if François was not so inattentive, what is it he would be doing?

How would you know he was more attentive?

Assessing Suicide Risk

As we have mentioned several times, assessment interviews are not like regular conversations. In assessment interviews, psychologists must be alert to client difficulties. Given the special risk for suicide among those suffering from a depressive disorder, in assessing a depressed client it is customary to ask questions to determine the risk that the client will make a suicide attempt. It is essential that those questions be based on what is known about the factors that increase the risk of suicidal behaviour. Psychologists ask direct questions about suicidal thoughts, plans, and access to the means to attempt suicide. Given the strong links between a history of suicidal behaviour and risk for future suicidal behaviour, questions must also focus on a history of suicide attempts. As some suicidal clients may make only a general statement about their level of unhappiness or hopelessness, it is the psychologist's responsibility to follow up such comments with questions assessing the current risk. **Table 6.8** gives examples of the kinds of questions psychologists ask in assessing suicide risk.

TABLE 6.8   Empirically Supported Suicide Risk Assessment

Sample Questions to Ask to Complete Suicide Risk Assessment

- Have you been thinking about suicide recently?

- When you think about suicide, what kinds of thoughts do you have?

- Have you made any plans for attempting suicide? For example, have you obtained the means necessary to complete suicide, like purchasing a gun or obtaining pills?

- Do you have confidence that you could attempt suicide?

- Have you ever attempted suicide previously?

- Have you ever harmed yourself intentionally? For example, cut yourself, swallowed pills, or burned yourself?

- What are some reasons that you would consider attempting suicide?

- Tell me about your support system. Do you feel isolated? Are you able to talk to friends and family about your problems?

- How do you feel when you think about the future? Are you hopeful that you can do something about your problems?

From Cukrowicz, Wingate, Driscoll, & Joiner (2004). With permission from Springer Science and Business Media.

Interviewing Couples

So far, we have described interviews with an individual. In some circumstances, psychologists may interview a couple. Couple interviews may be conducted to focus on the partner's impressions of the client's problems, on couple problems, or on the problems that the couple's child is experiencing. Interviewing a couple requires the psychologist to simultaneously engage with two people. As the two partners may differ in style, in opinions, and in willingness to attend the interview, the psychologist requires flexibility and interpersonal skills to ensure that each person has an opportunity to talk without the conversation becoming out of hand. After all, it is quite likely that each person

When interviewing a couple, the psychologist must remain flexible to accommodate each person's style and opinions.

has a different view of the situation and that the views may not be at all compatible. The couple interview allows the psychologist to observe the way the couple interacts, their warmth toward one another, the way they handle differences, and the way they communicate in general. The ability to direct and structure an interview is very important when there is a clear power differential in the couple, which may be evident from what is said by each partner or from one partner's reluctance to engage in the discussion. However, not all couple issues are best addressed in couple sessions. For example, it is impossible to screen for partner abuse in the presence of the partner. One person may be too intimidated by an abusive partner to respond honestly to questions about violence in the relationship. Screening for partner abuse must be conducted individually.

Interviewing Families

Just as couple interviews can be more challenging to conduct than individual interviews, family interviews can be even more taxing for the psychologist. The psychologist has the daunting task of establishing rapport with several people who have different styles and different agendas for the assessment. A psychologist who devoted undivided attention to Zak who wanted greater freedom from his parents would quickly lose rapport with Zak's parents Ethan and Lindy who wanted to explain their worries that their son was failing in school and interacting with delinquent peers. Similarly, if the psychologist devoted undivided attention to the parents, Zak would easily become disengaged. In assessing families, the psychologist ensures that over the course of the interview, attention is devoted to each person. At the beginning of the interview, the psychologist tells family members explicitly that he or she would like to hear from each person. However, to put that into practice, the psychologist often must diplomatically cut off one family member to ensure each has a turn: "I would like to hear more from you, but am conscious of time, and would also like to hear ideas from others in the family". Although each person is invited to speak, each also has the right to be silent. It may be necessary to remind parents of this. Family members are invited to comment from their own perspective.

VIEWPOINT BOX 6.2

ISSUES IN INTERVIEWING OLDER ADULTS

With an aging population it is inevitable that there will be an increasing need for psychological services for older adults. Demographic forecasts predict that older adults will comprise a large percentage of the population in the coming decades. There is considerable overlap between the needs of older adults and the needs of adults in mid-life so both geropsychologists and also generalist clinical psychologists may be able to offer effective psychological services to older adults. Like younger adults, older adults seek psychological services to deal with a range of emotional, behavioural, and cognitive issues. However, as we have emphasized in other chapters, the provision of effective psychological services requires sensitivity to developmental issues that influence clients' seeking services, as well as the nature of assessment and intervention services that are appropriate. A recent task force of the American Psychological Association laid out guidelines for psychological practice with older adults (American Psychological Association, 2004).

The APA guidelines encourage psychologists to become knowledgeable about adult development and aging. Psychologists should be aware of the problems in daily living that are commonly faced by older adults and, in addition to general knowledge of psychopathology, they should know about patterns of psychopathology that are evident in older adults. In assessing older adults, psychologists must tailor their strategies to the specific needs of that population. This means that assessment strategies should take into account the older person's health status and cognitive and emotional functioning.

Compared with the general population, older adults are more likely to face issues around declining health, loss of autonomy, relationships with caregivers, bereavement, and issues of mortality. Older adults are usually referred to psychological services by a primary health care provider. Given their declining health, older adults have more frequent contact with primary health care providers than do younger adults (La Rue & Watson, 1998). They may be referred to what seems to them a confusing array of health professionals. It is the psychologist's responsibility to ensure that the older adult is aware of the purpose of the psychological services and provides fully informed consent to any assessment procedure.

Although the majority of older adults enjoy sound cognitive functioning, a significant number suffer some degree of cognitive impairment. APA recommends that psychologists become skilled at recognizing cognitive changes in older clients. The extent of cognitive impairment varies from one person to another, with many people remaining capable of reaching decisions and acting autonomously despite some cognitive changes. The psychologist should ensure that the client understands the reason for referral, the nature of services offered, and the likely outcome of services. In offering services to older adults with serious cognitive impairment, the psychologist must pay particular attention to whether the person is capable of consent to services.

In interviewing older adults, the psychologist must be sensitive to the possible presence of cognitive impairment and to possible cohort effects. So, for example, the current population of older adults grew up in the time of the economic depression of the 1930s and of the Second World War. As one developmental task of later life is to reminisce about one's formative years, the socio-political influences these older adults experienced may figure prominently in their discussions of their lives. The interviewer must also be sensitive to the impact such events may have had on the interviewee.

The psychological assessment of older adults requires knowledge of the physical challenges that may affect the person. Issues around chronic illness and disability may be the reason that psychological services are required, but may also introduce special challenges in conducting the assessment. Psychologists must be well-informed about the possible effects of medication on client functioning. Skills in health psychology may be particularly important in working with older adults.

With declining health, some older adults may need to rely increasingly on both paid and unpaid caregivers. The cooperation of these caregivers may be essential in having the older adult attend an interview. The client may be unable to attend unless a caregiver agrees to provide transportation. Furthermore, when the older person suffers confusion or memory problems, it may be necessary to also gather important information from others. Like the challenges faced in integrating data from parents and children, the psychologist may face challenges in reconciling discrepant accounts from older adults and their caregivers. Unfortunately, some older adults are vulnerable to abuse by caregivers. Sensitive psychological services should include screening for maltreatment by family members or paid caregivers. The need for effective psychological services is bound to increase in the coming years. The provision of services will rely on the psychologist's sensitivity to the myriad health, cognitive, and social factors that affect the older adult.

INTERVIEWS WITH CHILDREN

In contrast to early approaches to the psychological assessment of children that relied primarily on adult accounts of child behaviour or on interpretations of children's play, current child assessment strategies often include the child as an important source of information about his or her thoughts and feelings. It is now recognized that children can provide unique information about aspects of their experience that are not fully tapped by measures completed by adult informants such as parents, teachers, or caregivers (Grills & Ollendick, 2002).

Interviews with children are designed to explore the child's perspective. They also allow the psychologist to assess the way the child interacts with an unfamiliar adult. The psychologist conducts the interview in a way that makes it seem like a conversation to the child, but that ensures the relevant topics are covered. Like adults, children are entitled to know about confidentiality and its limits. The psychologist must explain the purpose of the interview. As children may associate interviews with adults as evaluative in nature, it is important to reassure the child that there are no right or wrong answers to the questions, and that everyone has a different opinion. To engage the child in conversation, the psychologist maintains a varied voice tone and relaxed posture.

DEVELOPMENTAL ISSUES IN INTERVIEWING CHILDREN AND ADOLESCENTS

Interviewing techniques must be adapted when psychologists are interviewing children and adolescents. Developmental considerations affect cognitive functioning and the young client's understanding of what is being asked. Young children differ from adults in terms of their attention span and capacity to stay focused on the interview. Furthermore, children and adolescents differ from adults in their style of interaction. Think about a visit to the home of an adult friend and the way that you and your friend might talk together, perhaps seated at the kitchen table, or on the sofa. As adults, you may sustain conversation over a lengthy period of time, maintaining eye contact, asking questions, and clarifying your understanding of what was said. Now think about a conversation you might have if a child was present (perhaps your friend's younger sibling, or your friend's child). In what ways would your conversation be different with the child? It is quite likely that the range of topics you would talk about with a child would be substantially different. In addition, you'd probably change the way you asked questions. You would be surprised if 6-year-old Sarah joined in the conversation for a lengthy period—most likely she would chat for a while, then leave to do something she found more interesting. The type of conversation you would have would also depend on the child's age: in talking to a preschool age child, you'd probably talk about the immediate environment, such as the TV show the child had just watched, a toy the child was holding, the logo on a t-shirt, or the sport that the child was about to do. With an elementary school age child, you would be able to ask questions about the child's life—school, friends, activities, sports, or holidays. In other words, you would be able to talk about topics that were not in the child's immediate environment or planned activities. In general, with older children it becomes increasingly possible to have them reflect on patterns in their experiences and to discuss how other people might be feeling. Conversations with adolescents can cover a range of remote and abstract topics that younger children would be unable to discuss.

In interviewing children, psychologists must be careful not to use a sophisticated vocabulary that is incomprehensible to them. Although some children may announce they do not understand and ask for clarification, others may simply lose interest and become quiet. It is the psychologist's responsibility to ensure that a child client understands the questions that are being

Using drawings as aids to facilitate rapport between a psychologist and child is not the same as making interpretations about the child's drawing.

asked. A child who fails to understand a question may stare blankly, say "I don't know" or may give an answer based on erroneous understanding of what was being asked. Children find questions that relate to time particularly difficult. For example, a young child may be at a loss to say how many times over the last six months he or she has felt a certain way if the child has no concept of how long six months is. Generally it is helpful to use special events or occasions that are personally relevant to them such as the beginning of school, Hallowe'en, or a birthday. However, some strategies that are effective in helping children give more detailed responses such as using dolls may also increase the number of errors in children's statements (Salmon, 2001). Careful attention must be paid to ensure that the interviewer does not inadvertently prompt the child to give a particular response (Ceci & Bruck, 1993). Sometimes children may mistake a word for another that sounds similar. An 8-year-old girl who was asked if she ever thought about death, replied that she did, almost every day. When asked to tell more about this, she explained, "There's a girl in my class called Kirsten who is death and she has to sit at the front and wear a special hearing aid so she knows what the teacher says." Without this type of clarification, the psychologist might have wrongly assumed that this child felt suicidal, rather than recognizing that the child did not differentiate between the words death and deaf.

Whereas face-to-face contact and eye contact may be important ingredients of assessment interviews with most adults, we know that children and adolescents engage in some of their best conversations when they are not in eye contact. Teenagers who remain silent at the meal table may be much more talkative while being driven to an activity. Similarly, psychologists may invite child clients to play or draw while they are chatting. It is important to note, however, that using drawings and toys as aids to facilitate rapport is not the same as making interpretations about the child's drawings or play. In the first case, dolls and drawings are used to make the child at ease, whereas in the second they are used as projective material intended to reveal aspects of psychological functioning.

Psychologists may also have challenges in understanding what the child is talking about. As children's fashions change quickly, the psychologist may be uncertain whether Yu-Gi-Oh is the child's new friend, a TV show, or a new vaccination. No psychologist can expect to remain constantly up to date with the changing trends in children's expressions, activities, or movies, just as no psychologist can expect to be equally knowledgeable about the mores and customs of all cultures. Instead a psychologist must develop skills in listening to the child and in sensitively clarifying that he or she has properly understood what the child was saying. Children are different from adults, but they also differ from one another at different ages and developmental stages. Strategies that may be effective in engaging a young school age child such as bright décor, cheerful posters, and soft toys on the bookshelf may alienate the adolescent client. Psychologists must also alter their style when interviewing adolescents. If they treat the adolescent as an adult, there may be concepts and terms that the client doesn't understand (and may not admit to not understanding). On the other hand, adolescents may also be sensitive to what they perceive as simplistic baby talk, such as "When I use the word depression I mean when someone feels sad or kind of down" or a kindergarten teacher style of questioning, "Do you know what I mean when I say bulimia?"

STRUCTURED DIAGNOSTIC INTERVIEWS FOR ADULTS AND CHILDREN

In Chapter 3 we described the evolution of diagnostic systems used to categorize different types of psychopathology. You may remember that each version of the *Diagnostic and Statistical Manual of Mental Disorders (DSM)* provided more precise decision rules for the diagnosis of disorders. Researchers noted that although most mental health professionals agreed on the general features of a disorder, there was poor inter-rater reliability in assigning diagnoses; that is, there was low agreement between two interviewers about the precise diagnostic category. To address this problem, a number of **structured interviews** were developed. These interviews vary in their coverage of symptoms and life context. These interviews have a specific format for asking questions and a specific sequence in which questions are asked. Based on initial client responses the interviewer is then directed to use follow-up questions that help confirm or rule out possible diagnoses.

The most widely used clinical interview in North America, the **Structured Clinical Interview for Axis I Disorders** (SCID; First, Spitzer, Gibbon, & Williams, 1997), permits diagnosis of a broad spectrum of diagnoses. Two versions have been developed. The SCID-I is an interview designed for research that includes the entire spectrum of *DSM* Axis I disorders, whereas the shorter SCID-CV covers only the most common disorders. The SCID begins with an open-ended interview on demographic information, work history, chief complaint, history of present and past psychopathology, treatment history, and assessment of current functioning. The unstructured format is designed to develop rapport with the client prior to beginning the structured symptom-focused questions that are designed to yield diagnostic information. The structured portion includes required probe questions as well as recommended follow-up questions. Each probe corresponds to a specific *DSM* criterion. It is clear, therefore, that the SCID is not a completely standardized instrument. Reliability data on the SCID reflect its semi-structured format and reliance on clinical judgement. For some types of disorder, such as bipolar disorder, good inter-rater reliabilities have been reported, whereas for others, such as agoraphobia, the findings are poor (Groth-Marnat, 2003; Summerfeldt & Antony, 2002). The developers assumed that as the SCID criteria parallel *DSM* criteria, this provides sufficient evidence of its validity. The strength of the SCID lies in the breadth of the disorders it covers; the weakness, which may be related to the breadth of coverage, is the variable reliabilities that are obtained for different disorders and the lack of strong validity data. Because the SCID covers all of the Axis I diagnoses it also can be very time-consuming to administer—an important consideration in clinical use. A brief measure, the PRIME-MD, was developed for use in primary care settings (Spitzer et al., 1995). There is some evidence of the reliability of the PRIME-MD as well as support for its validity. The main advantage of the PRIME-MD is as a rapid screening device; however, it cannot be considered a substitute for a full diagnostic interview (Summerfeldt & Antony, 2002).

In contrast to the broad coverage of the SCID, the **Anxiety Disorders Interview Schedule for DSM-IV** (ADIS IV; Brown, Di Nardo, & Barlow, 1994) is a semi-structured diagnostic interview that focuses on anxiety disorders and disorders that are commonly comorbid with anxiety disorders (mood disorders, somatoform disorders, and substance-related disorders). There are two versions: one that addresses current diagnosis only and a longer version that assesses both current symptomatology and lifetime history of problems. Like the SCID, the ADIS includes general background information as well as questions that relate directly to DSM IV criteria. There is evidence of the reliability of the ADIS. Its main advantage over more general diagnostic interviews lies in the depth of coverage of the disorders that are assessed (Summerfeldt & Antony, 2002).

Table 6.9 presents information on the diagnostic interviews we have discussed. As you can see, the comprehensive interviews take at least an hour to administer, whereas the screening measures are completed more quickly. Most of these interviews can be administered by mental health professionals who have received additional specialized training.

Some of the structured diagnostic interviews that were originally developed for adults have been modified for use with children. For example, in adapting the ADIS for use with children and adolescents (ADIS Child and Parent Versions, Albano & Silverman, 1996), visual cues such as the Feelings Thermometer were introduced. On a Feelings Thermometer respondents are asked to indicate on a picture of a thermometer how they are feeling. 0 might represent totally calm and 100 might represent very afraid. The Feelings Thermometer is designed to enable children to better communicate

TABLE 6.9   Comparison of Features of Diagnostic Interviews

Name	Age range	Training required	Breadth of coverage	Time to administer	Correspondence to DSM-IV
Structured Clinical Interview for Axis I Disorders (SCID)	Adult	Trained mental health professional	Broad	60 minutes	Yes
Anxiety Disorders Interview Schedule (ADIS) IV	Adult	Trained mental health professional	Medium	45–60 minutes	Yes
Anxiety Disorders Interview Schedule (ADIS) IV Child-Parent Version	Child	Trained mental health professional	Medium	45–60 parent; 45–60 child	Yes
Primary Care Evaluation of Mental Disorders (PRIME-MD)	Adult	Trained health professional	Narrow	10–20 minutes	Somewhat
Dominic-R	6–11 years	Trained mental health professional	Broad	10–15 minutes	For screening only; no frequency and duration data

different gradations of feelings when their vocabulary for expressing these distinctions is limited. So, whereas a child might be able to verbalize only crude distinctions like "kind of scared" and "really scared," he or she may be able to convey that in some situations the level of fear is a 20, whereas on others it is a 60 or 80. Nevertheless, some features of diagnostic interviews are particularly problematic with children. These include the length of the interview, which often exceeds children's attention capacity, as well as questions requiring a more precise response than children are capable of providing. Diagnostic interviews for children and adolescents usually have parallel versions that are completed by parents. This of course raises the challenging issue of how to make sense of disagreements between different informants (Grills & Ollendick, 2002). To address some of the challenges of assessing very young children, some creative interview formats have been developed. Ablow and colleagues have used puppets in the assessment of children aged 4–8 (Ablow et al., 1999; Measelle,

Ablow, Cowan, & Cowan, 1998). Children are presented with two identical puppets, Iggy and Ziggy, who describe themselves in different ways. Children are then asked to indicate which puppet they are similar to. Ablow and colleagues have reported encouraging test-retest reliability and discriminant validity for the interview.

A group of Canadian researchers have developed a diagnostic interview for children aged 6–11 years, *Dominic*, which uses cartoon drawings as cues (Valla, Bergeron, & Smolla, 2000). Children are shown a series of drawings and asked to respond to a question whether they would or would not behave like the target child. The stimuli are available in different formats that vary in gender, age, ethnic background, and language. Given children's difficulties with the concept of time, there is no attempt to determine the frequency of behaviours, so the interview cannot yield full information required for diagnosis, nor does the information yield contextual data. Valla and colleagues have reported adequate test-retest reliability and criterion validity to support the use of the *Dominic* as an effective, brief screening instrument for mental disorders. Work is currently underway to validate an interactional version in which the stimuli are presented via computer and the child responds by clicking the appropriate box.

Figure 6.2   Illustrations from the Dominic Interview (www.dominicinteractive.com)

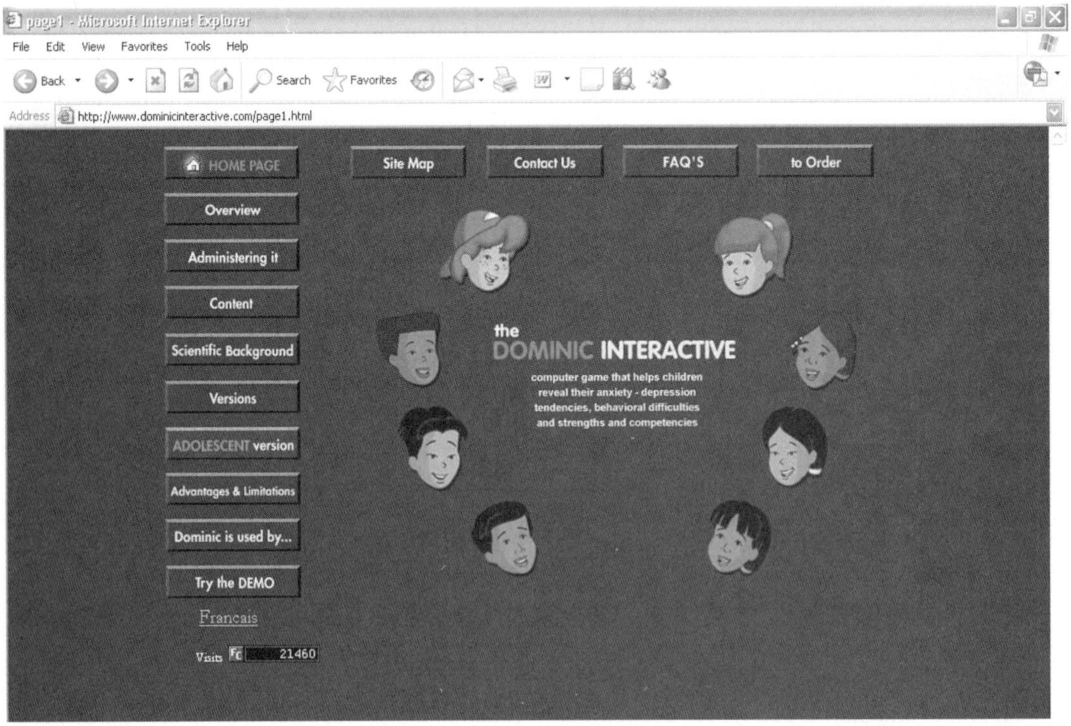

Reprinted with permission.

OBSERVATIONS

During the assessment interview, the psychologist is a keen observer of the client. In addition to the answers to questions, important data can be gathered by observing the client. Although clinical assessments traditionally included comments on the client's appearance and grooming, it is only necessary to report noteworthy features that are relevant to the assessment. Comments on clients' attractiveness are often not salient to the referral question and are considered offensive by some people. The psychologist notices the client's activity level, attention span, and impulsivity. Careful attention is paid to the client's speech, noting any difficulties or abnormalities. The psychologist observes the physical movements and behaviours of clients as well as the ease of interacting with them.

PROFILE BOX 6.1

DR. ERIC J. MASH

I obtained a Ph.D. at Florida State University, followed by specialized post-doctoral training in neurodevelopmental disabilities. I joined the faculty at the University of Calgary where I am a Professor in the Department of Psychology and a Chartered Psychologist in Alberta. Over the years my research and clinical activities have focused on the assessment and treatment of children with a variety of psychological disorders and their families, including attention-deficit disorder, autism, and child abuse, and I have written and edited a number of books and journal articles on these topics. I especially enjoy teaching under-

Dr. Eric J. Mash

graduate courses in abnormal child psychology and behaviour modification, and graduate courses in child psychopathology, child assessment, and child psychotherapy. During my career I have served as an editor, editorial board member, and consultant for numerous journals and granting agencies in Canada and the United States. I am a Fellow of the Canadian and American Psychological Associations. On those rare occasions when I am not working I enjoy hiking and bicycle riding in the Canadian Rockies and on the beaches of Oregon.

What made you choose to become a clinical psychologist?

I applied to graduate school in clinical psychology because I had a strong interest in understanding and helping people with problems—one that was stimulated by life experiences, psychology courses, and several inspiring professors. However, I could not have possibly anticipated what being a clinical psychologist would be like at that time since my later work as a clinical psychologist has been incredibly diverse, and continues to evolve in response to changing societal and economic forces. My interests in people have put me on a path where I have had the good fortune to pursue many different facets of clinical psychology including clinical practice, research, teaching, policy development, writing, editing, consulting, supervision, and public service. I'm glad I made this choice, even if I didn't know where it would take me at the time.

What is the most rewarding part of your job as a clinical psychologist?

Supporting children and families with problems and helping them find effective ways to overcome or cope with their difficulties. I particularly enjoy teaching and advising dedicated students who wish to become clinical psychologists, helping them explore evidence-based ways of assessing and treating children's problems, and of translating their ideas into actions that will benefit their future clients and society more generally. The opportunities I have had to collaborate with dedicated colleagues locally, nationally, and internationally around difficult clinical and research issues and challenges have also been especially rewarding.

What is the greatest challenge facing you as a clinical psychologist?

Keeping up with, and adapting to, the many rapid changes in the field. Every day seems to bring new knowledge from many disciplines about clinical problems, and about assessment, treatment, and prevention methods. Changing demographics, increasing client diversity, international perspectives, new societal stressors, health care economics, new technologies, and the rapid dissemination of information necessitate flexibility and the need to find new ways to quickly integrate new knowledge into clinical practice and training.

Tell us about the challenges of conducting standardized interviews and observations.

Because most of my work is with children and families, the use of standardized interviews and observations presents many special challenges. These include difficulties in assessing young children who don't always talk so well; assessing kids of different ages using methods that are sensitive to their level of development, ethnic background, and circumstances; and gathering information across multiple settings such as the home and school and from multiple informants such as the child, mother, father, and teachers. Integrating and making sense out of diverse information from these many sources, particularly when they don't agree, and using it to formulate clinical problems and to develop effective treatment strategies is always a challenge.

How do you integrate science and practice in your work?

In my practice, research, and teaching I rely heavily on the use of assessment and treatment methods for which there is empirical support. In the case of assessment this means using measures with established reliability, validity, clinical utility, and practicality for the clinical population that I am working with—when such measures are available. From a treatment standpoint this means using therapies that research has shown to be efficacious and effective, recognizing that these may not yet be available for many childhood disorders. My early training and later experiences led me to emphasize behavioural science values in my work, and these have contributed to my reliance on evidence-based practices. At the same time, there is still a great deal we don't know, and clinical data from individual clients provide a rich source of ideas that can be used to inform both research and practice.

What do you see as the most exciting changes in the profession of clinical psychology?

The explosion of new knowledge about mental health and wellness requires that clinical psychologists have a strong background not only in clinical psychology but also in the neurobiological and cognitive sciences. They need to be able to communicate and work with professionals from a wide range of disciplines, particularly in light of the increased use of combined psychological and pharmacological interventions. Another challenge is in translating our knowledge base in clinical psychology into real-world settings, by developing and disseminating effective assessment and treatment methods. Ultimately this will involve the development of coordinated systems of care rather than having a primary focus on individuals. Health care economics has and continues to challenge us to find evidence-based and cost-effective methods of helping people and a much greater emphasis on accountability in practice. Adapting current models and developing new models of clinical practice that are sensitive to the growing ethnic and cultural diversity in our society is a much needed and challenging new development. Also, following the adage that it is much easier to build a fence at the top of a cliff than to keep an ambulance waiting on the bottom, clinical psychology will need to place an even greater emphasis on prevention. The Internet and other technologies offer promising new methods for cost-effective assessments and interventions that will need to be explored in both practice and research. Finally, training models and practices in clinical psychology need to be recalibrated to accommodate these and many other new developments in the profession on an ongoing basis.

Home observation provides the psychologist with information about how the child and parent behave in a familiar setting.

Client behaviour in the psychologist's office may not always be representative of the way the person behaves. For example, children with ADHD often respond well in novel situations with the undivided attention of an unfamiliar adult. Therefore a psychologist could underestimate the extent of the child's problems by assuming that the child's behaviour during an intake interview was representative of how the child generally behaves. The purpose of naturalistic observations is to gather information that could not easily be obtained in the office. It allows observation of behaviours that clients may not describe in interviews or questionnaires because they are either unaware of them or uncomfortable about them. Home observations provide information about the ways the child and parents behave in a familiar setting. School observations provide information about the school context, teaching style, and the child's behaviour in a school context. Permission must be obtained to conduct observations outside the clinic. The parent (and the child if she or he is judged capable to consent) must give permission for the child to be observed. School personnel must also consent to observations at school. Naturalistic observations are scheduled at a time when the problem behaviour is most likely to occur. In many families with young children the hours around supper, homework, and preparation for bed are times of conflict and difficulty. Depending on the particular assessment question, school observations may be scheduled to see the child in both preferred and nonpreferred activities, with different teachers, in quiet study periods, and on the playground.

The observer's goal is to be like the proverbial fly on the wall, noticing everything, but not being noticed. Observers dress in a professional, but unobtrusive style. After brief introductions, the observer invites everyone to behave as they normally do. A clipboard and pen are reminders to both adults and children that this is not like a regular social visit. Even though adults may initially try hard to make a good impression and behave at their best, children are extraordinarily effective in leading adults to behave authentically. Children comment on unusual behaviours that the adults may engage in to impress the observer: "We're having dessert tonight?" "Why do you want us to eat at the table today?" "I really like the new toy you gave me." At the end of the observation period, the observer takes a few minutes to ask how typical this day was of their usual routine. "I know it's very strange having

VIEWPOINT BOX 6.3

WHY DON'T PSYCHOLOGISTS USE RESEARCH-BASED OBSERVATIONAL CODING SYSTEMS?

Research on marital functioning and on parent-child interaction has relied heavily on systematic observation of couples and families. From this research we have learned a great deal about the ways that couples interact; we have recognized the balance between positive and negative behaviour and have learned to identify patterns of interaction that are especially toxic in relationships. Observations of parents and their noncompliant children have identified the ways that each person in the interaction inadvertently reinforces in the other person the very behaviour that they most dislike.

Given the valuable insights that we have gained into parent-child and marital relationships by systematic observation, you might expect that clinicians would have borrowed these systematic observation systems for use in the clinic. This is not the case at all. Although clinicians use observation as an essential tool in assessment, they rarely use a form of assessment that has been standardized or that has established reliability and validity (Mash & Foster, 2001). Although structured diagnostic interviews that were originally developed in a research context have been modified for use in clinical practice, the same transfer from research to clinical practice has not occurred in terms of observations. One major obstacle is expense. Some of the most useful research coding schemes require as much as 20 hours of coding to analyse one hour of interaction. In a cost-conscious health care system, these costs could not be justified.

Assessments require the gathering of multiple sources of information. Observational data are integrated with results of interviews, collateral reports, and psychometric tests. How can psychologists improve the usefulness of observational data without using expensive coding schemes? First, psychologists can be informed by research evidence on the types of behaviours to observe. Research can guide us in what to observe in conducting assessments. Knowing, for example, that contemptuous behaviour has serious consequences in a relationship, they can sensitively observe whether partners treat one another with contempt; similarly, knowing the importance of parental supervision and monitoring in adolescent adjustment, they can be vigilant for signs that the parent tracks the adolescent's activities and requires divulging their whereabouts. As psychologists are so often called upon to make normative judgements, they must be certain to have an awareness of the range of behaviour that is commonly observed in different groups. Finally, the psychologist must be constantly aware of the ways that his or her biases affect both what is observed and the ways that observational data are interpreted.

someone watching." "How typical would you say today was?" "Was JP's behaviour the same as usual, worse than usual, or better than usual?" "In what way?" "What about your behaviour?"

Data from direct observations are used to generate hypotheses about the child's functioning that can be examined in light of other assessment data. It would obviously be inappropriate to draw diagnostic decisions solely based on observations, or to conclude that because a child appeared fine during the observation period that there were no difficulties. At most these observations provide a limited window on how the child behaves with significant others at home and at school. But when combined with information from interviews, testing, and other people's reports, observational data can provide data that confirm or attenuate the evolving picture of the child's strengths and weaknesses.

A large body of psychological research demonstrates that people are influenced by appearances (Garb, 1998). A well-known example is the assumption that people who wear glasses are more intelligent than those who do not wear glasses. Other biases relate to the way we cover or wear our hair, the formality of our clothes, levels of grooming, expressiveness of hand gestures, loudness of voice, and posture. Psychologists are not immune from these biases that may affect their decision-making. We are particularly prone to errors when interacting with an unfamiliar group. In some parts of Canada a greeting may entail a barely perceptible nod of the head, whereas elsewhere it may involve a handshake, kisses on both cheeks, or touching noses. Ethical guidelines require psychologists to become aware of the ways that their background influences their interactions with others and their interpretations of the behaviours of others.

SELF-MONITORING

In terms of data gathering, it would be ideal if a psychologist could observe a patient for many hours each day to see the precise nature of the symptoms or problems that are the focus of treatment. As this is not feasible psychologists rely on patients' retrospective reports of events to get a sense of how frequently a problem occurs and exactly how the problem is handled. As we all know, however, memories for events become clouded over time and, despite the patient's best efforts, he or she might not remember the important details of an event that occurred six days prior to an appointment with the psychologist. To obtain accurate information as economically as possible, psychologists have developed a number of strategies for patients to observe themselves that collectively are known as **self-monitoring** strategies.

Self-monitoring can take many forms. The client may be asked to simply record the occurrence of an event, such as when a cigarette was smoked, a meal was consumed, or a headache occurred. This kind of self-monitoring data can provide the type of information needed to establish baseline conditions for a behaviour or problem that will be the focus of treatment (such as using relaxation techniques to reduce the severity and frequency of headaches). With precise information about the frequency of these problems prior and during treatment it becomes possible to ascertain the degree to which treatment is effective or needs to be altered. Self-monitoring can also involve the client keeping daily records of thoughts or feelings. This is particularly useful information for the psychologist as it provides access to variables that are not amenable to direct observation. A client may be asked, for example, to record pertinent details each time he or she has thoughts of being a failure. For cognitive-behavioural psychologists, obtaining information about the context in which these thoughts occur can provide useful information about factors that may provoke or maintain dysfunctional or nonproductive behaviours. In developing intervention strategies for working with a client, self-monitoring involves recording occurrences of symptoms and also the efforts made to manage or curtail the symptoms. Compared with a simple series of interview questions in the psychologist's office requiring retrospective recall, this is likely to provide a fuller picture of the client's usual strategies, both successful and unsuccessful, for dealing with the symptoms. **Figures 6.3** and **6.4** provide

Figure 6.3   Self-Monitoring of Food Consumption

FOOD INTAKE RECORD

NAME: _____

DATE: _____

TIME	PLACE	FOOD CONSUMED	MEAL OCCASION	SITUATION
7:15 am	home	1 cup coffee, black 1 bran muffin	breakfast	For a change I actually got up in time to have breakfast.
1:30 pm	university cafeteria	Small salad, no dressing Diet coke, small	lunch	I tried putting off eating as late as possible
3:15 pm	class	chocolate bar Bag of peanuts	snack	I was so hungry in class that I had to eat something from my backpack
6:30 pm	home	2 cheese sandwiches, (light cheese slices) 1 apple, 1 bran muffin	dinner	I tried to have a nutritious meal
11:30 pm	home	1 litre chocolate ice cream, 3 glasses skim milk	snack	I couldn't sleep and I ended up bingeing

Figure 6.4   Self-Monitoring Worry

MY WORRY RECORD

DATE: _____

Please record every significant worry that you have during the day. As we discussed in our sessions, this would include anything that you find upsetting, difficult to stop thinking about, or that interferes with the things you are trying to do. Please be as specific as possible about each worry.

TIME	SITUATION	WORRY	ANXIETY LEVEL 0=calm 10=panicky	DURATION (minutes)
3:30 pm	at work	I will never get this done. I'm a failure. I won't be able to keep fooling them at work. I'm going to lose this job	8	45 minutes
7:40 pm	home, trying to relax	I know I can do it, but why do I have such a hard time with work deadlines? I spend so much time worrying and trying to understand my reaction. Why don't I just get things done! What is wrong with me!	6	30 minutes

examples of self-monitoring forms that might be used in the treatment of an eating disorder and an anxiety disorder, respectively.

Psychologists may choose to provide a client with a standard self-monitoring form that is appropriate for the symptom/behaviour to be reported. Alternatively the psychologist may decide to construct a form with the client that has the potential of ensuring that the client better understands the nature of the reporting task. In some clinics there may be aids used in self-monitoring. For example a watch with a timer may be given to the client, with the alarm set to sound at a preset time, thus indicating that the client should record the target behaviour. Palm computers or personal digital assistants (PDA) are used increasingly to provide both a prompt for recording an event and a convenient tool for entering the self-monitoring data. The use of a standard database program in a PDA also allows the client to keep track of changes over the course of treatment and even to graph treatment progress.

Despite the obvious strengths of the self-monitoring method, there are some challenges in implementation. Self-monitoring data are not always accurate, as the client may fail to record information at the appropriate time, may not have fully grasped the nature of the task given by the psychologist, or may be reluctant to report some undesirable thoughts or behaviours (Korotitsch & Nelson-Gray, 1999). The psychologist must take the time to ensure that the client understands both the importance of obtaining self-monitoring data and how to accurately record the necessary information. As with interviews, there may need to be procedural alterations in using self-monitoring with children (Shapiro & Cole, 1999). To ensure that children are clear on the behaviours to be recorded, the self-monitoring form may include reminders, either in the form of words, pictures, or stick figures. Training to do the self-monitoring properly also requires that the purpose of the task and the instructions be presented in an age appropriate manner. The issue of **reactivity** occurs in self-monitoring regardless of the client's age. Reactivity refers to a change in the phenomenon that is being monitored that is due specifically to the process of the self-monitoring. This has been found for a surprisingly wide array of symptoms and problems, including hallucinations, substance abuse, worry, and insomnia (Korotitsch & Nelson-Gray, 1999). In almost all cases such changes result in a decrease in the problem behaviour in question. Although this provides a therapeutic "bonus" it does undermine efforts to obtain the most accurate data possible.

SUMMARY AND CONCLUSIONS

Interviews and observations are used by all clinical psychologists in their assessment activities. Clinical interviews are different from other types of verbal interactions, as they are directed by one person with a specific set of goals in mind. In interviewing and observing, psychologists must be sensitive to diversity issues, including cultural, regional, and generational norms. Cognizant of these issues, psychologists must also find ways to obtain the type of information they need, even when asking about sensitive or painful topics. Because a number of factors affect the quality of an interview, structured interviews have been developed for a range of tasks, most notably for diagnostic purposes. Although these interviews provide a reliable approach to diagnosis, they can be very time-consuming and limited in scope. A final assessment method used by many psychologists is self-monitoring. Instead of relying on retrospective accounts of important events or behaviours, the patient is provided with a structured format to record events shortly after they occur. This information, when combined with that available from interviews and observations, helps fill out the emerging clinical picture of the client and his or her experiences.

Critical Thinking Questions

What are some of the major goals of assessment interviews?

What are some of the advantages and disadvantages of unstructured interviews?

How have psychologists adapted interview techniques to take into account developmental issues?

What are the major differences between assessment interviews and conversations with friends?

How can psychologists conduct culturally sensitive interviews?

What are the advantages of structured diagnostic interviews?

How can self-monitoring strategies add useful data to an assessment?

Key Terms

closed questions

limits of confidentiality

mental status examination

open questions

reactivity

self-monitoring

structured interviews

ADDITIONAL RESOURCES

Hersen, M., & Turner, S. M. (Eds). (2003). *Diagnostic interviewing* (3rd ed.). New York: Kluwer Publishers.

Rogers, R. (2001). *Handbook of diagnostic and structured interviewing.* New York: Guilford Press.

Sattler, J. M. (1998). *Clinical and forensic interviewing of children and families.* San Diego, CA: Jerome Sattler.

Sommers-Flanagan, J., & Sommers-Flanagan, R. (2003). *Clinical interviewing* (3rd ed). New York: John Wiley & Sons.

CHAPTER 7

Assessment: Intellectual and Cognitive Measures

INTRODUCTION

Because Western society places great value on intelligence, we have had a long-standing fascination with intelligence tests. In the 1940s, an elite organization called Mensa was founded in England. To become a member of Mensa, one must have an IQ score that is in the top 2% of the population. Today, more than 100,000 people worldwide are members of this organization. Hans Eysenck's best-selling book *Know Your Own I.Q.*, originally published in 1962, has gone into multiple editions and can still be purchased today. Intense public debate was reignited with the publication of *The Bell Curve* (Herrnstein & Murray, 1994), a review of the history of research on intelligence. Although many of the research-based conclusions presented in the book were not particularly original or controversial, the authors' attempts to link the results of research on intelligence to public policy initiatives (such as rescinding American affirmative action policies in education and hiring) drew the ire of many critics.

As you learned in Chapter 1, the history of assessment in clinical psychology and the history of intellectual assessment are closely connected, as both were greatly influenced by Binet and Simon's development of the first standardized test of intelligence. Many of the criteria that are now used to evaluate the qualities of any psychological test date back to efforts to develop the first tests in the early part of the 20th century. At that time, special education services were being designed and it was necessary to develop scientific instruments to identify those in need of such services. The vital importance of accurately identifying individuals who were unlikely to benefit from regular education led to the promotion of concepts such as standardization, reliability, validity, and norm-referenced interpretations. In the testing of intelligence and cognitive capacities there is a great deal at stake. Because of the important implications of the results of intellectual and cognitive assessment, efforts to reduce test bias and measurement error played a central role in the development of intelligence tests in the latter half of the 20th century. As a result, tests of intelligence and related cognitive abilities are among the best tests that psychologists have developed.

We begin this chapter by outlining theories of intelligence and some of the research relevant to understanding the influences on intelligence and intelligence tests. Psychologists working in many different settings are often asked to assess an individual's intellectual and cognitive abilities. After describing some of the more common situations in which such evaluations are required, we move to describe the most commonly used intelligence tests and other tests of cognitive functioning.

DEFINING INTELLIGENCE

We all have an intuitive idea of what intelligence is. We can point to individuals we consider highly intelligent; likewise we can probably identify examples of intelligent behaviour (and probably some examples of not so intelligent behaviour).

How can intelligence be defined in a manner that is appropriate across skills sets, areas of performance, and cultural contexts?

examples of not so intelligent behaviour). How can we define intelligence in a manner that is appropriate across skill sets, areas of performance, and cultural contexts? One option is to simply avoid the use of the term "intelligence," and to use other concepts such as ability or, more accurately, general mental ability. Although a number of theorists and test developers have taken this approach, it doesn't really get us any further in trying to tease out the meaning of intelligence, as it just substitutes one word or phrase for another.

Throughout the years psychologists have made many attempts to define intelligence. The range has included both broad definitions, such as the ability to learn or to adapt to the environment, and narrow definitions, such as the ability to engage in abstract thinking (cf. Aiken, 2003). Because Binet was working on the development of a tool to predict school performance, his definition focused on ability related to scholastic/academic tasks. You will probably agree that this yields a limited definition. More recent definitions of intelligence have focused on the context of life more generally. **David Wechsler** (1939) defined intelligence as a person's global capacity to act purposefully, to think in a rational manner, and to deal effectively with his or her environment. Wechsler devoted his career to the development of scales to assess a range of problem-solving skills. He assumed that these abilities were acquired through educational and life experiences. Wechsler's definition has influenced the way clinical psychologists evaluate intelligence. As we will see in the next section, theories of intelligence in the latter part of the 20th century explicitly acknowledge that intelligence is a combination of abilities in multiple areas of life.

THEORIES OF INTELLIGENCE

To provide a brief overview of the many theories of intelligence, we will categorize the dominant models into one of three domains: *factor models*, *hierarchical models*, and *information processing models*. Factor models involve two or more factors that are postulated to be at more or less the same structural level. In contrast, hierarchical models are based on the assumption that there are different levels of factors, with the higher-order or primary factors composed of lower-order or secondary factors. Information processing theories focus less on the organization of types of intelligence and more on identifying the processes and operations that reflect how information is handled by the brain.

Factor Models

The earliest and probably most influential factor model of intelligence was developed by **Charles Spearman** (1927). Based on the intercorrelations among tests of sensory abilities (sensory discriminations, reaction time, etc.), Spearman proposed that all intellectual activities share a single common core known as the *general factor* or **g**. The more highly correlated two tests of mental abilities are, the more they share a substantial loading on the g factor. However, because measures of intellectual abilities are not perfectly correlated, Spearman postulated that there are a number of *specific factors*, or s, that are responsible for unique aspects in the performance of any given task. The more a test is influenced by s, the less it represents the influence of g. Spearman's focus on g and s was known as the *two-factor model*.

The main alternative to Spearman's model was one proposed by Thurstone (1938). Although Thurstone did not dispute that mental ability measures were often intercorrelated, he did not think that the magnitude of these intercorrelations was particularly important. From his perspective these intercorrelations were low enough to indicate that many primary factors were involved across the range of tests. Based on his research, Thurstone proposed a group of factors known as *primary mental abilities*. Although the precise number and nature of these abilities changed over the course of his research, they involved factors such as spatial, perceptual, numerical, memory, verbal, word, reasoning, deduction, and induction abilities. These abilities, although relatively distinct, overlap to a very small extent and it was this small overlap that Thurstone suggested was Spearman's g. In contrast to the majority of researchers who developed a model of intelligence, Thurstone also developed a measure of intelligence based on his model.

A third factor model, the *structure of intellect model*, was proposed by Guilford (1956). In many ways, his model is a transition from a factor model to a hierarchical model. In Guilford's view, intelligence can be conceptualized along three independent axes (like the *x*, *y*, and *z* axes in three-dimensional graphs). The axes are contents, operations, and products. The content axis is used to describe the general nature of the information or task, be it visual, semantic, or behavioural. The operations axis describes what the person actually does in the task, such as memory retention, evaluation, or cognition. The final axis, products, describes the form in which the information is processed by the person, such as relations among variables, transformation of information, or implications. In total the subcategories within the three axes yield 180 unique cells or factors.

Hierarchical Models

Is intelligence composed of as few as 2 factors or as many as 180 factors? One response to this question is to determine whether there are actually relatively few main factors that are comprised of subfactors. This is the approach taken by theorists who have developed hierarchical models. One of the first models was proposed by **Raymond Cattell** (1963, Horn & Cattell, 1966). Cattell believed that existing intelligence tests were too focused on verbal, school-based tasks. In developing a test that assessed more perceptual aspects of intelligence, he proposed two general factors in intelligence: **fluid intelligence** (*Gf*) and **crystallized intelligence** (*Gc*). Fluid intelligence is the ability to solve novel problems and is best understood as representing one's innate intellectual potential. Crystallized intelligence is what we have learned in life, both from formal education and general life experiences.

Other hierarchical models represent attempts to reconcile many of the differences among the previous theories of intelligence. Both Vernon (1961) and Carroll (1993) presented a three-level model with Spearman's g as the highest order factor. The second order factors differ in the two models. For Vernon the second order factors are verbal/educational and spatial/mechanical; for Carroll there are 8 different second order factors, including Cattell's fluid and crystallized intelligence. For the lowest level of factors, Vernon simply suggested that these minor or subordinate factors existed, whereas Carroll explicitly listed and categorized the dozens of these lowest level factors.

Information Processing Models

Two influential information processing models of intelligence were proposed in the 1980s, both of which focus on the manner in which people process information and solve problems. Sternberg's (1985) *triarchic theory* involves three interrelated elements: componential, experiential, and contextual. The componential element deals with (a) the mental processes of planning, monitoring, and evaluating (referred to as executive functions), (b) performance, or the solving of a problem, and (c) knowledge acquisition, including encoding, combining, and comparing information. The experiential element addresses the influence of task novelty or unfamiliarity on the process of problem-solving. The third element, context, involves three different ways of interacting with the environment: adaptation, alteration of the environment, and selection of a different environment. Sternberg's model suggests that consideration of all these elements is necessary to understand intelligence. The explicit inclusion of the experiential and contextual elements sets it apart from other models as these elements underscore the need to incorporate learning history and environment in understanding intelligent behaviour.

Gardner's (1983, 1999) *theory of multiple intelligences* focuses on the use of symbolic mental systems in the processing of information. According to this theory, there are multiple forms of intelligence including linguistic, musical, logical-mathematical, spatial, bodily-kinaesthetic, intrapersonal, interpersonal, naturalist, spiritual, existential, and moral. These different types of intelligence are inadequately assessed by traditional intelligence tests. Gardner argued that a culturally unbiased assessment requires recognition of the full range of different types of intelligence. Although his theory has been embraced by many educators, psychologists have criticized its scientific underpinnings (e.g., Hogan, 2003).

Does this child's musical talent illustrate an aspect of Gardner's theory of multiple intelligences?

In summary, over the past century, a range of theories of intelligence has been proposed. Although it would be reasonable to assume a strong connection between theories and measures of intelligence, this has not consistently been the case. As you will see later in the chapter, the most commonly used measures of intelligence are not based on current models of intelligence.

ASSESSING INTELLIGENCE: THE CLINICAL CONTEXT

The assessment of intelligence is often an integral component of a psychological assessment. The following brief case examples provide an illustration of the range of situations in which an evaluation of intellectual functioning is required.

Natasha is a 63-year-old woman who has requested an evaluation of her cognitive functioning due to concerns about what she perceives to be recent memory problems. She is a senior manager in a successful marketing company and has always derived great satisfaction from her work. In the past year, Natasha has noticed that she often forgets her appointments and fails to complete her administrative duties on time because of a lack of attention to deadlines. Although she has purchased various aids to help her keep track of her work activities (such as a personal digital assistant), she fails to use them consistently. Occasionally she notices similar memory lapses in her home life, although they are less frequent with social appointments or activities with her husband. Natasha is concerned that the memory lapses are becoming more frequent and is concerned that they may be the initial stages of a more serious memory or cognitive disorder.

Kyle is a 47-year-old man who suffered a workplace accident two months ago. Kyle is a bricklayer who was working on a job site repairing damage to the brickwork of a shopping mall when a car hit the scaffolding on which he was standing. The scaffolding collapsed and Kyle fell from a height of two storeys onto a pile of bricks on the ground, injuring his back and breaking his wrist. He was also struck on the head by a falling brick. Although he did not lose consciousness at the time, he felt a bit dizzy for a couple of days after his fall. Initially he was primarily concerned about the potential effect of his back and wrist injury on his return to work. In the past month, though, Kyle has noticed that he often forgets where he is going and that he has a "fuzzy" feeling in his head that makes it difficult for him to concentrate. He was referred for an evaluation by the Workers' Compensation Board to determine if he is fit to return to work or if there are grounds for considering some form of disability pension stemming from his head injury.

Monica is an 8-year-old girl whose parents requested an assessment as part of their efforts to have her enrolled in a gifted program. Her parents report that she began reading words at the age of 2 years and that by the age of 5 she was reading books intended for those in Grade 2. Monica is currently in Grade 3 and is often being given additional work by her teacher because she rapidly completes the usual work assigned to the class. Despite being generally successful in school, Monica is described by her parents as being rather fearful of new situations and has a tendency to focus on her school work rather than playing with friends or getting involved in games or athletic activities.

Jamal is a 19-year-old university student who was referred for assessment because of academic problems. Although he reports always having had difficulty getting organized and completing his work on time, he found the first year of university extremely stressful because of consistently having to work through the night to complete assignments. In class Jamal refrains from asking any questions and borrows other people's notes because his own are poor and incomplete. Jamal is an avid reader who frequently forgets about his other commitments when he is in the middle of reading a novel. He reports that his friends describe him as a daydreamer. Jamal wonders if he has some type of learning problem that is interfering with meeting his academic goals.

In the preceding case examples, both Natasha and Kyle are experiencing changes in their usual level of cognitive functioning. In one instance there is a concern that this may be due to an underlying neurological condition and in the other there is a question about whether the changes are due to an injury. A common question addressed by psychologists in such cases is whether the current level of functioning represents a change from a previous level. Although it would be easy for a dentist to compare a person's dental status before and after an accident, people do not routinely have assessments of their intellectual functioning unless there is a problem. There can be conceptual and measurement problems associated with efforts to estimate what is known as a **premorbid IQ** (i.e., intellectual functioning prior to an accident or the onset of a neurological decline). However, psychologists have developed relatively effective strategies for making these estimates by consulting the client's achievement records, testing with measures of ability that are relatively insensitive to decline, and paying close attention to the intelligence scale subtests that are least affected by neurological impairment (Groth-Marnat, 2003). Both cases also present a challenge for the assessor as the extent and severity of the possible changes in functioning must be determined. In neither case will the assessment be limited to the use of an intelligence scale as, at a minimum, self-monitoring data and interviews with relevant others will be necessary to document any decrements in functioning. The use of multiple sources of data, including intellectual test results, is relatively standard for assessment questions that involve possible alterations in cognitive functioning, whether due to an accident, disease, or dementia.

The cases of Monica and Jamal present another common set of assessment questions that hinge on the use of intelligence tests. Questions related to giftedness, mental retardation, or learning disabilities rely heavily on the results of intelligence tests. Giftedness is defined, in most jurisdictions, as an intelligence test score in the top 2% of the population (IQ ≥ 130). A diagnosis of mental retardation requires that a person obtain an IQ score in the lowest 2% of the population (IQ ≤ 70) as well as have impairments in functioning in areas such as self-care, social skills, home living, and work. To diagnose a learning disability, or a learning disorder in DSM-IV-TR terminology, there must be a substantial discrepancy between scores on a standardized achievement test and the person's age and level of intelligence. It should be noted that questions about their validity make all these diagnoses controversial. For example, in a meta-analytic study of research on reading disabilities, Stuebing and colleagues (2002) found little evidence that poor readers with and without an IQ discrepancy perform differently from each other (which calls into question the validity of the reading learning disability). Nevertheless, the IQ-related criteria are the legal and professional standards that psychologists must use currently when assessing individuals for suspected intellectual deficits, giftedness, or learning problems.

In all cases, though, psychologists are careful to differentiate between intelligence test scores and intelligence *per se*. For reasons described in the following section, commonly used intelligence tests do not tap the full range of abilities that are included in modern theories of intelligence. Instead, they tend to focus on those abilities that are related to academic performance and are not designed to measure social, emotional, and other domains. Because our intelligence tests have only limited content validity for the broader construct of intelligence (as currently understood), any result on an intelligence test does not fully represent a person's total intelligence.

THE WECHSLER INTELLIGENCE SCALES

Background Issues

The Wechsler intelligence scales are the most commonly used individually administered measures of intelligence. There are three Wechsler scales: the Wechsler Adult Intelligence Scale–Third Edition (WAIS-III), which is designed for the age range of 16 to 89 years, the Wechsler Intelligence Scale for Children–Fourth Edition (WISC-IV), which is designed for the 6–16 age range, and the Wechsler Preschool and Primary Scale of Intelligence–Third Edition (WPPSI-III), designed for the age range from 2 years 6 months to 7 years 3 months. **Figure 7.1** provides information on the history of the three tests that all stem from the original Wechsler-Bellevue Intelligence Scale. As all three tests share common origins, it is hardly surprising that there is some overlap in the concepts and types of items. However, as we will see in the descriptions for each test, there are also differences between tests, partly due to the nature of how intelligence can be assessed at different ages and partly due to evolving notions about how best to conceptualize intelligence.

For psychologists, the name David Wechsler is synonymous with intelligence testing. Wechsler had extensive experience with early intelligence tests, as he studied under Spearman and was an intelligence examiner in the First World War. In the 1930s he became chief psychologist at the Bellevue Hospital in New York and it was in this context that he developed the Wechsler-Bellevue Intelligence Scale (1939), the first individually administered intelligence test intended for use in a general child and adult population. In constructing this intelligence scale,

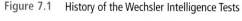

Figure 7.1   History of the Wechsler Intelligence Tests

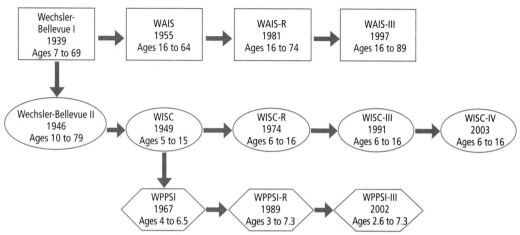

Note: WPPSI = Wechsler Preschool and Primary Scale of Intelligence; WISC = Wechsler Intelligence Scale for Children;
WAIS = Wechsler Adult Intelligence Scale. From A.S. Kaufman & E.O. Lichtenberger, *Essentials of WISC-III and WPPSI-R Assessment.*
Copyright 2000. John Wiley & Sons, Inc. This material is used by permission of John Wiley & Sons, Inc. Taken from Flanagan & Kaufman (2004).

Wechsler made little attempt to develop a theoretically informed test; rather, he borrowed the kinds of items included in the Stanford-Binet and the Army Alpha and Beta tests (Kaufman & Lichtenberger, 1999). In his scale, similar to the Alpha and Beta tests, equal weight was accorded Verbal intelligence subtests (i.e., those requiring verbal responses) and Performance intelligence subtests (i.e., those relying on nonverbal responses that are often timed).

An important innovation, introduced by Wechsler, was the use of deviation scores to measure intelligence. The Stanford-Binet relied on comparisons between the chronological age (CA) and the person's mental age (MA–defined as the average age in the normative sample of those who achieved the same test score as the person). The formula for the intelligence quotient (IQ) obtained from the scale is then IQ = (MA/CA)×100. Thus, everyone whose chronological age and mental age match has an IQ of 100. Although this is simple enough, there is a problem with this IQ ratio approach if the standard deviation of the IQ distribution differs with age. Let's assume, for a moment, that the standard deviation is 15 IQ points for 20-year-olds and 10 points for 50-year-olds. If someone scored one standard deviation above the age mean, this would result in an IQ of 115 for a 20-year-old and an IQ of 110 for a 50-year-old. Suddenly the meaning of a ratio IQ is not quite so clear-cut. To remedy this problem, Wechsler translated raw scores into *standard scores* based on a normal distribution with a mean of 100 and a standard deviation of 15, thus ensuring comparability in the meaning of IQ scores across ages. In other words, going back to our example, everyone who scores one standard deviation above the mean receives an IQ score of 115.

VIEWPOINT BOX 7.1

IQ AND ITS CORRELATES

There is probably no more controversial area of psychological research than that of intelligence and its correlates. This is partially due to a misunderstanding about psychological research. There is, for example, a common confusion about correlation and causation. The fact that a variable is correlated with an IQ score does not mean it has a causal connection with intelligence. A second source of error leading to controversy is the erroneous belief that intelligence (or any other psychological characteristic) must be due to *either* heredity *or* the environment. The results of decades of psychological research leave no question on this point: both heredity and environment interact in complex ways to influence intelligence.

Controversy and misunderstanding may also occur because of confusing an IQ score with the concept of intelligence. Remember that the content validity of most intelligence tests is related to performance in logical, educationally influenced tasks. Results of a study by Sternberg and colleagues (2001), who examined academic intelligence and practical intelligence in Kenyan children, nicely illustrate this point. These researchers used standard measures of fluid and crystallized intelligence (see the text section on *Theories of Intelligence*) along with a measure assessing practical intelligence for adaptation to the environment (primarily knowledge of natural herbal medicines). The correlation between the measure of practical intelligence and crystallized intelligence (i.e., academic intelligence) was -.31. The researchers speculated that this might reflect that the more time children devoted to school and school work, the less time they were able to devote to developing tacit knowledge about aspects of the indigenous environment.

So, with these points in mind, what do we know about the correlates of intelligence? The following conclusions are based on summaries of the research literature presented by Aiken (2003) and Hogan (2003).

- Approximately 50–60% of the variance in a population's IQ scores is attributable to genetic factors. This, however, does not reveal anything about genetic influence for any specific individual.

- Fetal and infant malnutrition is associated with persistent negative effects on IQ.

- Exposure to high levels of lead during early childhood has an adverse effect on IQ.

- Although there may be variability in a person's IQ during early childhood it becomes relatively stable during the school years.

- Mean IQ scores increase slightly during early adulthood and, for most people, reach a plateau by the age of 30 years. However, for those with above average IQs, small increases in IQ may be evident throughout middle age and even later.

- Declines in IQ are likely after the age of 70 years, but this does not occur for all individuals.

- Sex differences in IQ are minimal, but the variability of IQ scores is greater for men than it is for women.

- IQ is positively correlated with socio-economic status (i.e., parental income, education, and occupation).

- There tend to be ethnic differences in IQ, with the highest scores obtained by those whose ethnic heritage is identified as Asian, followed by Caucasian, Hispanic, and African. These differences are hypothesized to be due to a range of factors including test bias, differences in educational and social opportunities, and differences in brain structure.

- The IQ of first-born children is slightly greater than that of later-born children in a family. This may be related to the greater parental emphasis on language development for first-born children compared with later-born offspring.

The early versions of the WAIS, WISC, and WPPSI provided three main summary scores: Verbal IQ (VIQ), Performance IQ (PIQ), and **Full Scale IQ** (FSIQ; the sum of Verbal and Performance scales). This was in keeping with the manner in which the scales were originally constructed. However, there can be a substantial discrepancy between a test developer's assumptions about the interrelation between items and subtests and the pattern of interrelation revealed by the actual data. Over the years, numerous factor analytic studies of the Wechsler scales have found moderate intercorrelations among the various subscales in the three scales, suggesting they tap a g factor (e.g., Caruso & Cliff, 1999). However, very few factor analytic studies have found unqualified support for two separate Verbal and Performance factors. For example, the WAIS-III appears to have a four-component factor structure, including Verbal Comprehension, Perceptual Organization, Working Memory, and Processing Speed (Saklofske, Hildebrand, & Gorsuch, 2000). **Table 7.1** lists the factors (sometimes called indexes or composite scores) across the three tests. In the WISC-IV, the most recently revised of the scales, the FSIQ has been retained but the concepts of VIQ and PIQ have been replaced by summary scores based on the scale's factor structure (Verbal Comprehension and Perceptual Reasoning).

TABLE 7.1   Index/Composite Scores in the Wechsler Intelligence Scales

Verbal Comprehension
WAIS-III, WISC-IV, WPPSI-III

Perceptual Organization
WAIS-III, WISC-IV (now called Perceptual Reasoning), WPPSI-III

Working Memory
WAIS-III, WISC-IV

Processing Speed
WAIS-III, WISC-IV, WPPSI-III (only for ages 4 years to 7 years and 3 months)

General Language
WPPSI-III

The Wechsler-Bellevue was greatly criticized for its very limited set of norms. Since that early test, Wechsler and his collaborators have devoted enormous efforts to establishing a solid normative base for the Wechsler intelligence scales. The most recent versions of the three tests have all used normative samples of at least 1,700 participants. For all tests, great care was taken to ensure that the demographic characteristics of the normative samples matched the most up-to-date American census data. Although this ensures the **representativeness** of the normative sample for testing in the United States, it does not guarantee that the norms are appropriate for testing in other countries. A norm-referenced test is useful to the extent that it provides accurate information about a normative group that is relevant to the tested individual. Sattler (2001) suggested that the most salient characteristics that must be considered in making these normative comparisons are age, grade, gender, geographic region, ethnicity, and socio-economic status. Interpreting the test result from any individual who differs from the normative group on these characteristics may be problematic. There is evidence that the Wechsler norms are not always appropriate for use outside the United States. For example, Kamieniecki and Lynd-Stevenson (2002) found that Australian children under the age of 15 obtain slightly higher IQ scores than did American children of a similar age. If the American norms were used to classify giftedness or retardation among Australian children, for example, classification errors would occur.

There is, of course, another problem that may occur when testing someone who differs from the normative sample: the test itself may not be fair. For example, questions that are specific to an American context (e.g., "How many states were there when the United States was established?") may not be appropriate for assessing the general knowledge of a non-American test-taker. To eliminate the impact of American items on the tests scores of Canadians, a number of suggestions were made of ways to substitute Canadian items (e.g., Spreen & Tryk, 1970; Violato, 1986). Unfortunately these homemade items did not have a comparable level of difficulty to the American items and thus their use altered the meaning of the resulting test scores (Cyr & Atkinson, 1987). To address these issues, starting with the work on the WISC-III, recent revisions to all Wechsler scales include a Canadian standardization component. This involves ensuring that test items are appropriate to the Canadian context (and altering the items when necessary) and then establishing Canadian norms using a large sample of participants whose demographic characteristics are representative of Canadian national census data. As a result, psychologists in Canada can now use the Wechsler intelligence scales with great confidence—the same, however, cannot be said of psychologists working in other English-speaking countries, as no other national norms have been developed. Building on this foundation, efforts are currently underway to ensure that all subsequent editions of the Wechsler scales of intelligence have fair items and appropriate norms for testing French-speaking Canadians.

A final general point should be kept in mind with respect to the Wechsler intelligence scales. Wechsler modelled the original Wechsler-Bellevue scale on tests evaluating an examinee's abilities in academically related areas. This means that the tests are oriented to analytical forms of intelligence and do not measure abilities in the artistic, social, or emotional domains, among others. It also means that the focus of the Wechsler tests is on the examinee's current ability or some of the *products* of intelligence, with no attention directed to the *processes* that underlie intelligence. A person's performance on the Wechsler scales indicates a great deal about how well he or she can solve problems in a few important areas, but very little about exactly how he or she solves diverse problems (Groth-Marnat, 2003).

The Wechsler tests do not measure abilities in artistic, social, or emotional domains.

Administration, Scoring, and Interpretation Issues

Doctoral students in clinical psychology often spend an entire graduate course learning how to administer, score, and interpret the Wechsler scales. Standardized administration requires familiarity with all the subtests, ease in handling materials, and detailed knowledge of permitted prompts when an item is partially or incorrectly answered. Administration of the Wechsler scales should be conducted in a comfortable but relatively nondescript room (i.e., no distractions that influence the person's concentration). Typically the psychologist sits opposite the test-taker, or at a 90-degree angle to him or her—an important point if assessing an energetic youngster who is eagerly trying to peak at what the psychologist is getting ready to do next! The test-taker should be given information about the nature of the test (in an age appropriate manner) and should be allowed to ask questions. Testing with the scales can take up to two hours, so the psychologist should engage in small talk and reassuring comments to help the test-taker remain engaged throughout the testing. However, the assessor is not permitted to give the test-taker any feedback on performance, or whether answers are correct or incorrect, so the encouragement takes the form of noticing effort, concentration, and persistence, rather than suggesting that the person is doing well. In some cases, such as with children or individuals with brain damage, it is necessary to take breaks between subtests, otherwise the person's fatigue may interfere with the concentration necessary for the testing.

Extensive details about the administration, scoring, and interpretation of the Wechsler intelligence scales are provided in the manuals that accompany the measures. There are also many other sources available to aid psychologists in their use of these scales (e.g., Flanagan & Kaufman, 2004; Kaufman & Lichtenberger, 1999; Lichtenberger & Kaufman, 2004). As each new edition has some new procedures, psychologists attend training sessions to learn about them when a scale is revised. For the test scores to have meaning, clinicians must follow these guidelines—otherwise it is not possible to accurately use the normative data to interpret a person's test scores.

Administering and scoring these tests are not easy tasks. The consequences of administration and scoring errors can be substantial. In a series of studies Slate and colleagues (Slate, Jones, Coulter, & Covert, 1992; Slate, Jones, Murray, & Coulter, 1993; Whitten, Slate, Jones, & Shine, 1994) found evidence of numerous errors in the administration and scoring of all three Wechsler scales, with errors as great as 28 IQ points! Although in some cases such errors may be due to the psychologist's carelessness, these findings underscore just how complex it is to accurately use the Wechsler scales. To give you a sense of this, consider the following example, similar to an item on the WAIS-III. The test-taker is asked to indicate "In what way are a swimming pool and a baseball field alike?" The assessor must determine whether the person's response "You can have fun in both" is worth 2 points, 1 point, or 0 points. In the manual, information such as the following is provided: 2 points are awarded for answers that involve a recognition that both are used for sporting or athletic activities, 1 point is awarded for answers that indicate they are found in recreational areas or that both require maintenance, and 0 points are awarded for answers such as "You get wet in both" or "Both can be outside, but only a pool can be inside." Although the Wechsler manuals have been extensively tested and the most common responses (both good and poor) are listed, the assessor must know when to ask for more information in reaction to an answer that does not appear in the manual. For testing to proceed at a reasonable rate, the psychologist must be familiar with all the scoring rules to make rapid scoring decisions.

The general interpretive strategy, recommended by almost every source on the Wechsler tests, is to move from the general to the specific. Groth-Marnat (2003), for example, suggested that the FSIQ should always be interpreted first, followed by the VIQ and PIQ (including whether any differences between the two are statistically significant and meaningful), and then the factor scores (such as Verbal Comprehension, Working Memory). These steps allow the psychologist to understand the broad pattern of the examinee's IQ and his or her general strengths and weaknesses. FSIQ information, including the percentile rank, provides an overall indication of the person's mental abilities in comparison with the normative group. Interpretations of the other IQ scores and the factor scores allow for a more comprehensive picture of the examinee's cognitive abilities, including whether there are noteworthy aspects such as much superior functioning in the verbal domain compared with the performance domain. A difference such as this can be due to a host of factors, including educational background and brain damage. Careful consideration of these scores in the context of other assessment information can provide valuable information for determining the person's overall cognitive functioning and possible options for vocational or educational remediation.

The interpretation of a Wechsler scale then proceeds with an examination of additional factorial groupings of subtests that have been identified in the research literature. A common strategy is to use Horn and Cattell's (1966) distinction between crystallized and fluid intelligence. As we indicated earlier in the chapter, crystallized intelligence is defined as education-based knowledge and abilities and is measured by subtests such as Vocabulary and Information; fluid intelligence is the ability to solve novel problems and is measured by subtests such as Digit Span and Matrix Reasoning (see **Table 7.2** for information on these subtests on the WAIS-III). Most authorities then recommend that the psychologist interpret variability between and within the subtests of the scale. To this end, sources such as Flanagan and Kaufman (2004), Kaufman and Lichtenberger (1999), and Lichtenberger and Kaufman (2004) provide detailed descriptions, for each subtest, of the clinical considerations associated with each subtest and the factors that may influence each subtest. Although widely endorsed and practised, the analysis of subtest scatter is problematic, not least because the internal consistency reliability of each subtest is typically much lower than that associated with the summary scores (i.e., the IQ scores and factor scores). This translates into reduced assessment precision, which in turn means an increased likelihood of false positive and false negative statements about the person's ability as measured on each subtest. Moreover, decades of research have found that information contained in subtest profiles adds little to the prediction of academic achievement or of learning behaviours (Watkins, 2003).

PROFILE BOX 7.1

DR. DON SAKLOFSKE

I earned my Ph.D. from the University of Calgary and am now a Professor at the University of Saskatchewan. I am a registered psychologist in the provinces of Alberta and Saskatchewan and maintain a listing in the Canadian Register of Health Service Providers in Psychology. I am an elected Fellow of the Canadian Psychological Association. In addition to university teaching, professional association activities, and clinical work, a great deal of my professional time is devoted to research on intelligence and personality, resulting in a number of published articles, chapters, and books. I was the project director for the Canadian WAIS III study and an advisory panel member during the development of the WISC-IV.

Dr. Don Saklofske

What made you choose to become a clinical psychologist?

There are several reasons for this career choice. As an undergraduate, I was drawn to the scientist-practitioner perspective in clinically oriented courses and found the links among theory, research, and practice most compelling. As a graduate student I was fortunate to have been supported by a number of talented and brilliant faculty members at the University of Calgary who encouraged my interests.

What is the most rewarding part of your job as a clinical psychologist?

Being a psychologist is most exciting and rewarding. I participate daily in the search for the very factors that describe the wide diversity of human behaviour. The university setting provides a rich context to engage in such discovery and application of knowledge. Applying psychology in direct clinical service and in the training of both graduate and undergraduate students is the other side of my work that is most rewarding, and gives meaning to psychology as a scientific discipline and profession.

What is the greatest challenge facing you as a clinical psychologist?

There is no single answer to this question. One challenge is that, given all the unknowns in present-day psychological science and practice, our clinical efforts are not always successful. In addition, there is the ongoing concern that our resources are limited and we are constantly trying to do too much with too little. An important issue in years to come will be finding ways to provide psychology services outside of large cities. As well, we must become even more active in promoting psychological wellness and resiliency and developing prevention services to complement our skills in applying evidence-based therapies and interventions.

Tell us about the importance of Canadian norms for tests such as the Wechsler scales.

One of psychology's key contributions is the measurement of human characteristics. Psychologists have developed measures to assess numerous constructs including intelligence, personality variables such as extraversion, psychological symptoms of anxiety and depression, and various other factors such as self-concept and motivation. Standardized, norm-referenced tests allow us to compare the scores of one person with the scores of a relevant group. Some years ago, Canadian psychologists began to raise questions about differences in scores between Canadians and Americans on intelligence tests such as the Wechsler scales. Two important questions were: "Does this test that was developed in the United States work the same way in Canada?" and "Do Canadians score the same as Americans?" Although the way we measure intelligence appears to be similar in both countries, the norms from one country do not always fit in another country. As the Wechsler scales were developed in the United States they included several questions that had American content. Nevertheless, we found that when the WISC III was administered to Canadian children, they scored higher than did their counterparts in the United States. A similar pattern was found for adults in some of the age ranges in the WAIS III. These data provided a sound basis for developing Canadian norms. Our goal is to make these psychological tests as reliable and valid as possible for use in Canada, and this extends to developing Canadian norms if needed.

How do you integrate science and practice in your work?

The scientist-practitioner perspective is the foundation of my work and that of my colleagues. Although we must remain open to ideas from other fields, disciplines, and other cultures, the strength of psychology comes from being grounded in science. We must therefore search for evidence to determine whether our claims and efforts are supported or not, whether it be related to diagnosis, treatment, or the effectiveness of a prevention program.

What do you see as the most exciting changes in the profession of clinical psychology?

Everything! This is such an exciting time as advances in psychology are progressing at a very fast pace. The rapid growth of psychological knowledge and our collaboration with other fields such as the neurosciences and behaviour genetics and professions such as medicine and education holds great promise for humankind. Although psychologists will continue to be confronted by many emerging and still unanswered questions, our potential to provide evidence-based assessment, intervention, and prevention at the primary, secondary, and tertiary levels has never been greater.

Canadian Normative Data

Canadian standardization projects for the Wechsler intelligence scales began with the WISC-III (Wechsler, 1996). Since that time, Canadian norms have been developed for the WAIS-III, the WPPSI-III and, most recently, the WISC-IV. The general strategy for constructing the norms has been the same throughout these projects. It involves using recent Canadian census data to establish the sampling frame for the project and then developing a stratified random sampling plan to ensure that the resulting sample is representative of English-speaking Canadians. This plan has consistently included the demographic variables of age, gender, ethnicity, educational level, and geographical region. For example, with the WAIS-III (Wechsler, 2001) the final sample of 1,105 Canadian adults included those from ages 16 years to 89 years. Fifty-seven percent of the sample were women. With respect to ethnicity, 38% self-reported as British, 30% as French/European, 22% as having multiple ethnic origins, and 10% as other single ethnic origin. The range of educational levels of the sample was similar to the census data, as was the representation of geographical regions (with the exception of an over-sampling of the Maritime provinces and English-speaking regions of Quebec).

Using data from Canadian normative groups, the test developers then derived scaled scores (i.e., standardized scores) from the raw scores. As a first step the Canadian data were compared with the data from the American normative groups and the distribution of the scores for each age group were examined. Although there were some national differences in the mean raw scores in the normative groups, overall the distributions were similar. This similarity allowed the developers to apply the same statistical procedures employed with the American data to derive estimates of population values for the Canadian data. As a final step these estimates were transformed into standard scores so that each subtest has a mean of 10 and a standard deviation of 3.

WECHSLER ADULT INTELLIGENCE SCALE – THIRD EDITION (WAIS-III)

The WAIS-III was released in 1997, with the Canadian edition released a few years later (Wechsler, 2001). Compared with the previous version some new subtests were added, the age range was enlarged to include 16- to 89-year-olds, and, for the first time, the use of index scores (see Table 7.1) was incorporated into the test. In the American standardization sample 200 participants were administered, in a counterbalanced order, the WAIS-III and the previous edition of the WAIS. The correlations among the VIQ, PIQ, and FSIQ were all extremely high (.94, .86, and .93, respectively) and, consistent with the **Flynn effect** (Flynn, 1987; see **Viewpoint Box 7.2**), the scores on the old edition were slightly higher than on the new edition (Kaufman & Lichtenberger, 1999). **Table 7.2** provides details on the WAIS-III subtests. As part of the Canadian standardization project, only three potentially biased items were identified. These items involved aspects of American history and a calculation involving miles per hour. When Canadian data were analysed it was evident that the items were valid for Canadians (i.e., the level of difficulty of each item was comparable for the American and Canadian normative samples). As a result there is no altered content required to make the WAIS-III suitable for use with English-speaking Canadians.

The age range of the WAIS-III was enlarged so that it could be used to assess all these people.

TABLE 7.2   Wechsler Adult Intelligence Scale–Third Edition (WAIS-III)

Scales and Subtests

Verbal Scale

Vocabulary: The person defines a series of orally and visually presented words.

Similarities: After being presented with pairs of words (describing concepts or objects) the person provides an explanation about how the two concepts or objects are similar.

Arithmetic: The person solves arithmetic problems and provides the answer orally.

Digit Span: The person is presented with a series of numbers and must repeat them in the same sequence or in a reversed sequence.

Information: A set of orally presented questions that address knowledge of events, objects, people, and places.

Comprehension: Questions about common concepts and problems are presented orally and the person must provide the answer or solution.

Letter-Number Sequencing: Sequences of letters and numbers are presented orally and the person repeats them with the letters in alphabetical order and numbers in ascending order.

Performance Scale

Picture Completion: The person is presented with pictures of common objects and settings and must identify the missing part.

Digit Symbol Coding: Using a key that matches numbers to symbols, the person must rapidly provide the correct symbols to a list of numbers.

Block Design: The person uses coloured blocks to create three-dimensional representations of two-dimensional geometric patterns.

Matrix Reasoning: The person is presented with incomplete patterns and, from a list of five choices, must select the choice that completes the pattern.

Picture Arrangement: A series of pictures is presented and the person must put them in the correct, logical order.

Symbol Search: The person must indicate, by checking a box, whether target symbols occur in the group of symbols presented.

Object Assembly: The person must assemble a series of puzzles depicting common objects.

Adapted from Wechsler, (2001).

VIEWPOINT BOX 7.2

THE FLYNN EFFECT

Is your IQ increasing each year? Are you more intelligent than your parents or your grandparents? According to research conducted by James Flynn (1987), the answer to these questions is *yes*—at least at the population level. Flynn analysed changes in IQ scores in developed countries over the past few decades and found that, on average, there was an annual increase of .33 IQ score points. In other words, an average undergraduate student today has an IQ that is 1 standard deviation higher (i.e., 15 points) than that of the average undergraduate in the early 1960s. Not all IQ measures or subtests are rising at the same rate. Flynn found that measures of visuospatial abilities—usually treated as measures of fluid intelligence (see the text section on *Theories of Intelligence*)—increased more than measures of acquired knowledge (i.e., crystallized intelligence).

How can this be? The span of a few decades is certainly too brief for such dramatic changes to be due to genetic factors. Changes stemming from genetic alterations within a population take centuries, not generations, to be evident. Although it is always possible that these increases may be due to factors related to the tests themselves, this is rather unlikely. There is no evidence, for example, that people are generally aware of what the items are on IQ tests, or that they study for the tests prior to taking them, or that schools have altered their curricula to emphasize subjects related to *g*. After eliminating these possible explanations, environmental influences must be the primary driving forces behind this rise in IQ. But how exactly? Flynn speculated that improvements in educational systems are a contributory factor. This includes both increases in the number of people within a population who receive formal education as well as increases in the number of years of education completed. Flynn argued that other environmental influences must also be at work. These factors include improved nutrition, greater parental involvement with children, fewer severe childhood diseases, and rapid developments in technology that emphasize visuospatial skills such as television, video games, and computers (Neisser, 1998).

Yet, consider for a moment the fact that at least half of the variance in population IQ scores can be attributed to genetic factors. If these substantial rises in IQ are attributable to environmental factors, it might appear that alterations in these environmental factors over the past 50 years are absolutely enormous. In attempting to explain this "IQ paradox," Dickens and Flynn (2001) emphasized the importance of small but persistent alterations in the environment that, over generations, could influence IQ scores even though there is such a high genetic influence on IQ. For example, over the past century the cognitive complexity of most jobs has increased, leisure time has increased, technologies in the home have increased, and average family size has decreased (allowing more time for parents to focus their attention on each child). Cumulatively, year after year, generation after generation, these changes may be responsible for rising IQ scores by providing stimulating environments that match the intellectual potential of more and more people in a population. By optimizing the gene–environment fit, Dickens and Flynn speculated that a multiplier effect is occurring in which small environmental forces can yield large IQ effects. However, as appealing as such a model may be, it is unlikely to be the last word on the pattern of rising IQ. Rowe and Rodgers (2002) suggested that a recursive model (i.e., one in which environment and genes interact repeatedly) may well hold the key to explaining the pattern. They cautioned, however, that recursive models also predict an increase in the variability in IQ scores in a population. When the same data that demonstrate a rise in IQ are examined, there is little or no evidence for an accompanying increase in IQ variance. So, the search continues.

RELIABILITY AND VALIDITY

Previous versions of the WAIS were noted for their generally excellent reliability values. The WAIS-III continues this trend, with the internal consistency coefficients for the FSIQ, VIQ, and PIQ all exceeding .90. The reliability for the factor scores is also excellent, ranging from .88 to .96. Much greater variability is evident with the individual subtests, with values ranging from .68 to .93. The fact that 4 of 14 subtests have average reliability values below .80 underscores our earlier concerns about interpreting any apparent variability among the subtests. As so many validity studies were conducted over the years for earlier versions of the WAIS, it is important to note that, as described previously, there are very high correlations among the IQ scores for the WAIS-III and the WAIS-R. The pattern of subtest intercorrelations and factor analytic results reported in the test manual all support the continuing validity of the WAIS-III. An important question in using the WAIS-III is whether the scale's factor structure is the same for all age groups; for example, is it valid to interpret a Working Memory score for both 17-year-olds and 77-year-olds? To address this question Taub, McGrew, and Witta (2004) examined the factorial invariance of the scale across the 13 age groups used in the American normative data. They found clear evidence that the same four factors apply across all ages and, very importantly, that there is consistency across age groups regarding the subtests that contribute to each of these factors. Despite all the encouraging validity data for the WAIS-III, keep in mind that validity is not a property of a test, but rather a property that a test has when used for a particular purpose with a specific group of people. The WAIS-III must always be used and interpreted within the limits of the characteristics of the normative sample and the purposes for which it has established validity.

Wechsler Intelligence Scale for Children–Fourth Edition (WISC-IV)

The fourth edition of the WISC was released in 2003 (Wechsler, 2003). A description of the subtests and the four indexes (i.e., factors) is presented in **Table 7.3**. As you can see by comparing it with the information on the WAIS-III subtests in Table 7.2, there are a number of similarities in the type of tasks included in the WISC-IV. The WISC-IV is designed to provide age appropriate assessment of children/adolescents between the ages of 6 and 17. To increase the developmental appropriateness of the scale, the developers simplified the instructions, including sample and/or practice items within each subtest, and made the test material more attractive and engaging for children.

The WISC-IV was developed in the United States with a stratified sample of 2,200 children and adolescents. Subsequently the Canadian normative study for the WISC-IV collected data from 1,100 Canadian children between the ages of 6 and 17 years. A French-language research edition is also being prepared for release in Canada. It is slated to include a translation and adaptation of the American version of the scale, with the manual and all test materials translated and adapted for use with French-speaking Canadian children.

RELIABILITY AND VALIDITY

The mean internal consistency reliability of the WISC-IV subtests is very good, with only two of the subtests having reliability values below .80. The reliability of the FSIQ is .97, a rather remarkable accomplishment for the scale. All of the four index scores have outstanding reliability values, ranging from .88 to .94. As with previous versions of the WISC there is a great deal of validity information reported in the manual, including the intercorrelations among subtests and the factor structure of the scale. There are also numerous findings presented on the relation between the WISC-IV and other measures, including measures of similar and dissimilar constructs (i.e., convergent and discriminant validity). For example, the FSIQ correlates .89 with the FSIQ from the previous version of the WISC and with the FSIQ from the WAIS-III (based on data from 198 16-year-olds). In contrast, the correlations between a measure of emotional intelligence and the FSIQ and the 4 indexes ranged from .22 to .31, thus providing evidence of discriminant validity.

There is also a series of special group studies reported in the manual that document the scale's clinical value. These groups included samples of children identified as intellectually gifted, children with mild or moderate mental retardation, children with learning disabilities, children with autistic disorder, and children with traumatic brain injury. For each special group, a demographically matched sample of children from the normative sample was selected. The main purpose of these studies was to determine the ability of the WISC-IV to provide valid estimates of intellectual functioning in groups commonly encountered in the clinical use of the

TABLE 7.3   Wechsler Intelligence Scale for Children–Fourth Edition (WISC-IV)

Indexes and Subtests

Verbal Comprehension Index

Similarities: After being presented with pairs of words (describing concepts or objects) the child provides an explanation about how the two concepts or objects are similar.

Vocabulary: The child names pictures that are presented and defines words presented orally.

Comprehension: Questions about common concepts and social situations are presented orally and the child provides the answer or solution.

Information: A set of orally presented questions that address knowledge of a wide range of general topics.

Word Reasoning: After being presented a series of clues, the child describes the underlying common concept.

Perceptual Reasoning Index

Block Design: The person uses coloured blocks to create three-dimensional representations of three-dimension models and two-dimensional geometric patterns.

Picture Concepts: The child chooses pictures from rows of pictures in order to form a group that has a characteristic in common.

Matrix Reasoning: The child is presented with incomplete patterns and, from a list of five choices, must select the choice that completes the pattern.

Picture Completion: The child is presented with pictures of common objects and must point to or name the missing part.

Working Memory Index

Digit Span: The child is presented with a series of numbers and must repeat them in the same sequence or in a reversed sequence.

Letter-Number Sequencing: Sequences of letters and numbers are presented orally and the child repeats them with the letters in alphabetical order and numbers in ascending order.

Arithmetic: The child solves arithmetic problems and provides the answer orally.

Processing Speed Index

Coding: Using a key that matches numbers or geometric shapes to symbols, the child must rapidly provide the correct symbols to a list of shapes or numbers.

Symbol Search: The child indicates whether target symbols occur in the group of symbols presented.

Cancellation: The child marks target pictures in a series of pictures that include both random arrangements and structured arrangements.

Adapted from Wechsler, (2003).

scale. In all instances the observed patterns of group differences were consistent with the hypothesized group differences in intellectual ability. For example, the WISC-IV was administered to 45 children (8 to 13 years of age) who met *DSM-IV-TR* criteria for a learning disorder and attention-deficit/hyperactivity disorder. For all the index scores and the FSIQ, this group scored lower than did the matched control group of children.

The extensive information on the validity of the WISC-IV provided in the manual is a considerable strength of the test. However, this cannot not provide generic assurance about the test's psychometric soundness. It takes several years following the release of a test before research appears in the scientific literature. Accordingly the strengths and weaknesses of the WISC-IV based on the results of independently conducted studies will not be known for some time. Research on the previous version of the WISC does suggest some problem areas that may be evident in the newest edition. Watkins and Canivez (2004), for example, found major limitations with the temporal stability (i.e., test-retest reliability) of the subtests and the indexes. Moreover the reliability of index discrepancy scores (e.g., a difference between Verbal Comprehension and Perceptual Organization) was abysmal, with none of the reliability values attaining statistical significance. These data underscore the problems inherent in making interpretations at the level of the subtests or scatter among the subtests.

Wechsler Preschool and Primary Scale of Intelligence– Third Edition (WPPSI-III)

The Canadian version of the WPPSI-III was released just two years after the introduction of the American revision (Wechsler, 2004). There are a total of 14 subtests on the scale, but psychologists are likely to use only a subset of them in assessing an individual child. Subscales are selected according to the age of the child. For the youngest children (those aged 2 years 6 months to 3 years 11 months), there are four core subtests: Receptive Vocabulary, Information, Block Design, and Object Assembly. The FSIQ is comprised of all four subtests; the first two form the VIQ score and the latter two form the PIQ score. For older children (those 4 years to 7 years 3 months), six subtests are used: Information, Vocabulary, Word Reasoning (these three form the VIQ), Block Design, Matrix Reasoning, Picture Concepts (these three form the PIQ), and Coding. The subtests are similar to those described in Table 7.3 for the WISC-IV but are age appropriate in content, with even less emphasis on timed performance and reliance on verbal responses. There is also a series of subtests that can be administered to scores for Processing Speed and General Language (see Table 7.1).

RELIABILITY AND VALIDITY

For the younger age group, the internal consistency reliability of the 5 core subtests is uniformly good, with the lowest value being .83. The FSIQ reliability value is .95, with the reliability values for the composite (factor) scores exceeding .88. A similar reliability profile is evident for the older age group. All subtests have a mean reliability value of at least .81, the composite values are all at least

.90, and the FSIQ reliability is .96. The short-term test-retest reliability (over an average of 28 days) for the scale was determined in a sample of 104 children. The resulting stability values were excellent, with the values for all subtests exceeding .75 and the composite scores and FSIQ having values of at least .80. As with the other Wechsler scales, the manual reported validity data based on subtest intercorrelations and factor analytic results. Although comparable data are not available for the Canadian population, the use of matched special group comparisons in the American version of the WPPSI-III (like those we described for the WISC-IV) provided compelling evidence of test validity. Although peer-reviewed research on the WPPSI-III has yet to appear in the journals, the initial indications are that it is a substantial improvement over the previous edition (Hamilton & Burns, 2003).

OTHER INTELLIGENCE SCALES

Although we have focused on the Wechsler scales of intelligence, psychologists also use other scales to assess intellectual abilities. The Stanford-Binet Intelligence Scales is now in its 5th edition (Roid, 2003). It is designed to assess intelligence in individuals from 2 to 85 years. Like the Wechsler scales, it is standardized to have a mean of 100 and a standard deviation of 15. The subtests can be summed to provide a Full Scale IQ and various composite factor scores. A normative American sample of 4,800 was selected based on 2000 census data. The reliability data for this sample were very strong, with all subtests having internal consistency values ≥ .84 and the composite and FSIQ scores ≥ .92. Validity data were obtained by including a host of intelligence and achievement tests in the normative sample.

In developing tests of intellectual ability, Kaufman and Kaufman took a very different theoretical approach to that used in the Wechsler scales or the Stanford-Binet. Rather than focusing on content areas that measure intellectual functioning, they chose to construct measures that were process-based (Lichtenberger, Broadbooks, & Kaufman, 2000). In other words, their scales focused on how children and adults learn and assessed styles of learning rather than knowledge or skill areas. This resulted in the publication of the Kaufman Assessment Battery for Children (Kaufman & Kaufman, 1983), now in a second edition, and the Kaufman Adolescent and Adult Intelligence Test (Kaufman & Kaufman, 1993). The names of the scales from the child version— Sequential Processing, Simultaneous Processing, Mental Processing Composite, and Achievement—give a sense of how it differs from the Wechsler scales. By comparing the scores on the processing scales with those obtained on the achievement scale, it is possible to examine gaps between what the examinee has actually learned with the person's potential to learn. As is typical with intelligence scales, normative data were collected on a large nationally representative (American) sample and extensive psychometric data were presented in the test manuals.

Although the Kaufman scales were designed to be culturally fair and relevant to educational contexts, they do not seem to be widely used by clinical psychologists. This may be due as much to the limited number of training programs that teach the use of these scales as it is to the need for traditional IQ scores in making a range of clinical diagnoses.

SELECTED COGNITIVE ASSESSMENT SCALES

To address some of the assessment questions described earlier in the chapter, clinical psychologists usually need to supplement the results from an intelligence test with information obtained on other tests that address cognitive functioning. In this section, we describe two of the tests most commonly used for this purpose. The first test is the Wechsler Memory Scale–Third Edition, a test that is typically used if there is a question of brain injury or brain dysfunction due to causes such as dementias, temporal lobe epilepsy, or Parkinson's disease. The other test is a standardized achievement test: the Wechsler Individual Achievement Test–Second Edition. An achievement test is used, along with a measure of intellectual functioning, in assessments focused on diagnosing learning disabilities and making recommendations for educational plans to address any observed learning problem.

Wechsler Memory Scale–Third Edition (WMS-III)

The original WMS was published by Wechsler in 1945, revised in 1987, and revised again in 1997 (Wechsler, 1997). To help you understand the constructs that the WMS-III assesses, consider what we know about memory processes. Lichtenberger, Kaufman, and Lai (2002) distinguished between *procedural memory*—involving skills and complex motor actions (such as riding a bike)—and *declarative memory*—involving symbolic representations (such as a phone number). Declarative memory can be further subdivided into **semantic memory** and **episodic memory**. Semantic memory involves general knowledge of words, concepts, and events, whereas episodic memory deals with the person's direct experiences. Although all of these forms of memory may be relevant in clinical contexts, the WMS-III is designed to assess the episodic form of declarative memory. To that end the tasks involved in the WMS-III require the examinee to respond to a number of stimuli, both auditory and visual. **Table 7.4** provides details on the scale's primary subtests (there are optional subtests, which we will not describe). For each subtest, as with the Wechsler intelligence scales, the mean is 10 and the standard deviation is 3. The summary scores on the WMS-III (i.e., the indexes) have a mean of 100 and a standard deviation of 15, just like an IQ score.

TABLE 7.4   Wechsler Memory Scale–Third Edition (WMS-III)

Immediate Memory

Auditory Immediate

Logical Memory I: A story is read aloud and the examinee is asked to repeat back as much of the story as possible.

Verbal Paired Associates I: A set of word pairs is read out. Following this a single word is read and the examinee is asked to provide the paired word.

Visual Immediate

Faces I: The examinee is shown a set of pictures of faces and then must indicate whether each face in a second set was in the original set of faces.

Family Pictures I: Several scenes with characters in them are shown and the examinee is then asked who was in the scene and some questions about the activities of the characters in each scene.

General Memory (Delayed)

Auditory Delayed

Logical Memory II: The examinee is asked to recall stories presented in Logical Memory I and is then asked a series of questions about the stories (at least 25 minutes must have passed from doing Logical Memory I).

Verbal Paired Associates II: Same task as in Verbal Paired Associates I, but examinee must also indicate which word pairs were also in the Verbal Paired Associates I (at least 25 minutes must have passed from doing this subtest).

Visual Delayed

Faces II: A set of pictures of faces is presented and the examinee is asked whether each face appeared in the original set of faces in Faces I (at least 25 minutes must have passed from doing Faces I).

Family Pictures II: The examinee is asked to recall the characters from Family Picture I, where they were and what they were doing in each scene (at least 25 minutes must have passed from doing Family Pictures I). [/TA-T]

Auditory Recognition Delayed

Logical Memory II: see above

Verbal Paired Associates II: see above

Working Memory

Letter-Number Sequencing: Sequences of letters and numbers are read aloud and the examinee must repeat the sequences.

Spatial Span: Blocks are touched in specific sequences and the examinee must then repeat the sequences of touches (either forward or backward).

Adapted from Wechsler, (1997).

The WMS-III was normed with the WAIS-III in the United States. This resulted in a representative normative sample of 1,250 adults (between the ages of 16 and 89 years) who completed both scales. Internal consistency values for the subtests range from .74 to .93, with short-term stability values ranging from .62 to .82. For the primary indexes, the internal consistency values range from .74 to .93 and the stability values from .70 to .88. There is clear evidence that the WMS-III differentiates clinical groups (such as those with dementias or neurological disorders) from those with normal memory functioning and that the primary index scores can distinguish among the memory-impaired clinical groups (Groth-Marnat, 2003). Evidence of validity for these tasks is especially important as the WMS-III is the main measure used by clinical psychologists and neuropsychologists to assess memory impairment.

The WMS-III is often used with the WAIS-III to evaluate the presence and extent of brain dysfunction. Clinicians examine discrepancies in total scores between the two scales to determine the nature of any impairment. To provide empirically based guidance in this analysis Dori and Chelune (2004) used the WMS-III/WAIS-III normative data to construct base rate tables for the occurrence of statistically significant discrepancies in the general population. By stratifying these base rates by educational level, the researchers were able to provide clinicians with useful tables for establishing the likelihood that a discrepancy score observed in testing a person may be clinically relevant or, alternatively, may be fairly commonly found in the general population.

Wechsler Individual Achievement Test–Second Edition (WIAT-II)

The original WIAT was released in 1992. The revised test, the WIAT-II, was released in 2002, with a Canadian version released the following year (The Psychological Corporation, 2003). The WIAT-II is designed to evaluate a person's academic and problem-solving skills. The manual provides linkage with scores from the Wechsler family of intelligence tests, allowing easy identification of discrepancies between intellectual functioning and academic achievement. As a result, the WIAT-II, when used in conjunction with a Wechsler intelligence scale, can be used in the diagnosis of learning disabilities and can provide invaluable information that can be used for planning remedial educational efforts.

Table 7.5 provides information on the nine subtests of the WIAT-II. To give you a sense of the kinds of questions that are asked, a Written Expression question asks the person to write a response to a statement like: *My favourite thing to do is…* and a Reading Comprehension question involves the person reading a passage about kangaroos and then answering questions about how kangaroos move, where they live, and how kangaroos are born. The Canadian edition includes some items that differ from the American version of the WIAT-II. For example, pictures of coins used in some mathematics items were changed from American to Canadian currency, spelling changes were made to be consistent with Canadian usage, and units of measurement were changed from imperial to metric units. The nine subtests are organized into four composite scores: Reading, Mathematics, Written Language, and Oral Language. The composite scores have substantial applied value, as they map onto the four areas that the Learning Disabilities Association of Canada have defined as critical in assessing the precise nature of a learning disability.

TABLE 7.5   Wechsler Individual Achievement Test–Second Edition (WIAT-II)

COMPOSITE SCORES AND SUBTESTS

Reading Composite

Word Reading: Depending on age and grade, the person is required to identify letters, beginnings or ends of words, rhyming works, or to read as quickly as possible from a list of words.

Reading Comprehension: The person reads sentences and short passages, answers questions about the text, and draws conclusions and inferences from the text.

Pseudoword Decoding: The person uses phonetic skills to sound out unfamiliar or nonsense words.

Mathematics Composite

Numerical Operations: The person solves math problems of varying complexity.

Math Reasoning: The person solves problems related to areas such as time, measurement, geometry, and probability.

Written Language Composite

Spelling: The person spells a word based on its meaning as used in a sentence.

Written Expression: The person writes words, sentences, or a brief essay in response to a topic; the writing is evaluated based on spelling, punctuation, vocabulary, organization, and theme development.

Oral Language Composite

Listening Comprehension: The person must match words/sentences to pictures.

Oral Expression: The person provides words that match a topic, repeats sentences, tells a story based on presented pictures, or describes the necessary steps in completing a task.

Adapted from The Psychological Corporation, (2003).

As we described earlier in the chapter, research has found consistent American-Canadian differences in intelligence test scores. This fact, combined with different educational curricula in the two countries and national differences in the academic year (i.e., the Canadian school year is about 20 days longer than the American school year), led the developers of the WIAT-II to assume that there would be differences in achievement test scores in the two countries. Accordingly, extensive steps were taken to gather normative data for the Canadian version of the WIAT-II. A sampling strategy similar to that used in the United States for the WIAT-II was used to gather Canadian data. Data were collected across different regions of the country (37% from Western Canada, 51% from Central Canada, and 12% from Eastern Canada). Based on ethnic self-identification, data were collected for four ethnic categories (Caucasian, Asian, First Nations, and Other); the normative sample roughly approximated the percentage of each category found in Canadian census data. Care was also taken to ensure that a suitable proportion of those with learning disabilities and related disorders were also included in the normative group. The end result of this impressive sampling process was a sample of 865 English-speaking students for the age-based norms (i.e., 5–19 years) and 1,174 English-speaking students in the grade-based norms (i.e., kindergarten to fourth-year university).

As with the Wechsler scales of intelligence, the WIAT-II has strong internal consistency values. Across the age range of 5–19 years, five of nine subtests have average reliability values ≥ .90. For the two subtests that each yields only a single response, internal consistency cannot be calculated. For these subtests the test-retest data provide evidence of excellent reliability ($r = .86$ for the 5–19 year range). Only the Listening Comprehension subtest has relatively poor reliability for a clinical measure, with an internal consistency value of .78. Nevertheless, the composite scores all have reliability values ≥ .87, indicating a very high level of reliability. Although the WIAT-II included college and university students in the normative sample, the reliability data for these groups are mixed. Some subtests are highly reliable (e.g., a mean value of .90 for Numerical Operations) whereas others have unacceptably low reliability for an achievement test (e.g., a mean value of .60 for Written Expression), and even the composite scores vary greatly in reliability (from .77 to .90). As you may recall from Chapter 4, the higher the reliability, the lower the standard error of measurement (SEM) will be. As the size of the SEM influences the accuracy of classification of scores and any discrepancy score generated from comparisons to an intelligence test, normative reliability data suggest that considerable caution should be exercised when using the WIAT-II to assess college and university students.

There has been surprisingly little published research on the validity of the WIAT or the WIAT-II. Based on relatively small samples (i.e., < 100), there is evidence that the WIAT scores are associated with teacher-rated academic achievement (Michalki & Saklofske, 1996) and with another commonly used academic achievement test (Smith & Smith, 1998). Only a handful of studies have examined the validity of the WIAT/WIAT-II or the use of the WIAT-IQ discrepancy scores in assessing learning disorders (e.g., Brown, Giandenoto, & Bolen, 2000). As a result of (a) the inevitable measurement error involved in assessing intelligence and academic achievement and (b) the limited research base, it is difficult to know exactly how well the WIAT-II performs in this critical clinical task. It does seem, however, that the test has been commonly accepted by clinical psychologists as appropriate for such assessments.

SUMMARY AND CONCLUSIONS

Intelligence is a highly prized characteristic in our society. It is not surprising, therefore, that the measurement of intelligence is a sensitive topic that arouses heated debate. Decisions about access to services are frequently made based on the results of intellectual assessment. The assessment of intellectual and cognitive functioning has been an important professional activity for clinical psychologists for almost a century. Because significant decisions are made based on the results of intelligence tests, a great deal of effort has been made to ensure that tests are fair, that adequate normative data are gathered, and that assessments are both reliable and valid. The Wechsler scales are the most commonly used scales, allowing assessment of intelligence over different developmental periods, assessment of episodic memory, and assessment of academic achievement. In recent years, advances have been made in adapting the Wechsler scales for use in a Canadian context. The analysis of discrepancies between intellectual ability and achievement is the centerpiece of learning disabilities assessment. However, a number of common clinical practices in assessing intelligence are not supported by research. This indicates the importance of psychologists maintaining their knowledge and continuing their education throughout their professional lives.

Critical Thinking Questions

What are the problems in defining intelligence in terms of academic performance?

What types of questions can assessment of intelligence and cognitive functioning address?

What is the significance of having an appropriate normative group?

Why have psychologists developed Canadian versions of tests of intelligence and achievement?

What are some of the limitations of the Wechsler scales?

Key Terms

crystallized intelligence

episodic memory

fluid intelligence

Flynn effect

Full scale IQ

g

premorbid IQ

representativeness

semantic memory

Key Names

Raymond Cattell

James Flynn

Charles Spearman

David Wechsler

ADDITIONAL RESOURCES

Book

Sternberg, R. J. (Ed.). (2000). *Handbook of intelligence*. New York: Cambridge University Press.

Journal

Intelligence. The journal is published by Elsevier and includes articles on the nature and function of intelligence.

Websites

The Psychological Corporation, Canada, publishers of the Wechsler scales: http://harcourtassessment.com/haiweb/Cultures/en-CA/default.htm

Mensa International: http://www.mensa.org/home.php
Mensa Canada: http://www.canada.mensa.org

Learning Disabilities Association of Canada: http://www.ldac-taac.ca

CHAPTER 8

Assessment: Self-Report and Projective Measures

INTRODUCTION

Many people take psychology courses because they are interested in better understanding the differences in attitudes, beliefs, behaviours, and emotionality among people. Psychology examines the ways that we can identify differences among people and how we can use this knowledge to predict future behaviour. Having focused on differences in intelligence in Chapter 7, in this chapter we turn our attention to differences in personality. As social beings, people develop models for understanding and predicting other people's behaviour. If you were asked to describe the key psychological characteristics of your friends and family members, you probably wouldn't have difficulty coming up with a list. As you looked over your lists for the different people you know, you'd probably find that you used descriptors such as "friendly," "trustworthy," "sociable," "honest," "serious," "caring," and "fun-loving." These concepts refer to a person's tendency to consistently behave in a specific way—otherwise known as **personality traits** or dispositions. Moreover, we tend to use these concepts not just for those we know well, but also for ourselves, for people we barely know, characters in books and movies, and even for our pets. Over the course of a day we seek patterns in the behaviours of others (*Shane is grumpy today*), generate hypotheses about why those patterns occur (*I wonder whether he's worried about the midterm*), making inferences about other personal characteristics based on these patterns (*He's a pretty perfectionistic guy*), and predicting future behaviours from these patterns (*He'll probably be unbearable when he's doing his honours thesis next year*).

Over the past century, psychologists have constructed literally thousands of measures of individual differences. Many of these measures are designed to assess personality traits, which psychologists define as consistencies in behaviour, emotions, and attitudes that are evident across situations and across time. Personality theorists and researchers work to determine the influences of genetics and life experiences on the development and expression of traits (Mischel, 2004; Mischel, Shoda, & Smith, 2004). Clinical psychologists are active in both researching personality traits and in assessing personality traits for clinical purposes. Personality measures vary in the scope of the constructs they are designed to assess. Some are intended to measure very broad constructs such as extraversion or neuroticism; others focus on highly specific constructs, such as locus of control for health or motivation for academic tasks. Most personality measures are based on self-report data and are often called **objective personality tests** because they can be scored objectively (i.e., the same scoring system is always used). Other self-report measures are less complex than personality tests and are derived from descriptive characteristics of an experience or an event rather than from a personality theory. These **behaviour checklists** or **symptom checklists** are designed to provide information about the nature of an individual's experience (e.g., psychological distress, mood states, and feared situations) and the frequency or severity of the experience. **Projective personality tests** represent a very different approach to assessing personality characteristics. Projective tests require the test-taker to respond either to ambiguous stimuli such as pictures or incomplete sentences or to generate drawings according to the assessor's instructions. Projective tests are based on the assumption that valuable information on aspects of the test-taker's personality structure can be gleaned from responses to these ambiguous stimuli.

In this chapter we will review some of the major objective personality measures, behaviour and symptom checklists, as well as frequently used projective personality measures. To help you appreciate the strengths and weaknesses of these types of measures, we begin by discussing some of the factors that influence their clinical usefulness and accuracy.

THE PERSON-SITUATION DEBATE

Since the late 1960s, researchers and clinicians have struggled with a fundamental question about personality. Although most people (and most personality theorists) believe that personality traits influence the way people behave and are, therefore, responsible for the apparent stability of behaviour across time and situations, others have raised the question: what if this stability is illusory? In other words, what would happen if measures of personality couldn't accurately predict individual differences among people or the behaviour of an individual? This was the challenge—often called the **person-situation debate**—that Walter Mischel launched in his 1968 book *Personality and Assessment*. Mischel reviewed decades of research into personality assessment and the relation between personality and actual behaviour. At that time theorists and clinicians assumed a direct connection between personality traits or dispositions and actual behaviour. Therefore, it was believed that, the more an individual possessed a certain trait, the more likely that person was to behave in a manner consistent with the trait in any environment or situation. For example, Clarissa, who is an extraverted person, would be expected to always behave in an outgoing, confident way, at home, school, and with friends. However, Mischel's literature review revealed that the link between trait scores and actual behaviour rarely exceeded a correlation of .30! Moreover he also provided examples of research demonstrating that variations across situations seemed to be more important than personality measures in accounting for behavioural variability. To demonstrate this point, think about what is more likely to influence Clarissa's behaviour at a party—her personality characteristics or contextual factors such as whether it was a student party, a reception given by a potential employer, or a party to celebrate her grandparents' wedding anniversary.

Mischel's work, combined with some other conundrums personality researchers were facing (such as the limits to self-knowledge, see **Viewpoint Box 8.1**), led many clinical psychologists to question the clinical value of personality measures. This scepticism coincided with the rising influence of behavioural approaches to treatment. Clinical psychologists using a behavioural approach to treatment did not rely on traditional personality measures, preferring instead to use situation-specific or disorder-specific checklists and rating scales. The current use of such checklists in clinical practice largely developed from the activities of these early behavioural and cognitive-behavioural clinicians. Cross-situational variability in people's actions was seen as a source of important information by psychologists with a behavioural approach to assessment. For example, if Jacob, who is depressed, feels discouraged while on the job in an information technology company, but has great energy in his volunteer work at the animal shelter, it may be valuable to help him (a) learn about the conditions in which the symptoms are less severe and (b) use this knowledge to try to increase involvement in situations in which the symptoms are lower.

In the decades since the publication of Mischel's book there have been substantial developments in the science of personality. It now appears that variability across situations and stability across time co-exist. Those arguing for the power of situational influences and those arguing for the power of personality were both correct (Fleeson, 2004). However, as you will see later in the chapter, the most commonly taught and used personality measures have been available for well over 50 years. So, changes in clinical assessment tools have not kept pace with advances in personality research. On the other hand, these research developments appear to have influenced the way that most clinical psychologists interpret the results from personality measures. Yet, as you will see in the next chapter, there continue to be substantial concerns about how various biases—such as overestimating the influence of personality characteristics on actual behaviour—affect the process of clinical decision-making.

VIEWPOINT BOX 8.1

HOW WELL DO WE (AND CAN WE) KNOW OURSELVES?

We usually take for granted that we can know ourselves fairly well. Most people feel confident in their abilities to accurately describe themselves, their attitudes, and their personal preferences. Yet, for well over a century, psychological theorists and researchers have questioned the extent to which we can actually know our own mental states and the causes of our actions.

Based on early Freudian theories, many people view the nonconscious—or unconscious—aspect of our existence as something that can be accessed through a great deal of conscious effort. The metaphor often used is that of an archaeological dig that yields ever more fascinating material the deeper one digs into the past. In contrast, though, the contemporary view of the unconscious is rather less romantic than this. Most cognitive, social cognitive, and neuroscience researchers see the human mind as a collection of information processors that function largely out of our awareness and that probably developed long before consciousness emerged in our species (Wilson, 2002). According to this research-informed perspective, no amount of "digging" (i.e., introspection) is likely to result in a more accurate understanding of ourselves, our motives, or our past experiences.

Wilson and Dunn (2004) reviewed research relevant to the questions of (a) how well we can know and understand ourselves and (b) the obstacles that interfere with efforts to attain greater self-knowledge. Many of their conclusions may surprise you. First, despite decades of theorizing and research, there is little compelling evidence for the existence of the Freudian concept of repression by which information is kept out of consciousness but is stored in memory. Although there is no firm evidence for repression, there is substantial evidence for the existence of conscious suppression (i.e., trying not to think about or focus on something). Most research on suppression indicates that suppression often fails to accomplish the goal of rendering information unavailable to consciousness. Ironically, efforts to suppress thoughts, memories, or feelings can frequently result in people paying even more attention than usual to the information they are attempting to ignore (Wegner, 1994).

So if the unconscious is not the repository of unwanted and undesirable urges and experiences, what is it then? Psychological research has firmly established that a great deal of nonconscious processing does occur but, according to Wilson and Dunn, this processing is largely related to matters of perception, attention, learning, and automatic judgements. Contrary to Freud's hypotheses, current research indicates there are no motivational or emotional impediments to people easily accessing this unconscious content. Instead, much of the unconscious is simply inaccessible to conscious inspection, either because it was never processed in consciousness to begin (for example, we are not consciously aware of what we do to perceive depth) or because a simple, repetitive task has become automatic and removed from conscious awareness (for example, although when we learn to drive a car we are conscious of each action, as our skill develops, performing the various sub-tasks becomes automatic or unconscious).

If introspection cannot help us better understand ourselves, can we take other steps to increase the accuracy of our self-knowledge? Wilson and Dunn suggested that we could learn much about ourselves by attending to how others view us. However, research indicates that most people are unable to accurately learn about how others see them, especially if those views do not match their own views of themselves. Social cognitive research indicates that the best route to self-knowledge is to intentionally observe our own behaviours and decisions as they occur. But, before you decide to embark down this path toward greater self-awareness, there is one caution you should consider. Decades of psychological research has convincingly shown that there are real physical and psychological benefits to positive self-illusions, such as feeling you are more attractive, more intelligent, or more skilled than you really are (Taylor & Brown, 1988).

SELF-PRESENTATION BIASES

In many circumstances patients may be motivated to present themselves in a particular light. In some cases, such as those involving custody and access assessments or assessments to determine the suitability for police training, people may have a desire to downplay any personal problems and to appear as resilient and mentally healthy as possible. In other circumstances, such as when patients are seeking compensation for work or accident-related psychological problems, patients may be inclined to overemphasize their distress and difficulties.

To address these possible biases, most personality inventories designed for clinical use, such as the Minnesota Multiphasic Personality Inventory (MMPI), the Millon Clinical Multiaxial Inventory (MCMI), and the Personality Assessment Inventory (PAI), include "validity scales." Generally speaking the scales focus on three possible tendencies that could distort the answers given by test-takers: emphasizing positive characteristics ("faking good"), **malingering** or emphasizing negative characteristics ("faking bad"), and inconsistent or random responding to test items. Later in the chapter, we will briefly describe the evidence for the validity of these validity scales when we present information on these inventories. Other tests are specifically designed to evaluate possible malingering. The Test of Memory Malingering (Tombaugh, 1997), for example, was designed to assess whether an individual with established or suspected neurological impairments is exaggerating his or her memory deficits. This test has been demonstrated to be highly accurate in detecting attempts to simulate memory problems (Rees, Tombaugh, Gansler, & Mocyznski, 1998).

To avoid the problem of intentional misrepresentation, many clinical psychologists have advocated the use of projective personality tests, arguing that their ambiguous nature makes it difficult for clients to exaggerate or minimize psychological problems. The many studies on this issue have yielded inconclusive findings. In one study, Meisner (1988) instructed half of the sample of nondepressed undergraduate student participants to act as if they were depressed when responding to psychological tests. To assist them in this, he also provided them with a clinical description of depression and offered a cash incentive for convincingly displaying depression. Compared with the control group participants who completed the measures in an honest manner, those in the malingering condition had higher scores on the Beck Depression Inventory (a symptom checklist) as well as on several Rorschach indices of depression (a projective personality test). In contrast, Bornstein, Rossner, Hill, and Stepanian (1994) found that, when instructed to deliberately present as dependent or independent, undergraduate student participants could do so effectively on a self-report measure of dependency but not on a Rorschach dependency scale.

DEVELOPING CULTURALLY APPROPRIATE MEASURES

Given the multicultural nature of most countries, personality measures must be relevant and unbiased across cultural and ethnic groups. Unfortunately, few measures, with the possible exception of the MMPI (Butcher, 2004; Hall & Phung, 2001), have evidence of relevance and lack of bias across cultural and ethnic groups. Malgady (1996) proposed a radical change in the ways that clinical psychologists react when there is a paucity of research evidence. Rather than approaching these issues in the usual way that null hypotheses are generated—that no bias or differences exists—he argued that both practitioners and researchers should assume that measures *are* culturally biased unless there are data to suggest the opposite.

Tests can be biased or unfair in several ways. First, the test content may not be equally applicable or relevant to all cultural groups. Test items that accurately capture the essence of the underlying psychological construct for one cultural group may not be as appropriate for other cultural groups. In an early study on the influence of ethnicity on responses to the California Personality Inventory, for example, Cross and Burger (1982) found that African American and European American university students responded differently on more than a third of the test items. Second, the pattern of validity coefficients may not be similar across groups. For example, an association between a negative attribution style and depressive symptoms may be much larger for one group than for another.

Third, the use of a cut-off score on a scale to classify individuals may not be equally accurate across groups. As described in Chapter 5, many personality inventories use *T* scores (i.e., scores based on group means and standard deviations) of 65 or 70 to determine whether an individual's responses fall outside the normal range. Bias related to cut-off scores could mean that those in certain cultural and ethnic groups could be either over- or under-identified as having scores in the clinical range. Using the California Personality Inventory, Davis, Hoffman, and Nelson (1990) found that Native American women, compared with European American women, scored much higher on measures of passivity and assistance seeking. A clinical psychologist using this test with a Native American woman would, therefore, need to consider the impact of cultural influences when

Personality measures must be relevant and unbiased across cultural and ethnic groups.

interpreting the meaning of the obtained test scores. A fourth form of bias could occur with respect to the test's underlying structure. Researchers frequently use a statistical procedure called factor analysis to explore exactly how components of a construct relate to each other. For example, a measure of anxiety may have a factor structure that has cognitive and physical components for one group and only a physical component for another. If this pattern of results occurred, it would mean that the test is actually tapping different constructs in the two groups.

Few studies examine all of these possible forms of bias although it is common for researchers to test for more than one form. Blumentritt and VanVoorhis (2004), for example, tested for bias in the Millon Adolescent Clinical Inventory (MACI), a widely used self-report measure of adolescent psychopathology. In their sample of Mexican American youth, they found that the inventory had good reliability and construct validity. They also found that the cut-off scores used to determine clinical range scores provided information consistent with other available clinical data on their participants.

It may be necessary to alter self-report measures or to develop specific test norms if they are to be useful in assessing minority groups (Geisinger, 1994). These suggestions have substantial merit, but require that researchers conducting such studies know the types of variables that may influence the relation between culture and psychological test scores. Recommendations by Alvidrez, Azocar, and Miranda (1996) of the types of issues that must be considered when addressing ethnicity or culture in psychological research are presented in **Table 8.1**.

TABLE 8.1   Assessing Ethnicity and Culture in Psychology Research

Define Ethnicity and Culture

- Avoid overly broad researcher-generated definitions that may miss important subgroup differences.

- Allow participants to self-identify their cultural group and their parents' country of origin.

Examine Factors That May Confound the Role of Cultural Status

- Obtain information from participants about their experiences with respect to minority status (defined as the designation of members of particular groups as inferior or unwelcome).

- Obtain information from participants about their socio-economic status, income, and education.

Examine Information on Migration Experiences

- Obtain information from immigrant and refugee participants on their migration experiences. This includes factors that can affect psychosocial functioning, such as trauma, separation from social networks, loss of possessions, and unfamiliarity with the new cultural environment.

Examine Acculturation

- To evaluate the acculturation of research participants, researchers should use separate dimensions of exposure-adherence to traditional culture and exposure-adherence to the dominant culture.

Adapted from Alvidrez, Azocar, and Miranda (1996).

THE CLINICAL UTILITY OF SELF-REPORT AND PROJECTIVE MEASURES

Against the backdrop of challenges we described in the preceding sections, just how useful are self-report and projective measures in practice? The research base for personality measures and behaviour/symptom checklists is simply staggering in size, involving many tens of thousands of published studies. There is replicated, cumulative research on scores of personality traits and behaviour/symptom profiles that has greatly advanced our knowledge of human functioning. Whether the construct is state anxiety, sensation-seeking, ego strength, dependency, or optimism, psychologists have a wealth of empirical evidence to draw upon in understanding individual differences in human experience. In considering the impact of this research, it is essential to distinguish between basic and applied perspectives. In terms of the goals of basic research, our knowledge of personality has grown enormously in the past few decades. We now know a great deal about the manner in which personality traits are expressed and the ways in which they are reciprocally influenced by the person's life circumstances (Mischel, 2004; Mischel et al., 2004).

Addressing the applied value of this research literature is a different matter. Simply because psychologists know a great deal about personality determinants, structure, and expression it does not follow that all (or any) of this knowledge is useful in making changes in people's daily functioning. Instead there must be firm evidence that the measures, and the research on the measures, have clinical utility. Hunsley and Bailey (1999) defined **clinical utility** in three distinct and increasingly stringent ways. The simplest and least stringent approach to determine a measure's clinical utility is to see whether it is found useful by clinical practitioners. A second approach to clinical utility focuses on whether there is replicated evidence that the measurement data provide reliable and valid information about clients' psychological functioning. The third and most stringent definition of clinical utility requires that the use of the test and the resulting data improves upon typical clinical decision-making and treatment outcome. In other words, does using the measure eventually make a difference in terms of the client's functioning?

According to the first definition of clinical utility, it is indisputable that self-report and projective tests are seen as critical for general clinical practice. **Table 8.2** summarizes surveys of APA accredited clinical training programs (Childs & Eyde, 2002), APA accredited internships (Clemence & Handler, 2001), and clinical psychologist members of the APA (Camara, Nathan, & Puente, 2000) with respect to the most commonly taught or used psychological tests. In all three surveys, the Wechsler intelligence tests were consistently seen as the most important measures in clinical practice. However, as illustrated in Table 8.2, there is also remarkable consistency among endorsements of the self-report and projective measures. Among self-report personality measures, knowledge of the various versions of the MMPI and the MCMI was seen as essential. Two projective personality tests, the Rorschach inkblot test and the Thematic Apperception Test (TAT), were consistently ranked as being among the most important measures for students and practitioners. One self-report symptom checklist, the Beck Depression Inventory (BDI), was viewed as being important for both internship training and general clinical practice.

TABLE 8.2   Rank Ordering of Self-Report and Projective Measures among All Clinical Tests

Test	Taught in Clinical Graduate Courses[a]	Recommended for Internship[b]	Used by Clinical Psychologists[c]
MMPI	3	2	2
MCMI	8	8	10 (tied)
BDI	--	4	10 (tied)
Rorschach	4	3	4
TAT	5	5	6

[a]Childs & Eyde (2002); [b]Clemence & Handler (2001); [c]Camara, Nathan, & Puente (2000)

Let's move now to the second definition—whether there is evidence that the test can provide reliable and valid information about clients. Again, voluminous data indicate that many self-report tests and some projective tests provide psychometrically sound information. Some examples from the comprehensive report on psychological testing by Meyer and colleagues (2001) illustrate this point. These researchers drew data from more than 125 meta-analyses to illustrate the validity of a number of psychological tests. As we mentioned in Chapter 4, effect sizes in meta-analysis can be expressed as either differences between groups or as correlation coefficients. Meyer et al. chose to use correlations to present their results and reported the following type of results: thematic apperception scores (using TAT-like stimuli) of achievement motivation and achievement behaviour, $r = .22$; internal locus of control and subjective well-being, $r = .25$; attributions for negative events and depression, $r = .27$; MCMI scale scores and ability to detect depressive or psychotic disorders, $r = .37$; Rorschach-derived dependency scores and dependent behaviour, $r = .37$; MMPI scale scores and conceptually relevant criterion measures, $r = .39$; MMPI Validity scales and detection of known or suspected malingering, $r = .45$.

So what do these numbers mean? Is this good news or bad news? It may be useful to compare them with other validity findings in health care research. Meyer et al. (2001) reported that, for example, traditional electrocardiogram stress tests and coronary artery disease are correlated at $r = .22$, screening mammogram results and detection of breast cancer within a year are correlated at $r = .32$, and conventional dental x-rays and diagnosis of between-tooth cavities are correlated at $r = .43$. So, compared with the usefulness of other health care assessments, the results for many psychological tests are certainly noteworthy. Nevertheless, these results should be viewed with some caution, because in contrast to the situation for many medical or dental tests, there is surprisingly little evidence that psychological test results provide information that actually makes a difference in treatment provision or treatment outcome (Garb, Klein, & Grove, 2002; Hunsley, 2002).

This leads us to the third definition of clinical utility. Unfortunately, even though the need for evaluations of clinical utility has been apparent for many years (e.g., Mash, 1979) there are limited data supporting the clinical utility of psychological tests (Nelson-Gray, 2003). The only tools with broad supporting evidence of their utility are behaviourally oriented assessment strategies that rely on idiographic measurement or the use of behavioural checklists (Haynes, Leisen, & Blaine, 1997). Many of the psychological treatments that have been demonstrated to work well rely on behaviour and symptom checklists in assessing patient characteristics and experiences. It would be reasonable to assume, therefore, that these checklists have substantial clinical utility. Yet there is little research that has examined the degree to which these measures are really necessary for the success of these treatments. Indeed, the same can be said of the most commonly used personality tests. Despite decades of validity research and frequent clinical use, there is no scientific evidence that results from even the MMPI or the Rorschach have a meaningful impact on the outcome of psychological services (Hunsley & Bailey, 2001).

The fact that there is currently little evidence for the utility of self-report and projective tests is of great concern and makes it difficult to justify the need for time-consuming and expensive personality assessments in clinical practice. This gap in the literature could easily be addressed using straightforward research designs. For example, in an experimental design, all patients who are about to receive treatment could complete a personality measure. Half of the therapists would be randomly selected to receive the results of this test and the others would receive nothing. This would allow the researcher to determine whether the test results influence (a) therapists to alter the nature of the treatment offered to clients and (b) the actual outcome of the treatment. Lima and colleagues (in press) used just such a design to examine the value of clinicians' having access to patient MMPI-2 data at the beginning of treatment. They found that having these data available had no impact on the number of sessions patients attended, whether therapy ended prematurely, or overall patient improvement in functioning assessed in the end of treatment.

Over the years, there has been limited data supporting the clinical utility of psychological tests.

SELF-REPORT PERSONALITY MEASURES

In the following sections we present the most commonly used personality inventories in clinical psychology. The original major personality inventory, the Minnesota Multiphasic Personality Inventory, is now available in forms appropriate for adults (MMPI-2) and adolescents (MMPI-A). These inventories provide broad coverage of many clinical syndromes and other characteristics relevant for typical assessment and intervention purposes. Based on a distinct theoretical approach to psychopathology and keyed to *DSM* conditions, the Millon Clinical Multiaxial Inventory-III (for adults) and the Millon Adolescent Clinical Inventory (for adolescents) are frequently used by clinicians because of their emphasis on personality styles and disorders. One of the newest multiscale inventories, the Personality Assessment Inventory, is gaining support among clinical psychologists because its main scales are designed to address common *DSM* Axis I and Axis II diagnoses.

MMPI-2 and MMPI-A

BACKGROUND ISSUES

As described in the preceding pages, the Minnesota Multiphasic Personality Inventory (MMPI) and the revised versions of the test, the MMPI-2 (for use with adults) and the MMPI-A (for use with adolescents), are the most commonly taught and used self-report (or objective) personality measures in clinical psychology. The original MMPI was published in 1943 by Starke Hathaway and J. Charnley McKinley based on their test development research at the University of Minnesota Hospitals. Their original goal was to construct a self-report test that could provide accurate information on symptom severity and possible diagnoses for adult patients suspected of having mental disorders. Up until then, assessment data were collected via interviews by hospital staff, which entailed a great deal of time, effort, and expense. Also, as you may remember learning in Chapter 6, inter-rater reliability for unstructured interviews is generally poor. In developing the MMPI, the researchers relied on a test construction strategy known as an **empirical criterion-keying approach**, which involves generation and analysis of a pool of items. Items are retained if they discriminate between two clearly defined groups (in this case patients with mental disorders and a comparison group made up of patients' friends and family members, recent high school graduates, and patients with medical disorders). First, they established a pool of 1,000 items from existing personality tests, clinical reports, and other sources of clinical information. Following data analyses of group differences in item responses, almost 500 items were eliminated. With the later inclusion of scales measuring masculinity-femininity and social introversion, the final version of the original MMPI consisted of 550 items. Within years, the MMPI became widely used and researched; the MMPI was also translated and adapted for use in countries outside the United States (Butcher & Beutler, 2003; Groth-Marnat, 2003).

Addressing concerns about the potential for test-takers to either intentionally or unconsciously influence the way in which they answered the items on the test, Hathaway and McKinley developed several scales to assess possible threats to the validity of responses to the MMPI (such as answering in an unrealistically positive manner). Later, concerns were raised about wording problems, the outdated content of some items, the nonrepresentativeness of the original normative comparison group, and the test's technical shortcomings related to the use of empirical criterion-keying methods.

James Butcher headed a project to revise the MMPI that was begun in 1982. The researchers in this project faced a substantial challenge in attempting to (a) improve upon the original test by using better test construction strategies and obtaining representative normative data *and* (b) ensure continuity with the original test by retaining the MMPI's main scales. After some items were updated and a number of provisional new items were added, data were collected from more than 2,500 American adults. Extensive data analysis led to the elimination of some old and some new items, which resulted in the 567-item MMPI-2 (Butcher, Dahlstrom, Graham, Tellegen, & Kaemmer, 1989). The first 370 items on the test contain all of the original validity and clinical scales, with the remaining items providing information for a range of additional scales. Many of these new scales were formed by means of a **content approach** to test construction, which involves developing items specifically designed to tap the construct being assessed.

Many clinical psychologists who were familiar with the MMPI adopted the MMPI-2 slowly and cautiously. Changing from one version to the next involves purchasing new test and scoring materials, as well as learning the interpretation of the new measure. Eventually, despite ongoing criticisms about weaknesses in the test construction procedures used by the restandardization committee (e.g., Helmes & Reddon, 1993), the revised test became even more popular than the original because of its improved content, coverage of psychological symptoms, and standardization sample. The MMPI-2 is now available in more than two dozen languages (Butcher & Beutler, 2003).

Over the years, problems specific to test use with adolescents became apparent: for example, the MMPI was too long for many youth to complete, the reading level was too high, and the norms were not suitable for use in interpreting the scores obtained by adolescents (Groth-Marnat, 2003). This led to the development of the MMPI-Adolescent (MMPI-A; Butcher et al., 1992). This test includes a normative sample of adolescents, fewer items (478) than the MMPI-2, as well as reworded and additional items of particular relevance to youth.

Tables 8.3, 8.4, and 8.5 provide information on the main scales found in both the MMPI-2 and the MMPI-A. As shown in **Table 8.3**, the scales can assess potential biased responding in several ways, by detecting overly negative, overly positive, and careless, random, or otherwise biased responses. **Table 8.4** provides details on the traditional clinical scales that were part of the MMPI and that were retained for the revised tests. **Table 8.5** provides information about the most clinically relevant scales. These so-called Content scales were developed specifically to address some of the test users' needs (such as more thoroughly assessing anxiety and depressive symptoms and having information on factors related to family, work, and treatment contexts).

NORMS, RELIABILITY, AND VALIDITY

The normative sample for the MMPI-2 consisted of more than 1,400 American women and 1,100 American men. Participants were randomly selected within a sampling frame that was generally representative of the American population in terms of ethnicity, socio-economic status, and geographical location. The only limitation is a slight under-representation of adults with lower education and lower income. Consequently, for these individuals, the cut-off scores for determining the presence of clinical problems may be too low. This means that the test is likely to yield a high number of false positives (i.e., inaccurately identifying substantial clinical problems) in the evaluation of patients of lower socio-economic levels (Nichols, 2001). Clinicians therefore need to be aware of the possible tendency to **overpathologize** (i.e., tend to exaggerate and overestimate the extent of psychopathology) such patients. As for the MMPI-A, the normative sample consists of more than 800 female adolescents and 800 male adolescents who were representative of the American population of adolescents in terms of ethnicity and geographic location. Although there have often been efforts to establish new regional norms when the tests have been translated, there is surprisingly little research on the degree to which the original MMPI-2 and MMPI-A norms are appropriate for English-speaking populations outside the United States.

TABLE 8.3　MMPI Validity Scales

Cannot Say (?): This scale is the total number of unanswered items. A large number of unanswered items indicates defensive responding.

Lie Scale (L): A measure of self-presentation that is unrealistically positive.

Infrequency Scale (F): A measure of self-presentation that is very unfavourable. This can indicate a desire to present oneself as having severe psychopathology *or* it can be an accurate report of substantial distress, disorganization, and confusion.

Defensiveness Scale (K): A measure of unwillingness to disclose personal information and problems. The scores on some of the clinical scales are adjusted based on the test-taker's *K* score.

Back F Scale (FB): Similar to the *F* scale, the items for this scale all occur in the final third of the inventory. The scale measures a possible change in self-presentation, which may be due to a change in test-taking strategy.

Variable Response Inconsistency Scale (VRIN): A number of items have either similar or opposite content. The *VRIN* measures the tendency to answer these item pairs inconsistently and may reflect random or confused responding to the test.

True Response Inconsistency Scale (TRIN): The *TRIN* scale is based on answers to item pairs that are opposite in content. A very high score indicates a tendency to give "True" answers indiscriminately; a very low score indicates a tendency to give "False" answers indiscriminately.

TABLE 8.4　MMPI Clinical Scales

Scale 1 (Hs: Hypochondriasis): Measures the tendency to be preoccupied with one's health and to be unlikely to connect psychological problems to the experience of some physical symptoms.

Scale 2 (D: Depression): Measures common cognitive, physical, and interpersonal symptoms of depression.

Scale 3 (Hy: Hysteria): Measures the tendency to develop physical symptoms when stressed and to minimize the extent of interpersonal problems.

Scale 4 (Pd: Psychopathic Deviate): Measures the tendency toward rebellious attitudes, conflict with authorities and family, and engagement in antisocial activities.

Scale 5 (Mf: Masculinity-Femininity): Measures gender-stereotyped interests, beliefs, and activities.

Scale 6 (Pa: Paranoia): Measures interpersonal sensitivity, feelings of being mistreated, and, at the extreme, delusions of persecution.

Scale 7 (Pt: Psychasthenia): Measures the tendency toward worry, apprehension, rumination, and fears of loss of control.

Scale 8 (Sc: Schizophrenia): Measures the tendency to withdraw and experience social alienation, feel inferior, and, at the extreme, to experience delusions, hallucinations, and extreme disorganization.

Scale 9 (Ma: Hypomania): Measures the tendency toward hyperarousal, excessive energy, low frustration tolerance, and agitation.

Scale 0 (Si: Social Introversion): Measures introversion, lack of comfort in social contexts, and overcontrolled style of coping.

TABLE 8.5 MMPI Content Scales

Anxiety (ANX): A measure of general anxiety and worry.

Fears (FRS): A measure of the fear of specific objects, events, and situations.

Obsessiveness (OBS): A measure of indecisiveness and obsessiveness.

Depression (DEP): A measure of depressive symptoms.

Health Concerns (HEA): A measure of general health concerns.

Bizarre Mentation (BIZ): A measure of very peculiar or psychotic thought processes.

Anger (ANG): A measure of anger, aggression, and lack of control.

Cynicism (CYN): A measure of beliefs related to a general lack of trust in people and little faith in their intentions.

Antisocial Practices (ASP): A measure of antisocial attitudes and a history of engaging in antisocial acts such as stealing.

Type A Behavior (TPA): A measure of the Type A personality (i.e., characteristics of impatience, irritability, and being easily annoyed).

Low Self-Esteem (LSE): A measure of general self-esteem.

Social Discomfort (SOD): A measure of social introversion.

Family Problems (FAM): A measure of reported family conflict and the tendency to have characteristics that increase the likelihood of current interpersonal conflict.

Work Interference (WRK): A measure of work-related impairments.

Negative Treatment Indicators (TRT): A measure of negative attitudes toward health care professionals and mental health treatments.

Research on the original clinical scales yielded a wide range of reliability values, with some values being well below an alpha of .80. The median reliability values for the MMPI-2, as reported in the test manual, are .64 for the validity scales and .62 for the clinical scales. The higher median value for the reliability of the content scales, .86, is consistent with the improved approach to test construction used with the content scales. Nevertheless, it is evident that a number of MMPI scales have relatively weak internal consistency. As for test-retest reliability, the data are much more encouraging, with the median values for the validity, clinical, and content scales all exceeding .80.

With respect to validity, it is extremely difficult to meaningfully summarize the voluminous research on the various MMPI scales. Meta-analyses of these scales typically find support for the validity of many scales (e.g., Parker, Hanson, & Hunsley, 1988; Hiller, Rosenthal, Bornstein, Berry, & Brunell-Neuleib, 1999). However, there are so many scales and so many studies that it is necessary to consider cumulative validity data on a scale by scale basis. For example, Gross, Keyes, and

Greene (2000) reviewed the research on the validity of relevant clinical (Scale 2) and content (DEP) scales in predicting depression and found evidence of comparable validity for both scales. Further complicating the task of understanding MMPI validity is that, as we describe next, much of the interpretation of a test score involves a consideration of scale profiles (i.e., validity scale score, the highest two clinical scale scores, and the overall pattern of scores) rather than simply individual scales. **Figure 8.1** is an example of the profile obtained with MMPI validity and clinical scales.

Figure 8.1   MMPI-2™ Basic Service Profile Report

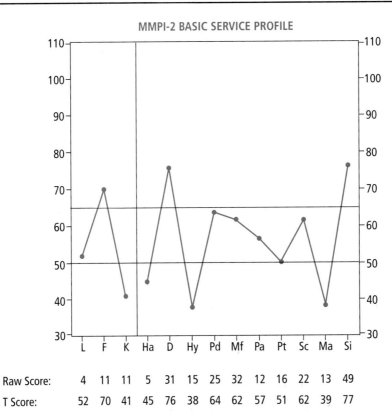

ADMINISTRATION, SCORING, AND INTERPRETATION ISSUES

Administering the MMPI-2 and MMPI-A is relatively straightforward. Nichols (2001) recommended that the assessor provide information on the overall purpose of the assessment and the nature of the MMPI. In providing test instructions the assessor encourages the patient to answer all the questions. Because the test requires reading ability, it is important to ensure that the patient has no visual impairment that interferes with test-taking (severely visually impaired patients typically use an audiotaped version of the test). The test requires reading comprehension at the Grade 8 or 9 level. Most people complete the test in 1 to 2 hours, although some psychiatric patients may require up to 4 hours.

Several standardized and objective scoring options are available. One option is to have the patient respond to the test using a computer scanning sheet that allows for direct entry and computerized scoring. Alternatively, the completed test response form may be sent to test scoring services that provide interpretive reports based on the patient's response. A third option is computerized administration and scoring (which has the additional advantage of reducing the time usually required to complete the test). The final and most cumbersome option is to hand score using templates available from the test publisher. Evaluators who use hand scoring must check carefully to ensure there are no scoring errors.

The MMPI-2 and MMPI-A provide a wealth of information on the patient's self-presentation, symptoms, severity of distress, personality style, and social functioning (Nichols, 2001). Several options are available to clinical psychologists for interpreting the test data, including interpretation by a test scoring service, the use of MMPI interpretation software, and reference to one of several professional books on the topic (e.g., Greene, 2000; Nichols, 2001). In most instances, psychologists use a combination of these sources of interpretive information.

Interpretation begins with examination of the validity scales to determine the degree to which responses to the clinical and content scales might be affected by response biases. The next stage involves categorizing the test profile into **code types**, which are summary codes for the highest two clinical scale elevations. Interpretive guidelines provide details on the possible meaning of code types, other high clinical scale scores, and high content scale scores. Regardless of the source of the interpretative information, it is imperative that factors related to age, ethnicity, and life context be taken into account when drawing conclusions from test data. Both individual circumstances and generational factors influence the nature of the patient's response. For example, Newsom, Archer, Trumbetta, and Gottesman (2003) found that the MMPI responses of typical adolescents have become more extreme over the past few decades, reflecting shifts in attitudes and experiences rather than increased distress and psychopathology. All guidelines for test interpretation, whether text-based or computer-based, are derived from expert summaries of the research literature, which vary in terms of completeness and accuracy (Butcher, Perry, & Atlis, 2000). Hence, for all these reasons, a computer-generated test report should never be used without careful review and analysis by a clinical psychologist who is knowledgeable about the test's strengths and limitations and about the current status of MMPI research.

Other Clinical Measures of Personality Functioning

THE MILLON MEASURES: MCMI-III & MACI

Personality and psychopathology researcher Theodore Millon has developed a set of personality inventories for use in a wide range of clinical settings. We will focus on two of these measures, the Millon Clinical Multiaxial Inventory-III (MCMI-III; Millon, 1997) and the Millon Adolescent Clinical Inventory (MACI; Millon, 1993). Both measures were developed from Millon's theory of psychopathology, are oriented toward *DSM* diagnostic categories, and contain scales to assess validity, clinical personality patterns, and clinical syndromes.

The MCMI-III is a 175-item true-false self-report measure designed to assess personality styles and disorders (e.g., avoidant personality pattern, passive-aggressive personality pattern, borderline personality pathology) and major clinical syndromes (e.g., mood disorders, anxiety disorders, and substance dependency). It is intended for use with clients seeking mental health services and is not appropriate for use with adults with no psychological problems. Like the MMPI tests, the MCMI-III can be hand-scored or computer-scored. Computer interpretation software or text guidelines (e.g., Strack, 2002) can be used to interpret the test scores, including both the validity indices and the personality and syndrome scales. Normative data for the test are based on responses from almost 1,000 American and Canadian adults with psychiatric diagnoses. The normative sample under-represents ethnic minorities but is otherwise representative in terms of demographic characteristics. A new set of norms based on data from more than 1,600 inmates in correctional facilities is available for use in correctional settings. The internal consistency values are quite variable for the MCMI scales, with most values in the .70 to .90 range; 1- to 2-week test-retest values are typically higher than .80 (Millon, 1997). In developing and validating the third edition of the measure, Millon drew upon research on the previous two editions. Although research has generally supported the validity of the MCMI-III scales, two major concerns are often expressed about the test (e.g., Retzlaff & Dunn, 2003). First, there are concerns about the item overlap among scales (i.e., the same item may appear on more than one scale), which can artificially inflate correlations between scales. Second, due in part to item overlap, it is common for test-takers to have high scores on several scales and, thus, the MCMI-III has a tendency to overpathologize test-takers.

The MACI is a 175-item self-report inventory designed to assess personality styles and disorders (e.g., inhibited personality pattern, dramatizing personality pattern, oppositional personality pattern), expressed concerns (e.g., body disapproval, peer insecurity, family discord), and major clinical syndromes (e.g., eating dysfunctions, anxious feeling, suicidal tendency). It is intended for use with adolescent clients aged 13 to 19 years who are seeking mental health services. Scoring and interpretation options are similar to those described for the MCMI-III. Data from more than 1,000 American and Canadian adolescents were used to develop the test norms. Separate norms are available for young adolescent girls, young adolescent boys, older adolescent girls, and older adolescent boys. Although the psychometric data published with the inventory are encouraging, there has been only limited subsequent research on the inventory (Strack, 2002). Additional research, especially studies conducted by investigators other than the test developer, is crucial for establishing the validity of the inventory. The limited research on the MACI also restricts the extent to which new information can be added to the knowledge base on which interpretation of the inventory is based.

PERSONALITY ASSESSMENT INVENTORY

Another broad-based personality inventory commonly used by clinical psychologists is the Personality Assessment Inventory (PAI; Morey, 1991). The PAI is a 344-item self-report measure designed for use with adults. Although it has many items, it requires only a Grade 4 reading level and can be completed in one hour. The PAI contains validity scales, clinical scales (e.g., somatic complaints, antisocial features, borderline features), treatment-oriented scales (e.g., aggression, stress, treatment rejection), and interpersonal scales (dominance and warmth). It was developed using modern test construction principles with extensive attention to both content validity and discriminant validity. The PAI norms are based on data from 1,000 American adults who were representative of American census data in terms of age, gender, and ethnicity. The overall reliability of the scales is superior to the inventories described thus far. Based on data from the normative sample and samples of more than 1,000 patients and more than 1,000 university students, median internal consistency and test-retest values are above .80. This relatively new inventory has an impressive amount of research supporting the validity of many of the scales. Like the other inventories we have presented, the PAI can be scored by hand or with computer software and interpretations can be based on information in the manual, test interpretation guides (Morey, 1996, 2003), or via computer software. As with the MMPI tests, the interpretation process involves an examination of validity indices, two-point code types, and then individual scales.

Self-Report Measures of Normal Personality Functioning

The self-report inventories we have discussed so far are intended for use with adolescents and adults who are likely to have some impairment in their psychosocial functioning. Some measures, such as the MMPI-A, are intended to provide information to help determine the presence and nature of the distress or disorder whereas others, such as the MACI, are only appropriate for use with individuals who have already been determined to have clinically relevant problems.

A host of inventories focused on normal personality assessment are available for use in clinical practice and research. We will present a few of the most commonly used measures below. These types of measures may be especially appropriate in assessing clients in vocational or counselling contexts,

PROFILE BOX 8.1

DR. PAUL L. HEWITT

Dr. Paul L. Hewitt

I received my Ph.D. in clinical psychology from the University of Saskatchewan. I am a Professor of Psychology in the Department of Psychology at the University of British Columbia in Vancouver, and am registered by the College of Psychologists of British Columbia. My work focuses on treatment of perfectionistic behaviour, personality disorders, interpersonal problems, and depression. My work has yielded more than 100 journal articles and chapters on perfectionism and the negative outcomes of perfectionistic behaviour as well as articles dealing with suicide and anorexia nervosa. I am regularly invited to present my research and clinical work in national and international symposia, workshops, and various media outlets. My current research examines treatment-related aspects of perfectionism, such as help-seeking, treatment process, and treatment outcome; how perfectionism influences suicide behaviour among adults, adolescents, and children; and how perfectionism influences athletic and other creative performance.

What made you choose to become a clinical psychologist?

I have always been fascinated by the complexity of people and their behaviour. This spawned an interest both in research and in clinical work. I became interested in doing research because it became clear to me that others often had explanations for behaviour that frequently were not based on any real evidence. When I read several books on psychotherapy and psychotherapists in high school, this truly captivated me, so I also had a fascination with attempting to treat people's problems.

What is the most rewarding part of your job as a clinical psychologist?

This is a difficult question to answer as there are numerous rewarding aspects of my work. Perhaps first and foremost is the reaction of those patients I have helped in my clinical work. To see the positive changes in individuals' lives—the enhancement of their relationships with others and their increased participation in their own lives—and to receive their heartfelt thanks truly touches me deeply. In addition, to hear from colleagues how my research has helped them to work with their own patients by aiding in understanding certain clinical problems is also extremely rewarding.

What is the greatest challenge facing you as a clinical psychologist?

One of the greatest challenges for clinical psychology is to maintain its scientist-practitioner identity. One the defining aspects of clinical psychologists is that they have both extensive clinical training and extensive research training. This allows them not only to conduct and evaluate research but, perhaps most importantly, provides them with a way of thinking, evaluating, and solving problems that differs from other disciplines.

Tell us about your interest in perfectionism.

My work on perfectionism started when I was an undergraduate doing a paper for a course. I had read a newspaper article about perfectionism and decided to look more closely at the construct and discovered that, although a large number of theorists had ideas and comments about what perfectionism is and what problems it created, there was virtually no research evidence that demonstrated the importance of the construct. In fact, there was only one very small correlational study published at the time. I began to address this issue by conducting some of my own studies, which resulted in an honour's thesis, master's thesis, Ph.D. dissertation, and, finally, a program of research that I have been engaged in ever since. Very generally, my research, in collaboration with numerous very gifted researchers, has focused on defining the multidimensional nature of perfectionism, examining the maladaptive outcomes of the different kinds of perfectionism in adults and children, attempting to provide a theoretical model of perfectionistic behaviour and the difficulties it creates, and, finally, to develop and hone a treatment approach that deals effectively with perfectionism and the attendant difficulties.

How do you integrate science and practice in your work?

My clinical work and research are very closely intertwined, mainly because both focus on perfectionistic behaviour. My clinical work has generated a multitude of research ideas and hypotheses and truly informs my research program. In addition, based on research findings, I have certainly altered my treatment approach over the years, but perhaps most importantly I have come to have a greater understanding of how perfectionism works in creating and maintaining difficulties, which aids tremendously in a treatment context.

What do you see as the most exciting changes in the profession of clinical psychology?

I would have to say that the return of the acceptance of more complex models of human behaviour is a very exciting change. Although parsimony is always the goal of research on human behaviour, at times, striving for parsimony lends itself to missing or not truly acknowledging how complex and multilayered people's behaviour is. We see more and more models incorporating what can be described as traditional concepts or ideas along with newer ideas. This synthesis, I believe, does pay homage to the multifaceted nature of human behaviour.

in which the goal of the assessment is to obtain data to help improve or optimize the client's adjustment, rather than to treat a mental disorder. For example, in dealing with a common event such as the ending of an intimate relationship, a person may seek psychological services as an aid to understanding what went wrong in the relationship and what could be done to enhance relationship functioning in the future. It may be advantageous in such a case for the psychologist to provide the client with research-based feedback on their personality as part of a discussion about personal preferences and styles that the client may wish to consider altering through treatment or through their own efforts. It is worth noting that, because of the focus on normal personality functioning, these types of inventories rarely include the types of validity scales that are common in the inventories we reviewed in the previous sections.

The California Psychological Inventory (CPI; Gough & Bradley, 1996), now in its third edition, is a 434-item inventory with a similar structure to the MMPI. In fact, roughly one-third of the CPI items also appear on the MMPI-2. Unlike the MMPI, though, the CPI largely focuses on normal interpersonal patterns and skills and is composed of scales that measure constructs such as dominance, empathy, tolerance, and flexibility. The research base for the CPI is enormous, involving more than 2,000 studies (Groth-Marnat, 2003). The inventory's norms and psychometric values are all generally acceptable and substantial information is available to assist clinicians in the use and interpretation of the CPI (e.g., Megargee, 2002).

The NEO Personality Inventory–Revised (NEO PI-R; Costa & McCrae, 1992) is based on the five-factor model of personality that is generally seen as the most scientifically supported personality theory (Wiggins & Trapnell, 1997). It is a 240-item test that measures the personality factors of neuroticism, extroversion, openness, agreeableness, and conscientiousness. The norms are based on data from more than 1,500 American adults. The internal consistency values for the factors all exceed .85, as do the 6-month test-retest reliability values. Validity data reported in the test manual provide extensive evidence for the factor scores. Because the factors assessed by the inventory tap the basic structure of personality, the evidence base for the inventory's validity continues to grow, with many studies on the NEO PI-R appearing each year.

The Myers-Briggs Type Indicator (MBTI; Myers & McCaulley, 1985) is a self-report personality test based on Jung's personality theory. This theory posits four basic personality preferences that are operationalized in the MBTI as bipolar, continuous constructs: extraversion-intraversion (oriented outwardly or inwardly), sensing-intuition (reliance on sensorial information versus intuition), thinking-feeling (tendency to make judgements based on logical analysis or personal values), and judgement-perception (preference for using either thinking-feeling or sensing-intuition processes for interacting with the world). Based on scores across these four preference dimensions, clients' test results are categorized into one of 16 different personality type categories. The MBTI is available in versions of different lengths and has been translated and normed in many languages. There are hundreds of studies relating the MBTI scores to a range of personality, educational, and vocational constructs. Most of this research uses data from the four preference dimensions. Unfortunately, as clinicians rarely use the four preference dimensions, this research has little relevance to the applied use of the test. Clinicians tend to base interpretations on the personality type revealed by test results. Because of the very limited research base on the reliability and validity of these 16 personality types and because research suggests only minimal correspondence between the MBTI and other personality measures, there are significant concerns about the validity of the test as it is used in clinical practice (Hunsley, Lee, & Wood, 2003).

SELF-REPORT CHECKLISTS OF BEHAVIOURS AND SYMPTOMS

Although traditionally most training in clinical assessment emphasized self-report personality inventories and (possibly) projective tests, current assessment practices of many clinicians reflect an important shift that involves less reliance on time-consuming broad-based tests (such as personality inventories and projective measures) and a greater use of self-report checklists of

behaviours and symptoms (Groth-Marnat, 1999; Mash & Hunsley, 2004; Piotrowski, Belter, & Keller, 1998). These changes are fuelled by a number of factors including changes in the reimbursement practices of insurance companies and health care organizations with respect to psychological assessments conducted as part of treatment provision (e.g., Stout & Cook, 1999) and clinicians' awareness of and demand for measures that aid in the formulation and evaluation of psychological services (Barkham et al., 2001; Bickman et al., 2000; Groth-Marnat, 2000).

As we discussed in the earlier section on clinical utility, there is very little evidence that traditional psychological assessments actually lead to better clinical outcomes. In the absence of compelling evidence of clinical utility, psychologists

Current assessment practices of many clinicians reflect a shift to greater usage of self-report checklists of behaviours and symptoms.

must consider the value of the resulting test information in light of the expense of hours spent in administering, scoring, and interpreting self-report inventories and projective tests. In contrast, behaviour and symptom checklists are very inexpensive and have direct and immediate relevance to treatment planning and monitoring. Consider a clinical psychologist who is tracking week by week changes in a patient's bingeing and purging. Based on checklist data, the psychologist is able to determine the success of treatment strategies and, if necessary, to discuss changes in treatment with the patient if there is no symptomatic improvement after several sessions of therapy.

There are literally dozens of well-developed, psychometrically sound checklists; in the following pages we provide only a small sample of the types of measures available to clinical psychologists for both research and clinical purposes. As you will see, some of these checklists cover a range of behaviours and symptoms whereas others are problem-specific or disorder-specific.

Achenbach System of Empirically Based Assessment

The Achenbach System of Empirically Based Assessment (ASEBA; Achenbach & Rescorla, 2000, 2001, 2003; Achenbach, Newhouse & Rescorla, 2004) is a family of questionnaires developed over many years by **Thomas Achenbach**. The original scale, the Child Behavior Checklist, is a standardized questionnaire completed by a child's parents that includes competence items as well as diverse problems. For each item the respondent is required to note whether it does not apply, applies occasionally, or applies frequently (Achenbach & Rescorla, 2001). The Child Behavior Checklist is one of the most widely used measures of child adjustment and has been demonstrated to be reliable and valid over hundreds of studies. Versions are available to be completed by parents of children aged 1.5–5 years and 6–18 years as well as by caregivers and teachers. The Youth Self-Report is a version of the Child Behavior Checklist that is completed by young people aged 11–18 years. Norms based on large national American samples are available for all the child and youth ASEBA measures. The ASEBA scales yield scores in the normal, clinical, or borderline range. Scales yield a total problem score, as well as scores for two broad-band types of problems: internalizing problems and externalizing problems. Internalizing problems relate to distressed feelings, social withdrawal, worry, and sadness. Externalizing problems refer to acting-out and aggressive behaviours. In addition, scores are generated for a number of DSM-oriented scales. Computerized scoring of the ASEBA scales also provides an analysis of the degree of agreement between two raters (e.g., mother and youth), as well as a comparison of their degree of agreement about a problem with that of a normative group. Most recently the ASEBA has expanded to include measures and norms for adults (18 to 59 years; Achenbach & Rescorla, 2003) and older adults (60 to 90 years; Achenbach et al., 2004): these measures are the Adult Self-Report, Adult Behavior Checklist, Older Adult Self-Report, and Older Adult Behavior Checklist.

SCL-90-R

The Symptom Checklist-90-Revised (SCL-90-R; Derogatis, 1994) is probably the most widely used general measure of distress in clinical service delivery settings. It is a 90-item measure with nine subscales that cover a range of symptom dimensions including interpersonal sensitivity, phobic anxiety, and hostility. Respondents are asked to indicate the extent to which they have been distressed by various symptoms over the past two weeks. Norms—although not nationally representative—are available for various groups, including nonpatient adults, nonpatient adolescents, psychiatric inpatients, and psychiatric outpatients. The internal consistency and test-retest reliability values (over 1 week) all exceed .75. The SCL-90-R has been used in hundreds of research studies. Although both the individual subscales and the global indices of distress available for the test have been demonstrated to be sensitive to treatment-related changes, there is considerable evidence that most subscales do not adequately measure the constructs they are designed to assess. Moreover, there is substantial intercorrelation among the subscales and little evidence for the divergent validity of the subscales (Groth-Marnat, 2003). As a result, the SCL-90-R is probably best conceptualized as a brief measure of general psychological distress.

Outcome Questionnaire 45

The 45-item Outcome Questionnaire (OQ-45; Lambert et al., 1996) is an increasingly popular measure for research and clinical purposes. The OQ-45 is composed of three subscales: symptom distress, interpersonal relations, and social role functioning. Taken together these subscales provide a good overview of a client's psychosocial functioning that takes only 5 minutes or so to complete. Because of high interscale correlation, it is probably most appropriate that the total score be used as an indicator of client distress. Although a relatively new measure, there is growing evidence that it is psychometrically strong (e.g., Umphress, Lambert, Smart, Barlow, & Clouse, 1997; Vermeersch, Lambert, & Burlingame, 2000). Designed for measuring therapeutic change, there is substantial evidence that it can accurately assess client progress. Even more importantly, meta-analytic results from more than 2,500 clients indicated that the use of the OQ-45 in monitoring treatment progress can both dramatically improve treatment success rates and reduce the rates of deterioration associated with treatment (Lambert et al., 2003). A version of the measure is also available for use with children and adolescents (Burlingame et al., 2001).

Beck Depression Inventory-II

The Beck Depression Inventory-II (BDI-II; Beck, Steer, & Brown, 1996) is a 21-item checklist with a multiple-choice format (i.e., several response options are available to describe each symptom).

The BDI-II has been identified as a reliable and valid symptom checklist for use with university students.

It is designed to evaluate the severity of depressive symptoms experienced in the past two weeks. Based on normative data, cut-offs are provided to classify the symptoms as minimal, mild, moderate, or severe. Although the BDI-II more closely maps onto DSM criteria than did the original BDI, it does not provide sufficient detail to determine whether a person meets diagnostic depression for a mood disorder. As one of the most frequently used symptom checklists in clinical research, there are studies of its reliability and validity in numerous populations, including psychiatric inpatients, patients with chronic pain, and university students. Although the precise factor structure and validity of the BDI-II varies somewhat across these groups, there is compelling evidence that the measure is a psychometrically strong tool for assessing depressive symptoms in adolescents and adults. It appears, though, that scores can drop appreciably simply due to repeated administration of the test (e.g., Sharpe & Gilbert, 1998). Such findings are concerning, as they indicate that the BDI-II may yield imprecise results when used for treatment monitoring purposes.

Children's Depression Inventory

Similar in content and structure to the BDI-II, the Children's Depression Inventory (Kovacs, 1992) is a self-report checklist designed to evaluate recent (the past one or two weeks) symptoms of depression in children. It has been shown to have good reliability and validity, especially in community samples (Sitarenios & Kovacs, 1999). The research evidence suggests that it does not distinguish between heightened levels of depressive and anxious symptoms, but no depression checklist is particularly good at making this distinction. A meta-analysis revealed no socio-economic status effects in CDI responses, although there may be effects due to ethnicity (Twenge & Nolen-Hoeksema, 2002). Unfortunately, consistent with data from the BDI, there is evidence that repeated testing with the CDI can result in substantial decreases in reported symptoms (Twenge & Nolen-Hoeksema, 2002).

PROJECTIVE MEASURES OF PERSONALITY

A variety of personality instruments used by clinical psychologists fall under the general category of projective measures. What these instruments have in common, and what makes them projective measures, is that the items or stimuli are ambiguous with respect to content and meaning. That is, regardless of whether the measure relies on pictures, colours, incomplete sentences, drawings, or puppets, there is no inherent meaning to the stimulus material, just as there are no obvious right and wrong answers. A core assumption is that the ambiguity of the material requires the individual to make sense of the stimulus and, in the process of doing this, aspects of the individual's personality are revealed. The original concept of projection was developed by Freud and was seen as a type of defence mechanism in which people unconsciously attribute to others undesirable or negative parts of themselves. There is little evidence to support the existence of projection and little doubt that the process involved in responding to projective tests doesn't rely on projection *per se*—rather, the process involves responses being influenced by a person's experiences and personality (Lilienfeld, Wood, & Garb, 2000).

There is some similarity between the methods used with projective measures and some of the techniques now used in cognitive sciences to examine unconscious mental processes (Westen, Feit, & Zittel, 1999). What is lacking, though, in the clinical use of projective measures is the standardization and rigorous attention to scientific principles that are the hallmarks of cognitive science techniques. As we noted in Chapter 1, projective tests such as the Rorschach inkblot test, the Thematic Apperception Test, and projective drawings were not developed in a manner consistent with psychological test construction guidelines. Consequently, most projective tests used in clinical settings do not have standardized administration, scoring, or interpretation guidelines, and only the Rorschach has normative data (Hunsley, Lee, & Wood, 2003).

Projective measures can be subdivided into five broad, but overlapping, categories (Lilienfeld et al., 2000). In the following sections we will present two examples from measures involving association techniques (i.e., those requiring people to report what a stimulus looks like) and construction techniques (i.e., those requiring the individual to produce a story or a drawing; see also **Viewpoint Box 8.2**). Other categories of projective measures are completion techniques (e.g., sentence completion tasks), arrangement/selection techniques (e.g., colour tests that require the rank ordering of preferred colours), and expression techniques (e.g., handwriting analysis). There is no denying the intuitive appeal of many of these techniques. For clinical psychologists with a psychodynamic orientation, projective measures hold a special appeal as they are assumed to provide information on unconscious processes. However, after many decades of research, there is no other assessment topic in clinical psychology as controversial as the use of projective techniques: clinical psychologists are likely to view these tests as indispensable clinical tools, professional embarrassments, or as invalid and potentially damaging measures.

VIEWPOINT BOX 8.2

ARE PROJECTIVE DRAWINGS WELCOME IN THE COURTROOM?

In the United States there has been a great deal of debate about the nature of expert testimony provided by health care professionals in legal cases. Based on a series of rulings in the 1990s, the U.S. Supreme Court established that, to be accepted, the expert testimony must be both scientifically valid and directly relevant to the matter under consideration by a court. To aid lower courts in determining the scientific validity of the testimony, the Supreme Court set out four criteria that must be met: (1) the theory or technique must be scientifically evaluated, (2) the theory or technique must have been reviewed by experts prior to its publication in professional journals, (3) the scientific community must have generally accepted the theory or technique, and (4) the theory or technique must have a known error rate and there must be standards in place to control the operation of the technique (Lally, 2001).

Survey data indicate that projective drawings of houses, trees, people, or families are commonly used by many psychologists in clinical practice. Given the evidence of their widespread use, Lally (2001) set out to determine whether projective human figure drawings meet the Supreme Court's criteria for a scientifically valid technique. To do this he began by categorizing the projective drawing tests into one of three groups based on the method used to interpret the drawings. The first group involved interpreting the drawings based on global impressions, with little or no formal scoring. Lally noted that this appeared to be the most commonly used interpretation method. The second group involved scoring criteria that linked specific aspects of a drawing to personality characteristics or diagnoses. The final group of tests relied on scoring criteria for the frequency with which multiple indicators of pathology were found in a drawing (as opposed to the interpretation of single indicators, as used in the second group). Lally then reviewed test manuals and the research literature to determine the nature of the scientific evidence for each scoring method.

Turning first to the *global impression* approach, Lally found little evidence of scientific validity. Although there are publications in peer-reviewed journals that used this scoring approach (the second criterion), he argued that the technique cannot really be evaluated *per se* (the first criterion). In the literature Lally reviewed, he found that errors in interpretation were consistently seen as mistakes made by the psychologists involved, rather than as evidence that the method itself was faulty. In other words, no amount of negative evidence could shake the faith of advocates of the global impression method. Accordingly this scoring approach failed the first criterion for acceptable expert testimony.

The *single sign* and the *frequency of pathological indicators* approaches fared somewhat better in Lally's analysis. Studies have been published in peer-reviewed journals and, at least occasionally, negative evidence has been taken by clinicians and researchers to mean that there may be flaws in the scoring methods (criteria two and one, respectively). At least some of these approaches use standardized administration procedures, which partly addresses the fourth criterion. However, neither scoring approach has been generally accepted by the scientific community (the third criterion). The other part of the fourth criterion—information on the error rates associated with these scoring methods—requires information on inter-rater reliability and discriminant validity. Lally found that there is insufficient evidence to determine just how accurate the single sign approach is, but there is possibly sufficient evidence for the frequency approach.

Based on his analysis, Lally concluded that neither the global impression nor the single sign approach to human figure drawing meets legal standards for admissibility. As for the frequency approach, he suggested that it partially meets the Supreme Court criteria and with additional research could meet more criteria. In Lally's own words "(a)lthough their validity is weak, their conclusions are limited in scope, and they appear to offer no additional information over other psychological tests, it can at least be argued that they cross the relatively low hurdle of admissibility (p. 146)."

With these conclusions in mind, imagine that you are a client who is told by a psychologist that the clinical interpretations based the drawings you just completed have only limited validity and questionable usefulness. Wouldn't you be concerned about the accuracy of the psychologist's interpretations? Would you want to continue services with this psychologist? Don't you think that clients deserve services that meet the highest standard of care, not just the "low hurdle of admissibility?"

Rorschach Inkblot Test

The Rorschach inkblots, developed by Swiss psychiatrist Hermann Rorschach, consist of 10 cards, each containing symmetrical inkblots, some coloured and some in black and white. Patients are asked to report what they see in these ambiguous stimuli. For much of the 20th century, several distinct approaches to the administration and scoring of the Rorschach existed, and many clinicians tended to use elements of different systems and to "personalize" the scoring and interpretation of the Rorschach based on their own experiences. However, John Exner's Comprehensive System (CS; Exner, 1993) is now considered the principal scoring system for the Rorschach. To his credit, Exner has always insisted that the Rorschach must meet the standards expected of a psychological test.

The Rorschach is a very complex measure to administer, score, and interpret. The CS offers very clear information on administration and scoring, with extensive tables and computer software available to aid the interpretation of the test results. Directions specify the seating arrangements, the instructions to be given to examinees, the sequence of card administration, as well as permissible responses to examinee questions. Unfortunately, research indicates that even if these standards are followed, relatively innocuous contextual factors in Rorschach administration, such as the layout of the testing room and the appearance of the assessor, affect the responses produced by examinees (Masling, 1992).

Since developing the CS, Exner has published norms for different age groups that have become a cornerstone of the system's scientific basis (e.g., Exner, 1993). For the adult norms, convenience sampling strategies were used to obtain Rorschach protocols from approximately 1,300 volunteers over a 20-year period. From this pool, 700 protocols were selected in an attempt to match key demographic variables reported in the 1980 U.S. census. Although members of some minority groups were included in this selected sample, this is not sufficient to ensure that the norms are relevant for the clinical use of the Rorschach with members of minority groups (Gray-Little & Kaplan, 1998).

A major problem for the CS norms is the likelihood that nonpatient norms overpathologize normal individuals—a phenomenon found for both child and adult samples (Wood, Nezworski, Garb, & Lilienfeld, 2001). The extent of this problem is vividly apparent in Hamel, Shaffer, and Erdberg's (2000) study involving data from 100 children who were selected for the absence of psychopathology and behaviour problems based on historical information and assessment of current functioning. When the Rorschach data from these children were scored and interpreted according to CS norms, a considerable number of children scored in the clinical range on Rorschach indices of psychopathology. As the authors wrote (p. 291): "(T)hese children may be described as grossly misperceiving and misinterpreting their surroundings and having unconventional ideation and significant cognitive impairment. Their distortion of reality and faulty reasoning approach psychosis. These children would also be described as having significant problems establishing and maintaining interpersonal relationships and coping within a social context." According to the interpretation of their responses to the Rorschach inkblots, these children sound very troubled, but remember—none of these children had had psychological problems in the past, none were currently experiencing psychological distress, and all were doing very well in school and in social activities.

Moving now to issues of scoring reliability, Acklin, McDowell, Verschell, and Chan (2000) reported inter-rater reliability values for most CS scores, for both normal and clinical samples. The median reliability value was slightly above .80, thus indicating (as with some of the self-report personality inventories described previously) that many, but not all scores meet the level commonly seen as indicative of good reliability. Of concern, Guarnaccia, Dill, Sabatino, and Southwick (2001) found that both graduate students and practising psychologists made numerous errors in scoring Rorschach data. These errors were so extensive that the overall mean accuracy in scoring the major components of the CS was only 65%!

The literature on the validity of the Rorschach, in general, and the CS, in particular, is so large that it is impossible to review it within a few paragraphs. There have been very heated debates over the past 50 years about the quality of Rorschach research and its adequacy for supporting the widespread clinical use of the test. A number of clinical psychology journals, such as *Psychological Assessment* (Meyer, 1999, 2001), have published special sections on this topic. Some general conclusions can be drawn, however, about the scientific status of the Rorschach. For example, global meta-analyses of Rorschach validity (Parker et al., 1988; Hiller et al., 1999) have demonstrated that some Rorschach scales have reasonable

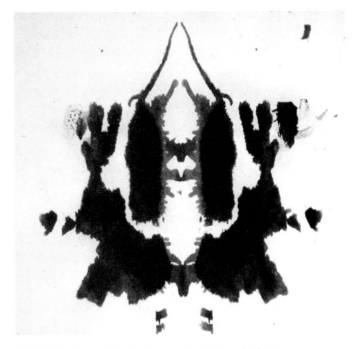

An inkblot pattern similar to those used in the Rorschach test.

validity, although typically lower than that found for MMPI scales. There is consensus that the Rorschach should not be used to provide diagnostic information. Wood, Lilienfeld, Garb, and Nezworski (2000) reviewed more than 150 studies on the use of the Rorschach and diagnoses of mental disorders and found almost no evidence that the Rorschach could consistently detect major depressive disorder, post-traumatic stress disorder, antisocial personality disorder, or many other psychiatric diagnoses. On the other hand, even the harshest critics of the Rorschach agree that the test can provide valid information about intelligence and thought disorder, although evidence of validity does not suggest that the Rorschach is necessarily the best method to assess these constructs (Wood, Nezworski, & Garb, 2003).

The Rorschach is likely to have some continuing value in research examining personality structure and correlates. However, as we have emphasized throughout the text, clinical psychologists have a responsibility to evaluate their assessment and treatment services in light of professional standards and scientific evidence. As we discuss in the next chapter, even when used with other measures, the Rorschach is likely to overpathologize patients. The evidence of both substantial problems with scoring accuracy and the significant limitations of the norms suggest that the Rorschach simply has too many shortcomings to be clinically useful. The potential for harming patients is likely to outweigh whatever assessment benefits may come from using Rorschach data.

Thematic Apperception Test

The Thematic Apperception Test (TAT; Murray, 1943) is a projective measure composed of 31 cards. The person being assessed is asked to tell stories about pictures printed on cards. The principle underlying the TAT is that, in creating these stories, the dominant needs, emotions, and conflicts of the person's personality are revealed. Moreover it is assumed that at least some aspects of personality cannot be assessed by self-report, as they may not be consciously accessible to the person being assessed. Although the TAT was the first apperceptive measure developed, there are a number of other such measures, including some designed for use with children, the elderly, and minority groups (Bellak & Abrams, 1997; Constantino, Malgady, Rogler, & Tsui, 1988).

There is little survey information available on the extent to which practitioners follow or modify the original instructions developed by Murray for the TAT. What is clear, though, is that there is little consistency across clinicians and researchers in terms of how many cards are used in an assessment, which cards are used, the order in which the cards are presented, the instructions used in administering the test, and the scoring and interpretive principles used with the test (Groth-Marnat, 2003; Keiser & Prather, 1990). Unlike the Rorschach, there is no single dominant scoring system and no norms are available for the measure. Even ardent proponents of the TAT admit that most clinicians using the TAT have abandoned a scientific approach to its use (Rossini & Moretti, 1997). Given this, any psychometric data on the measure available in the research literature are irrelevant to determining its actual reliability and validity as it is used by clinical psychologists. The current clinical status of the TAT is, therefore, best characterized as a measure that is taught and used in a manner that ignores scientific and professional standards (Hunsley et al., 2003).

The neglect of science in the routine clinical use of the TAT is very unfortunate. Most importantly, for those assessed with the TAT, there is absolutely no evidence to support the validity of the conclusions drawn by the psychologist. Nevertheless, there is substantial research to suggest that standardized apperceptive methods have the potential to provide valid personality information. For example, using selected TAT cards and adding other specially developed picture stimuli, McClelland and colleagues conducted a programmatic series of studies on achievement, power, and affiliative needs. The results of this research provided compelling evidence that, by using a standard set of cards and empirically supported scoring criteria, data from the modified TAT often outperformed self-report measures in predicting subsequent behaviour (McClelland, Koestner, & Weinberger, 1989; Spangler, 1992). Similarly Westen (1991) developed a psychodynamically oriented scoring system for TAT responses that focuses on the assessment of interpersonal relations (e.g., the complexity of representations of people, the capacity for emotional investment in relationships, and the understanding of causal factors in social relations). Using a detailed scoring manual and data from five to seven TAT cards, high inter-rater reliability has been obtained in several studies for this system and data from both nonpatient and patient samples have provided evidence of convergent validity with a range of self-report, interview, and other projective measures (Westen, 1991). Such findings with a carefully designed and validated scoring system stand in stark contrast to the repeated negative finding in the literature that many approaches to scoring the TAT are incapable of differentiating between research participants with mental disorders and those with no mental disorders (Lilienfeld et al., 2000). Although potentially useful systems are used in research contexts, they have not been adopted in clinical practice.

SUMMARY AND CONCLUSIONS

The self-report and projective measures described in this chapter represent some of the key measures within the clinical psychologist's kit of assessment tools. In graduate training, psychologists learn how to administer, score, and interpret various instruments that are used in the objective assessment of personality and in projective assessment. Although the scoring of objective assessment measures is more standardized and straightforward than the scoring of projective measures, it is not immune from administrative errors that can distort scores. In the interpretation of both objective and projective personality assessment measures, clinical psychologists are faced with a complex array of interpretation methods that vary in their degree of empirical support. The important advances in research on personality have not been reflected in comparable advances in the clinical assessment of personality. Perhaps the most important shift in recent years has been the recognition of the need to determine the suitability of measures developed in one population for use with another population. In addition to issues of standardization, reliability, validity, and norms, we must add the criterion that a test must be shown to be reliable and valid for the population in which it will be used. Without attention to these issues, there is a danger that psychological tests will overpathologize and have iatrogenic effects. A more fundamental question relates to the clinical utility of assessment tools. Although limited utility data are available, there is growing recognition of the usefulness of cost-effective, brief measures that allow tracking of symptoms in treatment planning and monitoring.

Critical Thinking Questions

What are the main differences between objective personality tests and symptom checklists?

How do some tests overpathologize test-takers and why is that a problem?

How can we ensure that tests are culturally sensitive?

What are criteria by which we can judge whether a test is useful?

What are the shortcomings of current practice in projective assessment?

K e y   T e r m s

behaviour checklists

clinical utility

code types

content approach

empirical criterion-keying approach

malingering

objective personality tests

overpathologize

personality traits

person-situation debate

projective personality tests

symptom checklists

K e y   N a m e s

Thomas Achenbach

James Butcher

John Exner

Starke Hathaway

J. Charnley McKinley

Theodore Millon

Walter Mischel

ADDITIONAL RESOURCES

Journals

Assessment

Journal of Clinical Psychology

Journal of Personality Assessment

Journal of Psychopathology and Behavioral Assessment

Psychological Assessment

Book

Wood, J. M., Nezworski, M. T., Lilienfeld, S. O., & Garb, H. N. (2003). *What's wrong with the Rorschach? Science confronts the controversial inkblot test.* New York: John Wiley & Sons.

Websites

MMPI-2, the publisher's site: http://www.pearsonassessments.com/tests/mmpi_2.htm

MMPI-A, the publisher's site: http://www.pearsonassessments.com/tests/mmpia.htm

MCMI-II, the publisher's site: http://www.pearsonassessments.com/tests/mcmi_3.htm

MACI, the publisher's site: http://www.pearsonassessments.com/tests/maci.htm

PAI, the publisher's site: http://www.parinc.com/product.cfm?ProductID=148

ASEBA, the publisher's site: http://www.aseba.org/

CHAPTER 9

Assessment: Integration and Clinical Decision-Making

INTRODUCTION

In Chapter 5 we described some of the general issues in psychological testing and assessment. Psychological assessment involves gathering and integrating multiple forms of information from multiple sources and perspectives. Based on the purposes of the assessment and the initial hypotheses to be explored, the clinical psychologist selects the most appropriate assessment methods and tools to conduct the assessment. As the psychologist gains a better understanding of the person (or couple or family) being assessed, additional assessment procedures may be used to narrow or expand the focus of the assessment. In Chapters 6, 7, and 8 we presented information on the most commonly used assessment methods and tools: interviews, observations, intellectual assessment measures, cognitive assessment measures, self-report measures, and projective measures.

It is now time to turn our attention to the final phases of the assessment process, namely the integration of the diverse data collected about the client and the clinical use of the completed assessment. As we described in Chapter 5, the clinical psychologist must examine all the assessment information, consider both consistencies and contradictions in the information, generate final hypotheses about the client, and formulate conclusions or clinical recommendations about the client based on the overall picture emerging from the assessment. These tasks are necessary whether the psychologist is providing an assessment-focused service or an intervention-focused assessment service. In this chapter we consider the process by which psychologists integrate assessment data and the product of this integration. To do this, we will examine research on the process of case conceptualization, threats to the validity of psychological assessments, and the use of assessment reports and feedback about the assessment findings. Because much of the focus of the chapter is on integration of data and addressing factors that can affect the assessment's accuracy, we will use an extended case example to illustrate how clinical psychologists work to achieve an assessment that is comprehensive, accurate, and clinically useful. Our goals are to convey to you both the challenges in integrating assessment data and the potential value for clients of an integrated psychological assessment.

TERESA

We described in Chapter 3 some of the problems that Teresa was experiencing. A new mother who had recently left her nursing career, Teresa reported a number of complaints related to worries about inadvertently injuring other people. These worries began in her work life after hearing media reports about errors in dispensing medication that had led to numerous deaths in hospitals in North America. She became increasingly preoccupied with the possibility of making such an error and spent excessive amounts of time checking and rechecking all of her work. Not surprisingly this led to her becoming very inefficient at work and, consequently, receiving a poor annual evaluation from her supervisor. Teresa tried to follow through on the supervisor's recommendations to work faster, but this led her to become even more concerned about the likelihood of making critical errors. Her anxiety mounted, she became irritable with patients and colleagues, and no longer looked forward to her workday. During her time away from work she became increasingly agitated and anticipated a call from work telling her that one of the patients in her care had died because of a mistake she had made. When Teresa became pregnant she and her husband Jeff decided that the stress she was experiencing at work was simply not worth the effect it was having on her—she quit the job that, only two years previously, she had cared so much about.

Both Teresa and Jeff had noticed that her concerns about hurting other people through inattention had spread to her life outside of work. They had assumed that her worries about hitting someone while driving would disappear once the stress of work was removed from her life. Unfortunately this did not occur. If anything her fears seemed to worsen, for she was frequently worried about how minor alterations in her diet, activities, and emotional state might injure the developing foetus. Although she would have preferred to stop driving altogether, she forced herself to continue driving because Jeff sometimes had business trips away from home.

Preparations for the baby's room and for the birth filled her with dread, for she imagined all the accidents that could occur during the birth and the baby's first weeks of life. Al though the delivery was uneventful and Teresa and Jeff had the help of family members in making the adjustment to their roles as new parents, Teresa became even more anxious and distressed. Teresa worried about the baby's eating and sleeping patterns. She was concerned about her capacity to feed the baby and was anxious that her diet might cause the baby gastric problems. Teresa was also vigilant for risk of sudden infant death syndrome. If she had to leave the baby's room, she turned the baby monitor on and, if she heard the slightest sound, she rushed back to check the baby. Teresa laundered the baby's clothes and bed linens on noticing the slightest mark. Exhausted from giving birth and from looking after a newborn, she spent much of her time when the baby was asleep going over the house to ensure that it was "babyproof." Although the couple had already done this prior to the birth, Teresa was convinced that they had forgotten something. She started using baby gates to block off access to the stairs in the house. The couple argued repeatedly about this, with Jeff pointing out that the baby was only a few weeks old and they were months away from needing to use the gates. Teresa also checked and rechecked all the cabinets in the kitchen, the bathrooms, the laundry room, and even the garage to make sure that all cleaning products, matches, and other hazardous materials were tightly sealed and stored at eye level.

Jeff's concern about his wife's health mounted during the first months after the birth of their child. He saw Teresa's distress and exhaustion grow. Although he felt that she was a wonderful and caring mother, he was starting to worry that her fatigue and distractibility might actually lead her to make the kind of mistake that she dreaded. As her checking for possible problems consumed more and more of her time, her involvement in pleasurable activities diminished and the number of arguments between the couple increased. Following a tearful discussion, Jeff and Teresa agreed she needed to talk to their family physician about her worries.

Teresa and Jeff met with the physician the following week. Ten minutes into their appointment the physician was convinced that the situation they were describing went beyond the typical cautiousness of new parents. She then asked questions about whether Teresa's anxiety was evident in other areas of her life. When she heard the litany of concerns, she knew that Teresa needed to be assessed by a specialist. She asked Teresa if she would be willing to meet with a psychologist who would be better able to diagnose her difficulties and possibly help her overcome them. Teresa quickly agreed to this and the physician said that she would make a referral to a psychologist. The physician then suggested that Jeff check about the extended health benefits he had through his work and, that afternoon, Jeff contacted someone in his company's human resources department and learned that he did have coverage for consultation with a psychologist. The next day the receptionist in the physician's office phoned Teresa to tell her that a referral had been made for her to see a psychologist the following month.

INTEGRATING THE ASSESSMENT DATA

The clinical psychologist has many tasks in integrating data obtained during an assessment. At the simplest level, it requires providing a descriptive account of the client's present psychological functioning. Even this "simple" account is a very complex task for any clinician. Depending on the nature of the assessment, this might involve a consideration of the client's personality structure, level of emotional distress, coping resources, and/or intellectual capacity. In many instances this description includes diagnosis using a classification system such as the *DSM-IV*. As comorbidity

Psychological assessments are conducted to answer a question, for example, determining a person's suitability to return to work.

is common with clinical diagnoses, many clients receive more than one diagnosis and the psychologist must indicate how these diagnoses are related to each other and to the person's overall psychosocial functioning. It is possible for someone to receive one or more diagnoses but to still function well in many life domains. This requires the psychologist to understand the person in his or her social and interpersonal environment. Examining the impact of diagnostic status on global psychosocial functioning is an important aspect of assessments conducted to determine a person's suitability to return to work or a parent's fitness to have primary physical custody of a child, for example.

All assessments are conducted to address a question. The question behind the assessment guides the psychologist in drawing together the various pieces of information available about the client. A question about a client's intellectual capabilities leads to the preparation of a report that highlights general intellectual functioning and more specific cognitive strengths and weaknesses. Emotional and interpersonal factors that affect the client's ability to achieve his or her potential also receive attention in such an assessment, but only after a clear presentation of the client's intellectual skills. On the other hand, an assessment report summarizing data relevant to the question of whether a depressed teacher is able to return to work would have a very different focus and structure. Symptom and diagnostic information would have to be discussed first. After that, the psychologist would address the factors that led to the teacher's burnout, the teacher's motivation and readiness to return to work, and possible impediments (both psychological and interpersonal) that could affect the return to work.

Unlike pieces of a jigsaw puzzle, data obtained in psychological assessments only infrequently fit together smoothly and neatly—rarely does one piece of information perfectly conform to a related piece of information. As described in the previous chapters, it is important for the psychologist to gather information using different methods and, often, from different informants. Yet each source of data has its own strengths, limitations, and potential biases that must be taken into account in when integrating the data and drawing conclusions. Assessments of children and adolescents typically require that, in addition to the information gathered directly from the young client, information is also obtained from significant others such as parents and teachers. In assessing adults, it is less common to obtain data from multiple informants, although for some assessment purposes (such as treatment planning for couples therapy or evaluating the daily impact of dementia on a patient) obtaining information from others can also be critical. **Viewpoint Box 9.1** describes some of the challenges in meaningfully integrating data obtained from different informants.

VIEWPOINT BOX 9.1

WHEN WORLDS COLLIDE (I): INTEGRATING DATA FROM MULTIPLE INFORMANTS

The psychological assessment of children and youth often involves collecting data from multiple informants. For example, in assessing 12-year-old Ahmed, who has been suspended from school for aggressive behaviour, data may be gathered from Ahmed, his parents, and his teachers. When the psychologist inspects the computer-generated profile based on Ahmed's responses, it reveals that he does not consider himself to have any problems with aggression, although he acknowledges feeling sad; in contrast, his father's profile shows that he sees Ahmed as having externalizing problems in the borderline range; his mother's profile indicates that she sees her son as having clinically significant externalizing problems and borderline problems with anxiety and depression; his teacher's profile suggests that she perceives Ahmed as having clinically significant externalizing problems and borderline problems with attention. It sounds as though we have four different descriptions of the same youth. How do we make sense of these apparently conflicting reports? Is Ahmed faking worry and sadness to avoid punishment? Is his father's perspective realistic or is he minimizing the problem? Is the mother realistic or is she over-sensitive to her son's distress? Did the teacher rate the correct child? Which report should the psychologist rely on?

A classic meta-analysis by Achenbach, McConaughy, and Howell (1987) found that such low agreement among informants is the norm rather than the exception. Rich data can be gathered by exploring the reasons for the discrepancies between different people's perspectives on the same person. Differences between raters are influenced by a host of variables including the contexts in which they interact with the person being assessed. For example, working in an academic environment, teachers are skilled in detecting difficulties in attention that parents may not be aware of. Ratings are also influenced by differences in the way the child behaves in each context. Ahmed may behave more aggressively toward women than he does toward men, so his father may have less exposure to Ahmed's aggressive behaviour. There may also be differences in what is considered acceptable behaviour. As sad or worried feelings are more private than are aggressive behaviours, not all adults will know Ahmed's feelings.

The ASEBA family of rating scales that were described in Chapter 8 are the only scales that provide data to assist the psychologist in making sense of discrepancies between raters. When data from different informants are scored, the correlation between different pairs of raters is calculated. The degree of concordance between raters is then compared with normative data on the average degree of agreement. To return to Ahmed, the psychologist might find that although these different raters have discrepant views on Ahmed's behaviour, the degree of agreement is average compared with other 12-year-old boys and their fathers, above-average compared with other 12-year old boys and their mothers, average compared with other mothers and fathers of 12-year-old boys; below average compared with other 12-year-old boys and their teachers; and average compared with other parents and teacher of 12-year-olds.

Combining information from multiple psychological tests or even from multiple scales within a self-report personality test can be a daunting task. Common psychological practice is to begin by examining the client's test responses at the most global level. This would mean, for example, that on the MMPI-2 the psychologist would first consider scores on the various validity scales and then move to examine the MMPI-2 code type (i.e., the highest two scores on the clinical scales). The validity score data allow the psychologist to evaluate the extent to which the other scale scores are likely to accurately reflect the client's personality and psychosocial functioning. With this in mind, the code type information serves as the foundation for generating hypotheses about the client, with other MMPI-2 scales and other sources of assessment data added to this foundation (Lewak & Hogan, 2003). Psychologists must be aware that data from other self-report tests and interviews are not independent sources of information than can be used to confirm initial hypotheses. Whether the client provides information about himself or herself during an interview, on one psychological test, or on many psychological tests, these data sources all represent client self-report. Additional assessment data from sources other than self-report (such as reports by significant others, clinical observation, or archival records such as hospitalization data) have the potential to independently corroborate or nuance hypotheses based on self-report data. However, if all the sources of assessment data are based on what is essentially the same source or form of information (such as different self-report measures completed by the same person) then the apparent convergence of data can lead to misplaced confidence regarding the validity or accuracy of the hypotheses or conclusions (Hunsley & Meyer, 2003).

Consider a situation in which a patient's depressive symptoms are being assessed. During a clinical interview the psychologist asks a number of questions related to symptoms such as sadness, loss of interest, or problems with eating or sleeping. These questions provide important descriptive information about the nature, extent, and severity of the patient's depressive symptoms and yield information that allows the psychologist to diagnose a mood disorder. The patient may also be asked to complete the BDI-II and the MMPI-2. After scoring these tests the psychologist finds that the patient scored in the moderate range of depressive symptom severity on the BDI-II and had clinically significant elevations on both the MMPI-2 clinical and content scales that measure depressive symptoms. The findings from the two psychological tests do not and cannot provide confirmation of a diagnosis of depression, as they are all based on the same source of data as the clinical interview (i.e., the patient's self-report). Of course it is important to know that there is consistency across the measures, but this is not the same as providing independent evidence to confirm a diagnosis. In order to address the potential problem of relying solely on self-report, some psychologists include projective measures in their assessments. Although this seems, on the surface, to be an appropriate approach for gathering assessment data independent of self-report, it is fraught with serious problems. **Viewpoint Box 9.2** deals with the specific difficulties associated in attempting to combine data from projective measures with other assessment data.

VIEWPOINT BOX 9.2

WHEN WORLDS COLLIDE (II): INTEGRATING SELF-REPORT AND PROJECTIVE TEST DATA

In Chapter 5 we reported that, for many decades, the Rorschach inkblot test and the MMPI have been among the most commonly taught and used assessment tools in clinical psychology. Over this same period, the empirical literature on these two measures has been remarkably consistent in demonstrating little or no meaningful relation between the two; even scales supposedly measuring the same construct have little in common (Archer, 1996). For example, Krishnamurthy, Archer, and House (1996) examined the convergent validity of conceptually related MMPI-A and Rorschach scales in a sample of 152 American adolescents. From a total of 237 correlations computed among conceptually related scales, only 8 (or 3.4%) were significantly correlated. Keeping in mind that the error rate typically set for statistical analyses is 5% (i.e., $p < .05$), it is highly likely that these significant correlations were simply due to chance.

In light of this lack of convergent validity, some psychologists have argued that combining MMPI and Rorschach data should lead to better assessments, as each test could contribute independent, non-redundant information to be used in addressing the assessment goals. The question of whether the addition of test data to other assessment information actually improves the outcome of the assessment is one of incremental validity. A number of studies have examined the incremental validity of the two measures relative to each other and, in general, the results suggest that adding Rorschach data to MMPI data does not improve assessment accuracy (Hunsley & Bailey, 1999). For example, using the same sample of adolescents as Krishnamurthy et al. (1996), Archer and Krishnamurthy (1997) reported that in no instance did adding data from a Rorschach variable to that of an MMPI-A scale improve the accuracy of the assessment. Moreover, the MMPI-A scales were consistently the best data to use in obtaining accurate assessment results.

Despite these empirical findings, many psychologists continue to advocate the conjoint use of the two tests in clinical assessments. Finn (1996), for example, suggested that three important outcomes could occur when the two tests are used: (a) the results of the two tests could agree, thus providing strong evidence for the validity of the assessment, (b) the Rorschach could show more disturbance than the MMPI, thus indicating underlying psychopathology in clients, or (c) the MMPI could show more disturbance than the Rorschach, thus indicating that clients are over-emphasizing problems and symptoms in order to draw attention to their situation. In most examples in the clinical literature, though, the dominant emphasis is on the ability of the Rorschach to "detect" psychopathology when the MMPI has failed to do so (e.g., Weiner, 1999). The problem with this stance is that it flies in the face of the empirical evidence regarding the incremental validity of the Rorschach. Most importantly, when psychologists use Rorschach data to augment the findings obtained from MMPI data, they are greatly increasing the likelihood that their assessment results yield false positives (i.e., inaccurately concluding that a problem exists). Remember that, in Chapter 8, we described the study by Hamel, Shaffer, and Erdberg (2000) in which many of the 100 children screened for an absence of psychopathology and behaviour problems were determined to have significant psychological impairments when data from the Rorschach were considered. As the Rorschach is likely to "detect" pathology when in fact no problems exist, there are very real dangers that those assessed with the test will be improperly diagnosed and unfairly described as having clinically significant psychological problems.

Case Formulation

Many assessment questions require the psychologist to go beyond a descriptive account of the client. Often the purpose of the assessment is to provide directions for possible alleviation or remediation of problems. This includes assessments to address educational concerns (e.g., does the client require some form of special education services?), vocational questions (e.g., are the client's career aspirations realistic in light of his or her intellectual abilities, personality, and interests?), rehabilitation services (e.g., does the client need assistance in developing new strategies for daily living to cope with the effects of a severe closed head injury?), and possible referrals for psychotherapy (e.g., are the client's problems amenable to treatment and how motivated is the client to engage in therapy?). In such cases the psychologist needs to formulate hypotheses about how the problems developed and what factors serve to maintain them. Typically the clinical psychologist is also expected to develop a fuller perspective on how the client's current functioning fits with his or her life history and how well the client may be able to function in the future. Then, based on these hypotheses and conclusions, the psychologist provides recommendations of ways to improve the client's functioning. These recommendations frequently, but not necessarily, include suggestions for psychological services. Other suggestions may include obtaining further assessment data from other health care specialists (such as internists, neurologists, or audiologists) or involving health care specialists or other professionals (e.g., teachers, lawyers, and residential care staff) in service planning.

As described in Chapter 5, the term **case formulation** refers to the task of both describing the patient in his or her life context and developing a set of hypotheses that pull together a comprehensive clinical picture in sufficient detail that the psychologist can make decisions about treatment options. **Table 9.1** summarizes the ways in which a good case formulation can aid in planning clinical services. A detailed case formulation is particularly useful when a patient has numerous or complex clinical problems, for it allows the psychologist to make informed decisions about the timing, sequence, duration, and specific focus of interventions (Mumma, 1998; Tompkins, 1999).

TABLE 9.1   The Benefits of Clinical Case Formulations

- Provides a way of understanding the connections between a patient's various problems
- Provides guidance on the type of treatment to consider (including whether the treatment should be conducted in an individual, couple, family, or group modality)
- Predicts the patient's future functioning if treatment is not sought and if treatment is successful
- Provides options to consider if difficulties are encountered in implementing and following through on treatment
- Indicates what options, outside of psychological services, might be worthwhile for the patient to consider
- Provides alternative treatment options to consider if the initial treatment is unsuccessful

Adapted from Persons (1989).

Clinical psychologists of all theoretical orientations use assessment data to develop case formulations. Eells, Kendjelic, and Lucas (1998) found that, across orientations, case formulations tended to include four major components: symptoms and problems, events or stressors that led to the symptoms and problems, predisposing life events or stressors (i.e., pre-existing vulnerabilities), and a hypothesized mechanism that linked the first four components together to offer an explanation for the development and maintenance of the problems and symptoms. **Table 9.2** summarizes the steps that Mariush (2002) suggested all psychologists should follow in developing a case formulation.

TABLE 9.2   Developing a Case Formulation

Step 1. Develop a comprehensive problem list, including the patient's stated problems and other problems indicated by referral agents or identified by other informants during the assessment.

Step 2. Determine the nature of each problem, including its origin, current precipitants, and consequences.

Step 3. Identify patterns or commonalities among the problems; this may yield an indication of previously unidentified factors that serve to maintain, exacerbate, or lessen the problem.

Step 4. Develop working hypotheses to explain the problems.

Step 5. Evaluate and refine the hypotheses, using all information gathered during the assessment and the patient's feedback on the hypotheses.

Step 6. If the psychologist moves from conducting an assessment to providing treatment, the hypotheses should be reconsidered, re-evaluated, and revised (as necessary) based on data gathered during treatment.

Adapted from Mariush (2002).

A major challenge in developing a case formulation is that the psychologist must accurately detect patterns in the wealth of data gathered during an assessment. Even if the assessment is limited to an interview with the client and some self-report measures completed by the client before the interview, detecting patterns is not an easy task. Then, assuming that the psychologist has been able to recognize patterns in the data, he or she must then try to relate these patterns to specific causes and outcomes. We address the challenges of this exercise more fully in the next section. At this point we will illustrate the difficulty of these tasks with one example. O'Brien (1995) presented clinical psychology graduate students with a very limited but clear set of assessment data: daily self-monitoring data (for 14 days) from a client who presented with frequent and severe headaches. Each day of self-monitoring data included information on the client's overall stress level, hours of sleep, interpersonal conflicts, number of headaches, severity and duration of the headaches, and the number of analgesics taken to deal with the headaches. The students' task was to estimate the magnitude of the relation between precipitating factors (such as reduced sleep, high stress, and frequency of arguments) and headache symptoms (such as frequency, severity, and duration). Across the 14 days of self-monitoring data the students were able to accurately detect the factors most highly correlated with symptoms only 50% of the time!

Thus far we have not directly addressed the influence of the clinical psychologist's theoretical orientation in the elaboration of a case formulation. Theoretical orientation plays a central role in all aspects of the assessment process, from the nature of the initial hypotheses made about the client, to the selection of assessment tools, to the manner in which the assessment data are used to build a full clinical picture of the client. Berman (1997) described case conceptualization as having two key features. The first is a succinct analysis of the client's core strengths and weaknesses, which she called the premise. The second is the supporting material, which involves an in-depth analysis of these strengths and weaknesses. Berman indicated that the premise of the case conceptualization is tied to the clinician's theoretical perspective. Indeed, the type of constructs to be included in both the premise and the supporting material are enormously influenced by orientation. Interpersonally oriented psychodynamic case formulations are likely to focus on dysfunctional relationship styles (called "cyclical maladaptive patterns") as the premise for the formulations, whereas process-experiential formulations are likely to use information about the client's emotional processing and insight into emotional issues in developing the main premise (Berman, 1997; Eells, 1997).

Given exactly the same clinical information, clinicians of differing orientations are likely to develop very different formulations. Plous and Zimbardo (1986) found, for example, that in developing hypotheses for the development of psychological symptoms, psychoanalysts emphasized dispositional and personality factors whereas behaviour therapists focused on either situational influences or on the interaction of situational and dispositional influences. Of course, this raises the question of just who is right: unfortunately there is very limited research on the validity of case formulations (Garb, 1997). There is, however, growing research on the reliability of case formulations. This line of research provides evidence on the extent to which clinical psychologists within an orientation are likely to formulate the same case conceptualization for a given patient. Jacqueline Persons has devoted considerable effort to develop an approach to case conceptualization that clinical psychologists can easily learn and use. Her *Cognitive-Behavioral Case Formulation approach* emphasizes the importance of identifying the patient's overt problems (such as psychological symptoms, interpersonal conflicts, or legal problems) and the longstanding beliefs (called "schemas") that, when activated by life events, are believed to cause the overt problems (Persons, 1989). She found that, when presented with detailed case information, clinicians accurately identified about two-thirds of a client's main presenting problems and that the mean inter-rater reliability of patient schemas was $r = 0.72$ (Persons & Bertagnolli, 1999). Similar reliability results have been reported for psychodynamic case conceptualizations that focus on core relationship conflicts (Barber & Crits-Christoph, 1993). Such findings suggest that, within an orientation, there can be considerable similarity in the case formulations developed by clinicians.

TERESA

The clinical psychologist to whom Teresa was referred specialized in providing cognitive-behavioural treatments for anxiety and related problems. Based on the referral from the physician, the psychologist assumed that a major part of the assessment would involve an evaluation of obsessive-compulsive symptoms. However, knowing from the empirical literature that patients who have an anxiety disorder often have a comorbid mood disorder or another anxiety disorder, the psychologist was prepared to assess a full range of potential anxiety and mood symptoms. As people with anxiety disorders often use alcohol or other drugs in an attempt to moderate their symptoms, the evaluation would also cover the possibility of a substance abuse problem. Finally, because individuals with Obsessive Compulsive Disorder (OCD) may not be fully aware of the extent or severity of their problems, the psychologist planned to briefly interview Jeff as part of the assessment. (More details on these assessment issues can be found in McLean and Woody [2001] and Taylor, Thordarson, and Söchting [2002].) An interview with Jeff would also provide an opportunity to determine (a) Jeff's perspective on the extent to which the baby might be in any significant danger because of Teresa's symptoms leading her to neglect or forget about the baby and (b) his willingness to assist in his wife's treatment (with his wife's agreement, of course). Accordingly, based on knowledge of both the psychopathology and treatment literatures, the psychologist planned to use the following assessment tools: an interview with Teresa, an interview with Jeff, self-monitoring diaries with Teresa (and possibly with Jeff), the MMPI-2, the Yale-Brown Obsessive Compulsive Scale (YBOCS; Goodman et al., 1989), the BDI-II, the Penn State Worry Questionnaire (Meyer, Miller, Metzger, & Borkovec, 1990), and the Fear Questionnaire (Marks & Mathews, 1979). Of course, tools might be dropped or added based on the psychologist's initial case formulation following the interviews.

Having reviewed criteria for OCD, major depressive disorder, and generalized anxiety disorder prior to the interview, the psychologist conducted an interview with Teresa that focused largely on her symptoms. Questions were also asked about her understanding of the development of her problems, her efforts to cope with her symptoms, and her concerns regarding the symptoms' effects on her baby and Jeff. After approximately 45 minutes, the psychologist concluded this first interview with Teresa. The importance of using standardized symptoms measures was then explained to Teresa and she was asked to complete the four symptom checklists (not including the MMPI-2) while Jeff was interviewed. During his interview Jeff was asked about how Teresa was coping with her problems, his understanding of her problems, and how his life was affected by Teresa's distress. The psychologist also made a point of asking Jeff how they were both dealing with the demands of being new parents and how Jeff saw Teresa in her role as a mother. After 30 minutes or so the psychologist concluded the interview with Jeff, checked that Teresa had completed the measures, and invited her to join Jeff in the psychologist's office.

At this point the psychologist shared some initial impressions with the couple. After commenting on how well they were dealing with the challenges they both faced, the psychologist stated that it appeared Teresa was indeed suffering from OCD. Although the tests would need to be scored and further information would be required to determine if other clinical problems were evident, it was clear that Teresa should consider treatment for this anxiety disorder. The psychologist briefly described the main evidence-based psychological and pharmacological treatments for OCD but emphasized that Teresa would not need to make any treatment-related decisions until the assessment was concluded. As a final step in this initial feedback session the psychologist provided Teresa with a simple self-monitoring form to record some information (duration of anxiety, level of anxiety, and efforts to cope with the anxiety) each time she noticed that she was anxious about inadvertently harming someone and about the possibility of having left dangerous materials in the house. Teresa understood that recording these details would help the psychologist better understand the nature of her anxiety and readily agreed to do the self-monitoring each day until the next assessment appointment 6 days later.

Between the first and second appointments with Teresa, the psychologist scored the symptom measures and summarized diagnostic hypotheses from the interviews. Teresa clearly met criteria for OCD and both the obsessions and the compulsions subscales of the YBOCS were in the OCD range. There were a number of situations that Teresa indicated on the Fear Questionnaire that she tended to avoid but, other than trying to avoid thoughts of injury or illness, none of the items indicated evidence of a clinical problem. On the worry measure she scored above the 70th percentile, but the interview data suggested that she did not meet criteria for generalized anxiety disorder as all of her worries were better accounted for by the OCD diagnosis. Teresa scored in the moderately depressed range on the BDI-II, but the interview data indicated that she did not currently meet criteria for a mood disorder—it did seem likely to the psychologist that such a disorder might develop if her OCD was not treated.

At the second appointment, the psychologist met with Teresa for 30 minutes to review the self-monitoring data and to ask Teresa about her symptoms over the past few days. The psychologist also checked whether she had any questions about the information discussed in their first meeting. After the interview, Teresa completed the MMPI-2. To allow sufficient time for the psychologist to review the assessment data, a full feedback session was scheduled for 2 weeks later. Teresa asked if Jeff could attend the meeting—the psychologist immediately agreed to this.

In interpreting the MMPI-2 the psychologist was particularly interested in the code type of Teresa's responses (i.e., her highest scores on the Clinical scales) and the scores on some of the Content scales. All Validity scale scores were in the normal range, indicating that she had responded in a consistent and forthright manner to the MMPI-2 items. This was in line with observations of Teresa during the two interviews, for she clearly took all the interview questions seriously and tried to give full and accurate answers even when she became upset in describing some of her difficulties. With respect to code type, Teresa's highest two scores in the clinical range were 7 (Pt) and 8 (Sc), with 7 being much higher than 8. This code type is typically found among people who are having problems with ruminations, obsessions, anxiety, and depression, who have frequent health concerns, and who are feeling stressed-out. On the Content scales, there were elevations with Anxiety, Obsessiveness, and Health Concerns—the Depression scale did not quite reach the clinical level. Finally the psychologist scored the test for the supplemental scores available to evaluate addiction and substance abuse: consistent with interview data there was no indication that Teresa was relying on alcohol or other substances to alleviate her anxiety.

THREATS TO THE VALIDITY OF ASSESSMENTS AND CASE FORMULATIONS

Patient/Client Factors

As you know from Chapter 8, clinical psychologists are well aware that people may selectively choose how they depict themselves during a psychological evaluation. To achieve certain ends, people may consciously highlight either their strengths or their weaknesses. Some people who are required to undergo an evaluation for court-mandated reasons may attempt to render their results invalid by purposely responding to test items in a random manner. As we described previously, there are measures to detect such attempts at impression management. There are also more subtle biases that can affect the validity of patient-provided data. These biases are not necessarily consciously intended and, therefore, are much less likely to be detected by responses to validity scales or measures of malingering.

A basic assumption underlying the use of interviews and self-report measures is that people accurately recall and report events in their lives. The truth of this assumption seems so obvious that, in our daily lives, we rarely have any reason to question it. After all, we are usually certain about what we were doing when important events occurred in our lives, whether they be events of personal significance (such as learning of the death of a family member) or of more global significance (such as what we were doing when we learned that planes had struck the World Trade Center in New York City in 2001). However, when psychologists study the accuracy of these recalled memories it appears that there is good reason to be sceptical about the general accuracy of memory. We will examine several lines of research bearing on the accuracy of self-report data that relies on **retrospective recall**.

Gosling, John, Craik, and Robins (1998) videotaped research participants in a group discussion. Following the interaction, each participant was asked to recall how frequently he or she had engaged in specific acts such as "I persuaded others to accept my opinion on the issue." Using the videotapes, observers recorded each instance of the participant engaging in these acts. Across 12 different acts that were coded with high reliability (an alpha > .80), the average correlation between participants' recall and observers' records was only .40! For highly observable acts (e.g., "The participant reminded the group of their time limit") there was much greater agreement than there was for acts that required some inference on the part of observers (e.g., "The participant took the opposite point of view just to be contrary"). The desirability of the acts also seemed to have an effect on the correlation between participant and observer data. Compared with observer act counts, participants tended to over-report the frequency with which they engaged in socially desirable acts (e.g., "Participant settled the dispute among other members of the group") and to under-report engaging in less desirable acts (e.g., "Participant yelled at someone"). Taken together, these results, which are consistent with prior research findings, suggest that there may be considerable variability in the accuracy of people's reports of how they acted in a particular situation, even when the reports are given shortly after the situation occurred. The clinical implications are clear: first, we should not assume complete accuracy when using checklists that ask clients to indicate the frequency of occurrence of behaviours, symptoms, or other experiences and, second, we should expect that the desirability of the experience being reported may influence the accuracy of the information provided by the client.

A second line of research relevant to the issue of memory effects on self-report measures compares people's recording of events as they happen (or shortly after they happen) with their later recall of the events. For example, Shiffman and colleagues (1997) asked people who recently had quit smoking to record on a hand-held computer their smoking lapses and temptations to smoke. Twelve weeks later participants were asked to provide retrospective accounts of these events. The overall pattern of results suggested that recalled information was highly inaccurate: only 57% of participants were able to accurately recall whether they had a lapse within a 2-week period and the recalled number of cigarettes smoked was three times greater than the number reported during the lapses. Perhaps most strikingly, people were highly confident in the accuracy of their recall but there was no statistically significant relation between confidence ratings and accuracy. Stone and colleagues (1998) also used palmtops to examine the relation between immediate reports of participants' attempts to cope with daily stressors and recall of their coping efforts two days later. On average approximately one-third of people failed to retrospectively report coping efforts they recorded using during the actual occurrence of their efforts; a similar number retrospectively reported using coping strategies that they did not report using during the events in question. As a final example, Halford, Keefer, and Osgarby (2002) asked 60 heterosexual couples to keep a daily diary of events in their relationship for one week. At the end of the week all participants were asked to describe the week overall and their descriptions were then coded in terms of positive and negative comments about the relationship. The researchers were particularly interested in whether participants' satisfaction with their relationship would colour their recall of events. Consistent with their hypotheses, when these summary comments were compared with the daily diaries, low relationship satisfaction was significantly related to a tendency to recall the relationship events in an overly negative manner.

Research indicates that it is not just minor daily events that are difficult to accurately recall. As part of an ongoing project based in New Zealand to track health and development, Henry, Moffit, Caspi, Langley, and Silva (1994) used data from more than 1,000 young adults to compare retrospectively recalled events at age 18 with data on these events that were obtained throughout the participants' childhood and adolescence. The researchers found enormous variability in the accuracy of the recollections, with correlations between recalled events and actual details of the events ranging from -.02 to .77! Although correlations were relatively high for such reports on the number of housing moves ($r = .76$) and height and weight just prior to puberty ($r \geq .59$), accuracy was very poor for recall of psychosocial variables such as the extent of conflict in the family prior to age 15 ($r \leq .25$), maternal depression prior to age 15 ($r \leq .20$), and the extent of depressive or hyperactive symptoms in participants prior to age 11 ($r \leq .12$). As these psychosocial variables are the ones that clinicians typically ask about during initial assessments, it appears that there are considerable grounds for doubting the veracity of these reports.

Studies suggest that a person's recall memory is not as accurate as he or she would believe when compared to their recording of events as they occurred.

As we described in previous chapters, clinical psychologists may be asked to assess individuals to determine their level of ability or functioning prior to an event such as a workplace injury or a motor vehicle accident. Many studies suggest that it is important to gather archival information, such as medical, school, or police records, as part of this assessment rather than relying on patient self-report. Greiffenstein, Baker, and Johnson-Greene (2002), for example, compared self-reported and actual academic performance among people with head injuries who were or were not involved in legal suits based on the accident that led to the injuries. Compared with the nonlitigating group, those who had filed legal suits showed a much greater tendency to overestimate their scholastic performance.

Clinician Factors

Since the groundbreaking work of cognitive psychologists Tversky and Kahneman (1974), there has been dramatic growth in our knowledge of how subtle influences can affect judgement, reasoning, and decision-making processes. We now know a great deal about how experience, expectations, attributions, and stereotypes all shape the ways in which people make both relatively minor and major decisions. For example, hundreds of studies have examined the tendency for people to see themselves in a generally positive light, even when such positivity may not be warranted. A meta-analysis conducted by Mezulis, Abramson, Hyde, and Hankin (2004) included 266 studies of the **self-serving attributional bias**. This bias involves people making more internal, stable, and global attributions for positive events in their lives than they do for negative events (e.g., "I got an A on the paper because I worked hard for it. I am always a hard worker, in every area of my life, so it is no wonder that good things occur in my life." versus "I really didn't deserve a C on the paper. It really wasn't my fault that my computer crashed. I usually get things done on time—I know that I left things late this time but if my hard drive hadn't crashed I would have been fine.").

Generally speaking **biases** involve judgements that are systematically different from what a person should conclude based on logic or probability. **Heuristics** are mental shortcuts that people often use to ease the burden of decision-making but which also tend to result in errors in decision-making and, thus, are at the heart of cognitive biases. Since the 1980s Howard Garb has contributed much to our understanding of how biases and heuristics influence routine clinical tasks (e.g., Garb, 1997) and his 1998 book provides an excellent summary of the large literature indicating that simply being trained to provide psychological services does not eliminate human information processing biases. **Table 9.3** provides a summary of common biases and heuristics that can affect clinical decision-making. Although we present this table in the section on clinician factors that affect the validity of assessment, these biases and heuristics apply equally to patients.

TABLE 9.3   Common Decision-Making Biases and Heuristics

Fundamental Attribution Error: In attempting to understand why a person acted in such a manner, there is a tendency to overestimate the influence of personality traits and to underestimate the influence of situational effects on the person's behaviour.

Inattention to Base Rates: A psychologist may believe that a certain pattern of responses on a test is indicative of a specific diagnosis and supports this belief with information on some relevant cases. However, without full knowledge of the base rate of (a) the pattern of test responses and (b) the diagnosis, it is not possible to determine the extent to which the test responses accurately predict the diagnosis.

Belief in the Law of Small Numbers: Results drawn from small samples are likely to be more extreme and less consistent than those obtained from large samples. Nevertheless, the clinical psychologist may be tempted to attend more to information gained from two or three patients with a specific disorder than to the results of research on the disorder. Direct experience with a small number of patients may feel more relevant and compelling, even though it is less likely to yield accurate information compared with data drawn from research samples.

Regression to the Mean: Because of the nature of measurement error, a person who obtains an extreme score on a test at one point in time is likely to obtain a less extreme score when next taking the test. This apparent change in test scores has nothing to do with real alterations in the person's life. (The standard error of measurement is available for many psychological tests so that psychologists can take this into account when comparing test scores from two time points.)

Inferring Causation from Correlation: A psychologist may note that there appears to be substantial co-occurrence of certain patient characteristics (such as a history of sexual abuse and the presence of borderline personality disorder) and infer that the earlier of the two characteristics causes the later characteristic (i.e., the abuse led to the development of the personality disorder). Before drawing causal inferences, though, other factors must be considered, including whether the later characteristic may influence the information provided about the earlier characteristic and the possibility that both characteristics stemmed from a third variable (e.g., severely dysfunctional family environment).

Hindsight Bias: As the saying goes, "Hindsight is 20/20." Most decisions (including clinical decisions) must be made without the benefit of all the pertinent information. After a decision has been made and, as a consequence, a certain course of action has been taken, new information may become available. It is tempting to validate or question the initial decision based on data gathered after the fact even though it was not possible to have these data inform the original decision.

continued...

Confirmatory Bias: Once a clinical hunch has been formed, it is tempting to gather information to support it. However, in testing a hypothesis it is important to evaluate evidence both for and against the hypothesis. The clinical psychologist must avoid simply looking for evidence to support the hypothesis (such as a diagnosis or an emerging case formulation) and also actively look for evidence that would refute or temper the strength of the hypothesis.

Representativeness Heuristic: Relying on biases such as the belief in the law of small numbers to draw conclusions about the degree to which a symptom or behaviour is representative of an underlying disorder or condition.

Availability Heuristic: Making a decision based on easily recalled information, such as recent or extreme or unusual examples that are relevant to the decision. Using only easily recalled examples (such as the last person assessed with similar symptoms) will lead to an incomplete evaluation of the elements that must be considered in the decision; by definition, extreme examples are atypical and likely to bias a decision.

Affect Heuristic: When reaching a decision the affective qualities (such as likeability, negativity, disgust, or pleasure) of cognitive representations of people or objects are rapidly considered. This usually occurs at an unconscious level and can lead to a judgement based solely on emotional considerations (such as the attractiveness of an individual), with only minimal attention paid to the full range of factors relevant to the decision.

Anchoring and Adjustment Heuristic: Initial conditions or characteristics determine a starting point for considering the nature of an individual or task (such as using the dealer's price when negotiating to buy a car). In clinical contexts this means that, for example, first impressions may serve as the (possibly inaccurate) basis for considering and integrating all subsequent information gathered about a person.

By definition, biases and heuristics lead to errors in decision-making. However, not all errors are created equal: some are potentially more damaging than others and small errors may not really make much of a difference. For example, inaccurately scoring one item on an intelligence test will definitely affect the overall total score, but is unlikely to affect the global interpretation of the client's score as being average or above average. In other words, not all errors result in mistakes that have real world consequences. We do know, however, that some clinician errors can have substantial consequences. Kim and Ahn (2002) found that when determining a diagnosis, clinical psychologists and graduate clinical psychology students are more likely to be influenced by their own causal theories than they are by the actual *DSM* criteria relevant to the diagnostic category. Compared with actual occurrences of violence, clinicians typically overpredict the violence of male patients and underpredict the violence of female patients; likewise black psychiatric inpatients and prison inmates are predicted to be more violent than are white psychiatric inpatients and prison inmates (Garb, 1997, 2005). Other ethnic biases have also been found in clinical practice: for example, minority patients diagnosed with schizophrenia are almost twice as likely as white patients to receive excessive dosages of antipsychotic medication (Wood, Garb, Lilienfeld, & Nezworski, 2002).

If some clinical errors are so important, what gets in the way of clinicians—psychologists, physicians, psychiatrists, and others—identifying and correcting their mistakes? One of the main obstacles seems to be that people tend to be overconfident in the accuracy or correctness of their decisions (Griffin, Dunning, & Ross, 1990). Ryan and Schnakenburg-Ott (2003), for example, found that despite making substantial errors in scoring a WAIS-III protocol, psychologists and graduate students were very confident about the accuracy of their scoring efforts. In an attempt to understand the factors that lead to overconfidence in clinical decisions, Smith and Dumont (2002) asked 36 clinical psychologists to "think aloud" while they read case file material about a patient (including life history data and information about current events in the patient's life). The researchers coded several aspects of the thoughts reported by participants during the task, including the confidence expressed in the accuracy of their conclusions. Among the variables they investigated, the sole factor that predicted psychologists' confidence was the extent to which dispositional (as opposed to contextual) information was used. In other words, it appears that the fundamental attribution error (see Table 9.3) may play a powerful role in leading clinicians to be overconfident in their interpretations, decisions, and conclusions.

Improving the Accuracy of Clinical Judgement

In light of the kinds of errors we have just described, it seems obvious that psychologists and other clinicians should be more cautious in their decision-making. Simply being aware of decision-making biases and the resultant errors is insufficient—clinical psychologists (and others who wish to reduce the role of biases in their decisions) must take concrete steps to tackle the potential for bias and error. In this regard, the evidence is overwhelming that the use of informal, unstructured strategies to integrate assessment data is inferior to strategies that rely on the structured application of empirical evidence (Grove, Zald, Lebow, Snitz, & Nelson, 2000). Accordingly, no one should interpret an MMPI-A profile by looking at individual items to generate a clinical formulation: the formulation should be informed by code type interpretations based on research studies. Measures designed to systematize clinical observations are being developed, which holds the possibility for structuring the data obtained from even the most unstructured clinical interviews (Westen & Weinberger, 2004). **Table 9.4** describes a host of other simple, practical strategies that many psychologists follow in order to minimize the impact of bias and error in their work.

TABLE 9.4   Improving the Accuracy of Clinical Judgement

- Use psychological tests that are directly relevant to the assessment task and that have strong psychometric qualities.
- Check for scoring errors when using test data.
- Use computers as aids in the collection, scoring, and interpretation of clinical data whenever possible.
- Use normative data and base rate information whenever available.
- Use *DSM* criteria when making diagnostic decisions.
- Use decision aids, such as decision trees or clinical guidelines.
- In unstructured tasks, such as conducting interviews and reviewing assessment data, be as systematic, structured, and as quantifiable as possible in order to obtain, consider, and use all relevant information.
- Be aware of relevant research in psychological assessment, psychopathology, and prevention/intervention.
- Be aware of personal biases and preconceptions.
- Be self-critical: search for alternative explanations for hypotheses and challenge evolving case conceptualizations.
- Seek consultation from other professionals when unsure of the accuracy of conclusions.
- Don't rely on memory and don't rush any conclusion or decision.

T E R E S A

The psychologist was concerned about a number of possible biases that might affect the validity of the assessment information. To deal with the possibility that Teresa might unwittingly underestimate the extent of her problems, symptom-related information was also collected from Jeff. As Teresa might consciously downplay her difficulties, a measure with established validity scales was used (the MMPI-2). Because both Teresa and Jeff's memories of her symptoms might be influenced by her most recent episodes of anxiety or by her most extreme episodes of anxiety, Teresa was asked to self-monitor her anxiety for a week. Finally, because both Teresa and Jeff might have concerns about how Teresa's anxiety was influencing her ability as a parent, the psychologist asked each of them separately about this issue. This point was particularly important as the psychologist had a duty to contact the Children's Aid Society if it appeared that the baby was in need of protection. After interviewing both parents, it was the psychologist's opinion that the baby was not in need of protection.

Several steps were taken to guard against biases that might affect the clinical psychologist's judgement; for example, DSM-IV-TR criteria were used to make diagnostic decisions. Because the psychologist specialized in anxiety disorders it was important to address the possibilities of overestimating the likelihood of an anxiety diagnosis and underestimating other diagnoses. To this end, several self-report measures were used to establish the nature of the anxiety and depressive symptoms. The MMPI-2 would also provide indications if other clinically significant disorders might be present. With respect to the possibility of errors in the assessment, standardized psychological tests were used that had relevant norms and solid psychometric properties. The psychologist checked all scoring of the measures and used software to generate interpretive statements for the MMPI-2. The psychologist obtained information from multiple informants and looked for independent confirmation of the main hypotheses generated early in the assessment with Teresa.

PSYCHOLOGICAL ASSESSMENT REPORTS AND TREATMENT PLANS

The assessment process culminates in writing a report and, usually, presenting the assessment findings to the individual or individuals who were the focus of the assessment. In addition to providing information to the agency or professional (or the client), the report serves as a record of the assessment that can be referred to subsequently and, in some instances, can also be a document used for legal purposes. In situations in which some form of treatment will follow the assessment, the report records the client's functioning prior to intervention. This baseline information is crucial in accurately determining the impact of any intervention.

Assessments may be requested by many people including clients, the parents of young clients, physicians, insurance companies, employers, lawyers, or the courts. Accordingly, when conducting the assessment and writing the report, the psychologist must be cognizant of the potential uses of the report and the "audiences" for the report. This is especially true when the person being assessed is in a potentially adversarial position with the agency that requested the assessment. As described previously in the text, this can happen when an individual is making a claim for compensation based on injuries suffered and the agency responsible for adjudicating the claim seeks an independent evaluation of the individual's psychological state. Issues of informed consent and confidentiality are always important in the provision of psychological services. However, when there may be competing interests involved, it is especially important for the psychologist to emphasize and reiterate the rights and options available to the person who is being assessed.

In almost all jurisdictions, privacy legislation allows clients access to their psychological records, so the psychologist should write a report with this in mind. Although this should not change any conclusions or recommendations, it should affect how the report is written. Care must be taken to minimize or eliminate any stigmatizing or objectionable terms or descriptions in the report. Moreover, in integrating information from multiple sources, it is also crucial that the psychologist clearly attribute who said what. Reports are always potential legal documents that may have ramifications far beyond the original reasons for which the assessment was conducted. If based solely on client self-report, a statement such as "*His father physically assaulted him on numerous occasions*" should be written as "*The client reported that his father had physically assaulted him on numerous occasions.*" Likewise, ambiguous terms should be avoided: in describing marital arguments, for example, the phrase "*the couple often fight*" could refer either to frequent arguments or physical violence. **Table 9.5** highlights some principles that clinical psychologists typically follow in order to maximize the validity and usefulness of their assessment reports.

TABLE 9.5   Report-Writing Principles

- Identify common themes, integrating the findings across assessment procedures.

- Use all relevant sources of information about the client (including reliable and valid test results, behavioural observations, individual test responses, interview data, and case history) in generating hypotheses, formulating interpretations, and making recommendations.

- Be definitive when the findings are clear; be cautious when the findings are inconsistent or problematic.

- Use concrete examples to enhance the report's readability.

- Interpret the meaning and implications of a test score rather than simply citing test names and scores.

- Refrain from making diagnoses solely on the basis of test scores; consider all sources of information.

- Communicate clearly and eliminate unnecessary technical material in order to enhance the report's readability.

Adapted from Sattler (1992).

Earlier in the chapter we described how computers could be used to improve the accuracy of some aspects of clinical decision-making. Despite the numerous benefits of using computers for various assessment-related tasks, clinical psychologists need to exercise considerable caution with **computer-based interpretations** (CBIs) when integrating the assessment data and writing the assessment report. Because CBIs are based on research using group level data, not all interpretative comments associated with, say, a specific MMPI-2 code type, apply to the patient being assessed. The clinician needs to review the CBI and select only those narrative statements that accurately describe the patient in question. Next the psychologist must examine the relevance of any statement given the reasons for the assessment (Kvaal, Choca, & Groth-Marnat, 2003). In most jurisdictions the regulatory bodies for psychologists have clear guidelines on the use of CBIs in psychological assessment. Most typically these include the need to ensure the relevance of the interpretations to the patients and to clearly identify any statements that come directly from the computer report and that are the sole source of information for a specific point or conclusion. For these reasons including an unedited computer report in an assessment report is not considered appropriate or responsible in routine practice.

Table 9.6 presents the sections typically found in most psychological assessment reports. There are no standards dictating the necessary components of a report; the content and structure depends on the reasons for the assessment. Most reports are several single-spaced pages in length, although reports prepared for legal or forensic purposes tend to be substantially longer. **Table 9.7** presents the sections usually included in assessment reports prepared for intervention purposes. These treatment plans differ from the typical assessment report: they primarily focus on using the assessment data to develop and structure a plan for intervening with the patient. This should also include some consideration of whether psychological treatment is warranted or appropriate at this time. Both types of reports serve to document the client's psychological functioning and to provide clinically informed conceptualizations that draw on the assessment data. A treatment plan report involves problem identification, delineation of the aims and goals of treatment, and the strategies and tactics involved in the planned treatment (Mariush, 2002). Specific attention is also paid to the need for ongoing evaluation of the patient's functioning, for the monitoring of treatment impact is important in determining whether treatment should be discontinued or whether alternative treatment options should be considered. A growing number of agencies now require a treatment plan prior to the commencement of therapy and sometimes require an updated plan if the clinical psychologist requests additional sessions for the patient's treatment. **Viewpoint Box 9.3** deals with one of the challenges psychologists are likely to encounter in developing a treatment plan.

TABLE 9.6   Sections of a Typical Psychological Report

- Identifying patient/client information
- Reason for referral
- Background information (including, as relevant, developmental history, educational history, employment history, family history, relationship history, medical history, history of symptoms and disorders)
- Assessment methods (including tests administered)
- Interview data and behavioural observations
- Test results (including interpretation of test scores)
- Diagnostic impressions
- Summary
- Recommendations

TABLE 9.7   Elements of a Typical Treatment Plan

- Identifying patient/client information
- Reason for referral
- Evaluation of primary symptoms and problems
- Diagnosis
- Patient strengths
- Treatment-related goals and objectives
- Proposed treatment(s)
- Potential barriers to treatment
- Criteria for treatment termination or transfer to other service provider
- Service provider responsible for treatment implementation and evaluation of treatment

Adapted from Mariush (2002).

VIEWPOINT BOX 9.3

WHEN WORLDS COLLIDE (III): INTEGRATING MULTIPLE PERSPECTIVES ON TREATMENT GOALS

One of the first steps in offering intervention services is for the psychologist to help the client establish treatment goals (Nezu & Nezu, 1993). Psychological interventions for adult clients involve at least two perspectives: that of the client and that of the therapist. The psychologist asks questions to discover what the person hopes to get out of psychological services. Clients vary in the extent to which they have clear ideas about what needs to change to resolve the problem. The goals identified by the psychologist depend on the way the psychologist formulates the case, which in turn is influenced by the theoretical model that the psychologist uses in understanding problems. The core of an effective therapeutic alliance is the agreement on goals by client and therapist (Horvath & Luborsky, 1993). Agreement on goals is even more of a challenge in the delivery of psychological services to children and families. Children rarely refer themselves for services (Kazdin, 1988). Over years of clinical practice, we have yet to receive a call from a young person saying "I realize that I am pretty tough to live with; my distractibility is getting in the way of meeting my academic goals and my impulsiveness leads to all kinds of trouble, so I think I need to see a psychologist." Adults are the ones to request psychological services for children. As you saw in Viewpoint Box 9.1, there is often limited overlap in the ways that young people and their parents view their behaviour. So, if parents and children do not agree on what the problem is, how can they agree on treatment goals?

Hawley and Weisz (2003) asked 315 children and their parents attending community mental health centres about the problem for which services were being sought. They also asked the children's therapists to identify the presenting problem. All three raters identified disobedience, temper tantrums, poor schoolwork, and difficulties getting along with other children as the most common reasons for seeking services. However, beyond such generalities, the level of agreement among children, parents, and therapists was low. Only 23.2% of triads (child-parent-therapist) agreed on the target problem for therapy; less than half of the triads agreed on the general area that needed to be addressed. Agreement was significantly higher for externalizing, or acting-out, problems (41.3%) than it was for internalizing problems, for which there was only 6.7% agreement. In general, there was higher agreement between therapists and parents than between children and either therapists or parents. Therapists offering services to children and families therefore face a dilemma: if they act according to the parents' identification of the problem, they are likely to set treatment goals that are not endorsed by the child. On the other hand, if they set goals according to what the child thinks is a problem, they risk alienating the parents, who may see the focus as misplaced. To engage both child and parents in psychological services, the psychologist must first find a way to formulate goals that are meaningful to both the child and parents. If the child does not see the point in services, he or she is unlikely to cooperate and although parents may sometimes force the child's attendance, they cannot force meaningful involvement. As the parents are the ones who control access to services, it is essential that they be convinced that the services offered are relevant. Psychologists working with children and families must therefore be sensitive to the different perspectives of those seeking services and of those child clients who are referred to them.

Assessment Feedback

For much of the history of psychological assessment, the results of the assessment process were delivered primarily to the medical or educational personnel who requested the assessment. In the assessment of child clients, parents often received some feedback on the results of the assessment. Opportunities to present assessment feedback are invaluable in assisting other professionals in developing remedial or intervention strategies to use with the assessed client. However, with changes in ethical codes and in legislation since the 1970s, it is now commonplace for those who were assessed to also receive feedback from the clinical psychologist involved. Indeed, current ethical requirements underscore the importance of psychologists providing such feedback in most circumstances. As indicated in **Table 9.8**, not only do clients have the right to receive feedback, the provision of feedback yields an opportunity for the psychologist to verify assessment findings and conclusions and to help clients begin to use the assessment findings in making modifications in their lives. For an assessment designed to address elements of a treatment plan, it is essential that client and psychologist work collaboratively during the initial assessment phase and throughout the following treatment phases. Therefore it is crucial that the psychologist explain the results of all assessments, including the initial assessment data and the data that are collected as part of the treatment monitoring and evaluation process.

TABLE 9.8   The Purposes of Providing Assessment Feedback

- Verify the general accuracy of the assessment results

- Refine the interpretation of the results to ensure an optimal fit with the individual's life circumstances

- Put the individual's symptoms, problems, and experiences in the context of his or her life history and current life circumstances

- Provide some psychological relief for the individual by presenting an integrated picture that helps make sense of the individual's difficulties

- Provide concrete information about steps the individual can take to address personal difficulties

- Help the individual identify potentially stressful situations that can exacerbate difficulties

- Collaborate with the individual in creating therapeutic goals that build on personal strengths

Adapted from Lewak and Hogan (2003).

Building on a range of research evidence that suggested assessment feedback can influence client emotional functioning, Stephen Finn developed a **therapeutic model of assessment** (e.g., Finn & Tonsager, 1997). In this model, clients are active participants in all phases of the assessment. This includes discussing the reasons for assessment, observing the test results, and interpreting the test scores. Particular efforts are made to (a) develop a strong working alliance with the client, (b) work collaboratively in defining the client's goals for the assessment, and (c) explore the assessment data with the client. Research evaluating aspects of this model has been encouraging: compared with assessment procedures focused solely on information-gathering (i.e., little active collaboration with clients), clients receiving therapeutic assessment developed stronger working alliances with the psychologists, which then carry over into the treatment phase (Hilsenroth, Peters, & Ackerman, 2004), and were less likely to prematurely terminate treatment (Ackerman, Hilsenroth, Baity, & Blagys, 2000). These studies were conducted in the context of providing short-term psychodynamic treatment to clients, but the results may also be relevant to other treatment forms. Therapist-client collaboration is a cornerstone of cognitive-behavioural treatments and findings such as these suggest that the collaborative approach to assessment and treatment may be instrumental in the well-documented success of the cognitive-behavioural therapies (see Chapter 14).

PROFILE BOX 9.1

DR. MARTIN M. ANTONY

I received my Ph.D. in clinical psychology from the University at Albany, State University of New York. I am a Professor in the Department of Psychiatry and Behavioural Neurosciences at McMaster University in Hamilton, Ontario. In addition I am Psychologist-in-Chief at St. Joseph's Healthcare in Hamilton, where I also direct the Anxiety Treatment and Research Centre and the Clinical Psychology Residency Training Program. I am licensed as a psychologist in the province of Ontario and am board certified in Clinical Psychology with the American Board of Professional Psychology.

Dr. Martin M. Antony

In addition to teaching and training, I maintain a clinical practice. I have published 12 books and more than 90 articles and book chapters in my research areas of cognitive behaviour therapy, panic disorder, social phobia, specific phobia, and obsessive compulsive disorder. I have received early career awards from the Society of Clinical Psychology (American Psychological Association), the Canadian Psychological Association, and the Anxiety Disorders Association of America. I am a Fellow of the American and Canadian Psychological Associations.

What made you choose to become a clinical psychologist?

Early in my undergraduate training, I was interested in a career in medicine. However, I found that as time went on, I enjoyed my psychology courses more than my biology and chemistry courses. I ended up switching from a major in biology to a major in psychology in my third year. By that point, I had decided to pursue a career in clinical psychology. I found the topic of mental illness fascinating, and my volunteer work at the Clarke Institute of Psychiatry in Toronto (now the Centre for Addiction and Mental Health) solidified my interest.

I fell into my work in anxiety disorders by accident. When I finished my undergraduate degree, I decided to take a year off to work full-time. I applied for two research assistant positions: one in schizophrenia and one in anxiety disorders. Though I really wanted the position in schizophrenia, I settled for the job in anxiety disorders when that was the only offer I received. In the end, it worked out very well. I loved the work in anxiety disorders, and as a result, I applied primarily to graduate schools where I could work in the area of anxiety.

What is the most rewarding part of your job as a clinical psychologist?

I love doing many different things and my career in clinical psychology has allowed me to do just that. I am actively involved in training psychologists and other professionals, conducting research, writing books, providing clinical service, and administration. My career has also allowed me to feed my entrepreneurial spirit. A portion of my income comes from providing continuing education to mental health professionals, consulting, and private practice. My work in anxiety disorders is particularly rewarding because (1) anxiety disorders are important (they are among the most prevalent of psychological problems, and they lead to significant impairment), and (2) because people with anxiety disorders can usually experience significant improvements in a relatively brief time.

What is the greatest challenge facing you as a clinical psychologist?

Perhaps the biggest challenge to me personally is trying to find the time to do all the things I want to do. For the first time, I have started to turn down some opportunities, with the long-term goal of achieving a better balance between work and other pursuits.

Tell us about the role of assessment tools in treatment planning.

In our centre, patients receive an evidence-based diagnostic interview to establish a diagnostic description that best captures their problems. Assignment to particular treatment programs is based on the results of the interview (for example, a principal diagnosis of social anxiety disorder would likely lead to an offer of treatment in our social anxiety disorder treatment program). In addition, specific symptom severity measures are used to plan particular components of the treatment. For example, data from the *Mobility Inventory for Agoraphobia* (Chambless et al., 1985) are used to help generate items for the exposure hierarchy, which in turn guides the behavioural component of treatment for people with panic disorder and agoraphobia.

How do you integrate science and practice in your work?

First, staying actively involved in research and writing allows me to be up to date with respect to scientific advances in the treatment of anxiety disorders and other problems. Over time, our assessment and treatment tools are updated in response to recent scientific findings. Second, many of our treatment programs are offered in the context of scientific research. For example, we recently completed a study comparing a home-based treatment for obsessive-compulsive disorder to a standard office-based treatment. While the study was going on, many of the individuals receiving services in our centre for obsessive-compulsive disorder were treated as part of this study. Finally, our centre takes an empirical approach to delivering clinical services. For example, we collect outcome data routinely, using standard, evidence-based assessment methods.

What do you see as the most exciting changes in the profession of clinical psychology?

One of the most exciting changes in the profession of clinical psychology is the move toward greater accountability. Increasingly, treatment facilities, funding agencies, and the public are demanding that assessment and treatment procedures be based on solid evidence. We still have a long way to go, but the situation has improved considerably compared to when I started my training. The publication of criteria for empirically supported psychological treatments by the Society of Clinical Psychology was an important step along the way. Although these criteria have generated much debate and controversy, they have also led to changes in the types of questions clinical researchers are asking.

TERESA

The psychologist drafted a report to be sent to Teresa and Jeff's family physician and to the company that managed Jeff's extended health care benefits. The psychologist summarized the reason for the assessment and Teresa's history of anxiety symptoms. The results of the testing, interviews, observations, and self-monitoring were described and a diagnosis of obsessive-compulsive disorder was indicated. Based on the nature of Teresa's symptoms and the treatment literature on OCD, the psychologist recommended that Teresa begin cognitive-behavioural treatment emphasizing exposure and response prevention. It was also recommended that, if the couple were willing, Jeff should participate in some sessions in order to assist Teresa with some of the exposure steps she would need to undertake.

The psychologist met with Teresa and Jeff to provide feedback on the full assessment and to review details of the report. The couple were encouraged to ask questions about the results—they had very few, as the findings were consistent with their own views. They were also encouraged to ask questions about the treatment options, including medication and partner-assisted exposure and response prevention. They had many questions on these matters and the psychologist took considerable time to explain the nature of the psychological treatment. They discussed, in particular, the symptoms that would be targeted in the treatment (e.g., thoughts about injuring people, checking for dangerous materials around the house, checking about pedestrian injuries when driving). The psychologist also emphasized that the treatment required substantial commitment from both Teresa and Jeff to work on anxiety-related assignments between treatment sessions.

After noting two minor errors in the information in the draft report (concerning the dates of work-related events), Teresa indicated that she felt comfortable with the report being sent to the physician and the health care company. Although the psychologist indicated that the couple could take their time to discuss treatment options between themselves, very little discussion was needed for Teresa and Jeff to decide to go ahead with the psychological treatment. Accordingly the psychologist booked an initial treatment appointment for both of them. Teresa was also asked to continue her self-monitoring activities, as these data would provide an important baseline for examining changes in anxiety symptoms during treatment.

SUMMARY AND CONCLUSIONS

In this chapter we have described the final stage of the assessment process in which the psychologist integrates diverse material from different sources into a sound formulation. The task of drawing together information requires the same kind of scientific thinking needed to make sense of research results. The psychologist draws on a wealth of knowledge about psychological functioning, psychopathology, risk, and protective factors, as well as solid understanding of psychometric issues in reaching a meaningful conclusion about a particular client. Like other types of decision-making, clinical decision-making is prone to a host of biases and errors. The psychologist must be flexible in generating hypotheses and cautious in weighing the evidence in support of them or against them. Overconfidence in one's own wisdom and experience may lead to a premature conclusion that fails to take into account all relevant data. Even-handed consideration of confirming and disconfirming data is as essential in clinical practice as it is in conducting research.

Students of clinical psychology may initially feel discouraged to learn of all the potential pitfalls in clinical decision-making. However, it is important to remember that these decision-making errors apply to everyone: they apply in our personal lives and they occur in other types of decision-making. Clinical psychologists are not immune from the same kinds of errors in decision-making that affect other people. However, awareness of these pitfalls can lead to the use of strategies that minimize the likelihood of errors. As we discussed in earlier chapters, the different types of assessment information all have advantages and disadvantages. There is no single test that will yield a meaningful clinical formulation—the task of the clinical psychologist is much more complex. Research has established that clinical psychologists can effectively combine data from several imperfect methods to reach a clinically meaningful formulation that can guide services. The move toward greater transparency and accountability in the delivery of health services fits well with the clinical psychology practices of providing feedback to clients following psychological assessment. A psychological assessment report is the product of careful analysis of a specific client: it draws on research evidence developed on large groups of individuals with particular attention to the client's specific circumstances.

Critical Thinking Questions

What common heuristics are operating when we assume that a person who has been exposed to trauma is likely to be psychologically vulnerable?

What are the advantages of reviewing reports with clients?

In what ways is the process of developing a case formulation a scientific endeavour?

Key Terms

biases

case formulation

computer-based interpretations

heuristics

retrospective recall

self-serving attributional bias

therapeutic model of assessment

Key Names

Stephen Finn

Howard Garb

Jacqueline Persons

ADDITIONAL RESOURCES
Books

Antony, M. M., & Barlow, D. H. (2002). *Handbook of assessment and treatment planning for psychological disorders.* New York: Guilford Press.

Eells, T. D. (Ed). (1997). *Handbook of psychotherapy case formulation.* New York: Guilford Press.

Garb, H. N. (1998). *Studying the clinician: Judgment research and psychological assessment.* Washington, DC: American Psychological Association.

Prevention

INTRODUCTION

Harry sits in a comfortable chair watching the clock. Since the death of his wife five years ago, Harry has lived alone. An avid reader and expert horticulturalist, Harry spends many hours reading and tending his plants. His adult children maintain regular contact with weekly phone calls, but live too far away to allow frequent visits. Over the years Harry, now 83, has been troubled by rheumatoid arthritis that causes him pain and debilitation. He has found it increasingly difficult to manipulate small objects as the joints in his hands are stiff and inflamed. Pain in his knees and hips makes walking difficult, although he attempts to be as active as possible. Harry adjusts his clothing, smoothing his tie and brushing lint off his jacket. He checks his watch, shaking it to make sure it has not stopped. On hearing a noise outside his door, Harry grasps his cane and pulls himself painfully to a standing position. As the door opens with a creak, Harry grumbles "I'm hungry, I thought you were supposed to be here at 12:30." The cheery face at his door belongs to Anne, a sprightly 76-year-old who has been a volunteer since her retirement from teaching 11 years ago. Anne sets out Harry's lunch, asks how he's enjoying the book he's reading, admires the blooms on his azalea, commiserates with his disappointment that his daughter has had to postpone her next visit, gathers up the tray and dishes from yesterday's meal, and leaves to deliver other meals.

The *Meals on Wheels* organization operates in many countries to provide wholesome meals to older adults whose nutrition might otherwise be poor. The benefits to recipients of *Meals on Wheels* may extend beyond the physical advantages of having a good meal. For Harry, the regular brief visits punctuate his day, reducing his isolation. For Harry's adult children who live far away, they provide reassurance that he is having at least one good meal a day and that he is seen by an informed and caring person on days that meals are delivered. For volunteers such as Anne, there may be a sense of satisfaction in contributing to the well-being of others. The *Meals on Wheels* program is a non-profit, volunteer-based organization in different countries. It is a good example of a program designed to offer services to a vulnerable population and prevent the development of serious problems. *Meals on Wheels* is committed to offering a sustainable service that is accountable to government and is sensitive to the needs of a diverse population.

Prevention programs were first established to prevent physical health problems. As we witnessed with the 2003 outbreak of severe acute respiratory syndrome (SARS), programs to prevent the spread of infectious diseases involve simple practices such as handwashing, more intrusive procedures such as quarantining and wearing masks, and challenging tasks such as the development and use of vaccines. According to the World Health Organization the provision of clean drinking water and the development of vaccination programs have been effective in preventing illness and death for millions of people worldwide every year (World Health Organization, 2003). Vaccinations are cost-effective in preventing such virulent diseases as smallpox, rabies, plague, diphtheria, pertussis (whooping cough), tuberculosis, tetanus, yellow fever, polio, measles, mumps, rubella, and hepatitis B. Tragically, these vaccines are under-used and two million children die each year from diseases that could be prevented at low cost (World Health Organization, 2003). Furthermore, although vaccines in general are effective, that does not mean that a particular vaccine will be effective. For example, many Canadians were shocked to discover that the innovative program in which free influenza vaccinations are provided to the entire population of Ontario (at an annual cost to the government of many million dollars) was in place for several years before evaluations of its impact were begun. Although the idea of a vaccination program makes sense, there are no data to indicate that the use of the 'flu vaccine has reduced rates of illness or death, or has yielded reductions in overall health care costs in Ontario.

Because lifestyle factors are associated with many health problems, many prevention efforts also focus on encouraging the development of healthy habits such as good nutrition, regular exercise, and adequate sleep. Efforts to introduce a healthy lifestyle are usually referred to as **health promotion**. Health promotion is usually designed to increase activities that are beneficial to many aspects of physical health.

As we discussed in Chapter 1, until recently clinical psychologists were not very involved in prevention activities. Community psychologists, on the other hand, have a longer history of developing services that are offered to a vulnerable population. For many years, the training of clinical psychologists focused on understanding problems at the level of the individual—it made sense then that interventions would also be designed at that level. Clinical psychologists reasoned that if problems were related to the way a person thought, felt, or acted, then it made sense to help the person by finding ways to change the dysfunctional thoughts, feelings, or behaviours. Consequently, clinical psychologists developed interventions at the level of the individual, couple, or family. Efforts to evaluate the effectiveness of those psychological services showed that the services were helpful for some people. Services to help parents manage their children's behaviour are a good example. We know from studies of many species, from flatworms to humans, that (a) when a behaviour is followed by a positive outcome, that behaviour is likely to be repeated and (b) when a behaviour is followed by a negative outcome it is less likely to be repeated. Early parent education programs based on these simple reinforcement principles were helpful to many parents. Nevertheless, some people did not come for psychological services, some dropped out after the first session, and others failed to do their between-session assignments designed to improve their parenting. Even though clinical psychologists knew effective ways to encourage appropriate behaviour, to help children manage their angry feelings and learn to share, etc., they were unable to reach some parents. Who are these people who are so difficult to reach? Parents who argued a lot tended to drop out of treatment, as did depressed mothers and women who felt isolated (Miller & Prinz, 1990). The recognition that potentially effective strategies were not accessible to parents who needed them the most forced clinical psychologists to think outside the box and to develop innovative ways to prevent problems and to head off more serious problems.

You may remember learning in Chapter 1 of the vast numbers of people who suffer from mental disorders, the severe psychological toll of these disorders on affected individuals and their families, and the escalating financial costs of mental health problems. Estimates for the United States suggest that the costs of mental disorders were at least $147 billion—more than the costs of cancer, respiratory disease, or AIDS (World Health Organization, 2004). Mental disorders also increase the risk of physical illness. Experts agree, therefore, that the only sustainable way to reduce the burden of mental disorders is through prevention (World Health Organization, 2004). Clinical psychologists working with people suffering from specific disorders are increasingly aware of

Parent education programs based on behavioural principles have been helpful to many parents.

the need to develop prevention programs (Dozois & Dobson, 2004). We admire the apparent simplicity of vaccination programs that allow the body to develop immunity to a virus before exposure to the actual virus. A trip to the clinic, tears of protest, and an afternoon with a slightly cranky child seem a small price to pay to protect a child from the dangers of smallpox! There is, however, no vaccine for child abuse, bullying, suicide, or eating disorders. Although we can all agree that prevention is a desirable goal, it is much more difficult to determine the most appropriate prevention program to develop, how it will be implemented, who will pay for it, and how we will measure its effectiveness.

In this chapter we outline different models that have guided the development of prevention programs. We present some key concepts in prevention science and illustrate them by briefly describing programs that have been found effective in addressing problems of substance abuse, promoting effective parenting, preventing violence, preventing internalizing disorders, and reducing the negative sequelae of trauma and loss. Because prevention is based on the principle of early intervention, a very large number of efforts focus on children and youth (Weissberg, Kumpfer, & Seligman, 2003). Although there are many innovative and promising prevention programs that target adults (Dozois & Dobson, 2004; Le, Muñoz, Ippen, & Stoddard, 2003; Zabinski, Wilfley, Winzelberg, Taylor, & Calfas, 2004) we focus most of our presentation on programs that target children and youth. **Profile Box 10.1** presents the Centre for Children and Families in the Justice System in London, Ontario, which serves vulnerable young people dealing with diverse stressors. The Centre has been at the forefront of the development of innovative prevention programs addressing both internalizing and externalizing problems.

PROFILE BOX 10.1

CENTRE FOR CHILDREN AND FAMILIES IN THE JUSTICE SYSTEM

The Centre is a non-profit, community-based organization whose mission is to help children and families involved with the justice system. The youth we serve may be victims of crime or abuse, youthful offenders, the subjects of custody/access disputes, the subjects of child welfare proceedings, parties in civil litigation, or residents of treatment or custody facilities. Our goal is to help vulnerable children achieve their full potential in life, through prevention programs, professional training, resource development, applied research, public education, community collaboration, and by the provision of clinical services.

Dr. Linda Baker

Psychological services are part of the multidisciplinary approach at the Centre and psychologists are involved in diverse activities. In addition to their administrative roles, psychologists conduct court-ordered assessments in youth justice, child welfare, child witness, custody and access, civil litigation, and victim services. Psychologists often are subpoenaed as expert witnesses to educate the court on areas of their expertise and to explain multidisciplinary assessments completed for court. Psychologists also play a key role in supervision, proposal writing, research, resource development, training, public education, and consultation.

Graduate students from a wide array of disciplines obtain training at the Centre. Opportunities exist for psychology students to come on practicum placements, internships, or postdoctoral programs. Working under the supervision of psychologists, students participate on multidisciplinary teams in a dynamic clinical environment and in a diversity of challenging cases.

The Centre's reputation for research and integrating evidence and practice is recognized internationally. Team members work with government agencies and professional organizations to help inform the development of legislation, policy, and practice standards. Needs and gaps in knowledge are identified through the Centre's clinical programs and consultation with professionals in the field. This information informs applied research conducted at the Centre, ranging from qualitative, exploratory research on the experience of children living with violence to multi-site, randomized effectiveness trials of Multisystemic Therapy with long-term follow-up. (You will learn more about Multisystemic Therapy in Chapter 13). The Centre also plays a key role in translating our research and that of others into implications for practice. Large bodies of literature are reviewed from multiple disciplines on a variety of children's issues (e.g., exposure to domestic violence; child and adolescent depression; and preventive interventions for antisocial behaviour in youth).

The Centre is involved in providing and evaluating all types of prevention programs. One of our universal prevention initiatives, *A School-based Anti-violence Program* (ASAP), is designed to promote healthy relationships in children and adolescents attending school. ASAP provides educators with a compendium of information on different types of violence, and most importantly, provides concrete strategies for promoting respectful relationships at the curriculum, classroom, school, and school board level. The importance of involving students, parents, educators, school administrators, and the broader community in promoting healthy relationships is stressed. The prevention strategy is to establish a caring school culture where all members of the school community are safe, and to build student competencies for meeting needs and resolving conflict in respectful ways.

The Centre helped develop an indicated prevention program for child witnesses to woman abuse. Research completed at the Centre in the early 1980s revealed that children exposed to woman abuse experienced higher rates of adjustment diffi-culties, including depression, anxiety, and externalizing behaviours. Also, these children were viewed to be at risk of injury because of the violence in their homes, as well as being vulnerable to short- and long-term adjustment difficulties, including later involvement in abusive relationships. The group program for child witnesses was designed to lower the risk for adjustment difficulties in children exposed to woman abuse, to increase their safety, and to increase healthy relationship skills (e.g., conflict resolution skills). Socializing with other children with similar experi-ences in a safe and nurturing environment was also an important component of this intervention. This pioneering prevention initiative has been implemented through-out Ontario and in many parts of Canada.

Another example of an indicated prevention program we offer is our *Adolescent Suicide Prevention* initiative. Adolescent suicide is the second leading cause of death among adolescents in Canada and youth in justice facilities have been shown to be at higher risk for suicidal behaviours. We were asked to develop a pro-gram to reduce suicide attempts and completions in young people in residential settings within the justice system. Based on consultation with leaders in the field, we selected to meet this objective by increasing the capacity of frontline staff teams to identify risk and implement preventive interventions. A three-day training program with a complementary resource was developed. The content of the training target-ed: recognizing risk and protective factors, increasing skills for de-escalating suicidal crises safely, increasing access to and the effective use of consultations from mental health service providers, and implementing effective safety contracting and longer term supportive interventions. Two staff members from every setting are trained and then train their co-workers in suicide prevention. The training initiative was piloted with two groups in southwestern Ontario. Based on the feedback, additions were made to the resource and plans to roll out the prevention initiative were designed. The train-the-trainer suicide prevention program is being delivered to representa-tives of all youth justice custody settings throughout Ontario.

Changes in the profession of clinical psychology that are particularly exciting for our agency include the recognition of the importance of interdisciplinary approaches in community-based services, the increased emphasis placed on preventive intervention programs and evaluation research on both risk and protective factors related to chil-dren's healthy development, the role that psychologists are playing in clinical administration, the increased number of and opportunities for women in psychology, and the increased demand for psychologists to play a role in gathering information to inform decision-making by those charged with governance and development of policy.

VIEWPOINT BOX 10.1

POVERTY

In 2003, UNICEF released troubling results indicating that more than one billion children worldwide suffer the severe effects of poverty and are deprived of basic human rights such as adequate shelter, food, water, sanitation, and education. There is, however, no internationally agreed on definition of poverty. As politicians and scholars point out, the definition of poverty varies according to a country's level of affluence. There are basically two ways to identify and track those who are vulnerable to the effects of poverty: in relative terms or in absolute terms. Relative definitions identify the proportion of the population whose income is significantly below the median income. This is a statistical definition. Absolute means identify those people whose incomes are insufficient to purchase goods and services that are considered essential. The Luxembourg Income Study (2000) developed methods for comparing poverty rates across 25 countries by calculating the proportions of people whose income was 50% of the median income. Data for 1994 indicated that the highest proportion of children living in poverty among the 25 countries evaluated was Mexico (26.1%), followed by the United States (24.5%). Levels of child poverty were similar in Australia (15.8%), Canada (15.4%), Ireland (14.6%), and the United Kingdom (13.9%). The pattern with respect to the elderly was somewhat different, with the bleakest statistics indicating that 31.0% of elderly Mexicans had incomes 50% of the median, followed by Australia (29.4%), the United States (20.6%), Ireland (17.3%), and the United Kingdom (15.1%). At 4.9%, the figures for older Canadians were dramatically lower than those for Canadian children living in poverty.

For decades, social scientists have recognized the deleterious consequences of child poverty on children's mental and physical health status. Scholars now see that children living in poverty are subject to multiple risk factors that have cumulative negative effects on their well-being. Poverty is harmful to the physical, socio-emotional, and cognitive well-being of children, youth, and their families (Evans, 2004). Compared with other children, children living in poverty are more likely to be exposed to family disruption and violence, their parents are less responsive, read to them less frequently, and are less involved with their school activities. These children are more likely to be exposed to environmental pollutants, live in more crowded housing, and attend poorer quality daycare.

So how is all of this relevant to clinical psychology? The most important message is that children living in poverty are being attacked on multiple fronts. They are compromised in all areas of their lives. Consequently, any efforts to prevent negative outcomes for these vulnerable children must take into account the effects not simply of one stressor or disadvantage, but of the pileup of stressors. Although it may be conceptually easier to study the effects of children witnessing violence in one study and the children of alcoholic parents in another study, we now understand that there is tremendous overlap in the different populations—the child whom we identify as exposed to violence in one study may be the same child identified as the child of an alcoholic parent in another study, and as an aggressive child in a third study. The serious, cumulative, and chronic risks to which children in poverty are exposed require high dosage prevention programs to buffer children from the pileup of challenges these children face. A meta-analysis of the effectiveness of preschool prevention programs (Nelson, Westhues, & MacLeod, 2003) provided encouraging data indicating that positive effects of intensive preschool interventions for multiply disadvantaged children are sustained in the short-, medium-, and long-term. Not surprisingly, the longer and the more intense the intervention, the greater the gains.

APPROACHES TO PREVENTION

The Commission on Chronic Illness (1957) identified three different types of intervention with respect to illness: primary, secondary, and tertiary. Primary intervention occurs before a disorder has developed and is designed to prevent the development of the disorder. Secondary intervention occurs when a disorder is evident; we usually refer to this type of intervention as treatment. Tertiary intervention occurs with respect to a chronic disorder and focuses on rehabilitation and long-term adaptation. The model of primary, secondary, and tertiary intervention that was originally designed to categorize services with respect to physical illness was then applied to mental disorders. Traditionally, the focus of psychological services has been at the level of secondary intervention or treatment. As described in Chapter 1, clinical psychologists also have extended their services both toward primary intervention in the prevention of problems and toward tertiary intervention in rehabilitation services.

It is also useful to think of distinctions among prevention programs. One distinction involves universal preventive interventions, selective preventive interventions, and indicated preventive interventions (Mrazek & Haggerty, 1994). As the name implies, **universal preventive interventions** are applied to an entire population. As a member of the general public you will have been exposed to several universal preventive interventions. You may, for example, remember television advertising campaigns designed to reduce undesirable activities such as wife assault or smoking, or to promote healthy activities such as regular physical exercise. Your parents probably remember the initial advertising campaigns to encourage the wearing of seat belts while driving. During the SARS crisis, universal programs reminded the public to reduce contagion by frequent and thorough hand-washing. **Selective preventive interventions**, on the other hand, target people who are at elevated risk of developing a particular disorder or problem. So, to continue with the SARS example, selective prevention programs required people entering hospitals to wear masks. **Indicated preventive interventions** target people who do not meet criteria for a disorder, but who have elevated risk and may show detectable, but subclinical signs of the disorder. Those who had come into contact with a confirmed case of SARS were targets for indicated preventive interventions requiring a period of quarantine. We can probably all agree that the goal of preventing SARS, a debilitating, contagious, and potentially fatal disease, is a good one. Nevertheless, there is controversy about the most effective prevention efforts. If you were a nurse in a hospital caring for patients with SARS, you would want compelling evidence that the prevention strategies were effective in protecting you from potentially fatal infection. Similarly, if your life was effectively put on hold for almost two weeks by imposed quarantine (missing school, recreation, and social life), you would probably want reassurance that this sacrifice was necessary to help contain the spread of the disease. This means that prevention programs should be evaluated to determine whether they are meeting their goals. A clear example of this: post-SARS crisis analysis of the usefulness of infrared cameras in airports revealed that this expensive and intrusive procedure was not effective in detecting a single case of SARS.

Some prevention scientists consider that these categories have an overreliance on a disease model and have proposed that psychologists think instead in terms of promoting health (e.g., Kaplan, 2000). This of courses raises the question of what we mean by health. Health is not simply the opposite of illness. There is no universal definition of health—it all depends on the person's context. Younger people often consider health in terms of fitness, energy, and strength. Older people tend to see health in terms of their inner strength and their ability to meet life's challenges (World Health Organization, 2004). The World Health Organization defines mental health promotion activities as those designed to increase well-being and resilience. Different types of prevention programs are designed to reduce the symptoms and burden of mental disorders. **Primary prevention** is based on a behavioural model of functioning and does not rely on the concept of disease. Primary prevention is focused on the provision of conditions conducive to good health. Primary prevention is similar to the concept of health promotion. **Secondary prevention** is more similar to selected and indicated prevention programs because it focuses on prevention in groups of people who are identified as being at high risk. The **risk reduction model** of prevention relies heavily on research to guide interventions (Mrazek & Haggerty, 1994). **Risk factors** are characteristics of the individual or the environment that render a person more vulnerable to the development of a problem or disorder, or that are associated with more severe symptoms. Once at-risk individuals are identified, they are the target of prevention programs designed to protect them from developing the problem or disorder. The other side of the coin is the identification of factors associated with resilience—those characteristics that protect high-risk individuals from developing the problem or disorder. If we understand the variables that are protective, then we can use such knowledge in developing effective prevention programs.

The science of prevention requires knowledge of a problem, its prevalence, variables that are causally involved in its development, the mechanisms of risk transmission, and particular subgroups that are at high risk. Obviously not all risk factors are equally malleable, so it makes sense to target those risk factors that can be changed. Some risk and **protective factors** are specific to disorders, whereas others are generic. Potential risk and protective factors associated with the development of psychopathology in children and youth are listed in **Tables 10.1** and **10.2**.

TABLE 10.1   Risk Factors Potentially Influencing the Development of Psychopathology in Children and Youth

Individual factors
- complications in pregnancy
- prenatal brain damage
- neurochemical imbalance
- premature birth
- birth injury
- low birth weight
- birth complication
- physical or intellectual disability
- learning disability
- physical health problems
- insecure attachment to caregiver
- low intelligence
- difficult temperament
- chronic illness
- poor social skills
- low self-esteem
- peer rejection
- impulsivity
- attentional deficits

School context
- bullying
- peer rejection
- no connection to school
- inadequate behaviour management
- deviant peer group
- school failure

Family/Social factors
- teenage mother
- single parent
- absent father in childhood
- large family size
- antisocial role models in family
- exposure to family or community violence
- marital discord or conflict
- poor supervision and monitoring of child, harsh or inconsistent discipline
- parental abuse or neglect
- long-term parental unemployment
- criminality in family
- parental substance use/abuse
- parental mental illness

Life events and situations
- physical, sexual, or verbal abuse
- frequent social changes
- family divorce or separation
- death of family member
- severe physical illness or injury to self or family member
- parental unemployment
- homelessness
- parental imprisonment
- poverty
- war or natural disasters
- witnessing trauma
- migration

continued...

Community and cultural factors

- socioeconomic disadvantage
- social or cultural discrimination
- isolation
- exposure to community violence or crime

- high-density living
- poor housing conditions
- isolated from support services including transport, shopping, recreational facilities

Reproduced with permission. Barrett & Turner, 2004.

TABLE 10.2   Protective Factors Potentially Influencing the Development of Psychopathology in Children and Youth

Individual factors

- easy temperament
- adequate nutrition
- positive attachment to family
- above-average intelligence
- school achievement
- problem-solving skills
- internal locus of control
- social competence
- social skills
- adequate coping skills
- proactive coping style
- optimism
- positive self-esteem

Family/Social factors

- supportive caring parents
- family harmony
- small family size
- more than two years between siblings
- responsibility within the family
- supportive relationship with another adult (aside from parents)
- strong family norms and prosocial values

School context

- sense of belonging
- positive school context
- prosocial peer group
- required responsibility and helpfulness
- opportunities for some success and recognition of achievement
- school norms against violence
- positive school-home relations
- quality schools

Life events and situations

- involvement with significant other person (e.g., mentor)
- availability of opportunities at critical turning points or major life transitions
- economic security

Community and cultural factors

- attachment to networks within the community
- participation in church or other community groups
- strong cultural identity and ethnic pride
- access to support services
- community/cultural norms against violence

Reproduced with permission. Barrett & Turner, 2004.

Once a program has been designed, the prevention scientist must carefully monitor its implementation to ensure that it is conducted as planned. This is especially important, as the prevention program is likely to be implemented in numerous agencies that vary in their resources and staff skills. Both the program's short- and long-term outcomes must be monitored in order to fully evaluate its impact. **Table 10.3** describes the process that a researcher follows in developing a prevention program.

TABLE 10.3   Designing and Evaluating Prevention Research

- Identifying the target: what do you want to prevent?

- Determine how serious the problem is. How many people are affected? What are the costs of the problem, in human suffering, health care costs, etc.?

- Review the research evidence about the problem. What do we know about how the risk factors develop? What variables make it more likely that a problem will develop?

- Identify high-risk groups. These are the factors that have been shown to moderate risk.

- What is known about protective factors?

- Designing the intervention: How will the target condition be prevented? Is there an evidence-based prevention program for this problem? If so, does it need to be modified for my community?

- Designing the study: How will you know if the intervention is effective?

Although more than 1,000 controlled studies have examined the effectiveness of programs designed to prevent mental health problems, very few have examined whether these programs are effective in reducing the incidence of new cases of a disorder (Cuijpers, 2003). In order to have the statistical power to detect a difference in the incidence of disorder, it would be necessary to have studies with very large samples. Alternative research strategies are to target high-risk samples, to offer the program at high intensity, or to rely on accumulating samples from different studies. Although used with increasing frequency, these strategies remain underutilized in evaluating the impact of prevention efforts.

Durlak and Wells (1997) conducted a comprehensive meta-analysis of 177 controlled outcome studies of programs designed to prevent a variety of problems. They concluded that programs designed to modify the school environment, individually focused mental health promotion programs, and programs to help children negotiate life transitions produced outcomes equal or superior to the effects of prevention programs in medicine. Meta-analytic reviews of prevention programs are very useful in identifying the types of programs that have demonstrated effectiveness. You may recall learning in Chapter 4 the distinction between efficacy and effectiveness. These concepts apply to the science of prevention just as they do to intervention research. Once a prevention program has been shown to be efficacious in controlled studies, it is likely to be adopted in other less strictly controlled settings. Effectiveness refers to the extent to which a prevention program achieves desired outcomes when used in an applied setting rather than in the original research conditions. Even if a program has been demonstrated to be effective in other settings and meta-analyses have yielded positive results, it is important that the program be evaluated to determine its usefulness in each setting in which it is applied.

PREVENTION OF SUBSTANCE ABUSE

The societal costs of smoking, alcohol abuse, and drug abuse are enormous. Alcohol, tobacco, and drug use during pregnancy are associated with a host of deleterious consequences such as premature delivery, low birth weight, perinatal mortality, and long-term neurological and cognitive-emotional problems (World Health Organization, 2004). It is estimated that tobacco is responsible for 4.1% of the total global economic costs due to disability, with alcohol accounting for another 4.0% (World Health Organization, 2004). Substance abuse is a leading cause of adolescent morbidity and mortality due to its links with motor vehicle accidents and with sexual behaviour leading to unplanned pregnancies and HIV infection (Essau, 2004). Problems with smoking, alcohol, and drug abuse emerge during adolescence. There is evidence that the early onset of consumption is associated with higher risk of abuse (Essau, 2004). **Table 10.4** provides data from Canadian national surveys indicating that in Grade 9 (age 14–15), 1 in 7 young people reported smoking in the past 30 days; 1 in 5 12- to 15-year-olds reported that they had been drunk, with a first episode occurring when they were just over 13; over a third of 15-year-olds had used marijuana, and 1 in 10 reported using other illegal substances.

Problems with smoking, alcohol, and drug abuse emerge during adolescence.

TABLE 10.4   Consumption of Cigarettes, Alcohol, and Marijuana by Canadian Teens

Substance	Findings
Cigarettes[1]	2002
	6.2% of youth in Grades 5–9 had smoked in the past 30 days; the percentage increases from 1.2% in Grades 5 and 6 to 13.6% in Grade 9.
Alcohol[2]	1998
	Average age of first drink: 12.4 years; 42% of 12- to 15-year-olds had consumed at least one drink; 66% of 15-year-olds had consumed at least one drink;
	Average age of first episode of drunkenness: 13.2 years; 22% of 12- to 15-year-olds said they had been drunk once; 44% of 15-year-olds said they had been drunk once
Marijuana	1998[2]
	Average age of first use 13.1 years; 19% of 12- to 15-year-olds reported having smoked marijuana; 38% of 15-year-olds said they had smoked marijuana;
	2002[3]
	29% of 15- to 17-year-olds said they had used marijuana in the past year; 38% of 18- to 19-year-olds said they had used marijuana in the past year
Other illegal drugs[2]	1998
	Average age of first use: 13.8 years; 11% of 14- and 15-year-olds reported having used hallucinogens; 4% of 14- and 15-year-olds reported having used other drugs such as ecstasy or cocaine

1. Data from Statistics Canada, 2004b.
2. Data from Statistics Canada, 2004a.
3. Data from Statistics Canada, 2003.

Between 2001 and 2002, the World Health Organization conducted a study of the health behaviour of school-aged children in 35 countries (World Health Organization Europe, 2004). Results from this study indicate large differences between countries and regions in the proportions of young people who smoke regularly, ranging from 11 to 57% of 15-year-olds. Similarly, there is variability in the consumption of alcohol. Having been drunk twice or more is more common in young people from Canada and northern European countries than it is in youth in southern European countries. Regular use of marijuana is highest in Canada, Spain, and Switzerland.

Although alcohol use is common in society, not all those who drink alcohol go on to abuse it. What factors are associated with greater risk? Risk can be considered at the level of the individual, the family, peer group, and community, and at a provincial or national level according to the laws governing access to cigarettes and alcohol. Individual level risks include temperamental factors, coping skills, psychopathology, and exposure to negative life events. A large-scale study in New Zealand followed a cohort of 1,037 children from birth to adulthood (Caspi, Moffitt, Newman, & Silva, 1996). This study indicated that boys categorized at age three as being either undercontrolled or as inhibited were at greater risk for developing alcohol problems in early adulthood. This finding should have important ramifications for the development of prevention programs because it implies that the risk factors are present many years before the young person starts drinking. Nevertheless, most prevention efforts focus on youth in high school. Unfortunately, some of the high-risk youth may also be at risk of school dropout and may therefore not receive the program (Zucker, 2003). Those at risk for one problem behaviour may also be at risk for others. For example, adolescent smoking is highly correlated with engagement in other problem behaviours including alcohol abuse, antisocial behaviour, high-risk sexual behaviours, and academic failure (Biglan & Severson, 2003).

Universal preventive interventions can focus on regulating young people's access to tobacco and alcohol as well as education about their harmful effects. A series of meta-analyses by Tobler and colleagues (Tobler et al., 2000) distinguished between two types of programs: interactive and noninteractive. *Interactive programs* that foster the development of interpersonal skills yielded higher effect sizes than did lecture-based *noninteractive programs*. The effective programs begin by providing multiple sessions early in adolescence and follow them with booster sessions in mid-adolescence (Coughlan, Doyle, & Carr, 2002). **Table 10.5** illustrates features of effective drug abuse prevention programs.

Although it makes sense to think that in selecting a prevention program, organizations would be guided by the results of meta-analyses of the scientific literature, unfortunately, this is not always the case. For example, Ennett and colleagues (2003) surveyed a national sample of public and private schools in the United States about the programs they used to prevent substance abuse. Although Tobler's series of meta-analyses clearly identified that programs are most effective when they include interactive teaching strategies, only 17.4% of surveyed programs delivered material in an interactive style. It is possible that sufficient time had not passed for Tobler's work to influence these school programs. On the other hand, the majority of the studies used in the meta-analyses had been available for many years with, apparently, limited effect on the nature of school-based prevention efforts. Psychologists' ethical codes dictate that they should strive to deliver programs that work, and taxpayers expect that funds should be directed toward those programs that are most cost-effective. It is essential therefore that priority be given to developing scientifically based programs that are effective in preventing problems and in promoting health.

Problems of substance abuse are particularly acute in some indigenous populations. Although risk and protective factors for the development of substance abuse may be similar in American Indian populations and in the general population, there has been little systematic study of any culture-specific risk and protective factors, or of the effectiveness of prevention programs in these populations (Hawkins, Cummins, & Marlatt, 2004). As a step toward addressing this shortcoming in our knowledge, a group of researchers from the University of Washington has collaborated with the Seattle Indian Health Board to develop a program based on empirically supported principles that will be delivered congruent with the culture of urban native youth (Hawkins et al., 2004). Evaluations of this *Journeys of the Circle* program are underway.

TABLE 10.5   Key Elements of Effective Drug Abuse Prevention Programs

Resistance skills and normative education	• skills to identify social pressure to use drugs and skills to resist such pressure • accurate knowledge about prevalence of drug use to help develop conservative drug use norms
Life skills	• assertiveness skills • skills for improving self-control and self-esteem • stress management skills • social communication and problem-solving skills • decision-making skills • skills for developing social alternatives to drug use
Multisystemic involvement	• peer-leader involvement in program delivery • peer group projects exploring alternatives to drug use • home-school liaison about drug use prevention policy • parent-child homework assignments about drug abuse prevention • parent training in parent-adolescent communication, limit-setting, and supervision • community involvement in drug abuse prevention task force
General design features	• adequate training, support and supervision of teachers, peer leaders and program staff • manualized program curricula • monitoring of accurate program implementation • active training methods (modelling, rehearsal, corrective feedback, reinforcement and extended practice) • begin at the transition from primary to secondary school when youngsters are aged 11–13 • extend over at least a school year and include booster sessions annually throughout high school • incorporated into existing school curriculum • developmentally staged • socially and culturally acceptable to the community, particularly where youngsters are from ethnic minorities • rigorously evaluated and feedback of evaluation given to implementation team and participants

Adapted from Coughlan, Doyle, & Carr, 2002.

PROMOTING EVIDENCE-BASED PARENTING

Parents play a key role in their children's socialization. The task of parenting children is a demanding one that requires no licence, training, or supervision. As shown in Table 10.1, harsh or inconsistent discipline, poor supervision and monitoring of a child, parental abuse, and neglect are risk factors that are associated with the development of child and adolescent psychopathology. On the other hand, the availability of supportive, caring parents can protect children and youth from the development of psychopathology (Table 10.2). Although the responsibilities of child-rearing can be daunting at times to all parents, some parents are particularly vulnerable due to their age, isolation, distress, conflict, or limited socio-economic resources. There is strong evidence that children's functioning is challenged by poor parenting, conflict in the family, and parental psychopathology (Biglan, 2003; World Health Organization, 2004). We describe below three evidence-based programs that have been developed to promote good parenting and therefore to decrease risk factors for diverse child problems.

Triple P

Developed by psychologist Matthew Sanders and his colleagues in Australia, the *Triple P Positive Parenting Program* is an evidence-based parenting program designed to (a) enhance knowledge, skills, and confidence of parents; (b) promote safe environments for young people; and (c) promote children's competence through positive parenting practices (Bor, Sanders, & Markie-Dadds, 2002; Sanders, 1999; Sanders, Cann, & Markie-Dadds, 2003; Sanders, Markie-Dadds, Turner, & Ralph, 2004). Consistent with the idea of adapting programs to offer different "dosages" of intervention according to participants' needs, the *Triple P* program is a multi-level system that provides interventions of gradually increasing intensity, according to the level of need (Collins, Murphy, & Bierman, 2004). **Table 10.6** illustrates the different "dosages" of *Triple P*.

The *Universal Triple P* program is offered to all interested parents using a variety of media to provide evidence-based information about general parenting strategies to deal with everyday issues and challenges. The next step in the program hierarchy is to offer brief (one- or two-session) individualized services by phone or face to face to address parents' specific concerns. Moving one step further, parents of children with mild to moderate problems may benefit from a program delivered over four sessions by a primary health care provider. Parents of children with more severe behaviour problems may require the *Standard Triple P* offered in either a group or self-directed format. The most intensive intervention is the *Enhanced Triple P* that includes not only parenting skills, but also additional sessions focused on parents' mood, coping, and partner support.

Program materials are designed for five different developmental stages (infants, toddlers, preschoolers, children in elementary school, and teenagers). The program is designed to enhance

TABLE 10.6   The Triple P Model of Parenting and Family Support

Level of intervention	Target population
1. Universal Triple P Media-based parenting information campaign	All parents interested in information about parenting and promoting their child's development
2. Selected Triple P Information and advice for a specific parenting concern	Parents with specific concerns about their child's behaviour or development.
3. Primary Care Triple P Narrow-focus parenting skills training	Parents with specific concerns about their child's behaviour or development who require consultations or active skills training.
4. Standard Triple P Group Triple P Self-Directed Triple P Broad-focus parenting skills training	Parents with specific concerns about their child's behaviour or development who require consultations or active skills training. Typically targets parents of children with more severe behaviour problems.
5. Enhanced Triple P Behavioural family intervention	Parents of children with concurrent child behaviour problems and family dysfunction

protective factors and to decrease risk factors for child problems. Consequently, parents are trained to develop positive relationships with their children, encourage desirable behaviour, teach new skills, and manage misbehaviour. Parents are encouraged to adopt developmentally appropriate expectations about their child's behaviour. The importance of taking care of oneself as a parent is also stressed. *The Triple P* approach involves intense training of practitioners as well as continuing education for those who deliver the program.

The developers of the *Triple P* approach have conducted a series of randomized controlled trials comparing *Triple P* interventions with wait-list control groups, as well as comparing different formats of *Triple P* (Sanders et al., 2004). Results of this research indicate that *Triple P* is effective in helping parents adopt positive parenting practices, which in turn is associated with fewer child problems, greater parental confidence, and enhanced parental well-being (Sanders et al., 2004). Currently the *Triple P* program is being adapted for use in diverse populations in several countries and evaluations of those programs are underway.

Intervention methods	Possible target areas
A coordinated information campaign using print and electronic media and other health promotion strategies to promote awareness of parenting issues and normalize participation in parenting programmes such as Triple P. May include some contact with professional staff (e.g., telephone information line)	• General parenting issues • Common everyday behavioural and developmental issues
Provision of specific advice on how to solve common child developmental issues and minor child behaviour problems. May involve face-to-face or telephone contact with a practitioner (about 20 min over two sessions) or (60-90-min) seminars.	• Common behaviour difficulties or developmental transitions, such as toilet training, bedtime problems
A brief programme (about 80 min over four sessions) combining advice with rehearsal and self-evaluation as required to teach parents to manage discrete child problem behaviour. May involve face-to-face or telephone contact with a practitioner.	• Discrete child behaviour problems, such as tantrums, whining, fighting with siblings
A broad-focus programme (up to 12 1-hour sessions) for parents requiring intensive training in positive parenting skills and generalization enhancement strategies. Application of parenting skills to a broad range of target behaviours, settings, and children. Programme variants include individual, group or self-directed (with or without telephone assistance) options.	• Multiple child behaviour problems • Aggressive behaviour • Oppositional defiant disorder • Conduct disorder • Learning difficulties
An intensive individually tailored programme (up to 11 1-hour sessions) for families with child behaviour problems and family dysfunction. Programme modules include home visits to enhance parenting skills, mood management strategies and stress coping skills, and partner support skills.	• Concurrent child behaviour problems and parent problems (e.g., relationship conflict, depression, stress)

From Sanders et al., 2003. Originally printed in: M. R. Sanders, C, Markie-Dadds, and K. M. T. Turner, 2001, *Practitioner's manual for stand Triple P*. Brisbane AU, Families International Publishing.

Home Visiting Programs

A number of programs have demonstrated impressive results in targeting at-risk parents. In a 25-year research program, Olds and his colleagues have developed, implemented, tested, and replicated a program offering services to low-income teenage single mothers expecting their first child (Olds, 2002). Home visits were conducted by trained nurses beginning during the pregnancy and continuing after the child's birth. During these visits nurses addressed women's concerns about the pregnancy, delivery, and care of the child. They taught skills in both self-care and child care and promoted women's use of the health care system. **Figure 10.1** illustrates the model of program influences on maternal and child health and development.

Figure 10.1 Model of Influences of Home Visit Program on Maternal and Child Health and Development

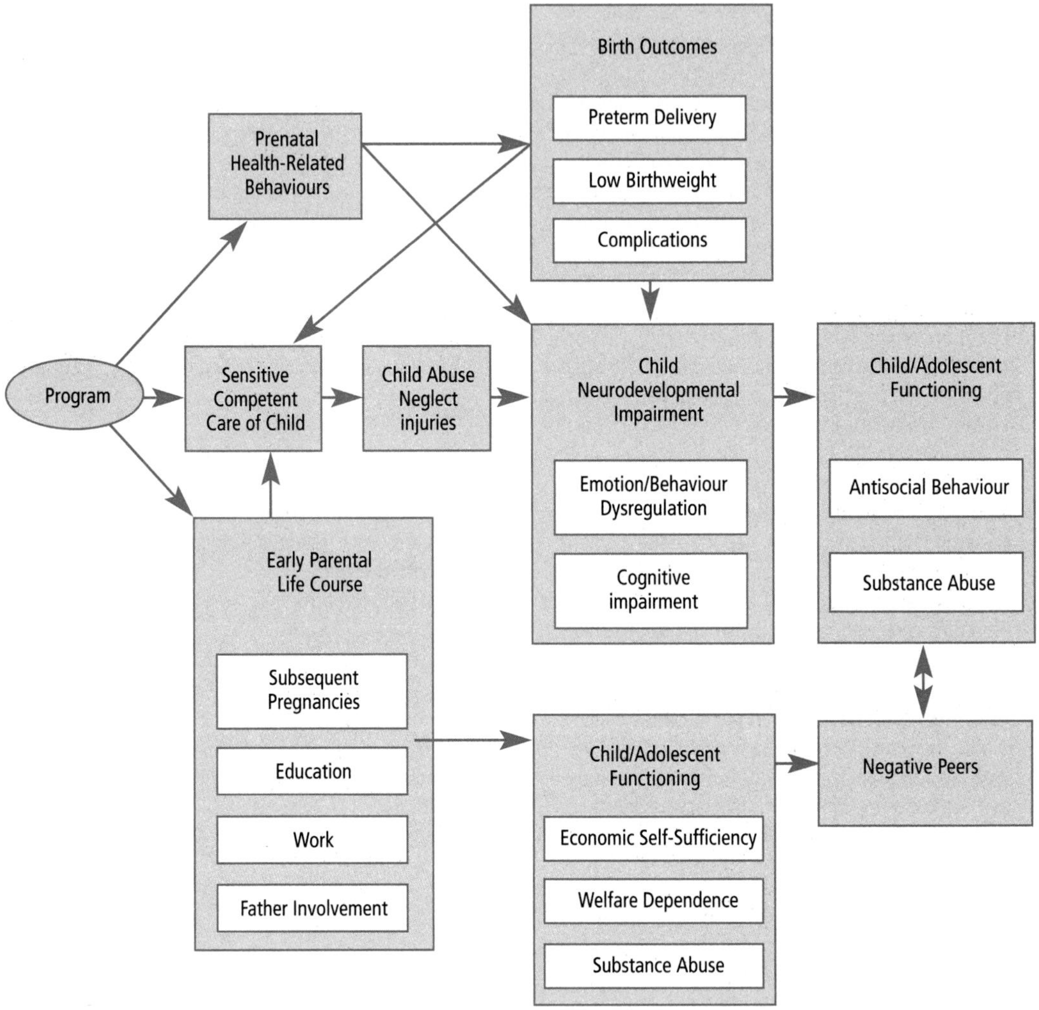

Reproduced from Olds (2002). With permission from Springer Science and Business Media.

In randomized controlled trials, Olds and his colleagues have found that the home visit program is effective in achieving the immediate goal of improving parental care. In the middle term, this has benefits for children in terms of reducing child abuse and neglect, and in the long-term, reducing the number of arrests, convictions, substance abuse problems, and sexual promiscuity in the children when they reached the age of 15. Furthermore, the program improves a young mother's life course by increasing labour force participation and her economic self-sufficiency.

These positive effects are all the more remarkable as nurses completed only an average of 8 visits during pregnancy and 25 visits during the child's first two years of life. Visits lasted up to an hour and a half. These short- and long-term gains were accomplished in a very high-risk group with the investment of under 50 hours of direct contact between nurses and teenage mothers. In general, the most beneficial effects were found for the families who were at greatest risk.

Incredible Years

Developed and refined over 20 years of research by psychologist **Carolyn Webster-Stratton**, the *Incredible Years* training program was originally designed to help children aged 3–8 who had been identified as having conduct problems (Webster-Stratton & Reid, 2003). As the program was found to be successful in treating conduct problems, it has been expanded to cover a wider age range and has been offered as a prevention program (Baydar, Reid, & Webster-Stratton, 2003). The program uses group discussion, videotaped modelling, and behavioural rehearsal techniques to promote adult-child interactions that will facilitate children's development of social competence. The primary goal of the *Incredible Years* program is to train parents in skills so that they can effectively play

with their child, provide praise for positive behaviours, and set limits on unacceptable behaviours using time-out, ignoring, appropriate consequences, and problem-solving. The basic program is available for different age ranges and includes a minimum of 12 sessions (although additional sessions may be required). An advanced 9- to 12-session program targets parents' interpersonal difficulties by teaching problem-solving, anger management, communication, emotional regulation skills, and support-seeking skills. A supplementary program, *Supporting Your Child's Education*, helps parents whose children are experiencing school difficulties. Complementary programs involve training teachers (Webster-Stratton, Reid, & Hammond, 2001) and a 22-week child training program (Webster-Stratton & Reid, 2004) that teaches emotional literacy, perspective-taking, friendship skills,

Dr. Carolyn Webster-Stratton and a young child using the materials in the *Incredible Years* program.

anger management, and problem-solving. The effectiveness of this selective prevention program has been tested with more than 1,000 multiethnic, socio-economically disadvantaged families. Results support the program's effectiveness in promoting good parenting, enhancing children's social competence, and preventing the development of conduct problems (Gross et al., 2003; Webster-Stratton & Reid, 2003).

PREVENTION OF VIOLENCE

Physical Abuse of Children

Physical abuse of children refers to the deliberate infliction of injury on a child. Estimates of the incidence of physical abuse vary, as there is considerable variability in the definition of the boundaries between acceptable discipline and abuse. For example, although a growing number of countries have banned the use of physical punishment, in both Canada and the United States parents are permitted to punish their children physically, as long as they do not inflict physical harm. A review of 20 methodologically sound studies of programs designed to prevent parents' physical abuse of children found that home visiting programs, behavioural parent training programs, and multimodal programs were effective in modifying the risk of physical abuse (O'Riordan & Carr, 2002). The risk of child abuse by poor, single teenage mothers who participated in the home visiting programs described in the previous section (Olds, 2002) was half that of comparison mothers who did not participate. Both behavioural training and stress management training were effective in improving maternal reports of their own well-being and child welfare; these positive effects were evident both in the short-term and at long-term follow-up. Unfortunately, improvements in parenting skills were evident in the short-term only and were not maintained at follow-up. Multimodal programs appear to blend the benefits of both home visits and skills-based programs and have the advantage of minimizing participant attrition (O'Riordan & Carr, 2002).

Programs designed to prevent parents' physical abuse of children have been effective in modifying the risk of physical abuse.

Youth Violence: Bullying and Delinquency

One of the most common reasons children are referred to mental health clinics stems from problems with aggressive and noncompliant behaviour (Miller & Prinz, 1990). A subgroup of children exhibits risk factors for the development of aggression from a very early age (Nagin & Tremblay, 1999). By the time these young people reach adolescence, their aggressive behaviour has brought them into conflict with the law and they are alienated from the school system (Fisher, 2003). Intervention at that stage has only limited success as these young people are very resistant to efforts to change their behaviour (Fisher, 2003). If we have such limited success in treating conduct disorder once it has developed, it makes much more sense then to try to prevent its development in the first place (Biglan, 2003; World Health Organization, 2004).

There is some overlap between the types of programs designed to prevent violence and delinquency and those designed to treat oppositional defiant disorder and conduct disorder in young children. In a previous section we described programs for families with very young children such as home visits, *Triple P*, and *Incredible Years* that have been successful in promoting parenting, enhancing child competence, and reducing child aggression.

School-based interventions that directly target aggression and violence by training students in anger management and conflict resolution have reported mixed success (Prinz & Dumas, 2004). For example, observers may note improvements in prosocial behaviours, but there may be no change in parent or teacher ratings of the youth's aggression. In other studies youth know-ledge of socially appropriate responses increases, but there is limited change in violent behaviour after participation in the program. More encouraging results were found in a comprehensive school-based program to reduce bullying in children aged 6–15 years developed in Norway following the suicide of two youth who were the victims of bullying (Olweus, 1993). The program is designed to reduce both the opportunities and the rewards for bullying. This comprehensive program encourages changes in the school (anti-bullying policy) and in the classroom (anti-bullying rules and discussion of alternatives to antisocial behaviour), and promotes links between family and schools. The program is effective not only in reducing bullying, but in reducing antisocial behaviour in general and in enhancing student satisfaction with school. A study of 37 schools and 89 teachers who used the *Olweus Bullying Prevention Program* to varying degrees revealed that teachers are the key agent of change: their recognition of a problem with bullying and their commitment to the program are essential to its effective implementation (Kallestad & Olweus, 2003). The Olweus program has been applied in many countries. McCarthy and Carr (2002) reviewed four studies of its effectiveness, including data from 110 schools and almost 20,000 youths. They concluded that the program is effective in reducing reports of bullying as well as reducing reports of being bullied. These effects are evident in the short-term and, importantly, are sustained over longer periods. Consistent with our previous comments about prevention program implementation, program effectiveness is determined by the extent to which program integrity is maintained. When the program is diluted, effects are reduced (McCarthy & Carr, 2002). The whole-school bullying prevention programs are described in **Table 10.7**.

TABLE 10.7   Components of a Whole-School Bullying Prevention Program

Goals	• To increase awareness and knowledge of bully–victim problems • To achieve active involvement on the part of parents and teachers • To develop clear rules against bullying • To provide support and protection for victims
Policy principles	• Parents and teachers co-operate in engaging in authoritative adult–child relationships with pupils • Firm limits to unacceptable behaviour • Non-physical sanctions consistently applied for rule violations
School strategies	• Develop joint long-term action plan for the school • Regular meetings of teachers together; parents together; and parents and teachers together, to develop anti-bullying social milieu of the school • Provide supervision of children during recess and lunchtime • Teachers to be contactable by children and parents in confidence
Class strategies	• Regular class meetings • Teachers and pupils jointly establish class rules and sanctions against bullying • Teachers praise pupils for pro-social behaviour • Teachers consistently apply sanctions for bullying • Teachers promote co-operative learning through group projects and activities where participation and effort are encouraged • Teachers use role-playing, rehearsal, and discussion of bullying-related videos and literature to support anti-bullying social milieu
Individual strategies	• Teachers talk with bullies and victims and their parents about bullying incidents as soon as incidents come to light • These meetings continue until the bullying is resolved • Parents and teachers co-operate in applying sanctions for bullying consistently • Parents and teachers support both victims and bullies as they move on from the bullying incident • Neutral pupils may be involved to aid this support process • Where the incident cannot be resolved within a class, the bully not the victim may be moved to another class • Assertiveness training for victims • Peer counselling where pupils run a helpline for victims • Bully courts in which peers hear both sides of the story
Materials	• Booklet for schools (37-page booklet in Olweus pack) • Booklet for parents (4-page booklet in Olweus pack) • Bullying questionnaire • Video of bullying events for classroom discussion (25 minutes on events in lives of victims in the Olweus pack)

McCarthy & Carr, 2002.

A multicomponent prevention program, the *Fast Track* Project was launched in 1990 by the Conduct Problems Prevention Research Group (CPPRG; 2002a). This trial project was based on available research on risk and protective factors in the development of conduct disorder. The program was designed to assess the feasibility of (a) engaging community stakeholders in the project; (b) maintaining the program's fidelity while responding to local needs; and (c) maintaining community engagement so that the program would be sustainable (CPPRG, 2002a). The *Fast Track* program expanded on a program developed in Montreal to target high-risk children in kindergarten (Tremblay, Pagani-Kurtz, Mâsse, Vitaro, & Pihl, 1995). Screening of more than 9,000 kindergarten children identified a very high-risk sample of 891 children who were then randomly assigned to an intervention group or to a control group. A multi-year program was offered in the schools attended by the intervention group children. The intervention included a child component designed to increase academic competence, emotion-regulation, and social skills. Discipline, support of constructive behaviour, and monitoring of activities were targeted in the parent component. Group discussions were followed up by home visits. The classroom component involved a curriculum designed to promote self-control, emotional awareness, and social problem-solving. At the end of the first year, the program had been delivered successfully to most families and the results were encouraging (CPPRG, 2002b). Compared with the control group, children in the intervention had more positive interactions with their peers and were less frequently rejected. Parents in the intervention group were more involved with their children, were more consistent in their discipline strategies, and were less reliant on harsh physical punishment. Teachers rated intervention parents as more involved with their children's education. School observations revealed that the intervention children had fewer behavioural problems than did the untreated control children. As the goal of a prevention program is to reduce the incidence of problems in the future, longer-term assessment is essential. An assessment of children at the end of Grade 3 revealed that some of the gains had been maintained, but some effects had disappeared. Children who received the intervention were less likely to show signs of serious conduct problems than were children in the control group. **Figure 10.2** shows that more than a third of the children in the intervention group (37%) were classified as "problem-free" at the end of Grade 3, whereas just over a quarter of children in the control group were considered problem-free.

At first glance these results may seem disappointing, as almost two thirds of the children in the program were classified as having conduct problems. However, there is another way to look at these data. Although the total elimination of disorders or illnesses would be ideal, prevention programs usually have a more realistic goal of reducing the incidence of disorders. So, another way to think of the results is that the children who received the program were 37% less likely to have serious problems than were children in the control group. Follow-up at the end of Grades 4 and 5 indicated that high-risk children who participated in the program had better social competence, fewer problems in social cognition, less involvement with deviant peers, and fewer conduct problems than did high-risk children who did not participate (CPPRG, 2004). Although

Figure 10.2   Proportion of Intervention and Control Children Classified as Problem-Free

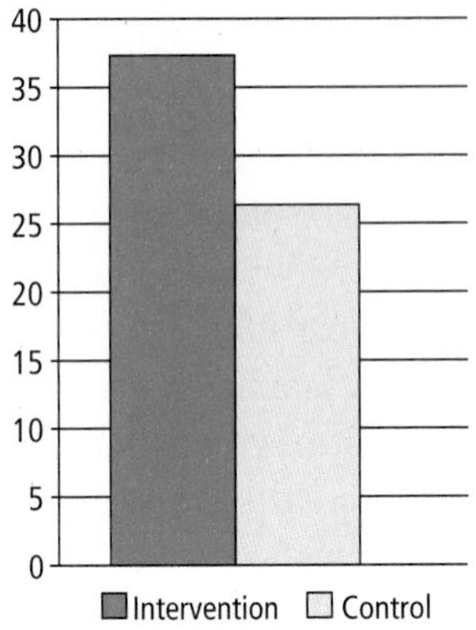

Conduct Problems Prevention Research Group. (2002b).
Reproduced with permission of Springer Science and Business Media.

significant, these effects were small. Ongoing evaluation of this program as the children progress toward adolescence will assess the long-term effectiveness of this intervention for children at very high risk of developing conduct problems.

PREVENTION OF INTERNALIZING DISORDERS

You may recall learning in Chapter 3 that researchers have found it useful to consider problem behaviours along two dimensions: internalizing problems and externalizing problems. So far in this chapter we have focused most of our discussion on the prevention of externalizing problems and on the promotion of good parenting. Externalizing problems are often dramatic and, when they result in injuries or damage to property, can yield sensational newspaper headlines. Internalizing problems, by definition, are more private. The person with internalizing problems may suffer quietly on his/her own without coming to anyone's attention. Internalizing problems are no less serious, however, and recent prevention efforts have also focused on ways to prevent the development of problems such as anxiety and depression.

The Canadian Community Health Survey is a national study of Canadians over the age of 15. Some key results are shown in **Table 10.8**. These data indicate that similar numbers of Canadians suffer from anxiety disorders or depressive disorders as from chronic physical disorders such as heart disease, diabetes, or a thyroid condition (Statistics Canada, 2003). In addition to their psychological toll, these disorders incur substantial costs to the health care system and to the economy. Internalizing problems are also evident in childhood. Some research suggests that anxiety problems in childhood may be related to the development of depression in young people (Cole, Peeke, Martin, Truglio, & Seroczynski, 1998). Psychologists have therefore been at the forefront of efforts to prevent anxiety and depression in children.

TABLE 10.8   Canadian Community Health Survey 2002: Mental Disorders in the Past 12 Months

Problem	Males	Females	Total
Any mood disorder	3.8%	5.9%	4.0%
Any anxiety disorder	3.6%	5.8%	4.7%

Anxiety Disorders

Risk factors for the development of anxiety include individual factors such as inhibited temperament and an avoidant coping style, as well as overprotective parenting practices and parental anxiety (Barrett & Turner, 2004). A group of Australian researchers, led by Paula Barrett, developed a prevention program that was adapted from an effective treatment program for children with anxiety disorders (Barrett & Turner, 2001; Dadds et al., 1999; Lowry-Webster & Barrett, 2001). In a selected prevention program, schoolchildren were screened to identify those with mild to moderate anxiety problems ($n = 128$) who were randomly assigned to an intervention group or to a monitoring group. The intervention was based on the *Coping Koala* program with 10 sessions offered to children in a group format as well as three sessions offered to parents, followed by booster sessions. Children who received the intervention were found to have lower rates of anxiety disorder at the end of treatment. At 12-month follow-up, differences between the intervention group and the comparison group had diminished, but by the 24-month follow-up, 39% of children in the untreated group met criteria for an anxiety disorder, whereas only 20% of children in the intervention group did so (Dadds et al., 1999). This means that participation in the program was associated with almost a 50% reduction in the incidence of anxiety disorders at two-year follow-up.

Barrett and Turner (2001) adapted the *Coping Koala* program to a format that could be used in a universal prevention program delivered by teachers (*Friends for Children* and *Friends for Youth*). Within a sample of 489 children, assignment was made to one of three conditions: psychologist-led preventive intervention, teacher-led preventive intervention, or standard curriculum. The intervention included 10 weekly sessions and two booster sessions as well as four parent sessions. Assessment at the end of the program revealed positive effects in both intervention conditions. These data suggest that the program can be effectively delivered by teachers. Longer-term follow-up evaluations and replications in other cultures are underway (Barrett & Turner, 2004).

Depression

Risk factors for the development of depression include individual variables such as interpersonal skills deficits and cognitive errors, family variables such as parental depression and marital conflict, as well as contextual factors such as negative life events (Barrett & Turner, 2004). A number of cognitive-behavioural programs have been designed to prevent the development of depression in adolescents (Essau, 2003). Because children of depressed parents are at elevated risk for developing a depressive disorder, prevention programs have examined the usefulness of a cognitive intervention to reduce rates of depressive symptoms in youth with a depressed parent (Clarke et al., 2001). The prevention program was an abbreviated version of an evidence-based treatment. Youth participated in 15 one-hour group sessions focused on cognitive restructuring and challenging unrealistic beliefs. In addition, parents participated in three meetings. Data indicated that following the program, participants had lower scores on measures of depressive symptomatology than did comparison youth who did not receive the program. At the 18- and 24-month follow-up assessments, the positive effects persisted but were not as large as at the post-program assessment.

A small-scale targeted prevention program was offered to 90 Grade 7 children with elevated scores on a measure of depressive symptoms (Roberts, Kane, Thomson, Hart, & Bishop, 2003). These children who attended elementary schools in rural Western Australia received a 12-session program taught by health education teachers addressing the links among thoughts and feelings, cognitive restructuring, coping skills, assertion, and social skills. Although no program effects were found for depressive symptoms, children who completed the program had lower anxiety and fewer internalizing problems than did comparison children who followed the regular health education curriculum. The positive effects for anxiety were maintained at 6-month follow-up.

A larger scale universal prevention program was offered as part of the regular curriculum to 751 Grade 8 students in the Brisbane region of Australia (Spence, Sheffield, & Donovan, 2003). Students who were randomly assigned to the *Problem Solving for Life* program learned cognitive restructuring and problem-solving in 8 40- to 50-minute sessions. Compared with untreated peers, youth in the high-risk group (with elevated depression scores pre-intervention) showed greater decreases in depressive symptoms post-program. Similar effects were found in the low-risk group, although the effects were smaller. The beneficial program effects were not maintained at 12-month follow-up, however. Follow-up assessments at 2, 3, and 4 years after the prevention program also indicated no differences between youth in the two groups on any of the outcome measures (Spence, Sheffield, & Donovan, 2005). Long-term results such as these underscore the importance of evaluating the impact of prevention programs.

Overall, these studies suggest that there is merit to developing programs to prevent the development of internalizing problems. Cognitive-behavioural principles are promising strategies to promote individual and interpersonal skills that will protect children and youth from developing internalizing disorders. School-based programs offer an appealing avenue to circumvent adolescents' avoidance of the stigma of mental health services. Researchers are working hard to identify the most cost-effective strategy to convey these skills to young people and to solicit the collaboration of their parents.

VIEWPOINT BOX 10.2

HEALTH PROMOTION AND PREVENTION PROGRAMS FOR OLDER ADULTS

Although most of the prevention and promotion programs we have presented target very young children, it would be a mistake to conclude that health promotion and the prevention of mental disorders focus exclusively on very young participants. With an aging population there have been growing efforts to identify ways to promote resilience and decrease the risk of problems in older adults. These include programs to promote exercise and social support, early screening efforts, and programs to support caregivers (World Health Organization, 2004).

Studies have provided evidence of the multiple mental and physical benefits of regular exercise for older adults. Li, McAuley, Chaumeton, and Harmer (2001), for example, reported from a randomized controlled trial of the effects of Tai Chi that participants scored higher than did controls on measures of life satisfaction and positive affect, and had fewer depressive symptoms. Various factors contribute to the social isolation of older adults, including their lack of involvement in the labour force, decreased mobility due to disability, and bereavement due to the death of a spouse or friend. Although befriending programs are believed to have positive effects on the well-being of older women, there have been few systematic attempts to assess whether such programs are effective in enhancing social support (World Health Organization, 2004). Early screening programs are designed to identify older adults requiring additional services. A small randomized controlled trial (Shapiro & Taylor, 2002) reported that provision of early in-home geriatric assessment to older adults at moderate risk for losing their ability to remain in their own homes was associated with higher subjective well-being and lower likelihood of institutionalization.

Family caregivers of older adults shoulder a significant financial, physical, and emotional burden in caring for their loved ones. Because the toll of such caregiving is substantial, a number of programs have been designed to ease caregiver burden. Sörensen, Pinquart, and Duberstein (2002) conducted a meta-analysis of 78 caregiver intervention studies. Sörensen and colleagues found that interventions yielded small to moderate effect sizes. Overall, programs were more effective in increasing knowledge than they were in reducing burden or depressed symptoms. The field of prevention of problems for older adults is an emerging one, with promising interventions. However, with the growing need for such programs to meet the demands of an aging population, it is essential that the evaluation of the usefulness of such programs be a priority.

PREVENTION OF PROBLEMS IN THOSE EXPOSED TO TRAUMA OR LOSS

Within the mental health field it is a commonly held belief that it is necessary to express and *work through* difficult experiences. This conviction has its origins in Freudian theories and has lead to the widespread belief that mental health services are required by everyone who is the victim of or witness to an unpleasant event (Bonanno, 2004). News reports of tragedies such as high school shootings, train derailments, or murder-suicides inevitably end with the phrase "counsellors will be available on site to assist the survivors." The strategy of *critical incident stress debriefing* was introduced as a preventive strategy to ensure that survivors and witnesses to tragedies had assistance in processing the details of the traumatic event at the time in order to avoid the dangers of a delayed stress reaction. In critical incident stress debriefing, counsellors work with groups of up to 15 participants whom they instruct to recount details of the event they have witnessed. Participants are then asked to describe their thoughts, emotional reactions, and symptoms in response to the event. Finally, counsellors provide psychoeducation on coping skills before sharing a snack and returning participants to their regular environment (Enright & Carr, 2002). The rationale for critical incident stress debriefing has an intuitive appeal. If indeed it were possible to protect people from developing posttraumatic stress disorder by devoting a couple of hours to hearing their stories, then it would certainly be time well-invested. Unfortunately, outcome data do not support the effectiveness of critical incident stress debriefing and suggest that sometimes it may even be harmful as it may impede natural recovery processes (Bonanno, 2004; World Health Organization, 2004). The basic problem with an approach such as critical incident stress debriefing is that it is based on the faulty assumption that there is only one path to recovery and that beneficial effects can be obtained by imposing the same solution on everyone. There is, however, ample evidence that there are multiple pathways to healthy functioning and that it is ineffective and sometimes harmful to insist that everyone be treated the same.

We see similarly faulty logic with respect to services for the bereaved. Although we assume that the death of a parent would be an appalling blow that would provoke serious mental health problems for children, research suggests that a substantial minority of bereaved children are resilient in the face of such deaths and do not show any signs of adjustment problems (Lin, Sandler, Ayers, Wolchik, & Luecken, 2004). The assumption that grief is resolved in a similar fashion by everyone led to the assumption that a person who does not show an overt grief reaction is an emotional time bomb who will inevitably one day experience a delayed grief reaction. There is no scientific evidence to support this assumption (Bonanno, 2004). It is clear that in our efforts to identify those who are suffering psychological pain, we have inadvertently overlooked the many people who are resilient in the face of adversity. By searching to better understand the qualities, behaviours, and resources of these individuals—who despite enduring suffering maintain their equilibrium and lead satisfying lives—we may be in a better position to mount effective prevention programs.

VIEWPOINT BOX 10.3

UNSUNG HEROES

It is easy to get discouraged when we read the data from the World Health Organization that despite the development of effective vaccines, millions of children die every year from infectious diseases and that despite the development of effective programs for the prevention of substance abuse, most programs are not delivered in an effective way. If you are contemplating a career in prevention science, you may be overwhelmed by the thought of having to master knowledge and skills not only in clinical psychology but in public health as well. You may doubt that you would have the charisma, vision, or persistence to become a member of a team that was successful in securing funding and getting cooperation from stakeholders in government, education, and the community. Does this mean you cannot contribute to the prevention of mental health problems? Let's consider Rachel's story.

Rachel's father, Daniel, was a Holocaust survivor, embittered by his suffering and haunted by guilt that he alone of all his family had survived the concentration camps of Nazi Germany. Daniel married, had two children, and built a life in Canada, working hard to provide safety for his son and daughter. His grief prevented him from ever experiencing much joy and he was a hard taskmaster to his children. He punished his son harshly with a strap and was critical and demanding toward Rachel. Rachel grew up with low self-esteem and poor coping skills. She married early and found herself in a relationship that mirrored the emotional abuse she suffered as a child. Nevertheless, she was a resourceful woman who was a devoted and loving mother to her own two children. Rachel sought psychological services for depression after leaving her abusive husband. During the intake assessment, the psychologist asked her about other adults who might have been sources of support during her childhood and adolescence. Sadly, Rachel saw her mother as having failed to protect her from her father's rages. The person she remembered was the father of a friend of hers. On a rare free evening after school in Grade 9, Rachel had gone home with her friend Hillary. As the girls prepared a snack in the kitchen, they heard Hillary's father call up from the basement: "Is that you Hillary? Could you give me a hand please?" To Rachel's horror, Hillary yelled back, "Sure Dad, in a few minutes when we're done our snack." Rachel felt her heart pound and her hands get clammy as she braced for Hillary's dad to burst out of the basement in a rage because Hillary had not immediately complied with his request. She could not believe her ears when he replied, "OK honey, no rush." Rachel treasured the opportunities to visit Hillary—she found Hillary's relationship with her father amazing. Hillary's father may have shaken his head sadly at his daughter's shy friend and may have felt helpless to make a difference in the life of this young woman whose home life was overshadowed by the suffering of the Holocaust. Although he did not know it, Hillary's father provided a lifeline for Rachel. He gave her hope that young people could be treated respectfully by parents. Rachel nurtured that hope and acted on it with her own children, treating them as she had seen Hillary's father behave, rather than as she had been treated.

Even if you do not choose a career in preventing mental health problems, you will have many opportunities to contribute to the prevention of emotional and behavioural difficulties. The principles for healthy development are relatively simple. You already learned in other psychology courses about the importance of positive reinforcement, of social support, of modelling prosocial behaviour, and of clear communication. As you put those principles into practice in your job, in your family, in your friendships, and in your community, you will be making an important step in preventing problems. The protective factors listed in Table 10.2 include many ways that you can contribute to mental health promotion.

SUMMARY AND CONCLUSIONS

We have summarized research on some of the many programs designed to prevent emotional and behavioural problems and to promote positive psychological functioning. As noted by Anthony Biglan, the most successful programs have several features in common. First, they are evidence-based (Biglan, Mrazek, Carmine, & Flay, 2003). Each effective program was designed to target known risk and protective factors in the development of psychopathology. These prevention programs drew on psychological research that has identified those factors that make a person vulnerable to develop psychopathology as well as those factors that act as a buffer against the development of problems. Second, many programs work to promote the same relatively simple principles such as promoting positive adult-child relationships; allowing children ample opportunities to be rewarded for appropriate behaviour; providing adequate monitoring and supervision; providing mild corrective feedback for inappropriate behaviour; helping children manage emotions, treat one another with respect, and act assertively rather than aggressively; and facilitating the development of supportive networks (Biglan, 2003; Carr, 2002). Third, they are usually multifaceted, involving different components or modules that operate at the level of the individual, family, school, community, or legal system. This allows the same message to be conveyed by parents, teachers, peers, community leaders, and government (Biglan, 2003; Weissberg et al., 2003).

A fourth common feature among some of the most successful programs is that they were developed as an expansion of an effective treatment intervention that was modified and offered in a slightly diluted format to those with subclinical problems. Programmatic research is then carried out over many years to determine the program's effectiveness (Nation et al., 2003). Fifth, successful programs are offered in convenient contexts. Services are offered in a milieu that minimizes obstacles to participation, by using schools, community centres, and home visits, as well as by offering childcare services so that parents can participate (Carr, 2002). Finally, the developers of effective prevention programs all stress the importance of program fidelity in adopting their interventions (e.g., Webster-Stratton, in press). This means that it is necessary to use the same materials and protocols and to deliver the same number of sessions as the original program.

To ensure that people are receiving effective services it is necessary to conduct outcome assessments of both competence and symptoms/risk factors. These programs are designed to reduce problems in the future, so it is essential that evaluations extend beyond the conclusion of a program in order to evaluate longer term functioning. As those who receive preventive services are led to believe that these services will make a difference in their lives, we owe it to them to be certain that this is really the case.

Critical Thinking Questions

Compared with prevention programs for physical health problems, what are the special challenges faced in prevention programs for mental health problems?

How do primary and secondary prevention programs differ in their focus? Are these approaches incompatible with one another?

Why is long-term systematic evaluation so important in prevention science?

Prevention programs seem to be relatively effective for many psychological problems, so why aren't they more commonly used in our health care and educational systems?

Key Terms

health promotion	risk reduction model
indicated preventive interventions	secondary prevention
primary prevention	selective preventive interventions
protective factors	universal preventive interventions
risk factors	

Key Names

Paula Barrett

Anthony Biglan

Matthew Sanders

Carolyn Webster-Stratton

ADDITIONAL RESOURCES
Websites

A Canadian website devoted to encouraging the understanding and use of economic evaluations in Canada's non-profit and public sectors. Includes useful links to Canadian and international prevention websites: http://www.prevention-dividend.com/

An American website providing information on the *Incredible Years Program*: http://www.incredibleyears.com

An Australian website providing information on the *Triple P* program: http://www.triplep.net/

Centre for Children and Families in the Justice System (described in Profile Box 10.1): http://www.lfcc.on.ca/

CHAPTER 11

Intervention: Overview

INTRODUCTION

Previous chapters have examined the ways that psychologists conduct assessments (Chapters 5 to 9) as well as efforts to prevent the development of psychological disorders (Chapter 10). In this chapter and the following three chapters, we discuss psychological interventions. As we described in Chapter 2, a major part of most psychologists' workload is devoted to providing psychological treatment; the vast majority of clinical psychologists report providing psychotherapy as part of their practices. Throughout the text we have drawn attention to the ethical principles that guide the delivery of psychological services. In this chapter we will discuss ethical issues in the selection of treatments, in informed consent to services, and in the requirement for ongoing assessment of treatment usefulness. We will also highlight issues related to confidentiality. Then we will examine some major models that inform current evidence-based psychological interventions. In Chapter 9 we explained that the theoretical model adopted by the psychologist guides the assessment process and informs clinical formulations. Rather than providing comprehensive coverage of theoretical approaches, we present those with the strongest empirical support, consistent with the focus on evidence-based practice throughout this book. We will not be covering two large categories of therapy: those with have a long history but scant empirical support (e.g., psychoanalysis, Jungian analysis) and more recently developed therapies that, likewise, are lacking empirical support (e.g., primal scream therapy, thought field therapy).

With the recognition of diverse client needs, psychologists are developing menus of effective treatments.

Next we will consider the characteristics of people who seek and receive psychological services. We will look at the paths by which people are referred (or self-refer) for psychological services. Although the majority of psychological interventions are delivered in one-to-one sessions in the psychologist's office, there is evidence that other modes of treatment delivery—such as couples therapy, family therapy, and group therapy—are also effective. With the recognition of diverse client needs, as well as concerns to offer the most cost effective services, psychologists are developing menus of effective treatments that can be calibrated according to the level of need. We will discuss the principles of this "stepped care" approach. Finally, we will highlight recent innovations in the use of computer technology and the Internet in the delivery of psychological interventions.

THE ETHICS OF INTERVENTION

See Pomerantz + Handelman's re: tx consent form

In Chapter 5 we highlighted ethical issues in obtaining consent to psychological assessment and in Chapter 6 we described confidentiality and the limits to confidentiality in psychological services. Given the central importance of these ethical principles in the delivery of all psychological services, it is critical to recognize their applicability in psychological interventions. A core ethical issue is that the psychologist cannot proceed with any psychological services without the client's agreement to receive the services. Furthermore, this agreement must be based on a reasonable understanding of what the services will entail and the likely outcomes of receiving or not receiving services. The process of obtaining informed consent recognizes the consumer's rights regarding psychological services. It is insufficient to simply obtain the client's signature at the bottom of a jargon-filled description of services; the psychologist must provide a comprehensible account so that the client can make an informed decision on whether to pursue services. Each person who is involved in services must understand the nature of those services and must consent. Guidelines proposed in the United Kingdom by the National Institute for Health and

Clinical Excellence for the treatment of anxiety and depression (NICE 2004a, 2004b) indicate that patients should be informed of the treatment options and invited to choose the one with which they are most comfortable. According to these guidelines, in the treatment of anxiety, patients should be informed that in descending order of long-term effectiveness, the treatment options are psychological therapy such as cognitive-behavioural therapy (CBT), medication such as a selective serotonin reuptake inhibitor (SSRI) approved for the treatment of generalized anxiety disorder, and self-help based on CBT principles. In different jurisdictions the issue of obtaining consent from children is treated in various ways, including setting chronological ages at which children are presumed competent to give consent, or requiring the psychologist to determine in each case whether a child is competent to give consent (Fisher, 2004). As we discussed in Chapter 6, clients must be assured of the confidentiality of the services they receive, as well as the limits to confidentiality when a person's safety is in danger. They must also receive clear descriptions of the steps taken by the psychologist to protect their privacy.

Many potential clients do not ask about confidentiality issues, financial arrangements, or treatment alternatives (Braaten, Otto, & Handelsman, 1993). When seeking psychological services, it is wise to prepare a list of questions to ask potential service providers. As psychological services are often offered outside of publicly funded health care, it is important to know the hourly rate for sessions, whether the psychologist offers a sliding fee scale, the extent to which any private health insurance will cover the fees, and the number and frequency of sessions. Questions about the clinical psychologist may include training, years of experience, and the types of problems for which he or she commonly offers services. Questions about services may include the menu of alternative services for the particular problem: Which treatment is most effective and what are its advantages and disadvantages?

Ethical issues are prominent at the beginning of psychological services. They do not end once consent has been obtained, confidentiality explained, and a course of services begun. As we have emphasized many times, the psychologist has an ethical responsibility to monitor the effectiveness of services. It would be unethical to persist in offering services to a client if those services did not prove helpful in addressing the problem. Although there is great merit in adopting an approach that has been shown to be effective in treating similar problems, the psychologist must be vigilant in monitoring its usefulness for each client. Ethical practice requires that the psychologist be attentive to the ongoing and potentially changing fit between the treatment plan, the client's needs, and the client's responses to treatment.

THEORETICAL APPROACHES

As we indicated in the chapter introduction, we will be focusing on the forms of psychotherapy that have the strongest empirical support. These include **short-term psychodynamic therapy**,

interpersonal therapy, **process-experiential therapy**, and **cognitive-behavioural therapy**. As you will see, each approach is based on a distinct theory of psychological functioning and change processes. All of these approaches have at least a moderate amount of supporting data for use with specific DSM IV Axis I disorders. All have also been applied to DSM IV Axis II disorders, although the evidence of their impact is rather limited at this time. In Chapters 12 and 13 we will provide more details about specific evidence-based versions of each approach.

Short-Term Psychodynamic Psychotherapies

In response to concerns about the cost and effectiveness of extended psychoanalytic and psychodynamic interventions, a number of short-term psychodynamic psychotherapies (STPPs) have been developed. STPPs are grounded in psychodynamic principles that originated in the work of Freud (Messer, 2001). As you may recall from Chapter 1 and from other psychology courses, Freud's drive theory emphasized the importance of innate, biological drives that the individual must control in order to adapt to society. Ego psychology, developed by Freud's daughter Anna, among others, focused on the process by which the very young child learns to construct a model of the world (Vakoch & Strupp, 2000). Themes from both drive and ego theories were blended in object relations theories that noted that infants tend to categorize their experiences into good and bad. As children mature, they learn that each person has both positive and negative qualities. If, however, they do not learn this, they are prone to chaotic relationships, because they act as though people are either all good or all bad (Vakoch & Strupp, 2000).

Psychodynamic theories assume that individuals are prone to conflicts between id and ego. These conflicts are resolved when the ego learns to accept and tolerate the id impulses. However, there is a tendency for these impulses to be suppressed so that they are not within conscious awareness. The unconscious conflict between id and superego is therefore re-enacted throughout the client's life. According to psychodynamic theorists, it is inevitable that the client's core interpersonal conflicts will be repeated in the relationship with the therapist through a process known as **transference** (Vakoch & Strupp, 2000).

Since the 1920s, there have been attempts to speed up the process of psychodynamic exploration. Rank and Ferenczi, for example, introduced a focus on the transference relationship as a strategy to provoke feelings in the client (Messer, 2001). Expanding on this idea a decade later, Alexander suggested that the relationship with a benign therapist offers the client a *corrective emotional experience* that heals the wounds of early emotional conflicts (Messer, 2001). Brief psychodynamic therapies were championed in the 1960s and 1970s by psychiatrists Malan, Davanloo, and Sifneos, who proposed theoretical models in which change is proposed to occur by the therapist challenging the client's defences. The 1980s witnessed the development of another generation of brief therapies including Lester Luborsky's supportive-expressive therapy (Luborsky, 1984) and Hans Strupp's time-limited dynamic therapy (e.g., Strupp & Binder,

1984). Although these forms of psychodynamic therapy have different emphases and assign differing importance to various intervention strategies, they have a great deal in common. Across the different types of STPPs, therapy is considered a process of understanding stages of psychological development, bringing to awareness unconscious processes, and re-enacting in the relationship with the therapist issues that have troubled the client in the past (Messer, 2001).

STPPs involve face-to-face sessions conducted once or twice a week for between 16 and 30 sessions (Leichsenring, Rabung, & Lebing, 2004). By setting a limit to the number of sessions, the therapist encourages the client to anticipate that change will occur relatively quickly (Messer, 2001). Compared with traditional psychoanalytic therapists, STPP therapists are relatively active, engaging in dialogue and challenging the client. The therapist's first task is to foster the development of a therapeutic alliance and positive transference, by adopting an open-minded, non-judgemental stance and displaying interest in the client's experience (Cutler, Goldyne, Markowitz, Devlin, & Glick, 2004). Among the techniques of the STPP therapist are reflection, clarification, interpretation, and confrontation of maladaptive patterns (Messer, 2001).

Like most forms of psychodynamic therapy, examination of the transference relationship is a central theme of STPP; however, attention is paid to the present relationship, without necessarily connecting patterns to the client's past (Leichsenring et al., 2004). Examination of the transference relationship is considered an important tool in understanding how the client views the world; it is designed to bring to awareness unconscious fantasies and to reveal the ways that the client thinks about relationships (Blagys & Hilsenroth, 2000). Counter-transference refers to the therapist's emotional reaction to the client. Although Freud viewed counter-transference as a breach in therapeutic neutrality caused by the therapist's unconscious conflicts, STPP therapists take a more benign view, seeing counter-transference as providing useful information about the way the client's interpersonal behaviours affect others (Vakoch & Strupp, 2000). **Table 11.1** lists the therapeutic tasks of the different STPP stages.

TABLE 11.1   Short-Term Psychodynamic Psychotherapy

Phase 1:	Developing positive transference relationship
	Identifying themes that are important for the patient
Phase 2:	Analysing transference relationship
	Exploring themes through clarification and confrontation
Phase 3:	Terminating therapy
	Dealing with loss
	Dealing with limits in life

Adapted from Vakoch & Strupp (2000).

Early in therapy the therapist identifies specific themes or conflicts that will be the focus of attention. This theme is individualized to capture the therapist's formulation of the conflict that underlies the presenting problem (Messer, 2001). Throughout therapy, the therapist maintains a focus on these themes, treatment goals, and termination issues. The therapist identifies defensive patterns that interfere with the client's life (Cutler et al., 2004). Consistent with their Freudian roots (Blagys & Hilsenroth, 2000), STPP theorists accord a central role to evoking emotions and to facilitating change through a process of catharsis (i.e., the release of previously suppressed emotional reactions). Goal-setting plays an important part of STPP, setting it apart from long-term psychodynamic therapy and making it similar to other short-term treatment approaches (Messer, 2000).

As therapy moves toward termination, gains are consolidated. During this phase, the client faces issues of loss (of the therapist), separation (from the therapeutic relationship), and individuation (moving toward independence from the therapist). As STPP is, by definition, brief and time-limited, issues of termination of services cannot be avoided. Theorists have proposed that the time-limited nature of therapy raises awareness of the time-limited nature of human life, making it particularly salient for clients who are dealing with mortality issues (Messer, 2000).

Interpersonal Psychotherapy for Depression

In contrast to the usual intrapsychic focus of psychodynamic theories, Sullivan (1953) drew attention to interpersonal factors in psychopathology, suggesting that psychiatric problems were often related to difficulties in communication and to dysfunctional relationships. This theoretical framework laid the foundation for studies of the interpersonal context of those suffering from disorders such as alcoholism, depression, eating disorders, panic disorder, and schizophrenia (Gotlib & Schraedley, 2000). Compelling evidence regarding the interpersonal difficulties experienced by those suffering from depression fuelled interest in developing a therapy that addressed interpersonal factors associated with this disorder (Klerman, Weissman, Rounsaville, & Chevron, 1984). Interpersonal psychotherapy (IPT) for depression focuses on changing interpersonal problems that are related to the onset, maintenance, and relapse of depressive symptoms.

IPT is a brief therapy that involves weekly meetings over three to four months. IPT is divided into distinct phases that are described in **Table 11.2**. The first phase involves assessment of the symptoms of depression as well as an examination of the patient's relationships. The construction of an inventory of current and past relationships is essential in identifying the interpersonal themes that will be the focus of therapy. At the end of this assessment phase, the IPT therapist diagnoses the patient and provides an interpersonal formulation of the patient's difficulties. The patient is explicitly absolved of responsibility for symptoms as these are ascribed to the disorder of depression. The IPT therapist explains the ways that interpersonal issues maintain the depression and invites the patient to participate actively in changing current relationships.

TABLE 11.2   Interpersonal Psychotherapy for Depression

Initial sessions (1–3):
Assessment of symptoms
Diagnosis and explanation of depressive disorder
Assessment of interpersonal context (current and past)
Presentation of IPT formulation of patient's problems

Intermediate sessions (4–12) addressing one or more of the following themes:
Grief
        -help patient deal with a loss; promote healthy mourning
        -facilitate the development of new relationships

Role disputes
        -identify dispute
        -formulate plan for dispute resolution
        -modify communication and/or change expectations to resolve dispute

Role transitions
        -leave old role and mourn its loss if necessary
        -develop skills, coping strategies, and support for transition

Interpersonal deficits
        -build social skills
        -increase social involvement

Termination phase (13–16)
Acknowledge worries and sadness related to ending therapy
Encourage awareness of and practise of new skills
Anticipate future challenges in which new skills will be employed

Adapted from Weissman, Markowitz, & Klerman (2000).

The focus of subsequent sessions is tailored to the client's specific needs and may include addressing one or all of the following themes: grief, role disputes, role transitions, and interpersonal deficits. In addressing grief issues the therapist facilitates mourning of a lost relationship as well as the development of a new social network. If role disputes are identified as contributing to depressive symptoms, the patient and therapist collaborate on a plan for resolving the difficulty, by renegotiating the problem, reaching an agreement that the dispute is insoluble, or dissolving the relationship. The patient is assisted in developing effective communication patterns and in developing realistic expectations about relationships. Both IPT and STPPs address aspects of interpersonal functioning. An important difference is that IPT is designed to alter relational functioning whereas STPPs use information about relationships to alter intrapsychic variables.

Research has established that people are often vulnerable at times of role transition. Even though some transitions such as marriage, the birth of a child, or starting a new job are considered positive and may be welcomed, they create a challenge as the person adapts to new role demands. In IPT, the patient is first encouraged to shed the old role (e.g., moving from being a student to a professional, from being single to married, or from being employed to retired); next the client is aided in developing skills that are required in the new role (e.g., adopting a more formal style, focussing on the challenges of living with another person, or finding ways to maintain an active social life). Some depressed patients may not be troubled by grief, role disputes, or role transitions, but may have an impoverished interpersonal network with few contacts and little opportunity for pleasant or supportive exchanges. In this case, the therapist focuses on the development of communication and relationship skills that are likely to promote the development of closer interpersonal ties. Within IPT the termination phase of therapy offers an opportunity to consolidate gains made in previous phases. The therapist helps the client recognize and take credit for the changes that have occurred as well as prepare for future challenges.

Some depressed patients may not be troubled by grief or role transitions but may have few contacts and little opportunity to develop an interpersonal network.

In therapy the client communicates any misgivings and anxieties about ending the therapeutic relationship.

As interpersonal difficulties are found in other age groups, the treatment protocol has been modified by Myrna Weissman and her colleagues to address the needs of other populations (Weissman, Markowitz, & Klerman, 2000). IPT-LL was developed to meet the needs of adults in late life (Sholomskas, Chevron, Prusoff, & Berry, 1983) by having brief sessions that included help with practical matters, and that focused on ways to tolerate negative affect in relationships rather than withdrawing from them. Mufson and her colleagues (Mufson, Dorta, Moreau, & Weissman, 2004; Mufson, Weissman, Moreau, & Garfinkel,

1999; Mufson & Dorta, 2004) developed IPT-A for adolescents by including attention to developmental issues such as separation from parents, exploration of parental authority, the development of dyadic relationships, and peer pressure. Recently IPT has been delivered in a group format to treat depression in rural Uganda (Bolton et al., 2003) and has been modified for use with eating disorders, anxiety disorders, and substance use disorders (Weissman, Markowitz, & Klerman, 2000).

Process-Experiential Therapies

With their origins as alternatives to psychodynamic and behavioural psychology, humanistic and experiential approaches to psychotherapy include client-centred therapy (Rogers, 1951), Gestalt therapy (Perls, Hefferline, & Goodman, 1951), and existential therapy (May, Angel, & Ellenberger, 1958). These approaches are based on the assumption that human nature is fundamentally growth-oriented, trustworthy, and guided by choice (Elliott, Greenberg, & Lietaer, 2004).

You may recall from Chapter 1 that Rogers was committed to psychotherapy research. During the 1970s and the 1980s, however, research on humanistic-experiential approaches dwindled. Given the emphasis on the uniqueness of each individual's subjective experience, humanistic-experiential approaches have not been the subject of much psychotherapy outcome research. For many decades humanistic-experiential theorists and therapists actively rejected any attempts to evaluate their treatments with experimental designs. Consequently, by the early 1990s there was only one experiential therapy (emotion-focused therapy for moderately distressed couples, Johnson & Greenberg, 1985) that was considered to have a strong evidence base (Elliott, 2001). In recent years, largely through the efforts of Robert Elliott and Leslie Greenberg, there has been a resurgence of well-designed research on the process-experiential (PE) approach that draws together elements of client-centred and Gestalt approaches into a strongly emotion-focused approach to treatment (Hill, 2001; Elliott et al., 2004).

A central characteristic of PE therapies is the emphasis on in-session experiencing. PE therapies are based on the assumption that change can be facilitated when clients are guided to focus their attention on their in-session experiences in order to intensify and make those experiences more vivid. PE emphasizes the therapeutic relationship and the process of reflecting on emotions to create new meaning for the client. The therapeutic relationship is considered to provide both support and guidance in the client's exploration of his or her experience. PE is a 12- to 20-session treatment in which the therapist facilitates the client's role as an active agent of self-change. This approach is clearly intrapsychic, placing emphasis on the client's self-exploration and understanding rather than on relationships with others. In contrast to early client-centred approaches, the PE therapist takes a more task-focused approach (Elliott, 2001). **Table 11.3** describes general features of process-experiential therapy.

TABLE 11.3   Process-Experiential Therapy

Treatment Principles

Fostering a therapeutic relationship

- Enter and track client's experiencing
- Express empathy and genuine prizing
- Facilitate mutual involvement in goals and tasks of therapy

Facilitating work on therapeutic tasks

- Facilitate optimal client experiential processing
- Foster client growth and self-determination
- Facilitate client completion of key therapeutic tasks

Experiential Response Modes

- Simple empathy responses
- Empathic exploration
- Process-directing responses
- Experiential presence
- Content directives

Therapeutic tasks

- Basic exploratory tasks
- Active expression
- Interpersonal tasks

Adapted from Elliott (2001).

Cognitive-Behavioural Therapies

The overwhelming vote in 2004 by members of the Association for the Advancement of Behavior Therapy to change the name of the association to the Association of Behavioral and Cognitive Therapies reflects the fact that behavioural, cognitive, and cognitive-behavioural therapies should be considered a single orientation. Behavioural approaches are based on the assumption that problem behaviours are learned behaviours and that faulty learning can be reversed through the application of learning principles. The earliest application of behaviour therapy was the use of operant conditioning in treating patients who were considered untreatable: those with psychotic disorders and those with mental retardation. From its roots in the application of classical and operant conditioning, the field of behaviour therapy has advanced to include procedures based on research findings from areas such as perception, cognition, and the biological bases of behaviour. Behavioural therapists focus on present functioning as opposed to childhood history. Accordingly,

Behavioural therapists focus on present functioning as opposed to childhood history. Accordingly, behavioural interventions focus on specific targets by reducing undesirable behaviours (e.g., intrusive thoughts about a traumatic event, self-harming behaviours, and avoidance), as well as increasing desirable behaviours (e.g., engaging in pleasant activities, calmly presenting a seminar, or assertively dealing with an angry customer). An essential feature is the application of scientifically derived principles in the treatment of problems. Throughout therapy, progress is assessed to determine whether the strategy should be modified. Behavioural treatment requires clear identification of goals and is oriented toward the future (Emmelkamp, 2004).

Albert Bandura's seminal findings that learning could take place by observation and imitation have been applied in the treatment of both adults and children (Naugle & Maher, 2003). **Self-efficacy**, which refers to a person's sense of competence to learn and perform new tasks, is often found to be the best predictor of behaviour, such as approaching a phobic stimulus or attempting a new behaviour. Bandura's work laid the foundation for approaches that emphasize the importance of cognitions in mediating behavioural responses (Craighead, Hart, Craighead, & Ilardi, 2002). Using models developed in information processing, D'Zurilla and Goldfried (1971) introduced a **problem-solving** approach that was applied in the treatment of diverse problems such as weight control, clinical depression, and social skills deficits. The key elements of problem-solving in cognitive-behavioural treatments are problem definition and formulation, generating alternative solutions to deal with the problem, deciding on the best solution to implement, and implementing and evaluating the solution (D'Zurilla & Nezu, 1999).

Purely cognitive approaches, such as **Albert Ellis's** Rational-Emotive Behavior Therapy and **Aaron Beck's** Cognitive Therapy, are based on the assumption that an individual's perception of events, rather than the events themselves, affect adjustment. Consequently, they focus on identifying automatic thoughts and changing maladaptive patterns of thinking that are associated with distress, anxiety, and depression (Hollon & Beck, 2004). Cognitive approaches foster a collaborative relationship in which the therapist and client work together to identify problems,

Dr. Albert Bandura developed influential social learning theories.

test hypotheses, and re-evaluate beliefs. Like their behavioural relatives, cognitive and cognitive-behavioural approaches rely on the application of empirically derived strategies in the treatment of diverse disorders, including depression, anxiety disorders, eating disorders, attention-deficit/hyper-activity disorder, chronic pain, personality disorders, and marital distress (Hersen, 2002). A cornerstone of all CBTs is that the treatment is tailored to the needs of individual clients and the client's responses to treatment are continuously monitored in order to evaluate the effect of intervention and the possible need to alter treatment plans. **Table 11.4** describes the typical phases of CBT.

TABLE 11.4   Phases of Cognitive Behavioural Therapies (8–30 sessions)

Assessment phase:	Integration of data from interview, direct observation, rating scales, and self-monitoring Establishment of concrete treatment goals

Intervention phase:	1. Skills learned in session:
	Behavioural
	  assertive behaviours
	  behavioural activation
	  exposure to feared stimulus
	  reinforcement
	  response shaping
	  self-soothing/relaxation
	Cognitive
	  cognitive restructuring
	  self-instructional training
	Cognitive-behavioural
	  problem-solving
	  communication
	  stress management
	2. Skills practised as homework assignments and reviewed in session
	3. Skills generalized to natural context and reviewed in session
	4. Session by session review of progress toward treatment goals

Termination phase:	Review of goal attainment Consolidation of skills Anticipation of future challenges
Booster session:	Review of goal attainment Consolidation of skills Anticipation of future challenges

> **VIEWPOINT BOX 11.1**
>
> **THE CASE OF MICHAEL**
>
> Cutler et al. (2004) described a client, Michael, who was referred for treatment of depression. Experts espousing different theoretical orientations (long-term psychodynamic, interpersonal, and cognitive-behavioural) provided their perspectives on treatment for Michael.
>
> Although he had been a successful student as an undergraduate, in law school Michael had developed a habit of procrastination and poor class attendance that led to him having to cram at exam time. He found this extremely stressful and started to feel increasingly depressed, began over-eating and over-sleeping, and had increasing trouble concentrating. Michael experienced prolonged feelings of sadness as well as decreased sexual desire and diminished pleasure in activities he used to enjoy.
>
> After his parents divorced when he was an infant, Michael's father remarried and began a new family; his mother did not date or remarry. His father maintained contact twice a year, but did not engage in any meaningful parenting. As a pre-adolescent, Michael was cared for by his grandmother while his mother sought training in another city. The only times in which his father became engaged in Michael's life were when he was in trouble for skipping classes. As a student, Michael had a supportive mentoring relationship with a professor, but felt disappointed that the professor did not maintain the relationship when Michael moved to law school. During law school Michael was troubled by phone calls from his mother expressing her distress and reproving him for not spending enough time with her. Another current stressor in his life was an unsatisfactory relationship with a student he had dated. Although the woman broke off the romantic relationship with Michael, she maintained regular contact with him.
>
> Michael's style toward the therapist was deferential. He apologized for arriving late for some of the intake assessment interviews. After a couple of sessions Michael reported that he had begun to feel better, had thrown away his prescription for antidepressant medication, and wished to engage in psychotherapy.
>
> Dr. Glick, whose orientation is psychodynamic, assumes that Michael's problems stem from conflicts of which he is not fully aware. The goal of therapy would be to promote Michael's exploration of the underlying meaning of his feelings. Dr. Glick would strive to respond to Michael in an open-minded manner to facilitate Michael's curiosity about himself and, eventually, his insight into the source of his problems. Dr. Glick assumes that in the context of a non-judgemental therapeutic relationship,

Michael will learn to tolerate painful feelings. Exploration of the transference relationship is designed to facilitate greater awareness of defensive responding. The therapist would comment on aspects of Michael's behaviour toward him, offering possible interpretations of their significance. For example, "you missed a big part of each session. And today you seem to be staying on the surface of things. Might you be avoiding painful or troubling feelings about you?" (Cutler et al. 2004, p. 1571). Dr. Glick assumes that a core issue is Michael's unconscious feelings of unresolved anger toward his parents, whom he perceives as rejecting. His ambivalence toward his mother is then played out in his current romantic relationship. Examination of the transference relationship allows exploration of Michael's need for a nurturing father-figure and his fears of being seen as needy and weak.

Dr. Markowitz, the interpersonal psychotherapist, would be sensitive to Michael's various difficulties. He would probe Michael's emotions in reaction to perceived rejection or disappointment and ask whether Michael has communicated his reactions to the people in his life. The therapist would explicitly present an interpersonal formulation of Michael's problems in which his reactions are normalized. "Coming to terms with losses can be hard, especially when you've had as many dislocations as you've already had…I suggest we work…on solving your law school role transition; as you gain greater comfort in your situation there, not only will that improve your life, but your mood symptoms should improve as well." (Cutler et al. 2004, p. 1570). Dr. Markowitz predicted that over the course of interpersonal psychotherapy, Michael would learn to respond more effectively to interpersonal challenges. Although no formal homework is given, Michael would be encouraged to increase his activity level. The final phase of services would allow Michael to consolidate his gains, taking credit for the new skills he has mastered. Termination would be a time to celebrate his gains as well as to be aware of the loss associated with end the therapeutic relationship.

Dr. Devlin, the cognitive behaviour therapist, would establish goals and collaborate to help Michael adopt a cognitive-behavioural formulation in which he understands the links between his thoughts, feelings, and behaviours. Homework tasks would be assigned to help track links between different feelings and procrastination behaviours, as well as to identify exceptional occasions on which Michael experiences pleasure. Michael would be encouraged to conduct behavioural experiments to determine whether his thoughts are accurate. For example, the thought that *I don't enjoy anything anymore* could be tested by monitoring his mood as he engages in different activities. Michael would be encouraged to shift from making characterological statements about himself to recognizing the choices that he makes to behave in specific ways. As he becomes more active, Michael would be in a position to identify and challenge his core beliefs about his inadequacy.

CBT therapists assume a very active role in service provision. They probe the precise nature of the problem, seeking information on its intensity, frequency, and duration as well as contextual factors that are associated with variation in the problem. They collaborate with clients in establishing concrete treatment goals and in translating vague complaints into measurable outcomes toward which the client will work. CBT therapists provide information about the process of treatment, explaining the central role of homework assignments in gathering data, carrying out experiments, and practising new skills.

CBT therapists take responsibility for structuring each session, setting an agenda, and teaching new skills. Throughout treatment, the therapist uses a blend of didactic teaching methods (i.e., directions and instructions) and Socratic questioning (i.e., questions that encourage the client to examine their beliefs and to be self-directed in skill acquisition) to help the client. To promote changes, the therapist engages in a process of collaborative empiricism with the client. This means that the client and therapist develop strategies to concretely test the client's dysfunctional beliefs. By encouraging self-examination and then working with the client to test the validity of his or her beliefs, the therapist actively encourages a process of guided discovery for the client. Thus, in contrast to many other forms of therapy, the most important changes are presumed to take place not in sessions but *between* sessions as the client completes and learns from homework assignments (Blagys & Hilsenroth, 2002).

The other theoretical orientations we have discussed consider termination in terms of the end of the therapeutic relationship. In CBT the termination phase is seen as a time for consolidating skills, anticipating future challenges, and preparing the client to face inevitable slip-ups. Termination is future-oriented. CBT also allows for the possibility of clients requiring one or two future "booster" sessions to help them get back on track.

SEEKING PSYCHOTHERAPY SERVICES

There are numerous reasons why people seek the services of a clinical psychologist. In some instances, those seeking therapy desire assistance and advice in managing the expectable challenges in life, such as problems in parenting or in handling workplace difficulties. The transition from one phase of life to another, such as becoming a parent, brings new demands as well as new joys. Dealing with other expectable, but painful, life events such as the death of a parent or a spouse may also lead some people to initiate therapy. In many cases the motivation for seeking treatment stems from the presence of significant emotional distress that interferes with daily functioning. Individuals often suffer from mental disorders for months or years before seeking professional services. Finally, some people who engage in therapy have only minimal levels of distress. These individuals are often seeking to address questions related to personal identity, values, or self-knowledge.

It may seem almost inconceivable that the same service—psychotherapy—can be applied to the myriad reasons people seek treatment. Psychotherapy is often defined as a process in which a professional systematically applies techniques derived from psychological principles to relieve another person's psychological distress or to facilitate growth. This rather broad definition becomes even more problematic because it also defines psychological counselling and, as we described in Chapter 1, there is a blurring of boundaries between counselling and psychotherapy. To clarify this situation—for clients, psychologists, and others working in health care system—Barlow (2004) suggested that the term *psychological treatments* be used for the growing number of specific, evidence-based interventions designed to treat clinically significant problems (i.e., Axis I and II diagnoses). By implication, the term *psychotherapy* would then be used to describe intervention efforts aimed at addressing difficulties of a subclinical intensity such as generic identity or relational problems. This does not resolve the boundary issue between psychotherapy and counselling, and only time will tell whether Barlow's proposal will gain acceptance among clinical psychologists and the other providers of psychotherapy.

It is important to recognize that psychotherapy is practised by professionals from many disciplines, including psychology, psychiatry, social work, medicine, and nursing. In most jurisdictions the title *psychotherapist* is not licensed or restricted in any fashion. Accordingly anyone can advertise his or her services as a psychotherapist. Those seeking psychotherapeutic services would be well-advised, therefore, to obtain treatment from a registered or licensed health care professional. The following statement from the College of Psychologists of Ontario (2004) nicely captures the reasons for seeking services from a regulated professional.

"As regulated health providers, psychologists and psychological associates are required by law to deliver competent, ethical and professional services and are accountable to the public, through the College, for their professional behaviour and activities. As members of the College, psychologists and psychological associates must meet rigorous professional entry requirements, adhere to prescribed standards, guidelines and ethical principles and participate in quality assurance activities to continually update and improve their knowledge and skill. In contrast, *the College has no jurisdiction over unregulated service providers*. There is no regulatory body to set minimum levels of education, training and competence or to establish and monitor professional and ethical standards of conduct. There is no regulatory body to protect the public interest and hold unregulated providers accountable for the services they provide."

Evidence suggests that the overall use of mental health services has been increasing in recent decades. Psychological services are not, however, the only form of treatment available for psychological problems and, in fact, they are used much less frequently than psychotropic medication. Data from a 1990 survey in Ontario indicated that 7.8% of those 15 to 64 years of age reported seeking mental health services, with almost 94% of these individuals having sought outpatient services, as opposed to inpatient hospital services (Lin, Goering, Offord, Campbell, & Boyle, 1996). Based on data from a large, nationally representative American survey, Kessler and colleagues (1999) reported that 13.3% of those between the ages of 15 and 54 reported receiving outpatient services for a psychiatric problem in the past year. They also indicated that these data, gathered in the early 1990s, demonstrate a somewhat greater percentage of people receiving services than in the 1980s. However, it seems that much of this increase may be due to the increased use of psychotropic medication. Comparing data from American surveys in 1987 and 1997, Olfson, Marcus, Druss, and Pincus (2002) reported no statistical change in the overall rates of psychotherapy during this period. In 1987, 3.2% of Americans reported receiving psychotherapy; in 1997 the figure was 3.6%. With respect to the treatment of depression, the proportion of those receiving antidepressant medication doubled, whereas the proportion of those receiving psychotherapy declined (Olfson, Marcus, Druss, Elinson, Tanielian, & Pincus, 2002). Based on a population survey in Great Britain, 6.7% of women and 6.2% of men reported receiving psychotherapy for an Axis I disorder in 1993 (Brugha et al., 2004). In 2000, there was no statistically significant change in this: 7.9% of women and 9.8% of men reported receiving psychotherapy. In stark contrast, the rates of psychotropic medication use during this period rose sharply for both women (9.6% to 20.1%) and men (9.7% to 19.1%).

Who are the people who decide to seek therapy as either an alternative or an adjunct to medication? American epidemiological surveys indicate that a number of socio-demographic characteristics are related to the use of psychotherapy (Vessey & Howard, 1993). Across all approaches to psychotherapy, two-thirds of psychotherapy clients are female, half have a college or university education, half are married, and the majority are young to middle-aged adults. Unfortunately, consistent with the information we presented early in the book, Vessey and Howard's analysis also suggested that many of those most in need of such services (i.e., those with a diagnosable condition) never seek professional help of any kind.

Responses to the Canadian National Population Health Survey showed similar socio-demographic characteristics among those who reported consulting a psychologist for physical or mental health reasons (Hunsley, Lee, & Aubry, 1999). This survey, conducted in 1994 and 1995, found that 2.2% of Canadians 12 years and older reported consulting a psychologist during the previous year. Not surprisingly, those who sought psychological services reported more stress and distress and lower life satisfaction than did the population at large. Consistent with the American data just described, many who might benefit from mental health services had not received it: for example, many Canadians suffering from depression had received neither therapy nor medication. **Table 11.5** provides some further details about the findings from this survey. One aspect we wish to highlight is the finding that Canadians living in rural areas were three times less likely to consult a psychologist compared with their counterparts in urban areas. Although the rates of psychological problems are no lower in rural settings, access to all health care professionals, including psychologists, is much lower. **Profile Box 11.1** describes an innovative training program designed to address the needs of those in underserved rural areas. **Profile Box 11.2** describes the work of Dr. Patrick McGrath, who develops and evaluates treatment services for children and families in remote areas.

TABLE 11.5   Characteristics of Canadians Receiving Psychological Services

- Women/girls are twice as likely as men/boys to consult a psychologist.

- People between the ages of 30 and 50 are most likely to see a psychologist.

- Canadians living in rural areas, compared with those in urban settings, are one-third as likely to consult a psychologist.

- 22% of those consulting a psychologist have a university education, compared with 13% of the Canadian population.

- Although parents and children in single-parent families make up 8% of the Canadian population, they make up 20% of those who see psychologists.

- People experiencing significant pain that interferes with daily activities are twice as likely as other Canadians to consult a psychologist.

- People who receive psychological services also tend to be frequent users of other health care services.

- Adolescents and adults who feel so unhappy that they believe life is not worthwhile are five times as likely as other Canadians to seek psychological services.

Adapted from Hunsley, Lee, & Aubry (1999).

PROFILE BOX 11.1

RURAL AND NORTHERN PSYCHOLOGY INTERNSHIP STREAM AT THE UNIVERSITY OF MANITOBA

Training Program Members

The Rural and Northern Community-Based Psychology Training Program was introduced in 1996 to increase the supply of potential recruits to provide psychological services in rural and northern practice. Psychology interns considering the possibility of a rural or northern career can experience the rewards and challenges of this type of work, learning the skills required for practice in small or remote communities with a supervisor always close by.

The program is based in the Department of Clinical Health Psychology within the Faculty of Medicine of the University of Manitoba. The location of a clinical health psychology department in a medical school is unique in Canada. Psychology pre-doctoral interns receive the same salary and benefits as do medical residents. The department's mission is to train psychologists who will provide services to the whole province of Manitoba. This is consistent with the outreach mission of the Faculty of Medicine at the University of Manitoba, which is a leader in the education of Aboriginal physicians.

The internship is accredited by both the Canadian Psychological Association and the American Psychological Association and has places for seven pre-doctoral interns. Of these, two are accepted into the Rural and Northern stream in which they spend their first six months in Winnipeg-based clinical rotations and relocate to rural or northern communities for the second half of their training year. In recent years six interns have completed northern rotations hundreds of kilometres away from Winnipeg in Thompson, The Pas, Flin Flon, and Dauphin. The program has also trained six rural interns in the Interlake region, close enough to Winnipeg for them to live in or near the city.

During their urban rotations, interns have several clinical supervisors and attend weekly seminars and case conferences with other interns. Through the province's MBTelehealth service (which uses two-way information technologies to link care providers and patients), psychologists in the north also participate in these case conferences; interns continue to participate in case conferences when they are based in the north. The ongoing case conferences supplement the supervision that interns receive in rural and northern rotations where there is typically only one psychologist supervising them. Consultation with other psychologists from Winnipeg is frequent, providing a range of expertise that contributes to the intern's learning and supports the staff psychologists in these regions.

The Department of Clinical Health Psychology also offers a one-year post-doctoral residency, based in one of the rural regions surrounding Winnipeg. The residency offers a greater degree of autonomy (still with regular supervision) and opportunities to become more involved in community health promotion and illness prevention projects or applied research.

Staff turnover is inevitable and expected in remote communities. Frequently the department has hired former trainees from this program into positions in rural and northern communities when these have become vacant. The early exposure helps prepare them for the reality of rural or northern practice.

All supervising psychologists in rural and northern rotations are academic faculty members of the Faculty of Medicine of the University of Manitoba and thus have ready access to colleagues, libraries, research support, and other university resources. The close collaborative relationship with the rest of the Department of Clinical

Health Psychology helps reduce professional isolation and burnout for staff dealing with the unusually varied caseloads encountered in rural and northern communities.

Psychologists working in rural and northern areas must be competent in a broader range of diagnostic, treatment, and administrative skills than are their counterparts in typical urban practice settings. In rural and northern practices, typical caseloads include adults, children, adolescents and families, medical, surgical, and rehabilitation patients, and both outpatient and inpatient mental health referrals. (The northern communities have 8- to 10-bed inpatient mental health units in their regional general hospitals). The psychologist's workload also includes consultation to community mental health workers, family physicians, home care staff, and self-help groups. Many patients and clients in some regions are Aboriginal. The rural and northern training model emphasizes the development of generalist clinical skills and cross-cultural competencies.

Telehealth is frequently used for case consultation and continuing education, but is rarely used for direct service to patients. The program's philosophy emphasizes the importance of a community-based multidisciplinary approach to treatment and prevention in which importance is placed on having psychologists who live in the rural or northern regions where they work. Telehealth treatment lends itself more to an individual-centred approach. If one does not understand the context of a patient's problem, there may be an unfortunate tendency to assume that the source of the problem is only in the individual, an assumption that providing assessment or treatment services only from a distance can encourage. Thus, the program uses Telehealth to support—not substitute for—services from psychologists in the north.

Another good reason for psychologists to be visible in these communities is to be role models for students who may consider future careers in psychology. Staff psychologists and interns are encouraged to participate in school career days and similar events. Life in small, remote communities is often difficult for young urban professionals, leading to staff turnover. The long-range strategy is to recruit interns and staff with rural backgrounds and lifestyle interests who will remain in rural or northern communities.

PROFILE BOX 11.2

DR. PATRICK McGRATH

Dr. Patrick McGrath

I received a Ph.D. from Queen's University in Kingston, Ontario. For 10 years, I worked as a clinical psychologist at the Children's Hospital of Eastern Ontario, where I became enthusiastic about research and especially about pediatric pain research because I saw research as a way of helping children. During my time at CHEO, I got my first grants and published many papers. In 1989, I moved to Dalhousie University to head a new clinical psychology doctoral program. My research is on pediatric pain and distance treatment of child mental health problems. I teach the Introductory Psychology class and work closely with graduate students and colleagues on research. I am licensed by the Board of Examiners in Psychology of Nova Scotia and have a small clinical practice.

What made you choose to become a clinical psychologist?

I became a psychologist because I wanted to help children. When I was a child, Canice Connors, a priest and psychologist who was studying at the University of Ottawa often visited our home. He was a great guy and I learned about clinical psychology from him. Serge Piccinin, my first-year psychology instructor, solidified my interest.

What is the most rewarding part of your job as a clinical psychologist?

When I publish a paper on pain in children, I help children around the world. I am lucky to have the intellectual stimulation and emotional satisfaction that the combination of clinical work, teaching, and research gives me.

What is the greatest challenge facing you as a clinical psychologist?

Having the time to do all of the interesting things that I am doing. I supervise many students, I have many research projects, I teach, and I usually have a small clinical practice.

Tell us about the innovations you have developed in offering psychological services to children and families.

My colleagues and I have really created the awareness of pain in infants, children, and adolescents and have changed the way the health system takes care of pediatric pain. We have shown that psychological interventions are effective in both acute pain and in chronic pain. We have also shown that it is possible to accurately measure pediatric pain. I am particularly pleased that our research has led to health care professionals' increasing awareness of the experience of pain in individuals with severe cognitive impairment.

Most recently, I have been working on bringing psychological treatments to more children who need them by using distance treatment methods. We have randomized trials underway on the treatment of oppositional defiant disorder, attention-deficit/hyperactivity disorder, anxiety disorders, recurrent pain, and enuresis (bedwetting). We treat the children in their home using the telephone, handbooks, and videos. Our goal is to increase access to treatments that work.

How do you integrate science and practice in your work?

All of my clinical work and teaching uses knowledge gained from research. Almost all of my research is on clinical problems. For example, our trials on distance treatment will make treatments that work available to children who need them.

What do you see as the most exciting changes in the profession of clinical psychology?

Psychology is now more aggressively using science to promote the public good. We work in all areas of health and well-being and infuse our practical work with a commitment to science.

Depending on the nature of the national health care system, there are many routes to receive treatment from clinical psychologists. In some countries, services provided by psychologists in hospitals or community clinics are covered by the national health care system; in other countries, such services may be covered by private insurance for most individuals, with only those in the lower income brackets receiving state-supported services. Across most health care systems, it is possible to obtain services from clinical psychologists in private practice settings. Typically this requires that clients directly pay for services; some clients have extended health care benefits through their workplace that may cover part or all of the costs. Although a referral from a physician may be necessary for psychological services delivered in publicly funded settings (such as a hospital), clients can usually self-refer when seeking the services of a private practitioner. The financial costs of psychological services are a major obstacle for many potential clients. This economic burden comes on top of the multiple obstacles that many people face when making a decision to seek therapy. Saunders (1993) conceptualized the process of seeking psychotherapy as involving a series of four inter-related decisions: realizing that there is a problem, deciding that therapy might be of value, actually deciding to seek therapy, and then contacting a therapist or a clinic. In Saunders' research, the majority of those who eventually sought therapy reported that it took several months to move from recognizing that a significant problem existed to deciding that therapy might be useful. Even then, over half of the clients indicated that it took at least several weeks to make the decision to seek treatment. The extent to which the potential client feels supported by significant others in this process can also influence decisions around seeking therapy (Saunders, 1996).

THE DURATION AND IMPACT OF PSYCHOTHERAPY

Mention the word psychotherapy to most people and their initial associations probably include a couch and a nodding therapist who says very little, but grunts enigmatically. As mentioned in Chapter 2, movies and television series frequently depict psychotherapy as a life-long form of treatment. Even if images such as these were accurate at one time, they do not correspond to current reality. The vast majority of people who receive psychotherapy attend fewer than 10 sessions and evidence-based treatment, across orientations, requires a very active therapist. Across practice settings, countries, and client presenting problems, the duration of psychotherapy has been remarkably consistent for decades (Garfield, 1994; Phillips, 1991): a large minority of clients come for only one or two sessions, and the median number of therapy sessions is typically in the range of 5 to 13 sessions. Over the years, several studies have examined clients' and therapists' expectations for a number of treatment-related factors, including the duration of treatment and reasons for the therapy termination (e.g., Hunsley, Aubry, Vestervelt, & Vito, 1999; Steenbarger, 1994). Ironically, compared with therapists' expectations, clients' expectations for treatment duration seem to be more in line with the actual duration of therapy. Likewise, clients generally report more benefits from treatment—even treatment of a brief duration—than do therapists. **Viewpoint Box 11.2** suggests a possible cognitive bias that may affect clinician's ability to accurately gauge the duration of treatment for the majority of their clients.

VIEWPOINT BOX 11.2

THE CLINICIAN'S ILLUSION

For decades there have been disagreements among researchers and clinicians regarding the severity and prognosis of many disorders. Cohen and Cohen (1984) suggested that part of this disagreement may be due to differences in the populations sampled. On the one hand, relatively optimistic estimates tend to be provided by researchers who use community-based samples, or those who combine multiple samples from community and clinical settings. In contrast, more pessimistic estimates are typically provided by practising clinicians and researchers who only use samples of patients receiving treatment. These differences in sampling strategies can lead to widely discrepant opinions, as we illustrated in Chapter 3 in discussing the possible association between childhood sexual abuse and later dissociative symptoms. Because information gathered solely from clinical samples is likely to be biased toward more severe problems, Cohen and Cohen labelled this bias the *clinician's illusion*.

The clinician's illusion has also been found when expectations about treatment duration are examined: psychotherapists consistently overestimate the duration of treatment. As an example, survey data from Knesper, Pagnucco, and Wheeler (1985) found that psychologists, psychiatrists, and social workers all overestimated, by up to 100%, the duration of treatment services they offered. Vessey, Howard, Lueger, Kächele, and Mergenthaler (1994) used a statistical technique known as stochastic modelling to better understand why this type of error occurs so consistently. Stochastic modelling is a technique that allows predictions to be made about if and when a steady state will occur in a process of operations. For example, in a retail context, the technique can be used to determine how many units of a product (such as televisions or computers) should be maintained in a warehouse to meet the needs of a large number of retailers, which vary in the size and frequency of their product orders.

Vessey and colleagues started their analyses by considering actual data on the duration of treatment and formed frequency estimates for types of patient, ranging from short-term patients (i.e., those attending 1–8 sessions) to long-term patients (i.e., those attending more than 52 sessions). They then applied these data to what happens in the months after a beginning therapist opens a new practice. They made assumptions about the number of treatment "slots" available each week and used the data on treatment duration to generate a series of models about the proportion of patient types in a developing practice. When a new practice opens, the mix of patient types resembles the population data on treatment duration, with most patients receiving fewer than 8 sessions and relatively few receiving more than 52 sessions. However, by definition, treatment termination occurs more rapidly for patients who have few treatment sessions. When these patients are replaced by new patients, the majority of the new patients are those who receive a small number of sessions; however, a minority of these new patients will be those who will continue for a greater duration. In the meantime, though, the initial long-term patients continue to receive treatment. As this process continues over time, there will be more long-term patients who replace short-term patients than there will be short-term patients who replace long-term patients. As a result, the case mix in the practice becomes increasingly weighted toward long-term patients. In fact, in terms of treatment duration, within two years the mix of patients in a typical practice will no longer be representative of the mix of patients waiting to receive treatment.

What this means, of course, is that the clinician's illusion isn't really an illusion *per se*. Rather, it is an accurate reflection of biased information that is derived from a limited and nonrepresentative set of data. Thus, when estimating the duration of treatment for a new patient (such as during the process of obtaining informed consent), clinicians should not base an estimate on the nature of their current practices. Instead, clinicians need to be aware of the larger picture—namely the empirical evidence regarding treatment duration—and use the most representative data to generate this estimate. Providing an accurate estimate is important for at least two reasons. First, for patients to give truly informed consent, they need to know about the likely duration of treatment. Second, with respect to treatment planning, psychologists and other providers of psychotherapy need to be realistic in matching the goals and pacing of therapy with the number of sessions that a patient is likely to attend.

Findings reported by Hansen, Lambert, and Forman (2002) nicely illustrate several aspects of what is known about the duration and impact of psychotherapy as it is typically practised. These American researchers provided summary information based on data from more than 6,000 adult patients seen in a range of settings including employee assistance programs, university counselling centres, community mental health clinics, and health maintenance organizations. Fully one-third of these patients attended only a single session of psychotherapy, with the median number of therapy sessions being three! Using data from the Outcome Questionnaire (OQ-45, see Chapter 8) and standard methods for calculating clinically significant changes in functioning, the researchers used four categories to classify treatment outcome: (a) *deterioration* meant that a patient's scores had reliably moved in a negative direction during the course of treatment, (b) *no change* meant that reliable change had not occurred in OQ-45 scores, (c) *improved* meant that the scores had reliably changed in a positive direction, and (d) *recovered* meant that a reliable, positive change had occurred that was large enough to move from the range of dysfunctional scores to the range of functional scores. Across settings, 8.2% of patients deteriorated during treatment, 56.8% experienced no change, 20.9% improved, and 14.1% recovered.

These numbers may seem very discouraging and, in many ways, they are. At first glance the data seem to suggest that psychotherapy, as routinely practised, only benefits slightly more than a third of those who enter treatment. Viewed with a sceptical eye, even that may be an exaggeration: without the use of an experimental design it is not possible to attribute changes in functioning solely to the impact of therapy. On the other hand, if you take into account that the median number of therapy sessions was only three, it is not entirely surprising that psychotherapy has such a limited impact. As you will see in Chapters 12 and 13 when we discuss specific evidence-based psychological treatments, most current treatments are designed to be short-term, ranging from 10 to 30 sessions. It seems obvious that if most people are not receiving a full "dose" of treatment, any therapeutic benefits are likely to be minimal. Keep in mind, however, that the data we just described came from the results of psychotherapy as it is usually delivered in practice settings. It is very unlikely that much of this therapy is of the evidence-based form, an issue we will return to in later chapters. In other words, the observed impact of routine psychotherapy may be weak for two separate reasons: most patients attend too few sessions and most therapists do not provide evidence-based treatments.

The "dose" of psychotherapy required to elicit clinically significant changes has become a focus of naturalistic psychotherapy research. The study that launched the investigation of the dose-effect relationship in psychotherapy was published in 1986 by Howard, Kopta, Krause, and Orlinsky. They defined dose as the number of therapy sessions and effect as the percentage of improved patients. These researchers used data from 15 independent treatment samples (with more than 2,400 patients) to plot effect against dose. They found a negatively accelerated curve: the effect of therapy is greatest early in treatment and increases only slowly as the dose increases. **Figure 11.1** depicts this relationship. The bottom line from this study is that 8 sessions of treatment were required to obtain a 50% patient improvement rate.

Other researchers have examined the dose-effect relationship in routine practice settings. As summarized by Hansen et al. (2002), the number of sessions required to achieve a 50% patient improvement rate has ranged from 5 to 18 sessions. It is important to note that the most common form of treatment in these studies was psychodynamic or interpersonal-psychodynamic. Earlier in the chapter we outlined short-term versions of these approaches to treatment and in Chapter 12 we will review the evidence for their efficacy. However, it is unlikely that most of the treatments included in dose-effect studies were evidence-based. Nevertheless, the reality remains: most adult patients receive little benefit from routine treatment. In contrast, it is informative to look at other data summarized by Hansen et al. They extracted data from randomized controlled trials (RCTs) of evidence-based treatments. Across 28 studies and more than 2,100 patients, the average dose of therapy was 12.7 sessions, with 57.6% of patients meeting criteria for recovery (and 67.2% meeting criteria for improvement or recovery). Put bluntly, with more treatment, and treatment that is evidence-based, the success rate of psychotherapy improves substantially compared with treatment as usual (67.2% versus 35.0%). The discerning reader might question

Figure 11.1 Relation of Number of Sessions of Psychotherapy and Percentage of Patients Improved

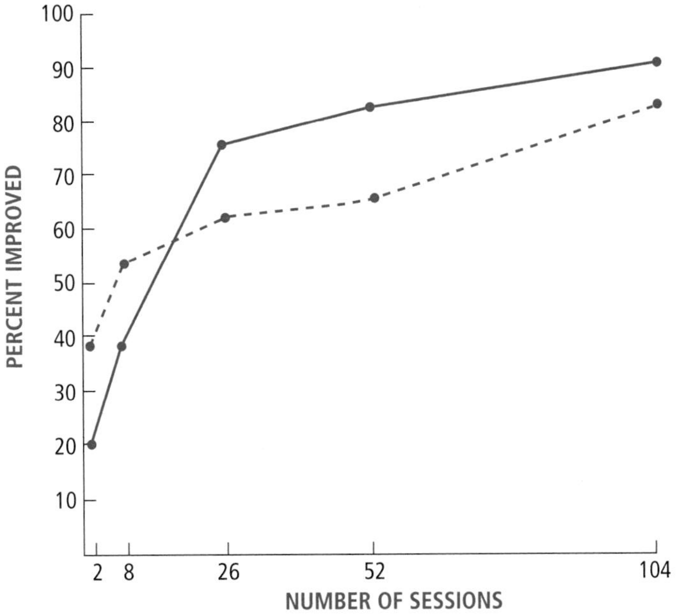

Note. Objective ratings at termination are shown by the solid line; subjective ratings during therapy are shown by the broken line.

Reproduced with permission.

whether the RCTs obtain better results because they are dealing with a less distressed sample of patients. In actual fact, the exact opposite is true: Stirman, DeRubeis, Crits-Christoph, and Brody (2003) reported that the average severity of symptoms reported in RCTs of evidence-based treatments is greater than that found in the patients seeking routine psychotherapy services. Evidence-based treatments do better than treatment as usual, even though the patients receiving the evidence-based treatments are more severely distressed.

ALTERNATIVE MODES OF SERVICE DELIVERY

Although the vast majority of psychological interventions are delivered in individual sessions in the psychologist's office, psychological services are also delivered in other formats. A variety of structured, brief couples therapies have been developed from different theoretical orientations including behavioural marital therapy, cognitive-behavioural marital therapy, insight-oriented marital therapy, and emotionally focused couple therapy. Although some of these approaches were originally labelled "marital therapies," the term "couple therapy" is now used as these

approaches apply to intimate relationships in married and co-habiting heterosexual, gay, and les-
bian couples. Behavioural and cognitive behavioural approaches draw heavily on research on
relationships, whereas insight-oriented and emotionally focused approaches originated in the
expansion of individually oriented approaches to couples. Each theoretical approach varies in the
weight given to affective, behavioural, and cognitive factors that disrupt relationships. Based on
mixed results of the efficacy of couple therapy, many approaches have been modified. So, for
example, behavioural marital therapy was modified from a solely skill-based, behavioural
exchange model designed to improve unsatisfactory relationships into Integrative Behavioral
Couple Therapy that also includes tasks designed to facilitate acceptance of an imperfect but adequate relationship (Jacobson, Christensen, Prince, Cordova, & Elridge, 2000).

Couple therapy is offered to treat distressed relationships and also to address psychological disorders that are associated with relationship dysfunction, such as depression (Baucom, Epstein, &
Gordon, 2000; Birchler & Fals-Stewart, 2002). Couple therapy is delivered primarily by means of
conjoint sessions in which both partners are present, but may also include individual sessions with
each partner. Although there is a wealth of research on couple therapy, there are no data on the
effectiveness of these approaches with ethnic minority couples (Gray-Little & Kaplan, 2000).

Like couple therapy, family interventions are practised by clinical psychologists of different orientations as well as by other mental health professionals such as social workers and psychiatrists.
However, whereas advocates of different theoretical approaches to couple therapy agree on a common goal of therapy such as reduced conflict and increased satisfaction, there is no single type of
family outcome that is sought across different approaches (Sexton, Alexander, & Mease, 2004).
Family therapy may be sought to address difficulties associated with transitions, as well as to address
Axis I problems in a family member. Although early family approaches viewed the family as the
source of a family member's problems, many current family approaches make no such assumption
but consider the family an important part of the solution to problems. A common aspect of family
approaches is to identify interactions between family members that may inadvertently contribute to
problems. Research supports the usefulness of a number of methods that integrate behavioural and
family approaches in the treatment of serious problems in adolescence (e.g., Barton & Alexander,
1981; Henggeler, Schoenwald, Borduin, Rowland, & Cunningham, 1998).

Given concerns over mounting health care costs, there are increasing pressures to find innovative ways to deliver services in as cost efficient a manner as possible. One obvious solution is to
bring together a group of people who are facing the same types of difficulties and to treat them as
a group. Like all other forms of psychotherapy, group approaches are based on a variety of theoretical models, including psychodynamic, interpersonal, experiential, and cognitive-behavioural. It is
useful to make a distinction between *process* groups that are designed to capitalize on the dynam-
ics of the group and *structured* group approaches that are extensions of treatments that are also
offered in an individual format (Burlingame, MacKenzie, & Strauss, 2004). Group approaches
should not be seen simply in terms of cost-savings as they also offer unique opportunities to promote change by exchanges between participants (Yalom, 1995). Group therapy is offered both as a

primary form of treatment for diverse types of problems, as well as an adjunct to individual therapy, as in the case of the treatment of substance abuse (Burlingame et al., 2004). Groups are offered at different stages of the lifespan to children, adolescents, adults, and the elderly (Brabender, Fallon, & Smolar, 2004). Group therapy offers many promising mechanisms of change, including universality, support, and modelling. Universality refers to the experience of recognizing that one is not alone in facing a particular difficulty and that others share similar challenges and reactions. Support may be provided in a group format, not only by the therapist but also by others in the group. Group contexts allow opportunities for modelling of behaviours, so that a client may learn new ways of coping by observing the efforts of another person. Unfortunately, groups allow the modelling of both positive and negative behaviours. Dishion, McCord, and Poulin (1999) reviewed evidence suggesting that when adolescents with significant problem behaviours received peer-group interventions, they learned aggressive behaviours from one another. Thus group treatment had an iatrogenic effect, in that youth who received the group treatment did more poorly than did youth who did not receive the treatment. This finding underlines the essential requirement to continuously evaluate the effects of therapy, to determine that therapy is helpful, and to ensure that, if therapy is harmful, it is terminated immediately.

Thus far we have discussed what might be termed "traditional" alternative modes of intervention. Since the 1980s, there has been dramatic growth in a new wave of alternative intervention options. These include **self-administered treatment** (also known as self-help), **computer-based treatment** (including virtual reality treatments), and computer-based treatment delivery systems.

It might seem unlikely that self-help books would be classified as a new development in treatment. After all, the shelves of any bookstore are replete with self-help books, with advice from a host of health care professionals, famous and formerly famous celebrities, and self-promoting lifestyle gurus. Whereas the sales of some of these books may lead to improvements in the financial well-being of their authors, there is little evidence that they do much for improving the quality of the readers' lives. What has changed, though, is that there is now a new generation of self-help materials that has been demonstrated to have a meaningful clinical impact. What these books have in

There has been dramatic growth in alternative interventions such as self-administered treatment, virtual reality treatments, and computer-based treatment delivery.

common is that they are based on both well-established psychological principles and treatment protocols for psychotherapies that are evidence-based.

Self-help materials can be used in different ways in treatment (Newman, Erickson, Przeworski, & Dzus, 2003). At one end of the continuum, treatment can be entirely self-administered, with the only therapist contact being an initial assessment of patient suitability. Alternatively, treatment can be predominantly self-administered with occasional therapist contact beyond an initial assessment to teach patients how to use the materials and check on their progress. The degree of therapist involvement can be further increased—but still below the level found in traditional therapy—in minimal-contact therapy where the therapist actively aids the patient in using the self-help materials (which still remain the central focus of therapy). Finally, at the other end of the continuum, in traditional, predominantly therapist-administered treatments, self-help materials can be used as an adjunct to treatment. There is evidence that self-administered treatments, across this continuum, can be clinically effective in treating depression, anxiety disorders, and substance abuse disorders (Scogin, 2003).

Since the early 1980s, researchers have experimented with the possibility of delivering individual treatments via computers. Early programs were rather primitive and limited in scope but, with the rapid growth in computing power in personal computers, more recent programs are incredibly sophisticated and flexible. In fact, in a number of experimental trials, computer-based treatments have been found to have efficacy comparable to that of traditional individual psychotherapy for some people and conditions (Marks, Shaw, & Parkin, 1998). For example, Proudfoot et al. (2004) reported on a large randomized controlled trial in England in which 274 primary care patients with anxiety and/or depression received, with or without medication, either computerized CBT or treatment as usual as directed by the patient's primary care physician. The *Beating the Blues* program involves a brief videotape introduction followed by 8 50-minute computer sessions, with homework assigned to be completed between sessions. Compared with the treatment as usual condition, the patients who followed the *Beating the Blues* program evidenced significant improvements in depression, anxiety, work adjustment, and social adjustment. Interestingly, even though the cost of the computer-based treatment was £40 higher per patient than the usual treatments, lost employment costs were £407 less per patient (McCrone et al., 2004).

Other computer-based treatments are now available through the Internet, thus greatly expanding service delivery options for those who are far from a psychologist or who are too impaired by anxiety symptoms to travel for treatment (Kenwright & Marks, 2004). This use of information technology and telecommunications to provide health care services at a distance is known as **telehealth**. Telehealth covers a range of delivery options, including videoconferencing and computer-mediated communications (including email, chat rooms, and Internet-based services). The possibility of providing appropriate evidence-based services at a distance is extremely exciting and opens up countless opportunities for reaching people who might otherwise be unable or unwilling to seek necessary psychological services. However, the use of these technologies also opens a host of ethical, legal, and training questions (Jerome & Zaylor, 2000; Glueckauf, Pickett, Ketterson,

Loomis, & Rozensky, 2003). What additional training is required to allow a psychologist who is competent at delivering evidence-based therapy to be prepared to deliver the same types of treatment via videoconferencing? Is it legal for a psychologist to deliver Internet-based treatment to a patient who lives in a jurisdiction other than the one in which the psychologist is licensed? In **Profile Box 11.3**, you will learn more about the work of Dr. Stéphane Bouchard, whose research investigates the promise and challenges of telehealth.

PROFILE BOX 11.3

DR. STÉPHANE BOUCHARD

I received my Ph.D. at the Université Laval in Quebec City. I also completed post-doctoral training in the genetic epidemiology of early onset schizophrenia at the Centre de recherche Robert-Giffard. I am a licensed psychologist in the province of Quebec and a member of the Canadian Register of Health Service Providers in Psychology. I am a full professor at the *Université du Québec* en Outaouais where I hold the Canada Research Chair in Clinical Cyberpsychology. My research examines the efficacy of treatments for anxiety disorders as well as the mechanisms by which they work. My current research examines the usefulness of virtual reality and videoconference telepsychotherapy in different populations.

Dr. Stéphane Bouchard

What made you chose to become a clinical psychologist?

Like many students, I went into psychology with the desire to help people. Later on I was drawn to the idea of a job that gives me autonomy and allows me to devote my energy to diverse activities including teaching, clinical practice, and research.

What is the most rewarding part of your job as a clinical psychologist?

Seeing clients getting better. This is true both for clients in my private practice and for the clients of students whose clinical work I am supervising.

What is the greatest challenge facing you as a clinical psychologist?

My greatest challenge is the dissemination of empirically supported treatments. Many mental health professionals, including some psychologists, are reluctant to use evidence-based treatments. The challenge is to find ways to disseminate these treatments so that more professionals can adopt evidence-based approaches.

What innovations have you developed in offering psychological services to people with anxiety disorders?

The innovations I have developed are in two related topics: telepsychotherapy and the use of virtual reality. There are already effective treatments for anxiety disorders. However, there is a serious problem in terms of limited accessibility of these treatments. My work suggests that offering complete psychotherapy services in one-on-one high-bandwidth videoconference (telepsychotherapy) is an effective solution to make treatments more accessible. Interestingly, we have found that the quality of the therapeutic alliance does not seem to be hindered by the use of this technology. I think in the future, telepsychotherapy will have a significant impact on our approach to treatment delivery. Another very innovative application of technology is the use of virtual reality to treat anxiety disorders, as well as other mental disorders. I am working to determine the usefulness of interactive 3-D computer-generated environments in creating standardized situations where people could have what psychologists call *emotionally corrective experiences*. For example, virtual environments can be used to help people with anxiety disorders progressively face their fears (e.g., spiders, public speaking, flying). Not only does virtual reality-based treatment work, but it has also raised many fascinating research questions about how both virtual and traditional treatments work. With these technologies in hand, our clinic is already offering full-time clinical services in telepsychotherapy and virtual reality to clients suffering from a large array of disorders, from specific phobias, to panic disorder with agoraphobia or post-traumatic stress disorder.

How do you integrate science and practice in your work?

In the ongoing debate about whether psychotherapy is a science or an art, my position is that psychotherapy is a science applied with art. To me, science and practice must be intertwined. As a therapist, I have to know what science tells us about mental disorders and their treatments, but it is clinical experience and empathy that help me understand a client's specific situation and tailor the treatment to the client's specific needs.

What do you see as the most exciting changes in the profession of clinical psychology?

I am thrilled when I think that our profession will probably be influenced by (a) the integration of technologies such as telehealth and virtual reality; (b) a more refined understanding of the neurobiology involved in the psychological treatment of mental disorders; and (c) a shift from a reliance on a specific school of psychotherapy to an approach that uses research evidence to determine the treatment that is most likely to help a specific client. Naturally, new technologies will influence the way mental health services are delivered, both by psychologists and other mental health professionals. The fact that the brain is modified by effective psychotherapeutic treatment is also fascinating, and a better understanding of this neuroplasticity will definitively change our profession. A better understanding of mental disorders will also help us identify the most effective factors to target in therapy. I expect that in the future, we will develop effective therapies based on a better understanding of the precise mechanisms of how change occurs in therapy.

With this growing range of treatment options, models of **stepped care**, long available in medicine, are now being applied to psychological treatments. In an attempt to make the most of scarce health care resources, lower cost interventions are offered first, with more intensive and more costly interventions provided only to those for whom the first-line intervention was insufficient (Haaga, 2000; Scogin, Hanson, & Welsh, 2003). Following a thorough assessment of the patient and the state of the empirical evidence for the available treatment options, self-help or computer-based treatments may be worth considering as initial treatments. If symptoms persist after the completion of such treatments, then individual therapy might be considered. If the likelihood is low that a patient will complete a treatment that does not involve ongoing contact with a health care professional, minimal contact treatments (i.e., 3 or 4 sessions) or group treatments might be the best initial options. With respect to providing services to children and families, less intense interventions may involve the use of therapeutic feedback, large group parenting training, or psychoeducational school-based programs (Stormshak & Dishion, 2002; see Table 10.6 for a description of the different dosages of the Triple P program). Many details need to be worked out, and much research needs to be done, before stepped care models will be viable and widely accepted by patients and psychologists. What is clear, though, is that individual, face-to-face psychotherapy is no longer the only choice for many individuals seeking psychological services.

SUMMARY AND CONCLUSIONS

In this chapter we have provided an introduction to psychological intervention. We described a number of psychological treatments that have some empirical support. These therapies share some features, such as their short-term nature, the establishment of treatment goals, and the active role played by the therapist. Similarly, they share the view that the therapist must establish a positive relationship with the client. Most important, there have been efforts to evaluate the efficacy and effectiveness of these approaches. They differ, however, in their assumptions about the nature of problems, the process by which change occurs, the importance of examining the past, and the relative benefits of insight, experimentation, and skills. These approaches differ in the role ascribed to the therapeutic relationship—whether it is seen as a mirror of the problems the client experiences, a support in exploration, or as a resource to experiment and learn new skills.

Although there has been an increase in the number of people seeking treatments for psychological problems, this is accounted for by increased psychopharmacology rather than increased psychotherapy or other psychological services. It is clear that the majority of people who require psychological services do not have access to them. Canadian data indicate that the needs for psychological services of those living in rural areas are woefully underserved. The popular stereotype of long-term psychotherapy does not match the data on the provision of psychotherapy. Important changes are made by many clients after weeks or months of psychological services. The short-term therapies we described are intended to create an expectancy of change as well as encouragement to think, behave, or feel in different ways. In addition to individual therapy, encouraging findings are reported from couple, family, and group therapy. Psychologists have begun to exploit the enormous potential of virtual reality and Internet technologies to extend services to sections of the population who have been underserved in the past. Rigorous evaluation of the effectiveness of psychological services allows the development of a range of interventions that can be offered according to clients' needs and preferences. Rather than imposing a one size fits all approach to psychotherapy, it makes sense to tailor approaches to meet the needs of a diverse population.

Critical Thinking Questions

What may account for the difficulty many people experience in deciding to seek psychological services?

Once people have decided to begin therapy, what kinds of questions should they raise in an initial session?

Four main evidence-based approaches to therapy are presented in the chapter. Where would you place them on a continuum with intrapsychic and interpersonal as endpoints?

Compared with individual treatment, are there some disorders for which group treatment might be especially appropriate?

For someone considering psychological treatment, what might the advantages be in considering self-administered treatments? What drawbacks might there be?

Key Terms

cognitive-behavioural therapy	self-efficacy
computer-based treatment	short-term psychodynamic therapy
interpersonal therapy	stepped care
problem-solving	telehealth
process-experiential therapy	transference
self-administered treatment	

Key Names

Albert Bandura	Leslie Greenberg
Aaron Beck	Lester Luborsky
Robert Elliott	Hans Strupp
Albert Ellis	Myrna Weissman

ADDITIONAL RESOURCES
Websites

Beating the Blues computer-based treatment of anxiety and depression: http://www.ultrasis.com/products/btb/btb.html

The *FearFighter* Internet-based treatment of phobias and panic, and other Internet-based treatments: http://www.ccbt.co.uk/CommercialHomeContent.htm

A sample of websites describing virtual reality treatments and treatment-related research. Keep in mind the importance of empirical evidence in reviewing self-help books and websites offering treatment options:

http://www.virtuallybetter.com/

http://www.vrphobia.com/

http://www.vrselfhelp.com

CHAPTER 12

Intervention: Adults and Couples

INTRODUCTION

- *Evidence-based psychotherapies are required by health care systems.*
- *Psychotherapy research provides prescriptive "treatments of choice" for certain disorders and people.*
- *Practice guidelines become a standard part of daily psychotherapy.*

Experts have predicted that by 2010, these trends in psychotherapy will be evident. Norcross, Hedges, and Prochaska (2002) asked 62 psychotherapy experts and editors of leading mental health journals to forecast trends in psychotherapy research and practice. In addition to these three main predictions, respondents predicted it was unlikely that psychotherapy would be regulated by federal agencies or that revolutionary new techniques would replace current treatments. The experts expected an increase in the use of cognitive-behavioural therapy (CBT), interpersonal therapy (IPT), and treatments sensitive to cultural factors, as well as a decrease in the popularity of psychoanalysis, Adlerian analysis, Jungian analysis, Gestalt therapy, and existential therapy. As for changes in specific interventions and techniques, the use of homework assignments, attention to relapse prevention, and the use of computerized treatments and virtual reality were all predicted to increase, with free association techniques, implosion/flooding treatments, and dream interpretation predicted to decrease.

Only time will tell the accuracy of these predictions. As we will see in this chapter, there has been a dramatic evolution in the nature of psychological treatment since the middle of the twentieth century. Significant questions about whether psychotherapy has any discernable effect provoked a veritable explosion of research on the impact of psychological treatments, which, in turn, led to the establishment of efficacious and (often) effective treatments for a wide range of disorders and presenting problems. In the first part of this chapter we summarize these important events and describe efforts to accurately review treatment studies. We outline recent efforts to establish criteria for evidence-based treatments. In a growing number of countries these efforts have culminated in the development of clinical practice guidelines that set out treatments of choice for both adult and child disorders.

In addition to presenting the big picture regarding the history and current state of empirically based efforts to develop and promote psychological intervention, we will also provide several detailed examples of current preferred treatments for a number of disorders. This will allow you to develop a clear sense of what is involved in modern treatments for significant and common clinical conditions such as depression, posttraumatic stress disorder (PTSD), and couple conflict. Because of the scope of the research and scholarly activity involved, it is not possible to do justice to all of this work in a single chapter. Accordingly, in this chapter we focus on treatments for use with adults and couples; the following chapter addresses treatments for use with children, adolescents, and families.

DOES PSYCHOTHERAPY WORK? A CONTROVERSY AND ITS IMPACT

PsycINFO, the searchable database of psychological literature developed by APA, covers the period from the second half of the 1800s to the present. If you search this database for empirical studies on psychotherapy for adults that were published in peer-reviewed journals prior to 1950, you will find zero entries. If you run the same search, but change the date to prior to 2005, your search will yield more than 17,000 entries! Many scholars have attributed this astonishing growth in empirical attention to the effects of psychotherapy to a single paper. In 1952 **Hans Eysenck** published an article in which he argued that the rates of improvement among clients receiving psychodynamic or eclectic therapy were comparable to, or even worse than, rates of remission of symptoms among untreated clients. At that time, there were no **randomized controlled trials** (RCTs) of psychotherapy. Instead, proponents of various schools of psychotherapy proclaimed the effectiveness of their treatments on the basis of authoritative clinical experience and, occasionally, case histories of successfully treated patients. Eysenck, an early proponent of applying learning principles to alleviate psychological distress, reviewed data from 24 uncontrolled evaluations of psychoanalytic and eclectic therapies. Summing across data sets, he concluded that 44% of patients receiving psychoanalysis improved and 64% of those receiving eclectic treatments improved. He compared these results with two data sets in which *spontaneous recovery* occurred for 72% of *untreated* patients.

As we discussed in Chapter 4, internal validity is an important aspect of any psychological research. If you look back at Table 4.7 in that chapter, you can see that Eysenck's analysis of the data probably suffered from several threats to internal validity, including history, maturation, statistical regression, and selection biases. Without the use of appropriate control groups, in which participants are randomly assigned to treatment conditions, it is incorrect to compare the results from the different data sets. Without randomization there is no way to determine whether the patients in the different samples were comparable in terms of disorder, or severity of distress. It is also important to note that the so-called *untreated* groups were patients in residential treatment settings and patients making psychologically based disability claims who were treated by general medical practitioners. In other words, although they did not receive formal psychotherapy services, these *untreated* patients would have received some guidance and suggestions on their psychological difficulties as part of their treatment regimen. Critics of Eysenck's work, such as Luborsky (1954), also claimed that Eysenck's criteria for establishing clinical improvement were arbitrary and biased against finding positive therapeutic effects.

From the late 1950s to the early 1970s a number of competing reviews of the effectiveness of psychotherapy were published. Those who advocated the use of learning principles in developing psychological interventions, such as Eysenck (1966) and Rachman (1971), maintained that there was no compelling evidence supporting the efficacy of psychodynamic and other "traditional" forms of treatment. In stark contrast, proponents of the traditional psychotherapies conducted reviews showing that not only did these therapies have positive effects but that their effects were comparable to those reported for the newly developed behavioural therapies (Bergin, 1971; Luborsky, Singer, & Luborsky, 1975). Because each research group used different criteria to select studies for review, there was little overlap in the studies on which conclusions were based. Furthermore, different criteria were used to evaluate whether therapy worked. On top of that, interpretation of results was coloured by pre-existing biases for and against the value of traditional psychotherapies. For example, Bergin (1971) concluded that significant results in 22 out of 60 studies indicated that psychotherapy had a moderately positive effect, whereas critics of traditional therapy could claim the exact opposite, noting that 38 out of 60 studies failed to demonstrate clear evidence of positive treatment effects.

META-ANALYSIS AND PSYCHOTHERAPY RESEARCH

Throughout the 1970s, as the debate about the impact of psychotherapy grew, so did the number of published treatment studies. The literature became so vast that anyone attempting to understand and integrate the research evidence on various forms of psychotherapy faced the daunting task of qualitatively reviewing hundreds of published studies. The publication of the first **meta-analysis** of the psychotherapy literature by Mary Smith and Gene Glass (1977) was a landmark in efforts to review scientific literature on treatment outcome.

As we described in Chapter 4, meta-analysis is a method for quantitatively reviewing research studies. To allow for the meaningful integration of data across studies, researchers convert the results of studies into **effect sizes**. When based on group comparison statistics (such as t or F), effect sizes are expressed in standard deviation units: an effect size of $d = .5$ means that there is a difference of one-half standard deviation between groups. When correlational analyses are used (e.g., r or R), the effect size is expressed as an r statistic. It is also possible to convert d effect sizes into r effect sizes, and vice-versa. Effect sizes using the d statistic can also be represented in another way that is even more compelling. Let's consider a psychotherapy outcome research study in which there is a treated and an untreated group, and let's assume that the distribution of outcome scores for each group is normal in shape. If there were no group difference, then d would equal 0, and the two group distributions would overlap perfectly. However, if the treated group had better outcomes than did the untreated group (for example, $d = .5$), then the distributions would only overlap partially as there is a half standard deviation difference between the means of the two groups. It is possible, therefore, to represent the d statistic as the percentage of participants in the untreated group whose scores are lower than that of the average participants in the treated group. **Table 12.1** provides information on the equivalency among d, r, and the percentage of those in the untreated group falling below the level of the mean treated participant.

Dr. Gene Glass co-authored the first meta-analysis of the psychotherapy literature in 1977.

TABLE 12.1   Equivalencies for Meta-Analytic Statistics

d	r	Percentage of untreated participants below the mean of treated participants
0.0	.00	50
0.2	.10	58
0.4	.20	66
0.6	.29	73
0.8	.37	79
1.0	.45	84
1.5	.60	93
2.0	.71	98

By current standards, the first attempt to employ meta-analytic techniques was rather crude. Nevertheless, based on data from more than 370 published and unpublished studies, Smith and Glass (1977) reported the average effect of psychotherapy to be $d = .68$. In percentage terms, this means that the average person receiving treatment was better off at the end of treatment than 74% of those who had not received treatment. Psychotherapy, in general, certainly seemed to have a substantial impact. In 1980, Smith, Glass, and Miller published a more extensive and more sophisticated meta-analysis of the psychotherapy literature (and the drug treatment literature). They reviewed 475 controlled studies of psychotherapy, including studies published in scientific journals and unpublished dissertations. Their overall finding was that psychotherapy had an average effect size of $d = .85$ (i.e., the average person receiving therapy was better off after therapy than 80% of people who did not receive therapy).

Smith and colleagues calculated the efficacy of various types of treatment. Cognitive and cognitive-behavioural treatments had the largest effect sizes (d values of 1.31 and 1.24, respectively), followed by behavioural (.91) and psychodynamic (.78) treatments, humanistic treatments (.63), and, finally, developmental treatments (including vocational-personal development counselling and *undifferentiated counselling* (.42). These effect sizes cannot be directly compared, however, as clients treated within each type of treatment were not necessarily equivalent in the type and severity of problems. Smith et al. also examined the effects of psychotherapy across different disorders. Some of the largest effect sizes were for anxiety and mood problems and, again, some significant differences between treatments were evident. A subset of the studies they reviewed included direct comparisons of different forms of treatment (i.e., comparative treatment outcome studies in which participants were randomly assigned to different treatments). We will discuss these and other findings from this landmark meta-analysis in Chapter 14.

Criticisms of meta-analysis emerged rapidly (e.g., Eysenck, 1978; Wilson & Rachman, 1983). One criticism referred to the problem of *garbage-in, garbage-out*; in other words, if poor quality studies were included in a meta-analysis they could negatively influence the results. Similarly, the *apples and oranges* argument raised concern about the meaningfulness of including different treatments and different measures in a meta-analysis. For example, in considering the general effect of treatment, meta-analysts might give equal weight to a measure of patients' satisfaction with treatment as to data on whether a diagnosable condition was still present after treatment. In early meta-analyses, some researchers made other mistakes such as not controlling for differences in sample sizes across studies or using all results from each study rather than an average of all results (which meant that studies with a large number of analyses had more influence on the results of the meta-analysis). Fortunately meta-analysts took these concerns seriously and current practices in meta-analysis address such shortcomings.

Throughout the 1980s and 1990s, the number of meta-analyses grew. Because Smith et al.'s (1980) general findings on the effectiveness of psychotherapy were replicated by other researchers (e.g., Landman & Dawes, 1982), meta-analyses became more focused in nature. Instead of dealing with whether or not therapy had an effect, questions were refined to: "How effective are the treatments for a specific disorder?" and "How effective is a specific treatment for a specific disorder?" Dobson (1989) and Robinson, Berman, and Neimeyer (1990), for example, examined research on treatments for depression and found that cognitive therapy had a very large effect size compared with waiting-list controls ($d > 1.5$) but only a small relative advantage over other treatments such as behaviour therapy. Chambless and Gillis (1993) reviewed research on the treatment of anxiety disorders, including agoraphobia, panic disorder, social phobia, and generalized anxiety disorders. Cognitive-behavioural treatments were, in general, very efficacious compared with no-treatment conditions, but the extent to which treatments differentially emphasized cognitive or behavioural elements had little impact on treatment outcome.

Today, a PsycINFO search would reveal hundreds of meta-analyses published in the adult psychotherapy literature. This quantitative approach to reviewing research is now the gold standard for evaluating treatment effects. However, sometimes even gold has impurities that mar its value. In a series of *multidimensional* meta-analyses, Drew Westen and his colleagues have examined treatment research for depression, bulimia nervosa, generalized anxiety disorder, panic disorder, PTSD, and obsessive-compulsive disorder (Bradley, Greene, Russ, Dutra, & Westen, 2005; Eddy, Dutra, Bradley, & Westen, 2004; Thompson-Brenner, Glass, & Westen, 2003; Westen & Morrison, 2001). These meta-analyses are distinct (and multidimensional) in that a number of elements other than treatment outcome were analysed. In order to consider the external validity and the clinical utility of treatment studies, Westen and colleagues also examined variables such as the number of patients excluded from the RCTs for failure to meet inclusion criteria, recovery rates, and the persistence of treatment benefits over time. By examining these types of variables, the researchers' intention was to determine (a) the clinical significance of obtained treatment results and (b) the applicability of the research results to the general population of patients receiving therapy.

To illustrate these points, we will consider their multidimensional meta-analysis on bulimia nervosa (Thompson-Brenner et al., 2003). The researchers found that, on average, more than 80% of patients who began the RCT completed the treatment—an important aspect to consider in understanding the potential impact of the treatments studied. When the usual effect sizes across treatments were calculated from 26 clinical trials, the average effect of therapy compared with no-treatment was substantial, with d values in the range of .9 to 1.0. But just how big an effect was this in the patients' lives? Approximately 40% of patients recovered completely, with the others continuing to experience some symptoms. Thirty-two percent of patients maintained their recovery a year after treatment. Although these findings indicate that treatments for this eating disorder can have a substantial impact on patients' functioning, it is clear that many patients continue to manifest some aspects of the disorder despite having received treatment.

Thompson-Brenner et al. were also concerned to find that, on average, 40% of patients were excluded from the RCTs they examined. Reasons for exclusion included the presence of psychotic disorders, substance abuse, or other major psychiatric problems. This raises an important issue: is it possible that the RCTs routinely exclude from treatment too many patients who normally seek treatment, thereby greatly reducing the generalizability of findings? Fortunately this does not appear to be the case. As we mentioned in the previous chapter, Stirman and colleagues (2003) found that the average severity of symptoms reported in RCTs of evidence-based treatments is greater than that found in the patients seeking routine psychotherapy services. Moreover, it appears that, even if a potential research participant might be excluded from an RCT because of the presence of a comorbid diagnosis, it is highly likely that the patient would meet commonly used inclusion criteria used in the RCTs for the comorbid diagnosis (Stirman, DeRubeis, Crits-Christoph, & Rothman, 2005). The implications of this are that (a) there are likely to be efficacious treatment options (based on RCTs) for most patients, even those with co-morbid diagnoses and (b) in working with patients with co-morbid diagnoses psychologists must decide which diagnosis or condition should be addressed first and which problems should be addressed only after some initial changes in functioning have occurred. So, for example, in treating a client experiencing both PTSD and bulimia nervosa, the psychologist might determine that the eating problem needs to be stabilized before initiating treatment for the trauma.

PROFILE BOX 12.1

DR. KEITH DOBSON

I completed my Ph.D. in 1980 at the University of Western Ontario and have been a Professor in the Clinical Psychology training program at the University of Calgary since 1989. My basic research has focused on both cognitive models and mechanisms in depression, and the treatment of depression, particularly using cognitive-behavioural therapies. Applied research has included efficacy analyses of cognitive therapy, trials of prevention programs in depression, and a large study investigating the relative efficacy of cognitive therapy, behavioural activation, and SSRI medications in the treatment of depression.

Dr. Keith Dobson

My research has resulted in more than 120 published articles and chapters, 7 books, and numerous conference and workshop presentations. In addition to research on depression, I have written about developments in professional psychology, and have been actively involved in organized psychology in Canada. For example, I was the President of the Canadian Psychological Association in 1993–1994. I am currently on the boards of the Academy of Cognitive Therapy and the International Association of Cognitive Psychotherapy, and am an Associate Editor of *Behaviour Research and Therapy*. Among other awards, I was recently given the Canadian Psychological Association's Award for Distinguished Contributions to the Profession of Psychology.

What made you choose to become a clinical psychologist?

My original interest in psychology developed during my undergraduate degree. I learned early in my graduate career that I really enjoyed research, and it was this realization that helped me choose a research-academic career in clinical psychology.

What is the most rewarding part of your job as a clinical psychologist?

It is working with graduate students. These extremely competent and highly motivated people have made a commitment to become professionals in the field. It is a genuine privilege for me to watch these people, over the course of 6 or so years, become trained and skilful, and ready to take their places as colleagues in the profession of clinical psychology

What is the greatest challenge facing you as a clinical psychologist?

My major challenge is that there is so much that I find of interest, it is easy to become somewhat unfocused. As a professor, I am often asked to do things that take me away from my primary interests, and so balancing my interests and activities, as against the other interesting things that are brought to me, is a challenge. One of the major skills I have had to learn is how to say "no" gracefully.

Tell us about the work you have done in promoting evidence-based services for depression.

I believe strongly that clinical psychology must move, as quickly as it can, to become an evidence-based profession. This is not to say that as an evidence-based profession, it will consist only of "cookie cutter" treatments applied in an unthoughtful or inflexible manner. Rather, I think that as our knowledge grows, we will learn more about where standard protocols for assessment and treatment work well, and where we need more reliance on clinical judgement. My own work has been to conduct research related to the efficacy of treatments, and in particular cognitive therapy for depression. This work has included understanding the relative success of various treatments for depression, and studying the mechanisms of change within cognitive therapy. I have given lectures and published on the virtues and limitations of evidence-based psychotherapy, and I urge the students I teach to both appreciate where the research evidence gives strong indications about treatments, and where the evidence is not as well developed.

How do you integrate science and practice in your work?

I definitely employ what I know about empirically supported treatments in the clinical work that I do. Most of my clinical practice is with clinically anxious and depressed patients, and I often use methods I have recently read about or I know are being developed with patients (with their consent, of course). I find that my work with patients also often provides ideas for further research. This kind of bi-directional synergy, between science and practice, is what I consider one of the hallmarks of the scientist-practitioner model of clinical psychology.

What do you see as the most exciting changes in the profession of clinical psychology?

I obtained my doctoral degree in 1980, and so have been working in the field for some time. Although clinical psychology has had strong theoretical bases for many years, I believe that the database related to practice has now developed to the point that we can make some very clear statements about treatments that work, for quite a range of clinical problems. Within the range of theories and methods that have had particular success are the cognitive-behavioural therapies, which I have had the good fortune to be involved with. The movement toward empirically supported therapies has definitely assisted the development of clinical psychology, and I think will continue to exert a strong influence for the foreseeable future.

EVIDENCE-BASED TREATMENTS: INITIATIVES AND CONTROVERSIES

Based on the efforts of psychotherapy researchers in numerous countries, there is now compelling evidence that psychotherapy has the potential to improve the psychosocial functioning of adult patients with a wide range of disorders. These include common psychological disorders—mood disorders, anxiety disorders, eating disorders, sleep disorders, sexual disorders, and substance-related disorders—and diseases and disorders that are routinely seen in primary care medical practices but that are typically difficult to medically manage, including type 1 diabetes, chronic tension-type headaches, rheumatoid arthritis, chronic low-back pain, and chronic fatigue syndrome (First & Tasman, 2004; Hunsley, 2003). Given this research, it is surprising that so little has been done to promote the use of treatments found to be efficacious.

Clinical practice guidelines, based on the best available empirical evidence, are a common way in which empirical evidence is used to assist clinicians in making assessment and treatment decisions. Many health professions, such as medicine, nursing, and psychiatry, have developed expert review panels to translate the knowledge gained from research into concrete guidelines intended to inform clinical practice. The American Psychiatric Association, for example, has over a dozen practice guidelines listed on its website that address the treatment of dementias, mood disorders, several anxiety disorders, borderline personality disorder, eating disorders, and schizophrenia.

Despite the extent and strength of psychotherapy research, organized clinical psychology has been very slow and seemingly reluctant to develop clinical practice guidelines. The first initiative in this direction in clinical psychology began in the early 1990s. **David Barlow**, then the president of the APA Society of Clinical Psychology, struck a task force on the promotion and dissemination of psychological procedures. The goal of the task force was to set a standard for defining treatment efficacy or effectiveness that was comparable to standards used in other areas of health care, such as approval criteria for pharmaceuticals. The impetus for this work came from increasing pressure in the United States for health care practices to be both demonstrably effective and cost-effective (Beutler, 1998). Legislation and state case law were being used to shape the nature of both federal and state health care policy, and there appeared to be a very real danger that access to mental health and behavioural health care services might be curtailed because of perceptions that such services were both expensive and relatively ineffective.

Members of the original task force, chaired by Dianne Chambless, came from a range of occupational settings and espoused a variety of theoretical orientations. The task force's strategy was to examine treatment research for specific disorders and conditions according to a number of criteria. The task force required that for a treatment to be designated as efficacious, there must be evidence of symptom reduction and/or improved functioning from either at least two independently conducted RCTs or from a large series of single-case studies. Furthermore, the studies must have included a clear description of the client sample (which allows clinicians to determine the generalizability of results to their own practices) and the utilization of a treatment manual describing the nature and process of the intervention (which allows clinicians a way to develop knowledge regarding the implementation of the intervention). Treatments meeting all these criteria were referred to as empirically validated treatments, a term that was subsequently changed to **empirically supported treatments** (ESTs).

A report of the task force criteria and an initial list of ESTs was published in 1995 (Task Force on Promotion and Dissemination of Psychological Procedures, 1995). As the task force continued its work, the membership was expanded and additional issues were addressed in subsequent reports. A statement was added clarifying that the list of treatments was preliminary and was not meant to guide decisions about payment (or nonpayment) for psychological services (Chambless et al., 1996). The next task force report expanded the list of treatments and presented some of the issues that would be examined in its future efforts to evaluate treatments (Chambless et al., 1998). The most recent report from the task force did not include an updated list of treatments. Rather, the committee members chose to focus on efforts to (a) improve the review and classification procedures, (b) promote improved treatment research, and (c) disseminate research findings (Weisz, Hawley, Pilkonis, Woody, & Follette, 2000). In a related effort, in 1998, a special section in the *Journal of Consulting and Clinical Psychology* was devoted to the topic of ESTs. To guide authors in reviewing the literature for the special section, Chambless and Hollon (1998) formulated a refined set of criteria for designating ESTs. **Table 12.2** presents these criteria.

Many vocal critics of the EST initiative expressed concerns about a multitude of issues, ranging from the scientific soundness of the endeavour to the potential negative impacts on practising clinicians (e.g., Garfield, 1996; Henry, 1998; Silverman, 1996; Wampold, 1997). **Table 12.3** provides a summary of concerns and objections raised most frequently by these and other commentators, along with a set of responses typically offered by EST proponents.

TABLE 12.2   Chambless and Hollon's (1998) Criteria for Empirically Supported Treatments

Methodological and Statistical Criteria for Treatment Studies

1. There must be a comparison of the treatment with no-treatment control group, alternative treatment group, or placebo in an RCT, controlled single-case experiment, or an equivalent time-series research design.

2. The treatment must be statistically significantly superior to the comparison groups described above *OR* the treatment is equivalent to another treatment that is already of established efficacy.

3. The research must have sufficient statistical power to detect moderate differences.

4. The research must have been conducted with (a) a treatment manual or its equivalent, (b) a population treated for specified problems, for whom inclusion criteria have been delineated in a reliable and valid manner, (c) reliable and valid treatment outcome measures that, at a minimum, assess the problems addressed in the treatment, and (d) appropriate data analysis.

Designation Criteria for Treatments

Efficacious: The superiority of the EST must have been shown in at least 2 independent research settings (for single-case experiments the sample size must have been at least 3 at each site). If the data from all studies of the treatment are conflicting, the preponderance of the well-controlled data must support the EST efficacy.

Possibly Efficacious: One study is sufficient for this designation, in the absence of conflicting evidence (for single-case experiments the study must have had a sample size of at least 3).

Efficacious and Specific: The EST must have been shown to be statistically significantly superior to pill, psychological placebo, or alternative *bona fide* treatment in at least 2 independent research settings. If there is conflicting evidence, the preponderance of the well-controlled data must support the EST's efficacy and specificity.

More recently, the series of meta-analyses by Westen and colleagues raised the question of the appropriateness of reliance on statistically significant differences on symptom measures between treated and untreated patients to determine the strength of a treatment. As we described earlier in the chapter, even a large effect size (such as $d = 1.0$) does not guarantee that the majority of patients are symptom-free by the end of treatment or that they remain symptom-free for years after treatment. On the other hand, the standard used by most health care professions in defining preferred treatments is evidence of significant group differences from RCTs. Is it appropriate to apply a higher standard for psychological treatments than for other health care interventions? Doing so could reduce utilization of these treatments in public health care systems, as psychological services would appear less effective than alternative treatments such as pharmacotherapy. At a minimum, clinical psychologists, along with other health care providers, need to remain aware of the important difference in all health care treatment research between *statistically significant differences* and *clinically significant differences* (as represented by such concepts as *improved quality of life, cure*, and *recovery*).

TABLE 12.3   Criticisms of the EST Initiative

❑ It is premature to come up with list of treatments with empirical support. *Given (a) the hundreds of treatment studies, (b) the millions of dollars spent on psychotherapy research to date, and (c) the fact that millions of people worldwide receive psychotherapeutic services it is hard to see listing ESTs as premature.*

❑ The EST criteria, for example requiring RCTs and treatment manuals, disadvantage some therapeutic orientations. *This may require some psychotherapy researchers to provide more details about the nature of the treatments they study, but researchers from psychodynamic, experiential, interpersonal, and cognitive-behavioural have been able to develop treatment manuals and conduct RCTs.*

❑ Patients in RCTs are not representative of patients in the "real world" who seek therapy. *This is an important issue that requires further empirical attention. Initial indications are that, by and large, patients in RCTs may have more severe problems than those typically found in clinical practice.*

❑ EST designations are based on efficacy trials, but do we really know that these treatments can work in the "real world" (i.e., what about effectiveness trials)? *This is an extremely important point, as effectiveness trials are critical for ensuring that treatments can be appropriately delivered in clinical practice. However, the relation between efficacy and effectiveness trials should be seen as evolutionary, as it only makes sense to mount an effectiveness trial for a treatment that has been repeatedly shown to work in efficacy trials.*

❑ Treatment manuals can never capture the subtle nuances necessary for clinical services. *True, but manuals are not intended to do this. Thorough clinical training is necessary for the appropriate application of treatment manuals.*

❑ Doesn't using an EST require the clinician to follow, step-by-step, the treatment manual, thus leaving no room to tailor therapy to the clients' individual needs? *This criticism may have been valid for the first wave of treatment manuals developed in the 1970s and 1980s. However, most manuals now outline the key elements of treatment and explicitly encourage clinicians to adjust treatment to clients' needs.*

❑ Why the exclusive emphasis on treatment techniques—what about the therapeutic relationship or client characteristics? *A good point—one that led to the development of a task force looking at these issues (see Chapter 14).*

❑ What about diversity issues—for example, have ESTs been developed for all ethnic groups? *This, too, is a good point, and one for which current research is inadequate. A growing number of RCTs include patients from various ethnic groups and, for some research granting agencies, the sample of patients must be broadly representative of the population in the area in which the study is conducted. Nevertheless, at this point in time, psychologists must rely on their clinical skills and sensitivity to determine how best to tailor ESTs to the realities of individual patients, including attention to all forms of diversity.*

Another critical distinction is between a treatment that is untested, which by definition could not meet EST criteria, and a treatment that has been demonstrated to be ineffective. It is highly likely that some existing, but untested, treatments work for some patients. From an evidence-based perspective, though, a treatment with existing research support should always be considered by health care professionals and patients before they turn to untested treatments. This is true whether the clinical condition requiring treatment is depression, back pain, or diabetes, and whether the health care provider is a psychologist, a physician, or an occupational therapist. However, in light of the undeniable fact that even the best evidence-based treatments are not 100% effective for all people, it is important to keep an open mind about other available treatments. Based on research evidence, ESTs are likely to be the best treatment option for most people, but they are not a panacea. Proponents of ESTs have underscored these points and have stressed the need for lobbying and public education efforts about psychological services to be sensitive to these considerations (e.g., Hunsley, Dobson, Johnston, & Mikail, 1999).

The EST initiative inspired other divisions within APA to examine the issue of evidence-based treatments. In the next chapter we describe some of the efforts to designate treatments for children and youth as empirically supported. The Section on Clinical Psychology of the Canadian Psychological Association struck a task force in 1996 to examine the EST issue. The task force produced a report that was generally supportive of the promotion and dissemination of ESTs as defined by the APA Society of Clinical Psychology (Hunsley et al., 1999; Hunsley & Johnston, 2000). Related to these efforts, both APA and CPA accreditation criteria require that clinical training programs and internships include training in ESTs.

In addition to the EST initiative in North America, there have been evidence-based treatment initiatives in other countries. For example, in Germany, the federal government commissioned an expert report on psychotherapy that was used to guide the writing of laws to regulate psychotherapy. An important element of this expert report was the emphasis on ensuring access to psychotherapy services for which there is empirical evidence of effectiveness (Schulte & Hahlweg, 2000). Another example comes from Australia and New Zealand, where the Quality Assurance Project has published several guidelines for the treatment of psychological disorders. These guidelines are based on the combined results of meta-analytic reviews of the empirical literature, surveys of practitioners, and the opinions of experts. An alternative to the EST approach was developed in the United Kingdom, when the National Health Service (NHS) commissioned a report to guide the strategic policy review of psychotherapy services. The authors of this report used similar, but less stringent, criteria to those used by the Society of Clinical Psychology (Roth & Fonagy, 1996). In the most recent edition of this work (Roth & Fonagy, 2005), three criteria were used to determine whether there is evidence of treatment efficacy, each of which is less demanding than the EST criteria presented in Table 12.2. First, there must be a minimum of a single, high-quality RCT showing treatment efficacy. Second, there must be a clear description of the treatment, preferably but not necessarily in the form of a therapy manual. Third, there must be a clear description of the recipients of the therapy.

Nathan and Gorman (1998, 2002) adopted a different approach to reviewing and evaluating the therapy literature. Expert contributors were asked to provide indications of the methodological adequacy of outcome studies that supported the various treatments for a specific disorder. This allowed experts to provide empirically based guidance on the treatment of conditions for which the research was limited or was in an early stage of development. Three types of clinical trials were identified. In descending order of quality, Type 1 studies are high-quality RCTs, Type 2 studies are imperfect RCTs (e.g., very limited treatment duration, incomplete patient randomization), and Type 3 studies are **open trials** or pilot studies in which there are no control conditions. Additionally, experts could draw on the conclusions from quantitative literature reviews (Type 4), qualitative literature reviews (Type 5), and case studies or professional consensus statements not based on research evidence (Type 6).

Clearly there are strengths and weaknesses to all of these approaches to defining an evidence-based treatment. Most efforts to operationalize the concept of evidence-based practice rely heavily on a ranking system such as that used by Nathan and Gorman (1998, 2002) to establish a hierarchy of evidence. This is an important feature of evidence-based practice because, as we described in Chapter 4, research designs vary in the extent to which they address threats to internal and external validity. Accordingly, basing treatment recommendations for a patient on the results of a single, non-replicated study is less desirable than basing the recommendations on the results from numerous studies of the same treatment. Similarly, though, making treatment decisions based on uncontrolled or correlational research is better than basing it solely on professional opinion (sometimes facetiously referred to as *eminence-based treatment*). The establishment of a hierarchy of research evidence allows decisions to be made using the best available data with respect to a given disorder or condition.

The latest initiative to address the nature of evidence-based treatment in psychology comes from an APA presidential task force that was constituted to determine APA policies and practices with respect to evidence-based practice (APA Presidential Task Force on Evidence-Based Practice, 2005). Members of the task force were selected from academic, institutional health care settings and private practice settings to provide representation for all views on evidence-based practice issues. In its draft report the task force defined evidence-based practice in psychology as the integration of the best available research and clinical expertise within the context of patient characteristics, culture, values, and treatment preferences. In contrast to most statements about evidence-based practice issued by health care professions, the draft statement was extremely cautious about the use of research evidence in planning psychological services and said little about how different forms of research evidence should be weighted in making treatment decisions. The task force's position that treatment should be informed by research evidence but determined on the basis of other clinical information, patient choice, and the likely costs and benefits of available treatment options suggests that research evidence is the least important factor to consider in practising in an evidence-based manner. With respect to patient values, the draft statement was silent on the need for psychologists to ensure that patient views were based on accurate information and not on mistaken assumptions about the nature of psychological disorders and psychological treatments. At the time of the writing of this book, the task force was receiving feedback from individual psychologists and psychological associations, so it is likely that the final policy statement on evidence-based practice adopted by APA will be more in line with those found in other health care professions.

The most comprehensive list of evidence-based psychotherapies is one compiled by Chambless and Ollendick (2001), who incorporated lists of treatments from numerous sources, including some of those described above. Because their list is several years old, we have drawn upon more recent sources (Lambert, 2004; Nathan & Gorman, 2002; Roth & Fonagy, 2005) to supplement the Chambless and Ollendick work. Our updated list, focusing primarily on *DSM-IV* diagnoses for adults, is presented in **Table 12.4**.

TABLE 12.4   List of Evidence-Based Treatments for Adults

Mood Disorders

Major Depressive Disorder

- Cognitive-Behavioural Treatments
- Interpersonal Psychotherapy
- Short-Term Psychodynamic Therapy
- Process-Experiential Therapy

Bipolar Disorder

- Psychoeducation (including family members)
- Cognitive-Behavioural Treatments

Anxiety Disorders

Specific Phobias

- Cognitive-Behavioural Treatments

Social Phobia

- Cognitive-Behavioural Treatments

Panic Disorder with and without Agoraphobia

- Cognitive-Behavioural Treatments

Generalized Anxiety Disorder

- Cognitive-Behavioural Treatments

Obsessive-Compulsive Disorder

- Cognitive-Behavioural Treatments

Posttraumatic Stress Disorder

- Cognitive-Behavioural Treatments
- Eye Movement Desensitization and Reprocessing

Eating Disorders

Anorexia Nervosa

- Cognitive-Behavioural Treatments
- Short-Term Psychodynamic Therapy
- Systemic Family Therapy

Bulimia Nervosa

- Cognitive-Behavioural Treatments
- Interpersonal Psychotherapy

Binge-Eating Disorder

- Cognitive-Behavioural Treatments
- Interpersonal Psychotherapy

Substance-Related Disorders

Alcohol Abuse

- Psychoeducation (including Motivational Interviewing)
- Cognitive-Behavioural Treatments
- 12-Step Programs

Cocaine Abuse

- Cognitive-Behavioural Treatments
- 12-Step Programs

Opiate Abuse

- Cognitive-Behavioural Treatments
- Short-Term Psychodynamic Therapy

Sleep Disorders

- Cognitive-Behavioural Treatments

Sexual Disorders

- Cognitive-Behavioural Treatments

Schizophrenia

- Cognitive-Behavioural Treatments
- Psychoeducation (including family members)

Marital/Couple Conflict

- Cognitive-Behavioural Treatments
- Process-Experiential (Emotion-Focused Therapy)
- Short-Term Psychodynamic Therapy (Insight-Oriented Marital Therapy)

Personality Disorders

Avoidant Personality Disorder

- Cognitive-Behavioural Treatments

Borderline Personality Disorder

- Cognitive-Behavioural Treatments
- Psychodynamic Therapy

Somatoform Disorders

Pain Disorders

- Cognitive-Behavioural Treatments

Body Dysmorphic Disorder

- Cognitive-Behavioural Treatments

Hypochrondriasis

- Cognitive-Behavioural Treatments

Note: There are also evidence-based treatments for a range of health problems and illnesses, such as irritable bowel syndrome, chronic fatigue syndrome, Raynaud's disease, tinnitus, and smoking, to name only a few.

Two features in this table are striking. The first is the scope of conditions: there are evidence-based therapies for almost all commonly encountered Axis I conditions for adults. Axis II conditions fare less well in this regard. This is partially due to the difficulties in treating personality disorders (which by definition are chronic and pervasive problems) and partially due to the difficulty in obtaining research funds and conducting clinical trials that are of a duration sufficient to address these disorders (i.e., typically over one year). A second striking feature is that the majority of evidence-based treatments are Cognitive-Behavioural Treatments (CBT). Indeed, in many instances there is more than one form of CBT demonstrated to be efficacious in treating a condition, which is the reason for using the term Cognitive-Behavioural Treatments in the table. Despite this, it is clear that there are Process-Experiential, Interpersonal, and Psychodynamic treatments that have been demonstrated to be efficacious in the treatment of some clinical conditions. Treatment evaluation research has always been a central aspect of CBT, which explains, at least in part, why so many evidence-based treatments are cognitive-behavioural in nature. As this evaluation ethos is adopted by psychologists espousing other orientations, it is likely that there will be more non-CBT therapies added to the list of evidence-based treatments. Indeed, one could argue that one of the most important spinoffs from the EST initiative is that proponents of non-CBT approaches to psychotherapy are attending more to the need to empirically determine the impact of their treatments (cf. Elliott, Greenberg, & Lietaer, 2004). Psychoanalysts, too, are urged to conduct RCTs to establish an empirical basis for their treatment (Gabbard, Gunderson, & Fonagy, 2002).

VIEWPOINT BOX 12.1

THE EMDR CONTROVERSY

As indicated in **Table 12.4**, there is sufficient research on Eye Movement Desensitization and Reprocessing (EMDR) to list it as an efficacious, empirically supported treatment for PTSD. What is EMDR? In essence, it involves the patient imagining aspects of the traumatic event while visually tracking a quickly moving stimulus that goes back and forth across the patient's visual field. That stimulus is usually the therapist's first two fingers. Shapiro (1989) developed this treatment after a personal experience in which she found that, while thinking of an anxiety-provoking stimulus, her eyes made rapid, saccadic movements and, shortly thereafter, her anxiety was eliminated (Shapiro, 1995). Many thousands of mental health professionals have now been trained to provide EMDR. Although originally used to treat traumatic memories, EMDR has been promoted as a rapid cure for a host of psychological problems, including substance abuse, sexual dysfunction, dissociative disorders, and personality disorders (Devilly, 2002).

What is the controversy about EMDR? There are several areas of debate, including (a) the theory behind EMDR, (b) the utility or necessity of eye movements in EMDR, (c) the efficacy of EMDR, and (d) the likely mode of action responsible for treatment efficacy. With respect to theory, Shapiro initially claimed that the eye movements in EMDR were similar to those occurring in rapid eye movement (REM) sleep and that somehow these eye movements trigger a change in neurological functioning that allows the traumatic memories to be fully processed. There is no scientific evidence to support this position. Moreover, several studies have demonstrated that EMDR without the accompanying eye movements has results comparable to those obtained with EMDR with eye movements (e.g., Feske & Goldstein, 1997). In response to this research (which seems to call into question the main underlying premise of EMDR), proponents of EMDR then claimed that any external stimuli (such finger snapping or finger tapping) were sufficient to achieve successful treatment outcomes (Devilly, 2002).

Within a decade of the introduction of EMDR, numerous case reports and single-subject studies were published, along with approximately two dozen group treatment studies. Many studies found evidence for the efficacy of EMDR in treating trauma and other anxiety problems. In their review of the literature, Lohr, Lilienfeld, Tolin, and Herbert (1999) concluded that (a) eye movements were not necessary in EMDR, (b) EMDR was not more efficacious than existing exposure-based treatments, and (c) it was likely that the mode of therapeutic action in EMDR was through exposure (i.e., by repeatedly thinking about the trauma) rather than through any direct alterations in neurological functioning caused by the external visual or auditory stimuli. A subsequent meta-analytic review of this research substantiated these conclusions (Davidson & Parker, 2001).

The weight of evidence at this time is that EMDR is, at best, comparable in clinical impact to exposure-based treatments for PTSD and that it probably works because of the inclusion of some exposure elements in the treatment (e.g., repeatedly thinking about and imagining the traumatic events for extended periods). Despite empirical evidence to the contrary, proponents of EMDR continue to claim that the treatment works better and faster than CBT treatments utilizing exposure (see the claims on the EMDR Institute's website at http://www.emdr.com). Based on a review of the scientific evidence, critics of EMDR conclude that what is new and innovative about EMDR (i.e., eye movements triggering neurological changes) is not effective, and what is effective (i.e., exposure) is not particularly new or innovative.

CLINICAL PRACTICE GUIDELINES

As we indicated earlier in the chapter, clinical practice guidelines are used increasingly by many health care professions to promote evidence-based practice. To illustrate these initiatives, we will present information from several British programs. Health care professionals in the United Kingdom have been at the forefront of efforts to promote evidence-based health care. It is hardly surprising, therefore, that the UK National Health Service (NHS) has been actively involved in efforts to translate research evidence into recommendations and priorities for health care services. Compared with the limited attention accorded mental health issues in most countries, the inclusion of mental health services in these efforts is especially noteworthy. We have already briefly described the work of Roth and Fonagy (1996). Following that, a multidisciplinary guideline development group led by the British Psychological Society (BPS) developed lists of effective treatments and factors shown to affect treatment outcome. The report was designed to identify the main therapies that are most appropriate for specific adult patients (U.K. Department of Health, 2001). **Table 12.5** summarizes some of the conclusions from this group. It is interesting to compare the conclusions of this group with the information in Table 12.4 with respect to the availability of evidence-based treatments for anorexia nervosa. Such discrepancies are likely to occur due to advances in research and to variability in criteria used to determine what constitutes an evidence-based treatment.

TABLE 12.5   Treatment Choice in Psychological Therapies and Counselling

Principal Recommendations

- Psychotherapy should be routinely considered as an option when assessing mental health problems in patients.

- Patients adjusting to difficult life events, illnesses, disabilities, or losses may benefit from brief therapies, including counselling.

- Posttraumatic stress symptoms may be helped by psychotherapy, with most evidence supporting the use of CBT. The routine use of debriefing techniques following traumatic events is not recommended.

- A number of brief, structured therapies may be used to treat depression, including CBT, Interpersonal Therapy, and Psychodynamic Therapy.

- Patients with anxiety disorders are likely to benefit from CBT.

- Psychological intervention should be considered for somatic complaints having a psychological component. The strongest evidence is for the use of CBT in treating chronic pain and chronic fatigue.

- The best evidence for treating bulimia nervosa is for CBT, Interpersonal Therapy, and family therapy for adolescents. There is little evidence regarding the best treatment for anorexia nervosa.

- Structured psychological therapies delivered by skilled clinicians can contribute to the longer-term treatment of personality disorders.

Adapted from U.K. Department of Health (2001).

This group also identified treatments that should **not** be used, based on replicated evidence of nonsignificant effects and possible harm to clients. The identification of *stress debriefing* (also known as *Critical Incident Stress Debriefing*, described in Chapter 10) as a contraindicated treatment has been controversial, but is consistent with research evidence. Subsequent to the British report, McNally, Bryant, and Ehlers (2003) reviewed the scientific evidence for what is known about trauma, the development of PTSD, and debriefing strategies. They found that, although many people receiving debriefing services described them as helpful, the research evidence indicates that (a) those not receiving debriefing do not subsequently exhibit worse psychosocial functioning than do those who received debriefing, (b) debriefing does not reduce the incidence of subsequent PTSD, and (c) in some instances, debriefing may have an iatrogenic effect (i.e., result in decreased psychosocial functioning). Such results underscore the importance of an evidence-based approach to health care, for well-intentioned interventions delivered by caring and committed professionals can be ineffective or even harmful.

Because of a commitment to the translation of scientific findings into the provision of health care services, the NHS in England and Wales developed the National Institute for Health and Clinical Excellence (NICE) to guide health care professionals and patients in making decisions about health care treatment options. Independent from the NHS, NICE conducts extensive consultations with stakeholder organizations (both professional and consumer groups) in developing evidence-based clinical guidelines. Guidelines are reviewed and updated after several years to ensure their accuracy and completeness. There are clinical guidelines for assessment and treatment services for approximately 40 conditions.

With respect to psychological/psychiatric conditions, there are currently guidelines for the treatment of some anxiety conditions, depression, eating disorders, and schizophrenia, with several others in development. To develop guidelines related to these conditions, NICE draws upon the expertise of the National Collaborating Centre for Mental Health, which is a joint venture between the BPS and the Royal College of Psychiatrists that also involves consumer groups and other professional organizations (e.g., those representing occupational therapists, nurses, pharmacists, and general medical practitioners). The involvement of a wide range of stakeholders is intended to ensure that the guidelines are comprehensive and professionally viable. NICE serves as an exemplary model that could be adopted by health care systems in other countries.

Because of the prevalence of depression, we have selected the NICE guideline for the management of depression to illustrate the essence of an evidence-based clinical guideline. **Figure 12.1** illustrates the decision-making process that clinicians should follow in determining whether to implement this guideline. Consistent with the information we presented in Chapter 11, **Figure 12.2** provides an overview of the stepped care model recommended in the NICE guideline. The model incorporates the involvement of common primary care practitioners (i.e., nurses and general medical practitioners), primary care mental health professionals, and speciality mental health care. Finally, **Table 12.6** provides details on the evidence-based steps recommended in the model. It is important to note the variability in the strength of evidence supporting each of these recommended steps, ranging from relatively strong (meta-analyses of RCTs) to relatively weak (expert committee reports or opinions of respected authorities). Moreover, there is currently no evidence to support the entire stepped care model. It is essential that as guidelines such as these are disseminated, researchers evaluate the validity and usefulness of recommended steps within the model and the service models themselves (cf. Bower & Gilbody, 2005).

Figure 12.1   Which NICE Guideline?

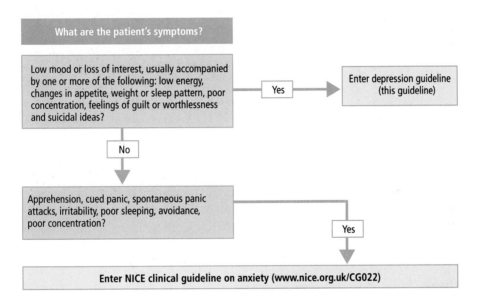

Source: NICE (2004a).

Figure 12.2   The Stepped Care Model

The recommendations in this guideline are presented within a stepped care framework that aims to match the needs of people with depression to the most appropriate services, depending on the characteristics of their illness and their personal and social circumstances. Each step represents increased complexity of intervention, with higher steps assuming interventions in previous steps.

Step 1: Recognition in primary care and general hospital settings

Step 2: Treatment of mild depression in primary care

Step 3: Treatment of moderate to severe depression in primary care

Step 4: Treatment of depression by mental health specialists

Step 5: Inpatient treatment for depression

	Who is responsible for care?	What is the focus?	What do they do?
Step 5:	Inpatient care, crisis teams	Risk to life, severe self-neglect	Medication, combined treatments, ECT
Step 4:	Mental health specialists, including crisis teams	Treatment-resistant, recurrent, atypical and psychotic depression, and those at significant risk	Medication, complex psychological interventions, combined treatments
Step 3:	Primary care team, primary care mental health worker	Mild depression	Medication, psychological interventions, social support
Step 2:	Primary care team, primary care mental health worker	Moderate or severe depression	Watchful waiting, guided self-help, computerised CBT, exercise, brief psychological interventions
Step 1:	GP, practice nurse	Recognition	Assessment

Source: NICE (2004a).

self-help?

TABLE 12.6   Key Priorities for Implementation

Screening in primary care and general hospital settings
- Screening should be undertaken in primary care and general hospital settings for depression in high-risk groups—for example, those with a past history of depression, significant physical illnesses causing disability, or other mental health problems such as dementia.

Watchful waiting
- For patients with mild depression who do not want an intervention or who, in the opinion of the healthcare professional, may recover with no intervention, a further assessment should be arranged, normally within 2 weeks ('watchful waiting').

Antidepressants in mild depression
- Antidepressants are not recommended for the initial treatment of mild depression, because the risk-benefit ratio is poor.

Guided self-help
- For patients with mild depression, healthcare professionals should consider recommending a guided self-help programme based on cognitive behavioural therapy (CBT).

Short-term psychological treatment
- In both mild and moderate depression, psychological treatment specifically focused on depression (such as problem-solving therapy, brief CBT and counselling) of 6 to 8 sessions over 10 to 12 weeks should be considered.

Prescription of an SSRI
- When an antidepressant is to be prescribed in routine care, it should be a selective serotonin reuptake inhibitor (SSRI), because SSRIs are as effective as tricyclic antidepressants and are less likely to be discontinued because of side effects.

Tolerance and craving, and discontinuation/withdrawal symptoms
- All patients prescribed antidepressants should be informed that, although the drugs are not associated with tolerance and craving, discontinuation/withdrawal symptoms may occur on stopping, missing doses or, occasionally, on reducing the dose of the drug. These symptoms are usually mild and self-limiting but can occasionally be severe, particularly if the drug is stopped abruptly.

Initial presentation of severe depression
- When patients present initially with severe depression, a combination of antidepressants and individual CBT should be considered as the combination is more cost-effective than either treatment on its own.

Maintenance treatment with antidepressants
- Patients who have had two or more depressive episodes in the recent past, and who have experienced significant functional impairment during the episodes, should be advised to continue antidepressants for 2 years.

Combined treatment for treatment-resistant depression
- For patients whose depression is treatment resistant, the combination of antidepressant medication with CBT should be considered.

CBT for recurrent depression
- CBT should be considered for patients with recurrent depression who have relapsed despite antidepressant treatment, or who express a preference for psychological interventions.

Source: NICE (2004a).

EVIDENCE-BASED TREATMENTS: SOME EXAMPLES

CBT for Depression

In the previous chapter we provided details on Interpersonal Psychotherapy for depression. We now turn to a brief presentation of another efficacious treatment for depression: cognitive-behavioural therapy. Many variants of CBT for depression have been extensively researched, ranging from those that are predominantly behavioural to those that are primarily cognitive (Emmelkamp, 2004; Hollon & Beck, 2004). A good example is a general form of CBT for depression described by Persons, Davidson, and Tompkins (2001).

The focus of CBT for depression is on altering the behaviours, negative automatic thoughts, and dysfunctional beliefs that are associated with the condition. In working with a depressed individual client using CBT, the psychologist conducts an initial assessment to determine the client's diagnostic status (including comorbid conditions) and to obtain a sense of the client's current life circumstances. Particular attention is paid to the client's relationships and social functioning, the client's psychological resources and strengths, recent events that may have precipitated the depressive episode, and the potential for suicidal behaviour. For example, Persons et al. (2001) described the case of Garrett, a musician who had lost a recording contract and a series of concert bookings. Based on initial assessment information, and in order to guide treatment, a case formulation was developed that related precipitating life events (e.g., loss of the contract and concert dates) to longstanding dysfunctional beliefs (e.g., *I'm a loser*). The case formulation also provided a framework for understanding Garrett's affective, cognitive, and behavioural symptoms. By spending time at home alone, instead of his usual socializing, and by spending hours watching television, instead of working on his music, Garrett felt increasingly depressed, discouraged, and listless.

Early in the treatment process the client is provided basic information about the nature of depression, the evolving case formulation, and the possible treatment options for addressing the depressive symptoms. As we described in Chapter 11, a CBT model emphasizes a collaboration in which the client participates actively in decision-making throughout treatment, which means that the therapist frequently provides information and lays out the options for addressing the agreed-upon targets for treatment. Throughout treatment, the client is asked to monitor symptoms and changes in functioning to determine the impact of therapy.

Initial sessions tend to focus primarily on behavioural activation tasks, such as getting the client to re-engage in some of the pleasurable activities that he or she used to do prior to the depressive episode. In order to do this, clients are first asked to self-monitor their activities during the day. In the typical case, this yields information that indicates that the client engages in very few pleasurable activities of any kind. To combat the lethargy and dysphoria common in depression, clients are encouraged to actively plan to increase their daily involvement in pleasant activities. This might involve activities such as exercise, going to a movie with a friend, reading a book, or making a special meal. Engaging in any of these pleasant activities is likely to reduce depressed feelings, whereas dwelling on past failures and ruminating about current problems are likely to increase depressed feelings.

As clients attempt to follow through on activity scheduling assignments, they typically express doubts about the point of the assignments and/or their abilities to carry them out. This provides an opportunity for the psychologist to point out the tendency to automatically focus on negative aspects of experiences and reasons for not attempting activities. Usually in the first few sessions this leads to the development of another form of homework assignment for clients that involves thought monitoring. This requires recording the types of thoughts that typically occur around upsetting or difficult situations. Persons et al. (2001) suggest the use of a thought record that includes a description of the situation (e.g., an event, a memory, or an attempt to do something), associated behaviours (e.g., getting into an argument and yelling at someone), associated emotions (e.g., frustration, sadness, and discouragement), and associated thoughts (e.g., *What's the point, I'm such a push-over, I'm such a total failure.*). You can find some examples of self-monitoring records in Figures 6.3 and 6.4. At the next stage in treatment, the therapist and client work together to examine how these thoughts influence decisions around behaviours (e.g., yelling rather than acting in a more assertive manner) and the resulting emotional states. The client is then coached to challenge the accuracy of these negative thoughts. Usually it is easy for clients to acknowledge the link between thoughts such as *I'm a loser* and feelings of discouragement and disengagement from an activity. It takes a great deal of effort and repeated practice, however, for a client to counter this thought with a response such as *No, I'm not a loser, I'm just not very comfortable about handling conflict.* However, once the client is able to do this, it usually opens up a whole range of options for responding differently to a situation than was previously evident. At this point, depending on the client's needs, the psychologist may help the client develop skills in areas such as assertiveness, problem-solving, or time management.

In the next stage of treatment, the primary focus is on examining and challenging the long-standing beliefs or schemas held by the client that render the client vulnerable to depression when confronted by negative life events. This involves helping the client to see patterns in the assumptions they make about themselves and events in their lives. These assumptions are often along the lines of beliefs such as *There is something basically wrong with me, Good things never happen to me, I can never succeed at anything important,* and *I'm not a loveable person.* Building on the behavioural and cognitive skills honed earlier in treatment, the client is encouraged to challenge these beliefs both cognitively and by engaging in personal experiments to test the accuracy of the assumption.

The final stage of treatment focuses on relapse prevention. The gains achieved by the client are reviewed, as are the specific skills the client learned or rediscovered. The clinician encourages the client to imagine events that might cause self-doubt and helps the client explore the most adaptive ways (both behavioural and cognitive) to respond to such events.

CBT (Prolonged Exposure) for PTSD

There are some general similarities in the CBT approach to treating depression and PTSD (and other conditions for that matter). These include the importance of a thorough initial assessment to develop a case formulation to guide treatment, the provision of information to the patient throughout treatment (both about the patient's condition and the rationale for specific treatment strategies), the development of a collaborative relationship between psychologist and patient, the use of between-session assignments, the ongoing monitoring of treatment impact, and attention to relapse prevention issues. Beyond these similarities, there are several treatment components that are different in the treatment of PTSD (Cook, Schnurr, & Foa, 2004; Foa & Rothbaum, 1998; Rothbaum & Schwartz, 2002).

Treatment typically begins with an assessment of the patient's condition and the provision of psychoeducational information about the nature of PTSD and the nature of the CBT approach. There are three broad components to CBT for PTSD: use of relaxation skills, imaginal exposure, and in vivo exposure. Because patients are asked to confront images and situations that cause them severe emotional upset, it is important that the psychologist help patients develop or enhance their relaxation skills. This can involve the use of progressive muscle relaxation, breathing retraining, and/or cognitive strategies for self-soothing. In many instances patients are given reading materials or audiotapes and CDs to assist them in practising these relaxation skills at home.

The use of progressive muscle relaxation, breathing retraining, and other self-soothing strategies can be used by patients when confronting the images and memories that cause them severe emotional upset.

In most cases treatment then moves to the use of imaginal exposure. As part of the initial assessment process, patients will have already described the events, situations, and memories that are most disturbing to them. During treatment sessions patients are asked to close their eyes and to recount these traumatic experiences for an extended period (typically more than 30 minutes), using the present tense and providing as much contextual details as possible (e.g., smells, sounds, their own thoughts and physical reactions). This imaginal exposure encourages the patient to begin to fully emotionally process the trauma that was experienced. This allows patients to (a) revisit details of the trauma and gain new perspective on what happened and what might have occurred, (b) distinguish between remembering the event (which is not inherently dangerous) and re-encountering the event (which could be dangerous), (c) develop a consistent, organized narrative of what occurred, (d) learn that remembering the events can lead to an overall reduction in anxiety and other symptoms, and (e) develop a new appreciation for what they did to survive the trauma (Cook et al., 2004). These imaginal exposure sessions are usually audiotaped and the patient is asked to listen to the tape repeatedly between sessions in order to promote emotional processing.

In vivo exposure is used to assist patients in reducing distress associated with encountering stimuli that remind them of the trauma. This can include stimuli such as sounds (for a patient traumatized in a car accident, this could be hearing a car braking hard) and smells (for a patient who was raped, this could be the smell of the rapist's cologne), as well as common situations such as driving a car (for the car accident victim) or walking by a body of water (for someone who almost died in a flash flood). The psychologist develops a hierarchy of feared stimuli with the patient and encourages the patient to intentionally expose himself or herself to increasingly fearful stimuli. By having patients repeatedly expose themselves to these stimuli, anxiety is reduced, a sense of self-efficacy is developed, and the opportunity for engaging in a broader range of activities (instead of avoiding certain situations) is enhanced.

EFT for Couple Distress

Emotionally Focused Therapy (EFT) combines an experiential approach to affect with a systemic focus on the way in which relationship behaviours can develop into cyclical, self-perpetuating interactional patterns. The key factors in relational distress are assumed to be the ongoing construction of absorbing states of negative affect and destructive interactional sequences that arise from, reflect, and then prime this distressing affect (Johnson, Hunsley, Greenberg, & Schindler, 1999). Accordingly, the main goals of EFT for couple distress are to (a) modify emotional responses and constricted, rigid interactional patterns and (b) foster the establishment or enhancement of a secure emotional bond in the couple (Johnson, 1996). The following description is drawn from Johnson et al. (1999).

The psychologist providing EFT for couple distress must address each partner's affect and each partner's perspective on interactional problems. Partners are not seen as deficient in their ability to manage interpersonal issues but, rather, as needing assistance in formulating and presenting their attachment-related needs and fears to each other. To bring about change in the couple, the psychologist must find ways to generate new emotional experiences and new interactional experiences for both partners. As with any form of couple treatment, this can be very challenging as partners in distressed relationships typically develop habitual strategies for protecting themselves and attributing the lion's share of responsibility for their problems to the other partner.

There are nine steps in EFT designed to bring about the necessary changes in the couple. In mildly distressed couples it is common for both partners to work quickly through the nine steps at a similar pace. In couples with greater distress, the more withdrawn or passive partner is encouraged to go through the steps ahead of the other partner. It is assumed that as the more passive partner becomes engaged in the process, it will be easier for the more active or critical partner to trust that the passive partner is truly committed to the change process.

The first four steps involve assessment and the de-escalation of problematic interpersonal cycles. Step 1 involves the formation of an alliance with each partner and the development and presentation of a case conceptualization of the couple's core conflicts from an attachment perspective. Step 2 is devoted to the identification of the problematic interpersonal cycle that maintains the insecure attachment and the affective distress. The third and fourth steps focus on accessing the emotions underlying each partner's position in the relationship and then presenting their core relationship conflicts as stemming from these underlying emotions and attachment needs.

The next three steps are designed to promote change in each partner's interactional position. In Step 5, each partner is encouraged to identify and accept psychological needs that they have disowned or suppressed and to integrate these needs into their relationship. Step 6 requires each partner to learn to accept the other's new approach to their relationship. As partners adjust to these changes, Step 7 focuses on facilitating this adjustment by ensuring emotional engagement in the couple. The final two steps focus on developing new solutions to old relationship problems (Step 8) and consolidating these new solutions and the partners' new relationship positions (Step 9).

PROFILE BOX 12.2

DR. SUE JOHNSON

Dr. Sue Johnson

I received my doctorate in Counselling Psychology from the University of British Columbia in 1984. I am a Professor of Psychology and Psychiatry at the University of Ottawa and Director of the Ottawa Couple and Family Institute. I am a registered psychologist in the province of Ontario, and a member of the editorial boards of the *Journal of Marital and Family Therapy*, the *Journal of Couple and Relationship Therapy*, and the *Journal of Family Psychology*. Together with Leslie Greenberg, I developed Emotionally Focused Couple Therapy (EFT). My research has been devoted to evaluating the usefulness of this approach for helping couples who are dealing with diverse problems. My research has yielded numerous articles and chapters. In addition, I have written several books. I have received awards from the American Association of Marital and Family Therapy, the American Psychological Association, the University of Ottawa, and the YMCA.

What made you choose to become a clinical psychologist?

The choice to become a clinical psychologist was an easy one for me. I have always been fascinated by people, their relationships, and how people change and grow. I was a special education teacher and counsellor in a treatment centre for emotionally disturbed children and I just wanted to know more about how to reach people and help create change in their lives.

What is the most rewarding part of your job as a clinical psychologist?

Seeing people move through the process of changing themselves, putting their experience together in a new way, or really transforming the way they connect to the people they love. There is always a sense of discovery for me: I learn something from every couple and every client I see. There is also the reward of piecing together the puzzle of how we get stuck in and how we can repair close relationships.

What is the greatest challenge facing you as a clinical psychologist?

The greatest challenge for me is being able to teach in a way that makes EFT accessible and relevant to clinicians; to simplify without losing the significance of the complex drama you are trying to address.

Tell us about how you developed Emotionally Focused Couples Therapy (EFT).

EFT came together as a model when Leslie Greenberg and I watched tapes of distressed couples fight to repair their relationship and began to formulate what the therapist did that worked. The model we came up with was unfashionable at the time as therapists did not focus on emotions in couple relationships. The first outcome study, my dissertation, was a leap of faith to see whether we could find evidence for the power of the changes we saw couples making. We did not expect to find such powerful results.

After this, we conducted more outcome studies with different populations and process studies to understand the way the change process evolved. A key element for me was that we were dealing with attachment. Although John Bowlby had drawn attention to attachment in children, at that point, it had not been examined in adult relationships. Adult attachment theory and research exploded in the 1990s and offers, at last, an explanatory framework for adult love and for the repair of love relationships. The application of EFT to different populations, such as families of bulimic and depressed adolescents and especially to traumatized couples, has also been guided by our understanding of adult attachment. EFT gradually became more and more systematized. Because of the consistently positive outcome results—in studies 70–73% of couples rate their relationship as recovered from distress by the end of therapy—EFT is now taught in graduate schools all over North America and beyond. We are now busy studying the impact of EFT on the relationships of sexual abuse survivors and on maritally distressed cancer patients.

How do you integrate science and practice in your work?

For me therapy is always an art and a science. Science begins with the observation of patterns and this is how the EFT model started, by observing tapes of couples and noting the process steps and the moves they made that led to a more positive connection. Research knowledge then guides intervention. Practice also opens my eyes to new phenomena. For example, we observed that partners who refused to risk and trust spoke of injuries that destroyed their ability to count on and reach for their partner. We then systematically studied examples of those injuries and how some couples resolved them. We have now just completed the first study of resolving these attachment injuries. We found we can, in a systematic way, help people forgive, reconcile, and trust again. The research also then feeds back into and refines our clinical interventions.

What do you see as the most exciting changes in the profession of clinical psychology?

Clinical psychology is taking on and struggling with some of the key factors that influence people's lives—factors that were ignored until very recently. For example, it is time psychologists studied love and how to sustain it rather than leaving it to philosophers and talk show hosts. New frontiers are opening up. We are beginning to understand the nature of emotion and adult attachment—areas that prior to the 1990s were not even in the clinical psychology textbooks but that ordinary people knew shaped their lives. The study of relationships and trauma is expanding the field of psychology, placing individual problems in context rather than studying the individual in isolation.

EFFECTIVENESS TRIALS

Throughout the text we have highlighted the distinction between efficacy and effectiveness several times. As we mentioned earlier in the book, it is important to know about the effectiveness of usual clinical treatments (Hansen, Lambert, & Forman, 2002). So far, we have presented a sample of the substantial literature on treatment efficacy. However, it is vital to consider evidence that efficacious treatments (developed in controlled research studies) are effective in clinical settings. As we discussed previously, reservations have been voiced about the representativeness of the patients included in typical efficacy trials (e.g., Westen & Morrison, 2001).

It is encouraging that accumulating data indicate many treatments demonstrating positive results in efficacy trials also have a substantial impact in effectiveness trials. In other words, contrary to some initial concerns, it now appears that many efficacious treatments can be transported into routine clinical practice without much loss of treatment impact. Equally important, there is accumulating evidence that these treatments can be effective for patients from differing ethnic backgrounds (Miranda, Bernal, Lau, Kohn, Hwang, & LaFromboise, 2005). The strongest evidence for the transportability of a treatment to clinical settings is for CBT for depression. A number of studies, both in the United States (e.g., Merrill, Tolbert, & Wade, 2003; Persons, Bostrom, & Bertagnolli, 1999) and the United Kingdom (e.g., Cahill et al., 2003), have found that the treatment can be as effective in clinical settings (such as community mental health clinics and private practice settings) as it is in efficacy trials. These studies were conducted with patients who were seeking treatment for depression and services were provided by clinicians who differed in (a) their background training (including both doctoral and master's level clinicians) and (b) their experience in providing CBT for depression.

In effectiveness studies it is common to use what is known as a **benchmarking strategy** to evaluate the impact of a treatment. This involves using the results of efficacy trials to form a standard (or a benchmark) against which the services provided to *regular* patients by *regular* clinicians can be compared. Based on the benchmarking strategy there is evidence from various countries that CBT for a number of disorders can be clinically effective. Examples include the treatment of panic disorder (Wade, Treat, & Stuart, 1998), OCD (Warren & Thomas, 2001), and bulimia nervosa (Tuschen-Caffier, Pook, & Frank, 2001). As with efficacy research, effectiveness research with CBT is much more advanced than with other approaches to treatment. It is certain, however, that as the efficacy of other treatment approaches becomes established, researchers will turn their attention to evaluating treatment effectiveness.

ADOPTION OF EVIDENCE-BASED TREATMENTS

Rarely a day goes by without a media announcement of a breakthrough in the treatment of some health condition or disease. For example, around the time we wrote this chapter, there was a flurry of media attention on the possibility of a new drug that could be used to help with smoking cessation efforts and a new combination of drugs that could positively affect survival time in patients with brain tumours. Hearing such news reports, the average person realizes that it will take time for many of the breakthroughs to find their way into routine health services. It is unlikely, however, that the average person realizes all of the barriers that can impede the introduction of innovations into health care systems. In some cases, such as the introduction of a new 'flu vaccine, there are established laboratory and public health systems that facilitate the relatively rapid development and distribution of the vaccine. Unfortunately, this is rarely the case for evidence-based innovations in psychological interventions.

There are a number of reasons for this state of affairs. One reason is that psychological interventions, unlike pharmaceutical interventions, cannot be patented. Pharmaceutical companies typically devote enormous amounts of money to advertising and promoting their treatments. This includes targeting the health care professionals who prescribe the product and, in some countries, directly advertising to potential consumers. When a psychological treatment has been found to be efficacious (and even effective), there is no comparable process for disseminating the information and rapidly training psychologists to provide the treatment. Ethical codes and professional guidelines also prohibit most types of advertising of psychological services. A second reason is that there is often more to learning how to provide an efficacious psychological treatment than there is to learning how to appropriately prescribe a new medication. In this regard the training necessary to appropriately provide the intervention is akin to what is required for surgeons to learn and use new surgical procedures. Reading the research reports and details on the indications and contraindications for a new drug may be sufficient for responsible prescribing, but such steps are unlikely to be sufficient for surgery or psychotherapy. To effectively provide psychological services, the clinician requires background preparatory work, specialized training, and closely supervised experience in providing the intervention. Calhoun, Moras, Pilkonis, and Rehm (1998), for example, recommended that a clinical psychologist wishing to attain adequate skill in the delivery of an EST should be supervised in providing the treatment to at least three or four *typical* patients and a comparable number of *atypical* (i.e., those with more complex or chronic problems) patients. At this time, even though many jurisdictions require clinical psychologists to engage in continuing education activities, there are few structured opportunities for practising psychologists to obtain this intensity of training (cf. Arnow, 1999).

VIEWPOINT BOX 12.2

DOES TRAINING IN EVIDENCE-BASED TREATMENTS REALLY MAKE A DIFFERENCE FOR PATIENT CARE?

The main thrust of this chapter, and a consistent theme in this book, is that psychological services must be based on scientific evidence. So just how likely is it that patients will receive treatments that are evidence-based? To address this question we will focus on data regarding the treatment of anxiety disorders.

As indicated in Tables 12.4 and 12.5, CBT services are the treatments of choice for anxiety disorders. The majority of these CBT services have been available since the 1980s. Since their development, they have been applied in the successful treatment of a range of anxiety disorders. Despite this, Goisman, Warshaw, and Keller (1999) reported survey results indicating that the proportion of patients receiving CBT actually declined from 1991 to 1996. Fewer than 40% of patients in their study reported receiving behavioural, cognitive, or relaxation/meditation interventions to address their anxiety symptoms. The single most common form of therapy received by patients at both time points was psychodynamic treatment.

Most anxiety disordered patients receive treatments from primary care physicians, rather than from mental health specialists. In a nationally representative American sample, Young, Klap, Sherbourne, and Wells (2001) found that only 20% of patients with anxiety disorders received appropriate medications to treat their symptoms from their physicians, and only 10% received counselling about nonpharmacological steps they could take to alleviate symptoms. Almost identical findings were reported by Stein et al. (2004), who examined the quality of care for anxiety disordered patients in university-affiliated primary care clinics in the western United States. You might expect that physicians and other health care professionals working in these clinics would be, on average, more up to date in their treatment methods. However, Stein and colleagues found that, even when referrals in these clinics were made to mental health specialists, fewer than 10% of patients reported receiving treatment that included elements of quality CBT services. Deficiencies in the application of pharmacological treatments were also evident, as only 25% of patients received medications at an adequate dose and of sufficient duration.

Thus far the evidence does not look particularly encouraging, for it appears that most people with anxiety problems are unlikely to receive the most appropriate treatments. But let's take this a step further—is there any evidence that it makes a difference for people to receive the most appropriate treatment? In fact, there is, and the data are compelling. Howard (1999) used data from an American managed care organization to determine if anxiety disordered patients who received cognitive-behavioural treatments fared better than those who receive other forms of psychotherapy. During a two-year period, 86 patients received treatment from clinicians who used cognitive-behavioural treatments and who had training in providing these services, whereas 79 patients received treatment from other clinicians. Patients seen by CBT-oriented and trained clinicians had, on average, significantly fewer sessions of treatment than those seen by other clinicians (6.4 sessions versus 8.4 sessions). Compared with the other patients, the patients who received CBT reported significantly less anxiety at the termination of treatment—despite having had less treatment. Most importantly, the relapse rate among CBT patients was significantly lower than among the other group of patients: within two years of having received brief treatment, 19% of CBT patients relapsed, whereas 39% of the other patients relapsed.

The bottom line is that, even though evidence-based treatments don't work for all patients, they are the best that psychological science has to offer. So, if you are ever seeking psychological services for yourself, a family member, or a friend, please be sure to do your homework. First, check out some of the websites we list at the end of the chapter to identify the best treatments. After that, find out whether there are psychologists in your area who provide these treatments.

Beyond the issue of the availability of training, there are myriad potential barriers to the adoption of evidence-based treatments by psychologists and other health care professionals. These include systems level factors such as the extent of organizational support for learning and providing cutting-edge interventions, and individual level factors such as motivation, knowledge, and skill. Given the clear indication that there are evidence-based treatments for many (if not most) disorders, it is important to understand the barriers to their application. At the systems level, many institutions employing clinical psychologists are under great pressure to reduce waiting lists. There is, as a result, often a tension between the need to devote time to developing new skills and the need to devote this professional time to immediate patient care. Even in doctoral training, where the expectation is that proportionally more time is devoted to skill development than to patient services, there are significant restrictions in opportunities to learn evidence-based treatments. A 1995 survey found that, on average, APA accredited doctoral clinical psychology training programs included coursework and practicum training on slightly less than half of the ESTs available at that time (Crits-Christoph, Frank, Chambless, Brody, & Karp, 1995). Researchers were astonished to find that most APA accredited internship training programs were unlikely to require that interns develop competence in at least one EST. A more recent survey suggests that, although some progress has been made in this regard, there is still substantial room for improvement. Hays et al. (2002) reported that, in their survey of APA accredited internships, 19% of internships reported little or no time spent on providing training and supervision in ESTs, with only 28% reporting that they spent more than 15 hours of training and supervision in ESTs during the internship year.

Addis, Wade, and Hatgis (1999) summarized many of the individual level factors that obstruct the widespread adoption of evidence-based treatments by psychologists. These include concerns about the feasibility of implementing manual-based treatments, the possible lack of fit between client needs and available evidence-based treatments, the impact that manual-based treatments might have on the therapeutic relationship with clients, and the possibility for decreased job satisfaction among psychologists. In a survey of almost 900 psychologists, Addis and Krasnow (2000) found consistent associations between experience with offering manual-based treatments and attitudes toward such treatments: the psychologists with the strongest negative views on these treatments were those least likely to have familiarity with the nature of manual-based treatments.

Despite these individual and systems-level challenges, many psychologists provide evidence-based treatments and are motivated to learn to use such treatments. For example, in a survey of clinical psychologists who provide treatments for eating disorders, Mussell et al. (2000) found that, although 70% of respondents reported using empirically supported therapy techniques, approximately 75% of these psychologists reported having received no formal training in the provision of CBT or IPT for eating disorders. For many of these psychologists this probably indicated a commitment on their part to learn these treatments on their own after graduation. Importantly, though, more than 80% of respondents indicated a desire to obtain formal training in the approach. Commitment to the use of evidence-based treatments appears to be influenced by the nature of the clients' presenting problems and the nature of the treatment. As discussed earlier in the chapter, exposure is a key component of efficacious treatments for PTSD. A survey of psychologists providing PTSD treatments found that only 1 in 4 had received training in the use of exposure and only 17% reported using any form of exposure in their treatments of clients with PTSD (Becker, Zayfert, & Anderson, 2004). Numerous reasons for not using exposure were reported, including lack of familiarity with the technique, concerns about the appropriateness of the technique (e.g., clients presenting with comorbid disorders), and concerns about complications that could arise from using exposure (e.g., increased symptoms, dissociation). Although concerns about client suitability and well-being strongly influenced psychologists' perceptions about the usefulness of exposure, few, if any, of their concerns are likely to be valid when exposure is used in a clinically sensitive manner (Cook et al., 2004). Indeed exposure-based treatment for PTSD has been successfully adapted for use in other cultures, such as in the treatment of traumatized Ugandan refugees (Neuner, Schauer, Klaschik, Karunakara, & Elbert, 2004).

Clearly much more must be done in the education and continuing education of clinical psychologists to promote the use of evidence-based practices. Accreditation requirements for training in these practices should continue to influence what is taught in both doctoral training programs and internships. Beyond that, many psychologists are working on developing models to develop, disseminate, and implement evidence-based treatments (e.g., Gotham, 2004; Stirman, Crits-Christoph, & DeRubeis, 2004). A key element of such models is that psychologists who conduct treatment research and psychologists who provide real world services must both be involved as active and equal participants in efforts to adapt and implement these treatments in clinical settings. Psychological science has much to offer patients suffering from diverse health conditions, but efforts to disseminate treatment breakthroughs must take into account the challenges facing the frontline clinicians who, ultimately, have the task of providing psychological services.

SUMMARY AND CONCLUSIONS

The second half of the twentieth century was a period of rapid growth in psychological interventions for a variety of disorders. Passionate debates pitted proponents of one school of thinking against another. All of this occurred against a backdrop of shrinking health care budgets, increasing concerns about accountability, and growing reliance on practice guidelines. Psychologists used a range of strategies of varying methodological sophistication to examine whether or not their treatments worked. Meta-analysis became an important tool in integrating findings from the growing body of literature. Because meta-analysis requires an explicit statement about the decision rules for including a study and for weighting its findings, meta-analysis itself has been the subject of fierce debate. Many of the original criticisms of meta-analysis led to important modifications of the procedure.

There are many interdisciplinary efforts that have focused on achieving consensus about (a) the criteria for determining when a treatment is evidence-based and (b) routes for disseminating information about efficacious treatments. Overall, the results with respect to psychological treatments are encouraging, as there appear to be effective treatments for many Axis I disorders. Cognitive-behavioural approaches are prominent in the lists of evidence-based treatments. This can be explained in part by CBT's emphasis on establishing clear treatment goals and requiring the ongoing monitoring of treatment efficacy. The armamentarium of effective treatments also includes interpersonal approaches and process-experiential interventions. Nevertheless, a significant number of people drop out of treatment and others do not find it helpful. There is an urgent need to address the usefulness of various treatments in diverse populations.

Despite the encouraging data on treatment efficacy and growing evidence from effectiveness studies, it is premature to conclude that evidence-based approaches are now the routine standard of care in clinical psychology services. Barriers to the implementation of evidence-based services occur at many levels, including the lack of graduate and postgraduate training opportunities.

Critical Thinking Questions

How has meta-analysis affected the field of psychotherapy?

What are the advantages to the client of receiving evidence-based services?

What are the challenges in establishing a list of evidence-based treatments?

If we know that a treatment is successful, what are the barriers to its routine implementation?

Key Terms

behavioural activation	empirically supported treatments
benchmarking strategy	meta-analysis
clinical practice guidelines	open trials
effect size	randomized controlled trials

Key Names

David Barlow

Dianne Chambless

Hans Eysenck

Gene Glass

Mary Smith

Drew Westen

ADDITIONAL RESOURCES

Books

First, M. B., & Tasman, A. (2004). *DSM-IV-TR mental disorders: Diagnosis, etiology, and treatment.* New York: John Wiley & Sons.

Nathan, P., & Gorman, J. M. (Eds.). (2002). *A guide to treatments that work* (2nd ed.). New York: Oxford University Press.

Roth, A., & Fonagy, P. (2005). *What works for whom? A critical review of psychotherapy research* (2nd ed.). New York: Guilford Press.

Journals

Journal of Consulting and Clinical Psychology

Behavior Therapy

Clinical Psychology: Science and Practice

American Journal of Psychiatry

Websites

Empirically Supported Treatments:
http://pantheon.yale.edu/%7Etat22/empirically_supported_treatments.htm
http://www.apa.org/divisions/div12/rev_est/index.html

Treatment choice in psychological therapies and counselling: Evidence-based clinical practice guideline:
http://www.dh.gov.uk/assetRoot/04/05/82/45/04058245.pdf

NICE Clinical Guidelines:
http://www.nice.org.uk/page.aspx?o=guidelines.completed

American Psychiatric Association Practice Guidelines:
http://www.psych.org/psych_pract/treatg/pg/prac_guide.cfm

Centre for Evidence-Based Mental Health:
http://www.cebmh.com/

Best Treatments (from *British Medical Journal*):
https://www.besttreatments.org/Unified/CDA/HP/tmpl/HPIndex/

CHAPTER 13

Intervention: Children and Adolescents

INTRODUCTION

In Chapter 12 we described the debates over the effectiveness of psychotherapy for adults, the development of psychotherapy research, issues and controversies over evidence-based practice, as well as the emergence of clinical practice guidelines. Many issues in the psychological treatment of childhood disorders mirror the themes that were presented with respect to adults. Because we assume that you are now familiar with the material in Chapter 12, we will first explore ways that child services are different from services with respect to adults. Next we will highlight landmarks in the evolution of effective psychological treatments for childhood disorders. We will illustrate some efficacious treatments for common childhood problems, and finally we will consider issues related to generalizing from efficacy trials to regular clinical practice.

In Chapter 9 we used the extended case example of Teresa to illustrate how clinical psychologists conduct assessments that are comprehensive, accurate, and clinically useful. In this chapter we return to the case of Carl, the adolescent boy who had been traumatized by the genocide in his country of origin, to illustrate how clinical psychologists apply their knowledge of interventions to alleviate emotional distress. This case also allows us to describe how evidence-based strategies can be applied in situations for which there is currently no comprehensive empirically supported treatment package.

WHO IS THE CLIENT IN PSYCHOLOGICAL SERVICES FOR CHILDHOOD DISORDERS?

Adult psychotherapy usually involves an individual client working with a mental health professional to address an identified problem. In most cases, the adult seeks services after recognizing that there is a problem. As you may remember learning in Chapter 11, psychological services cannot be imposed on a client: informed consent is required. Children and youth rarely refer themselves for psychological services. Instead, young people are brought for psychological services by adults who are troubled or concerned by the young person's behaviour. In Chapter 9 (Viewpoint Box 9.1), we pointed out that there is an imperfect match between the views of young people, their parents, and their teachers on the nature of the problem; similarly, there is poor agreement between parents and youth about the goals for psychological services (Viewpoint Box 9.2). The child or youth may not believe there is a problem: according to 9-year-old Tyler, for example, the only problem is that his mom is picky and his teacher is strict and, if only both those adults would get off his case and stop grumbling about the importance of tidying up his room and doing his homework, then there would be no problem. For his mother and teacher, though, Tyler's non-compliance has reached the point where both are frustrated about how to positively influence him. Fifteen-year-old Cheryl, who has been feeling very low and who cuts her arms when she is distressed, may know that there is a problem. Despite her parents' insistence that she see some doctor they found, she is far from confident that it would make any difference to talk to some old person of 35 who has a boring office with certificates on the wall and who couldn't possibly understand what she is feeling.

Children and youth do not have the resources to seek, attend, and pay for psychological services independently. Unless services are provided within the school context or parents facilitate attendance by seeking a referral, arranging transportation, and paying for services, it is unlikely that children and youth will receive psychological services. Data from the United States indicate that only a small proportion of children with mental health needs receive any services (Kataoka, Zhang, & Wells, 2002).

Miller and Prinz (2003) reported evidence that, in the treatment of childhood conduct problems, when treatment did not match parents' understanding of the child's problem, parents were less likely to engage in treatment. This was underscored in a study in which young people receiving outpatient mental health services and their parents rated the alliance with the therapist (Hawley & Weisz, 2005). The *parent*-therapist alliance was related to participation in therapy, with those parents who reported a stronger alliance participating more in services and cancelling fewer sessions. The *youth*-therapist alliance was related to reports of improvements in symptoms. The results of this study illustrate that unless parents are convinced that the therapy is useful, it will be difficult for the youth to participate, but unless the young person is collaboratively engaged with the therapist, there will be limited change in his or her symptoms.

The legal issues with respect to consent for psychological services for a child or adolescent are complex. Depending on the context in which services are offered (e.g., through schools, mental health clinics, hospitals, child protection agencies, or in the office of private psychologists), consent laws may be included in legislation with respect to education services, health services, or child protection. That means that the psychologist must be knowledgeable about the specific legislation that covers psychological services in the type of agency in which he or she works. In some jurisdictions, consent procedures are determined by the young person's chronological age; according to an age criterion, for example, children under 12 can only receive psychological services with the consent of a parent or legal guardian. In other jurisdictions, there is no age criterion and the psychologist must determine whether each young client can understand what is involved in treatment and therefore can legally consent to services.

Jorge's situation illustrates how difficult these issues can be. Jorge is a 14-year-old who suffers from moderately severe symptoms of Tourette's disorder (frequent facial and vocal tics). He has developed severe social phobia because of his embarrassment about his tics. His parents, who are very concerned about his emotional and social functioning, brought him to see a clinical psychologist. Jorge's diagnostic status was clear to the psychologist based on interviews with the parents and an interview with Jorge. It was also clear to the psychologist, however, that Jorge generally understood the nature of his problems and was not willing to be involved in any treatment aimed at ameliorating his distress. The psychologist explained both the likely benefits of therapy and the likely prognosis if his problems went untreated. Again, Jorge understood these things. According to the laws regarding competency to consent to health services in the jurisdiction, the psychologist had no choice but to explain to the distraught parents that their son was not willing to engage in treatment. The only option available for the family at that point was for the parents to consider involvement in a local family support group for Tourette's disorder or involvement in family-focused services (without Jorge) aimed at helping them encourage Jorge to increase his social activities.

Adolescents and their parents often differ in their views on the need for treatment

It should not surprise you to learn that although legal consent to receive services is a necessary condition for treatment, it is not sufficient to ensure cooperation with the services. You can probably easily imagine the scene in which Cheryl's parents have insisted that she come to a mental health clinic; not wanting to create a scene in front of a stranger, Cheryl has signed a consent to services, but she effectively communicates disinterest in the process by sitting hunched in the chair, her hair concealing most of her face, rolling her eyes, and answering most questions with "I dunno."

Confidentiality issues are complex in services with children and youth. The psychologist must clarify from the outset of services the circumstances under which confidentiality will be maintained and what information will be shared with parents. As we described in Chapter 6, child protection laws require the psychologist to report situations in which a child is in need of protection. At the outset of services, the psychologist also explains who has access to material in the client's file.

In Chapter 10 (Table 10.1), we presented risk factors for the development of psychopathology in children and youth. As you can see, many of the risk factors involve conditions over which the young person has very limited control, such as antisocial role models in the family, poor parental supervision, parental mental illness, bullying, or poverty. The protective factors (Table 10.2) suggest some possible avenues for psychological services in the development of problem-solving skills, social competence, supportive family relationships, positive school-home relations, strong cultural identity, and ethnic pride. An examination of risk and protective factors influencing the development of psychopathology underlines that psychological services for children's psychological disorders must address the context in which the child's problem developed and is maintained. Child psychotherapy has traditionally focused on intrapsychic factors but, as you will see later in the chapter, decades of research on developmental psychopathology have led to the development of treatments that attend to both intrapsychic and interpersonal factors.

PSYCHOTHERAPY WORKS: NARRATIVE REVIEWS AND META-ANALYSES

You will recall from Chapter 12 that the debates over the efficacy of psychotherapy began with Eysenck's stinging review in 1952 and were fuelled by the meta-analyses of the 1980s and 1990s. Since that time, various researchers and organizations have undertaken systematic reviews of the empirical literature to identify efficacious treatments. In general, the process of reviewing the literature on psychological services for childhood disorders has followed a similar path. However, the progress with respect to the treatment of children and adolescents has generally lagged behind the progress with respect to adult treatments. There are simply fewer studies to examine in meta-analyses and, accordingly, compared with the adult literature, more limited and tentative conclusions must be drawn from the youth literature.

Echoing Eysenck's 1952 report, Levitt (1957, 1963) concluded that there was no evidence for the efficacy of child psychotherapy. During the subsequent two decades, a variety of new approaches to the treatment of disorders of childhood was developed and numerous studies examined the efficacy of different types of child psychotherapy. Details of the four largest scale meta-analyses are presented in **Table 13.1**. The first meta-analysis of the child psychotherapy outcome literature included 75 studies covering services to treat diverse clinical problems using a large range of therapeutic approaches for young people under the age of 13 (Casey & Berman, 1985). Across all techniques, Casey and Berman reported an effect size of .71, which is comparable to the .69 effect size reported by Smith and Glass (1977) based on their review of 370 studies of the adult psychotherapy literature. When Casey and Berman found that behavioural interventions yielded larger effect sizes than did nonbehavioural approaches, they wondered if this was because behavioural studies tended to use as outcome measures variables that were very similar to the variables targeted in therapy. To address this, they removed from their analyses data stemming from therapy-like outcome measures. This adjustment reduced the effect size for behavioural treatments from .91 to .55 and for nonbehavioural treatments from .40 to .34.

TABLE 13.1.   Meta-Analyses of Psychological Treatments for Disorders of Childhood and Adolescence

Meta-Analysis and Child Age Range	Number of Studies	Mean Effect Size	Major Finding
Casey & Berman, 1985 Under 13	75 studies published 1952–1983	.71	Effect sizes comparable to adult literature
Weisz, Weiss, Alicke, & Klotz, 1987 4–18 years	108 studies published 1958–1984	.79	Greater effects for behavioural than nonbehavioural approaches
Kazdin, Bass, Ayers, & Rodgers, 1990 4–18 years	223 studies published 1970–1988	.88 for treatment versus no treatment & .77 treatment versus active control	Discrepancy between treatment in research and in regular clinical practice
Weisz, Weiss, Han, Granger, & Morton, 1995 1.5–17.6 years	150 studies published before 1993 and not included in Casey & Berman or in Weisz et al., 1987	.54 using weighted least squares .71 using unweighted least squares	Greater effects of behavioural than nonbehavioural approaches

A subsequent meta-analysis by Weisz, Weiss, Alicke, and Klotz (1987) examined 108 controlled studies (less than a third of which were also reviewed by Casey & Berman, 1985). Psychotherapy researcher John Weisz and his colleagues reasoned that it made sense to remove from analyses some therapy-like outcomes, but not others. For example, they argued that if a treatment uses an artificial activity (like a computer task) to train a skill (like paying attention) then it is simply not fair to use a score on that same computer activity as a measure of treatment outcome. However, they pointed out that if the therapy is designed to treat fear of dogs, then a behavioural approach would focus on helping the child to approach dogs and an appropriate outcome measure would be the extent to which the child was able to comfortably interact with dogs. Using this reasoning, they excluded from analyses of outcome any artificial or analogue activities that had been used in the treatment, but retained as outcome measures real-world activities that had been targeted in treatment. Based on their analyses, Weisz and his colleagues reported a mean effect size of .79, with larger effects found for behavioural approaches than for nonbehavioural approaches.

A subsequent meta-analysis by Kazdin, Bass, Ayers, and Rodgers (1990) yielded a very similar effect size to those reported by Casey and Berman (1985) and Weisz et al. (1987). However, although the effect sizes looked encouraging, Alan Kazdin and his colleagues drew attention to a troubling discrepancy between the nature of psychotherapy research and the nature of clinical practice. They found that treatment studies often relied on volunteer samples recruited through schools and treated in a group format. In contrast, surveys indicated that clinical practice more commonly involved individual treatment in outpatient clinics of referred patients. Furthermore, Kazdin and his colleagues recommended that treatment researchers pay greater attention to characteristics of the child, parent, family, or therapist that might influence treatment outcome.

You learned in Chapters 4 and 12 that the use of meta-analysis has revolutionized the field by offering an explicit set of decision rules for synthesizing data from diverse studies and reporting findings using a common metric. Like other research tools, meta-analysis is not perfect. As problems in the procedure are identified, refinements are introduced. The fourth major meta-analysis of the effects of child psychotherapy (Weisz, Weiss, Han, Granger, & Morton, 1995) introduced a more conservative way of calculating effect sizes, using a statistical technique known as the *weighted least squares method*. As you know from your statistics courses, when sampling data from a population, there will always be some error involved (i.e., deviations from the true population values). Generally speaking, data from larger samples have less error variance and, therefore, are closer to population values. The weighted least squares method takes this into account by assigning less weight in the meta-analysis to studies with greater error variance and more heavily weighting those with less error variance. Based on a meta-analysis of 150 outcome studies that had not been previously reviewed, Weisz et al. (1995) reported a similar effect size to all the previous meta-analyses when they used unweighted least squares methods, and a lower effect size of .54 using the weighted strategy. The effects were more positive for behavioural than for nonbehavioural approaches. Furthermore, treatment effects were evident not only at the end of services, but at follow-up six months later as well. **Figure 13.1** illustrates the effect sizes reported in these four meta-analyses and compares them with the effect sizes reported by Smith and Glass (1977) and Shapiro and Shapiro (1982) for the literature on adult psychotherapy.

Figure 13.1   Mean Effect Sizes Reported in Meta-Analyses of Psychotherapy Outcome Studies

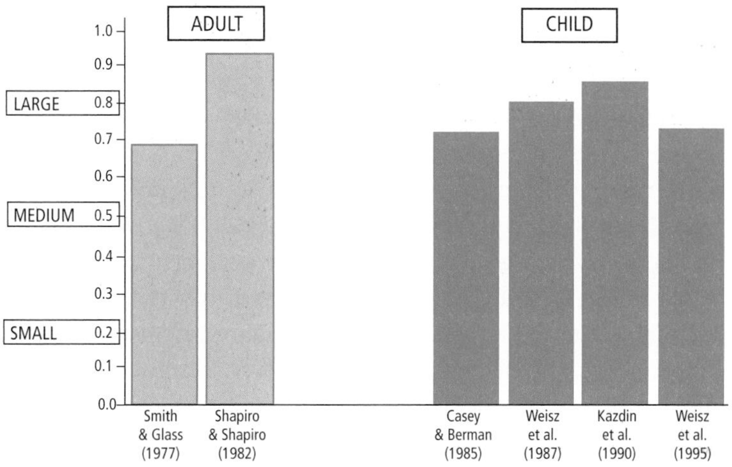

Weisz, Donnenberg, Han, & Weiss (1995).

You will notice that the four meta-analyses in Table 13.1 all relied on published studies. Unfortunately, this may bias the results because journals are more likely to publish studies that report statistically significant findings than those that report nonsignificant results. McLeod and Weisz (2004) compared 134 published studies with 121 dissertations in terms of both their methodological adequacy and their findings. Overall, they found that the unpublished dissertations were stronger methodologically, but obtained lower effect sizes than did the published studies. This suggests that meta-analyses based on published studies may lead us to overestimate the effect sizes from child psychotherapy studies. McLeod and Weisz therefore recommended that future meta-analyses also include data from unpublished dissertations.

Although it is encouraging to know that psychological treatments can be efficacious in treating childhood disorders, the most important questions need much more precise answers.

Researchers have focused, therefore, on examining the research on efficacious treatments for different types of childhood disorders. In parallel with the trend in adult psychotherapy research, there have been numerous narrative reviews and meta-analyses examining the outcome research for different types of children's problems.

THE IDENTIFICATION OF EVIDENCE-BASED TREATMENTS

Psychotherapy researchers in various countries have developed psychosocial interventions and demonstrated that they can help children and adolescents who are dealing with diverse disorders and problems. These include DSM IV Axis I disorders such as anxiety disorders (Kendall, Aschenbrand, & Hudson, 2003), depression (Clarke, DeBar, & Lewinsohn, 2003), ADHD: Anastopoulos & Farley, 2003), oppositional defiant disorder (Brinkmeyer & Eyberg, 2003), and conduct disorder (Kazdin, 2002), as well as problems that are seen in primary care or medical practice such as obesity (Epstein, 2003) or enuresis (Houts, 2003). Unfortunately, although there are numerous efficacious psychological treatments for various mental disorders and problems of childhood and adolescence, they are not routinely offered in standard care (Connor-Smith & Weisz, 2003). One obstacle to the adoption of efficacious treatments is that clinicians may simply be unaware of them. The field of clinical psychology is constantly evolving, with exciting new research being published daily. Reviewing the literature in 2003, Kazdin conservatively estimated that more than 1,500 controlled outcome studies for psychotherapy with children and adolescents have been published, and the number is now even higher. The average clinician is unable to consult the literature and synthesize new findings into meaningful recommendations on a regular basis. In addition, the average parent who is a potential consumer of psychological services can be faced with a bewildering array of contradictory messages about the most appropriate solution to the child's problem. If you browse through the parenting sections of bookstores or search the term *children's behaviour* on the Internet, you will see books advocating diverse ways to address children's problems. It is a challenge for parents to distinguish between experts whose message is based on solid research and those who are simply proposing something that makes sense to them but that lacks a solid empirical foundation.

Among the health disciplines, psychology is not alone in facing this dilemma of how to translate research findings into practice. Similar challenges are faced by clinicians trying to keep up to date with rapid advances in the knowledge base in professions such as nursing and medicine. As we explained in Chapter 12, a number of expert review panels have been set up to evaluate research findings and to develop clear evidence-based practice guidelines. Some of these review panels are organized within a particular discipline, whereas others are multidisciplinary. Some are sponsored by a professional organization, whereas others are the independent enterprise of a small number of researchers.

Discipline-Based Reviews

You learned in Chapter 12 that the first report of the Task Force on Promotion and Dissemination of Psychological Procedures from the Division of Clinical Psychology of the American Psychological Association included treatments for adults. Subsequently, a task force was charged with reviewing the research literature on the treatment of childhood disorders. This task force used slightly different but similar criteria to those used in reviewing the literature with respect to adults. The Society of Clinical Child and Adolescent Psychology (Division 53 of the American Psychological Association) published a series of reviews in the *Journal of Clinical Child Psychology* in 1998 and in the *Journal of Pediatric Psychology* in 1999. The most recent published list of empirically supported treatments (Chambless & Ollendick, 2001) identified 37 efficacious treatments for children.

Building on the work of these psychology-based reviews, McCellan and Werry (2003) reviewed the literature on evidence-based psychopharmacological and psychosocial treatments in child and adolescent psychiatry. They reported that, among the psychopharmacological studies, the best evidence supports the use of psychostimulants in the treatment of ADHD and the use of selective serotonin reuptake inhibitors (SSRIs) in the treatment of obsessive-compulsive disorder. McCellan and Werry concluded that, among the psychosocial interventions, those best supported by well-controlled studies are cognitive-behavioural and behavioural interventions to address anxiety, mood, and behavioural disorders. In addition, they found some evidence for the efficacy of interpersonal therapy for depressed adolescents and multisystemic interventions for adolescents with serious behaviour disorders.

Interdisciplinary Reviews

Interdisciplinary reviews have been conducted under the auspices of national organizations as well as being conducted independently and then published as books. As described in Chapter 12, Nathan and Gorman (2002) invited experts from psychology and psychiatry to contribute to an edited book on treatments that "work." All authors were asked to use the same criteria to categorize the evidence in support of various treatments (see Chapter 12 for details). Although the majority of chapters addressed adult disorders, three focused on problems of childhood, including ADHD (Hinshaw, Klein, & Abikoff, 2002; Greenhill & Ford, 2002) and conduct disorder (Kazdin, 2002).

In a similar initiative in the United Kingdom, Fonagy and his colleagues (Fonagy, Target, Cottrell, Phillips, & Kurtz, 2002) identified many efficacious treatments for childhood disorders. Furthermore, a second edition of the volume on adult disorders included a summary chapter on child and adolescent psychiatric disorders (Target & Fonagy, 2005). However, not all experts use the same set of criteria to categorize the evidence base for treatments. This is typically the case when reviews are undertaken by a group of authors, rather than as part of a national organization.

For example, Kazdin and Weisz (2003) and Barrett and Ollendick (2004) invited experts with extensive knowledge on particular disorders and problems to write chapters describing the research and drawing conclusions about what is currently known and what we need to examine in the future. Not surprisingly, experts differed in the standards they used to describe the scientific status of treatments across problem areas.

In the United States, an influential review of children's mental health services was initiated in response to a class action lawsuit on behalf of children with special needs. The settlement of the lawsuit involved an agreement by the state of Hawaii to develop a comprehensive system of care for those aged 0–20 years with mental health needs (Chorpita et al., 2002). As a first step, the Hawaii Department of Health established a task force to identify the empirical basis for services. This multidisciplinary group included health administrators, parents of children with special needs, clinical service providers, and academics in psychology (including anxiety and depression researcher Bruce Chorpita), psychiatry, nursing, and social work. The task force conducted a literature review of studies in psychology, psychiatry, and related mental health disciplines, adopting the criteria that had been developed by APA Division 12 and highlighting the findings of the Division 53 task force. The mandate of the Hawaii task force was to identify not only efficacious treatments, but also effective treatments; that is, they wanted to know which treatments would work in the challenging context of isolated rural areas with multi-ethnic populations.

It is clear, then, that over the last decade there have been concerted efforts in different countries and across different disciplines to draw conclusions about the current state of knowledge of psychological treatments for childhood disorders. Based on our review of these diverse efforts (Chambless & Ollendick, 2001; Chorpita et al., 2002; Kazdin, 2003; Kazdin & Weisz, 2003; Target & Fonagy, 2005), we have compiled a list of the major evidence-based treatments for children and adolescents that is presented in **Table 13.2**. As with all such lists, this should be considered to reflect the state of knowledge in the area at the time of writing. The field is constantly evolving, so a list presented in the next edition of this book may look somewhat different. You will notice that most of the evidence-based approaches are behavioural and cognitive-behavioural. In contrast to treatments for adults that are offered to individuals, many of the efficacious treatments involve parents learning strategies to manage their children's behaviour. Treatments for externalizing problems often include others who are trained to respond in a way that encourages desirable behaviour. Although treatments for internalizing problems usually focus directly on the child, there is evidence that in some cases, it is also helpful to include parents in treatment (Barrett & Shortt, 2003). In the treatment of adolescent depression, attention is focused on interpersonal issues. Thus most effective treatments of childhood disorders fall under the umbrella of cognitive-behavioural and interpersonal approaches. The involvement of parents is consistent with our earlier discussion of the importance of attending to protective factors in designing psychological interventions for youth. Due to developmental changes, in examining the usefulness of different treatment strategies (such as parental involvement), it is also important to take into account the child's age.

TABLE 13.2   A List of Evidence-Based Treatments for Disorders in Child and Youth

Autistic Disorder
- Applied behaviour analysis and communication training

Attention-Deficit/Hyperactivity Disorder
- Behavioural Parent Training
- Behaviour Modification in the classroom

Anxiety Disorders
- CBT (exposure, modelling, relaxation)
- CBT including parents

Chronic Pain
- CBT

Conduct Problems and Oppositional Defiant Disorder
- Behavioural Parent Training
- CBT (anger control; assertiveness)
- Multisystemic Therapy for adolescents

Major Depressive Disorder
- CBT
- CBT including parents
- Interpersonal Therapy

Elimination Disorders
- Behaviour Modification

Obesity
- CBT

Recurrent Pain
- CBT

CLINICAL PRACTICE GUIDELINES

In Chapter 12 you learned about the wealth of treatment guidelines that are available with respect to adult disorders; in contrast, the development of treatment guidelines for childhood disorders has lagged behind significantly. A number of professional organizations have sponsored reviews of the scientific literature to identify efficacious treatments that should be offered as routine care in the treatment of a specific problem. Unfortunately no guidelines have yet been developed by psychological organizations. Since 1997, the American Academy of Child and

Adolescent Psychiatry has published 20 practice parameters and guidelines in the *Journal of the American Academy of Child and Adolescent Psychiatry*, addressing topics including the treatment of anxiety disorders, ADHD, autistic disorder, conduct disorder, obsessive-compulsive disorder, and PTSD. The Canadian Paediatric Society (CPS) has prepared research-based position statements on a number of psychosocial topics including early intervention for children with autism, effective discipline for children, and promoting the mental health of children whose parents are separating. These statements can be downloaded from the CPS website. The Royal Australian and New Zealand College of Psychiatrists (RANZCP) has developed six evidence-based clinical practice guidelines designed to inform practitioners, consumers, and carers about treatment for various disorders. A version of these guidelines for clinicians and another version for consumers can be downloaded from the RANZCP website. Although the majority of these guidelines address treatment of adults suffering from mental disorders, the guideline on treatment of deliberate self-harm is available in two formats, one for adults and one for youth. If you check the documents on the RANZCP website, you will notice that, like many products in the grocery store, these guidelines are identified with a *best before* date. This is an explicit acknowledgement that although they represent the best recommendation based on available knowledge at the time they are released, research is ongoing, our understanding is constantly evolving, and guidelines must not be seen as the final word. Thus ongoing updates of clinical practice guidelines based on new research are essential to the promotion of evidence-based practice.

It is inevitable that guidelines developed by one professional body may be seen to promote the approach favoured by that profession and may be seen to downplay the benefits of other approaches. There are, therefore, benefits to collaboration between different disciplines in identifying practices that are most helpful. One of the earliest multidisciplinary review panels on children's mental health was convened in the United States by the National Institutes of Health (NIH) to identify evidence-based treatment of ADHD (NIH, 1998). This resulted in the *NIH Consensus Statement on the Diagnosis and Treatment of Attention-Deficit/Hyperactivity Disorder* that sets out standards for the evidence-based assessment and treatment of this condition. In Chapter 12 we described the development in England and Wales of the National Institute for Health and Clinical Excellence (NICE) whose mandate is to guide health care professionals and patients in making decisions about health care treatment options. Although to date, the bulk of the work in the mental health field has focused on adult disorders, in 2005 NICE sought consultation on two draft documents: one concerning the use of medication in the treatment of ADHD (NICE, 2005a) and another on the assessment and treatment of depression in children (NICE, 2005b). Although it is only in its infancy, the movement to develop interdisciplinary, evidence-based guidelines for the assessment and treatment of diverse childhood disorders has the potential to inform policy-makers, consumers, and the mental health professionals who serve children with emotional and behavioural problems. The widespread application of research-based services has the potential to streamline services so that a greater proportion of the children in need can be helped.

PROFILE BOX 13.1

DR. DAN WASCHBUSCH

I received a Ph.D. from the University of Pittsburgh. I am currently an Associate Professor in the Clinical Psychology Program at Dalhousie University in Halifax and Director of the Child Behaviour program. My research interests are in developmental psychopathology, ADHD, antisocial behaviour, and peer relations. I am licensed as a psychologist by the Nova Scotia Board of Examiners in Psychology.

Dr. Dan Waschbusch

What made you choose to become a clinical psychologist?

As an undergraduate, I was interested in both science and in children. I decided to explore fields that combined these two interests and psychology was the best fit. Once in psychology, I became interested in clinical primarily because I felt it was the most challenging field of psychology in terms of gaining admissions into graduate school. I figured I'd try the most difficult graduate school application process first and see how it went. Much to my delight, I was accepted and have never looked back.

What is the most rewarding part of your job as a clinical psychologist?

One of the best parts of my job, one part I really love, is when I've conducted a study and I get to sit down at a computer, analyse the data, and find out the answer to the research question I've posed. Equally rewarding is when I get to talk about my research with others, either informally (e.g., over lunch) or formally (e.g., at a scientific conference).

What is the greatest challenge facing you as a clinical psychologist?

Clinical problems are often very complex, with multiple contributing factors. Gaining an understanding of this complexity as a researcher or clinician is very challenging. Communicating that complexity to non-psychologists, such as parents of children with ADHD, can also be challenging.

Tell us about evidence-based services for the treatment of childhood ADHD.

There are two types of treatments that research has shown are effective for the treatment of ADHD: stimulant medication, like methylphenidate (better known under the brand name Ritalin®), and behaviour modification. The key question facing researchers and clinicians is which one to use first. Most parents prefer to start with behavioural approaches, but most physicians recommend medication first. There is surprisingly little science that we can use to answer this question. Many other treatments for ADHD have been tried, ranging from biofeedback to cognitive therapy to pet therapy, but there is no evidence to support these and other approaches.

How do you integrate science and practice in your work?

I view science and practice as two sides of the same coin; they truly cannot be separated. I use science to select and evaluate treatments and I use treatment questions to guide my science.

What do you see as the most exciting changes in the profession of clinical psychology?

Psychology is moving out of therapy offices and out of academia and into the real world. Clinicians and researchers are realizing that it makes more sense to bring our treatments to patients, rather than waiting for patients to seek our treatments. For example, rather than treating children with ADHD in a psychologist's office, children with ADHD are now treated in their classrooms, playgrounds, and summer camp settings. This move has not only made treatments more accessible and practical, but it has also led to greater collaboration between psychologists and other experts, such as educators, social workers, physicians, physical therapists, speech therapists, and so on.

EXAMPLES OF EVIDENCE-BASED TREATMENTS

It is clearly beyond the scope of this chapter to present all the evidence-based interventions that are listed in Table 13.2. Instead we will examine some of the efficacious treatments for different types of common problems of childhood. As disruptive behaviour disorders are the most frequent reason for referral to mental health services, we will examine some treatments that are helpful for oppositional defiant disorder and conduct disorder. Next we will examine a treatment for adolescent depression.

Disruptive Behaviour Disorders

As we discussed earlier in the chapter, children do not refer themselves for treatment. It is perhaps not surprising that disruptive behaviour constitutes the most common reason for which adults refer children and youth for mental health services (Kazdin, 2004). Oppositional defiant disorder (ODD) reflects a pattern of persistent negativistic and hostile behaviour that is usually evident before the age of 8 years (American Psychiatric Association, 2000). Although all children sometimes fail to comply with parental requests, argue with adults, and are easily upset, children diagnosed with ODD behave like this consistently and their behaviour interferes with normal functioning. Children with ODD have problems in several contexts, such as home and school. ODD often precedes conduct disorder (CD), which involves a pattern of serious violation of the rights of others including aggression, destructiveness, deceitfulness, and serious violation of rules (APA, 2000). Young people diagnosed with ODD and CD are at risk for other mental health problems such as ADHD, learning problems, depression, and substance abuse. There is evidence that, left untreated, these problems persist into adolescence and adulthood.

The research on treatment for disruptive behaviour disorders has been the subject of many reviews. Brestan and Eyberg (1998) identified two treatment programs as well-established and efficacious: the *Incredible Years Program* developed by Carolyn Webster-Stratton (Webster-Stratton & Reid, 2003) and *Parent Management Training* (PMT) developed and refined by Gerald Patterson and his colleagues (Patterson, 1982). Other reviews, including one by T. K. Taylor and Biglan (1998), identified these two programs as having produced exemplary material for clinicians. As the *Incredible Years* program was described in Chapter 10, we will focus in this chapter on Patterson's PMT program. We will also describe a program identified by Brestan and Eyberg as probably efficacious, *Multisystemic Therapy* (MST) for seriously disordered adolescents, developed by Scott Henggeler and his colleagues (Henggeler & Lee, 2003; Henggeler, Schoenwald, Borduin, Rowland, & Cunningham, 1998).

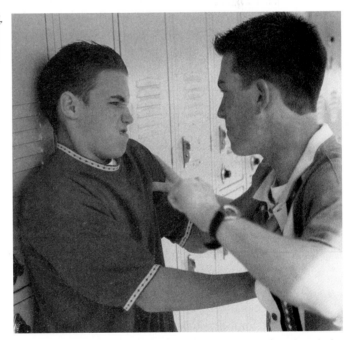

Conduct disorder involves a pattern of serious violation of the rights of others including aggression and destructiveness.

PARENT MANAGEMENT TRAINING

Parent Management Training (PMT) is based on social learning theory and the assumption that oppositional child behaviour can be changed by modifying the child's social environment rather than by working directly with the child. According to this theory, maladaptive patterns of parent-child interaction inadvertently encourage both parents and children to engage in inappropriate behaviours. During **coercive exchanges** the parent unintentionally rewards the child for whining or aggression (by withdrawing a demand or providing attention) and the child rewards the parent for giving in to his or her complaints (by ceasing the aversive behaviour). Patterson's team has conducted more than 30 years of systematic observations of families (Chamberlain & Smith, 2003; Patterson, 2005) and has found that in all families there are disagreements and conflicts that must be managed. In well-functioning families, children learn pro-social ways to resolve conflict (such as discussion and compromise), whereas in families with aggressive children, the child learns coercive ways to get what he or she wants. You have probably observed the classic example of a coercive exchange at the grocery store checkout. You first see a child grab a chocolate bar. The parent reminds the child that it is soon time for a meal, or that he or she has already had enough sugar. The child then launches into a routine that begins with wheedling, "Please, just one…" then rapidly escalates in volume and aversiveness as the parent repeats quietly "I said no." The child may protest loudly that he or she is hungry, that the parent had promised, or that the parent allowed another sibling to have a chocolate bar the last time they were in the grocery store. The child may also demand an explanation for the parent's refusal ("Why are you always so mean to me?"). As the child's protests draw the attention of a growing number of onlookers, the parent's embarrassment mounts and he or she gives in to the child's demands. This sequence has rewarded the child for grabbing, whininess, yelling, and persistence as well as increasing the likelihood that the child will do the same thing the next time. The parent's giving in is briefly rewarded by the short-term relief of the child's tantrum ending. Unfortunately, the coercive behaviours reinforced in the home are then applied in other contexts, so that the child behaves in a noncompliant and disruptive way with teachers, babysitters, coaches, and other children.

Patterson and his colleagues identified five parenting practices that are associated with the development of prosocial or deviant behaviour: skill encouragement, discipline, monitoring, problem-solving, and positive involvement (Patterson, 2005). Based on these research findings, Patterson and his colleagues developed a program designed to train parents to encourage appropriate behaviour and to discourage unacceptable behaviours. Parents meet with a therapist who teaches them the core skills listed in **Table 13.3**. An essential aspect of behavioural training is that complex skills are broken into small steps. First parents must establish a few simple rules on which they agree and which they are willing to impose consistently. Rules for child behaviour are basic guidelines about daily living, including the child's responsibilities and chores, daytime routines, and respectful ways of interacting. Lists of rules must be realistic, taking into account the child's developmental level, circumstances, and any special needs.

TABLE 13.3   Core Parenting Skills

❑ Skill encouragement

- Breaking behaviours into small steps
- Prompting appropriate behaviour through clear rules and cues
  Put your toys away

- Contingent positive reinforcement (praise and incentives)
  Wow, you tidied up your toys—that's great!
  I like the way you played with Tyler and shared your toys. Would you like to pick a sticker?
  You've done your homework carefully, now you can have 30 minutes on the computer.

❑ Discipline

- Limit setting
  Complete homework after school.
  No hitting.

- Mild sanctions (time out, removal of privileges)
  Because you did not complete your homework, you cannot have screen time.
  Because you hit your brother, you must take a time out for 10 minutes.

❑ Monitoring

- Tracking child's whereabouts and activities

❑ Problem-solving

- Establishing clear rules
- Establishing consequences
- Negotiating

❑ Positive involvement

- Loving attention

Because research has consistently found that distressed families engage in fewer positive interactions than do nondistressed families, an important goal in treatment is to increase reinforcement for positive behaviour. As you have learned in other psychology courses, **positive reinforcement** is any consequence that increases the likelihood of a behaviour being repeated. Parents seeking mental health services for their children's oppositional behaviours often report that their interactions with their children are very negative. They feel at a loss in coming up with potential reinforcers. In fact, the list of potential reinforcers is very long. The benefits of social reinforcement through smiles, attention, verbal encouragement, and touch are often overlooked. In coming up with other potential reinforcers, the parent must put themselves in the child's position, so that he or she can appreciate the range of stickers, activities, and freedoms that can possibly serve as reinforcers of desirable behaviour. Parents may also worry about the long-term consequences of what they see as paying their children to behave well. By learning to use social reinforcers and by understanding the importance of fading out the use of material reinforcers, parents learn to intentionally use reinforcers without being haunted by the unrealistic fear of turning their child into a monster who will only behave well if bribed.

Although establishing a system of positive reinforcement can go a long way toward resolving some behaviour problems, parents need to also develop skills in dealing with non-compliance. Patterson's approach offers mild punishment as an effective response to misbehaviour. Basically, punishment involves the withdrawal of reinforcers—this can include a range of losses according to the child's age and preferences. Punishment for a very young child may involve not being allowed to play with a favourite toy that he or she has just used to hurt another child or turning off the TV after the child has yelled and disturbed a sibling; for an older child, it may include an earlier curfew, or loss of computer time. Parents learn to use **time out** procedures in which the child does not have access to reinforcers for a brief period following misbehaviour.

PMT is not offered as a quick fix for child behaviour problems. It is an approach to parenting in which the adult assumes an active role in monitoring and responding to the child's behaviours. With very young children, monitoring may include close physical supervision of the child's activities. As the child grows older, parental monitoring shifts so that parents learn to maintain a relationship with the young person, who informs parents about his or her whereabouts and activities. An essential component of parenting is recognizing that as children get older they should become more involved in decision-making. Therefore, parents learn negotiation and how to alter their expectations based on developmental changes.

PMT is delivered in a structured format, using a treatment manual and repeated practice. The number of sessions varies according to the child's age and the severity of the disruptive behaviour: from 4-8 weeks with young mildly oppositional children to 12-25 weeks for clinically referred youth diagnosed with conduct disorder (Kazdin, 2003). During sessions, parents practise skills through behaviour rehearsal and role-playing. Between sessions they complete homework assignments related to the skills they have learned. Patterson's work has also inspired many variations of PMT that were described in Chapter 10, including the work of Webster-Stratton and the Triple P program.

Recent innovations in PMT have highlighted the importance of cognitive and affective variables that are related to treatment outcome. For example, if parents believe that the young person *intentionally* engages in misbehaviour, then they are less likely to adopt effective discipline strategies and are more likely to continue with strategies that actually increase the likelihood of misbehaviour. It is therefore necessary for PMT to focus not only on parents' behaviours toward the child, but also on the ways that parents understand the child's misbehaviour (Patterson, 2005). A core element of PMT is to increase the amount of positive interaction between parent and child. The importance of this affective dimension has been underlined in recent studies that have shown that parent-child warmth is associated with **parental monitoring** and that adolescent-parent contempt is associated with inconsistent and disrupted parental monitoring, which in turn is associated with delinquency (Patterson, 2005).

MULTISYSTEMIC THERAPY

Multisystemic Therapy (MST) is an approach designed to treat seriously disturbed delinquent adolescents by intervening in an integrated way in the multiple systems in which they are involved (Henggeler et al., 1998). These youth who are at risk of being placed in out-of-home care require costly services that consume a disproportionate amount of mental health resources (Henggeler & Lee, 2003). Grounded in an **ecological theory** of psychosocial functioning (Bronfenbrenner, 1979), MST works with these youth within the context of numerous systems including the nuclear family, extended family, neighbourhood, school, peer, community, juvenile justice, child welfare, and mental health (Henggeler et al., 1998). This treatment approach is consistent with research findings that delinquent behaviour is not simply caused by one factor but, rather, is multiply determined. Within this model the caregiver (usually, but not always, a parent) plays a key role in the young person's short- and long-term adjustment. **Table 13.4** describes the nine principles that guide MST. The goals of the approach are positive and future-oriented. MST uses a behavioural approach that is designed to integrate services, so that gains in one area will generalize to other contexts. A fundamental characteristic of this approach is that treatment effectiveness is evaluated continuously from the perspective of multiple stakeholders, including the youth, parents, and others in the educational, health, and justice systems.

MST therapists work in teams of three to five people. Each therapist works with a very small caseload of four to five families. The therapist coordinates all the services that the youth and family receive. To reduce barriers to participation, services are offered in homes, schools, and neighbourhood centres rather than in hospitals or court clinics. Treatment is time limited, lasting only three to five months. It is, however, very intense, with therapists available 24 hours a day and 7 days a week to respond to crises.

The first phase of services involves an explanation of the MST model. The therapist works hard to develop a collaborative relationship with the caregiver. Assessment involves identification of the risk factors that contribute to the problem as well as strengths that can be drawn upon in every system in which the young person is involved. As you learned in Chapter 10, risk factors include low caregiver monitoring, low warmth, ineffective discipline, high conflict, caregiver psychopathology, and family criminal behaviour. Protective factors include secure attachment, a

444   **Chapter 13** ■ Intervention: Children and Adolescents

---

TABLE 13.4   MST Treatment Principles

Principle 1:	The primary purpose of assessment is to understand the fit between the identified problems and their broader systemic context.
Principle 2:	Therapeutic contacts emphasize the positive and use systemic strengths as levers for change.
Principle 3:	Interventions are designed to promote responsible behaviour and decrease irresponsible behaviour among family members.
Principle 4:	Interventions are present focused and action oriented, targeting specific and well-defined problems.
Principle 5:	Interventions target sequences of behaviour within and between multiple systems that maintain the identified problems.
Principle 6:	Interventions are developmentally appropriate and fit the developmental needs of the youth.
Principle 7:	Interventions are designed to require daily or weekly effort by family members.
Principle 8:	Intervention effectiveness is evaluated continuously from multiple perspectives with providers assuming accountability for overcoming barriers to successful outcomes.
Principle 9:	Interventions are designed to promote treatment generalization and long-term maintenance of therapeutic change by empowering caregivers to address family members' needs across multiple systemic contexts.

Adapted from Henggeler, Schoenwald, Borduin, Rowland, & Cunningham, (1998).

---

supportive family environment, and a harmonious couple relationship between the parents. At an early stage in services the therapist works with the family to establish measurable long-term goals that can be broken down into measurable weekly goals. The therapist makes contact with any person or system that can affect the attainment of these goals in order to ensure their co-operation. In collaboration with the caregiver and youth, the therapist then selects evidence-based treatments for each goal. As you can imagine, services to establish clear rules, to reward pro-social behaviour, and to encourage appropriate monitoring are very similar to PMT approaches. Caregivers are not always able to implement the recommendations and their stress or psychopathology may pose a serious obstacle to successful treatment. Therefore the MST therapist also targets for intervention any caregiver characteristics that significantly limit the capacity to parent effectively.

Interventions that target the peer system depend on the nature of the problem. Peers can serve as a risk factor if they are antisocial, or as a protective factor if they are socially competent. Youth lacking in social skills or assertiveness receive training in these areas. On the other hand, if the peer group is an antisocial one that encourages delinquent behaviour, the intervention focuses on limiting access to those peers, increasing parental monitoring, and developing more appropriate peer contacts through other activities.

Risk factors in the school system include learning problems, a chaotic school environment, and poor contact between family and school. Protective factors include strong intellectual functioning, a commitment to education, and good contact between family and school. MST therapists can play a key role in facilitating the development of a collaborative relationship between school and family to ensure a consistent approach between the two environments.

Individually oriented services target specific difficulties the youth may be experiencing using evidence-based approaches. For example, cognitive-behavioural strategies may be used to address problems with anxiety or depression. A referral may be made for a trial of medication in the treatment of ADHD. As MST is a short-term intervention, considerable emphasis is placed on developing a supportive network so that the youth and family will be able to maintain the gains that they made when working directly with the therapist, after the therapist is no longer actively involved.

The developers of MST have established a quality assurance system to ensure that the approach is faithfully applied according to a manual by trained therapists who receive adequate supervision and consultation. Given the promising data on the efficacy of MST in reducing delinquent behaviour among seriously troubled youth, it is encouraging to learn that licensed MST programs operate in 30 of the U.S. states and in several countries (Henggeler & Lee, 2003). Ongoing research is examining the usefulness of this approach to treat other serious problems in adolescents.

VIEWPOINT BOX 13.1

TREATMENT OF CHILDHOOD ATTENTION-DEFICIT/HYPERACTIVITY DISORDER

As ADHD is a neurological disorder and reviews have consistently found evidence for the efficacy of stimulant medication in reducing symptoms of inattention, hyperactivity, and impulsivity (NICE, 2005a; NIH, 1998; Schachar et al., 2002), you may wonder why there is any need for psychosocial interventions to treat children with ADHD. There are many significant reasons why psychosocial treatment should be considered. First, although problematic parent-child interaction does not cause ADHD, there is evidence that the presence of child ADHD is associated with disrupted parenting, and this in turn affects the management of ADHD symptoms and the development of oppositional symptoms. Second, stimulants should not be prescribed to children under age 6 (Greenhill & Ford, 2002). Third, a number of parents are unwilling to consider giving their children medication (Waschbusch & Hill, 2003). Fourth, although stimulant medication is effective in suppressing the symptoms of ADHD, the effect lasts only while the child is taking medication, with a return to regular functioning within 3–10 hours of a ingesting a dose (Greenhill & Ford, 2002; NIH, 1998; NICE, 2005a). Fifth, 30% of children with ADHD do not respond to the medication (Greenhill & Ford, 2002). Sixth, although stimulants are associated with reduction of core symptoms of ADHD, there is little evidence that medication is associated with improvement in academic or social skills (NIH, 1998). Seventh, although stimulants are not associated with serious side effects, there are minor unpleasant physiological symptoms, the most common of which is appetite suppression (NICE, 2005a). Eighth, over time, there is a gradual decline in the numbers of children who adhere to their medication (Charach, Ickowicz, & Schachar, 2004). Unfortunately, it is impossible to predict which children will respond positively to medication (Greenhill & Ford, 2002).

Given the fact that medication is not suitable for all children and that its positive effects are limited to the hours shortly after it has been administered, it is not surprising that behavioural approaches that have been used to treat other disruptive behaviour disorders have also been used to treat childhood ADHD. Similar to PMT for oppositional behaviour, behavioural treatments for children with ADHD are designed to help adults (parents and teachers) provide a structured, consistent environment in which the child is reinforced for appropriate behaviour and misbehaviour is ignored or mildly punished. Pelham, Wheeler, and Chronis (1998) found evidence of positive treatment effects both at home and school regardless of whether the intervention used parents, teachers, or behavioural experts. However, echoing the findings for medication, although behavioural approaches have been demonstrated to be efficacious in the short term, the treatment effects are not sustained in the long run and have not been found to generalize well to other settings (Farmer, Compton, Burns, & Robertson, 2002; Hinshaw et al., 2003; Waschbusch & Hill, 2003). Furthermore, not all parents benefit from behavioural parent training (Chronis, Chacko, Fabiano, Wymbs, & Pelham, 2004). Similar to findings with respect to treatment of children with oppositional behaviour, parents facing environmental stressors such as low family income, single parenthood, marital discord, and parental psychopathology are least likely to benefit from standard behavioural parent training. For example, Sonuga-Barke, Daley, and Thompson (2002) found that mothers who themselves had high levels of ADHD symptomatology demonstrated no improvement in parenting following training, whereas mothers with low or moderate ADHD symptoms demonstrated substantial improvement in parenting.

Given the promising but imperfect results from studies examining the separate effects of medication and of psychosocial treatment, a large group of researchers launched the Multimodal Treatment Study of Children with Attention-Deficit/Hyperactivity Disorder (MTA: Richters et al., 1995). In this collaborative study

579 children diagnosed with ADHD-combined type were recruited across six North American sites. Children were randomly assigned to 14 months of treatment in one of four treatment conditions: (1) medication management only (in which the dose of medication was adjusted in double-blind trials); (2) behavioural treatment with parents, child, and school; (3) a combination of medication management and behavioural treatment; and (4) a comparison of regular treatment in the community (which included medication for about two-thirds of the group). The behavioural treatment included 35 individual and group training sessions for parents, up to 24 teacher contacts (face-to-face or by phone), as well as an intensive 8-week summer camp program for children. A daily report card was used to maintain links between home and school. As research has already established that there are efficacious treatments for ADHD, it would have been unethical to assign any children to a condition in which they received no treatment at all for the 14 months of the study (Swanson et al., 2002).

The results from the MTA study are complex and vary according to the type of outcome measure as well as to characteristics of the child and family. Across all four types of treatment, there were positive results. In terms of reducing ADHD symptoms, medication management only and combined medication management/behavioural treatments were superior to behavioural only or standard community care (MTA Cooperative Group, 1999a). It would be wrong, however, to conclude that stimulant medication is all that is required in treating children with ADHD. Children in the combined group achieved the same positive effects as did children in the medication management only group, but received 20% less medication—that is, the addition of a psychosocial component was associated with children requiring less medication. Treatment changes in three-quarters of the children in the behavioural group were successfully maintained without medication. For children who also suffered anxiety disorders, behavioural treatment was superior to community care and equivalent to medication management only and combined treatment (MTA Cooperative Group, 1999b). For families receiving public assistance, medication management only was associated with a decrease in the quality of parent-child interactions, whereas combined treatment yielded greater benefit in terms of social skills than did the other treatments (MTA Cooperative Group, 1999b). Furthermore, in the treatments that included medication, child treatment response was poorer when the parent suffered depressive symptoms (Owens et al., 2003). Using cut-off scores that combined parent and teacher ratings to define excellent treatment response, Swanson et al. (2001) reported success rates of 68% for combined treatment, 56% for medication management, 34% for behavioural treatment, and 25% for standard community care.

The results of the MTA study suggest that there is there is no one size fits all treatment for all children with ADHD, but there is a menu of effective treatments.

Quite simply, because ADHD is a chronic disorder that causes serious debilitation in multiple contexts, as well as frequent comorbidity (oppositional behaviour, learning problems, and depression), it is unlikely that a single approach to treatment will be sufficient to address the problem for all children. A multidimensional approach is therefore recommended (Farley, 2003). Researchers continue to develop enhancements to psychosocial interventions that will help a greater number of families benefit from this approach (Chronis et al., 2004).

Adolescent Depression

Epidemiological studies indicate that major depressive disorder is almost as common in adolescence as it is in adulthood (Lewinsohn & Clarke, 1999). Data from the United States indicate that, by the age of 18, 1 in 5 young people will have experienced an episode of major depressive disorder (Clarke et al., 2003). Depression is a chronic recurrent disorder that is associated with difficulties in peer relationships, poorer school functioning, and troubled family relationships (Seligman, Goza, & Ollendick, 2004). It is also associated with an increased rate of suicide (Clarke et al., 2003).

Although adolescent depression is a serious problem, in contrast to the wealth of research on the treatment of adult depression, the literature with respect to depression in young people is less extensive. Reviews of this literature have concluded that there is support for CBT as an efficacious treatment and for Interpersonal Therapy (IPT) as a probably efficacious approach in the treatment of adolescent depression (Chorpita et al., 2002; Kazdin, 2003, 2004).

Draft guidelines for the treatment of depression in children (NICE, 2005b) recommend that the initial assessment address risk and protective factors in the child's social networks. If there is evidence that the young person is exposed to bullying, school and health professionals should develop strategies to deal with the bullying. Mental health professionals should consider whether it is necessary that parental psychopathology be treated in parallel with the services offered to the young person. The young person should be advised of the benefits of lifestyle factors including regular exercise, adequate sleep, and good nutrition. The draft NICE guidelines recommend that antidepressant medication *not* be prescribed to treat mild depression. Instead, monitoring, non-directive supportive therapy, or group CBT are recommended. The first line of treatment for youth with moderate or severe depression is individual CBT, IPT, or short-term family therapy. According to the draft guidelines, antidepressant medication should only be offered in combination with a psychological treatment.

In Chapter 11 we described the ways that IPT, which was originally developed to treat depression in adults, has been modified to meet the needs of adolescents (Mufson & Dorta, 2003; Mufson, Weissman, Moreau, & Garfinkel, 1999). In Chapter 12 we described CBT for adult depression. In order to give you a sense of how CBT can be provided to youth, we will describe a CBT approach developed for adults that has been modified specifically to treat adolescent depression.

COPING WITH DEPRESSION IN ADOLESCENCE

Coping with Depression in Adolescence (CWDA) is a program developed by Peter Lewinsohn and his colleagues (Lewinsohn & Clarke, 1999; Clarke et al., 2003) as an adaptation of the *Coping with Depression Course* (Lewinsohn, Antonuccio, Steinmetz, & Teri, 1984) that had been found to be efficacious in the treatment of depressed adults. The two coping programs are based on a model of depression that applies to both adults and adolescents. It is assumed that there are genetic risk factors for depression that, when combined with maladaptive learned thoughts and behaviours, heighten the chances of experiencing clinically significant depressive symptoms (Clarke et al., 2003). In CWDA, treatment focuses on behaviours, cognitions, and management of affect. Behavioural interventions include increasing pleasant activities and developing problem-solving skills, assertiveness skills, communication skills, and conflict resolution skills. Cognitive techniques include promoting the use of positive self-talk, self-monitoring, coping, and cognitive restructuring. The affective component involves learning strategies for dealing with negative emotions, including relaxation and anger management. Parents may be involved to develop their parenting, conflict resolution, and communication skills. Just as with CBT for adult depression, **mood monitoring** is a central activity that is introduced at the beginning of the program and is continued throughout the course of services. The focus of initial sessions is on behavioural change, with an emphasis on the practice of social skills and an increase in pleasant activities. This flows logically into an examination of dysfunctional cognitions. The end of the program focuses on strategies to ensure the maintenance of gains, progress toward goals, and the prevention of relapse. Participants are told that not every skill will be equally useful to all participants, but they are required to attempt every activity. Booster sessions can be offered at four-month intervals for two years after completing the program.

The CWDA program is delivered according to a treatment manual in a group format. Between 6 and 10 depressed adolescents (aged 13–18) take part in each group. The **psychoeducational** approach presents material in a similar way to the way other subjects are taught in school. This style of conveying material is assumed to be less stigmatizing to young people who may feel very uncomfortable with the idea of receiving treatment of a mental disorder. Treatment includes 16 two-hour sessions that are scheduled over an 8-week period. The course uses a workbook with readings, quizzes, and forms for homework. Materials are designed to be engaging for young people, using popular newspaper cartoons such as Calvin and Hobbes, Peanuts and Garfield to illustrate common dysfunctional thoughts. Therapists are active and engage participation by seeking examples and facilitating the exchange of ideas between group members. Skills are presented in the session and are practised using role plays. Participants are then assigned homework tasks that involve the application of the skills in their everyday lives. As you can see, there are more similarities than dissimilarities between the treatment of adult and youth depression. The major difference is in adapting the psychoeducational material to make it more engaging to young people and in developing modules that include parents.

VIEWPOINT BOX 13.2

PSYCHOLOGICAL TREATMENT FOR CARL

In Chapter 3 we introduced Carl, a 12-year-old boy exposed to the trauma of genocide. Carl suffered from diverse symptoms, including anxiety, persistent re-experiencing of the events, avoidance of stimuli associated with the trauma, somatic complaints, and sleep disturbance. Carl's symptoms were consistent with a diagnosis of PTSD. The initial assessment lead to a formulation of Carl's problems in terms of his initial exposure to genocide when he was three years old as well as the re-emergence of threat when he was nine years old. Counterbalancing these serious risk factors were the protective factors of his strong attachment to his mother and twin sister. Carl's mother did not connect her son's symptoms of anxiety to his horrific experiences. She was bewildered that, now the family was safe in Canada, her son was showing signs of "craziness." In understanding the mother's reaction, it is important to bear in mind that she, too, had been exposed to trauma, with the murder of her husband and threats to herself and her children. She, too, suffered from PTSD and experienced characteristic numbing and avoidance of stimuli that made it hard for her to acknowledge the source of Carl's difficulties.

In treatment planning, psychologists must first consider whether there are evidence-based treatments for the client's problem. Although there are efficacious treatments for adults with PTSD, the treatment of childhood and adolescent PTSD is not as well developed (Feeny, Foa, Treadwell, & March, 2004; Roberts, Lazicki-Puddy, Puddy, & Johnson, 2003; Target & Fonagy, 2005; T. L. Taylor & Chemtob, 2004). There is evidence of the usefulness of some approaches in treating childhood PTSD resulting from a single traumatic event such as a car accident (Scotti, Morris, Ruggiero, & Wolfgang, 2002). However, Carl was exposed to unremitting trauma over the course of months. There is some preliminary evidence of the usefulness of CBT approaches in treating children who suffer PTSD as a result of sexual abuse (T. L. Taylor & Chemtob, 2004), and case studies of exposure in the treatment of Lebanese children suffering war-related PTSD (Feeny et al., 2004), but no studies on the treatment of children and adolescents exposed to genocide. As you learned in Chapter 12, efficacious treatments for adults with PTSD include relaxation, imaginal exposure, and in vivo exposure. Important pre-requisites for treatment are that the person must be safe and there must be people available to support him or her during the painful period of habituation to the stimuli associated with symptoms. Although Carl was safe in Canada, his refugee claim was pending. In the event that his family's claim for refugee status was denied and they were forced to return to their home country, he would again be exposed to danger. Carl's mother was devoted to her children's well-being, but she also suffered from PTSD, so her capacity to support him emotionally was diminished.

In the absence of an evidence-based treatment package that matches the client's needs, the psychologist must consider whether there are elements of evidence-based approaches that are relevant (Connor-Smith & Weisz, 2003). Fortunately, the treatment of anxiety disorders in childhood includes many efficacious strategies (Cartwright-Hatton, Roberts, Chitsabesan, Fothergill, & Harrington, 2004; Kazdin, 2003; Roberts et al., 2003). Accordingly, the treatment goals for Carl included the development of relaxation and stress management strategies, as well as the accurate identification of emotions and changes in his belief systems. A critically important goal was the reduction of avoidance of stimuli associated with the trauma. In a feedback session with Carl and his mother, the psychologist provided information about PTSD, linking it to the events they had experienced. Carl and his mother agreed to parallel services in which each would work on PTSD symptoms and develop effective stress management skills.

Carl attended 13 sessions. Initial sessions focused on the development of a collaborative relationship through non-threatening activities. For example, Carl learned to expand his vocabulary of emotions by Internet-based activities in which he had to match facial expressions to emotion labels (e.g., scared, disappointed, frustrated, grumpy, worried). Next he worked to generate possible explanations for emotions (e.g., worried because a test is coming up, embarrassed because he does not want o look stupid). Carl agreed to keep a sleep log in which he recorded his nighttime routine and any awakening as well as the thoughts he had when unable to sleep. Subsequently he learned relaxation activities including both breathing exercises and progressive muscle relaxation; at the same time, his mother was also learning relaxation strategies. Carl then practised these relaxation activities when he went to bed and whenever he awoke in the night. Carl observed that the relaxation strategies were helpful in reducing the time spent awake.

In the next phase of services, Carl's cognitions were targeted. Following an episode in which he lay awake for hours having heard what he thought was an intruder in the house, Carl learned to distinguish between "real" emotional alarms and "false" emotional alarms. The therapist used the example of firefighters to illustrate this. Carl learned that when the bell sounds in the fire hall, the firefighters get ready to fight a fire; as they put on their gear and travel to the possible fire, they are ready for action. Once at the site, they check carefully whether there is a fire. In the event that there is a fire, they work to extinguish it. However, in the event that there is a false alarm, they return to the fire hall and resume their activities. Applying this analogy in his own life, Carl was able to remind himself that, like the firefighters, he should check to see whether there was a reason for the alarm, by checking that the doors were locked and that no one had access to the house; once he had established that it was a false alarm, he could use the relaxation strategies to fall back to sleep.

As the anniversary of the genocide approached, Carl talked about his ambivalence in participating in memorial activities. Equipped with his expanded vocabulary of feelings he communicated his desire to avoid the extreme sadness and anger of remembering the horror, balanced by his desire to connect to other people who had shared the experience. Carl recognized that participation did not have to be an all-or-nothing decision, and chose to be involved in some activities, such as a candlelight vigil, but to limit others, such as watching hours of television footage of the carnage. With the psychologist, Carl practised communicating his preferences to his mother. Subsequently Carl reported satisfaction that he was able to make choices, exhaustion at the emotional toll of the memorial, but appreciation of a greater feeling of connectedness with others in his extended family and community. At the end of services, Carl reported that he no longer suffered from sleep disturbance or somatic complaints. The persistent re-experiencing of the trauma had diminished and he was less avoidant of stimuli associated with it.

In adapting treatment for this young client, it was essential to deliver material in a developmentally appropriate fashion; whereas a younger child might be engaged in cutting pictures from a magazine and pasting a collage that illustrates different emotions, Carl found it cool to point and click at images on a website. As a young man on the verge of adolescence, Carl was most comfortable with individual services in which he could enjoy privacy with the therapist. Nevertheless, from the provision of information about PTSD that reduced the mother's intolerance of her son's anxious behaviour, to the encouragement that both practise relaxation exercises, the coordination of services for mother and youth was essential.

EFFICACY, EFFECTIVENESS, AND THE DISSEMINATION OF EVIDENCE-BASED TREATMENTS

In Chapter 12 we discussed the challenges of moving from efficacy in clinical trials to establishing effectiveness in clinical practice. The issues raised with respect to adults are equally important with respect to children and adolescents. In the previous sections of this chapter we have described the progress that has been made in identifying efficacious treatments for children and adolescents. Mean effect sizes in efficacy studies for treatment of child and adolescent problems can exceed .70 (Connor-Smith & Weisz, 2003). However, there is growing evidence that standard community care for child and adolescent disorders is generally not effective (Ollendick & King, 2004). For example, Weersing and Weisz (2002) compared the outcomes of depressed youth receiving care in community mental health centres with those obtained in clinical trials. It is very troubling that the effects of community-based services were more similar to what is found for youth in no-treatment control conditions than what is found in the treatment condition of RCTs. The two crucial issues confronting the field are therefore: (1) whether efficacious treatments established in methodologically sound studies are also effective when they are applied as part of regular clinical practice; and (assuming the first question is answered affirmatively) (2) how these evidence-based treatments can be disseminated so that they are more widely available.

There is a small but growing body of research that demonstrates efficacious treatments for youth can also be effective in routine practice. The best example of this comes from community-based research on Webster-Stratton's *Incredible Years Program*. For example, T. K. Taylor, Schmidt, Pepler, and Hodgins (1998) randomly assigned 108 parents seeking help at a Canadian children's mental health clinic for managing the problem behaviours of their 3- to 8-year-old children to one of three conditions: Webster-Stratton parenting groups, the eclectic approach to treatment typically offered at the clinic, or a wait-list control group. Both treatments were effective, relative to the no-treatment condition, in reducing problem behaviours, but the Webster-Stratton intervention was more effective than the usual treatment provided at the clinic. Scott, Spender, Doolan, Jacobs, and Aspland (2001) conducted a controlled study at four child and adolescent mental health services in the United Kingdom. One hundred and forty-one children aged 3–8 years were referred to these services with problems of antisocial behaviour. Their parents were randomly assigned to either 13 to 16 weeks of the Webster-Stratton parenting groups or to a waiting list control group. Based on their analysis of the treatment outcome data, the researchers concluded that the parenting groups offered in real world conditions effectively reduced the serious antisocial behaviour of the referred children.

A recent review indicated that there is a growing body of research indicating that evidence-based treatments for anxiety, depression, ADHD, and disruptive disorders appear to be equally effective for African American and Latino youths as they are for Caucasian youths (Miranda et al.,

2005). Unfortunately, despite progress in the identification of efficacious treatments, dissemination of those treatments appears slower with respect to treatment of childhood disorders than for adult disorders (Herschell, McNeil, & McNeil, 2004). For example, Herschell et al. found that the proportion of journal articles devoted to treatment dissemination for adult disorders was double that for disorders of childhood and adolescence. **Table 13.5** lists some of the strategies proposed by Herschell and colleagues to improve dissemination of evidence-based treatments. As you can see, some of the strategies require action on the part of the developers of interventions (e.g., making treatment manuals widely available, providing opportunities for training and supervision). Other recommendations target graduate training programs that are in the business of educating future psychologists. In addition, licensing bodies could contribute to the dissemination of evidence-based treatments by requiring that psychologists engage in continuing education so that the process of learning does not end with the awarding of the Ph.D. but is a career-long process.

TABLE 13.5   Strategies to Facilitate the Dissemination of Evidence-Based Treatment

- Development of manuals that allow flexible implementation

- Graduate education in evidence-based treatment

- Continuing education in evidence-based treatment

- Training protocols such as workshops, supervision, and consultation

- Increased research on effective dissemination strategies.

Adapted from Herschell, McNeil, & McNeil, 2004.

The concerns first raised by Kazdin and his colleagues in their 1990 meta-analysis (Kazdin et al., 1990) are echoed in recent reviews of the literature (Kazdin, 2003; Weisz, Doss, & Hawley, 2005). Kazdin (2003) highlighted the ongoing need to conduct research to identify the ingredients in treatment that are responsible for change, as well as on identifying particular subgroups for which a treatment is helpful. Weisz et al. (2005) reviewed published, methodologically sound RCTs for anxiety (82 studies), depression (18 studies), ADHD (40 studies), and conduct problems (96 studies). These authors highlighted a number of threats to both internal validity and external validity that limited the extent to which results could be generalized. For example, in many studies there was no reliable determination of the diagnosis. Most studies were underpowered: they had too few participants in each condition to provide the statistical power to detect meaningful group differences. Few studies were clinically representative: in the majority of studies, participants were recruited rather than being drawn from contexts in which were seeking treatment. Furthermore, they reported that two-thirds of the studies were conducted in the United States and that learning-based treatments were 8 to 10 times more likely to be studied than were insight-based treatments (i.e., psychodynamic treatments). Thus, although there has been progress in the study of psychological treatments for children and adolescents, it is essential that research be conducted to determine the extent to which promising treatments are useful for the populations who require services.

SUMMARY AND CONCLUSIONS

Compared with the evidence base for adult treatments, far less is known about the effects of psychotherapy for children and adolescents. Nevertheless, meta-analytic estimates do indicate that treatments for youth can have substantial effects on psychological symptoms, with some estimates indicating almost comparable treatment effects for adults and youth. Various organizations have worked to develop listings of evidence-based interventions for children and adolescents and, at present, there are scientifically supported psychosocial treatments for the most commonly occurring Axis I disorders. Clinical practice guidelines for addressing mood disorders, anxiety disorders, ADHD, and externalizing disorders are now available for both clinicians and patients and their families. Despite these advances, much more work needs to be done to encourage treatment research that is more clinically representative, to understand exactly what the ingredients of successful treatment are, and to promote the use of evidence-based treatments in real world settings.

Critical Thinking Questions

What are some of the major differences between services for children and adolescents and services for adults?

What are some of the factors that might be responsible for the existence of less youth treatment research than adult treatment research?

Is there currently evidence that psychotherapy can work in the treatment of childhood and adolescent disorders?

Why is it so important to have parents involved in many forms of child treatment?

How do services for children and services for adolescents differ?

Key Terms

coercive exchanges

ecological theory

mood monitoring

parental monitoring

positive reinforcement

psychoeducation

time out

Key Names

Bruce Chorpita   Gerald Patterson

Alan Kazdin   Carolyn Webster-Stratton

Peter Lewinsohn   John Weisz

ADDITIONAL RESOURCES

Books

Fonagy, P., Target, M., Cottrell, D., Phillips, J., & Kurtz, Z. (2002). *What works for whom? A critical review of treatments for children and adolescents.* New York: Guilford.

Kazdin, A. E., & Weisz, J. R. (Eds). (2003). *Evidence-based psychotherapies for children and adolescents* (pp. 101-119). New York: Guilford.

Websites

The APA's Society of Clinical Child and Adolescent Psychology: http://www.effectivechildtherapy.com/

The *British Medical Journal*, providing reviews of the literature on the treatment of physical and mental disorders: http://www.clinicalevidence.org

The Canadian Paediatric Society, providing position statements on the treatment of psychosocial problems: http://www.cps.ca/english/publications/Psychosocial.htm

The Royal Australian and New Zealand College of Psychiatrists, providing clinical practice guidelines: http://www.ranzcp.org/publicarea/cpg.asp

The American Academy of Child and Adolescent Psychiatry, providing Practice Parameters: http://www.aacap.org/clinical/parameters/index.htm

Multisystemic Therapy: http://www.mstservices.com/

CHAPTER 14

Intervention: Identifying Key Elements of Change

INTRODUCTION

Consistent with our emphasis that clinical psychology is an *evidence-based* discipline, Chapters 12 and 13 examined the empirical evidence on interventions that work in the treatment of a variety of disorders and problems. However, it is important also to consider the large body of evidence that focuses on patient, therapist, and therapeutic process variables that influence treatment outcome. As we described in the previous chapters, hundreds of studies have examined the outcome of treatments and the comparative outcome of different types of treatment. There are also, however, hundreds of studies that examine elements of psychotherapy such as the alliance between patient and therapist and how these process elements are related to the impact of treatment. Such approaches to studying psychotherapy are known as, respectively, process research and process-outcome research. In the first part of this chapter, we illustrate what can be learned about psychotherapy from **process-outcome research**.

As we mentioned in Chapter 2, many clinical psychologists describe their theoretical orientation as combining two or more of the major approaches to treatment, such as experiential and cognitive-behavioural. When asked to explain their use of multiple approaches to treatment, these psychologists may indicate that there are **common factors** in successful treatment that cut across specific approaches to therapy (e.g., Garfield, 1994; Norcross & Goldfried, 1992). In the latter part of the chapter we examine both theories and research on these common (or nonspecific) factors. Common factors are sometimes presented as responsible for most of the impact of any form of psychotherapy, so we review evidence with respect to the claim that all forms of psychotherapy have equivalent effects.

As you saw in the previous two chapters, findings from treatment outcome research have been used to develop evidence-based recommendations for the treatment of specific health conditions. The results of process research and process-outcome research have also been used to formulate clinical guidelines for psychologists and, in the final part of this chapter, we examine these initiatives in detail. The first initiative involves explicitly emphasizing client characteristics and therapy relationship factors that have been found to be related to treatment outcome. The second and more integrative initiative involves combining research findings on client, therapist, client-therapist relationship, and treatment characteristics to develop evidence-based principles of therapeutic change that can be applied to all forms of treatment.

PSYCHOTHERAPY PROCESS-OUTCOME RESEARCH

To understand the relation between treatment outcome research and process-outcome research, it is useful to consider a sports analogy. A team's performance over a season can be analysed in a number

of ways. For example, you can simply count the number of wins during a season, the number of wins when a team plays at home, the number of wins when a team plays on natural or synthetic surfaces, or the team's record against specific opponents. Like treatment outcome research, all of these examples focus on outcomes, outcomes under varying conditions, or how the team fared compared with other teams. None of this reveals much about how the team achieved its record. To do this, we need to examine processes within each game and then examine the consistency of these processes across all games the team played. For example, how well does the team do if they score first, what happens if the star offensive player has a poor game, or what is the effect on the outcome if there are a greater than average number of penalties

Just as a team's play can be analyzed in different ways (such as number of wins, points scored versus points allowed, or points scored by individual players), the effects of psychological treatment can also be examined at multiple levels (e.g., treatment outcome, use of different techniques, the relation between client characteristics and treatment outcome).

called against the team? All of these questions explore the issue of what is occurring during a game that is associated with the team being relatively successful or unsuccessful. Such questions are similar to those posed by process-outcome psychotherapy researchers.

Both ways of examining the record of a sports team (or of psychotherapy) provide valid answers to different questions. Identifying the best team or comparing teams to one another requires different data and a different approach to data analysis than does determining the factors that contribute to a team's success or whether these same factors account for the performance of all the teams in the league. In a review of the history of process-outcome research, David Orlinsky and colleagues (Orlinsky, Rønnestad, & Willutzki, 2004) traced the development of this line of psychotherapy research over the past 50 years. In the 1950s and 1960s psychologists started to use two important sources of data: recordings of psychotherapy sessions and standardized measures of clients' and therapists' experience of the treatment process. Since then, the strategies for studying what transpires in therapy and how it is related to client change have grown dramatically. **Table 14.1** provides an overview of the different levels at which psychotherapy researchers have addressed these important questions.

TABLE 14.1   Levels of Analysis for Psychotherapeutic Process and Outcome Studies

TIMEFRAME	TIMESCALE	PROCESS FOCUS	OUTCOME FOCUS
Level 1: Liminal	Split-seconds	*Micromomentary processes* (gaze shifts; facial expressions)	None
Level 2: Momentary	Large fractions to small multiples of minutes	*Moment-by-moment processes* (tactical moves, e.g., specific utterances; interactive turns)	*In-session impacts* (emergent helpful or hindering experiences, e.g., insight, catharsis)
Level 3: Situational	Large fractions to small multiples of hours	*Session processes* (strategic change events, rupture and repair of alliance; dynamics of whole sessions)	*Postsession outcome* (immediate improvements in mood, motivation, and cognition, e.g., resolution of "splitting")
Level 4: Daily	Large fractions to small multiples of days	*Session-sequential process* (intersession experiences; use of homework assignments; very brief treatment episodes, e.g., emergency therapy)	*Micro-outcome* (enhancement of current functioning, e.g., boost in morale; communication skills; better handling of problem situations)

continued...

TIMEFRAME	TIMESCALE	PROCESS FOCUS	OUTCOME FOCUS
Level 5: Monthly	Large fractions to small multiples of months (weeks)	*Phase/short course process* (formation and evolution of a therapeutic alliance; or whole short-term treatment episode, e.g., 12–26 weeks)	*Mini-outcome* (upgrading of week-to-week psychological state, e.g., symptom reduction, lessening of irrational cognitions)
Level 6: Seasonal	Large fractions to small multiples of years (months)	*Medium-course processes* (work on recurrent interpersonal, cognitive, and motivational conflicts; medium-term treatment episodes, e.g., 6–24 months)	*Meso-outcome* (change in personal adaptation, e.g., increase in self-ideal congruence, resolution of of dysfunctional attitudes and cognitions)
Level 7: Perennial	Large fractions to small multiples of decades (years)	*Long course processes* (long-term treatment episodes, e.g., 2–7 + years)	*Macro-outcome* (personality change, e.g., methods of defense; removal of neurotic blocks to growth)
Level 8: Developmental	Life trajectory vectors and stage transitions	*Multitreatment processes* (sequential treatment episodes)	*Mega-outcome* (character change, e.g., modification of Axis-II personality disorder)
Level 9: Biographic	Life course	*Therapeutic career* (total treatment history)	*Meta-outcome* (retrospective view of life course as influenced by treatment experience)

Adapted from Orlinsky, Rønnestad, & Willutzki, 2004.

As you will see throughout this chapter, by examining process questions, and then relating this information to treatment outcome, psychotherapy researchers have learned a great deal about what makes therapy work. By using this research to influence therapeutic practices, clinical psychologists can improve the services they offer clients. In the following pages we describe some of the interesting results obtained in process-outcome research. Our description of the research on **sudden client gains** in treatment in **Viewpoint Box 14.1** is an example of the important discoveries that have been made in process-outcome research.

VIEWPOINT BOX 14.1

SUDDEN GAINS IN THERAPY

After reading the chapters on psychological treatment you may be wondering what the process of therapeutic change looks like. What happens to indicate that the client is improving? Is it a steady progression of small, barely perceptible but important changes that cumulatively result in altered psychosocial functioning? Or is it the case that, as often portrayed in movies, after weeks of non-productive sessions, a client experiences a dramatic breakthrough that results in a qualitatively different view of him- or herself?

This was the question that Tang and DeRubeis (1999) addressed when they undertook a session-by-session review of the treatment progress of depressed patients in two cognitive-behavioural therapy (CBT) efficacy trials. Although they found different patterns of progress across patients, they noticed that more than one-third of patients experienced large reductions in depressive symptoms early in treatment. Closer examination revealed that these patients made sudden large gains in functioning around session 4, 5, or 6. The sudden gains in functioning were very large—they involved at least a 25% reduction in pre-treatment symptom levels—and were made during a single period of time between two sessions. Those who experienced these sudden gains were less depressed than other patients at the end of treatment and they tended to maintain their gains up to 18 months after treatment. Using a different CBT efficacy trial data set, Tang, DeRubeis, Beberman, and Pham (2005) attempted to replicate their original findings. They found clear evidence of the same pattern of sudden gains and they also found evidence that, prior to the sudden gains, substantial cognitive changes occurred among the patients who experienced sudden gains. They hypothesized that these changes in the way in which patients thought about themselves and their life situations were causally related to the observed changes in symptoms. Such an interpretation is certainly consistent with the cognitive theory of change proposed by cognitive therapists (see Chapter 11).

Tang, Luborsky, and Andrusyna (2002) also reported sudden gains in depressed patients in an efficacy trial of short-term psychodynamic treatment. These sudden gains were of similar magnitude to those originally reported by Tang and DeRubeis (1999), and occurred for a similar percentage of patients early in treatment. Although patients with sudden gains were, in comparison with those without sudden gains, significantly better at the end of treatment, the two groups had similar levels of depression six months after treatment ended. Evidence of sudden gains has also come from two British studies using data from routine treatment settings. Hardy et al. (2005) examined the progress of clients receiving cognitive therapy for depression in a National Health Service clinic: 40% of clients experienced changes almost identical to those reported by Tang and DeRubeis (1999). Stiles et al. (2003) examined data from 135 clients with a variety of disorders and problems who were treated with a variety of approaches (including cognitive therapy, psychodynamic therapy, and experiential therapies). Seventeen percent of clients experienced the sudden gains, with half of the clients achieving them by the fifth treatment session. As in other studies, by the end of treatment these clients were significantly improved relative to the clients who did not experience sudden gains. Finally, Vittengl, Clark, and Jarrett (2005) found evidence of sudden treatment gains in two data sets that involved cognitive therapy of major depressive disorder. Sudden gain patterns similar to those reported by Tang and DeRubeis (1999) were found using both patient data and therapist data. What is particularly noteworthy, though, is that Vittengl and colleagues also found evidence of sudden gains in patients who received pill placebos and those who received antidepressant medication.

The repeated independent replication of the sudden gains pattern lends credibility to the validity of the phenomenon. However, the fact that the pattern is evident in different forms of intervention has fuelled speculation that there may be a common, single cause responsible for the pattern, regardless of whether treatment involves psychotherapy, medication, or a placebo. In future studies, researchers will attempt to address the important questions of what is responsible for the sudden gains and whether all sudden gains can be accounted for by the same cause.

Examining Client Factors

As you learned in Chapters 12 and 13, the vast majority of randomized controlled trial (RCT) psychotherapy research examines treatment outcomes for different groups of clients classified on the basis of diagnoses or presenting problems. However, there is far more to people than just their psychological symptoms. No psychotherapy researcher believes that diagnosis is the primary factor that determines treatment outcome. Client characteristics other than diagnosis may be very important predictors of treatment success or failure. Consequently, a large literature has examined the influence of client variables on psychotherapy. Much of this research comes from studies of treatments provided in real world clinic settings, but a growing number of studies are derived from RCTs in which investigators have sought to identify mediators and moderators of treatment efficacy.

The first challenge in examining client variables is determining which variables to evaluate. Which client characteristics should be taken into account? Among the myriad potential variables are personality characteristics, current life circumstances, life experiences, family of origin characteristics, ethnicity and cultural factors, beliefs about psychological problems, and expectations regarding treatment. Efforts to synthesize results of the voluminous research on client factors in therapy are hampered by the non-systematic nature of the studies. In other words, different researchers have often examined a variable, such as clients' treatment expectations, in different ways across studies. It is extremely difficult to detect patterns across studies that used different types of measures (e.g., completion of a self-report measure versus coding of statements made during a therapy session) and different timing of the assessment (e.g., prior to commencing treatment or after one session of therapy). The consequence of this variability, as succinctly summarized by Petry, Tennen, and Affleck (2000), is that after thousands of empirical studies we have only a rudimentary appreciation of how client variables affect treatment responses. **Table 14.2** provides a summary of the most consistent findings in the empirical literature.

Although the list in Table 14.2 is short, it provides clear guidance to therapists. Let's take the example of socio-economic status. Knowing that a client with a lower socio-economic status is at heightened risk for premature termination, psychologists can take steps early in treatment to enhance the likelihood that the client will engage in treatment. So, in providing services to Shari, a single mother of two young children who has a part-time job with irregular working hours, the psychologist could explicitly discuss options to help Shari fit therapy appointments into her schedule. Rather than a regular appointment during standard office hours, the psychologist could offer appointments that do not require Shari to take time off work or to make arrangements for extra childcare. Furthermore, many psychologists in private practice have sliding fee scales that allow patients with lower incomes (and limited private insurance coverage) to pay reduced fees. By enhancing access to affordable services, the psychologist may make the difference between Shari engaging in therapy and prematurely ending services.

Awareness of a client's life circumstances may help the psychologist to respond sensitively early in treatment, reducing the likelihood of early dropout.

TABLE 14.2   Client Variables that Influence Treatment

Sociodemographic Characteristics

Socio-economic Status
- evidence that higher socio-economic status is associated with a greater likelihood of engaging in and staying in treatment

Ethnicity
- some evidence that similarity in client and therapist ethnicity is associated with a greater likelihood of clients staying in treatment and of making therapeutic change

Gender
- evidence that women are more likely to seek therapy than are men, but there is no gender difference in premature termination of services
- matching of client and therapist gender seems to have little influence on treatment outcome or treatment satisfaction

Age
- evidence indicates client age is unrelated to treatment outcome

Psychological Functioning

Symptom Severity
- consistent evidence that the severity of psychological symptoms is related to poorer treatment outcome

Functional Impairment
- consistent evidence that greater overall impairment in functioning (i.e., in various social roles and health status) is related to poorer treatment outcome

Personality Characteristics

Personality Disorders
- evidence that the presence of an Axis II diagnosis is associated with premature termination, problems in the process of therapy, and less therapeutic change during treatment

Ego Strength
- ego strength (broadly defined as the capacity to use personality resources to manage negative emotional states and threats to personal identity) is consistently related to positive treatment outcome

Psychological Mindedness
- psychological mindedness (broadly defined as the ability to understand people and problems in psychological terms) is usually found to be related to positive treatment outcome

Psychological Reactance
- psychological reactance (broadly defined as the tendency to react against attempts to directly influence one's behaviour) has been found to be a treatment moderator, in that clients low in reactance tend to experience greater therapeutic gains in more directive treatments whereas clients high in reactance tend to experience greater therapeutic gains in less directive treatments

Treatment Expectations
- positive expectations for treatment are associated with remaining in treatment and greater therapeutic gains

Adapted from Clarkin & Levy (2004) and Petry, Tennen, & Affleck (2000).

It is important to keep in mind that pre-existing client variables, such as current life context, life experiences, and personality may have their greatest impact on client decisions about seeking and engaging in therapy. Once treatment starts, the dynamic interplay between client and ther-apist is likely to generate a far more powerful influence on the course and outcome of treatment (cf. Clarkin & Levy, 2004). The ultimate outcome of treatment is affected by the way the client feels about the therapist, therapist response to client questions and challenges, the degree of benefit the client expe-riences early in treatment, and the extent to which treatment influences the client's daily life. In a large scale study of the treatment of depression, for example, patients who initially expected treat-ment to be effective remained in therapy and engaged actively and constructively in therapy sessions, which resulted in reductions in their symptoms (Elkin et al., 1999; Meyer et al., 2002).

Examining Therapist Factors

Just as researchers have explored the impact of *client* variables on treatment processes and out-come, so too have they addressed the ways in which *therapist* characteristics affect aspects of psychotherapy. This research has yielded subtle and nuanced findings about the impact of the psychotherapist on the patient's response to treatment. As mentioned previously with respect to client variables, this is partly because of the manner in which interactions between patient and therapist occur and evolve over the course of treatment as well as the power such interactions exert on the process of therapeutic change. **Table 14.3** summarizes the main findings on the con-tribution of therapist factors to psychotherapy process and outcome.

The research described in Table 14.3, like that summarized for client variables in Table 14.2, is based on an examination of the individual contribution of specific therapist variables on the therapeutic process. However, many therapist variables may interact in therapy. It seems intuitive-ly obvious that the "sum" of the therapist's personal qualities should be an important ingredient in any recipe for good therapy. After all, there must be considerable knowledge, technical skills, interpersonal sensitivity, and tolerance for distress that go into the making of a good psychother-apist. For example, Lafferty, Beutler, and Crago (1989) studied trainee therapists working in an outpatient clinic, including trainees in clinical psychology, psychiatry, clinical social work, and psychiatric nursing. Based on the treatment results for two randomly selected clients for each trainee, 30 therapists were categorized as less effective (i.e., neither patient improved) or as more effective (i.e., both patients improved). Data from patients and therapists were used to examine differences in the therapists between these two groups. Although there were only small differences between the less effective and more effective groups of therapists in terms of emotional adjustment of or general life values, analyses revealed an important group difference in what transpired dur-ing treatment. Specifically, patients of the more effective therapists reported feeling more understood in treatment than did the patients of the less effective therapists.

TABLE 14.3   Therapist Variables that Influence Treatment

Sociodemographic Characteristics

Ethnicity
- there is virtually no research examining the main effect of therapist ethnicity or cultural background on treatment outcome

Gender
- therapist gender has no consistent effect on treatment outcome

Age
- therapist age is unrelated to treatment outcome
- similarity in age between client and therapist does not contribute significantly to treatment outcome

Professional Background

Professional Discipline
- therapists trained in mental health discipline tend to have better treatment outcomes than those trained in health discipline (i.e., general practitioners)
- research is inconclusive regarding the relative effectiveness of therapists trained in different mental health disciplines (i.e., clinical psychologists, psychiatrists, social workers, marriage and family counsellors)

Professional Experience
- although the variability in the evidence is considerable, overall the research indicates that therapist experience (measured in years or number of clients treated) is positively related to treatment outcome

Personality Characteristics

Personality Traits
- therapist personality traits have little association with treatment outcome

Emotional Well-Being
- therapist emotional well-being is consistently positively associated with treatment outcome

Values, Attitudes, and Beliefs
- no consistent pattern of results is available regarding the influence of therapists' values, attitudes, and beliefs on the process and outcome of therapy

Use of Self-Disclosure
- self-disclosure (broadly defined as the therapist's judicious sharing of personal experiences or views in the process of therapy) has been found to be a small but positive effect on treatment outcome

Adapted from Beutler et al. (2004) and Teyber & McClure (2000).

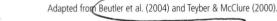

But what do we know about overall differences in therapeutic effectiveness among fully qualified and practising therapists? An early study by Orlinsky and Howard (1980) examined 23 practising therapists, 6 of whom had high success rates with patients (defined as > 70% of patients improved) and 5 had lower success rates (defined as < 50% of patients improved). Moreover, in examining the various components responsible for patient change in RCTs, Lyon and Howard (1991) found that the effects on patient outcome due to specific therapists are typically greater than the effects due to specific treatments. Even though systematic training based on explicit treatment manuals improves the overall effectiveness of therapists, it does not eliminate important variability among specific therapists (Teyber & McClure, 2000).

Unfortunately, we know very little about what consistently differentiates more and less effective therapists or what sets the exceptional therapist apart from his or her colleagues. In the Orlinsky and Howard (1980) study, few variables distinguished the two groups. Similarly, in a large scale study of treatment for alcohol problems (more than 1,700 patients), 4 out of 54 therapists accounted for most of the poorest treatment outcomes (Project MATCH Research Group, 1998). The researchers were unable, however, to identify characteristics that discriminated these 4 therapists from the others. As there is evidence of important variability in therapist impact, even in RCTs, psychotherapy researchers are concerned to examine therapist characteristics and behaviours that may be responsible for variability in patient outcome.

Examining Treatment Factors

In previous chapters we described some of the characteristics of the current main approaches to psychotherapy and presented evidence for their efficacy and effectiveness in treating specific conditions. Researchers have examined, both within specific treatment orientations and across orientations, whether some aspects of therapy are especially important in achieving therapeutic change. Is it important for therapists to explicitly interpret clients' behaviour? Is it better to focus on symptom reduction or on achieving insight? Does the use of between-session assignments make any difference in treatment? Process-outcome researchers have investigated these questions and many others. In this section, drawing on the comprehensive review by Beutler et al. (2004), we consider some of the main findings from this line of inquiry.

INTERPRETATION

Interpretation of client behaviour often occurs in psychodynamic and experiential approaches to therapy. This can include explanations for the client's problems as well as the labelling of unconscious processes that are believed to influence thoughts, emotions, and behaviours. In their review of the research on interpretations, Beutler and colleagues found no consistent pattern of results across studies. Although the weighted average effect size was a nonsignificant $r = .07$, there were a number of studies in which interpretations were strongly correlated with positive outcome. In general, these studies suggested that therapist interpretations were most successful with clients who had good interpersonal skills. You can well imagine the mixed reactions people would have to frequent comments on the reasons for their behaviours and emotions. A high degree of interpersonal competence would probably be important in helping the client to openly discuss such affectively charged therapist comments.

DIRECTIVENESS

How directive should the therapist be? Is it better to have an active, guiding therapist or is a neutral, reflective stance more conducive to positive outcomes? Based on their review, Beutler et al. (2004) reported a weighted average effect size of $r = .06$, which was statistically nonsignificant. However, the range of effect sizes across studies varied enormously, from -.17 to .79. With such wide variation, it is obvious that calculating the mean across studies is likely to obscure some important information. In all likelihood, in this instance, there are moderating variables that influence the extent to which therapist directiveness is appropriate. When we consider the evidence summarized in Table 14.2, it seems likely that the optimal degree of therapist directiveness is determined, at least in part, by the client's level of psychological reactance. Psychological **reactance** is the tendency to react against attempts to directly influence one's behaviour. Low reactant clients usually experience greater therapeutic gains in more directive treatments, whereas clients high in reactance tend to experience greater therapeutic gains in less directive treatments.

Across all treatment approaches it is possible for therapists to flexibly adjust their interactional style in order to differentially emphasize the provision of direct guidance versus client self-exploration and self-directedness. So what would this actually mean for psychologists in providing services? Let's consider the initial appointment for Florio, a middle-aged man referred because of recent panic attacks. When the clinic receptionist called to make the appointment with Florio, he insisted on talking to the psychologist directly. When the psychologist later phoned him back, Florio proceeded to ask a series of questions about the psychologist's training, her experience with treating people with problems similar to his, and whether she could guarantee that the treatment would help. During the first session, the psychologist's attempts to structure the interview and to gather information about his anxiety and panic and his family history were met with frequent comments such as "Just let me tell you my story in my own time," "Not so fast, I don't think I want to answer that question," and "So why do you want to know that?" Whenever the psychologist made an empathic statement about how Florio seemed to be feeling, he rebuffed her with statements such as "Not at all" and "You're off the mark there, doc." Halfway through the session, the psychologist concluded that her usual approach to gathering information was simply not going to work with Florio. She told Florio that, in order to try to help him with his panic attacks, she needed precise information about what was going on in his life that seemed to be related to the panic. She said that, although she normally asked a series of questions to help gather this information, as he was a "take charge" kind of person she was willing to be guided by Florio in how she gathered this information. She invited Florio to tell her what he thought was important and stated that she would only ask an occasional question if she needed something clarified. At this point Florio laughed and said "Well, you've got my number doc. I just don't like being bossed around and told what to do. But don't worry—I don't bite, just ask whatever you want when you want. Don't push too hard though." The interview then proceeded more smoothly, with the psychologist gathering less information than was usual in a first session, but with Florio making a commitment to come to a second assessment session.

A psychologist's level of directiveness should be influenced by the client's level of psychological reactance.

INSIGHT VERSUS SYMPTOM REDUCTION

For the relative merits of treatments focused on achieving patient insight or patient symptom reduction, Beutler et al. (2004) reported overall effect sizes of zero in this literature. However, patient coping style may be an important moderator of the relation between the focus of treatment and treatment outcome. By and large, focusing on enhancing patient self-awareness and understanding of their problems works best for patients who are introspective or introverted. In contrast, patients who are impulsive and undercontrolled respond best to a focus on symptom alleviation. As with the degree of therapist directiveness, regardless of orientation, it is possible for therapists to adjust the focus of treatment to best match these patient characteristics.

BETWEEN-SESSION ASSIGNMENTS

Between-session assignments (also known as homework assignments) are a central component of cognitive-behavioural treatments and are used by many clinical psychologists regardless of orientation (APA, 2003). But does it really matter whether a therapist assigns homework in order to consolidate something addressed in the session and does it matter whether the clients actually do the homework? The answer to both these questions is "yes." In a meta-analysis of 27 CBT studies, Kazantzis, Deane, and Ronan (2000) reported an effect size of $r = .36$ for the association between the use of homework assignments and positive treatment outcomes and an effect size of $r = .22$ for the association between the degree of patient completion of assignments and positive treatment outcomes. Furthermore, Burns and Spangler (2000) found a large causal impact of homework completion on reductions in symptoms in the treatment of depression.

Some Methodological Cautions Regarding Process-Outcome Research

Jones and Pulos (1993) reported some intriguing results from their analysis of the therapeutic process in psychodynamic and cognitive-behavioural treatments. Based on expert judges' ratings of therapy transcripts from treatment studies using these two forms of therapy, the researchers developed a list of descriptors that characterized each treatment. So, for example, descriptors of psychodynamic techniques included "Therapist is neutral," "Therapist points out patient's use of defensive manoeuvres," "Therapist interprets warded-off or unconscious wishes, feelings, or ideas," and "Memories or reconstructions of infancy and childhood are topics of discussion." Some of the descriptors of cognitive-behavioural techniques were "Therapist explains rationale behind his/her technique or approach to treatment," "Therapist acts to strengthen defences," "Therapist self-discloses," and "Therapist gives explicit advice and guidance." So far this should seem consistent with our descriptions of these treatment approaches in Chapter 11. The incongruence arose when the researchers correlated the ratings of these techniques with patient outcome. Generally speaking, the treatments were successful in treating the majority of patients. In the cognitive-behavioural treatment, the use of cognitive-behavioural techniques was not significantly associated with any of the five patient outcome measures, but the use of psychodynamic techniques (by the cognitive-behavioural therapists) was significantly correlated with patient change on four of the five measures. In the psychodynamic treatment, the use of psychodynamic techniques was significantly correlated with change on only one of four measures, and similarly, use of CBT techniques (by the psychodynamic therapists) was correlated with one of four patient outcomes.

How can this be? How is it possible that the use of psychodynamic techniques—but not cognitive-behavioural techniques—by cognitive-behavioural therapists is related to patient improvement? How is it possible that the use of psychodynamic techniques (or CBT techniques either, for that matter) in psychodynamic treatment was unrelated to patient improvement? Although Jones and Pulos (1993) offered some intriguing theoretical explanations for their findings, we think that the answers can be found elsewhere. A careful reading of the study reveals two methodological issues that may explain the rather strange pattern of results.

First, researchers rated transcripts from the 1st, 5th, and 14th therapy sessions. Like any other relationship, the therapy relationship evolves over time. Just as you would expect different behaviours on a first date compared with a date in an established relationship, what transpires during the first therapy session is likely to be very different from what occurs at the 5th or 14th. By combining information about what therapists and patients do when starting treatment with information about what they do part-way through, and when they have almost completed treatment, the researchers are likely to end up with a hodgepodge of therapist and client behaviours that are not at all representative of what occurs during most of the treatment process.

A second questionable assumption made in this research is that the more therapists or clients engage in a specific strategy, the better it is for client outcome. By correlating the use of specific techniques with client outcome, that is essentially what the researchers assumed. Is this a valid assumption about therapy? Returning to the date analogy, although you may appreciate your date self-disclosing on some topics, you would probably not respond positively to a person who spent the entire evening providing a revealing account of himself or herself. Likewise, in the realm of psychotherapy, it is relevant to ask whether more therapist self-disclosure in cognitive-behavioural treatment is always better than less. Similarly, is more therapist neutrality in psychodynamic treatment always better than less? As a final example, it might be a good thing for a psychodynamic therapist to frequently point out a patient's use of defence mechanisms in the 5th session of therapy, but if the therapist still needs to do this in one of the final sessions this may actually be an indication that treatment is *not* going well.

Unfortunately these methodological problems are relatively common in the process-outcome treatment literature. As pointed out by Stiles (1988) and Stiles and Shapiro (1989), it is inappropriate to assume that a significant correlation necessarily means that a process component (such as a cognitive-behavioural therapist explaining the rationale for the treatment) is crucial in achieving the desired outcome (as you know, it is also not appropriate to assume causation on the basis of correlation). Likewise, they argued that a nonsignificant correlation does not necessarily mean that the process component is irrelevant to successful outcome. Clinical skill involves adapting the frequency and strength of certain techniques to match the patient's individual needs. Jones and Pulos (1993) found that explaining the rationale for an intervention was characteristic of CBT—but if the patient clearly understands the rationale, why would frequent (and unnecessary) explanations of the rationale be expected to correlate positively and significantly with patient outcome? Presumably repeated explanations would only be necessary if there were consistent indications that the patient had not fully grasped the nature of the treatment.

Keijsers, Schaap, Hoogduin, and Lammers' (1995) study is a good illustration of how these pitfalls can be avoided in attempts to uncover what transpires in psychotherapy. The researchers were interested in better understanding the nature of patient-therapist interactions in the 12-session behavioural treatment of panic disorder with agoraphobia. Rather than obtaining data by collapsing across therapy sessions, these researchers developed hypotheses that were tested separately with data from the 1st, 3rd, and 10th sessions. For example, compared with the frequency of empathic therapist statements and requests for information in the initial session, the frequency of these statements and requests were hypothesized to decline over the course of treatment. This hypothesis reflects sensitivity to the changing context of therapy: early in treatment the focus is on establishing rapport and conducting an assessment and, as treatment progresses, there should be less of a need to spend as much time in sessions on these activities. The researchers found the results of their data analyses were consistent with these hypotheses. In session 1, 16% of all therapist statements were expressions of empathy; this declined significantly to 10% in session 3 and 11% in session 10. Likewise, in the first session 37% of the therapist's comments involved exploration of the client's problem; by sessions 3 and 10 such statements had declined significantly (to 28% and 29%, respectively).

It is always important to carefully read the methods and results sections of research articles. The information contained in these sections is crucial for a complete understanding of the nature of the data and analyses used in the study. Because the results of treatment research (whether process-outcome research or treatment outcome research) can have a significant impact on the provision of clinical services, it is essential that consumers of the scientific literature exercise critical and informed judgements in evaluating the relevance and applicability of this research.

COMMON FACTORS IN PSYCHOTHERAPY

Despite clear differences in guiding theory and preferred intervention techniques among the major approaches to psychotherapy, many clinical psychologists maintain that the effectiveness of all approaches stems from a common set of therapeutic factors. Rosenzweig (1936) is credited with being the first to identify a common set of therapeutic factors. He presented two broad propositions about psychotherapy: first, all therapies share common therapeutic elements that are responsible for client improvement (in particular, the therapeutic relationship and an explanation for the existence of the client's problems) and, second, because all therapies rely on these common factors to bring about change, all therapies should be equivalent in outcome. In considering Rosenzweig's assertion, it is important to note that treatments at that time were all variations on psychoanalytic treatment and that Rosenzweig provided no evidence supporting his claim. Nevertheless, both of these claims have greatly influenced subsequent psychotherapy researchers. We examine the common factors proposition first and consider the equivalency proposition in a later section.

For much of the middle of the last century, the common factors proposition lay dormant and, as described in Chapter 1, there was a proliferation of new theoretical approaches to treatment. In the 1970s Jerome Frank revisited the common factors perspective. Drawing on such diverse sources of data as studies of psychiatric practices, the placebo effect, and anthropological reports of the practices of shamans (or "witch doctors"), Frank developed an intriguing and compelling model to explain all treatment effects (Frank, 1973, 1982). His model begins with a demoralized individual who is distressed and unable to resolve his or her problems. The individual seeks help from a socially sanctioned healer, who provides the healing services that, if successful, result in the restoration of the individual's morale. This occurs by virtue of the healer working in a recognized healing setting, providing a rationale for the person's difficulties, instilling hope that improvement is possible, and using a set of healing rituals to resolve the problems. Frank argued that this model applies to all health care treatments, irrespective of differences in healers (psychologists, mystics), settings (hospitals, religious shrines), or rituals (free association while reclining on a couch, doing between-session assignments, or sacrificing animals to appease angry spirits).

Inspired by Frank's model, psychologists began to develop generic models of psychotherapy that cut across theoretical orientations, to develop lists of possible common factors shared by psychotherapies, and to search for evidence of the influence of these factors. By the 1990s, the common factors perspective had become so

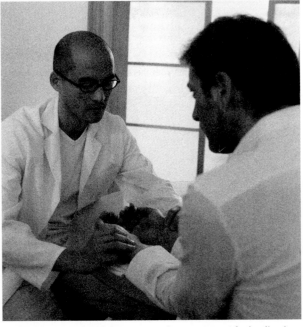

Jerome Frank proposed that common factors account for healing in diverse health care treatments, irrespective of differences in healers, settings, or rituals.

popular that Weinberger (1995) identified an interesting dilemma: few proponents of the common factors explanation for psychotherapeutic changes agreed on what actually constituted the set of hypothesized common factors. Or, as Weinberger wryly noted in the title of his literature review, "common factors aren't so common." In attempting to bring order to the common factors perspective, Weinberger emphasized the importance of the therapeutic relationship, client expectations, confronting problems in therapy, the client's development of a sense of mastery, and the client's attributions for the treatment outcome. Taking a different approach, Lambert and Ogles (2004) used three main dimensions of common factors (support factors, learning factors, and action factors) to categorize the most commonly suggested common factors. Their framework is presented in **Table 14.4**.

The intuitive appeal of the common factors approach and its potential to harness the power of psychotherapy led to the promotion of models described as **integrative treatment models**. These models borrow theories and techniques from the major therapeutic approaches to optimize the influence of the common factors regardless of the nature of the patient's problems or characteristics (e.g., Hubble, Duncan, & Miller, 1999; Lampropoulos, 2000). There is little doubt that many of the common factors are found in a variety of treatments, but how do we know that they are the *main* elements of treatment responsible for client improvement? The diversity evident among the list of common factors and the inconsistencies in operationalizing the factors have resulted in little cumulative

TABLE 14.4   Common Factors in Psychotherapy

Support Factors	Learning Factors	Action Factors
Catharsis	Advice	Behavioural regulation
Identification with therapist	Affective experiencing	Cognitive mastery
Mitigation of isolation	Assimilating problematic	Encouragement of facing fears
Positive relationship	experiences	Taking risks
Reassurance	Cognitive learning	Mastery efforts
Release of tension	Corrective emotional experience	Modelling
Structure	Feedback	Practice
Therapeutic alliance	Insight	Reality testing
Therapist/client active participation	Rationale	Success experience
Therapist expertness	Exploration of internal frame of	Working through
Therapist warmth, respect,	reference	
empathy, acceptance,	Changing expectations of	
genuineness	personal effectiveness	
Trust		

Lambert & Ogles (2004).
Reproduced with permission.

research addressing the importance of these common factors in achieving treatment outcome. There is one notable exception to this state of affairs, a *common* common factor that has received extensive attention from researchers—the **therapeutic alliance**—and it is to this research that we now turn.

Research Perspectives on Common Factors: The Therapeutic Alliance

The therapeutic alliance refers to the quality and strength of the collaborative relationship between client and therapist (Horvath & Bedi, 2002). It includes positive affective bonds (e.g., mutual trust, liking, respect, and caring), consensus about and commitment to the goals of therapy, and a shared sense of partnership in the therapeutic process. Although originally developed within psychodynamic approaches, the construct of therapeutic alliance applies to all approaches to psychotherapy. A series of meta-analyses on the relation between therapeutic alliance, typically measured in the first few sessions of treatment, and treatment outcome have all found the alliance to be a consistent predictor of the impact of treatment. This holds for treatments for adults (e.g., Beutler et al., 2004; Horvath & Bedi, 2002; Martin, Garske, & Davis, 2000) and for youths (Shirk & Karver, 2003). There are numerous measures of the therapeutic alliance, many of which are not highly intercorrelated. The alliance can be assessed from the perspective of the patient, the therapist, and an observer rating videotaped sessions. However, despite these disparities in measurement, all meta-analyses yield essentially the same general effect size, typically close to a weighted r of .20.

PROFILE BOX 14.1

DR. ADAM HORVATH

Dr. Adam Horvath

I was born in Hungary. In the fall of 1956 there was a popular uprising against the Soviet-dominated Hungarian puppet regime; I perceived this development as an exceptional opportunity to skip school for a few days, so I joined the revolution. The politicians who took over after the revolution failed had a poor sense of humour and invited the high school truant and would-be revolutionary to discuss his recent activities in court. I declined the invitation, escaped to Canada, and settled in Montreal. After starting university as a pre-engineering student in 1959 I finished as a Sociology/Psychology major in 1964. In 1967 I received an MSW from McGill and worked as a therapist in Quebec until 1969 when the winds of revolution caught up with me there. One direct experience with violent social movements was sufficient for me, so I moved to Vancouver where I continued to work in the mental health field. I earned a doctorate from the University of British Columbia in 1981 and joined the faculty of Simon Fraser University counselling psychology program in 1985. I am licensed as a psychologist by the College of Psychologists of British Columbia. I divide my professional time among teaching, supervision, research, and clinical practice. I am the past president of the North American Society for Psychotherapy Research.

What made you choose to become a clinical psychologist?

Curiosity has been a character trait of mine since early childhood. I recall wanting to understand how things worked and what caused things to happen. The dominant themes of my adolescence were sputniks and space exploration, thus the quest for understanding translated to interest in science. However, as a recent immigrant in Canada I needed to be practical, study something that would lead to a secure job. Engineering was a logical choice. I started to reconsider my goals as a result of my first assignment in Psy100. The professor wrote comments nearly as long as my essay, on the margin, across the top, even on the back of some of the pages. The professor took issue with my ideas, challenged my assumptions, and questioned my arguments. I headed back to the library, wrote a "rebuttal" that I knew better than to hand in, and took my seat at the front of the class. Though in retrospect it is evident to me that my interest in people—how they think, act, and feel—long pre-dated this particular event, until this class I did not think of the study of human behaviour as something that could be rigorously examined or explained. I had a long investment in seeing myself in the role of an engineer and it was not until I had encountered another inspiring psychology professor in the next semester that I made an appointment with the career counsellor. In retrospect the key ingredients in my decision seem to be a combination of two main factors: I have found the topics that will never cease to feed and challenge my curiosity of "how things work," and a good fortune to meet an excellent role model who demonstrated the possibility of combining science with a passion for humans.

What is the most rewarding part of your job as a clinical psychologist?

I have the exceptional good fortune that my position at the university provides me with an opportunity to combine teaching, research, and clinical practice. The most exciting and rewarding aspect of this multi-faceted job is the synergy between these different aspects of my professional life. I have also chosen to devote some of my energies to a professional organization, the Society for Psychotherapy Research, an international group that brings together from all over the world psychologists, psychiatrists, and other scientists interested in psychotherapy-related research. We meet annually to exchange ideas and discuss the latest findings from our research projects. I find interacting with colleagues from different backgrounds, cultures, and research traditions exciting and intellectually invigorating.

What do you see as the most important elements in successful psychotherapy?

Therapy is a complex process with diverse variables playing significant roles depending on the kind of problem, client, and the helping context. There are interpersonal elements that, in my view, play a necessary role in the helping process: (a) we need to make connections with our clients at a personal level, (b) we have to engage our clients in visioning a meaningful goal that therapist and client will strive for in a collaborative fashion, and (c) we need to reach agreement on a mutually meaningful set of therapeutic tasks. It is, I believe, very important to remember that the therapist's work needs to represent a logical and cohesive sequence of interventions based on credible evidence of efficacy. The psychologist has to have a thorough understanding of the theory the intervention is based on, feel comfortable with the demands of the method, and be mindful of engaging the client only in work that will likely yield results within the limits of the treatment parameters. Finally, one of the hardest challenges for a therapist is to make a sound and careful judgement when and how treatment should be ended or suspended. As helpers, our task is to leave the client with greater sense of efficacy and confidence of being better able to manage life's challenges.

How do you integrate science and practice in your work?

The questions that drive my research have to do with the way persons relate to one another as they combine their resources to accomplish difficult tasks. These questions arose from my work as a therapist with clients: how do I contribute to their change processes? As I began to research different aspects of the therapist-client relationship, my practice began to reflect what I had learned from research and in turn new, more focused questions arose that inspired my subsequent research process.

What is the greatest challenge facing clinical psychology?

The most obvious one is the urgent need to provide quality service to our clients in a climate of diminishing resources. Psychologists, along with other health care providers, will have to do a better job in documenting the results of their intervention and finding ways to deliver care more efficiently. As part of adjusting to the changing landscape of the health care system, we will need to increase our efforts to work collaboratively with the medical community and to think of our services as part of a complex and integrated professional team. I think we will also need to better address the issue of serving a multicultural population. The great majority of our theories, assessments, and practices rest on Euro/American cultural values. To provide service to the growing number of clients who were raised in communities with diverse traditions, we need to reach beyond the concept of cultural sensitivity and develop methods of assessments and interventions that are compatible with the values and beliefs of diverse cultures. Although I do not believe that to provide effective psychological service, client and helper need to have an identical cultural background, the profession needs to engage in an internal dialogue about this issue. Such dialogue needs the voices that represent a true cross-section of the population, with a particular emphasis on the voices of the First Nations who are underrepresented in our ranks.

What do you see as the most exciting changes in the profession of clinical psychology?

I believe it is the opportunity for us to contribute to the emerging concept of community-based comprehensive health care, in which we can participate in the area of prevention, lifestyle education, wellness services, and community planning, to name a few. Another important new challenge is to bridge the gap between ongoing discoveries in neurology, psychopharmacology, and clinical psychology. A further important area of growth and challenge is the development of family and community-based treatments, both as an alternative and as a complement to the more traditional individual therapies. Clinical psychology will increase its contributions to health management on an ever-broadening front linking physical and psychological aspects of health and performance, possibly becoming an important link between the fields of health education, medicine, and social policy.

One of the problems in interpreting the research on the alliance-outcome link is the importance of not inferring causation from correlation. Although it seems obvious that a good alliance is necessary for a good outcome, methodological factors may temper this conclusion. First, a poor alliance can lead to the premature termination of treatment by clients. So, because clients with good alliances are more likely to complete therapy, researchers have a greater chance of obtaining data on treatment effects in clients reporting a strong alliance. In other words, the detrimental effect of a poor therapeutic alliance may be stronger than the treatment benefits derived from a good therapeutic alliance. Second, as alliance is typically assessed after initial treatment sessions, it is possible that early client improvement may confound the relation between alliance and treatment outcome. Studies designed to test this possibility have found that early alliance significantly predicts outcome even after statistically controlling for the effects of early improvement (e.g., Barber, Connolly, Crits-Christoph, Gladis, & Siqueland, 2000).

Before leaving this section on the therapeutic alliance, there is a final point to consider. The research on the alliance-outcome link appears compelling, which lends credence to claims about the power of common factors in therapy. But think back to Chapter 11, in which we described alternatives to traditionally delivered psychotherapy such as telehealth, self-administered, and computer-administered treatments. As we indicated in that chapter, there is growing evidence that these forms of psychological intervention, when grounded in evidence-based therapist-administered treatments, can be very helpful treatments for many people. One could make the case that a therapeutic alliance can be established with a health service provider who is hundreds of kilometres away and who is known to the patient only by video link or a voice on the telephone line. But what about the user of a self-help manual or a computer therapy program—can there be a form of therapeutic alliance with the materials or the "invisible" developer of the materials? Such a proposition would seem to stretch the definition of therapeutic alliance (i.e., affective bond, consensus on goals, partnership) so much as to render it meaningless. Accordingly, it is important to be mindful that a good therapeutic alliance, this most common of all common factors, is not actually always necessary for psychological treatment to be successful.

Lewis Carroll's Dodo bird.

Research Perspectives on Common Factors: Psychotherapy Equivalence

As mentioned previously in the chapter, Rosenzweig (1936) proposed that, because all psychotherapies are based on common curative factors, they must be equivalent in their effects. He referred to this hypothesized equivalence of psychotherapies as the **Dodo bird verdict**.

This is an allusion to Lewis Carroll's *Alice in Wonderland* in which an argument about who had won a race was resolved by the Dodo bird, who announced: "*Everybody* has won, and *all* must have prizes." Lewis Carroll's Dodo bird verdict was a satirical jab at political committees, as it described the outcome of a caucus race in which competitors started at different points and ran in different directions for half an hour.

Like the common factors perspective itself, the concept of psychotherapy equivalence received little attention during the decades in which many forms of psychotherapy were being developed. However, the Dodo bird verdict was revitalized by Luborsky, Singer, and Luborsky's (1975) review of treatment research in which they concluded there was no substantial evidence of differential treatment effects. In subsequent literature reviews, **Lester Luborsky** and colleagues (Luborsky et al., 1993; Luborsky et al., 1999; Luborsky et al., 2002) reiterated this position and concluded there was overwhelming evidence that all therapies were equal and that psychotherapies did not have distinct, specific effects. As efforts to establish empirically supported treatments began, some psychologists argued that psychotherapy itself is empirically supported (e.g., Elliott, 1998) and that, for effective treatment, all that is needed is a therapeutic alliance and efforts to mobilize the client's capacity to resolve problems and distress (Bohart, O'Hara, & Leitner, 1998).

To properly consider the evidence on the impact of different psychotherapies, it is important to impose some rules. Otherwise, like Carroll's caucus race, it is comparable to having competitors in a race start at different points and run in different directions. The first rule in evaluating the accuracy of the Dodo bird verdict is that empirical evidence must be considered. Rosenzweig's claim of general therapy equivalence was based solely on the hypothesis that all curative effects in therapy are due to common factors. By applying this first rule to current forms of psychotherapy, it is easy to see that this broad claim of equivalence (i.e., that any treatment provided by a psychotherapist, regardless of the nature of the client's problem or life context, is likely to be as effective as any other possible treatment) is simply untenable because not all forms of psychotherapy have been empirically evaluated. The second rule deals with the type of evidence that can be considered in evaluating the impact of different psychotherapies. In this regard, both treatment outcome studies and comparative treatment studies are relevant. Treatment outcome studies are experiments in which the impact of a treatment is compared with a control condition in which no services are provided (typically a wait-list control group). In contrast, comparative treatment studies are experiments in which the differential impact of at least two treatments are compared, and a no-treatment control group may or may not be included. Of course, if there was evidence for psychotherapy equivalence from these types of studies it would mean that only the psychotherapies that were evaluated in the studies could be assumed to be equivalent, as the subset of therapies that have been evaluated are by no means a representative sample of those therapies offered by clinicians (Kazdin, 1995).

As described at several earlier points in the book, to accurately consider the huge amount of treatment research we must use meta-analyses. In Chapter 12, we described the general findings from the important Smith, Glass, and Miller (1980) meta-analysis. As we indicated, Smith et al. calculated the efficacy of various types of treatment based on treatment outcome studies and reported that cognitive and cognitive-behavioural treatments had the largest effect sizes (d values of 1.31 and 1.24, respectively), followed by behavioural (.91), psychodynamic (.78), and humanistic treatments (.63), and, finally, developmental treatments (including vocational-personal development counselling and "undifferentiated counselling" (.42). This evidence certainly suggests that treatments are not equivalent.

Proponents of the psychotherapy equivalence perspective point to the importance of other analyses conducted by Smith et al., specifically comparisons of therapy "classes" in which behavioural ($d = .98$) and verbal ($d = .85$) treatments were found to produce comparable effects. In their categorization system, Smith et al. included cognitive-behavioural, behaviour modification, systematic desensitization, and other behavioural treatments in the behavioural class; they included psychodynamic, humanistic, and cognitive treatments in the verbal class. As the researchers themselves noted, this categorization scheme was arbitrary but, they argued, defensible (e.g., all behavioural treatments focused primarily on attaining behavioural change). Given our description of the various orientations in Chapter 11 and the fact that cognitive therapies routinely include behavioural elements, it is extremely difficult to justify not including cognitive treatments with behavioural treatments. In other words, the apparently compelling evidence for equivalence of therapy classes in the Smith et al. meta-analysis is undermined by the reliance questionable classification of the classes of treatment.

Smith et al. also conducted analyses on data from 56 comparative outcome studies of the behavioural and verbal classes of treatment. Even with the classification error, there were significant differences between the two classes of therapy ($d = .96$ for behavioural treatments and $d = .77$ for verbal treatments). However, when the researchers then adjusted results for something they called *measurement tractability* (measures of anxiety, self-esteem, and global adjustment were rated as more tractable than were such measures as somatic complaints and life adjustment), the group differences disappeared. The basis for this statistical adjustment is hard to determine, as the researchers did not use this in any of the hundreds of other analyses they reported.

Although frequently cited as evidence in support of the Dodo bird verdict, the influential meta-analysis published by Smith et al. yielded numerous results that do not support a verdict of psychotherapy equivalence. Whether examined by therapy subclasses (i.e., cognitive, cognitive-behavioural, behavioural, psychodynamic, humanistic, and developmental) or by client conditions within therapy subclasses, clear differences among treatment effects were evident. Only by first (mis)classifying the cognitive therapies with psychodynamic and humanistic therapies (rather than with behavioural therapies) and then statistically adjusting for supposed measurement problems did some of their results suggest equivalence across forms of psychotherapy (Hunsley & Di Giulio, 2002).

The results of other meta-analyses are relevant to an examination of the possibility of psychotherapy equivalence. As we described in Chapter 13, meta-analyses examining treatment effects in the child and adolescent treatment literature have found clear orientation differences, with behavioural treatments being more effective than other treatments (e.g., Weiss & Weisz, 1995). In a meta-analysis focused specifically on ensuring the clinical representativeness of their results, Shadish, Matt, Navarro, and Phillips (2000) selected studies in which clients, treatments, and therapists were representative of typical clinical settings. In the 90 studies they examined, the cognitive-behavioural family of treatments was more efficacious than other treatment approaches. There have also been numerous focused meta-analyses dealing with the treatment of such specific conditions as depression, insomnia, smoking cessation, and bulimia. Reviewing the results of more than 40 such meta-analyses, Reid (1997) concluded that approximately three-quarters showed evidence of differential treatment effects. Consistent with other results we have reported, Reid noted that behavioural, cognitive, and cognitive-behavioural treatments demonstrated superiority to other forms of treatment for child maladjustment, child abuse, juvenile delinquency, and panic/agoraphobia.

Like Luborsky, Bruce Wampold has been a vocal proponent of the psychotherapy equivalency position. He has been highly critical of evidence-based treatment initiatives because, in his view, they have tended to overemphasize differences among treatments (e.g., Wampold 2001; Wampold & Bhati, 2004). In a direct test of the Dodo bird verdict, Wampold et al. (1997) conducted a meta-analysis with data from adult treatment studies published between 1970 and 1995 that compared at least two treatments. Wampold et al. reported an average d of .19 which, despite statistical significance, was described as a small and relatively unimportant difference. Accordingly, they interpreted their results as strongly supporting the Dodo bird verdict. They did explicitly caution, however, that their results should not be taken as evidence that all psychotherapies are equally efficacious or as efficacious as those included in their sample. It has been pointed out, though, that the majority of the studies included in their analyses were comparisons among different forms of CBT, not different orientations (Crits-Christoph, 1997). Furthermore, a d of .19 can be practically important, as it means that, for every 1,000 treated patients, more than 90 would experience greater improvement by receiving the significantly more efficacious treatment (Hunsley & Di Giulio, 2002).

In their most recent meta-analysis, Luborsky and colleagues (2002) examined 17 meta-analyses of the comparative treatment literature and found a d value of .20, almost identical to the value found by Wampold et al. (1997). Again, this effect size was described as small and unimportant. In commenting on this meta-analysis, Beutler (2002) suggested that, just as it would be meaningless to look for the average efficacy of drug treatments across various illnesses and types of medication, so too it is meaningless to look at average effects of psychotherapy or the average effects of certain classes of psychotherapy. In a similar vein, Chambless (2002) warned that it is erroneous to conclude that a relatively small average difference among treatments necessarily indicates that the difference between treatment options for a specific disorder is also small. Even if the average effect is relatively small, she pointed out that there could be considerable variability in the size of differential treatment effects for a specific disorder.

We now return to the rules we originally described to evaluate the Dodo bird verdict, as there is an important hidden issue about comparative treatment studies that warrants attention. In order to mount a comparative treatment study, researchers need adequate financial resources to cover the costs of training and/or paying therapists, paying for the work of research assistants over several years, and the costs of equipment (e.g., computers, recording equipment) used in the study. In most instances these costs amount to at least many tens of thousands of dollars, which means that researchers need financial support from a granting agency. This is likely to exert a critical, but typically unrecognized, effect on the nature of the study. For a granting agency to approve the funds for a comparative treatment study, there must be convincing evidence that the proposed study is worthwhile—it must address a relevant question with a set of methods that are appropriate. Accordingly, to build the strongest possible case for the study, plans for comparative treatment studies almost always involve the head to head comparison of treatments that have already been shown to be efficacious. After all, the research is intended to determine which treatment is the best one. Research comparing a treatment with established efficacy to one that has no empirical support, on the other hand, is unlikely to be funded—in addition to being unethical it would be seen as a waste of time and money to compare a strong treatment with one that has no existing empirical support. The net result of this is that the comparative treatment literature largely consists of comparisons among treatments that are known to be efficacious. If all the studied treatments are efficacious, it is hardly surprising that only small differences among the treatments emerge from comparative treatment studies.

In sum, it is clear that there is still no consensus on the question of psychotherapy equivalence. There is an alternative to the diametrically opposed positions of absolute equivalency or absolute specificity (Chambless, 2002; Hunsley & Di Giulio, 2002). The evidence seems to indicate that for most conditions, the outcomes of different treatments are not equivalent. However, in a small number of cases, such as adult depression, several different treatments have sufficient evidence to be considered as first line options for clients, including several forms of cognitive-behavioural treatment, interpersonal therapy, short-term psychodynamic therapy, and process-experiential therapy.

EMPIRICALLY SUPPORTED THERAPY RELATIONSHIPS

As we described at the outset of the chapter, research on psychological interventions comprises both studies of treatment outcome and studies of the relation between process and outcome. If you quickly glance back at the evidence-based treatment initiatives we presented in Chapters 12 and 13, you will see that all of these efforts have been based solely on the results of treatment outcome studies. To highlight the relevance of process-outcome research for evidence-based psychological practice, the APA Psychotherapy Division (Division 29) established a task force in 1999 to identify, operationalize, and disseminate information on **empirically supported therapy relationships** (ESRs).

The two aims of the task force were to (a) identify elements of effective therapy relationships and (b) determine methods of tailoring therapy to individual patient characteristics. The results of the task force, chaired by John Norcross, were published in a special issue of the Division's journal, *Psychotherapy* (Norcross, 2001a), with a more detailed report subsequently published as a book (Norcross, 2002).

As with other evidence-based initiatives, some of the key decision points addressed by the task force involved determining what type of evidence (experimental studies, correlational studies, or both) and how much evidence was required to conclude that a treatment element was empirically supported. In the end, the decision was made to include both experimental and correlational studies and to categorize treatment elements as *demonstrably effective, promising and probably effective*, and *insufficient research to judge* (Norcross, 2001b). Unfortunately, as with most process-outcome research, this initiative was limited to studies of treatments for adults. **Table 14.5** presents the listings developed by this task force for general elements of the therapy relationship. Given the evidence presented previously in this chapter, some of the elements listed in these tables will already be familiar to you.

TABLE 14.5   Empirically Supported Therapy Relationship Task Force Listing of General Elements of the Therapy Relationship

Demonstrably Effective Elements

- Therapeutic Alliance
- Cohesion in Group Therapy
- Empathy
- Goal Consensus and Collaboration

Promising and Probably Effective Elements

- Positive Regard (treating clients in a warm and accepting manner)
- Congruence/Genuineness (the therapist being himself/herself in the therapy and being fully involved in the treatment process)
- Feedback
- Repair of Alliance Ruptures (addressing any problems that develop in the therapeutic relationship)
- Self-Disclosure
- Management of Countertransference (therapist appropriately managing both negative and positive feelings toward the client)
- Quality of Relational Interpretations (the accuracy and appropriateness of the therapist's interpretations of interpersonal themes in the client's life)

Alliance and Cohesion

With respect to the general elements of the therapy relationship (Table 14.5), there is little doubt that the quality of the therapeutic alliance is positively linked to good treatment outcome. As you know from our earlier discussion, the extent to which alliance and outcome are causally linked is a matter of intense investigation. Nevertheless, evidence indicates that efforts to establish and maintain a good working relationship with clients are important for all therapists. In group therapy, there are numerous relationships, between each client and therapist, as well as among clients. The totality of all these relationships is referred to as **cohesion**. Thus the promotion of cohesion in a group treatment modality also makes good sense. Unresolved interpersonal conflicts, unexamined tensions between group members, and feelings of exclusion or rejection among group members can all undermine the impact of group treatment.

Empathy

Empathy is typically defined as the ability to understand another person's experience. The meta-analytic finding that effect size of therapist empathy on outcome is $r = .32$ (Greenberg, Elliott, Watson, & Bohart, 2001) underlines the importance of the therapist's interpersonal sensitivity in both understanding patients and effectively communicating with them. This is true regardless of therapeutic orientation or the nature of the patient's presenting problem. As discussed in relation to the Lafferty et al. (1989) study, the patient's sense of being understood by the therapist appears to be directly related to the effectiveness of the therapist.

Goal Consensus and Collaboration

The final demonstrably effective element, goal consensus and collaboration, highlights the critical need for patient and therapist to work together to set and achieve the goals of therapy. Explicit agreement on the nature and direction of treatment seems essential if therapy is to have an optimal influence on the patient.

Client Reactance and Functional Impairment

The ESR task force concluded there were two main client characteristics that require the tailoring of treatment in order to achieve therapeutic gains. Resistance or reactance, as already discussed, requires that the therapist adapt a style that either emphasizes therapist directiveness (for low reactant clients) or client self-direction (for high reactant clients). Skilful therapists should be able to make such modifications to treatment, assuming of course that they have accurately gauged the client's level of reactance. When dealing with clients presenting with significant functional impairment (i.e., severe distress and disruptions in functioning that are likely manifested across several life domains), therapists must appreciate the limits that such impairment may place on what gains are possible in treatment. However, the negative effects of functional impairments can be partially overcome by increasing the frequency or the duration of treatment (Beutler, Rocco, Moleiro, & Talebi, 2002). This allows the client and therapist expanded opportunities to address specific client concerns and to ensure the generalization of gains across problematic life situations.

Recommendations

As a final step, the task force issued a number of practice, training, research, and policy recommendations based on its findings. For our purposes, we will highlight the practice and training recommendations from the task force, which are listed in **Table 14.6**. Consistent with the strength of evidence they found in the literature, the task force recommended that mental health training programs, including those in clinical psychology, provide specific training on elements of ESRs. Likewise they encouraged mental health practitioners, including clinical psychologists, to actively use ESRs in their clinical work. It is especially noteworthy that the task force encouraged clinicians to (a) routinely monitor their treatment services and (b) strive to integrate aspects of ESRs and ESTs in their clinical work in order to provide the best services possible to clients. This integrated approach to intervention brings together much of what research on clinical psychology has to offer patients seeking help for psychological problems. It also avoids the unnecessary tendency, sometimes evident in clinical psychology, to pit evidence for common or non-specific treatment factors against what we have learned from treatment outcome research (Beutler, 2002).

TABLE 14.6   Empirically Supported Therapy Relationship Task Force Practice and Training Recommendations

For Practice

1. Clinicians are encouraged to make the creation of a therapy relationship characterized by the elements found to be demonstrably and probably effective a primary aim in treating patients.

2. Clinicians are encouraged to adapt the therapy relationship to specific patient characteristics shown to enhance therapeutic outcome.

3. Clinicians are encouraged to routinely evaluate patients' responses to the therapy relationship and ongoing treatment. Such monitoring can lead to increased opportunities to improve the process and outcome of treatment.

4. Concurrent use of empirically supported therapy relationships and empirically supported treatments tailored to the patient's disorder and characteristics is likely to result in the best outcomes for the patient.

For Training

1. Psychotherapy training programs are encouraged to explicitly train students in the effective elements of the therapy relationship.

continued...

2. Accreditation and certification organizations are encouraged to develop criteria for assessing the adequacy of training in empirically supported therapy relationships.

Adapted from the Steering Committee of the ESR Task Force, 2001.

EMPIRICALLY BASED PRINCIPLES OF THERAPEUTIC CHANGE

In an effort to provide clear and unambiguous guidance to clinicians on how best to integrate the EST and the ESR perspectives, psychotherapy researchers Louis Castonguay and Larry Beutler developed an initiative to identify **empirically based principles of therapeutic change** (Castonguay & Beutler, 2006a). Their starting point was the assumption that psychotherapy research is sufficiently advanced to allow definition of the basic principles of therapeutic change in a manner that is not tied to any specific orientation or narrowly defined set of concepts. According to Beutler and Castonguay (2006), such principles should be general statements that identify participant characteristics (i.e., both therapist and patient), relational conditions, therapist behaviours, and types of intervention that are likely to lead to therapeutic change. Principles should be more general than a description of techniques and more specific than theoretical models.

In forming their task force, Castonguay and Beutler went to great lengths to ensure representation of a variety of perspectives by selecting experts in the adult treatment of each of four problem areas (mood disorder, anxiety disorders, personality disorders, and substance abuse disorders) who were also strongly affiliated with either the ESR or the EST perspectives. To adequately cover the relevant literature, they planned a 3 × 4 matrix with the domains of participant factors, relationship factors, and treatment factors cutting across the four problem areas. Those experts focusing on participant factors were asked to review what was known about the patient and therapist characteristics covered in the ESR report (Norcross, 2002) and other relevant reviews of this literature. Task force members working on relationship factors were also asked to assess the status of research by reviewing these sources of information. Finally, those working on treatment factors were asked to review Nathan and Gorman (1998, 2002), the EST chapter by Chambless and Ollendick (2001), and other relevant sources.

On completion of these reviews, members discussed the principles of change that emerged from the work. By comparing these emergent sets of principles, members distinguished between principles that were similar across the problem areas and those that were relatively unique to a specific problem area. Once common principles were identified, task force members worked on identifying and refining the list of principles that were specific to each problem area. Beutler and Castonguay (2006) cautioned that none of these principles has been empirically tested, which is why the term *empirically based* rather than *empirically supported* was used to describe them. The main common principles that resulted from this process are presented in **Table 14.7**.

TABLE 14.7   Common Empirically Based Principles of Therapeutic Change

Client variables hypothesized to reduce the likelihood of benefiting from therapy
- greater pre-treatment impairment
- presence of a personality disorder
- financial/occupational difficulties
- significant interpersonal problems during early development
- unfavourable expectations about problems and their treatment

Relational conditions hypothesized to increase the likelihood of benefiting from therapy
- a strong therapeutic alliance established and maintained during treatment
- strong level of group cohesion developed and maintained during group therapy

Therapist behaviours hypothesized to increase the likelihood of benefiting from therapy
- a high degree of collaboration with clients
- empathic response
- attitude of authenticity, caring, warmth, and acceptance
- a limited number of accurate relational interpretations
- sensitivity to alliance ruptures and addressing these ruptures in an empathic and flexible way
- provision of a structured treatment and with a consistent but flexible focus on the application of his/her interventions
- skillful use of nondirective techniques

Intervention targets hypothesized to lead to therapeutic change
- intrapersonal issues
- interpersonal issues related to client's clinical problems
- problematic cognitions
- maladaptive behavioural, emotional, or physiological responses
- client self-exploration
- acceptance, tolerance, and full experience of emotions
- controlling extreme emotions

Adapted from Castonguay & Beutler (2006b).

Although lengthy and, at times, rather too general in nature, the information presented in Table 14.7 is the first attempt in the history of clinical psychology to use empirical evidence in fully considering the roles of participant, relationship, and techniques in therapy. This will serve as an important starting point for future evidence-based initiatives and could be applied to the research on treatments for children and adolescents. As Castonguay and Beutler (2006b) cautioned, the principles governing these factors do not operate in isolation, as the successful implementation of an effective technique is based on a collaborative process within a well-established relationship in which the therapist is empathic and genuine. Researchers have just begun to examine these complex interactions, and the future of psychotherapy research holds the promise of many exciting findings that will lead to improvements in the quality and impact of our treatments.

SUMMARY AND CONCLUSIONS

Having identified in Chapters 12 and 13 that there are psychological interventions that are helpful in treating diverse disorders in adults and children, in this chapter we considered the elements of psychotherapy that facilitate change. The identification of common factors that cut across treatments holds an intuitive appeal. However, the task of examining these common factors in a systematic and consistent fashion has proved challenging. Over time, research has become more sophisticated in attending to the relative significance of different factors in influencing the change process at different stages. Among the sea of inconsistency and contradiction, one robust finding stands out: across all types of psychotherapy, the nature of the therapeutic relationship is an important ingredient facilitating change. The establishment of a collaborative relationship in which the client feels understood and in which therapist and client agree on goals sets the stage for facilitating change.

In general, clients with long-standing serious interpersonal difficulties and current acute stressors face greater challenges in benefiting from psychotherapy. Considerable progress has been made in identifying other client characteristics that moderate the effects of different therapeutic approaches. In matching interventions to best meet client needs, psychologists must be sensitive to psychological variables such as reactance. We have highlighted some of the intense debates over interpretation of meta-analytic findings concerning the equivalence or differential effectiveness of different types of therapy. Advances in psychotherapy research rely on clear theorizing, methodological rigour, the establishment of clear decision-making rules, openness to input, and willingness to put cherished hypotheses to the empirical test. Efforts have been made to draw up principles that reflect the combined wisdom and expertise of proponents of ESRs and ESTs. Such efforts enable us to better understand the ways that psychological interventions can assist a diverse clientele with diverse problems.

C r i t i c a l   T h i n k i n g   Q u e s t i o n s

How important is it that clients and therapists are similar in terms of key demographic variables? Can a male therapist possibly help a female client, or can a young therapist possibly help an elderly client?

How should the therapeutic alliance evolve over the course of successful psychological intervention?

Are good therapists born or trained?

How can we explain the apparent effectiveness of different types of treatment for the same disorder?

K e y   T e r m s

cohesion

common factors

Dodo bird verdict

empirically based principles of therapeutic change

empirically supported therapy relationships

integrative treatment models

process-outcome research

reactance

sudden client gains

therapeutic alliance

K e y   N a m e s

Larry Beutler

Louis Castonguay

Jerome Frank

Lester Luborsky

John Norcross

David Orlinsky

Bruce Wampold

ADDITIONAL RESOURCES
Journals

Psychotherapy Research

Psychotherapy

Journal of Clinical Psychology

Books

Castonguay, L. G. & Beutler, L. E. (Eds.). (2006a). *Principles of therapeutic change that work*. New York: Oxford University Press.

Lambert. M. J. (Ed.). (2004). *Bergin and Garfield's handbook of psychotherapy and behavior change* (5th ed). New York: John Wiley & Sons.

Norcross, J. C. (Ed.). (2002). *Psychotherapy relationships that work: Therapist contributions and responsiveness to patients. London*: Oxford University Press.

CHAPTER 15

Health Psychology, Clinical Neuropsychology, and Forensic Psychology

INTRODUCTION

Throughout this book we have emphasized the diversity of issues addressed by clinical psychologists, the range of settings in which they are employed, and the growing number of populations with which they work. Across all these types of work, clinical psychologists rely on their knowledge of normal functioning, research methods, professional issues, assessment, diagnosis, case formulation, and intervention. As an example of the requirements in one jurisdiction, **Table 15.1** provides a list of the areas in which candidates must be knowledgeable for licensure as a psychologist in the province of Ontario.

As you learned in earlier chapters, clinical psychology has expanded its boundaries from an early focus on mental health to address a broad array of issues including physical health (Arnett, 2001), brain-behaviour links (Rourke, Ahmad, Collins, Hayman-Abello, & Warriner, 2002), and forensic work (Brown & Dean, 2001). In this chapter, we will examine in greater depth three areas of clinical practice: health psychology, clinical neuropsychology, and forensic psychology. There is great variability in the definitions and scope of these areas of practice. Some jurisdictions have specialty requirements to practise in these areas, whereas in other jurisdictions, practice in these areas is subsumed under the umbrella of clinical psychology.

We have touched on some of these areas of practice in earlier chapters. You may recall the profiles of two scientist-practitioners whose work addresses the problem of pain:

Dr. Heather Hadjistavropoulos, who works with older adults (Chapter 2), and Dr. Patrick McGrath, who works with children (Chapter 11). In the chapter on intellectual assessment (Chapter 6), we introduced cognitive assessment, a central component of many clinical neuropsychological services; and in the chapter on prevention (Chapter 10), we profiled the Centre for Children and Families in the Justice System, an organization that addresses many forensic psychology issues.

TABLE 15.1   Areas of Knowledge Required for Registration as a Psychologist in the Province of Ontario

Normal functioning
- biological bases of behaviour
- cognitive affective bases of behaviour
- social bases of behaviour
- psychology of the individual
- learning
- lifespan development
- personality/individual differences

Scientific issues
- research design and methodology
- statistics
- psychological measurement

Professional issues
- ethical, legal, and professional issues

Assessment and case formulation
- psychopathology
- psychological assessment
- psychodiagnostics

Intervention
- intervention procedures; psychotherapy
- evaluation of change

In addition, there are specialized skills listed for practice in the area of health psychology (Table 15.3), clinical neuro-psychology (Table 15.7), and forensic psychology (Table 15.10).

All clinical psychologists must be knowledgeable about the links between physical and mental health, be sensitive to the possibility of organic problems contributing to psychological impairment, and be aware that their work may be subpoenaed and they may be required to testify in court. In this chapter, we profile psychologists who practise health psychology (Dr. Michael Vallis), clinical neuropsychology (Dr. Sally Kuehn), and forensic psychology (Dr. Stephen Wormith). Practice in these three areas involves collaboration with other professionals including physicians, occupational therapists, lawyers, and judges. To highlight the core knowledge and skills of these three practice areas, we present the requirements for licensure in these areas in the province of Ontario. Our presentation is most representative of practice in North America. Where possible we underscore similarities and differences with practice in other countries. We then highlight assessment and intervention issues in each area.

HEALTH PSYCHOLOGY

Twentieth century advances in sanitation and in medicine dramatically reduced the effects of infectious diseases on morbidity and mortality, so that lifestyle factors replaced germs as the major threat to a person's health (Poole, Hunt Matheson, & Cox, 2005). Research has established links between psychosocial stress and health outcomes (Schneiderman, Ironson, & Siegel, 2005). In addition, advances in medical technology greatly increased the life expectancy of people living with serious illnesses such as cardiovascular disease, cancer, and HIV/AIDS (T. W. Smith, Kendall, & Keefe, 2002). These developments within public health, medicine, and psychology set the stage for psychologists to play a significant role in health promotion, treatment of disease, and rehabilitation (T. W. Smith, Nealey, & Hamann, 2000).

Lifestyle factors have replaced germs as the major threat to health. Research has established links between psychosocial stress and health outcomes.

Definitions of Health and Disability

In 1980, the World Health Organization (WHO) developed the *International Classification of Functioning, Disability and Health* (ICF) to provide a standard language to describe health (see Chapter 3). The most recent update of the ICF defines *functioning* in terms of body functions, activities, and participation. In parallel, the ICF defines **disability** as impairment, activity limitation, and participation restriction (WHO, 2002). Within a medical model, disability is considered a characteristic of a person, requiring treatment of that person to correct the problem. In contrast, within a social model, disability is viewed as a function of both the physical environment and the social environment. WHO has adopted an integrated or **biopsychosocial model** that takes into account biological, individual, and social factors associated with the individual's participation in various activities. According to this model (represented in **Figure 15.1**), an individual's functioning or disability is determined by the interaction between health conditions (diseases, disorders, and injuries) and contextual factors. Contextual factors include individual characteristics such as gender, age, coping style, social background, education, occupation, temperament, and behaviour, as well as variables that are external to the individual including climate, physical environment, societal attitudes, and finally, legal and social structures. Impairment can, but does not necessarily, lead to restrictions in activity and in diminished participation. For example, Chantalle, who has juvenile diabetes, has a bodily impairment (pancreatic dysfunction) that is controlled by insulin injections, so she has no limitation in activities; however, because she is anxious about independently monitoring her blood sugar levels (individual contextual variable) and no teacher has offered to support her (environmental contextual variable), she is unable to participate in a school trip. Interventions to help Chantalle could focus on diminishing her anxiety as well as on strategies to mobilize environmental supports. Edward, who sustained a spinal injury in a motorcycle accident, has a serious impairment (paralysis) as well as an activity limitation in that he is unable to drive or to use public transport; however, he is a determined person who uses a specially adapted transportation system as he participates in a wide range of activities.

Figure 15.1   The International Classification of Functioning, Disability, and Health Model Developed by the World Health Organization

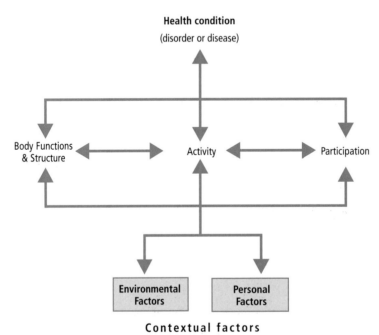

From: World Health Organization. (2002).

To get an idea of the scope of health-related problems, it is useful to look at national data on the numbers of people whose lives are affected by health problems. As part of the Census, Statistics Canada asks a screening question on limitation of everyday activities due to a health-related condition or problem. This is followed by a detailed survey, the *Participation and Activity Limitation Survey* (PALS). PALS data from 2001 revealed a 12.4% disability rate, indicating that 3.6 million Canadians reported that their activities were limited by health-related problems (Statistics Canada, 2002). Not surprisingly, the disability rate increases with age. **Figure 15.2** shows the disability rate by age and gender. The disability rate was lowest among children (3.3%), for whom the most common disability was related to a chronic health condition such as asthma. In adults aged 15–64, the disability rate rose to 10%. Among working age adults, the most common type of disability was related to pain (7.5%): 2.4 million Canadian adults reported having activity limitations due to chronic pain and a further 0.8 million Canadians experienced chronic pain that did not limit their activities. In older adults (aged 65+), the disability rate rose sharply to 40%; the most common disability in those aged over 65 (31.5%) was mobility problems. More than half of those over 75 (53.3%) report some kind of disability. In the next section, we examine the different roles that psychologists play in assisting people suffering from health-related problems.

Figure 15.2   A Profile of Disability in Canada

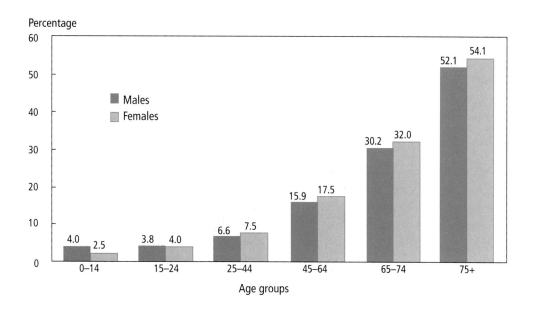

Adapted from Statistics Canada (2002).

Although it is important to recognize the extent of disability, it is also important to consider the positive aspects of functioning. The concept of **quality of life** has been used by many health professions to assess various aspects of well-being for those living with diverse disorders, as well as for their caregivers. Many quality of life assessment tools have been developed for use with people suffering from mental and physical problems, and for people of different ages. Although there is concern over the lack of standardization of these measures (Barbotte, Guillemin, Chau, & the Lorhandicap Group, 2001), quality of life measures appear to be sensitive to change (Selwood, Thorgrimsen, & Orrell, 2005) and to have predictive validity in some populations (Frisch et al., 2005).

Licensure and Training

Table 15.2 provides definitions of health psychology used in different countries. You will note that all reflect a biopsychosocial view of health. Common to all the definitions is a reliance on knowledge of psychological research with respect to health in efforts to promote healthy lifestyles as well as to help people adjust to health problems. To conduct health psychology research it is not necessary to have clinical training; however, within North America, practising health psychologists have generalist training in clinical psychology as well as knowledge of psychological issues related to health. Some jurisdictions, such as Ontario, require specialized knowledge to practise health psychology. **Table 15.3** describes the additional knowledge beyond that described in Table 15.1 that is required to practise in the area of health psychology in the province of Ontario. You will notice that practice with children requires knowledge in developmental psychology as well as knowledge of issues related to the health of children. In some other Canadian provinces, there are no explicit requirements concerning knowledge related to health. The role of health psychologists in Britain and Ireland can also include elements related to the improvements in health care systems. In these countries, psychologists may receive training that focuses entirely on health psychology, rather than on training in health psychology as a practice area under the umbrella of clinical psychology. Health promotion activities include efforts to reduce smoking, reduce obesity, and encourage regular exercise. Initiatives to promote a healthy lifestyle and to prevent the development of health problems are key activities for a growing number of health psychologists. As we discussed issues related to health promotion in Chapter 10, we focus our discussion here on the activities of health psychologists in providing psychological services to individuals with health problems.

Health psychologists can work with patients dealing with any type of health problem. For example, a special issue of the *Journal of Consulting and Clinical Psychology* on behavioural medicine and clinical health psychology (T. W. Smith et al., 2002) included reviews of work in psychoneuroimmunology (the links between psychological functioning and the immune system), essential hypertension, coronary heart disease, cancer, diabetes, arthritis, recurrent headaches, asthma, end-stage renal disease, peptic ulcers, irritable bowel syndrome, women's reproductive health (menstruation, fertility, pregnancy, birth, and menopause), organ transplant, genetic testing, and somatoform disorders. Within a biopsychosocial model, psychologists can assess and treat patients with any type of health problem. As it would be impossible to address the research in all of these areas in a single chapter we will focus on general issues that apply across the spectrum of health problems. **Profile Box 15.1** introduces Dr. Michael Vallis, a Canadian clinical psychologist whose clinical work and research all focus on health problems.

TABLE 15.2   Definitions of Health Psychology

American Psychological Association

The biopsychosocial model views health and illness as the product of a combination of factors including biological characteristics (e.g., genetic predisposition), behavioral factors (e.g., lifestyle, stress, health beliefs), and social conditions (e.g., cultural influences, family relationships, social support). Psychologists who strive to understand how biological, behavioral, and social factors influence health and illness are called health psychologists. The term "health psychology" is often interchanged with the terms "behavioral medicine" or "medical psychology".

British Psychological Society

Health psychologists apply psychological research and methods to:
- the promotion and maintenance of health;
- the prevention and management of illness;
- the identification of psychological factors contributing to physical illness;
- the improvement of the health care system;
- the formulation of health policy

Irish Psychological Society

Health Psychology is the application of psychological theory, methods and research to health, physical illness and health care. It is concerned with the behavioural and psychological aspects of promotion, improvement and maintenance of health. The promotion and maintenance of health involves behavioural and psychosocial processes at the interface between the individual, the health care system and society.

Australian Psychological Society

Health psychologists specialise in understanding the effects of psychological factors related to health and illness. They practice in two main areas: health promotion and clinical health. Many health psychologists are engaged in the prevention of illness and the promotion of health-related behaviours. They also work in clinical health and the application of psychology to illness assessment, treatment and rehabilitation.

College of Psychologists of Ontario

Health Psychology is the application of psychological knowledge and skills to the promotion and maintenance of health, the prevention and treatment of illness, and the identification of determinants of health and illness.

TABLE 15.3   College of Psychologists of Ontario: Additional Knowledge Requirements to Practise Health Psychology

Health Psychology
- behavioural medicine and psychological issues related to health

Pediatric Health Psychology
- behavioural medicine and psychological issues related to the health of children
- developmental psychology

PROFILE BOX 15.1

DR. MICHAEL VALLIS

I obtained my Ph.D. in clinical psychology from the University of Western Ontario in London in 1983. I am a registered clinical psychologist employed at the Queen Elizabeth II Health Sciences Centre, Halifax, and cross-appointed as an Adjunct Professor in Psychology and Associate Professor in Psychiatry at Dalhousie University. I am a clinical health psychologist with a main area of expertise in diabetes, gastroenterology, cardiovascular risk reduction, and obesity. My office is located in the Diabetes Management Centre, where I spend half of my clinical time. I see gastroenterology patients in my

Dr. Michael Vallis

office on the gastro-intestinal (GI) Unit. I have always believed strongly that it is important for health psychologists to become integrated into the medical units they service, and not to have patients sent from these medical units to a psychology department. I spend about 60% of my time seeing patients individually or in groups, 20% doing research, 15% of my time teaching, and 5% in administration.

A typical week

My week is fairly structured. Monday mornings are spent in the GI unit seeing patients. This Monday I saw three patients with serious GI disease. The focus of psychological treatment is to help them cope and maximize their quality of life. Monday afternoons are in the Diabetes Management Centre, also seeing patients. Today I serve as secretary for our monthly departmental meeting, so I can only see three patients. These individuals are benefiting from stress management and motivational enhancement interventions that help them cope with the demands of managing diabetes day-in, day-out. I finish the day with a one-hour supervision session with a pre-doctoral intern.

Tuesday is a busy clinical day spent in the GI unit. I begin with an inpatient visit to a young woman with ulcerative colitis who just had her large bowel removed and must now live with an ostomy. Needless to say, she's struggling to cope with this adjustment. I return to the clinic (fortunately the inpatient unit is just down the hall) to see two follow-up patients before attending Hepatitis C rounds. We are meeting with *Direction 180*, a community based high-tolerance methadone clinic that has begun to treat Hepatitis C with our help. We discuss ways to help patients deal with the stress of treatment and its side effects. I agree to a staff request to provide monthly backup support, although I know it will be hard for me to schedule it in. My afternoon is filled with three follow-up patients and a Hepatitis C coping group. Five people show up to focus on coping with the side effects of medical treatment.

Wednesday is my research day. I meet with the Capital District Health Authority (CDHA) Research Director to discuss the results of the most recent competition to the CDHA Research Fund. I am Co-Chair of this committee and we must decide who will receive funding and who will not. We allocate $350,000 worth of funds to new research projects. I then return to my office to meet with a colleague from Dalhousie Continuing Medical Education and a professional actor to discuss an upcoming training workshop to Nova Scotia Family Physicians entitled "Lifestyle Counselling." We go over the session and how we will use the professional actor to help us out with role plays in the session. The rest of my day is spent reviewing literature on another physician counselling program to promote physical activity, called the PACE program (*Physician-Assisted Counselling for Exercise*). I have been asked to develop my workshop into a larger program and I want to determine the evidence-based effectiveness of PACE so I can best decide how to modify my program. I also deal with several requests by phone and email. I am invited to present on psychological issues in diabetes to the Juvenile Diabetes Association in Toronto next May. Another person in Toronto wants to use a scale I developed for a research project looking at self-care in diabetes. Next I have some time to work on two of my research projects; I am beginning study 2 of a project in which we are assessing how fatigue in those with Hepatitis C differs from normal fatigue. Also, I spend some time preparing for a research meeting on Thursday; along with colleagues from medicine, nursing, social work, and pharmacy, and including representatives from all Atlantic provinces, we have just received three years of funding from the Canadian Institutes of Health Research to form the Atlantic Interdisciplinary Research Network (AIRN) to study social and behavioural issues in HIV and Hepatitis C.

Thursday is another clinical day in the Diabetes Management Centre. I begin with an 8:30 am supervision session with a pre-doctoral intern, and then see patients until my 10:30 AIRN conference call. Then it's a steady flow of five patients until my 4 p.m. diabetes

coping group. Six people show up to discuss the psychological issues of living with diabetes. I leave at 5:45, really quite tired.

Friday is a "catch-all" day. I book patients from 9 till 1. During this time I see a couple of patients from the cardiovascular risk reduction clinic (I carry only a small
caseload due to other commitments) and also one diabetes and one GI patient who
couldn't be booked earlier in the week. I then have a supervision session with a
psychologist who is on the temporary register of the Nova Scotia Board of Examiners
in Psychology. I am her Board supervisor and see her two hours per month. I then
return to my office to spend a few hours catching up on email and working through
a to-do list before leaving for the weekend. I keep very busy but I never doubt that
what I do is worthwhile and appreciated by others.

Activities of Health Psychologists

Table 15.4 presents an outline for assessment and intervention in the clinical application of the
biopsychosocial model. Health psychologists must be knowledgeable about the physical disorders from which their patients suffer. They need to know about the characteristics of the disorder,
risk factors, and prognosis, as well as diagnostic and treatment procedures. In addition to these
biological variables, the health psychologist must also consider psychological issues, whether the
patient meets diagnostic criteria for a mental disorder in addition to a physical disorder, the
patient's understanding of the condition, and how it is likely to affect his or her life. As the social
context determines the demands that will be placed on the patient and his or her resources, the
health psychologist must consider the quality of the person's relationships, the extent to which
others are available to provide instrumental and emotional support, the nature of the relationship with health care professionals, as well as cultural issues. Finally, the patient's concerns must
be considered in the context of the health care system to which the patient has access.

Health psychologists may be employed within a hospital, a community health clinic, or a private practice setting—issues related to health problems don't just occur in hospitals. For example,
a family sought private services from a psychologist due to concerns about their seven-year-old
daughter, Laila, who was becoming fearful and reluctant to attend school. Laila's father, David, had
had an unsuccessful kidney transplant and had recently been diagnosed with cancer. Physicians
had informed him that he could expect to deteriorate steadily over the coming months and that
there was virtually no hope of slowing the rate of his decline. Although David was resigned to having a terminal illness, he felt guilty and anxious at the thought of leaving his daughter. Laila's

TABLE 15.4   Outline for Assessment and Intervention in the Clinical Application of the Biopsychosocial Model

I. The illness
  A. Pathophysiology
  B. Risk factors
  C. Prognosis
  D. Diagnostic procedures
  E. Treatment procedures

II. The patient
  A. DSM Axis I disorders
  B. Disease history
  C. Personality traits and coping styles or mechanisms
  D. Conceptualization of disease and treatment
  E. Educational and vocational issues
  F. Impact of illness on subjective distress, social functioning, activity level, self-care, and overall quality of life

III. Social, family, and cultural contexts
  A. Quality of marital and family relationships
  B. Use and efficacy of social support
  C. Patient-physician relationship
  D. Patient's cultural background

IV. The health care system
  A. Medical organization
  B. Insurance coverage for diagnostic and treatment procedures
  C. Geographical, social, and psychological barriers to accessing health services
  D. Existence of disability benefits for medical condition

Adapted from T.W. Smith, Nealey, & Hamann (2000).

mother, Anna, was a tower of strength for the entire family. Since her husband's diagnosis she had supplemented the family income by additional hours at work. A psychological assessment revealed David was suffering from a dysthymic disorder, Laila met criteria for a diagnosis of separation anxiety disorder, and Anna, although fatigued and distressed, did not meet criteria for any mental disorder. The psychologist identified three foci for intervention: (a) addressing David's depressive symptoms; (b) addressing Laila's anxious symptoms and facilitating regular attendance at school; and (c) helping Anna to mobilize supports by reducing her work hours and taking care of her emotional needs.

ASSESSMENT AND INTERVENTION RELATED TO PAIN

Pain serves a useful function in alerting us to potential harm. The sharp pain you feel when you twist an ankle is an important signal that you need to take weight off the ankle, a scorching sensation warns you to move away from a fire, chafing lets you know that clothing is too tight, and stinging reminds you to keep away from certain plants or insects. Although most of us consider pain an unpleasant experience that we would rather avoid, the very rare individual who is insensitive to pain is vulnerable to life-threatening injuries because he or she does not experience the warning signals of pain. Because pain is a subjective experience, we rely on individual reports to let us know how much pain a person is suffering: there is no objective scale on which we can judge another person's pain. This poses an important challenge in understanding the pain experiences of those who are incapable of verbalizing pain. Until relatively recently, many health care professionals assumed that babies and very young children did not feel pain (Poole et al. 2005). Consequently, it was considered reasonable to conduct procedures such as circumcision on male infants without using local anaesthesia, whereas such procedures would not be applied to an older male without some intervention to block or dull the pain. Patrick McGrath and his colleagues have developed innovative strategies to measure pain in infants and children, as well as in adults who are incapable of expressing pain verbally (McGrath & Finley, 2003; McGrath & Unruh, 1999). These include research-based strategies for asking children about pain, observing their behaviour, and watching facial expressions (Breau, McGrath, Camfield, & Finley, 2002; Chambers, Finley, McGrath, & Walsh, 2003).

It is important to distinguish between **acute pain** and **chronic pain**. Acute pain is a short-term sensation that serves an unpleasant, but useful, function; it can usually be relieved in different ways including the application of heat or cold, rest, distraction, or the administration of analgesics. Pain that persists for more than six months is considered chronic. We will briefly outline ways that psychologists are involved in the treatment of acute pain in children and chronic pain in adults.

Children experience acute pain due to injuries, illness, and medical procedures. All children are exposed to procedures such as vaccination, many experience minor surgery, and a few must face pain associated with invasive procedures associated with the treatment of serious conditions such as cancer. Pain management is multi-dimensional, including physical measures such as the administration of medication and psychological interventions such as training in distraction strategies. As children are discharged from hospital very rapidly following minor surgery, parents are often responsible for managing the child's pain. McGrath and his colleagues (McGrath, Finley, Ritchie, & Dowden, 2003) prepared a booklet to help parents help children. **Table 15.5** includes strategies they suggest can be helpful in addressing children's acute pain and some commonly used strategies that are not helpful.

TABLE 15.5   Methods to Manage Children's Acute Pain

Psychological
- Presence of a parent or other special person
- Encouragement to ask questions and express feelings
- Provision of simple, accurate information about a medical procedure
- Provision of some control (e.g., sit on a lap or in a chair)
- Distraction: talking, videogames, music, books
- Imagination: thinking of activities associated with being relaxed and calm
- Suggestion that the child let the pain slip away
- Play and silliness
- Encouragement that the child is doing well

Physical
- Deep breathing
- Comforting touch: stroking, swaddling, holding, rocking, cuddling
- Medication

Unhelpful strategies
- Denying the pain: *you won't feel a thing*
- Ridiculing or shaming: *only babies cry*
- Giving false reassurance: *it only takes a second*
- Focusing too much on pain: *I know you are worried it will hurt a lot*

Adapted from McGrath, Finley, Ritchie, & Dowden (2003).

More than three million Canadians experience chronic pain and, for 2.6 million Canadians, chronic pain interferes with their activities in significant ways (Statistics Canada, 2002). Chronic pain is associated with a host of other problems including sleep disturbances, depression, and anxiety (Ohayon, 2005). The person's beliefs about pain influence the experience of pain: those who attribute their pain to a traumatic injury, who are fearful of causing further pain by engaging in activity, and who feel unable to control their pain report more intense pain symptoms (Turk & Okifuji, 2002). Psychological factors play an important role in determining whether the person will recover from the pain or will experience long-term disability. Dysfunctional beliefs about pain, lack of social support, heightened emotional reactivity, low job satisfaction, and the possibility of compensation are associated with the experience of chronic problems (Turk & Okifuji, 2002). Psychologists may be consulted to conduct assessments in claims for disability due to pain-related injuries. This type of work involves knowledge of health psychology and forensic issues.

Psychological services to deal with pain may be offered within multidisciplinary services that include physicians and physiotherapists. Psychological treatment may be directed at various goals, including the adoption of active coping strategies to manage pain, reduction of avoidance behaviours, improved sleep (see **Viewpoint Box 15.1**), adherence to a medication regimen, stress management, reduction of anxiety related to pain, resolution of interpersonal issues related to pain (e.g., communication difficulties and conflict with family members), and vocational issues (Hadjistavropoulos & Williams, 2004). **Table 15.6** lists cognitive-behavioural strategies frequently used in managing chronic pain. These interventions can be offered individually or in a group format. Well-established treatments include behaviour therapy for headache and multi-component CBT for pain associated with rheumatic disease (Chambless et al., 1998); CBT is considered a probably efficacious treatment for chronic low back pain (Chambless et al., 1998).

VIEWPOINT BOX 15.1

INSOMNIA: NO NEED TO LOSE SLEEP OVER IT!

We all need sleep. As you may know from direct experience, without adequate sleep, both children and adults suffer cognitive and physical impairments (Streisand & Efron, 2003). Sleep can be affected by many variables including age, parental status, stress, and shift work (Williams, 2001), as well as by a host of physical variables including chronic pain (Ohayon, 2005). Results of Statistics Canada's 1998 *General Social Survey* revealed that 25% of adults reported regular difficulty in either falling asleep or in staying asleep (Williams, 2001).

Everyone occasionally suffers from insomnia triggered by life events, stressors, or an illness. Normal sleeping patterns usually return once the stressor or illness is over. However, an occasional bout of insomnia can develop into a chronic sleep disorder that takes on a life of its own, independent of the original trigger. Within the *DSM-IV* system, insomnia is a disorder of initiating and/or maintaining sleep that is accompanied by fatigue-related impairment during the day (American Psychiatric Association, 2000). Chronic insomnia is often maintained by faulty behaviours and beliefs (Morin, 2004). Although the problem of insomnia is well-recognized by the medical profession, the topic is not routinely covered in training in clinical psychology (Streisand & Efron, 2003).

With roots in basic psychological research and its existence on the boundary between general clinical psychology and health psychology, the topic of sleep disorders can be overlooked by applied psychologists (De Koninck, 1997). Nevertheless, there is increasing evidence that psychological interventions may be very useful in the treatment of this common disorder, especially when the insomnia is chronic. As pharmacological interventions can lead to poor quality sleep, possible addiction, and rebound insomnia on withdrawal of the medication, there is a pressing need for effective psychological interventions.

Dr. Charles Morin of Laval University has been at the forefront of research in this area (Morin, Colecchi, Stone, Sood, & Brink, 1999; Morin, 2004). CBT interventions include three components: educational, behavioural, and cognitive (Morin, 2004). Educational strategies focus on knowledge of the physiology of sleep and on understanding the mechanics of how insomnia develops into a chronic problem. Education also focuses on the principles of sleep hygiene (i.e., good sleep practices): avoid caffeine and other stimulants in the evening; avoid smoking close to bedtime; avoid exercising too close to bedtime; and reduce noise, light, and excessive temperature (Morin, 2004). Behavioural strategies focus on stimulus control with five simple instructions: (a) go to bed only when sleepy; (b) use bed or bedroom only for sleeping; (c) get out of bed when unable to sleep and return only when sleepy; (d) get up at the same time every day no matter how little you have slept; and (e) do not take daytime naps. Two additional behavioural strategies include restricting sleep time and learning relaxation strategies. Cognitive interventions target and attempt to alter dysfunctional beliefs about sleep including unrealistic expectations, feelings of lack of control, and catastrophic thinking about the consequences of being unable to sleep. Cognitive-behavioural interventions yield an average of 50–60% symptom reduction in those suffering from insomnia, a figure that is comparable with that obtained with pharmacotherapy (Morin, 2004). Furthermore, the effects of cognitive behavioural interventions are better maintained over time.

A meta-analysis of studies comparing cognitive-behavioural interventions to pharmacotherapy revealed that, whereas medication produced superior results in terms of sleep duration, cognitive behavioural interventions were associated with greater improvement in quality of sleep (M. T. Smith et al., 2002). Despite evidence that psychological interventions are efficacious, they have been underused, as some people consider medication an easier alternative. Researchers have therefore focused their efforts on ways to deliver psychological interventions in brief and inexpensive ways. For example, a recent randomized controlled trial found that a brief (two-hour) cognitive-behavioural intervention for young and middle-aged adults was more efficacious than either pharmacotherapy or combined cognitive-behavioural treatment and pharmacotherapy in the treatment of insomnia (Jacobs, Pace-Shott, Stickgold, & Otto, 2004). Bastien, Morin, Ouellet, Blais, and Bouchard (2004) compared three different ways to deliver a cognitive behavioural intervention to middle-aged adults with insomnia. These investigators found that participants who received services via individual sessions, groups, or telephone consultation all reported improvements in sleep that were maintained six months after completion. This preliminary study suggests that CBT can be effectively delivered in inexpensive ways to address a common and troubling disorder.

TABLE 15.6   Cognitive-Behavioural Approaches to the Management of Chronic Pain

Intervention	Strategy	Goal
Education about pain	Provide a rationale for the treatment	Motivate patients to take an active role in treatment
Goal-setting	Short- and long-term goals; activity scheduling; pacing	Realistic goals; recognition of gradual progress
Relaxation	Training and rehearsal of skills and achieve calm state	Develop capacity to reduce muscle tension
Contingency management	Self-reinforcement of healthy behaviours	Reduce use of analgesics; increase appropriate exercise; increase balanced response to pain
Exercise and fitness	Collaborate with physiotherapist/trainer	Address fears and avoidance of more active lifestyle
Cognitive restructuring	Identify and challenge catastrophizing thoughts	Realistic appraisals of pain
Problem-solving	Address limitations and conflicts	Awareness of choices; capacity to activate support; clear communication
Generalization and maintenance	Practise skills in relation to diverse issues; anticipate difficulties	Lifestyle changes so that skills are applied consistently

Adapted from Hadjistavropoulos & Williams (2004).

In sum, the application of psychological knowledge to address issues related to health is a growing area of practice. Over the relatively brief history of behavioural medicine and health psychology, psychologists have made an important contribution to the understanding of health, the promotion of healthy lifestyles, and the adjustment to health problems. Given the aging of our population and the increasing need for services to help people adjust to chronic health problems, it is highly likely that health psychology will become an even more important psychological service area in the coming years (Arnett, 2001).

CLINICAL NEUROPSYCHOLOGY

Neuropsychology is the study of brain-behaviour relationships; clinical neuropsychology is the application of this knowledge in the assessment and remediation of neurological injury or illness (Groth-Marnat, 2000). Clinical neuropsychology addresses the effects on functioning of neurological problems, including genetic problems such as Williams syndrome, birth-related injuries, head injuries resulting from sports accidents and car accidents, brain tumours, infections, demyelinating diseases such as multiple sclerosis, cerebrovascular diseases, epilepsy, neurodegenerative diseases such as Alzheimer's disease or Parkinson's disease, the effects of exposure to environmental toxins, and the effects of chemotherapy (Cairns, 2004).

Clinical neuropsychology developed after the Second World War, building on the work of Ward Halstead and Ralph Reitan in the United States and Aleksandr Luria in the Soviet Union (Groth-Marnat, 2000). Halstead, who was trained in physiological psychology, studied the behaviour of patients with neurological impairment. Dissatisfied with the academic focus of intelligence tests, he developed tests to assess specific adaptive deficits (Broshek & Barth, 2000). Over the course of his career, Reitan conducted numerous studies comparing performance on these tests between patients with brain damage and nondisordered individuals and examining the usefulness of the battery in identifying the precise area of the brain that had been damaged (Broshek & Barth, 2000). The Halstead-Reitan battery is the most extensively investigated neuropsychological test and is widely considered a useful tool in evaluating cognitive functioning (see Table 15.12 below). However, the Halstead-Reitan is not without its flaws. Criticisms include the length of time required for administration; the failure to take into account differences according to age, education, and gender; and the lack of studies on diverse populations (Broshek & Barth, 2000). Luria's approach was a qualitative one that yielded a profile of the patient's strengths and weaknesses, but that lent itself less readily to standardization in administration or scoring (Golden, Freshwater, & Vayalakkara, 2000). Current neuropsychological practices reflect an integration of the two traditions so that use of tests is complemented by careful analysis of functioning (Groth-Marnat, 2000).

Licensure and Training

In addition to the knowledge base required for all clinical psychologists (see Table 15.1), clinical neuropsychologists require additional specialized knowledge as listed in **Table 15.7**. To practise clinical neuropsychology, one must understand normal brain functioning (neuroanatomy); the ways that environmental toxins, chemotherapy, or recreational drugs affect brain functioning (pharmacology); and the ways that injuries and diseases affect the brain (neuropathology). In addition, clinical neuropsychologists must be knowledgeable about a wide array of assessment strategies to identify neuropsychological problems, as well as ways to adapt to these limitations.

TABLE 15. 7   College of Psychologists of Ontario: Additional Knowledge Requirements to Practise Clinical Neuropsychology and Child Clinical Neuropsychology

Clinical Neuropsychology	Child Clinical Neuropsychology
• neuroanatomy	• neuroanatomy
• physiology	• physiology
• pharmacology	• pharmacology
• human neuropsychology	• human neuropsychology
• human neuropathology	• human neuropathology
• neuropsychological assessment	• pediatric neuropsychological assessment
• neuropsychological intervention techniques	• pediatric neuropsychological intervention techniques
	• developmental psychology

Clinical neuropsychologists work with clients across the lifespan and must be sensitive to issues in working with children (Middleton, 2004) and older adults (American Psychological Association Working Group on the Older Adult, 1998; Morris, 2004). Those working with children require knowledge of assessment and intervention that is suitable for children and must have a strong background in developmental psychology. **Profile Box 15.2** describes Dr. Sally Kuehn, a pediatric clinical neuropsychologist. In assessing older adults, the clinical neuropsychologist must take into account the physical and sensory changes that accompany aging, in addition to the cognitive changes that are the focus of the assessment (APA Working Group on the Older Adult, 1998; Lichtenberg, Murman, & Mellow, 2003).

Training in clinical neuropsychology can be obtained in several ways: within generalist training in clinical psychology, in a small number of specialist clinical neuropsychology doctoral programs, or in post-doctoral training. The Division of Clinical Neuropsychology of the American Psychological Association identifies fulfillment of the requirements of the American Board of Clinical Neuropsychology as clear evidence of competence. The Division of Neuropsychology of the British Psychological Society has also developed professional practice guidelines such that chartered clinical psychologists who have met the criteria for membership in the Division of Neuropsychology are considered competent as clinical neuropsychologists (BPS, 2003).

PROFILE BOX 15.2

DR. SALLY KUEHN

After completing a Ph.D. at the University of Waterloo, I obtained postdoctoral training in the Neonatal Follow-up Program at the Hospital for Sick Children (HSC) in Toronto. During my period of supervised practice for provincial registration, I completed a course on neuroanatomy at the University of Toronto. I was employed as a staff psychologist within the same program at HSC for approximately six months before accepting a position in the Neurocognitive Program at the Children's Hospital of Eastern Ontario (CHEO) in Ottawa. Over the course of my

Dr. Sally Kuehn

career, I have provided neuropsychological assessment services to diverse populations of children including those with brain tumours, epilepsy, a history of traumatic brain injury, and those who experienced complications of a premature birth. I have recently begun working on the Attention-Deficit/Hyperactivity Disorder (ADHD)/Disruptive Behaviour Disorder Team at CHEO. My positions as a registered psychologist have entailed the provision of diagnostic assessment services, teaching of interns, supervision of psychometrists, and research.

A typical week

As a registered psychologist employed at CHEO, my routine activities can be grouped into four broad categories. The first of these are the activities associated with conducting diagnostic assessments. This entails interviews with parents to obtain relevant background information and to clarify their concerns regarding their child. During assessment sessions I administer a series of standardized tests examining cognitive, academic, social, and behavioural aspects of their functioning. For some assessments, I supervise a psychometrist who administers the tests. I then interpret results and integrate them in a written report. In feedback sessions with the family, I review the results and provide the rationale for the recommendations. These activities commonly consume 80% of my weekly hours.

The second aspect of my routine activities pertains to administrative responsibilities. These entail attending team meetings to review and assist with the assignment of new cases. In the past, I have also been asked to represent the discipline on various hospital committees, and to act as the head of professional teams. Administrative commitments can be very time-consuming. Fortunately, in my current position they consume only 10% of my weekly hours.

A third category of activities pertains to teaching and continued learning. I am expected to attend bimonthly meetings of the discipline within this setting and bimonthly professional development meetings. There are also ample opportunities to attend teaching rounds. On average, I attend conferences twice yearly. On occasion, I am responsible for giving teaching rounds. These activities consume 5 to 10% of my week. I am also responsible for the supervision of an intern for a six-month rotation. This supervision entails a commitment of several hours per week for discussion of cases, assessment procedures, legislation, and ethical issues. The frequency with which interns are assigned to a specific psychologist varies. It is often necessary to reduce the amount of time spent on other activities while supervising an intern.

A fourth category of activities is research. In this setting, the research activities of psychologists must be directly linked to their clinical activities. Thus, reading related to the conditions of the patients being served may also be relevant to research with the same population. In some instances, psychologists are given "protected time" for research (i.e., money is awarded to cover the cost of the clinical time spent conducting research). For those without protected time, the true challenge lies in finding enough time to write research proposals, prepare manuscripts, and hold the meetings necessary for effective collaboration with other professionals. Although I have not had protected time to date, I have collaborated on a number of projects with psychologists, neurologists, neurosurgeons, and oncologists.

Activities of Clinical Neuropsychologists

Like other areas of clinical psychology, clinical neuropsychology has expanded and evolved over recent decades (Hayman-Abello, Hayman-Abello, & Rourke, 2003). As noted above, early clinical neuropsychology was primarily a diagnostic activity in which tests were developed to aid in the localization of lesions. Neuropsychological assessment was used to determine whether there was an organic basis for observed psychological and behavioural problems, and if so, to identify the precise area of the brain that was affected (Goldstein & McNeil, 2004). With the development of effective imaging techniques such as magnetic resonance imaging (MRI) and functional magnetic resonance imaging (fMRI), there are now alternative ways to identify the precise nature of brain dysfunction (Mellers, 2004). Clinical neuropsychology, in turn, has expanded its focus to apply neuropsychological methods in treatment planning and therapeutic interventions (Lemsky, 2000).

ASSESSMENT

Neuropsychological assessment examines memory, abstract reasoning, problem-solving, spatial abilities, and the emotional consequences of brain dysfunction (Groth-Marnat, 2000). In Chapter 5 we noted that psychological assessment can be conducted for screening, diagnosis and case formulation, prognosis, treatment design and planning, treatment monitoring, and treatment evaluation (cf. Hunsley, Crabb, & Mash, 2004). Similarly, neuropsychological assessment can address many different questions (see **Table 15.8**).

TABLE 15.8   Purposes of Neuropsychological Assessment

- **Diagnosis**
  Does this child show signs of having been exposed to a toxic substance?
  Are this patient's memory complaints related to dementia or to depression?

- **Prognosis**
  To what extent will this child's acquisition of language be affected by her head injury?
  How long is it reasonable to expect this person to live alone, given his declining memory and executive functioning?

- **Treatment Planning and Rehabilitation**
  What kind of special learning aids will this child with a learning disability require?
  If this patient who has had a stroke returns to work, what kinds of adaptations will need to be made to compensate for deficits related to the stroke?
  What can be done to help this person with mild memory loss?

- **Legal Proceedings**
  Is there evidence of brain dysfunction that could be related to the person committing a violent act?
  What is the extent of damage to this employee who sustained an electric shock?

Screening for organic problems may be conducted by a generalist clinical psychologist who then refers the patient for a full neuropsychological assessment if the screening indicates possible neuropathology. As you can see in Table 15.8, the most common reasons for neuropsychological assessment are to address issues around diagnosis, prognosis, treatment planning, and legal issues. Diagnostic issues include determining whether the person's problem is primarily neurological or psychological. To conduct such an assessment, the clinical neuropsychologist must understand neuropathology and psychopathology.

Neuropsychologists are often required to predict a patient's prognosis (Lemsky, 2000). For example, the neuropsychologist may be asked whether or not a person can return to work following a brain injury, and if so, to identify the types of tasks that may be difficult. Prediction of future functioning requires an understanding of the neuropathology and its course, as well as the person's developmental level. Some forms of neuropathology are progressive, so that the person can expect a process of deterioration.

Other problems, such as those caused by a blow to the head, may lead to different problems at different ages. For example, following a mild concussion, a child may exhibit fewer symptoms than an adult would. However, there is some evidence that damage occurring at times of rapid development causes more harm than does damage occurring at times of slow development (Middleton, 2004). Counter-balancing this is the fact that the child's brain is in the process of development, so it may be possible for a child to recover from some types of injuries more easily than an adult could (Middleton, 2004). In assessing an adult who had difficulties with language following a head injury, the clinical neuropsychologist predicts the extent of recovery of functioning that can be expected. In assessing a three-year-old with a similar injury, the child clinical neuropsychologist predicts whether the child will acquire language at the same rate as noninjured peers or whether language delays can be expected (Middleton, 2004). In conducting neuropsychological assessment for the purposes of planning treatment and rehabilitation, the clinical neuropsychologist draws on knowledge of normal processes in memory, language, and executive functioning to make predictions that a person with a particular deficit could benefit from a particular intervention (Lemsky, 2000).

In Chapter 5 we emphasized that psychological assessment and psychological testing are not synonymous. Similarly, neuropsychological assessment includes, but is not limited to, neuropsychological testing. The toolkit of the clinical neuropsychologist contains assessment strategies and instruments that we presented in earlier chapters, including interviews (Chapter 6) and psychometric tests such as the Wechsler Adult Intelligence Scale III, Wechsler Memory Scale III, and Wechsler Individual Achievement Test II (Chapter 7). In choosing a neuropsychological test, the psychologist must consider the core psychometric elements that are required for all types of psychological tests: standardization (of stimuli, administration, and scoring), reliability, validity, and norms. There is no simple correspondence between performance on a neuropsychological test and performance of the activities of daily living (Goldstein & McNeil, 2004). The context of neuropsychological testing may actually mask some types of deficits (Lemsky, 2000). For example, an individual may perform better in the brief, structured one-to-one environment of a testing session than in the home setting with multiple distractions and simultaneous demands on attention. Therefore, it is essential that data be gathered from the individual and from others who are knowledgeable about his or her functioning, to determine his or her functional status in various domains.

In interpreting a score on a particular test, the clinical neuropsychologist refers to normative data. However, the usefulness of this comparison depends on the appropriateness of the normative group. Some widely used tests have norms for older adults. The WAIS III (Wechsler, 1997), for example, provides normative data for the 74- to 89-year age range. Unfortunately, other commonly used neuropsychological tests were normed on small samples of convenience, so that an extreme score may represent a difference between the individual and the normative sample, rather than a clinically meaningful difference (Crawford, 2004). Of particular concern, many norms for neuropsychological tests are based on samples that under-represent minority groups. **Viewpoint Box 15.2** describes the development of new scales for use with diverse populations of older adults.

VIEWPOINT BOX 15.2

SENAS: A NEW TOOL FOR THE ASSESSMENT OF COGNITIVE FUNCTIONING IN OLDER ADULTS OF VARYING ETHNIC BACKGROUNDS

With an aging population, there is an urgent need for sound tools to assess cognitive functioning and dementia in the elderly. Many commonly used tools were developed for use with an English-speaking population. Over the years, as tests have been translated into other languages, little attention has been focused on ensuring that the translation has the same psychometric properties as the original version. Furthermore, performance on tests of cognitive functioning is affected by language and education. It is possible to overestimate cognitive impairment when testing an elderly person with limited education using a translated version of a neuropsychological test. It is essential that tools be developed for use with an ethnically and linguistically diverse population. Such tools must also allow for equally sensitive and reliable measurement in different domains (Crawford, 2004).

To address these psychometric concerns, Mungas and colleagues began developing the *Spanish and English Neuropsychological Assessment Scales* (SENAS; Mungas et al., 2004). The SENAS were designed as tests of cognitive abilities in older individuals from diverse ethnic groups. Mungas and his colleagues used sophisticated test construction techniques to develop and systematically test a set of new scales.

Mungas, Reed, Marshall, and González (2000) developed 12 new neuropsychological scales that included both verbal and nonverbal measures. Item selection was guided by the research literature on cognition and intelligence, cognitive effects of aging, and cognitive effects of neuropathology. The instrument was designed to assess six areas: conceptual thinking, semantic memory, attention span, episodic memory, non-verbal spatial ability, and verbal ability. For each scale, 90–100 potential items were generated. Verbal items were translated into Spanish and then back-translated from Spanish to English to ensure that the translation was sound. Items were then tested with 21 English-speaking and 21 Spanish-speaking individuals aged 60 and over. Results from pilot testing lead to refining the items and the translation. Next the items were administered to 408 community dwelling elderly participants (208 in English and 200 in Spanish). Item response theory was used to identify and eliminate linguistically biased items, yielding scales with 40–50 items that were (a) well-matched across English and Spanish forms, (b) reliable, and (c) sensitive to cognitive impairment.

Mungas et al. (2004) reported on additional evaluations of the SENAS. The scales developed with the previous sample were modified to address shortcomings and an additional scale was added. The 13 scales were then tested in a sample of 1,374 participants over the age of 60 (Study 1: 345 Caucasian Americans tested in English, 353 Hispanic Americans tested in English, and 676 Hispanic Americans tested in Spanish). Once again, item response theory was used to ensure the scales were well-matched in terms of the psychometric properties of the English and Spanish versions and that the scale had strong psychometrics at different levels of ability. Matching within language groups was good for 7 of the 13 scales; minor differences were found in the precision of measurement across language groups for 4 of the scales; 2 scales did not yield similar psychometric properties across language groups. Analyses in a second study provided support for the model of functioning on which the scales were based. Results suggested that the different domains were correlated with one another, reflecting an underlying dimension of cognitive ability. Nevertheless, the degree of correlation was moderate, suggesting that each scale contributes unique measurement variance. Finally, in a third set of analyses using data from Study 1, the researchers examined the possibility that responses would be affected by demographic characteristics. They found responses were relatively unaffected by education, ethnicity, gender, and age, suggesting that the SENAS will be useful in evaluating both Caucasian and Hispanic older adults.

The work of Mungas and his colleagues is noteworthy for the scrupulous application of state of the art test construction techniques in the development of sound tools that can be used in diverse populations. They plan to continue construct validation of the scales.

INTERVENTION

Compared with the history of treatments for mental disorders, the history of treatments for individuals with neurocognitive impairment is relatively brief. However, with an aging population, there are increasing numbers of people living with dementia (Turner, 2003). In addition, due to improvements in medical care, many people now survive strokes and serious head injuries. There is a clear need to offer effective services to help the growing numbers of people who are faced with the challenge of living with the effects of neurological problems (B. A. Wilson, 2004). Although these interventions include services to deal with the psychological consequences of the problem, such as depression, a growing number of interventions are designed to remediate the problems that are identified in neuropsychological assessment. **Viewpoint Box 15.3** provides a case example of neuropsychological assessment conducted to aid in treatment planning.

VIEWPOINT BOX 15.3

NEUROPSYCHOLOGICAL ASSESSMENT TO AID IN DIFFERENTIAL DIAGNOSIS AND TREATMENT PLANNING

Peter (age 25) was referred for a neuropsychological assessment by a neurologist. He had difficulties with memory and concentration, slept poorly, suffered headaches, and felt anxious. Six months earlier, Peter had been a passenger in a car accident in which he sustained a mild head injury with loss of consciousness for 10-15 minutes. His close friend, who was the driver, was killed in the accident. A neuropsychological assessment was requested to determine whether Peter's symptoms were related to posttraumatic stress disorder (PTSD), a psychological disorder related to the effects of the severe accident in which a friend died, or to post-concussion syndrome (PCS), a physiological disorder due to a brain injury during the accident.

The neuropsychological assessment included an interview, as well as tests of intelligence, memory, perceptual and visual skills, and executive functioning. Results revealed Peter experienced some symptoms of anxiety related to the accident, as well as grief over the death of his friend. However, he did not meet criteria for a diagnosis of PTSD, as he did not report re-experiencing the accident or intrusive thoughts about it. He did evidence significant cognitive difficulties in formal testing that were consistent with the problems he reported in daily living. These cognitive symptoms were more pronounced than those that would be seen after exposure to a traumatic event. The clinical neuropsychologist therefore concluded that Peter's symptoms reflected the residual effects of the brain injury (i.e., PCS), which were compounded by his emotional reaction to the accident and his friend's death. To address these issues, Peter was provided with information about head injury and given strategies to address his memory and attention difficulties. He was advised to attempt a gradual return to work and was offered counselling to address the emotional sequelae of the accident.

Adapted from Goldstein & McNeil (2004).

Despite the potential usefulness of neuropsychological assessment in treatment planning, it is not routinely available to all patients with neurological problems. A recent survey of rehabilitation programs within the American Hospital Association (Stringer, 2003) revealed that most patients were under 65 and had been hospitalized for a stroke or a brain injury. The majority of these patients received individualized cognitive rehabilitation services over a period of one to six months, at a cost of $130 (U.S.) per session. These services were often delivered by speech therapists and occupational therapists. Few of these programs incorporated neuropsychological testing.

Different theoretical models of **cognitive rehabilitation** lead to different strategies to help a person deal with the real-life problems caused by neurological problems (Lemsky, 2000). Using the terminology of the World Health Organization, some interventions are designed to overcome impairments by teaching the patient new strategies; other interventions are designed to compensate for impairments by modifying the environment or by using aids so that the patient is capable of carrying out an activity, and others address social, psychological, and physical barriers to the person's participation (Lemsky, 2000). The development of effective treatments relies on a solid understanding of cognitive processes such as memory and learning. One type of treatment focusing on impairments is cognitive rehabilitation for memory difficulties or for attention deficits. In the treatment of memory deficits, efforts to retrain memory have been found to be ineffective and external memory aids such as lists, calendars, electronic agendas, pagers, and personal digital assistants are widely used (Evans, 2004).

The Committee on Empirically Supported Programs (COESP) of the Division of Clinical Neuropsychology of the American Psychological Association commissioned a review of literature on treatments for attentional problems (Riccio & French, 2004). Across all treatment programs and populations reviewed, the existing research does not provide evidence of the efficacy of the approach. Quite simply, there has not yet been methodologically adequate research conducted to demonstrate that the treatments make a difference. Similarly, a review of cognitive rehabilitation for people with early stage Alzheimer's disease concluded that although single case reports provided encouraging data, no randomized control trials have been conducted, so there is no empirical basis that individualized cognitive rehabilitation programs are efficacious for people with early-stage Alzheimer's disease (Clare & Woods, 2004). There is clearly an urgent need for these relatively costly interventions to be studied so that we can identify the most efficacious programs for people dealing with impairment and disability related to neurological injury and disease.

FORENSIC PSYCHOLOGY

Forensic psychology, broadly defined, is the application of psychology in the legal and criminal justice systems. Within the scope of forensic psychology, there are clinical psychologists who provide services in correctional facilities. Like other types of clinical psychology, forensic psychologists engage in services related to prevention, assessment, treatment, and research. In earlier chapters we raised issues that are important in forensic psychology, such as assessing whether a person making an insurance claim for injuries sustained in an accident is accurately reporting symptoms or is malingering (Chapter 8), developing programs to prevent the emergence of delinquent behaviour (Chapter 10), and treating victims of accidents or abuse (Chapters 12 and 13). We indicated that psychologists do not have client privilege, so that their work may be subpoenaed, and they must explain the limits of confidentiality to clients (Chapter 6). Forensic psychologists provide services to many stakeholders including victims of crime, witnesses of crimes, offenders, parties in a legal dispute, police forces, and the courts. Other mental health professionals such as psychiatrists also offer forensic services based on interviews and examination of collateral data such as reports from schools, employers, or previous therapists. With their expertise in using data from psychological tests, psychologists are well-positioned to offer expert opinion (Lally, 2003).

Forensic psychologists are employed in myriad settings, including hospitals, private practice, court clinics, maximum security federal penitentiaries, provincial jails, provincial correctional centres, minimum security camps (both adult and youth), specialized treatment facilities, community probation and parole offices, and Aboriginal healing lodges. The vast majority of these psychologists are directly engaged in providing psychological services, but others are research psychologists or psychologists who work in the fields of policy and administration (Magaletta & Verdeyen, 2005).

Licensure and Training

In Canada, most forensic psychologists have a doctorate in clinical psychology and field training in forensic psychology. **Table 15.9** lists additional areas beyond those listed in Table 15.1 in which a psychologist must be knowledgeable in order to practise forensic psychology in the province of Ontario. Given the nature of the problems with which they work, forensic psychologists must be knowledgeable about strategies for assessing and managing risk. In addition, those working with children must understand the criminal justice and legal systems with respect to children. Training in corrections is available through a few clinical psychology programs in Canada and in several clinical internship sites. Research forensic psychologists do not require training in clinical psychology.

TABLE 15.9   College of Psychologists of Ontario: Additional Knowledge Requirements to Practise Forensic Psychology

Forensic Psychology	Child and Adolescent Forensic Psychology
• criminal justice/legal systems	• criminal justice/legal systems with respect to children and adolescents
• criminal behaviour	• criminal behaviour
• application of psychological principles within the federal and provincial legal systems	• application of psychological principles within the federal and provincial legal systems
• risk assessment	• risk assessment
• risk management	• risk management

Activities of Forensic Psychologists

Table 15.10 lists some of the activities in which forensic psychologists engage. As you can see, the potential scope of activities is very broad. As noted above, within the field of forensic psychology, a number of psychologists are employed within the correctional system. **Profile Box 15.3** presents Dr. Stephen Wormith, a psychologist who has worked in the correctional system for many years.

TABLE 15.10   The Scope of Forensic Psychology Services

Prevention Programs
To reduce violence and bullying

Court-Related Assessment
Witness
- Credibility issues

Victim
- Impact of an assault or injury
- Credibility versus malingering

Accused
- Evaluation of mental status at the time of an offence
- Competence to stand trial

Disputing Parties
- Child custody evaluation

Offender Assessment
Risk of violence
Risk of sexual violence

Treatment Services
To address mental health issues such as depression and anxiety
To address criminal behaviour

Research
To identify the best strategies to predict criminal behaviour
To identify the most effective treatments

PROFILE BOX 15.3

DR. STEPHEN WORMITH

I earned a Ph.D. in psychology at the University of Ottawa and then worked as a correctional psychologist and researcher with the Correctional Service of Canada, both in institutions and in the community. Formerly, I was Psychologist-in-Chief for the Ontario Ministry of Community Safety and Correctional Services and Deputy Superintendent (Treatment) at Rideau Correctional and Treatment Centre. I am currently Chair of Forensic Psychology in the Psychology Department of the University of Saskatchewan. My research activities have concentrated on the assessment, treatment, and thera-

Dr. Stephen Wormith

peutic processes of offenders, including various special offender groups, such as young offenders, sexual offenders, and mentally disordered offenders. I am a registered psychologist in the provinces of Saskatchewan and Ontario. I provide forensic clinical consultation services to the Regional Psychiatric Centre, Saskatoon (Correctional Service of Canada) and psychological assessments for youth and adult court. I provide forensic research consultation services to the Saskatchewan Department of Corrections and Public Safety, the Ontario Ministry of Community Safety and Correctional Services, and the Correctional Service of Canada. I am also active in the voluntary sector as president of Crime Prevention Saskatchewan, vice-president of the Canadian Training Institute, and the Canadian Psychological Association's representative on the National Associations Active in Criminal Justice.

A typical workday

A typical workday for a correctional psychologist in the field includes a combination of clinical and administrative duties. The first step is often to determine whether there have been any significant events in the last 24 hours that must be addressed. This can include anything from individual issues pertaining to an offender on the psychologist's caseload or major events and disruptions that affect the larger institution. If an offender has presented a problem to correctional staff, she or he may have been removed to a special segregation cell and may require psychological assistance. New admissions to prison are frequently depressed and their potential for self-harm, suicide, or violence must be assessed. Other sudden and unexpected events may have transpired and require attention. An offender may have received upsetting information, such as the loss of a family member or a negative response from the parole board, and may have submitted a request to be seen as soon as possible. In a prison setting, incidents such as these take on even larger proportions because of the offender's feeling of helplessness and inability to take any kind of action. Therefore, a correctional psychologist must always be prepared for crisis intervention activities with his or her clientele even before settling into a day's work.

A recent survey of more than 800 psychologists in American state and federal prisons (Boothby & Clements, 2000) revealed that correctional psychologists spend most of their time performing direct clinical activities. This includes treatment and counselling of inmates (26%) and offender psychological assessment (18%). In addition, a considerable amount of their time is consumed by administrative matters (26%), with a small portion of time devoted to research (6%). Comparable Canadian survey data are not available. Canadian correctional psychologists devote considerable time to conducting risk assessments of offenders. Risk assessments are requested to advise decision-making groups, such as parole boards, in determining the degree of risk an offender poses in the community and under what circumstances this risk might be altered. Canadian psychologists have taken a leadership role in the development of specialized risk assessment measures. With respect to the treatment of the offender, most services provided by psychologists have moved away from the nondirective approaches of the 1960s and 1970s to behavioural and cognitive-behavioural treatments that conform to the empirical evidence concerning *what works* in corrections.

Survey statistics represent averages across many different settings and types of psychologists. My own experience working in a correctional setting has been in various capacities, where the mix of these different activities varied greatly. Early in one's career, one can expect to work primarily as a clinician, interacting directly with offenders, conducting assessments and providing individual and group therapy. Some settings have the luxury of having correctional research psychologists who devote most, if not all, of their efforts to in-house research. These are often clinical or social psychologists whose operational research is designed both to assist the correctional administration and whose clinical and programmatic research is designed to evaluate clinical practice and improve client services. Finally, some psychologists are active in the policy and management aspects of the organization. These psychologists have typically risen through the ranks and work either at the local level, managing clinical services and, in some cases, the larger institutional activities, or at the corporate level, liaising with senior management and policy personnel as they contribute their psychological expertise to the planning and direction of the organization's future.

ASSESSMENT

A recent survey of expert forensic psychologists (Lally, 2003) identified the psychological assessment measures considered appropriate for different types of assessments. **Table 15.11** lists the measures that were deemed *recommended, acceptable,* or *unacceptable* in evaluating risk of violence and in evaluating competency to stand trial. Many of the assessment tools should be familiar to you from previous chapters. You will also notice that an instrument designed specifically for an offender population, the Psychopathy Checklist-Revised (Hare, 1991), is the most highly recommended tool for assessing risk of violence. The majority of expert forensic psychologists who responded to the survey did not consider projective tests acceptable in assessing the risk of violent behaviour or in determining competence to stand trial. A similar survey about instruments used in assessing young offenders' competence to stand trial indicated that (a) intelligence tests such as the Wechsler scales were used by the majority of experts in juvenile forensic assessment (82%), (b) around half of the survey respondents (56%) reported using the MMPI-A, and (c) only a small minority reported using projective tests such as the Rorschach (16%), TAT (12%), or sentence completion tests (10%) (Ryba, Cooper, & Zapf, 2003).

TABLE 15.11 Expert Opinion on Tests for Forensic Evaluations

	Risk for Violence	Competency to Stand Trial
Recommended	Psychopathy Checklist-Revised	WAIS III
		MacArthur Competence Assessment Tool
Acceptable	MMPI-2	MMPI 2
	Psychopathy Checklist–Screening version	Halstead-Reitan
		Stanford-Binet
	Violence Risk Appraisal Guide	Luria-Nebraska
	WAIS III	Interdisciplinary fitness interview
	Personality Assessment Inventory	Personality Assessment Inventory
Unacceptable	Projective drawings	Projective drawings
	TAT	TAT
	Sentence completion	Sentence completion
	Rorschach	Rorschach
	16 PF	16 PF
		MCMI II

Adapted from Lally (2003).

There are important similarities and differences between regular clinical practice and clinical practice within the corrections system. For example, correctional psychologists, like other clinical psychologists, should use evidence-based strategies in their assessment, treatment, and prevention activities. Any psychological assessment can have serious consequences for the well-being of the individual and of society. However, one of the differences in a correctional context is that assessments usually involve public safety issues. This is especially evident in the context of risk assessments that focus on the likelihood of an individual re-engaging in violent criminal behaviour. **Viewpoint Box 15.4** highlights issues in conducting these assessments.

INTERVENTION

Correctional psychology is not simply clinical practice with people who happen to live in a prison (Magaletta & Verdeyen, 2005). For example, for a correctional psychologist, treatment outcome is more likely to be measured in terms of recidivism (committing crimes after release from incarceration) rather than reduction in symptoms. This means that programs are more likely to target factors associated with risk of criminal behaviour (e.g., association with delinquent peers, antisocial attitudes, anger and control of impulsivity) than they are to target variables that are distressing to the offender, but unrelated to criminal behaviour (e.g., low self-esteem) (Dowden & Andrews, 2004). In the 1970s and 1980s, it was assumed that offender treatment had little chance of facilitating change. However, with the introduction of cognitive behavioural programs that target risk factors, the portrait has changed considerably. A series of meta-analyses have supported the utility of CBT interventions for offenders (Dowden & Andrews, 2004).

Unfortunately, the methodological quality of outcome studies in this area is relatively poor, with few randomized control trials. In a recent meta-analysis, D. B. Wilson, Bouffard, and MacKenzie (2005) examined studies using a range of cognitive behavioural interventions including problem-solving, social skills training, cognitive restructuring, and impulse control. Wilson et al. found that the methodologically strongest studies yielded a moderate effect size ($d = .51$). Translating this effect size into recidivism rates, treated offenders had a recidivism rate of 46%, whereas for untreated offenders, the rate was 54% (D. B. Wilson et al., 2005). As in all therapy outcome research, it is important to examine not only the efficacy of research treatment programs but also the effectiveness of these programs when they are widely applied. Wormith (2002), for example, underlined the importance of developing programs for offenders of Aboriginal ancestry who are particularly likely to drop out of treatment programs. Dowden and Andrews (2004) have emphasized the importance of considering correctional staff practices in the delivery of effective treatment. It is clear that the considerable impact of environmental constraints and influences (e.g., restrictiveness of the setting, staff practices, what constitutes normative behaviour in a correctional setting) sets clinical practice in corrections apart from other types of mental health services provided by clinical psychologists.

VIEWPOINT BOX 15.4

RISK ASSESSMENT

One of the primary reasons for requesting a psychological assessment is to obtain a sci-entifically informed prediction about a person's behaviour. Psychological assessments may be used in predicting diverse outcomes such as suicidal risk, the ability to benefit from a social skills group, or the likelihood that the person will adhere to a medical reg-imen. When making predictions, the psychologist draws on research knowledge of risk and protective factors. The risks associated with making errors are carefully weighed. Although most psychological predictions are important, they are rarely the focus of public scrutiny. However, in the case of predictions of violent behaviour, the repercus-sions of errors are very serious. You may recall the media outcry that occurs when news breaks of a violent offence perpetrated by someone recently released from prison or on parole. There are often recriminations that mental health professionals have failed to predict and prevent the violent behaviour. The failure to predict that a person with a violent history will re-offend can have deadly consequences. On the other hand, over-ly conservative predictions based on single episodes of violence that are unlikely to be repeated can lead to the prolonged and unjust incarceration of an offender beyond the time when a sentence has been served.

Twenty-five years ago, mental health professionals were ill-equipped to predict dangerousness (Monahan, 1981). Since that time a number of effective, evidence-based approaches have been developed to aid psychologists in making predictions (Hanson, 2005; Webster & Bailes, 2004). Armed with research-based assessment tools that allow reasonably accurate prediction of violent behaviour, numerous correctional policies have been introduced in North America to protect the public from dangerous offenders. Canadian researchers such as Robert Hare have been at the vanguard of these research efforts. Hare's groundbreaking work on the construct of psychopathy has described the capacity of charming psychopaths to manipulate others without remorse. Hare's *Psychopathy Checklist-Revised* (PCL-R) is considered the single best predictor of violent behaviour (Fulero, 1995; Lally, 2003). The PCL-R has also been demonstrated to be use-ful in diverse cultural contexts (Hare, Clark, Grann, & Thornton, 2000). Another commonly used measure, the *Violence Risk Appraisal Guide* (VRAG; Harris, Rice, & Quinsey, 1993), uses empirically derived combinations of common clinical variables to predict long-term recidivism. Specialized measures have also been developed for sub-populations such as young offenders or men who assault their wives (Hanson, 2005). There is a high degree of correlation between the different measures and many are moderately accurate in predicting recidivism in violent offenders (Hanson, 2005).

SUMMARY AND CONCLUSIONS

In addition to offering traditional mental health services, a growing number of clinical psychologists work in health psychology, clinical neuropsychology, and forensic psychology. Practice in these areas is based on the core skill set found in clinical psychology, with additional specific knowledge and skills taught in graduate training, in internships, and on the job. Health psychologists, with their focus on health maintenance, illness prevention, assessment, and intervention, have a broad scope of practice applicable to all age groups in all health care settings. Clinical neuropsychologists, with their knowledge of brain-behaviour connections, have been and continue to be key contributors to the health care of people with a wide range of neurological impairments. Forensic psychologists, working within and outside correctional facilities, have developed an increasingly efficacious and effective set of assessment and intervention procedures. Across these areas of practice, psychologists strive to apply the science of psychology to the improvement of the lives of young and old alike.

Critical Thinking Questions

Across the different applied areas of practice described in the chapter, what knowledge and skill elements are common to all?

Do you think it could be possible for a clinical psychologist to be a generalist who covers the areas of health psychology, neuropsychology, and forensic psychology? What would be the challenges involved for such a professional?

How does the role of a health psychologist differ from that of a physician?

With the advent of advanced imaging techniques in neurology, what can clinical neuropsychologists contribute to the care of those with neurological impairments?

What are the roles for psychologists in dealing with those involved in the criminal justice system?

Key Terms

acute pain	neuropathology
biopsychosocial model	quality of life
chronic pain	recidivism
cognitive rehabilitation	risk assessments
disability	sleep hygiene
neuroanatomy	

Key Names

Ward Halstead	Patrick McGrath
Robert Hare	Charles Morin
Aleksandr Luria	Ralph Reitan

ADDITIONAL RESOURCES

Books

Goldstein, L. H., & McNeil, J. E. (Eds.). (2004). *Clinical neuropsychology: A practical guide to assessment and management for clinicians.* Chichester, UK: John Wiley & Sons.

Hollin, C. R. (Ed.). (2004). *The essential handbook of offender assessment and treatment.* Chichester, UK: John Wiley & Sons.

Llewelyn, S. (2003). *Handbook of clinical health psychology.* New York: John Wiley & Sons.

Websites

American Board of Clinical Neuropsychology: http://www.theabcn.org/

Canadian National Crime Prevention Strategy: http://www.prevention.gc.ca/en/index.asp

IWK Health Centre and the Pediatric Pain Laboratory of the Psychology Department of Dalhousie University: http://www.pediatric-pain.ca

Major Journals Relevant to Clinical Psychology

American Journal of Psychiatry

This journal is the official publication of the American Psychiatric Association. It includes articles on developments in biological psychiatry as well as on treatment innovations and forensic, ethical, economic, and social topics.

American Psychologist

This is the official journal of the American Psychological Association. Articles address current issues in psychology, the science and practice of psychology, and psychology's contribution to public policy

Annual Review of Clinical Psychology

New in 2005, this journal contains reviews in clinical psychology.

Annual Review of Psychology

This journal presents authoritative, analytic reviews by eminent psychologists covering the entire range of psychological research.

Archives of Clinical Neuropsychology

This journal includes articles in psychological aspects of the etiology, diagnosis, and treatment of disorders arising out of dysfunction of the central nervous system.

Archives of General Psychiatry

This journal contains studies and commentaries of general interest to clinicians, scholars, and research scientists in psychiatry, mental health, behavioural science, and allied fields.

Assessment

This journal covers studies on the use of assessment measures within the domain of clinical and applied psychology, including practical applications of measurement methods, test development and interpretation strategies, and advances in the description and prediction of human behaviour.

Behavior Therapy

This journal is one of the two official publications of the Association for Behavioral and Cognitive Therapies (formally the Association for the Advancement of Behavior Therapy). It includes reports and reviews of studies on the application of behavioural and cognitive sciences to clinical problems.

Behavioral Sciences and the Law

This journal covers topics at the interface of the law and the behavioural sciences, with theoretical, legal, and research articles on psycholegal topics, including mental health.

Behaviour Research and Therapy

This journal contains articles on cognitive behaviour therapy applied to clinical disorders, behavioural medicine, and medical psychology.

British Journal of Clinical Psychology

Published by the British Psychological Society, this journal includes original contributions to scientific knowledge in clinical psychology. Articles include descriptive studies as well as studies of the etiology, assessment, and amelioration of disorders of all kinds, in all settings, and among all age groups.

British Journal of Psychiatry

Published by the Royal College of Psychiatrists, this journal includes editorials, review articles, and commentaries on contentious articles. The target readership is psychiatrists, clinical psychologists, and other mental health professionals.

Canadian Psychology

The official journal of the Canadian Psychological Association, this journal has articles in areas of theory, research, and practice that are potentially of interest to a broad cross-section of psychologists.

Clinical Child and Family Psychology Review

This journal includes research reviews and conceptual and theoretical papers related to infants, children, adolescents, and families. Topics covered include etiology, assessment, description, treatment and intervention, prevention, methodology, and public policy.

Clinical Psychology Review

This journal presents reviews of research on topics such as psychopathology, psychotherapy, behaviour therapy, behavioural medicine, community mental health, assessment, and child development.

Clinical Psychology: Science and Practice

This is the official publication of the Society of Clinical Psychology (Division 12) of the American Psychological Association. It includes reviews of research related to assessment, intervention, service delivery, and professional issues.

Cognitive and Behavioral Practice

This journal is one of the two official publications of the Association for Behavioral and Cognitive Therapies (formally the Association for the Advancement of Behavior Therapy). It contains clinically rich accounts of assessment and intervention procedures that are clearly grounded in empirical research.

Cognitive Therapy and Research

This is an interdisciplinary journal on the role of cognitive processes in human adaptation and adjustment. The journal includes experimental studies; theoretical, review, technical, and methodological articles; case studies; and brief reports.

Criminal Justice and Behavior

This is the official publication of the American Association for Correctional and Forensic Psychology. It includes scholarly evaluations of assessment, classification, prevention, intervention, and treatment programs.

Evidence Based Mental Health

This multidisciplinary journal provides a digest of the most important clinical research relevant to clinicians in mental health.

Health Psychology

Published by the American Psychological Association, this journal is designed to further an understanding of the links between behavioural principles and physical health and illness.

Journal of Abnormal Child Psychology

This is the journal of the International Society for Research in Child and Adolescent Psychopathology. It includes research on psychopathology in childhood and adolescence with an emphasis on empirical studies of the major childhood disorders (the disruptive behaviour disorders, depression, anxiety, and pervasive developmental disorders).

Journal of Abnormal Psychology

This journal, published by the American Psychological Association, includes articles on basic research and theory in psychopathology, normal processes in abnormal individuals, pathological or atypical features of the behaviour of normal persons, experimental studies relating to disordered emotional behaviour or pathology, the influence of gender and ethnicity on pathological processes, and tests of hypotheses from psychological theories that relate to abnormal behaviour.

Journal of Behavioral Medicine

This interdisciplinary journal is devoted to furthering our understanding of physical health and illness through the knowledge and techniques of behavioural science.

Journal of Clinical Child and Adolescent Psychology

Formerly published as the *Journal of Clinical Child Psychology*, this is the official journal of the Society of Clinical Child and Adolescent Psychology (Division 53) of the American Psychological Association. It includes research on development and evaluation of assessment and intervention techniques, studies on the development and maintenance of problems, cross-cultural and socio-demographic variables that influence clinical child and adolescent psychology, training and professional practice issues, and child advocacy.

Journal of Clinical Psychology

This journal includes research studies, articles on contemporary professional issues, single case research, dissertations in brief, notes from the field, and news and notes. Topics include psychopathology, psychodiagnostics, and the psychotherapeutic process, as well as articles focusing on psychotherapy effectiveness research, psychological assessment and treatment matching, and clinical outcomes.

Journal of Consulting and Clinical Psychology

This journal, published by the American Psychological Association, includes articles on the development, validity, and use of techniques of diagnosis and treatment of disordered behaviour; studies of populations of clinical interest, such as hospitals, prison, rehabilitation, geriatric, and similar samples; cross-cultural and demographic studies of interest for behaviour disorders; studies of personality and of its assessment and development where these have a clear bearing on problems of clinical dysfunction; studies of gender, ethnicity, or sexual orientation that have a clear bearing on diagnosis, assessment, and treatment; and methodologically sound case studies pertinent to the preceding topics.

Journal of Family Psychology

This is the official publication of the Division of Family Psychology of the American Psychological Association (Division 43) and is devoted to the study of the family system from multiple perspectives and to the application of psychological methods to advance knowledge related to family research, intervention, and policy.

Journal of Marital and Family Therapy

This is the official journal of the American Association of Marital and Family Therapy. It has articles on research and clinical innovations.

Journal of Personality Assessment

This is the official publication of the Society for Personality Assessment. It contains articles dealing with the development, evaluation, refinement, and application of personality assessment methods. Articles address empirical, theoretical, instructional, and professional aspects of using psychological tests, interview data, and the applied clinical assessment process.

Journal of Psychopathology and Behavioral Assessment

This journal includes research investigations and clinical case summaries on psychopathology and mental disorders applicable to all ages, deviant or abnormal behaviours (including those related to medical conditions and trauma), and personality constructs.

Neuropsychology

Published by the American Psychological Association, this journal focuses on basic research, the integration of basic and applied research, and improved practice in the field of neuropsychology.

Professional Psychology: Research and Practice

This journal, published by the American Psychological Association, has articles on the application of psychology, including data-based and theoretical articles on techniques and practices.

Psychological Assessment

This journal, published by the American Psychological Association, presents empirical research on measurement and evaluation relevant to the broad field of clinical psychology. Topics include clinical judgement and the application of decision-making models; paradigms derived from basic psychological research in cognition, personality–social psychology, and biological psychology; and development, validation, and application of assessment instruments, observational methods, and interviews.

Psychological Bulletin

Published by the American Psychological Association, this journal includes evaluative and integrative research reviews and interpretations of issues in scientific psychology.

Psychotherapy

This is the official publication of the Division of Psychotherapy of the American Psychological Association (Division 29). The journal includes theoretical contributions, research studies, novel ideas, controversies, and examples of practice-relevant issues. The journal is designed to be of interest to theorists, researchers, and/or practitioners.

Psychotherapy Research

This journal includes research findings relevant to practice, education, and policy formulation. The journal presents reports of original research on all aspects of psychotherapy, as well as methodological, theoretical, and review articles of direct relevance to psychotherapy research.

Scientific Review of Mental Health Practice

This journal is devoted exclusively to distinguishing scientifically supported claims from scientifically unsupported claims in clinical psychology, psychiatry, social work, and allied disciplines.

Applications to Graduate School

1. DO YOU WANT TO BE A CLINICAL PSYCHOLOGIST?

We hope that the descriptions we have provided of the diverse activities in which clinical psychologists engage help you imagine what it would be like to be a clinical psychologist. As you have learned, the term "clinical psychologist" covers many different types of professional activities, so that, for example, Dr. Maggie Mamen's week is very different from a week in the life of Dr. Heather Hadjistavropoulos, whose work is different again from that of Dr. Kerry Mothersill. Nevertheless, the work lives of these three psychologists have many features in common: (a) their work is based on a foundation of knowledge about human psychological functioning; (b) their work activities are diverse—they spend their work days in a variety of professional activities; (c) their work is demanding and they rarely feel they have enough hours in the day to do everything they wish to; and most importantly, (d) their work is rewarding; they feel a passionate commitment to what they do. These three psychologists are characterized by dynamism, energy, and a commitment to lifelong learning.

As you read the other chapters in this book, you will meet many clinical psychologists at different stages of their careers. When we asked them to tell us how they chose clinical psychology as a career, many described having discovered a passion for this field when they were undergraduates. They were drawn to clinical psychology by the promise it offered to understand and treat health and mental health problems using research-based tools. All the clinical psychologists profiled in this book have varied jobs that require balancing the various activities in learning about new research developments, delivering services, training others, and contributing to the administration of the agency in which they work, as well as serving the broader community. If this appeals to you, then you may be interested in a career in clinical psychology. If your career goal is to spend a much larger proportion of your professional time delivering direct services to clients, you may wish to consider other professions including social work, counselling, or psychiatric nursing.

Many undergraduate students taking a course in clinical psychology are attracted to career possibilities in other areas of psychology. If you find that you have a passion for social psychology or for cognitive psychology, you should follow the steps we suggest in this appendix, but adapt them for the area of psychology that most interests you. In the past it was possible for those with doctorates in non-applied areas of psychology to be registered as clinical psychologists. Due to the growing number of accredited clinical psychology training programs, the increasingly specialized nature of clinical training, and changes in registration requirements, this route for obtaining registration is closing. If you are interested in a career in clinical psychology, but decide to pursue training in a different area of psychology, you should be fully aware that your chances of switching to work as a clinical psychologist are extremely limited. The best option for becoming a clinical psychologist is to complete a doctorate in an accredited clinical program.

2. DO YOU WANT TO GO TO GRADUATE SCHOOL?

Some students apply to graduate school without really taking the time to think about whether it is something that they want to do. As training in clinical psychology in Canada and the United States usually requires around six years of further training after the completion of an honours baccalaureate, it is not something to be taken lightly. If you have high grades, you may have been encouraged by professors to apply to graduate school; however, you need to carefully consider whether this is something that you wish to do.

You must consider your short- and long-term goals for both career and personal life. Are you willing to move? Are you willing to delay earning a good salary? Although clinical psychologists are typically well-paid, there will be many years during graduate school when you will probably be earning much less than your peers who decided to enter the workforce. What kind of job do you hope to have 10 years from now? Graduate training does not occur in a vacuum. At the same time you are considering whether or not you wish to go to graduate school, you may also be reflecting on other decisions, for example, about relationships and when (or whether) you wish to become a parent. Although you may be fairly confident that parenthood is not in your plans in the next year or so, you may be less sure about your plans in three or four years' time. The decision to go to graduate school does not rule out having a family for the next six years. However, it does introduce challenges. Some programs have explicit policies with respect to parental leaves so that, for example, students are allowed one year longer to complete the program for each parental leave taken. If you are a mature student who already has a family, you will no doubt be considering the ways that you can meet the financial and time demands of your multiple roles.

3. ARE YOU ELIGIBLE FOR ADMISSION TO A PROGRAM IN CLINICAL PSYCHOLOGY?

Competition for places in clinical psychology programs is fierce. As programs accept only a very small proportion of the people who apply, all programs have demanding academic standards. As research is such a strong component of the training, programs ensure that candidates admitted to their programs have the intellectual capacity to conduct original research. The selection system can be an unforgiving one: a bad grade in a single course may not sink your application, but a bad year just might. Most programs prefer to accept students who are likely to receive major scholarship funding, which means that places are offered to those candidates who have earned high grades in the baccalaureate degree. As we mentioned early in the book, programs in counselling psychology are often somewhat less demanding in terms of the academic grades required.

Canadian Psychological Association criteria for accredited programs in clinical psychology require students to have completed an honours baccalaureate degree in psychology or its equivalent (CPA, 2002). The honours thesis provides an excellent opportunity to learn about the various steps in conducting research. If you enjoy the process of reviewing the literature to formulate meaningful hypotheses, the intellectual challenge of designing a feasible study that will test those hypotheses, the careful consideration of ethical issues involved in the study, painstaking data collection, rigorous data analysis, and the satisfaction of writing it all up in a coherent report, then the chances are good that you will savour the opportunity to conduct a doctoral dissertation. If, on the other hand, you find completing the honours thesis a tedious process, then you should think very carefully about whether you are attracted to a graduate program in clinical psychology in which one of the key requirements is the completion of a doctoral dissertation.

4. FINDING OUT ABOUT PROGRAMS IN CLINICAL PSYCHOLOGY

What do you need to know about clinical training programs? The Canadian Psychological Association and the American Psychological Association require accredited programs to make available information that will be useful to you in selecting the programs to which you wish to apply. Specifically, CPA and APA require accredited programs to provide information on the program's philosophy and mission, the theoretical orientation and research interests of faculty members, the goals set by the program (as well as outcome data on the extent to which those goals have been met), the requirements and expectations of students in the program, the activities for which the program prepares students, the training resources at the program's disposal, the usual size of the applicant pool, acceptance and attrition rates, percentages of male and female students, students with disabilities, and the diversity of students, age distribution of students, availability of financial and other support, as well as evidence of accreditation. All of this information should be helpful to you in choosing the programs to which you will apply.

The websites of the Canadian Psychological Association and American Psychological Association provide lists of accredited clinical programs. At the time of writing, Canada has 20 accredited clinical psychology programs and one accredited clinical neuropsychology program. Surfing a program website is probably the best strategy to get a general sense of what the program is like. Although all programs include training in the basics of clinical psychology, programs differ in their areas of strength. For example, some programs offer separate training in adult or child clinical psychology, whereas other programs offer combined training in both adult and child clinical psychology. Some programs have faculty members with a strong profile in clinical health psychology, others have special expertise in issues related to older adults, and some provide opportunities to learn about forensic psychology.

Accredited clinical psychology programs differ in the process by which students are selected. In some universities, students are accepted into the program and during the first year of study are matched to work with a particular thesis supervisor. In other programs, there must be a match with a thesis supervisor at the time of admission. You should become aware of the process for each program and tailor your application to each one you are considering. You should also be aware that there are differences among training programs in the sequence of degrees granted. Some universities accept students into a masters program that is then followed by a doctoral program; other universities accept students directly into a doctoral program. Both sequences require comparable course work, research training, practica, and internship. The main difference is that students in the former programs must complete a masters thesis, which is required for the awarding of a masters degree.

5. THE APPLICATION PROCESS

The process of applying to graduate school consumes both time and money. The process consists of several phases including gathering information and deciding whether you wish to apply to graduate school, choosing the programs to which you will apply, studying for and completing the *Graduate Record Examination*, preparing the application materials, obtaining letters of reference and submitting a full application, and finally, (hopefully) making a decision about offers you have received. It is probably fair to say that the application process will take the same amount of your time as a one-term course.

Gathering Information

The information gathering stage begins in your second or third year of undergraduate study. You can probably gather enough information from websites to generate a list of programs that you wish to consider. You can increase your chances of obtaining a place by applying to several different programs. However, it is probably a waste of your time to apply to any programs that you know you do not wish to attend. In addition to the information from websites, you can gather informal information by asking professors for their opinion about different programs.

The Graduate Record Examination

Once you have decided to apply to graduate school and have selected a number of programs that interest you, you will have a better idea of the application requirements for each program. Most programs require candidates to submit scores on the *Graduate Record Examination* (GRE). As the GRE is available in English only, it is not usually required by programs providing instruction in French. The GRE includes both a general test and a subject test. The tests are completed at a licensed test centre either via computer or in a paper and pencil format. The general test takes up to three and a half hours and assesses analytical writing, verbal, and quantitative skills. A CD-ROM containing practice material is sent to applicants for the general test. The subject test lasts up to four hours and includes about 210 multiple choice questions of which 40% are oriented to experimental or natural science, 43% are oriented to social or social science, and 17% are general. In preparation for taking the GRE you should review materials from psychology courses and download a practice test from the GRE website.

Curriculum Vitae

Your *curriculum vitae* (CV) should provide contact information and detail educational accomplishments, honours and awards, scholarly conference presentations, publications, manuscripts submitted for publication, as well as work and volunteer experience. Volunteer experience in the mental health field can provide important opportunities to learn about different populations, the challenges they face, and the resources available to them. Paid or volunteer research experience provides the opportunity to learn research methods, to work more closely with a professor, and in some cases to gain valuable experience in conference presentations and the submission of manuscripts to scholarly journals.

Application Forms and Transcripts

Universities and programs all have different application forms. Ensure that your form is completed accurately. Printed or typed application forms are preferable to hand-written forms. There is also variability in the deadline by which all materials should be submitted ranging from early December to the end of January, so check each date carefully. Most programs require you to arrange for official transcripts to be forwarded to the admission office. Allow plenty of time so that the materials arrive prior to the application deadline. It is prudent to contact the admissions office a couple of weeks before the final deadline to request confirmation that all the application materials have arrived safely and that your file is complete. As this is a busy time of year for all admissions offices, it is probably easiest to do this via email rather than by phone.

Statements of Interest and Research Plans

Many programs ask candidates to submit a written statement about the areas in which they are interested, as well as their research plans. Programs do not expect candidates to have mapped out the study they will conduct for the doctoral dissertation. These written statements should describe your general areas of interest. If your statements are too specific, then you reduce the likelihood of finding a good match with a professor. It probably makes more sense to think in terms of whether you can imagine yourself joining in a professor's research group, than whether you can find someone whose ideas match yours perfectly.

Letters of Reference

All applications for graduate school require reference letters. In general, these letters should be from psychology professors. Although you may obtain a glowing letter from a person in a community agency in which you have volunteered, the opinions of psychology professors are usually given greater weight in the selection process. Whereas professors in small universities may know undergraduate students by name, in larger universities, this occurs less frequently. So in your second or third year, you need to plan to make contact with professors who will be potential referees. You may wish to consider volunteering your services in a research project. Inform the professor that your goal is to apply to graduate programs in clinical psychology and that you are eager to obtain relevant experience.

Table 1 highlights issues in obtaining a letter of reference. It is to your advantage to ask the professor whether she or he is willing to write a reference letter well ahead of the deadline. As you are aware, professors have numerous responsibilities, so if you make a request for a letter that is due in a week's time, you risk getting a brief letter, a late letter, or none at all. Once the professor has agreed to write the letter, you must prepare a complete package that contains all the material the professor will need in order to prepare letters to be sent to the various programs to which you are applying. It is beneficial for you to make the professor's task as straightforward as possible. Avoid asking for a series of letters as you decide to apply to different programs. A week or so before the deadline, contact the professor to inquire politely whether the letters are ready. Most professors who have gone to the trouble of preparing letters of reference for you will appreciate receiving a message of thanks and a message reporting the final outcome of the application process.

TABLE 1   Letters of Reference

Who to ask

Psychology professors who are familiar with your work

- Supervisor of honours thesis
- Instructor in a small class
- Supervisor of research assistantship or volunteer research

When to ask

- Once the professor is familiar with your work
- At least two months in advance

What to provide

- Full list of programs to which you are applying with addresses and deadlines
- Your *curriculum vitae*
- Copy of your transcript

Before the deadline

- Polite inquiry whether the letter is prepared

After you receive results

- Inform the professors who have written letters of the results and thank them

---

Universities have different policies concerning letters of reference. Some require the referee to send a letter directly to the university, others require the letters of reference to be given to the candidate in signed, sealed envelopes and included in the application package. Check the required procedure for each university.

Contacting Potential Supervisors

Email is a very easy way to contact potential supervisors. However, prior to contacting the potential supervisor, do your homework: find out all you can about the program in general and the work of that professor in particular. **Table 2** describes possible contact with potential supervisors. Professors often receive many emails a week in the fall term from potential students, so it is helpful to keep an initial email relatively brief. It is wise to verify whether the supervisor is planning on accepting a new student that year. It is important to know, for example, whether the professor is on parental leave, sabbatical leave, or close to retirement and not accepting a student.

As published material is easily available electronically, it does not make sense to request copies of the professor's publications. You should do a bit of homework and read several of the professor's recent publications. If you are truly interested in working with this person you may wish to ask to see a copy of work that is in press. Avoid clogging a professor's inbox with documents such as a transcript, your CV, and a copy of your honours thesis. However, it may be helpful to offer to send any of those materials if the professor would like to read them.

TABLE 2   Contacting Potential Supervisors

Prior to Application
- Find out information from university website
- Search for materials on PsycINFO
- Express interest via email
- Confirm that professor is eligible to take a new student
- Offer to send materials (CV, transcript)
- Ask for copies of articles that are in press
- Inquire about future research planned by the professor
- Inquire about interviews
- Ask specific questions if the information is not available elsewhere

If you are contacted by a potential supervisor
- Ask questions that would give information to help you choose between two offers
- Ask about supervision style
- Ask to speak to current or recent graduate students

Once you have made a decision
- Inform professor that you intend to accept offer
- Inform professor if you have accepted a place elsewhere

If you live within easy travelling of the university to which you are applying, you may wish to express your willingness to come for an interview. Many professors do not conduct interviews until after the deadline for admission (they simply do not have time to interview all potential candidates, so focus their energies on a few candidates who have met all the eligibility criteria and who are interested in research in their area). You may wish to ask a professor whether it is possible to meet or contact other graduate students.

6. FINANCING YOUR TRAINING

Unless you are independently wealthy, your planning should include consideration of how you will finance the years you will be in graduate school. On average, students take over six years after the bachelor's degree to complete a Ph.D. in clinical psychology. Expenses include tuition fees as well as living expenses. Accredited programs in clinical psychology require full-time registration as a student for at least four years. That means that you are not allowed to work more than a small number of hours a week (e.g., 10 hours a week in many universities). Part of your planning and decision-making should include finding out about all your potential sources of income.

Scholarships and Bursaries

You may be eligible to receive scholarships and bursaries from diverse sources including the university in which you will be enrolled, and from provincial or federal funding agencies. Most scholarships are awarded on the basis of merit, which means that they are given to the students who have high grade point averages; if you have made a presentation at a scholarly conference, or have submitted a manuscript for publication, that will also strengthen your application. Applications for federal and provincial funding are made a year in advance, so it is important to gather information and submit your application in plenty of time.

In addition to major funding, there may be many small scholarships for which you may be eligible. Some of these may be offered to students whose work is in a certain area, or to those in serious financial need. Some students are proficient in finding out about potential sources of funding and become competent at preparing application packages. Although a $500 scholarship will not solve all your financial concerns, it will help, and will of course be an important item to add to your CV.

Research Assistantships

You may be eligible to work part-time as a research assistant. The rates for research assistants vary from university to university. In addition to earning money, you will also be gaining experience in various research tasks. In addition, the professor who supervises your research assistantship will be in a good position to observe your research skills and may be a good person to ask to prepare letters of reference for you in the future.

Teaching Assistantships and Teaching Courses

Many graduate students work part-time as teaching assistants with responsibilities in conducting laboratories, marking assignments, and even teaching a class or two. In some universities, graduate students also have the opportunity to teach a full course.

Practica and Internships

In Canada it is rare for students to be paid for completing practica. However, accredited clinical programs include a full one-year accredited paid internship. The salaries for internships vary tremendously from site to site. You will not be able to retire on your year's salary, but it will probably pay your living expenses for the internship year.

7. DECISION-MAKING

Unsuccessful Applications

The number of qualified applicants to programs in clinical psychology far exceeds the number of spaces available in accredited clinical psychology programs. That means that each year a number of candidates with high grade point averages, excellent letters of reference, and a passionate commitment to become a clinical psychologist fail to receive an offer of admission to an accredited clinical program. This is often a very disheartening experience—it may be the first sense of academic failure that you have experienced.

If your application is unsuccessful, it is important that you carefully examine the base rates. Across clinical programs there are about 10 applicants for every position. In deciding what to do next, you must consider your chances for future years. If, for example, your grade point average is above the official cut-off, but much lower than that of students admitted to clinical programs, then you may wish to consider alternative programs of study that are less stringent in terms of academic criteria. If you have highly specialized research interests in an area in which there are few supervisors, you may wish to broaden your interests. If you have applied to only one program, then you have seriously limited the odds of acceptance. If you decide to reapply next year, it makes sense to investigate strategies to enhance the chance of success next year. You may wish to consider ways to boost your GPA, or you may wish to study harder and re-take the GRE. If you are involved with a research laboratory, you could inquire about opportunities to become involved in a conference presentation or a manuscript submission.

Successful Applications

Although receiving a rejection letter is stressful, so too is receiving more than one offer of admission. Fortunately, all graduate programs allow candidates until mid-April to accept offers of admission. Unfortunately, that can lead to chains of people waiting: candidate A has an offer from university 1, but really wants to go to university 2; candidate B has an offer from university 2, but really wants to go to university 3, and candidate C has an offer from university 3, but is not sure whether she or he wants to go into psychology or to law school. Although there is no fool-proof way to avoid this kind of situation, it can be minimized if candidates gather all the information they need to make informed choices and develop a list of preferences.

ADDITIONAL RESOURCES

Websites

Listing of all Canadian graduate programs in psychology: http://www.cpa.ca/graduate/guide.pdf

Listing of all graduate programs accredited by the Canadian Psychological Association:

http://www.cpa.ca/accredlist.htm

The *Graduate Record Examination*: http://www.gre.org

Books

Keith-Spiegel, P., & Wiederman, M. W. (2000). *Complete guide to graduate school admission: Psychology, counseling and related professions.* (2nd ed.) Mahwah, NJ: Erlbaum.

Sayette, M. A., Mayne, T. J., & Norcross, J. C. (2004). *Insider's guide to graduate programs in clinical and counseling psychology.* New York. Guilford.

References

Ablow, J. C., Measelle, J. R., Kraemer, H. C., Harrington, R., Luby, J., Smider, N., et al. (1999). The MacArthur three-city outcome study: Evaluating multi-informant measures of young children's symptomatology. *Journal of the American Academy of Child and Adolescent Psychiatry, 38,* 1580–1590.

Abramowitz, J. S. (1997). Effectiveness of psychological and pharmacological treatments for Obsessive-Compulsive Disorder: A quantitative review. *Journal of Consulting and Clinical Psychology, 65,* 44–52.

Achenbach, T. M. (2002). *Manual for the Assessment Data Management Program (ADM) CBCL, YSR, TRF, YASR, YCBCL, SCICA, CBCL/2-3, CBCL/1.5-5 and C-TRF.* Vermont: University Medical Associates.

Achenbach, T. M., McConaughy, S. H., & Howell, C. T. (1987). Child/adolescent behavioral and emotional problems: Implications of cross-informant correlations for situational specificity. *Psychological Bulletin, 101,* 213–232.

Achenbach, T. M., Newhouse, P. A., & Rescorla, L. A. (2004). *Manual for ASEBA Older Adult Forms & Profiles.* Burlington, VT: University of Vermont, Research Center for Children, Youth, & Families.

Achenbach, T. M., & Rescorla, L. A. (2000). *Manual for ASEBA Preschool Forms & Profiles.* Burlington, VT: University of Vermont, Research Center for Children, Youth, & Families.

Achenbach, T. M., & Rescorla, L. A. (2001). *Manual for ASEBA School-Age Forms & Profiles.* Burlington, VT: University of Vermont, Research Center for Children, Youth, & Families.

Achenbach, T. M., & Rescorla, L. A. (2003). *Manual for ASEBA Adult Forms & Profiles.* Burlington, VT: University of Vermont, Research Center for Children, Youth, & Families.

Ackerman, M. J., & Ackerman, M. C. (1997). Custody evaluation practices: A survey of experienced professionals (revisited). *Professional Psychology: Research and Practice, 28,* 137–145.

Ackerman, S. J., Hilsenroth, M. J., Baity, M. R., & Blagys, M. D. (2000). Interaction of therapeutic process and alliance during psychological assessment. *Journal of Personality Assessment, 75,* 82–109.

Acklin, M. W., McDowell, C. J., Verschell, M. S., & Chan, D. (2000). Interobserver agreement, intraobserver reliability, and the Rorschach Comprehensive System. *Journal of Personality Assessment, 74,* 15–47.

Addis, M. E., & Krasnow, A. D. (2000). A national survey of practicing psychologists' attitudes towards psychotherapy treatment manuals. *Journal of Consulting and Clinical Psychology, 68,* 331–339.

Addis, M. E., Wade, W. A., & Hatgis, C. (1999). Addressing practitioners' concerns about manual-based psychotherapies. *Clinical Psychology: Science and Practice, 6,* 430–441.

Aiken, L. R. (2003). *Psychological testing and assessment* (11th ed.). Toronto: Pearson.

Albano, A. M., & Silverman, W. K. (1996). *Anxiety Disorders Interview Schedule for Children for DSM-IV (ADIS IV): Clinician manual for parent and child versions.* San Antonio, TX: Psychological Corporation.

Alvidrez, J., Azocar, F., & Miranda, J. (1996). Demystifying the concept of ethnicity for psychotherapy researchers. *Journal of Consulting and Clinical Psychology, 64,* 903–908.

American Educational Research Association, American Psychological Association, & National Council on Measurement in Education. (1999). *Standards for educational and psychological testing.* Washington, DC: American Educational Research Association.

American Indian and Alaska native youth: Promising strategies for healthier communities. *Psychological Bulletin, 130,* 304–323.

American Psychiatric Association. (1952). *Diagnostic and statistical manual of mental disorders.* Washington, DC: Author.

American Psychiatric Association. (1968). *Diagnostic and statistical manual of mental disorders* (2nd ed.). Washington, DC: Author.

American Psychiatric Association. (1980). *Diagnostic and statistical manual of mental disorders* (3rd ed.). Washington, DC: Author.

American Psychiatric Association. (1987). *Diagnostic and statistical manual of mental disorders* (3rd ed., revised). Washington, DC: Author.

American Psychiatric Association. (1994). *Diagnostic and statistical manual of mental disorders* (4th ed.). Washington, DC: Author.

American Psychiatric Association. (2000). *Diagnostic and statistical manual of mental disorders* (4th ed., text revision). Washington, DC: Author.

American Psychological Association, Division 12 Presidential Task Force. (1999). Assessment for the Twenty-first century: A model curriculum. *The Clinical Psychologist, 52(4),* 10–15.

American Psychological Association. (1994). Guidelines for child custody evaluations in divorce proceedings. *American Psychologist, 49,* 677–680.

American Psychological Association. (2002). Ethical principles of psychologists and code of conduct. *American Psychologist, 57,* 1060–1073.

American Psychological Association. (2002). *Guidelines on multicultural education, training, research, practice, and organizational change for psychologists.* Washington, DC: Author.

American Psychological Association. (2003). Guidelines on multicultural education, training, research, practice, and organizational change for psychologists. *American Psychologist, 58,* 377–402.

American Psychological Association. (2004). Guidelines for psychological practice with older adults. *American Psychologist, 59,* 236–260.

American Psychological Association. (2003). PracticeNet survey: Clinical practice patterns. Retrieved April 8, 2005, from http://www.apapracticenet.net/results/Summer 2003/1.asp

American Psychological Association Practice Directorate. (2003). PracticeNet survey: Clinical practice patterns. Retrieved April 8, 2005 from http://www.apapracticenet.net/results/

American Psychological Association Working Group on the Older Adult. (1998). What practitioners should know about working with older adults. *Professional Psychology: Research and Practice, 29,* 413–427.

Anastasi, A., & Urbina, S. (1997). *Psychological testing* (7th ed.). Upper Saddle River, NJ : Prentice-Hall, Inc.

Anastopoulos, A. D., & Farley, S. E. (2003). A cognitive-behavioral training program for parents of children with Attention-Deficit/Hyperactivity Disorder. In A. E. Kazdin & J. R. Weisz (Eds.), *Evidence-based psychotherapies for children and adolescents* (pp. 187–203). New York: Guilford.

APA Presidential Task Force on Evidence-Based Practice. (2005). *Draft policy statement on evidence-based practice in psychology.* Retrieved on March 3rd 2005, from http://forms.apa.org/members/ebp/

Archer, R. P. (1996). MMPI-Rorschach interrelationships: Proposed criteria for evaluating explanatory models. *Journal of Personality Assessment, 67,* 504–515.

Archer, R. P., & Krishnamurthy, R. (1997). MMPI-A and Rorschach indices related to depression and conduct disorder: An evaluation of the incremental validity hypothesis. *Journal of Personality Assessment, 69,* 517–533.

Arnett, J. L. (2001). Clinical and health psychology: Future directions. *Canadian Psychology, 42,* 38–48.

Arnow, B. A. (1999). Why are empirically supported treatments for Bulimia Nervosa underutilized and what can we do about it? *Journal of Clinical Psychology, 55,* 769–779.

Aspinwall, L.G., & Staudinger, U. M. (Eds.). (2003). *A psychology of human strengths: Fundamental questions and future directions for a positive psychology.* Washington, DC: APA Books.

Association of Family and Conciliation Courts. (1994). Model standards of practice for child custody evaluations. *Family and Conciliation Courts Review, 32,* 504–513.

Association of State and Provincial Psychology Boards. (2005). *ASPPB code of conduct.* Montgomery, AL: Author.

Barber, J. P., Connolly, M. B., Crits-Christoph, P., Gladis, L., & Siqueland, L. (2000). Alliance predicts patients' outcome beyond in-treatment change in symptoms. *Journal of Consulting and Clinical Psychology, 68,* 1027–1032.

Barber, J. P., & Crits-Christoph, P. (1993). Advances in measures of psychodynamic formulations. *Journal of Consulting and Clinical Psychology, 61,* 574–585.

Barbopoulos, A., & Clark, J. M. (2003). Practising psychology in rural settings: Issues and guidelines. *Canadian Psychology, 44,* 410–424.

Barbotte, E., Guillemin, F., Chau, N., & the Lorhandicap Group. (2001). Prevalence of impairments, disabilities, handicaps and quality of life in the general population: A review of the literature. *Bulletin of the World Health Organization, 79,* 1047–1055.

Barkham, M., Margison, F., Leach, C., Lucock, M., Mellor-Clark, J., Evans, C., et al. (2001). Service profiling and outcomes benchmarking using the CORE-OM: Toward practice-based evidence in the psychological therapies. *Journal of Consulting and Clinical Psychology, 69,* 184–196.

Barkley, R. et al. (2002). International Consensus Statement on ADHD. *Clinical Child and Family Psychology Review, 5,* 89–111.

Barlow, D. H. (2004). Psychological treatments. *American Psychologist, 59,* 869–878.

Barlow, D. H., Allen, L. B., & Choate, M. L. (2004). Toward a unified treatment for emotional disorders. *Behavior Therapy, 35,* 205–230.

Barrett, P. M., & Ollendick, T. H. (Eds.). (2004). *Interventions that work with children and adolescents: Prevention and treatment.* New York: John Wiley & Sons.

Barrett, P. M., & Shortt, A. L. (2003). Parental involvement in the treatment of anxious children. In A. E. Kazdin & J. R. Weisz (Eds.), *Evidence-based psychotherapies for children and adolescents* (pp. 101–119). New York: Guilford.

Barrett, P., & Turner, C. (2001). Prevention of anxiety symptoms in primary school children: Preliminary results from a universal school-based trial. *British Journal of Clinical Psychology, 40,* 399–410.

Barrett, P., & Turner, C. (2004). Prevention of childhood anxiety and depression. In P. M. Barrett & T. H. Ollendick (Eds.), *Interventions that work with children and adolescents: Prevention and Treatment* (pp. 429–474). Chichester, UK: John Wiley & Sons.

Barton, C., & Alexander, J. F. (1981). Functional family therapy. In A. Gurman & D. Kniskern (Eds.), *Handbook of family therapy* (pp. 403–443). New York: Brunner/Mazel.

Bastien, C. H., Morin, C. M., Ouellet, M-C., Blais, F. C., & Bouchard, S. (2004). Cognitive-behavioral therapy for insomnia: Comparison of individual therapy, group therapy, and telephone consultations. *Journal of Consulting and Clinical Psychology, 72,* 653–659.

Baucom, D. H., Epstein, N., & Gordon, K. C. (2000). Marital therapy: Theory, practice and empirical status. In C. R. Snyder & R. E. Ingram (Eds.), *Handbook of psychological changes: Psychotherapy processes and practices for the 21st century* (pp. 280–308). New York: John Wiley & Sons.

Bauer, S., Lambert, M. J., & Nielsen, S. L. (2004). Clinical significance methods: A comparison of statistical techniques. *Journal of Personality Assessment, 82,* 60–70.

Baydar, N., Reid, J., & Webster-Stratton, C. (2003). The role of mental health factors and program engagement in the effectiveness of a preventive parenting program for Head Start mothers. *Journal of Consulting and Clinical Psychology, 74,* 1433–1453.

Beach, S. R. H., & Amir, N. (2003). Is depression taxonic, dimensional, or both? *Journal of Abnormal Psychology, 112,* 228–236.

Beck, A. T., Rush, A. J., Shaw, B. F., & Emery, G. (1979). *Cognitive therapy of depression.* New York: Guilford.

Beck, A. T., Steer, R. A., & Brown, G. K. (1996). *Beck Depression Inventory manual* (2nd ed.). San Antonio, TX: Psychological Corporation.

Becker, C. B., Zayfert, C., & Anderson, E. (2004). A survey of psychologists' attitudes towards and utilization of exposure therapy for PTSD. *Behaviour Research and Therapy, 42,* 277–292.

Bekhit, N. S., Thomas, G. V., Lalonde, S., & Jolley, R. (2002). Psychological assessment in clinical practice in Britain. *Clinical Psychology and Psychotherapy, 9,* 285–291.

Bellak, L., & Abrams, D. M. (1997). *The Thematic Apperception Test, the Children's Apperception Test, and the Senior Apperception Technique in clinical use* (6th ed.). Boston, MA: Allyn & Bacon.

Benton, S. A., Robertson, J. M., Tseng, W. C., Newton, F. B., & Benton, S. L. (2003). Changes in counseling center client problems across 13 years. *Professional Psychology: Research and Practice, 34,* 66–72.

Bergin, A. E. (1971). The evaluation of therapeutic outcomes. In A. E. Bergin & S. L. Garfield (Eds.), *Handbook of psychotherapy and behaviour change* (pp. 217–270). New York: John Wiley & Sons.

Berman, P. S. (1997). *Case conceptualization and treatment planning.* Thousand Oaks, CA: Sage.

Beutler, L. E. (1998). Identifying empirically supported treatments: What if we didn't? *Journal of Consulting and Clinical Psychology, 66,* 113–120.

Beutler, L. E. (2002). The dodo bird is extinct. *Clinical Psychology: Science and Practice, 9,* 30–34.

Beutler, L. E., & Castonguay, L. G. (2006). The task force on empirically based principles of therapeutic change. In L. G. Castonguay & L. E. Beutler (Eds.), *Principles of therapeutic change that work* (pp. 1–10). New York: Oxford University Press.

Beutler, L. E., Malik, M., Alimohamed, S., Harwood, T. M., Talebi, H., Noble, S., et al. (2004). Therapist variables. In M. J. Lambert (Ed.), *Bergin and Garfield's handbook of psychotherapy and behavior change* (5th ed., pp. 227–306). New York: John Wiley & Sons.

Beutler, L. E., Rocco, F., Moleiro, C. M., & Talebi, H. (2002). Resistance. *Psychotherapy, 38,* 431–442.

Bickman, L. (1996). A continuum of care: More is not always better. *American Psychologist, 51,* 689–701.

Bickman, L., Rosof-Williams, J., Salzerm M. S., Summerfelt, W. T., Noser, K., Wilson, S. J., et al. (2000). What information do clinicians value for monitoring adolescent client progress and outcomes? *Professional Psychology: Research and Practice, 31,* 70–74.

Biglan, A. (2003). The generic features of effective childrearing. In A. Biglan, M. Wang, & H. J. Walberg (Eds.), *Preventing youth problems* (pp. 145–162). New York: Kluwer Academic.

Biglan, A., Mrazek, P. K., Carnine, D., & Flay, B. R. (2003). The integration of research and practice in the prevention of youth behaviour problems. *American Psychologist, 58,* 433–440.

Biglan, A., & Severson, H. H. (2003). The prevention of tobacco use. In A. Biglan, M. Wang, & H. J. Walberg (Eds.), *Preventing youth problems* (pp. 63–85). New York: Kluwer: Academic.

Birchler, G. R., & Fals-Stewart, W. S. (2002). Marital dysfunction. In M. Hersen (Ed.), *Clinical behavior therapy with adults and children* (pp. 216–235). New York: John Wiley & Sons.

Blagys, M. D., & Hilsenroth, M. J. (2000). Distinctive features of short-term psychodynamic interpersonal psychotherapy: A review of the comparative psychotherapy process literature. *Clinical Psychology: Science and Practice, 7,* 167–188.

Blagys, M. D., & Hilsenroth, M. J. (2002). Distinctive activities of cognitive-behavioral therapy: A review of the comparative psychotherapy process literature. *Clinical Psychology Review, 22,* 671–706.

Blashfield, R. K. (1991). Models of psychiatric classification. In M. Hersen & S. M. Turner (Eds.), *Adult psychopathology and diagnosis* (2nd ed., pp. 3–22). New York: John Wiley & Sons.

Blumentritt, T. L., & VanVoorhis, C. R. W. (2004). The Millon Adolescent Clinical Inventory: Is it valid and reliable for Mexican American youth? *Journal of Personality Assessment, 83,* 64–74.

Bohart, A. C., O'Hara, M., & Leitner, L. M. (1998). Empirically violated treatments: Disenfranchisement of humanistic and other psychotherapies. *Psychotherapy Research, 8,* 141–157.

Bolton, P., Bass, J., Neugebauer, R., Verdeli, H., Clougherty, K. P., Wickramaratne, P., et al. (2003). Group interpersonal psychotherapy for depression in rural Uganda. *Journal of the American Medical Association, 289,* 3117–3124.

Bonanno, G. A. (2004). Loss, trauma, and human resilience. *American Psychologist, 59,* 20–28.

Bongers, I. L., Koot, H. M., van der Ende, J., & Verhulst, F. C. (2003). The normative development of child and adolescent problem behavior. *Journal of Abnormal Psychology, 112,* 179–192.

Boothby, J. L., & Clements, C. B. (2000). A national survey of correctional psychologists. *Criminal Justice and Behavior, 27,* 716–732.

Bor, W., Sanders, M. R., & Markie-Dadds, C. (2002). The effects of the Triple-P Positive Parenting Program on preschool children with co-occurring disruptive behaviour and attentional/hyperactive difficulties. *Journal of Abnormal Child Psychology, 30,* 571–587.

Bornstein, R. F., Rossner, S. C., Hill, E. L., & Stepanian, M. L. (1994). Face validity and fakability of objective and projective measures of dependency. *Journal of Personality Assessment, 63,* 363–386.

Bower, P., & Gilbody, S. (2005). Stepped care in psychological therapies: Access, effectiveness, and efficiency. *British Journal of Psychiatry, 186,* 11–17.

Bowman, M. L. (2000). The diversity of diversity: Canadian-American differences and their implications for clinical training and APA accreditation. *Canadian Psychology, 41,* 230–243.

Braaten, E. B., Otto, S., & Handelsman, M. M. (1993). What do people want to know about psychotherapy? *Psychotherapy, 30,* 565–570.

Brabender, V. A., Fallon, A. E., & Smolar, A. I. (2004). *Essentials of group therapy.* New York: John Wiley & Sons.

Bradley, R., Greene, J., Russ, E., Dutra, L., & Westen, D. (2005). A multi-dimensional meta-analysis of psychotherapy for PTSD. *American Journal of Psychiatry, 162,* 214–227.

Breau, L. M., McGrath, P. J., Camfield, C. S., & Finley, G. A. (2002). Psychometric properties of the non-communicating children's pain checklist-revised. *Pain, 99,* 349–357.

Brestan, E. V., & Eyberg, S. M. (1998). Effective psychosocial treatment of conduct disordered children and adolescents: 29 years, 82 studies, and 5257 kids. *Journal of Clinical Child Psychology, 27,* 180–189.

Brinkmeyer, M. Y., & Eyberg, S. M. (2003). Parent-child interaction therapy for oppositional children. In A. E. Kazdin & J. R. Weisz (Eds.), *Evidence-based psychotherapies for children and adolescents* (pp. 204–223). New York: Guilford.

British Psychological Society. (2003). *Professional Practice Guidelines: Division of Neuropsychology.* Retrieved January 15, 2005, from http://www.bps.org.uk

Brockington, I., & Mumford, D. (2002). Recruitment into psychiatry. *British Journal of Psychiatry, 180,* 307–312.

Bronfenbrenner, U. (1979). *The ecology of human development: Experiments by design and by nature.* Cambridge, MA: Harvard University Press.

Broshek, D. K., & Barth, J. T. (2000). The Halstead-Reitan Neuropsychological Test Battery. In G. Groth-Marnat (Ed.), *Neuropsychological assessment in clinical practice* (pp. 223–263). New York: John Wiley & Sons.

Brown, G. W., & Harris, T. O. (1978). *The social origins of depression: A study of psychiatric disturbance in women.* London: Tavistock Institute.

Brown, M. B., Giandenoto, M., & Bolen, L. M. (2000). Diagnosing written language disabilities using the Woodcock-Johnson Tests of Educational Achievement—Revised and the Wechsler Individual Achievement Test. *Psychological Reports, 87,* 197–204.

Brown, P., & Dean, S. (2001). Assessment as an intervention in the child and family forensic setting. *Professional Psychology: Research and Practice, 33,* 289–293.

Brown, T. A., Campbell, L. A., Lehman, C. L., Grisham, J. R., & Mancill, R. B. (2001). Current and lifetime comorbidity of the DSM-IV anxiety and mood disorders in a large clinical sample. *Journal of Abnormal Psychology, 110,* 585–589.

Brown, T. A., Di Nardo, P. A., & Barlow, D. H. (1994). *Anxiety Disorders Interview Schedule for DSM-IV (ADIS IV).* San Antonio, TX: Psychological Corporation.

Brugha, T. S., Bebbington, P. E., Singleton, N., Melzer, D., Jenkins, R., Lewis, G., et al. (2004). Trends in service use and treatment for mental disorders in adults throughout Great Britain. *British Journal of Psychiatry, 185,* 378–384.

Buchanan, T. (2002). Online assessment: Desirable or dangerous? *Professional Psychology: Research and Practice, 33,* 148–154.

Burlingame, G. M., MacKenzie, K. R., & Strauss, B. (2004). Small-group treatment: Evidence for effectiveness and mechanisms of change. In M. L. Lambert (Ed.), *Bergin and Garfield's Handbook of psychotherapy and behavior change* (5th ed., pp. 647–696). New York: John Wiley & Sons.

Burlingame, G. M., Mosier, J. I., Wells, M. G., Atkin, Q. G., Lamber, M. J., Whooery, M., et al. (2001). Tracking the influence of mental health treatment: The development of the Youth Outcome Questionnaire. *Clinical Psychology and Psychotherapy, 8,* 361–379.

Burns, D. D., & Spangler, D. L. (2000). Does psychotherapy homework lead to improvements in depression in cognitive-behavioral therapy or does improvement lead to increased homework compliance? *Journal of Consulting and Clinical Psychology, 68,* 46–56.

Butcher, J. N. (2004). Personality assessment without borders: Adaptation of the MMPI-2 across cultures. *Journal of Personality Assessment, 83,* 90–104.

Butcher, J. N., & Beutler, L. E. (2003). The MMPI-2. In L. E. Beutler & G. Groth-Marnat (Eds.), *Integrative assessment of adult personality* (2nd ed., pp. 157–191). New York: Guilford Press.

Butcher, J. N., Dahlstrom, W. G., Graham, J. R., Tellegen, A., & Kaemmer, B. (1989). *Manual for administration and scoring: MMPI-2.* Minneapolis, MN: University of Minnesota Press.

Butcher, J. N., Perry, J. N., & Atlis, M. M. (2000). Validity and utility of computer-based test interpretations. *Psychological Assessment, 12,* 6–18.

Butcher, J. N., Williams, C. L., Graham, J. R., Archer, R., Tellegen, A., Ben-Porath, Y. S., et al. (1992). *MMPI-A: Manual for administration, scoring, and interpretation.* Minneapolis, MN: University of Minnesota Press.

Cahill, J., Barkham, M., Hardy, G., Rees, A., Shapiro, D.A., Stiles, W.B., et al. (2003). Outcomes of patients completing and not completing cognitive therapy for depression. *British Journal of Clinical Psychology, 42,* 133–143.

Cairns, N. J. (2004). Neuroanatomy and neuropathology. In L. H. Goldstein & J. E. McNeil (Eds.), *Clinical neuropsychology: A practical guide to assessment and management for clinicians* (pp. 23–55). Chichester, UK: John Wiley & Sons.

Calhoun, K. S., Moras, K., Pilkonis, P. A., & Rehm, L. P. (1998). Empirically supported treatments: Implications for training. *Journal of Consulting and Clinical Psychology, 66,* 151–162.

Camara, W. J., Nathan, J. S., & Puente, A. E. (2000). Psychological test usage: Implications in professional psychology. *Professional Psychology: Science and Practice, 31,* 141–154.

Canadian Association of University Teachers. (2005). *CAUT almanac of post-secondary education in Canada.* Ottawa, ON: Author.

Canadian Institute for Health Information. (2004). *Health personnel trends in Canada 1993–2002.* Ottawa, ON: Author.

Canadian Psychological Association. (1999). *Geographic locations survey of clinical psychologists in Canada.* Ottawa, ON: Author.

Canadian Psychological Association. (2000). *Canadian code of ethics for psychologists* (3rd ed.). Ottawa, ON: Author.

Canadian Psychological Association. (2001). *Guidelines for non-discriminatory practice.* Ottawa, ON: Author.

Canadian Psychological Association. (2002). *Accreditation standards and procedures for doctoral programmes and internships in professional psychology* (4th revision). Ottawa, ON: Author.

Carr, A. (2002). Conclusions. In A. Carr (Ed.), *Prevention: what works with children and adolescents? A critical review of psychological prevention programmes for children, adolescents and their families* (pp. 359–372). Hove, UK: Brunner-Routledge.

Carroll, J. B. (1993). *Human cognitive abilities: A survey of factor analytic studies.* New York: Cambridge University Press.

Cartwright-Hatton, S., Roberts, C., Chitsabesan, P., Fothergill, C., & Harrington, R. (2004). Systematic review of the efficacy of cognitive behaviour therapies for childhood and adolescent anxiety disorders. *British Journal of Clinical Psychology, 43,* 421–436.

Caruso, J. C., & Cliff, N. (1999). The properties of equally and differentially weighted WAIS-III factor scores. *Psychological Assessment, 11,* 198–206.

Casey, R. J., & Berman, J. S. (1985). The outcome of psychotherapy with children. *Psychological Bulletin, 98,* 388–400.

Cashel, M. L. (2002). Child and adolescent psychological assessment: Current clinical practices and the impact of managed care. *Professional Psychology: Research and Practice, 33,* 446–453.

Caspi, A., Moffitt, T. E., Newman, D. L., & Silva, P. A. (1996). Behavioral observations at age 3 years predict adult psychiatric disorders. Longitudinal evidence from a birth cohort. *Archives of General Psychiatry, 53,* 1033–1039.

Castonguay, L. G., & Beutler, L. E. (Eds.). (2006a). *Principles of therapeutic change that work.* New York: Oxford University Press.

Castonguay, L. G., & Beutler, L. E. (2006b). Common and unique principles of therapeutic change: What do we know and what do we need to know? In L. G. Castonguay & L. E. Beutler (Eds.), *Principles of therapeutic change that work* (pp. 353–369). New York: Oxford University Press.

Cattell, R. B. (1963). Theory of fluid and crystallized intelligence: A critical experiment. *Journal of Educational Psychology, 54,* 1–22.

Ceci, S. J., & Bruck, M. (1993). Suggestibility of the child witness: A historical review and synthesis. *Psychological Bulletin, 113,* 403–439.

Chaimowitz, G. (2004). *Psychotherapy in psychiatry.* Ottawa, ON: Canadian Psychiatric Association.

Chamberlain, P., & Smith, D. K. (2003). Antisocial behaviour in children and adolescents: The Oregon multidimensional foster care model. In A. E. Kazdin & J. R. Weisz (Eds.), *Evidence-based psychotherapies for children and adolescents* (pp. 282–300). New York: Guilford.

Chambers, C. T., Finley, G. A., McGrath, P. J., & Walsh, T. M. (2003). The parents' postoperative pain measure: replication and extension to 2-6-year old children. *Pain, 105,* 437–443.

Chambless, D. L. (2002). Beware the dodo bird: The dangers of overgeneralization. *Clinical Psychology: Science and Practice, 9,* 13–16.

Chambless, D. L., Baker, M. J., Baucom, D. H., Beutler, L., Calhoun, K. S., Crits-Christoph, P., et al. (1998). Update on empirically validated therapies, II. *The Clinical Psychologist, 51,* 3–16.

Chambless, D. L., Caputo, G., Jasin, S. E., Gracely, E. J., & Williams, C. (1985). The Mobility Inventory for Agoraphobia. *Behaviour Research and Therapy, 23,* 35–44.

Chambless, D. L., & Gillis, M. M. (1993). Cognitive therapy of anxiety disorders. *Journal of Consulting and Clinical Psychology, 61,* 248–260.

Chambless, D. L., & Hollon, S. D. (1998). Defining empirically supported therapies. *Journal of Consulting and Clinical Psychology, 66,* 7–18.

Chambless, D. L., & Ollendick, T. H. (2001). Empirically supported psychological interventions: Controversies and evidence. *Annual Review of Psychology, 52,* 685–716.

Chambless, D. L., Sanderson, W. C., Shoham, V., Bennett Johnson, S., Pope, K. S., Crits-Christoph, P., et al. (1996). An update on empirically validated therapies. *The Clinical Psychologist, 49(2),* 5–18.

Chambless, D. L., et al. (1998). Update on empirically validated therapies, II. *The Clinical Psychologist, 51,* 3–16.

Charach, A., Ickowicz, A., & Schachar, R. (2004). Stimulant treatments over five years: Adherence, effectiveness, and adverse effects. *Journal of the American Academy of Child and Adolescent Psychiatry, 43,* 559–567.

Cherry, D. K., Messenger, L. C., & Jacoby, A. M. (2000). An examination of training model outcomes in clinical psychology programs. *Professional Psychology: Research & Practice, 31,* 562–568.

Childs, R. A., & Eyde, L. D. (2002). Assessment training in clinical psychology doctoral programs: What should we teach? What do we teach? *Journal of Personality Assessment, 78,* 130–144.

Chorpita, B. F., Yim, L. M., Donkervoet, J. C., Arensdorf, A., Amundsen, M. J., McGee, C., et al. (2002). Towards large-scale implementation of empirically supported treatments for children: A review and observations by the Hawaii Empirical Basis to Services Task Force. *Clinical Psychology: Science and Practice, 9,* 165–190.

Chronis, A. M., Chacko, A., Fabiano, G. A., Wymbs, B. T., & Pelham, W. E. (2004). Enhancements to the behavioural parent training paradigm for families of children with ADHD: Review and future directions. *Clinical Child and Family Psychology, Review, 7,* 1–27.

Clare, L., & Woods, R. T. (2004). Cognitive training and cognitive rehabilitation for people with early-stage Alzheimer's disease: A review. *Neuropsychological Rehabilitation, 14,* 385–401.

Clark, L. A., Watson, D., & Reynolds, S. (1995). Diagnosis and classification of psychopathology: Challenges to the current system and future directions. *Annual Review of Psychology, 46,* 121–153.

Clarke, G. N., DeBar, L. L., & Lewinsohn, P. M. (2003). Cognitive-behavioural group treatment for adolescent depression. In A. E. Kazdin & J. R. Weisz (Eds.), *Evidence-based psychotherapies for children and adolescents* (pp. 120–134). New York: Guilford.

Clarke, G., Hornbrook, M., Lynch, F., Polens, M., Gale, J., Beardslee, W., et al. (2001). A randomized trial of group cognitive intervention of preventing depression in adolescent offspring of depressed parents. *Archives of General Psychiatry, 58,* 1127–1134.

Clarkin, J. F., & Levy, K. N. (2004). The influence of client variables on psychotherapy. In M. J. Lambert (Ed.), *Bergin and Garfield's handbook of psychotherapy and behavior change* (5th ed., pp. 194–226). New York: John Wiley & Sons.

Clemence, A. J., & Handler, L. (2001). Psychological assessment on internship: A survey of training directors and their expectations for students. *Journal of Personality Assessment, 76,* 18–47.

Cohen, J. (1992). A power primer. *Psychological Bulletin, 112,* 115–159.

Cohen, P., & Cohen, J. (1984). The clinician's illusion. *Archives of General Psychiatry, 41,* 1178–1182.

Cole, D. A., Peeke, L. G., Martin, J. M., Truglio, R., & Seroczynski, A. D. (1998). A longitudinal look at the relation between depression and anxiety in children and adolescents. *Journal of Consulting and Clinical Psychology, 66,* 451–460.

Cole, D. A., Tram, J. M., Martin, J. M., Hoffman, K. B., Ruiz, M. D., Jacquez, F. M., et al. (2002). Individual differences in the emergence of depressive symptoms in children and adolescents: A longitudinal investigation of parent and child reports. *Journal of Abnormal Psychology, 111,* 156–165.

College of Psychologists of Ontario. (2004). *Why choose a regulated service provider?* Retrieved December 21, 2004, from http://www.cpo.on.ca /AboutCollege/College.htm

Collins, L. M., Murphy, S. A., & Bierman, K. L. (2004). A conceptual framework for adaptive preventive interventions. *Prevention Science, 5,* 185–196.

Commission on Chronic Illness. (1957). *Chronic illness in the United States.* (Vol. 1). Cambridge, MA: Harvard University Press.

Conduct Problems Prevention Research Group. (2002a). The implementation of the Fast Track Program: An example of a large-scale prevention science efficacy trial. *Journal of Abnormal Child Psychology, 30,* 1–17.

Conduct Problems Prevention Research Group. (2002b). Evaluation of the first 3 years of the Fast Track prevention trial with children with high risk for adolescent conduct problems. *Journal of Abnormal Child Psychology, 30,* 19–35.

Conduct Problems Prevention Research Group. (2004). The effects of the Fast Track program on serious problem outcomes at the end of elementary school. *Journal of Clinical Child and Adolescent Psychology, 33,* 650–661.

Connor-Smith, J. K., & Weisz, J. R. (2003). Applying treatment outcome research in clinical practice: Techniques for adapting interventions to the real world. *Child and Adolescent Mental Health, 8,* 3–10.

Cook, J. M., Schnurr, P. P., & Foa, E. B. (2004). Bridging the gap between Posttraumatic Stress Disorder research and clinical practice: The example of exposure therapy. *Psychotherapy, 41,* 374–381.

Cook, T. D., & Campbell, D. T. (Eds.). (1979). *Quasi-experimentation: Design and analysis issues for field settings.* Chicago, IL: Rand McNally.

Costa, P. T., & McCrae, R. R. (1992). *Revised NEO Personality Inventory (NEO PI-R) and NEO Five-Factor Inventory (NEO-FFI) professional manual.* Odessa, FL: Psychological Assessment Resources.

Costantino, G., Malgady, R. G., Rogler, L. H., & Tsui, E. C. (1988). Discriminant analysis of clinical outpatients and public school children by TEMAS: A thematic apperception test for Hispanics and Blacks. *Journal of Personality Assessment, 52,* 670–678.

Coughlan, B. J., Doyle, M., & Carr, A. (2002). Prevention of teenage smoking, alcohol use and drug abuse. In A. Carr (Ed.), *Prevention: what works with children and adolescents? A critical review of psychological prevention programmes for children, adolescents and their families* (pp. 267–286). Hove, UK: Brunner-Routledge.

Craighead, W. E., Hart, A. B., Craighead, L. W., & Ilardi, S. (2002). Psychosocial treatments for major depressive disorder. In P. E. Nathan & J. M. Gorman (Eds.), *A guide to treatments that work* (2nd ed., pp. 245–261). New York: Oxford University Press.

Crawford, J. R. (2004). Psychometric foundations of neuropsychological assessment. In L. H. Goldstein & J. E. McNeil (Eds.), *Clinical neuropsychology: A practical guide to assessment and management for clinicians* (pp. 121–140). Chichester, UK: John Wiley & Sons.

Crits-Christoph, P. (1997). Limitations of the dodo bird verdict and the role of clinical trials in psychotherapy research: Comment on Wampold et al. (1997). *Psychological Bulletin, 122,* 216–220.

Crits-Christoph, P., Frank, E., Chambless, D. L., Brody, C. & Karp, J. F. (1995). Training in empirically validated treatments: What are clinical psychology students learning? *Professional Psychology: Research and Practice, 26,* 514–522.

Cross, D. T., & Burger, G. K. (1982). Ethnicity as a variable in responses to California Psychological Inventory items. *Journal of Personality Assessment, 46,* 153–158.

Cuijpers, P. (2003). Examining the effects of prevention programs on the incidence of new cases of mental disorders: The lack of statistical power. *American Journal of Psychiatry, 160,* 1385–1391.

Cukrowicz, K. C., Wingate, L. R. W., Driscoll, K. A., & Joiner, T. E. (2004). A standard of care for the assessment of suicide risk and associated treatment. *Journal of Contemporary Psychotherapy, 34,* 87–100.

Cutler, J. L., Goldyne, A., Markowitz, J. C., Devlin, M. J., & Glick, R. A. (2004). Comparing cognitive behaviour therapy, inter-

personal psychotherapy, and psychodynamic psychotherapy. *American Journal of Psychiatry, 161,* 1567–1573.

Cyr, J. J., & Atkinson, L. (1987). Test item bias in the WISC-R. *Canadian Journal of Behavioural Sciences, 19,* 101–107.

D'Zurilla, T. J., & Goldfried, M. R. (1971). Problem solving and behaviour modification. *Journal of Abnormal Psychology, 78,* 101–126.

D'Zurilla, T. J., & Nezu, A. M. (1999). *Problem-solving therapy: A social competence approach to clinical intervention* (2nd ed.). New York: Springer.

Dadds, M. R., Holland, D. E., Barrett, P. M., Laurens, S. K., & Spence, S. (1999). Early intervention and prevention of anxiety disorders in children: Results at 2-year follow-up. *Journal of Consulting and Clinical Psychology, 67,* 145–150.

Davidson, P. R., & Parker, K. C. H. (2001). Eye movement desensitization and reprocessing (EMDR): A meta-analysis. *Journal of Consulting and Clinical Psychology, 69,* 305–316.

Davis, G. L., Hoffman, R. G., & Nelson, K. S. (1990). Differences between Native Americans and Whites on the California Personality Inventory. *Psychological Assessment, 2,* 238–242.

De Koninck, J. (1997). Sleep, the common denominator for psychological adaptation. *Canadian Psychology, 38,* 191–195.

Derogatis, L. R. (1994). *SCL-90-R: Administration, scoring, and procedures manual.* Minneapolis, MN: National Computer Systems.

Devilly, G. J. (2002). Eye movement desensitization and reprocessing: A chronology of its development and scientific standing. *Scientific Review of Mental Health Practice, 1,* 113–138.

Dickens, W., & Flynn, J. R. (2001). Hereditability estimates versus large environmental effects: The IQ paradox resolved. *Psychological Review, 108,* 346–369.

Dishion, T. J., McCord, J., & Poulin, F. (1999). When interventions harm: Peer groups and problem behavior. *American Psychologist, 54,* 755–764.

Dobson, K. S. (1989). A meta-analysis of the efficacy of cognitive therapy for depression. *Journal of Consulting and Clinical Psychology, 57,* 414–419.

Dori, G. A., & Chelune, G. J. (2004). Education-stratified base-rate information on the discrepancy scores within and between Wechsler Adult Intelligence Scale–Third Edition and the Wechsler Memory Scale–Third Edition. *Psychological Assessment, 16,* 146–154.

Dowden, C., & Andrews, D. A. (2004). The importance of staff practice in delivering effective correctional treatment: A meta-analytic review of core correctional practice. *International Journal of Offender Therapy and Comparative Criminology, 48,* 203–214.

Doyle, A. B., Edwards, H., & Robinson, R. W. (1993). Accreditation of doctoral training programmes and internships in professional psychology. In K. S. Dobson & D. G. Dobson (Eds.), *Professional psychology in Canada* (pp. 77–105). Toronto, ON: Hogrefe & Huber.

Dozois, D. J. A., & Dobson, K. S. (Eds.). (2004). *The prevention of anxiety and depression: Theory, research, and practice.* Washington, DC: American Psychological Association.

Durlak, J. A., & Wells, A. M. (1997). Primary prevention mental health programs for children and adolescents: A meta-analytic review. *American Journal of Community Psychology, 25,* 115–152.

Eddy, K. T., Dutra, L., Bradley, R., & Westen, D. (2004). A multidimensional meta-analysis of psychotherapy and pharmacotherapy for obsessive-compulsive disorder. *Clinical Psychology Review, 24,* 1011–1030.

Eells, T. D. (Ed.). (1997). *Handbook of psychotherapy case formulation.* New York: Guilford Press.

Eells, T. D., Kendjelic, E. M., & Lucas, C. P. (1998). What's in a case formulation? Development and use of a content coding manual. *Journal of Psychotherapy Practice and Research, 7,* 144–153.

Elkin, I., Yamaguchi, J. L., Arnkoff, D. B., Class, C. R., Sotsky, S. M., & Krupnick, J. L. (1999). "Patient-treatment fit" and early engagement in therapy. *Psychotherapy Research, 9,* 437–451.

Ellenberger, H. F. (1970). *The discovery of the unconscious: The history and evolution of dynamic psychiatry.* New York: Basic Books.

Elliott, R. (1998). Editor's introduction: A guide to the empirically supported treatments controversy. *Psychotherapy Research, 8,* 115–125.

Elliott, R. (2001). Contemporary brief experiential psychotherapy. *Clinical Psychology: Science and Practice, 8,* 38–50.

Elliott, R., Greenberg, L. S., & Lietaer, G. (2004). Research on experiential psychotherapies. In M. L. Lambert (Ed.), *Bergin and Garfield's Handbook of psychotherapy and behavior change* (5th ed., pp. 493–539). New York: John Wiley & Sons.

Emmelkamp, P. M. G. (2004). Behavior therapy with adults. In M. L. Lambert (Ed.), *Bergin and Garfield's Handbook of psychotherapy and behavior change* (5th ed., pp. 393–446) New York: John Wiley & Sons.

Ennett, S. T., Ringwalt, C. L., Thirne, J., Rohrbach, L. A., Vincus, A., Simons-Rudolph, A., et al. (2003). A comparison of current practice in school-base substance use prevention programs with meta-analysis findings. *Prevention Science, 4,* 1–14.

Enright, S., & Carr, A. (2002). Prevention of post-traumatic adjustment problems. In A. Carr (Ed.), *Prevention: what works with children and adolescents? A critical review of psychological prevention programmes for children, adolescents and their families* (pp. 314–335). Hove, UK: Brunner-Routledge.

Epstein, L. H. (2003). Development of evidence-based treatments for pediatric obesity. In A. E. Kazdin & J. R. Weisz (Eds.), *Evidence-based psychotherapies for children and adolescents* (pp. 374–388). New York: Guilford.

Essau, C. A. (2003). Primary prevention of depression. In D. J. A. Dozois & K. S. Dobson (Eds.), *The prevention of anxiety and depression: Theory: research, and practice* (pp. 185–204). Washington, DC: American Psychological Association.

Essau, C. A. (2004). Prevention of substance abuse in children and adolescents. In P. M. Barrett & T. H. Ollendick (Eds.), *Interventions that work with children and adolescents: Prevention and Treatment* (pp. 517–539). Chichester, UK: John Wiley & Sons.

Evans, G. W. (2004). The environment of child poverty. *American Psychologist, 59,* 77–92.

Evans, J. J. R. (2004). Disorders of memory. In L. H. Goldstein & J. E. McNeil (Eds.), *Clinical neuropsychology: A practical guide to assessment and management for clinicians* (pp. 143–163). Chichester, UK: John Wiley & Sons.

Exner, J. E. (1993). *The Rorschach: A comprehensive system. Vol. 1. Basic foundations* (3rd ed.). New York: John Wiley & Sons.

Eysenck, H. J. (1952). The effects of psychotherapy: An evaluation. *Journal of Consulting Psychology, 16,* 319–324.

Eysenck, H. J. (1962). *Know your own I.Q.* London: Penguin Books.

Eysenck, H. J. (1966). *The effects of psychotherapy.* New York: International Science Press.

Eysenck, H. J. (1978). An exercise in meta-silliness. *American Psychologist, 33,* 517.

Farmer, E. M. Z., Compton, S. N., Burns, B. J., & Robertson, E. (2002). Review of the evidence base for treatment of childhood psychopathology: Externalizing disorders. *Journal of Consulting and Clinical Psychology, 70,* 1267–1232.

Feeny, N. C., Foa, E. B., Treadwell, K. R. H., & March, J. (2004). Posttraumatic stress disorder in youth: A critical review of the cognitive and behavioural outcome literature. *Professional Psychology: Research and Practice, 35,* 466–476.

Feifel, D., Moutier, C. Y., & Swerdlow, N. R. (1999). Attitudes toward psychiatry as a prospective career among students entering medical school. *American Journal of Psychiatry, 156,* 1397–1402.

Feske, U., & Goldstein, A. (1997). Eye movement desensitization and reprocessing treatment for panic disorders: A controlled outcome and partial dismantling study. *Journal of Consulting and Clinical Psychology, 65,* 1026–1035.

Finn, S. E. (1996). Assessment feedback integrating MMPI-2 and Rorschach findings. *Journal of Personality Assessment, 67,* 543–557.

Finn, S. E., & Tonsager, M. E. (1997). Information-gathering and therapeutic models of assessment: Complementary paradigms. *Psychological Assessment, 9,* 374–385.

First, M. B., Pincus, H. A., Levine, J. B., Williams, J. B. W., Ustun, B., & Peele, R. (2004). Clinical utility as a criterion for revising psychiatric diagnoses. *American Journal of Psychiatry, 161,* 946–954.

First, M. B., Spitzer, R. L., Gibbon, M., & Williams, J. B. W. (1997). *Structured Clinical Interview for Axis I DSM –IV Disorders (SCID-I)-Clinician Version.* Washington, DC: American Psychiatric Press.

First, M. B., & Tasman, A. (2004). *DSM-IV-TR mental disorders: Diagnosis, etiology, and treatment.* New York: John Wiley & Sons.

Fisher, C. B. (2004). Informed consent and clinical research involving children and adolescents: implications of the Revised APA Ethics Code and HIPAA. *Journal of Clinical Child and Adolescent Psychology, 33,* 832–839.

Fisher, P. A. (2003). The prevention of antisocial behaviour: Beyond efficacy and effectiveness. In A. Biglan, M. Wang, & H. J. Walberg (Eds.), *Preventing youth problems* (pp. 5–31). New York: Kluwer Academic.

Flanagan, D. P., & Kaufman, A. S. (2004). *Essentials of WISC-IV assessment.* New York: John Wiley & Sons.

Fleeson, W. (2004). Moving personality beyond the person-situation debate: The challenge and opportunity of within-person variability. *Current Directions in Psychological Science, 13,* 83–87.

Floyd, F. J., & Widaman, J. F. (1995). Factor analysis in the development and refinement of clinical assessment instruments. *Psychological Assessment, 7,* 286–299.

Flynn, J. R. (1987). Massive IQ gains in 14 nations: What IQ tests really measure. *Psychological Bulletin, 101,* 171–191.

Foa, E. B., & Rothbaum, B. O. (1998). *Treating the trauma of rape: A cognitive-behavioral therapy for PTSD.* New York: Guilford Press.

Fonagy, P., Target, M., Cottrell, D., Phillips, J., & Kurtz, Z. (2002). *What works for whom? A critical review of treatments for children and adolescents.* New York: Guilford.

Frank, J. D. (1973). *Persuasion and healing.* Baltimore: Johns Hopkins University Press.

Frank, J. D. (1982). Therapeutic components shared by all psychotherapies. In J. H. Harvey & M. M. Parks (Eds.), *The Master Lecture Series: Vol. 1. Psychotherapy research and behavior change* (pp. 5–38). Washington, DC: American Psychological Association.

Frisch, M. B., Clark, M. P., Rouse, S. V., Rudd, M. D., Paweleck, J. K., Greenstone, A., et al. (2005). Predictive and treatment validity of life satisfaction and the Quality of Life Inventory. *Assessment, 12,* 66–78.

Fulero, S. M. (1995). The Psychopathy Checklist-Revised. In J. C. Conoley & J. C. Impara (Eds.), *Twelfth mental measurements yearbook* (pp. 453–454). Lincoln, NE: Buros Institute.

Gabbard, G. O., Gunderson, J. G., & Fonagy, P. (2002). The place of psychoanalytic treatments within psychiatry. *Archives of General Psychiatry, 59,* 505–510.

Garb, H. N. (1997). Race bias, social class bias, and gender bias in clinical judgment. *Clinical Psychology: Science and Practice, 4,* 99–120.

Garb, H. N. (1998). *Studying the clinician: Judgment research and psychological assessment.* Washington, DC: American Psychological Association.

Garb, H. N. (2005). Clinical judgment and decision making. *Annual Review of Clinical Psychology, 1,* 67–89.

Garb, H. N., & Boyle, P. A. (2003). Understanding why some clinicians use pseudoscientific methods: Findings from research on clinical judgment. In S. O. Lilienfeld, S. J. Lynn, & J. M. Lohr (Eds.), *Science and pseudoscience in clinical psychology* (pp.17–38). New York: Guilford Press.

Garb, H. N., Klein, D. F., & Grove, W. M. (2002). Comparison of medical and psychological tests. *American Psychologist, 57,* 137–138.

Gardner, H. (1983). *Frames of mind: The theory of multiple intelligences.* New York: Basic Books.

Gardner, H. (1999). *Intelligence reframed: Multiple intelligences for the 21st century.* New York: Basic Books.

Garfield, S. L. (1994). Eclecticism and integration in psychotherapy: Developments and issues. *Clinical Psychology: Science and Practice, 1,* 123–137.

Garfield, S. L. (1994). Research on client variables in psychotherapy. In A. E. Bergin & S. L. Garfield (Eds.), *Handbook of psychotherapy and behavior change* (4th ed., pp. 190–228). New York: John Wiley & Sons.

Garfield, S. L. (1996). Some problems associated with "validated" forms of psychotherapy. *Clinical Psychology: Research and Practice, 3,* 218–229.

Geisinger, K. F. (1994). Cross-cultural normative assessment: Translation and adaptation issues influencing the normative interpretation of assessment instruments. *Psychological Assessment, 6,* 304–312.

Glueckauf, R. L., Pickett, T. C., Ketterson, T. U., Loomis, J. S., & Rozensky, R. H. (2003). Preparation for the delivery of telehealth services: A self-study framework for expansion of practice. *Professional Psychology: Research and Practice, 34,* 159–163.

Goisman, R. M., Warshaw, M. G., & Keller, M. B. (1999). Psychosocial treatment prescriptions for Generalized Anxiety Disorder, Panic Disorder, and Social Phobia, 1991–1996. *American Journal of Psychiatry, 156,* 1819–1821.

Golden, C. J., Freshwater, S. M., & Vayalakkara, J. (2000). The Luria-Nebraska Neuropsychological Battery. In G. Groth-Marnat (Ed.), *Neuropsychological assessment in clinical practice* (pp. 263–289). New York: John Wiley & Sons.

Goldstein, L. H., & McNeil, J. E. (2004). General introduction: What is the relevance of neuropsychology for clinical psychology practice? In L. H. Goldstein & J. E. McNeil (Eds.), *Clinical neuropsychology: A practical guide to assessment and management for clinicians* (pp. 3–20). Chichester, UK: John Wiley & Sons.

Goodman, W. K., Price, L. H., Rasmussen, S. A., Mazure, C., Delgado, P., Heninger, G. R., et al. (1989). The Yale-Brown Obsessive Compulsive Scale. II: Validity. *Archives of General Psychiatry, 40,* 1012–1016.

Gosling, S. D., John, O. P., Craik, K. H., & Robins, R. W. (1998). Do people know how they behave? Self-reported act frequencies compared with on-line codings by observers. *Journal of Personality and Social Psychology, 74,* 1337–1349.

Gosling, S. D., Vazire, S., Srivastavas, S., & John, O. P. (2004). Should we trust web-based studies? *American Psychologist, 59,* 93–104.

Gotham, H. J. (2004). Diffusion of mental health and substance abuse treatments: Development, dissemination, and implementation. *Clinical Psychology: Science and Practice, 11,* 160–176.

Gotlib, I. H., & Schraedley, P. K. (2000). Interpersonal psychotherapy. In C. R. Snyder & R. E. Ingram (Eds.), *Handbook of psychological changes: Psychotherapy processes and practices for the 21st century* (pp. 258–279). New York: John Wiley & Sons.

Gough, H. G., & Bradley, P. (1996). *California Psychological Inventory manual* (3rd ed.). Palo Alto, CA: Consulting Psychologists Press.

Gray-Little, B., & Kaplan, D. (2000). Race and ethnicity in psychotherapy research. In C. R. Snyder & R. E. Ingram (Eds.), *Handbook of psychological changes: Psychotherapy processes and practices for the 21st century* (pp. 591–613). New York: John Wiley & Sons.

Gray-Little, B., & Kaplan, D. A. (1998). Interpretation of psychological tests in clinical and forensic evaluations. In J. Sandoval, C. L. Frisby, K. F. Geisinger, J. D. Scheuneman, & J. R. Grenier (Eds.), *Test interpretation and diversity: Achieving equity in assessment* (pp. 141–178). Washington, DC: American Psychological Association.

Greenberg, L. S., Elliott, R., Watson, J. C., Bohart, A. C. (2001). Empathy. *Psychotherapy, 38,* 380–384.

Greene, R. L. (2000). *The MMPI-2: An interpretive manual* (2nd ed.). Boston: Allyn & Bacon.

Greenhill, L. L., & Ford, R. E. (2002). Childhood attention-deficit/hyperactivity disorder: Pharmacological treatments. In P. E. Nathan & J. M. Gorman (Eds.), *A guide to treatments that work* (2nd ed., pp. 25–55). New York: Oxford University Press.

Greiffenstein, M. F., Baker, W. J., & Johnson-Greene, D. (2002). Actual versus self-reported scholastic achievement of litigating postconcussion and severe closed head injury claimants. *Psychological Assessment, 14,* 202–208.

Griffin, D. W., Dunning, D., & Ross, L. (1990). The role of construal processes in overconfident predictions about the self and others. *Journal of Personality and Social Psychology, 59,* 1128–1139.

Grills, A. E., & Ollendick, T. H. (2002). Issues in parent-child agreement: The case of structured diagnostic interviews. *Clinical Child and Family Psychology Review, 5,* 57–83.

Gross, D., Fogg, L., Webster-Stratton, C., Garvey, C., Julion, W., & Grady, J. (2003). Parent training with multi-ethnic families of toddlers in day care in low-income urban communities. *Journal of Consulting and Clinical Psychology, 71,* 261–278.

Gross, K., Keyes, M. D., & Greene, R. L. (2000). Assessing depression with the MMPI and MMPI-2. *Journal of Personality Assessment, 75,* 464–477.

Groth-Marnat, G. (1999). Financial efficacy of clinical assessment: Rational guidelines and issues for future research. *Journal of Clinical Psychology, 55,* 813–824.

Groth-Marnat, G. (2000). Introduction to neuropsychological assessment. In G. Groth-Marnat (Ed.), *Neuropsychological assessment in clinical practice* (pp. 3–25). New York: John Wiley & Sons.

Groth-Marnat, G. (2000). Visions of clinical assessment: Then, now, and a brief history of the future. *Journal of Clinical Psychology, 56,* 349–365.

Groth-Marnat, G. (2003). *Handbook of psychological assessment* (4th ed.). Hoboken, NJ: John Wiley & Sons.

Grove, W. M., Zald, D. H., Lebow, B. S., Snitz, B. E., & Nelson, C. (2000). Clinical versus mechanical prediction: A meta-analysis. *Psychological Assessment, 12,* 19–30.

Guarnaccia, V., Dill, C. A., Sabatino, S., & Southwick, S. (2001). Scoring accuracy using the Comprehensive System for the Rorschach. *Journal of Personality Assessment, 77,* 464–474.

Guilford, J. P. (1956). The structure of intellect. *Psychological Bulletin, 53,* 267–293.

Gunderson, J. G., Bender, D., Sanislow, C., Yen, S., Rettew, J. B., Dolan-Sewell, R., et al. (2003). Plausibility and possible determinants of sudden "remissions" in borderline patients. *Psychiatry, 66,* 111–119.

Haaga, D. A. F. (2000). Introduction to the special section on stepped care models in psychotherapy. *Journal of Consulting and Clinical Psychology, 68,* 547–548.

Hadjistavropoulos, H., & Williams, A. C. (2004). Psychological interventions and chronic pain. In T. Hadjistavropoulos & K. D. Craig (Eds.), *Pain: Psychological treatment perspectives* (pp. 271–301). New Jersey: Lawrence Erlbaum.

Halford, W. K., Keefer, E., & Osgarby, S. M. (2002). "How has the week been for you two?" Relationship satisfaction and hindsight memory biases in couples' reports of relationship events. *Cognitive Therapy and Research, 26,* 759–773.

Hall, G. C. N., & Phung, A. H. (2001). Minnesota Multiphasic Personality Inventory and Millon Clinical Multiaxial Inventory. In L. A. Suzuki, J. G. Ponterotto, & P. J. Meller (Eds.), *Handbook of multicultural assessment: Clinical, psychological, and educational applications* (2nd ed., pp. 307–330). San Francisco: Jossey-Bass.

Hamel, M., Shaffer, T. W., & Erdberg, P. (2000). A study of nonpatient preadolescent Rorschach protocols. *Journal of Personality Assessment, 75,* 280–294.

Hamilton, W., & Burns, T. G. (2003). WPPSI-III: Wechsler Preschool and Primary Scale of Intelligence (3rd ed.). *Applied Neuropsychology, 10,* 188–190.

Hammen, C., Shih, J. H., & Brennan, P. A. (2004). Intergenerational transmission of depression: Test of an interpersonal stress model in a community sample. *Journal of Consulting and Clinical Psychology, 72,* 511–522.

Hansen, N. B., Lambert, M. J., & Forman, E. M. (2002). The psychotherapy dose-response effect and its implications for treatment delivery services. *Clinical Psychology: Science and Practice, 9,* 329–343.

Hanson, R. K. (2005). Twenty years of progress in violence risk assessment. *Journal of Interpersonal Violence, 20,* 212–217.

Hardy, G. E., Cahill, J., Stiles, W. B., Ispan, C., Macaskill, N., & Barkham, M. (2005). Sudden gains in cognitive therapy for depression: A replication and extension. *Journal of Consulting and Clinical Psychology, 73,* 59–67.

Hare, R. D. (1991). The Hare Psychopathy Checklist-Revised. Toronto, ON: Multihealth Systems.

Hare, R. D., Clark, D., Grann, M., & Thornton, D. (2000). Psychopathy and the predictive validity of the PCL-R: an international perspective. *Behavioral Sciences and the Law, 18,* 623–645.

Harris, C. (2003). Editorial. *Psychological Bulletin, 129,* 3–9.

Harris, G. T., Rice, M. E., & Quinsey, V. L. (1993). Violent recidivism of mentally disordered offenders: The development of a statistical prediction instrument. *Criminal Justice and Behavior, 20,* 315–335.

Harvey, A. G., & Bryant, R. G. (2002). Acute Stress Disorder: A synthesis and critique. *Psychological Bulletin, 128,* 886–902.

Hathaway, S. R., & McKinley, J. C. (1943). *Minnesota Multiphasic Personality Inventory.* New York: Psychological Corporation.

Hawkins, E. H., Cummins, L. H., & Marlatt, G. A. (2004). Preventing substance abuse in

Hawley, K. M., & Weisz, J. R. (2003). Child, parent, and therapist (dis)agreement on target problems in outpatient therapy: The therapist's dilemma and its implications. *Journal of Consulting and Clinical Psychology, 71,* 62–70.

Hawley, K. M., & Weisz, J. R. (2005). Youth, versus parent working alliance in usual clinical care: Distinctive associations with retention, satisfaction, and treatment outcome. *Journal of Clinical Child and Adolescent Psychology, 34,* 117–128.

Hayes, S. C., Barlow, D. H., & Nelson-Gray, R. O. (1999). *The scientist practitioner: Research and accountability in the age of managed care* (2nd ed.). Needham Heights, MA: Allyn & Bacon.

Hayman-Abello, B. A., Hayman-Abello, S. E., & Rourke, B. P. (2003). Human neuropsychology in Canada: The 1990s (A review of research by Canadian neuropsychologists). *Canadian Psychology, 44,* 100–138.

Haynes, S. N., Leisen, M. B., & Blaine, D. D. (1997). Design of individualized behavioral treatment programs using functional analytic clinical case methods. *Psychological Assessment, 9,* 334–348.

Hays, K. A., Rardin, D. K., Jarvis, P. A., Taylor, N. M., Moorman, A. S., & Armstead, C. D. (2002). An exploratory survey on empirically supported treatments: Implications for internship training. *Professional Psychology: Research and Practice, 33,* 207–211.

Hearn, M. T., & Evans, D. R. (1993). Applications of psychology to health care. In K. S. Dobson & D. G. Dobson (Eds.), *Professional psychology in Canada* (pp. 248–284). Toronto, ON: Hogrefe & Huber.

Helmes, E., & Reddon, J. R. (1993). A perspective on developments in assessing psychopathology: A critical review of the MMPI and the MMPI-2. *Psychological Bulletin, 113,* 453–471.

Henggeler, S. W., & Lee, T. (2003). Multisystemic treatment of serious clinical problems. In A. E. Kazdin & J. R. Weisz (Eds.), *Evidence-based psychotherapies for children and adolescents* (pp. 301–324). New York: Guilford.

Henggeler, S. W., Schoenwald, S. K., Borduin, C. M., Rowland, M. D., & Cunningham, P. B. (1998). *Multisystemic treatment of antisocial behaviour in children and adolescents.* New York: Guilford.

Henry, B., Moffitt, T. E., Caspi, A., Langley, J., & Silva, P. A. (1994). On the "Remembrance of Things Past": A longitudinal evaluation of the retrospective method. *Psychological Assessment, 6,* 92–101.

Henry, W. P. (1998). Science, politics, and the politics of science: The use and misuse of empirically validated treatment research. *Psychotherapy Research, 8,* 126–140.

Herrnstein, R. J., & Murray, C. A. (1994). *The bell curve: Intelligence and class structure in American life.* New York: Free Press.

Herschell, A. D., McNeill, C. B., & McNeill, D. (2004). Clinical child psychology's progress in disseminating empirically supported treatments. *Clinical Psychology: Science and Practice, 11,* 267–288.

Hersen, M. (Ed.). (2002). *Clinical behaviour therapy: Adults and children.* New York: John Wiley & Sons.

Hertzsprung, E. A. M. & Dobson, K. S. (2000). Diversity training: Conceptual issues and practices for Canadian clinical psychology programs. *Canadian Psychology, 41,* 184–191.

Hill, C. E. (2001). *Helping skills: The empirical foundation.* Washington, DC: American Psychological Association.

Hiller, J. B., Rosenthal, R., Bornstein, R. F., Berry, D. T. R., & Brunell-Neuleib, S. (1999). A comparative meta-analysis of Rorschach and MMPI validity. *Psychological Assessment, 11,* 278–296.

Hilsenroth, M. J., Peters, E. J., & Ackerman, S. J. (2004). The development of therapeutic alliance during psychological assessment: Patient and therapist perspectives across treatment. *Journal of Personality Assessment, 83,* 332–344.

Himelein, M. J., & Putnam, E. A. (2001). Work activities of academic clinical psychologists: Do they practice what they teach? *Professional Psychology: Research and Practice, 32,* 537–542.

Hinshaw, S. P., Klein, R. G., & Abikoff, H. B. (2002). Childhood Attention-Deficit Hyperactivity Disorder: Nonpharmacological treatments and their combination with medication. In P. E. Nathan & J. M. Gorman (Eds.), *A guide to treatments that work* (2nd ed., pp. 3–55). New York: Oxford University Press.

Hogan, T. P. (2003). *Psychological testing: A practical introduction.* Hoboken, NJ: John Wiley & Sons.

Hoge, M. A., Tondora, J., & Stuart, G. W. (2003). Training in evidence-based practice. *Psychiatric Clinics of North America, 26,* 851–865.

Hollon, S. D., & Beck, A. T. (2004). Cognitive and cognitive behavioral therapies. In M. L. Lambert (Ed.), *Bergin and Garfield's Handbook of psychotherapy and behavior change* (5th ed., pp. 447–492). New York: John Wiley & Sons.

Holmbeck, G. N. (1997). Toward terminological, conceptual, and statistical clarity in the study of mediators and moderators: Examples from the child-clinical and pediatric literatures. *Journal of Consulting and Clinical Psychology, 65,* 599–610.

Horn, J. L., & Cattell, R. B. (1966). Refinement and test of theory of fluid and crystallizaed intelligence. *Journal of Educational Psychology, 57,* 253–270.

Horvath, A. O., & Bedi, R. P. (2002). The alliance. In J. C. Norcross (Ed.), *Psychotherapy relationships that work: Therapist contributions and responsiveness to patients* (pp. 37–69). London: Oxford University Press.

Horvath, A. O., & Luborsky, L. (1993). The role of the therapeutic alliance in psychotherapy. *Journal of Consulting and Clinical Psychology, 61,* 561–573.

Horvath, L. S., Logan, T. K., & Walker, R. (2002). Child custody cases: A content analysis of evaluations in practice. *Professional Psychology: Research and Practice, 33,* 557–565.

Houts, A. C. (2003). Behavioral treatment for Enuresis. In A. E. Kazdin & J. R. Weisz (Eds.), *Evidence-based psychotherapies for children and adolescents* (pp. 389–406). New York: Guilford.

Howard, K. I., Kopta, S. M., Krause, M. S., & Orlinsky, D. E. (1986). The dose-effect relationship in psychotherapy. *American Psychologist, 41,* 159–164.

Howard, R. C. (1999). Treatment of anxiety disorders: Does specialty training help? *Professional Psychology: Research and Practice, 30,* 470–473.

Hoyle, R. H., & Smith, G. T. (1994). Formulating clinical research hypotheses as structural equation models: A conceptual overview. *Journal of Consulting and Clinical Psychology, 62,* 429–440. http://journals.apa.org/prevention/volume6/pre0060010a.html

http://www.who.int/mental_health/evidence/en/prevention_of_mental_disorders_sr.pdf

Hubble, M. A., Duncan, B. L., & Miller, S. (Eds.). (1999). *The heart and soul of change.* Washington, DC: American Psychological Association.

Humble, K. L., Brown, D. L., Welder, A. N., Fillion, D. T., Dobson, K. S., & Arnett, J. L. (2004). A survey of hospital psychology in Canada. *Canadian Psychology, 45,* 31–41.

Hunsley, J. (2002). Psychological testing and psychological assessment: A closer examination. *American Psychologist, 57,* 139–140.

Hunsley, J. (2003). Cost-effectiveness and cost off-set considerations in psychological service provision. *Canadian Psychology, 44,* 61–73.

Hunsley, J. (2003). Introduction to the special section on incremental validity and utility in clinical assessment. *Psychological Assessment, 15,* 443–445.

Hunsley, J., Aubry, T. D., Vestervelt, C. M., & Vito, D. (1999). Clients' and therapists' perspectives on reasons for psychotherapy termination. *Psychotherapy, 36,* 380–388.

Hunsley, J., & Bailey, J. M. (1999). The clinical utility of the Rorschach: Unfulfilled promises and an uncertain future. *Psychological Assessment, 11,* 266–277.

Hunsley, J., & Bailey, J. M. (2001). Whither the Rorschach? An analysis of the evidence. *Psychological Assessment, 13,* 472–485.

Hunsley, J., Crabb, R., & Mash, E. J. (2004). Evidence-based clinical assessment. *The Clinical Psychologist, 57(3),* 25–32.

Hunsley, J., & Di Giulio, G. (2002). Dodo bird, phoenix, or urban legend? The question of psychotherapy equivalence. *Scientific Review of Mental Health Practice, 1,* 11–22.

Hunsley, J., Dobson, K. S., Johnston, C., & Mikail, S. F. (1999). Empirically supported treatments in psychology: Implications for Canadian professional psychology. *Canadian Psychology, 40,* 289–302.

Hunsley, J., & Johnston, C. (2000). The role of empirically supported treatments in evidence-based psychological practice: A Canadian perspective. *Clinical Psychology: Science and Practice, 7,* 269–272.

Hunsley, J., Lee, C. M., & Aubry, T. (1999). Who uses psychological services in Canada? *Canadian Psychology, 40,* 232–240.

Hunsley, J., Lee, C. M., & Wood, J. (2003). Controversial and questionable assessment techniques (pp. 39–76). In S. O. Lilienfeld, S. J. Lynn, & J. Lohr (Eds.), *Science and pseudoscience in clinical psychology.* New York: Guilford.

Hunsley, J., & Lefebvre, M. (1990). A survey of the practices and activities of Canadian clinical psychologists. *Canadian Psychology, 31,* 350–358.

Hunsley, J., & Meyer, G. J. (2003). The incremental validity of psychological testing and assessment: Conceptual, methodological, and statistical issues. *Psychological Assessment, 15,* 446–455.

Institute of Medicine. (2002). *Medical innovation in the changing healthcare marketplace: Conference summary.* Washington, DC: National Academy Press.

Jacobs, G. D., Pace-Shott, E. F., Stickgold, R., & Otto, M. W. (2004). Cognitive behavior therapy and pharmacotherapy for insomnia. *Archives of Internal Medicine, 164,* 1888–1896.

Jacobson, N. S., Christensen, A., Prince, S. E., Cordova, J., & Elridge, K. (2000). Integrative behavioral couple therapy: An acceptance based, promising new treatment for couple discord. *Journal of Consulting and Clinical Psychology, 68,* 351–355.

Jacobson, N. S., & Truax, P. (1991). Clinical significance: A statistical approach to defining meaningful change in psychotherapy research. *Journal of Clinical and Consulting Psychology, 59,* 12–19.

Jerome, L. W., & Zaylor, C. (2000). Cyberspace: Creating a therapeutic environment for tele-health applications. *Professional Psychology: Research and Practice, 31,* 478–483.

Johnson, S. M. (1996). *The practice of emotionally focused marital therapy: Creating connection.* New York: Brunner/Mazel.

Johnson, S. M., Hunsley, J., Greenberg, L., & Schindler, D. (1999). Emotionally focused couples therapy: Status and challenges. *Clinical Psychology: Science & Practice, 6,* 67–79.

Johnson, S., & Greenberg, L. (1985). Emotionally focused couples therapy: An outcome study. *Journal of Marriage and the Family, 11,* 313–317.

Johnston, E. A., & Stewart, D. W. (2000). Clinical supervision in Canadian academic and services settings: The importance of education, training, and workplace support for supervisor development. *Canadian Psychology, 41,* 124–130.

Jones, E. E., & Pulos, S. M. (1993). Comparing the process in psychodynamic and cognitive-behavioral therapies. *Journal of Consulting and Clinical Psychology, 61,* 306–316.

Kallestad, J. H., & Olweus, D. (2003). Predicting teachers' and schools' implementation of the Olweus Bullying Prevention Program: A multilevel study. *Prevention and Treatment, 6, Article 21.* Retrieved October 21, 2004, from http://journals.apa.org/prevention/volume6/pre0060021a.html

Kamieniecki, G. W., & Lynd-Stevenson, R. M. (2002). Is it appropriate to use United States norms to assess the "intelligence" of Australian children? *Australian Journal of Psychology, 54,* 67–78.

Kaplan, R. M. (2000). Two pathways to prevention. *American Psychologist, 55,* 382–396.

Kaplan, R. M., & Saccuzzo, D. P. (2001). *Psychological testing: Principles, applications, and issues* (5th ed.). Belmont, CA: Wadsworth/Thomson Learning.

Karney, B. R., Davila, J., Cohan, C. L., Sullivan, K. T., Johnson, M. D., & Bradbury, T. N. (1995). An empirical investigation of sampling strategies in marital research. *Journal of Marriage and the Family, 57,* 909–920.

Kataoka, S. H., Zhang, L., & Wells, K. B. (2002). Unmet needs for mental health care among U.S. children: Variation by ethnicity and insurance status. *American Journal of Psychiatry, 159,* 1548–1555.

Katz, L. E., & Gottman, J. M. (1993). Patterns of marital conflict predict children's internalizing and externalizing behaviors. *Developmental Psychology, 29,* 940–950.

Kaufman, A. S., & Kaufman, N. L. (1983). *Manuals for the Kaufman Assessment Battery for Children.* Circle Pines, MN: American Guidance Service.

Kaufman, A. S., & Kaufman, N. L. (1993). *Manual for the Kaufman Adolescent and Adult Intelligence Test.* Circle Pines, MN: American Guidance Service.

Kaufman, A. S., & Lichtenberger, E. O. (1999). *Essentials of WAIS-III assessment.* New York: John Wiley & Sons.

Kazantzis, N., Deane, F. P., & Ronan, K. R. (2000). Homework assignments in cognitive and behavioral therapy: A meta-analysis. *Clinical Psychology: Science and Practice, 7,* 189–202.

Kazdin, A. E. (1981). Drawing valid inferences from case studies. *Journal of Clinical and Consulting Psychology, 49,* 183–192.

Kazdin, A. E. (1988). *Child psychotherapy: Developing and identifying effective treatments.* New York: Pergamon.

Kazdin, A. E. (1993). Evaluation in clinical practice: Clinically sensitive and systematic methods of treatment delivery. *Behavior Therapy, 24,* 11–45.

Kazdin, A. E. (1995). Scope of child and adolescent psychotherapy research: Limited sampling of dysfunctions, treatments, and client characteristics. *Journal of Clinical Child Psychology, 24,* 125–140.

Kazdin, A. E. (1999). Overview of research design issues in clinical psychology. In P. C. Kendall, J. N. Butcher, & G. N. Holmbeck (Eds.), *Handbook of research methods in clinical psychology* (2nd ed., pp. 3–30). New York: John Wiley & Sons, Inc.

Kazdin, A. E. (2002). Psychosocial treatments for Conduct Disorder in children and adolescents. In P. E. Nathan & J. M. Gorman (Eds.), *A guide to treatments that work* (2nd ed., pp. 57–85). New York: Oxford University Press.

Kazdin, A. E. (2003). Psychotherapy for children and adolescents. *Annual Review of Psychology, 54,* 253–276.

Kazdin, A. E. (2004). Psychotherapy for children and adolescents. In M. L. Lambert (Ed.), *Bergin and Garfield's Handbook of psychotherapy and behavior change* (5th ed., pp. 543–589). New York: John Wiley & Sons.

Kazdin, A. E., & Bass, D. (1989). Power to detect differences between alternative treatments in comparative psychotherapy outcome research. *Journal of Consulting and Clinical Psychology, 57,* 138–147.

Kazdin, A. E., Bass, D., Ayers, W. A., & Rodgers, A. (1990). Empirical and clinical focus of child and adolescent psychotherapy research. *Journal of Consulting and Clinical Psychology, 58,* 729–740.

Kazdin, A. E., & Weisz, J. R. (Eds.). (2003). *Evidence-based psychotherapies for children and adolescents.* New York: Guilford.

Keijsers, G. P. J., Schaap, C. P. D. R., Hoogduin, C. A. L., & Lammers, M. W. (1995). Patient-therapist interaction in the behavioral treatment of Panic Disorder with Agoraphobia. *Behavior Modification, 19,* 491–517.

Keiser, R. E., & Prather, E. N. (1990). What is the TAT? A review of ten years of research. *Journal of Personality Assessment, 55,* 800–803.

Kendall, P. C., Aschenbrand, S. G., & Hudson, J. L. (2003). Child-focused treatment of anxiety. In A. E. Kazdin & J. R. Weisz (Eds.), *Evidence-based psychotherapies for children and adolescents* (pp. 81–100). New York: Guilford.

Kendell, R., & Jablensky, A. (2003). Distinguishing between the validity and utility of psychiatric diagnoses. *American Journal of Psychiatry, 160,* 4–12.

Kennedy, M. L., Faust, D., Willis, W. G., & Piotrowski, C. (1994). Social-emotional assessment practices in school psychology. *Journal of Psychoeducational Assessment, 12,* 228–240.

Kenwright, M., & Marks, I. M. (2004). Computer-aided self-help for phobia/panic via internet at home: A pilot study. *British Journal of Psychiatry, 184,* 448–449.

Kessler, R. C., Merikangas, K. R., Berglund, P., Eaton, W. W., Koretz, D. S., & Walters, E. E. (2003). Mild disorders should not be eliminated from the DSM-V. *Archives of General Psychiatry, 60,* 1117–1122.

Kessler, R. C., Zhao, S., Katz, S. J., Kouzis, A. C., Frank, R. G., Edlund, M., et al. (1999). Past-year use of outpatient services for psychiatric problems in the National Comorbidity Survey. *American Journal of Psychiatry, 156,* 115–123.

Kim, N. S., & Ahn, W. (2002). Clinical psychologists' theory-based representations of mental disorders predict their diagnostic reasoning and memory. *Journal of Experimental Psychology: General, 131,* 451–476.

Kirk, S. A. (2004). Are children's DSM diagnoses accurate? *Brief Treatment and Crisis Intervention, 4,* 255–270.

Klerman, G. L., Weissman, M. M., Rounsaville, B. J., & Chevron, E. S. (1984). *Interpersonal psychotherapy for depression.* New York: Basic Books.

Knesper, D. J., Pagnucco, D. J., & Wheeler, J. R. C. (1985). Similarities and differences across mental health service providers and practice settings in the United States. *American Psychologist, 40,* 1352–1369.

Korotitsch, W. J., & Nelson-Gray, R. O. (1999). An overview of self-monitoring research in assessment and treatment. *Psychological Assessment, 11,* 415–425.

Kovacs, M. (1992). *Manual for the Children's Depression Inventory.* North Tonawanda, NJ: Multi-Health Systems.

Kraemer, H. C., Morgan, G. A., Leech, N. L., Gliner, J. A., Vaske, J. J., & Harmon, R. J. (2003). Measures of clinical significance. *Journal of the American Academy of Child & Adolescent Psychiatry, 42,* 1524–1529.

Kraemer, H. C., Wilson, G. T., Fairburn, C. G., & Agras, W. S. (2002). Mediators and moderators of treatment effects in randomized clinical trials. *Archives of General Psychiatry, 59,* 877–883.

Krishnamurthy, R., Archer, R. P., & House, J. J. (1996). The MMPI-A and Rorschach: A failure to establish convergent validity. *Assessment, 3,* 179–191.

Krishnamurthy, R., VandeCreek, L., Kaslow, N. J., Tazeau, Y. N., Miville, M. L., Kerns, R., et al. (2004). Achieving competency in psychological assessment: Directions for education and training. *Journal of Clinical Psychology, 60,* 725–739.

Krueger, R. F., Caspi, A., Moffitt, T. E., & Silva, P. A. (1998). The structure and stability of common mental disorders (DSM-III-R): A longitudinal-epidemiological study. *Journal of Abnormal Psychology, 107,* 216–227.

Krueger, R. F., Chentsova-Dutton, Y. E., Markon, K. E., Goldberg, D., & Ormel, J. (2003). A cross-cultural study of the structure of comorbidity among common psychopathological syndromes in the general health care setting. *Journal of Abnormal Psychology, 112,* 437–447.

Kvaal, S., Choca, J., & Groth-Marnat, G. (2003). The integrated psychological report. In L. E. Beutler & G. Groth-Marnat (Eds.), *Integrative assessment of adult personality* (2nd ed., 398–433). New York: Guilford Press.

La Rue, A., & Watson, J. (1998). Psychological assessment of older adults. *Professional Psychology: Research and Practice, 29,* 5–14.

Lafferty, P., Beutler, L. E., & Crago, M. (1989). Differences between more and less effective psychotherapists: A study of select therapist variables. *Journal of Consulting and Clinical Psychology, 57,* 76–70.

Lally, S. J. (2001). Should human figure drawings be admitted into court? *Journal of Personality Assessment, 76,* 135–149.

Lally, S. J. (2003). What tests are acceptable for use in forensic evaluations? *Professional Psychology: Research and Practice, 34,* 491–498.

Lambert, M. J. (Ed.). (2004). *Bergin and Garfield's handbook of psychotherapy and behavior change* (5th ed.). New York: John Wiley & Sons.

Lambert, M. J., Hansen, N. B., Umphress, V., Lunnen, K., Okiishi, J., Burlingame, G., et al. (1996). *Administration and scoring manual for the Outcome Questionnaire (OQ 45.2)*. Wilmington, DE: American Professional Credentialing Services.

Lambert, M. J., & Ogles, B. M. (2004). The efficacy and effectiveness of psychotherapy. In M. J. Lambert (Ed.), *Bergin and Garfield's handbook of psychotherapy and behavior change* (5th ed., pp. 139–193). New York: John Wiley & Sons.

Lambert, M. J., Whipple, J. L., Hawkins, E. J., Vermeersch, D. A., Nielsen, S. L., & Smart, D. W. (2003). Is it time for clinicians to routinely track patient outcome? A meta-analysis. *Clinical Psychology: Science and Practice, 10,* 288–301.

Lampropoulos, G. K. (2000). Evolving psychotherapy integration: Eclectic selection and prescriptive applications of common factors in therapy. *Psychotherapy, 37,* 285–297.

Landman, J. T., & Dawes, R. M. (1982). Psychotherapy outcome: Smith and Glass' conclusions stand up under scrutiny. *American Psychologist, 37,* 504–516.

Le, H., Muñoz, R. F., Ippen, C. G., & Stoddard, J. L. (2003). Treatment is not enough: We must prevent major depression in women. *Prevention and Treatment, 6, Article 10.* Retrieved October 21, 2004.

Leichsenring, F., Rabung, S., & Lebing, E. (2004). The efficacy of short-term psychodynamic psychotherapy for specific psychiatric disorders. *Archives of General Psychiatry, 61,* 1208–1216.

Lemsky, C. M. (2000). Neuropsychological assessment and treatment planning. In G. Groth-Marnat (Ed.), *Neuropsychological assessment in clinical practice* (pp. 535–574). New York: John Wiley & Sons.

Levitt, E. E. (1957). The effects of psychotherapy with children: An evaluation. *Journal of Consulting Psychology, 21,* 189–196.

Levitt, E. E. (1963). The results of psychotherapy with children: A further evaluation. *Behaviour Research and Therapy, 60,* 326–329.

Lewak, R. W., & Hogan, R. S. (2003). Integrating and applying assessment information: Decision making, patient feedback, and consultation. In L. E. Beutler & G. Groth-Marnat (Eds.), *Integrative assessment of adult personality* (2nd ed., 356–397). New York: Guilford Press.

Lewinsohn, P. M., Antonuccio, D. O., Steinmetz, J. L., & Teri, L. (1984). *The coping with depression course: A psychoeducational intervention for unipolar depression.* Eugene, OR: Castilia.

Lewinsohn, P. M., & Clarke, G. N. (1999). Psychosocial treatments for adolescent depression. *Clinical Psychology Review, 19,* 329–342.

Li, F., McAuley, E., Chaumeton, N. R., & Harmer, P. (2001). Enhancing the psychological well-being of elderly individuals through Tai Chi exercise: A latent growth curve analysis. *Structural Equation Modeling, 8,* 53–83.

Lichtenberg, P. A., Murman, D. L., & Mellow, A. M. (2003). Integrated case studies. In P. A. Lichtenberg, D. L. Murman, & A. M. Mellow (Eds.), *Handbook of dementia* (pp. 403–412). New York: John Wiley & Sons.

Lichtenberger, E. O., Broadbooks, D. Y., & Kaufman, A. S. (2000). *Essentials of cognitive assessment with KAIT and other Kaufman measures.* New York: John Wiley & Sons.

Lichtenberger, E. O., Kaufman, A. S., & Lai, Z. C. (2002). *Essentials of WMS-III assessment.* New York: John Wiley & Sons.

Lichtenberger, E. O., & Kaufman, A. S. (2004). *Essentials of WPPSI-III assessment.* New York: John Wiley & Sons.

Lilienfeld, S. O., Lynn, S. J., & Lohr, J. M. (2003). Science and pseudoscience in clinical psychology: Initial thoughts, reflections, and considerations. In S. O. Lilienfeld, S. J. Lynn, & J. M. Lohr (Eds.), *Science and pseudoscience in clinical psychology* (pp. 1–14). New York: Guilford Press.

Lilienfeld, S. O., Wood, J. M., & Garb, H. N. (2000). The scientific status of projective techniques. *Psychological Science in the Public Interest, 1,* 27–66.

Lima, E. N., Stanley, S., Kaboski, B., Reitzel, L. R., Richey, J. A., Castro, Y., et al. (in press). The incremental validity of the MMPI-2: When does therapist access not enhance treatment outcome? *Psychological Assessment.*

Lin, E., Goering, P., Offord, D. R., Campbell, D., & Boyle, M. H. (1996). The use of mental health services in Ontario: Epidemiologic findings. *Canadian Journal of Psychiatry, 41,* 572–577.

Lin, K. K., Sandler, I. N., Ayers, T. S., Wolchik, S. A., & Luecken, L. J. (2004). Resilience in parentally bereaved children and adolescents seeking preventive services. *Journal of Clinical Child and Adolescent Psychology, 33,* 673–683.

Lohr, J. M., Lilienfeld, S. O., Tolin, D. F., & Herbert, J. D. (1999). Eye movement desensitization and reprocessing (EMDR): An analysis of specific and non-specific treatment factors. *Journal of Anxiety Research, 13,* 185–207.

Lopez, S. J., & Snyder, C.R. (2003). (Eds.). *Positive psychological assessment: A handbook of models and measures.* Washington, DC: American Psychological Association.

Lowry-Webster, H. M., & Barrett, P. M. (2001). A universal prevention trial of anxiety and depressive disorders in childhood: Preliminary data from an Australian study. *Behaviour Change, 18,* 36–50.

Luborsky, L. (1954). A note on Eysenck's article "The effects of psychotherapy: An evaluation." *British Journal of Psychology, 45,* 129–131.

Luborksy, L. (1984). *Principles of psychoanalytic psychotherapy: A manual for supportive expressive (SE) treatment.* New York: Basic Books.

Luborsky, L., Diguer, L., Luborsky, E., Singer, B., Dickter, D., & Schmidt, K. A. (1993). The efficacy of dynamic psychotherapies: Is it true that "Everyone has won and all must have prizes"? In M. E. Miller, L. Luborsky, J. P. Barber, & J. P. Docherty (Eds.), *Psychodynamic treatment research: A handbook for clinical practice* (pp. 497–516). New York: Basic Books.

Luborsky, L., Diguer, L., Seligman, D. A., Rosenthal, R., Krause, E. D., Johnson, S., et al. (1999). The researcher's own therapy allegiance: A "wild card" in comparisons of treatment efficacy. *Clinical Psychology: Science and Practice, 6,* 95–106.

Luborsky, L., Rosenthal, R., Diguer, L., Andrusyna, T. P., Berman, J. S., Levitt, J. T., et al. (2002). The dodo bird verdict is alive and well—mostly. *Clinical Psychology: Science and Practice, 9,* 2–12.

Luborsky, L., Singer, B., & Luborsky, E. (1975). Comparative studies of psychotherapies: Is it true that "Everybody has won and all must have prizes"? *Archives of General Psychiatry, 32,* 995–1008.

Luxembourg Income Study (2000). *Relative poverty rates for the total population, children and the elderly.* Retrieved on October 22, 2004, from http://www.lisproject.org/keyfigures/povertytable.htm

Lyon, J. S., & Howard, K. I. (1991). Main effects analysis in clinical research: Statistical guidelines for disaggregating treatment groups. *Journal of Consulting and Clinical Psychology, 59,* 745–748.

MacCallum, R. C., & Austin, J. T. (2000). Applications of structural equation modeling in psychological research. *Annual Review of Psychology, 51,* 201–226.

MacCallum, R. C., Zhang, S., Preacher, K. J., & Rucker, D. D. (2002). On the practice of dichotomization of quantitative variables. *Psychological Methods, 7,* 19–40.

Magaletta, P. R., & Verdeyen, V. (2005). Clinical practice in corrections: A conceptual framework. *Professional Psychology Research and Practice, 36,* 37–43.

Malgady, R. G. (1996). The question of cultural bias in assessment and diagnosis of ethnic minority clients: Let's reject the null hypothesis. *Professional Psychology: Research and Practice, 27,* 73–77.

Malloy, D. C., Hadjistavropoulos, T., Douaud, P., & Smythe, W. E. (2002). The codes of ethics of the Canadian Psychological Association and the Canadian Medical Association: Ethical orientation and functional grammar analysis. *Canadian Psychology, 43,* 244–253.

Mariush, M. E. (2002). *Essentials of treatment planning.* New York: John Wiley & Sons.

Marks, I. M., & Mathews, A. M. (1979). Brief standard self-rating for phobic patients. *Behaviour Research and Therapy, 17,* 263–267.

Marks, I., Shaw, S., & Parkin, R. (1998). Computer-aided treatments of mental health problems. *Clinical Psychology: Science and Practice, 5,* 151–170.

Martin, D. J., Garske, J. P., & Davis, M. K. (2000). Relation of the therapeutic alliance with outcome and other variables: A meta-analytic review. *Journal of Consulting and Clinical Psychology, 68,* 438–450.

Martin, L., Saperson, K., & Maddigan, B. (2003). Residency training: challenges and opportunities in preparing trainees for the 21st century. *Canadian Journal of Psychiatry, 48,* 225–231.

Mash, E. J. (1979). What is behavioral assessment? *Behavioral Assessment, 1,* 23–29.

Mash, E. J., & Foster, S. L. (2001). Exporting analogue behavioral observation from research to clinical practice: Useful or cost-defective? *Psychological Assessment, 13,* 86–98.

Mash, E. J., & Hunsley, J. (1993). Assessment considerations in the assessment of failing psychotherapy: Bringing the negatives out of the darkroom. *Psychological Assessment: A Journal of Consulting and Clinical Psychology, 5,* 292–301.

Mash, E. J., & Hunsley, J. (2004). Behavioral assessment: Sometimes you get what you need. In S. N. Haynes & E. M. Heiby (Eds.), *The comprehensive handbook of psychological assessment, Volume 3: Behavioral assessment* (pp. 489–501). New York: John Wiley & Sons.

Mash, E. J., & Hunsley, J. (in press). Evidence-based assessment of child and adolescent disorders: Issues and challenges. *Journal of Clinical Child and Adolescent Psychology.*

Masling, J. M. (1992). The influence of situation and interpersonal variables in projective testing. *Journal of Personality Assessment, 59,* 616–640.

May, R., Angel, E., & Ellenberger, H. (Eds.). (1958). *Existence: A new dimension in psychiatry and psychology.* New York: Basic Books.

McCarthy, O., & Carr, A. (2002). Prevention of bullying. In A. Carr (Ed.), *Prevention: what works with children and adolescents? A critical review of psychological prevention programmes for children, adolescents and their families* (pp. 205–221). Hove, UK: Brunner-Routledge.

McCellan, J. M., & Werry, J. S. (2003). Evidence-based treatments in child and adolescent psychiatry: An inventory. *Journal of the American Academy of Child and Adolescent Psychiatry, 42,* 1388–1400.

McClelland, D. C., Koestner, R., & Weinberger, J. (1989). How do self-attributed and implicit motives differ? *Psychological Bulletin, 96,* 690–702.

McCrone, P., Knapp, M., Proudfoot, J., Ryden, C., Cavanagh, K., Shapiro, D. A., et al. (2004). Cost-effectiveness of computerised cognitive-behavioural therapy for anxiety and depression in primary care: Randomised controlled trial. *British Journal of Psychiatry, 185,* 55–62.

McFall, R. M. (1991). Manifesto for a science of clinical psychology. *The Clinical Psychologist, 44,* 75–88.

McGrath, P. J., & Finley, G. A. (Eds.). (2003). *Pediatric pain: Biological and social context.* Seattle, WA: IASP Press.

McGrath, P. J., Finley, G. A., Ritchie, J., & Dowden, S. J. (2003). *Pain, pain, go away: Helping children with pain.* Halifax, NS: Dalhousie University.

McGrath, P. J., & Unruh, A. (1999). The measurement and assessment of paediatric pain. In P.D. Wall & R. Melzack (Eds.), *Textbook of Pain* (4th ed., pp. 371–384). London: Churchill Livingstone.

McLean, P. D., & Woody, S. R. (2001). *Anxiety disorders in adults: An evidence-based approach to psychological treatment.* New York: Oxford University Press.

McLellan, F. (2003). Research by US psychiatrists in danger of extinction. Expert committee recommends steps to strengthen research training in psychiatry residency. *Lancet, 362,* 1732.

McLeod, B. D., & Weisz, J. R. (2004). Using dissertations to examine potential bias in child and adolescent clinical trials. *Journal of Consulting and Clinical Psychology, 72,* 235–251.

McNally, R. J., Bryant, R. A., & Ehlers, A. (2003). Does early psychological intervention promote recovery from posttraumatic stress? *Psychological Science in the Public Interest, 4,* 45–79.

Measelle, J. R., Ablow, J. C., Cowan, P. A. & Cowan, C. P. (1998). Assessing young children's views of their academic, social and emotional lives: An evaluation of the self-perception scales of the Berkeley Puppet Interview. *Child Development, 69,* 1556–1576.

Megargee, E. I. (2002). *The California Psychological Inventory handbook* (2nd ed.). San Francisco: Jossey-Bass.

Meichenbaum, D. (1977). *Cognitive-behavior modification: An integrative approach.* New York: Plenum.

Meisner, S. (1988). Susceptibility of Rorschach distress correlates to malingering. *Journal of Personality Assessment, 52,* 564–571.

Mellers, J. D. C. (2004). Neurological investigations. In L. H. Goldstein & J. E. McNeil (Eds.), *Clinical neuropsychology: A practical guide to assessment and management for clinicians* (pp. 57–77). Chichester, UK: John Wiley & Sons.

Merrill, K. A., Tolbert, V. E., & Wade, W. A. (2003). Effectiveness of cognitive therapy for depression in a community mental health center: A benchmarking study. *Journal of Consulting and Clinical Psychology, 71,* 404–409.

Messer, S. B. (2001). What makes brief psychodynamic therapy time efficient? *Clinical Psychology: Science and Practice, 8,* 5–22.

Meyer, B., Pilkonis, P. A., Krupnick, J. L., Egan, M. K., Simmens, S. J., & Sotsky, S. M. (2002). Treatment expectancies, patient alliance, and outcome: Further analyses from the National Institute of Mental Health Treatment of Depression Collaborative Research Program. *Journal of Consulting and Clinical Psychology, 70,* 1051–1055.

Meyer, G. (Ed.). (1999). The utility of the Rorschach in clinical assessment [Special section: I]. *Psychological Assessment, 11,* 235–302.

Meyer, G. (Ed.). (2001). The utility of the Rorschach in clinical assessment [Special section: II]. *Psychological Assessment, 13,* 419–502.

Meyer, G. J., Finn, S. E., Eyde, L., Kay, G. G., Moreland, K. L., Dies, R. R., et al. (2001). Psychological testing and psychological assessment: A review of evidence and issues. *American Psychologist, 56,* 128–165.

Meyer, T. J., Miller, M. L., Metzger, R. L., & Borkovec, T. D. (1990). Developmental validation of the Penn State Worry Questionnaire. *Behaviour Research and Therapy, 28,* 487–496.

Mezulis, A. H., Abramson, L. Y., Hyde, J. S., & Hankin, B. L. (2004). Is there a universal positivity bias in attributions? A meta-analytic review of individual, developmental, and cultural differences in the self-serving attributional bias. *Psychological Bulletin, 130,* 711–747.

Michalki, K. T., & Saklofske, D. H. (1996). A psychometric investigation of the Wechsler Individual Achievement Test with a sample of Saskatchewan school children. *Canadian Journal of School Psychology, 12,* 44–54.

Middleton, J. A. (2004). Clinical neuropsychological assessment of children. In L. H. Goldstein & J. E. McNeil (Eds.), *Clinical neuropsychology: A practical guide to assessment and management for clinicians* (pp. 275–300). Chichester, UK: John Wiley & Sons.

Miller, G. E., & Prinz, R. J. (1990). Enhancement of social learning family interventions for childhood conduct disorder. *Psychological Bulletin, 108,* 291–307.

Miller, G. E., & Prinz, R. J. (2003). Engagement of families in treatment for childhood conduct problems. *Behavior Therapy, 34,* 517–534.

Millon, T. (1993). *Millon Adolescent Clinical Inventory manual.* Minneapolis, MN: National Computer Systems.

Millon, T. (1997). *Millon Clinical Multiaxial Inventory-III manual.* Minneapolis, MN: National Computer Systems.

Minke, K. M., & Brown, D. T. (1996). Preparing psychologists to work with children: A comparison of curricula in child-clinical and school psychology programs. *Professional Psychology: Research and Practice, 27,* 631–634.

Miranda, J., Bernal, G., Lau, A., Kohn, L., Hwang, W.-C., & LaFromboise, T. (2005). State of the science on psychosocial interventions for ethnic minorities. *Annual Review of Clinical Psychology, 1,* 113–142.

Mischel, W. (1968). *Personality and assessment.* New York: John Wiley & Sons.

Mischel, W. (2004). Toward an integrative science of the person. *Annual Review of Psychology, 55,* 1–22.

Mischel, W., Shoda, Y., & Smith, R. E. (2004). *Introduction to personality: Toward an integration.* New York: John Wiley & Sons.

Mokdad, A. H., Marks, J. S., Stroup, D. F., & Gerberding, J. L. (2004). Actual causes of death in the United States, 2000. *Journal of the American Medical Association, 291,* 1238–1245.

Monahan, J. (1981). *Predicting violent behaviour: An assessment of clinical techniques.* Beverly Hills, CA: Sage.

Morey, L. C. (1991). *The Personality Assessment Inventory professional manual.* Odessa, FL: Psychological Assessment Resources.

Morey, L. C. (1996). *An interpretive guide to the Personality Assessment Inventory.* Odessa, FL: Psychological Assessment Resources.

Morey, L. C. (2003). *Essentials of PAI assessment.* New York: John Wiley & Sons.

Morgan, D. L., & Morgan, R. K. (2001). Single-participant research design: Bringing science to managed care. *American Psychologist, 56,* 119–217.

Morin, C. M. (2004). Cognitive-behavioral approaches to the treatment of insomnia. *Journal of Clinical Psychiatry, 65 (suppl 16),* 33–40.

Morin, C. M., Colecchi, C., Stone, J., Sood, R., & Brink, D. (1999). Behavioral and pharmacological therapies for late-life insomnia: A randomized controlled trial. *Journal of the American Medical Association, 281,* 991–999.

Morley, S., & Adams, M. (1989). Some simple statistical tests for exploring single-case time-series data. *British Journal of Clinical Psychology, 28,* 1–18.

Morris, R. G. (2004). Neuropsychology of older adults. In L. H. Goldstein & J. E. McNeil (Eds.), *Clinical neuropsychology: A practical guide to assessment and management for clinicians* (pp. 301–318). Chichester, UK: John Wiley & Sons.

Mrazek, P. J., & Haggerty, R. J. (1994). *Reducing risks for mental disorders: Frontiers for preventive research.* Washington, DC: National Academy Press.

MTA Cooperative Group. (1999a). A 14-month randomized clinical trial of treatment strategies for Attention-Deficit/Hyperactivity Disorder. *Archives of General Psychiatry, 56,* 1073–1086.

MTA Cooperative Group. (1999b). Moderators and mediators of treatment response for children with Attention-Deficit/Hyperactivity Disorder. *Archives of General Psychiatry, 56,* 1088–1096.

Mufson, L., & Dorta, K. P. (2003). Interpersonal psychotherapy for depressed adolescents. In A. E. Kazdin & J. R. Weisz (Eds.), *Evidence-based psychotherapies for children and adolescents* (pp. 148–164). New York: Guilford.

Mufson, L., & Dorta, K. P. (2004). Interpersonal psychotherapy for depressed adolescents. In A. E. Kazdin & J. R. Weisz (Eds.), *Evidence-based psychotherapies for children and adolescents* (pp. 148–164). New York: Guilford.

Mufson, L., Dorta, K. P., Moreau, D., & Weissman, M. M. (2004). *Interpersonal psychotherapy for depressed adolescents* (2nd ed.). New York: Guilford.

Mufson, L., Weissman, M. M., Moreau, D., & Garfinkel, R. (1999). Efficacy of interpersonal psychotherapy for depressed adolescents. *Archives of General Psychiatry, 56,* 573–579.

Mullen, E. J., & Streiner, D. L. (2004). The evidence for and against evidence-based practice. *Brief Treatment and Crisis Intervention, 4,* 111–121.

Mumma, G. H. (1998). Improving cognitive case formulation and treatment planning in clinical practice and research. *Journal of Cognitive Psychotherapy, 12,* 251–274.

Mungas, D., Reed, B. R., Crane, P. K., Haan, M. N., & González, H. (2004). Spanish and English Neuropsychological Assessment scales (SENAS): Further development and psychometric characteristics. *Psychological Assessment, 16,* 347–359.

Mungas, D., Reed, B. R., Marshall, S. C., & González, H. (2000). Development of psychometrically matched English and Spanish language neuropsychological tests for older persons. *Neuropsychology, 14,* 209–223.

Murray, H. A. (1943). *Thematic Apperception Test manual.* Cambridge, MA: Harvard University Press.

Mussell, M. P., Crosby, R. D., Crow, S. J., Knopke, A. J., Peterson, C. B., Wonderlich, S. A., et al. (2000). Utilization of empirically supported psychotherapy treatments for individuals with Eating Disorders: A survey of psychologists. *International Journal of Eating Disorders, 27,* 230–237.

Myers, I. B., & McCaulley, M. H. (1985). *Manual: A guide to the development and use of the Myers-Briggs Type Indicator.* Palo Alto, CA: Consulting Psychologists Press.

Myers, L. L., & Thyer, B. A. (1997). Should social work clients have the right to effective treatment? *Social Work, 42,* 288–297.

Nagin, D., & Tremblay, R. E. (1999). Trajectories of boys' physical aggression, opposition, and hyperactivity on the path to physically violent and nonviolent juvenile delinquency. *Child Development, 70,* 1181–1196.

Naglieri, J. A., Drasgow, F., Schmit, M., Handler, L., Prifitera, A., Margolis, A.M., et al. (2004). Psychological testing on the Internet, *American Psychologist, 59,* 150–162.

Nathan, P. E. (2004). When science only takes us so far. *Clinical Psychology: Science and Practice, 11,* 216–218.

Nathan, P., & Gorman, J. M. (Eds.). (1998). *A guide to treatments that work.* New York: Oxford University Press.

Nathan, P., & Gorman, J. M. (Eds.). (2002). *A guide to treatments that work* (2nd ed.). New York: Oxford University Press.

Nation, M., Crusto, C., Wandersman, A., Kumpfer, K. L., Seybolt, D., Morrissey-Kane, E., et al. (2003). What works in prevention: Principles of effective prevention programs. *American Psychologist, 58,* 449–456.

National Institute for Clinical Excellence. (2004a). *Anxiety: management of anxiety (panic disorder, with or without agoraphobia, and generalized anxiety disorder) in adults in primary, secondary and community care.* Retrieved December 8, 2004, from http://www.nice.org.uk/CG022quickrefguide

National Institute for Clinical Excellence. (2004b). *Depression: management of depression in primary and secondary care.* Retrieved December 8, 2004, from http://www.nice.org.uk/CG023quickrefguide

National Institute for Clinical Excellence. (2005a). *Appraisal consultation document: Methylphenidate, atomoxetine and desamfetamine for attention deficit hyperactivity disorder (ADHD) in children and adolescents.* Retrieved March 15, 2005, from http://www.nice.org.uk

National Institute for Clinical Excellence. (2005b). *Depression in children: identification and management of depression in children and young people in primary, community and secondary care.* Retrieved February 15, 2005, from http://www.nice.org.uk

National Institutes of Health. (1998). *Diagnosis and treatment of Attention Deficit Hyperactivity Disorder (ADHD), NIH Consensus Statement, 16,* 1–37. Kensington, MD: Author.

National Opinion Research Center. (2004). Doctorate recipients from United States universities: Summary report 2002. Retrieved on May 28, 2004 from http://www.norc.uchicago.edu/issues/docdata/htm

Naugle, A. E., & Maher, S. (2003). Modeling and behavioral rehearsal. In W. O'Donohue, J. E. Fisher, & S. C. Hayes (Eds.), *Cognitive behavior therapy: Applying empirically supported techniques in your practice* (pp. 238–246). New York: John Wiley & Sons.

Neisser, U. (Ed.). (1998). *The rising curve: Long-term gains in IQ and related measures.* Washington, DC: American Psychological Association.

Nelson, G., Westhues, A., & MacLeod, J. (2003, December 18). A meta-analysis of longitudinal research on preschool prevention programs for children. *Prevention and Treatment, 6, Article 31.* Retrieved October 21, 2004, from http://journals.apa.org/prevention/volume6/pre0060031a.html

Nelson-Gray, R. O. (2003). Treatment utility of psychological assessment. *Psychological Assessment, 15,* 521–531.

Neuner, F., Schauer, M., Klaschik, C., Karunakara, U., & Elbert, T. (2004). A comparison of narrative exposure therapy, supportive counseling, and psychoeducation for treating posttraumatic stress disorder in an African refugee settlement. *Journal of Consulting and Clinical Psychology, 72,* 579–587.

Newman, D. L., Moffitt, T. E., Caspi, A., & Silva, P. A. (1998). Comorbid mental disorders: Implications for treatment and sample selection. *Journal of Abnormal Psychology, 107,* 305–311.

Newman, M. G., Erickson, T., Przeworski, A., & Dzus, E. (2003). Self-help and minimal-contact therapies for anxiety disorders: Is human contact necessary for therapeutic efficacy? *Journal of Clinical Psychology, 59,* 251–274.

Newsom, C. R., Archer, R. P., Trumbetta, S., & Gottesman, I. I. (2003). Changes in adolescent response patterns on the MMPI/MMPI-A across four decades. *Journal of Personality Assessment, 81,* 74–84.

Nezu, A. M., & Nezu, C. M. (1993). Identifying and selecting target problems for clinical interventions: A problem-solving model. *Psychological Assessment, 5,* 254–263.

Nichols, D. S. (2001). *Essentials of MMPI-2 assessment.* New York: John Wiley & Sons.

Norcross, J. C. (Ed.). (2002). *Psychotherapy relationships that work: Therapist contributions and responsiveness to patients.* London: Oxford University Press.

Norcross, J. C. (Ed.). (2001a). Empirically supported therapy relationships: Summary report of the Division 29 task force [Special issue]. *Psychotherapy, 38(4).*

Norcross, J. C. (2001b). Purposes, processes, and products of the Task Force on Empirically Supported Therapy Relationships. *Psychotherapy, 38,* 345–356.

Norcross, J. C., & Goldfried, M. R. (1992). *Handbook of psychotherapy integration.* New York: Basic Books.

Norcross, J. C., Hedges, M., & Prochaska, J. O. (2002). The face of 2010: A Delphi poll on the future of psychotherapy. *Professional Psychology: Research and Practice, 33,* 316–322.

Norcross, J. C., Karg, R. S., & Prochaska, J. (1997). Clinical psychologists in the 1990s: Part I. *The Clinical Psychologist, 50(2),* 4–9.

Norcross, J. C., Sayette, M. A., Mayne, T. J., Karg, R. S., & Turkson, M. A. (1998). Selecting a doctoral program in professional psychology: Some comparisons among Ph.D. counselling, Ph.D. clinical, and Psy.D. clinical psychology programs. *Professional Psychology: Research and Practice, 29,* 609–614.

Nunnally, J. C., & Bernstein, I. H. (1994). *Psychometric theory* (3rd ed.). New York: McGraw-Hill.

O'Brien, W. H. (1995). Inaccuracies in the estimation of functional relationships using self-monitoring data. *Journal of Behavior Therapy and Experimental Psychiatry, 26,* 351–357.

Ogles, B. M., Lambert, M. J., & Fields, S. A. (2002). *Essentials of outcome assessment.* New York: John Wiley & Sons.

Ohayon, M. M. (2005). Relationship between chronic painful physical conditions and insomnia. *Journal of Psychiatric Research, 39,* 151–159.

Olds, D. L. (2002). Prenatal and infancy home visiting by nurses: From randomized trials to community replication. *Prevention Science, 3,* 153–172.

Olfson, M., Marcus, S. C., Druss, B., & Pincus, H. A. (2002). National trends in the use of outpatient psychotherapy. *American Journal of Psychiatry, 159,* 1914–1920.

Olfson, M., Marcus, S. C., Druss, B., Elinson, L., Tanielian, T., & Pincus, H. A. (2002). National trends in the outpatient treatment of depression. *Journal of the American Medical Association, 287,* 203–209.

Ollendick, T. H., & King, N. J. (2004). Empirically supported treatments for children and adolescents: Advances toward evidence-based practice. In P. M., Barrett, P. M., & T. H. Ollendick (Eds.), *Interventions that work with children and adolescents: Prevention and treatment* (pp. 3–25). New York: John Wiley & Sons.

Olweus, D. (1993). *Bullying at school: What we know and what we can do.* Oxford: Blackwell.

Ontario Psychological Association. (1998). *Ethical guidelines for psychological practice related to child custody and access.* Toronto, ON: Author.

O'Riordan, B., & Carr, A. (2002). Prevention of physical abuse. In A. Carr (Ed.), *Prevention: what works with children and adolescents? A critical review of psychological prevention programmes for children, adolescents and their families* (pp. 154–180). Hove, UK: Brunner-Routledge.

Orlinsky, D. E., & Howard, K. I. (1980). Gender and psychotherapeutic outcome. In A. M. Brodsky & R. T. Hare-Mustin (Eds.), *Women in psychotherapy* (pp. 3–34). New York: Guilford Press.

Orlinsky, D. E., Rønnestad, M. H., & Willutzki, U. (2004). Fifty years of psychotherapy process-outcome research: Continuity and change. In M. J. Lambert (Ed.), *Bergin and Garfield's handbook of psychotherapy and behavior change* (5th ed., pp. 307–389). New York: John Wiley & Sons.

O'Rourke, N. (2004). Reliability generalization of responses by care providers to the Center for Epidemiologic Studies-Depression (CES-D) Scale. *Educational and Psychological Measurement, 64,* 973–990.

Owens, E. B., Hinshaw, S. P., Kraemer, H. C., Arnold, L. E., Abikoff, H. B., Cantwell, D. P., et al. (2003). Which treatments work for whom for ADHD? Moderators of treatment response in the MTA. *Journal of Consulting and Clinical Psychology, 71,* 540–522.

Palmiter, D. J. (2004). A survey of the assessment practices of child and adolescent clinicians. *American Journal of Orthopsychiatry, 74,* 122–128.

Parker, K. C. H., Hanson, R. K., & Hunsley, J. (1988). MMPI, Rorschach, and WAIS: A meta-analytic comparison of reliability, stability, and validity. *Psychological Bulletin, 103,* 367–373.

Patterson, G. R. (1982). *Coercive family process.* Eugene, OR: Castilia.

Patterson, G. R. (2005). The next generation of PMTO models. *The Behavior Therapist, 28,* 27–33.

Pelham, W. E., Wheeler, T., & Chronis, A. (1998). Empirically supported psychosocial treatment for Attention-deficit/Hyperactivity disorder. *Journal of Clinical Child Psychology, 27,* 190–205.

Perls, F. S., Hefferline, R. F., & Goodman, P. (1951). *Gestalt therapy.* New York: Julian Press.

Persons, J. B. (1989). *Cognitive therapy in practice: A case formulation approach.* New York: Norton.

Persons, J. B., & Bertagnolli, A. (1999). Inter-rater reliability of cognitive-behavioral case formulations of depression: A replication. *Cognitive Therapy & Research, 23,* 271–283.

Persons, J. B., Bostrom, A., & Bertagnolli, A. (1999). Results of randomized controlled trials of cognitive therapy for depression generalize to private practice. *Cognitive Therapy and Research, 23,* 535–548.

Persons, J. B., Davidson, J., & Tompkins, M. A. (2001). *Essential components of cognitive-behavior therapy for depression.* Washington, DC: American Psychological Association.

Peterson, D. R. (2004). Science, scientism, and professional responsibility. *Clinical Psychology: Science and Practice, 11,* 196–210.

Peterson, R., McHolland, J., Bent, R., David-Russell, E., Edwall, G., Polite, K., Singer, D., & Stricker, G. (1991). *The core curriculum in professional psychology.* Washington, DC: American Psychological Association.

Petry, N. M., Tennen, H., & Affleck, G. (2000). Stalking the elusive client variable in psychotherapy research. In C. R. Snyder & R. E. Ingram (Eds.), *Handbook of psychological change: Psychotherapy processes & practices for the 21st century* (pp. 88–108). New York: John Wiley & Sons.

Pew Internet. (2003). *Internet activities.* Retrieved September 21, 2004 from http://www.pewinternet.org/reports/chart/asp?img=Internet_A8.htm

Phillips, E. E. (1991). George Washington University's international data on psychotherapy delivery systems: Modeling new approaches to the study of therapy. In L. E. Beutler & M. Crago (Eds.), *Psychotherapy research: An international review of programmatic studies* (pp. 263–273). Washington, DC: American Psychological Association.

Phillips, E. L. (1991). George Washington University's international data on psychotherapy delivery systems: Modeling new approaches to the study of therapy. In L. E. Beutler & M. Crago (Eds.), *Psychotherapy research: an international review of programmatic studies* (pp. 263–273). Washington, DC: American Psychological Association.

Piotrowski, C., Belter, R. W., & Keller, J. W. (1998). The impact of "managed care" on the practice of psychological testing: Preliminary findings. *Journal of Personality Assessment, 70,* 441–447.

Plomin, R., & McGuffin, P. (2003). Psychopathology in the postgenomic era. *Annual Review of Psychology, 54,* 205–228.

Plous, S., & Zimbardo, P. G. (1986). Attributional biases among clinicians: A comparison of psychoanalysts and behavior therapists. *Journal of Consulting and Clinical Psychology, 54,* 568–570.

Poole, G., Hunt Matheson, D., & Cox, D. N. (2005). *The psychology of health and health care: A Canadian Perspective* (2nd ed). Toronto, ON: Pearson, Prentice Hall.

Pope, K. S. (2003). Logical fallacies in psychology: 18 types. Retrieved July 8, 2004, from: http://www.kspope.com/fallacies/fallacies.php

Prinz, R. J., & Dumas, J. E. (2004). Prevention of oppositional defiant disorder and conduct disorder in children and adolescents. In P. M. Barrett & T. H. Ollendick (Eds.), *Interventions that work with children and adolescents: Prevention and Treatment* (pp. 475–488). Chichester, UK: John Wiley & Sons.

Project MATCH Research Group. (1998). Therapist effects in three treatments for alcohol problems. *Psychotherapy Research, 8,* 455–474.

Proudfoot, J., Ryden, C., Everitt, B., Shapiro, D. A., Goldberg, D., Mann, A., et al. (2004). Clinical efficacy of computerised cognitive-behavioural therapy for anxiety and depression in primary care: Randomised controlled trial. *British Journal of Psychiatry, 185,* 46–54.

Psychology Today and PacifiCare Behavioral Health. (2004). *Therapy in America 2004.* Retrieved May 19 2004 at http://cms.psychologytoday.com/pto/topline_report_042904.pdf

Psychological Corporation, The. (2003). *Wechsler individual achievement test* (2nd ed.): *Canadian scoring and normative supplement for grades K–16.* Toronto: Author.

Rachman, S. (1971). *The effects of psychotherapy.* Oxford: Pergamon Press.

Rae, W. A., & Sullivan, J. R. (2003). Ethical considerations in clinical psychology research. In M. C. Roberts & S. S. Ilardi (Eds.), *Handbook of research methods in clinical psychology* (pp. 52–70). Oxford: Blackwell Publishing Ltd.

Raimy, V. C. (Ed.). (1950). *Training in clinical psychology.* New York: Prentice-Hall.

Rapaport, C., Gill, M., & Shafer, J. (1968). *Diagnostic psychological testing* (rev. ed.). Chicago: Year Book.

Rees, L. M., Tombaugh, T. N., Gansler, D. A., & Moczynski, N. P. (1998). Five validation experiments of the Test of Memory Malingering (TOMM). *Psychological Assessment, 10,* 10–20.

Regier, D. A., Kaelber, C. T., Rae, D. S., Farmer, M. E., Knauper, B., Kessler, R. C., et al. (1998). Limitations of diagnostic criteria and assessment instruments for mental disorders: Implications for research and policy. *Archives of General Psychiatry, 55,* 109–115.

Reid, W. J. (1997). Evaluating the dodo's verdict: Do all interventions have equivalent outcomes? *Social Work Research, 21,* 5–16.

Retzlaff, P. D., & Dunn, T. (2003). The Millon Clinical Multiaxial Inventory-III. In L. E. Beutler & G. Groth-Marnat (Eds.), *Integrative assessment of adult personality* (2nd ed., pp. 192–226). New York: Guilford Press.

Riccio, C. A., & French, C. L. (2004). The status of empirical support for treatments of attention deficits. *The Clinical Neuropsychologist, 18,* 528–558.

Richters, J. E., Arnold, L. E., Jensen, P. S., Abikoff, H., Conners, C. K., Greenhill, L. L., et al. (1995). The National Institute of Mental Health Collaborative Multisite Multimodal Treatment Study of Children with Attention-deficit Hyperactivity Disorder (MTA) I: background and rationale. *Journal of the American Academy of Child and Adolescent Psychiatry, 34,* 987–1000.

Roberts, C., Kane, R., Thomson, H., Hart, B., & Bishop, B. (2003). The prevention of depressive symptoms in rural school children: A randomized controlled trial. *Journal of Consulting and Clinical Psychology, 71,* 622–628.

Roberts, M. C., Lazicki-Puddy, T. A., Puddy, R. W., & Johnson, R. J. (2003). The outcomes of psychotherapy with adolescents: A practitioner-friendly research review. *Journal of Clinical Psychology/In session, 59,* 1177–1191.

Robinson, L. A., Berman, J. S., & Neimeyer, R. A. (1990). Psychotherapy for the treatment of depression: A comprehensive review of controlled outcome research. *Psychological Bulletin, 108,* 30–49.

Rogers, C. R. (1951). *Client centered therapy.* Boston: Houghton Mifflin.

Roid, G. (2003). *Stanford-Binet Intelligence Scales* (5th ed.). Itasca, IL: Riverside Publishing.

Romanow, R. J., & Marchildon, G. P. (2003). Psychological services and the future of health care in Canada. *Canadian Psychology, 44,* 283–295.

Rosenthal, R., & DiMatteo, M. R. (2001). Meta-analysis: Recent developments in quantitative methods for literature reviews. *Annual Review of Psychology, 52,* 59–82.

Rosenzweig, S. (1936). Some implicit common factors in diverse methods of psychotherapy. *American Journal of Orthopsychiatry, 6,* 412–415.

Rossini, E. D., & Moretti, R. J. (1997). Thematic Apperception Test (TAT) interpretation: Practice recommendations from a survey of clinical psychology doctoral programs accredited by the American Psychological Association. *Professional Psychology: Research and Practice, 28,* 393–398.

Roth, A., & Fonagy, P. (1996). *What works for whom? A critical review of psychotherapy research.* New York: Guilford Press.

Roth, A., & Fonagy, P. (2005). *What works for whom? A critical review of psychotherapy research* (2nd ed.). New York: Guilford Press.

Rothbaum, B. O., & Schwartz, A. C. (2002). Exposure therapy for posttraumatic stress disorder. *American Journal of Psychotherapy, 56,* 59–75.

Rourke, B. P., Ahmad, S. A., Collins, D. W., Hayman-Abello, B. A., & Warriner, E. M. (2002). Child clinical/pediatric neuropsychology: Some recent advances. *Annual Review of Psychology, 53,* 300–339.

Rowe, D. C., & Rodgers, J. L. (2002). Expanding variance and the case of historical changes in IQ means: A critique of Dickens and Flynn (2001). *Psychological Review, 109,* 759–763.

Rumstein-McKean, O., & Hunsley, J. (2001). Interpersonal and family functioning of female survivors of childhood sexual abuse. *Clinical Psychology Review, 21,* 471–490.

Ruscio, J., & Ruscio, A. M. (2000). Informing the continuity controversy: A taxometric analysis of depression. *Journal of Abnormal Psychology, 109,* 473–487.

Ryan, J. J., & Schnakenberg-Ott, S. D. (2003). Scoring reliability on the Wechsler Adult Intelligence Scale–Third Edition (WAIS-III). *Assessment, 10,* 151–159.

Ryba, N. L., Cooper, V. G., & Zapf, P. A. (2003). Juvenile competence to stand trial evaluations: A survey of current practices and test usage among psychologists. *Professional Psychology: Research and Practice, 34,* 499–507.

Sabin-Farrell, R., & Turpin, G. (2003). Vicarious traumatization: implications for the mental health of health workers. *Clinical Psychology Review, 23,* 449–480.

Sackett, D. L., Rosenberg, W. M., Gray, J. A., Haynes, R. B., & Richardson, W. S. (1996). Evidence-based medicine: What it is and what it isn't. *British Medical Journal, 312,* 71–72.

Saklofske, D. H., Hildebrand, D. K., & Gorsuch, R. L. (2000). Replication of the factors structure of the Wechsler Adult Intelligence Scale–Third Edition with a Canadian sample. *Psychological Assessment, 12,* 436–439.

Salmon, K. (2001). Remembering and reporting by children: The influence of cues and props. *Clinical Psychology Review, 21,* 267–300.

Sanders, M. R. (1999). Triple-P Positive parenting program: Towards an empirically validated multilevel parenting and family support strategy for the prevention of behavior and emotional problems in children. *Clinical Child and Family Psychology Review, 2,* 71–90.

Sanders, M. R., Cann, W., & Markie-Dadds, C. (2003). The Triple-P Positive Parenting Programme: A universal population-level approach to the prevention of child abuse. *Child Abuse Review, 12,* 155–171.

Sanders, M. R., Markie-Dadds, C., Turner, K., & Ralph, A. (2004). Using the Triple P system of intervention to prevent behavioural problems in children and adolescents. In P. M. Barrett & T. H. Ollendick (Eds.), *Interventions that work with children and adolescents: Prevention and Treatment* (pp. 489–516). Chichester, UK: John Wiley & Sons.

Santor, D. A., & Coyne, J. C. (2001). Evaluating the continuity of symptomatology between depressed and nondepressed individuals. *Journal of Abnormal Psychology, 110,* 216–225.

Sattler, J. M. (1992). *Assessment of children* (3rd ed.). San Diego, CA: Jerome Sattler.

Sattler, J. M. (2001). *Assessment of children: Cognitive applications* (4th ed.). San Diego, CA: Author.

Sattler, J. M., & Mash, E. J. (1998). Introduction to clinical assessment interviewing. In J. M. Sattler, *Clinical and forensic interviewing of children and families* (pp. 2–44). San Diego, CA: Jerome Sattler.

Saunders, S. M. (1993). Applicants' experience of the process of seeking therapy. *Psychotherapy, 30,* 554–564.

Saunders, S. M. (1996). Applicants' experience of social support in the process of seeking psychotherapy. *Psychotherapy, 33,* 617–627.

Schachar, R., Jadad, A. R., Gauld, M., Boyle, M., Booker, L., Snider, A., et al. (2002). Attention-deficit hyperactivity disorder: Critical appraisal of extended treatment studies. *Canadian Journal of Psychiatry, 47,* 337–348.

Schneiderman, N., Ironson, G., & Siegel, S. D. (2005). Stress and health: Psychological, behavioral and biological determinants. *Annual Review of Clinical Psychology, 1,* 607–628.

Schulte, D., & Hahlweg, K. (2000). A new law for governing psychotherapy for psychologists in Germany: Impact on training and mental health policy. *Clinical Psychology: Science and Practice, 7,* 259–263.

Scogin, F. (2003). Introduction: The status of self-administered treatments. *Journal of Clinical Psychology, 59,* 247–249.

Scogin, F. R., Hanson, A., & Welsh, D. (2003). Self-administered treatment in stepped-care models of depression treatment. *Journal of Clinical Psychology, 59,* 341–349.

Scott, S., Spender, Q., Doolan, M., Jacobs, B., & Aspland, H. (2001). Multicentre controlled trial of parenting groups for childhood antisocial behaviour in clinical practice. *British Medical Journal, 323,* 194–197.

Scotti, J. R., Morris, T. L., Ruggiero, K. J., & Wolfgang, J. (2002). *Post-traumatic stress disorder.* In M. Hersen (Ed.), *Clinical behaviour therapy: Adults and children* (pp. 361–382). New York: John Wiley & Sons.

Sechrest, L. (1963). Incremental validity: A recommendation. *Educational and Psychological Measurement, 23,* 153–158.

Seitz, J., & O'Neill, P. (1996). Ethical decision-making and the code of ethics of the Canadian Psychological Association. *Canadian Psychology, 37,* 23–30.

Seligman, L. D., Goza, A. B., & Ollendick, T. H. (2004). Treatment of depression in children and adolescents. In P. M. Barrett & T. H. Ollendick (Eds.), *Interventions that work with children and adolescents: Prevention and treatment* (pp. 301–328). New York: John Wiley & Sons.

Selwood, A., Thorgrimsen, L., & Orrell, M. (2005). Quality of life in dementia—a one year follow-up study. *International Journal of Geriatric Psychiatry, 20,* 232–237.

Sexton, T. L., Alexander, J. F., & Mease, A. L. (2004). Levels of evidence for the models and mechanisms of therapeutic change in family and couple therapy. In M. L. Lambert (Ed.), *Bergin and Garfield's Handbook of psychotherapy and behavior change* (5th ed., pp. 590–646). New York: John Wiley & Sons.

Shadish, W. R., Matt, G. E., Navarro, A. M., & Phillips, G. (2000). The effects of psychological therapies under clinically representative conditions: A meta-analysis. *Psychological Bulletin, 126,* 512–529.

Shapiro, A., & Taylor, M. (2002). Effects of a community-based early intervention program on the subjective well-being, institutionalization, and mortality of low-income elders. *The Gerontologist, 42,* 334–341.

Shapiro, D. A., & Shapiro, D. (1982). Meta-analysis of comparative therapy outcome studies: A replication and refinement. *Psychological Bulletin, 92,* 581–604.

Shapiro, E. S., & Cole, C. L. (1999). Self-monitoring in assessing children's problems. *Psychological Assessment, 11,* 448–457.

Shapiro, F. (1989). Eye movement desensitization: A new treatment for post traumatic stress disorder. *Journal of Behavior Therapy and Experimental Psychiatry, 20,* 211–217.

Shapiro, F. (1995). *Eye movement desensitization and reprocessing: Basic principles, protocols, and procedures.* New York: Guilford Press.

Sharpe, J. P., & Gilbert, D. G. (1998). Effects of repeated administration of the Beck Depression Inventory and other measures of negative mood states. *Personality and Individual Differences, 24,* 457–463.

Shea, S. (1991). Practical use of DSM-III-R. In M. Hersen & S. M. Turner (Eds.), *Adult psychopathology and diagnosis* (2nd ed., pp. 23–43). New York: John Wiley & Sons.

Sherman, M. D., & Thelen, M. H. (1998). Distress and professional impairment among psychologists in clinical practice. *Professional Psychology: Research & Practice, 29,* 79–85.

Shiffman, S., Hufford, M., Hickcox, M., Paty, J. A., Gnys, M., & Kassel, J. D. (1997). Remember that? A comparison of real-time versus retrospective recall of smoking lapses. *Journal of Consulting and Clinical Psychology, 65,* 292–300.

Shirk, S. R., & Karver, M. (2003). Prediction of treatment outcome from relationship variables in child and adolescent therapy: A meta-analytic review. *Journal of Consulting and Clinical Psychology, 71,* 452–464.

Sholomskas, A. J., Chevron, E. S., Prusoff, B. A., & Berry, C. (1983). Short-term interpersonal therapy (IPT) with the depressed elderly: Case reports and discussion. *American Journal of Psychotherapy, 37,* 552–566.

Silverman, W. H. (1996). Cookbooks, manuals, and paint-by-numbers: Psychotherapy in the 90s. *Psychotherapy, 33,* 207–215.

Sinclair, C. (1993). Codes of ethics and standards of practice. In K. S. Dobson & D. G. Dobson (Eds.), *Professional psychology in Canada* (pp. 167–224). Toronto, ON: Hogrefe & Huber.

Sinclair, C. (1998). Nine unique features of the Canadian code of ethics for psychologists. *Canadian Psychology, 39,* 167–176.

Sitarenios, G., & Kovacs, M. (1999). Use of the Children's Depression Inventory. In M. E. Maruish (Ed.), *The use of psychological testing for treatment planning and outcomes assessment* (2nd ed., pp. 267–298). Mahwah, NJ: Erlbaum.

Slate, J. R., Jones, C. R., Coulter, C., & Covert, T. L. (1992). Practitioners' administration and scoring of the WISC-R: Evidence that we do err. *Journal of School Psychology, 30,* 77–82.

Slate, J. R., Jones, C. R., Murray, R. A., & Coulter, C. (1993). Evidence that practitioners err in administering and scoring the WAIS-R. *Measurement and Evaluation in Counseling and Development, 25(4),* 156–161.

Smith, J. D., & Dumont, F. (2002). Confidence in psychodiagnosis: What makes us so sure? *Clinical Psychology and Psychotherapy, 9,* 292–298.

Smith, M. L., & Glass, G. V. (1977). Meta-analysis of psychotherapy outcome studies. *American Psychologist, 32,* 752–760.

Smith, M. L., Glass, G. V., & Miller, T. I. (1980). *The benefits of psychotherapy.* Baltimore: Johns Hopkins University Press.

Smith, M. T., Perlis, M. L., Park, A., Smith, M. S., Pennington, J., Giles, D. E., et al. (2002). Comparative meta-analysis of pharmacotherapy and behaviour therapy for persistent insomnia. *American Journal of Psychiatry, 159,* 5–11.

Smith, T. D., & Smith, B. L. (1998). Relationship between the Wide Range Achievement Test 3 and the Wechsler Individual Achievement Test. *Psychological Reports, 83,* 963–967.

Smith, T. W., Kendall, P. C., & Keefe, F. J. (2002). Behavioral medicine and clinical health psychology: Introduction to the special issue, a view from the Decade of Behavior. *Journal of Consulting and Clinical Psychology, 70,* 459–462.

Smith, T. W., Nealey, J. B., & Hamann, H. A. (2000). Health psychology. In C. R. Snyder & R. E. Ingram (Eds.), *Handbook of psychological change: Psychotherapy processes and practices for the 21st century* (pp. 562–590). New York: John Wiley & Sons.

Sommers-Flanagan, J., & Sommers-Flanagan, R. (2003). *Clinical interviewing* (3rd ed). New York: John Wiley & Sons.

Sonuga-Barke, E. J. S., Daley, D., & Thompson, M. (2002). Does maternal ADHD reduce the effectiveness of parent training for preschool children's ADHD? *Journal of the American Academy of Child and Adolescent Psychiatry, 41,* 696–702.

Sörensen, S., Pinquart, M., & Duberstein, P. (2002). How effective are interventions with caregivers? *The Gerontologist, 42,* 356–372.

Spangler, W. D. (1992). Validity of questionnaire and TAT measures of need for achievement: Two meta-analyses. *Psychological Bulletin, 112,* 140–154.

Spearman, C. (1927). *The abilities of man.* New York: Macmillan.

Spence, S. H., Sheffield, J. K., & Donovan, C. L. (2003). Preventing adolescent depression: An evaluation of the Problem-Solving for Life program. *Journal of Consulting and Clinical Psychology, 71,* 3–13.

Spence, S. H., Sheffield, J. K., & Donovan, C. L. (2005). Long-term outcome of a school-based universal approach to prevention of depression in adolescents. *Journal of Consulting and Clinical Psychology, 71,* 3–13.

Spitzer, R. L., Kroenke, K., Linzer, M., Hahn, S. R., Williams, J. B., deGruy, F. V., et al. (1995). Health-related quality of life in primary care patients with mental disorders: Results from the PRIME-MD 1000 study. *Journal of the American Medical Association, 282,* 1511-1517.

Spreen, O., & Tryk, E. (1970). WISC Information subtest in a Canadian population. *Canadian Journal of Behavioural Science, 2,* 295–298.

Statistics Canada. (2002). *A profile of disability in Canada.* Catalogue no. 89-577-XIE. Ottawa, ON: Minister of Industry.

Statistics Canada. (2002). Computer access at school and at home. *The Daily, October 29, 2002.* Retrieved September 17, 2004 from http://www.statcan.ca

Statistics Canada. (2003, September 3). *The Daily: Canadian Community Mental Health Survey: Mental health and well-being.* Retrieved November 11, 2004, from www.statcan.ca/Daily/English/030903/d030903a.htm

Statistics Canada. (2003a, September 3). Canadian Community Health Survey: Mental health and well-being 2002. *The Daily.* http://www.statcan.ca/Daily/English/030903/d030903a.htm

Statistics Canada. (2003b, September 5). Canadian Community Health Survey: Canadian Forces supplement on mental health 2002. *The Daily.* http://www.statcan.ca/Daily/English/030905/d030905b.htm

Statistics Canada. (2004a, May 18). *The Daily: Alcohol and drug use in early adolescence.* Retrieved October 20, 2004, from http://www.statcan.ca/Daily/English/040518/d040518b.htm

Statistics Canada. (2004b, June 14). *The Daily: Youth smoking survey.* Retrieved October 21, 2004, from http://www.statcan.ca/Daily/English/040614/d040614b.htm

Statistics Canada. (2005). *The Daily: March 22, 2005: Canada's visible minority population in 2017.* Retrieved on March 22, 2005 from http://www.statcan.ca/Daily/English/050322/d050322b.htm

Steenbarger, B. N. (1994) Duration and outcome in psychotherapy: An integrative review. *Professional Psychology: Research and Practice, 25,* 111–119.

Steering Committee of the Empirically Supported Therapy Relationship Task Force. (2001). Empirically supported therapy relationships: Conclusions and recommendations of the Division 29 Task Force. *Psychotherapy, 38,* 495–497.

Stein, M. B., Sherbourne, C. D., Craske, M. G., Means-Christensen, A., Bystritsky, A., Katon, W., et al. (2004). Quality of care for primary care patients with anxiety disorders. *American Journal of Psychiatry, 161,* 2230–2237.

Sternberg, R. (1985). *Beyond IQ: A triarchic theory of human intelligence.* New York: Cambridge University Press.

Sternberg, R. J., Nokes, K., Geissler, P. W., Prince, R., Okatcha, F., Bundy, D. A., et al. (2001). The relationship between academic and practical intelligence: A case study in Kenya. *Intelligence, 29,* 401–418.

Stiles, W. B. (1988). Psychotherapy process-outcome correlations may be misleading. *Psychotherapy, 25,* 27–35.

Stiles, W. B., & Shapiro, D. A. (1989). Abuse of the drug metaphor in psychotherapy process-outcome research. *Clinical Psychology Review, 9,* 521–543.

Stiles, W. B., Leach, C., Barkham, M., Lucock, M., Iveson, S., Shapiro, D. A., et al. (2003). Early sudden gains in psychotherapy under routine clinic conditions: Practice-based evidence. *Journal of Consulting and Clinical Psychology, 71,* 14–21.

Stirman, S. W., Crits-Christoph, P., & DeRubeis, R. J. (2004). Achieving successful dissemination of empirically supported psychotherapies: A synthesis of dissemination theory. *Clinical Psychology: Science and Practice, 11,* 343–359.

Stirman, S. W., DeRubeis, R. J., Crits-Christoph, P., & Rothman, A. (2005). Can the randomized controlled trial literature generalize to nonrandomized patients? *Journal of Consulting and Clinical Psychology, 73,* 127–135.

Stirman, S. W., DeRubeis, R. J., Crits-Christoph, P., & Brody, P. E. (2003). Are samples in randomized controlled trials of psychotherapy representative of community outpatients? A new methodology and initial findings. *Journal of Consulting and Clinical Psychology, 71,* 963–972.

Stone, A. A., Schwartz, J. E., Neale, J. M., Shiffman, S., Marco, C. A., Hickcox, M., et al. (1998). A comparison of coping assessed by ecological momentary assessment and retrospective recall. *Journal of Personality and Social Psychology, 74,* 1670–1680.

Stormshak, E. A., & Dishion, T. J. (2002). An ecological approach to child and family clinical and counseling psychology. *Clinical Child and Family Psychology Review, 5,* 197–215.

Stout, C. E., & Cook, L. P. (1999). New areas for psychological assessment in general health care settings: What to do today to prepare for tomorrow. *Journal of Clinical Psychology, 55,* 797–812.

Strack, S. (2002). *Essentials of Millon Inventories assessment* (2nd ed.). New York: John Wiley & Sons.

Streiner, D. L. (2002). Breaking up is hard to do: The heartbreak of dichotomizing continuous data. *Canadian Journal of Psychiatry, 47,* 262–266.

Streiner, D. L. (2003). Being inconsistent about consistency: When coefficient alpha does and doesn't matter. *Journal of Personality Assessment, 80,* 217–222.

Streisand, R., & Efron, L. A. (2003). Pediatric sleep disorders. In R. M. Roberts (Ed.), *Handbook of pediatric psychology* (3rd ed., pp. 578–598). New York: Guilford.

Stringer, A. Y. (2003). Cognitive rehabilitation practice patterns: A survey of American Hospital Association rehabilitation programs. *The Clinical Neuropsychologist, 17,* 34–44.

Strupp, H. H., & Binder, J. (1984). *Psychotherapy in a new key.* New York: Basic Books.

Stuebing, K. K., Fletcher, J. M., LeDoux, J. M., Lyon, G. R., Shaywitz, S. E., & Shaywitz, B. A. (2002). Validity of IQ-discrepancy classifications of reading disabilities: A meta-analysis. *American Educational Research Journal, 39,* 469–518.

Sullivan, H. S. (1953). *The interpersonal theory of psychiatry.* New York: Norton.

Summerfeldt, L. J., & Antony, M. M. (2002). Structured and semistructured diagnostic interviews. In M. M. Antony, & D. H. Barlow (Eds). *Handbook of assessment and treatment planning for psychological disorders* (pp. 3–37). New York: Guilford.

Swanson, J. M., Arnold, L. E., Vitiello, B., Abikoff, H. B., Wells, K. C., Pelham, W. E., et al. (2002). Response to commentary on the Multimodal Treatment Study of ADHD (MTA): Mining the meaning of the MTA. *Journal of Abnormal Child Psychology, 30,* 327–332.

Swanson, J. M., Kraemer, H. C., Hinshaw, S. P., Arnold, L. E., Conners, C. K., Abikoff, H. B., et al. (2001). Clinical relevance of the primary findings of the MTA: Success rates based on severity of ADHD and ODD symptoms at the end of treatment. *Journal of the American Academy of Child and Adolescent Psychiatry, 40,* 168–179.

Takushi, R., & Uomoto, J. M. (2001). The clinical interview from a multicultural perspective. In Suzuki, L. A., Ponterotto, J. G., & Meller, P. J. (Eds). *Handbook of multicultural assessment: Clinical, psychological, and educational applications* (2nd ed. pp. 47–66). San Francisco, CA: Jossey-Bass.

Tamaskar, P., & McGinnis, R. A. (2002). Declining student interest in psychiatry. *Journal of the American Medical Association, 287,* 1859.

Tang, T. Z., & DeRubeis, R. J. (1999). Sudden gains and critical sessions in cognitive-behavioral therapy for depression. *Journal of Consulting and Clinical Psychology, 67,* 894–904.

Tang, T. Z., DeRubeis, R. J., Beberman, R., & Pham, T. (2005). Cognitive changes, critical sessions, and sudden gains in cognitive-behavioral therapy for depression. *Journal of Consulting and Clinical Psychology, 73,* 168–172.

Tang, T. Z., Luborsky, L., & Andrusyna, T. (2002). Sudden gains in recovering from depression: Are they also found in psychotherapies other than cognitive-behavioural therapy? *Journal of Consulting and Clinical Psychology, 70,* 444–447.

Target, M., & Fonagy, P. (2005). The psychological treatment of child and adolescent disorders. In A. Roth & P. Fonagy (Eds.), *What works for whom? A critical review of psychotherapy research* (pp. 385–424). New York: Guilford.

Task Force on Promotion and Dissemination of Psychological Procedures. (1995). Training in and dissemination of empirically-validated psychological treatments: Report and recommendations. *The Clinical Psychologist, 48,* 3–23.

Taub, G. E., McGrew, K. S., & Witta, E. L. (2004). A confirmatory analysis of the factor structure and cross-age invariance of the Wechsler Adult Intelligence Scale–Third Edition. *Psychological Assessment, 16,* 85–89.

Taylor, S. E., & Brown, J. D. (1988). Illusion and well being: A social-psychological perspective on mental health. *Psychological Bulletin, 103,* 193–210.

Taylor, S., Thordarson, D. S., & Söchting, I. (2002). Obsessive-Compulsive Disorder. In M. M. Antony & D. H. Barlow (Eds.), *Handbook of assessment and treatment planning for psychological disorders* (pp. 182–214). New York: Guilford.

Taylor, T. K., & Biglan, A. (1998). Behavioral family interventions for improving child-rearing: A review of the literature for clinicians and policy makers. *Clinical Child and Family Psychology Review, 1,* 41–60.

Taylor, T. K., Schmidt, F., Pepler, D., & Hodgins, C. (1998). A comparison of eclectic treatment with Webster-Stratton's Parents and Children series in a children's mental health center: A randomized controlled trial. *Behavior Therapy, 29,* 221–240.

Taylor, T. L., & Chemtob, C. M. (2004). Efficacy of treatment for child and adolescent traumatic stress. *Archives of Pediatric and Adolescent Medicine, 158,* 786–791.

Teyber, E., & McClure, F. (2000). Therapist variables. In C. R. Snyder & R. E. Ingram (Eds.), *Handbook of psychological change: Psychotherapy processes & practices for the 21st century* (pp. 62–87). New York: John Wiley & Sons.

Tharyan, P., John, T., Tharyan, A., & Braganza, D. (2001). Attitudes of "tomorrow's doctors" towards psychiatry and mental illness. *National Medical Journal of India, 14,* 355–359.

Thomas, J. C., & Rosqvist, J. (2003). Introduction: Science in the service of practice. In J. C. Thomas & M. Hersen (Eds.), *Understanding research in clinical and counseling psychology* (pp. 3–26). Mahwah, NJ: Lawrence Erlbaum Associates.

Thompson-Brenner, H., Glass, S., & Westen, D. (2003). A multidimensional meta-analysis of psychotherapy for Bulimia Nervosa. *Clinical Psychology: Science and Practice, 10,* 269–287.

Thurstone, L. L. (1938). *Primary mental abilities.* Chicago: University of Chicago Press.

Tobler, N. S., Roona, M. R., Ochsborn, P., Marshall, D. G., Streke, A. V., & Stackpole, K. M. (2000). School-based adolescent drug prevention programs: 1998 Meta-analysis. *Journal of Primary Prevention, 20,* 275–336.

Tombaugh, T. N. (1997). The Test of Memory Malingering (TOMM): Normative data from cognitively intact and cognitively impaired individuals. *Psychological Assessment, 9,* 260–268.

Tompkins, M. A. (1999). Using a case formulation to manage treatment nonresponse. *Journal of Cognitive Psychotherapy, 13,* 317–330.

Tremblay, R. E., Pagani-Kurtz, L., Mâsse, L. C., Vitaro, F., & Pihl, R. O. (1995). A bimodal preventive intervention for disruptive kindergarten boys: Its impact through mid-adolescence. *Journal of Consulting and Clinical Psychology, 63,* 560–568.

Truax, C. B. (1966). Reinforcement and nonreinforcement in Rogerian psychotherapy. *Journal of Abnormal Psychology, 71,* 1–9.

Tryon, G. S. (2000). Doctoral training issues in school and clinical child psychology. *Professional Psychology: Research and Practice, 31,* 85–87.

Turk, D. C., & Okifuji, A. (2002). Psychological factors in chronic pain: Evolution and revolution. *Journal of Consulting and Clinical Psychology, 70,* 678–690.

Turner, R. J., & Lloyd, D. A. (2004). Stress burden and the lifetime incidence of psychiatric disorders in young adults. *Archives of General Psychiatry, 61,* 481–488.

Turner, R. S. (2003). Neurologic aspects of Alzheimer's disease. In P. A. Lichtenberg, D. L. Murman, & A. M. Mellow (Eds.), *Handbook of dementia* (pp.1–24). New York: John Wiley & Sons.

Tuschen-Caffier, B., Pook, M., & Frank, M. (2001). Evaluation of manual-based cognitive-behavioral therapy for bulimia nervosa in a service setting. *Behaviour Research and Therapy, 39,* 299–308.

Tversky, A., & Kahneman, D. (1974). Judgments under uncertainty: Heuristics and biases. *Science, 185,* 1124–1131.

Twenge, J. M., & Nolen-Hoeksema, S. (2002). Age, gender, race, socioeconomic status, and birth cohort differences on the Children's Depression Inventory: A meta-analysis. *Journal of Abnormal Psychology, 111,* 578–588.

U. K. Department of Health. (2001). *Treatment choice in psychological therapies and counselling: Evidence based clinical practice guidelines.* London: Author.

U.S. Department of Health and Human Services. (1999). *Mental health: A report of the Surgeon General.* Rockville, MD: Author.

Umphress, V. J., Lambert, M. J., Smart, D. W., Barlow, S. H., & Clouse, G. (1997). Concurrent and construct validity of the Outcome Questionnaire. *Journal of Psychoeducational Assessment, 15,* 40–55.

Unicef (2003, October 21). *New study shows one billion children suffer effects of poverty.* Retrieved October 22, 2004, from http://www.unicef.org.media/media_15082.html

Vakoch, D. A., & Strupp, H. H. (2000). Psychodynamic approaches to psychotherapy: Philosophical and theoretical foundations of effective practice. In C. R. Snyder & R. E. Ingram (Eds.), *Handbook of psychological changes: Psychotherapy processes and practices for the 21st century* (pp. 200–216). New York: John Wiley & Sons.

Valla, J-P., Bergeron, L., & Smolla, N. (2000). The Dominic-R: A pictorial interview for 6-11-year-old children. *Journal of the American Academy of Child and Adolescent Psychiatry, 39,* 85–93.

Vallis, T. M., & Howes, J. L. (1996). The field of clinical psychology: Arriving at a definition. *Canadian Psychology, 37,* 120–127.

Vermeersch, D. A., Lambert, M. J., & Burlingame, G. M. (2000). Outcome Questionnaire 45: Item sensitivity to change. *Journal of Personality Assessment, 74,* 242–261.

Vernon, P. E. (1961). *The structure of human abilities* (2nd ed.). London: Methuen.

Vessey, J. T., & Howard, K. I. (1993). Who seeks psychotherapy? *Psychotherapy, 30,* 546–553.

Vessey, J. T., Howard, K. I., Lueger, R. J., Kächele, H., & Mergenthaler, E. (1994). The clinician's illusion and the psychotherapy practice: An application of stochastic modeling. *Journal of Consulting and Clinical Psychology, 62,* 679–685.

Violato, C. (1986). Canadian versions of the Information subtests of the Wechsler tests of intelligence. *Canadian Psychology, 27,* 69–74.

Vittengl, J. R., Clark, L. A., & Jarrett, R. B. (2005). Validity of sudden gains in acute phase treatment of depression. *Journal of Consulting and Clinical Psychology, 73,* 173–182.

Wade, W. A., Treat, T. A., & Stuart, G. L. (1998). Transporting an empirically supported treatment for panic disorder to a service clinical setting: A benchmarking strategy. *Journal of Consulting and Clinical Psychology, 66,* 231–239.

Waehler, C. A., Kalodner, C. R., Wampold, B. E., & Lichtenberg, J. W. (2000). Empirically supported treatments (ESTs) in perspective: Implications for counseling psychology training. *The Counseling Psychologist, 28,* 657–671.

Wakefield, J. C. (1992). The concept of mental disorder: On the boundary between biological facts and social values. *American Psychologist, 47,* 373–388.

Wakefield, J. C. (1997). Diagnosing DSM-IV—Part 1: DSM-IV and the concept of disorder. *Behaviour Research and Therapy, 35,* 633–649.

Wampold, B. E. (1997). Methodological problems in identifying efficacious psychotherapies. *Psychotherapy Research, 7,* 21–43.

Wampold, B. E. (2001). *The great psychotherapy debate: Models, methods, and findings.* Mahwah, NJ: Lawrence Erlbaum Associates.

Wampold, B. E., & Bhati, K. S. (2004). Attending to the omissions: A historical examination of evidence-based practice movements. *Professional Psychology: Research and Practice, 35,* 563–570.

Wampold, B. E., Mondin, G. W., Moody, M., Stich, F., Benson, K., & Ahn, H. (1997). A meta-analysis of outcome studies comparing bona fide psychotherapies: Empirically, "All must have prizes." *Psychological Bulletin, 122,* 203–215.

Warner, R. E. (1991). A survey of theoretical orientations of Canadian clinical psychologists. *Canadian Psychology, 32,* 525–528.

Warren, R., & Thomas, J. C. (2001). Cognitive-behavior therapy of obsessive-compulsive disorder in private practice: An effectiveness study. *Journal of Anxiety Disorders, 15,* 277–285.

Waschbusch, D. A., & Hill, G. P. (2003). Empirically supported, promising, and unsupported treatments for children with Attention-Deficit/Hyperactivity Disorder. In S. O. Lilienfeld, S. J. Lynn, & J. M. Lohr (Eds.), *Science and Pseudoscience in Clinical Psychology* (pp. 333–362). New York: Guilford.

Watkins, M. W. (2003). IQ subtest analysis: Clinical acumen or clinical illusion? *The Scientific Review of Mental Health Practice, 2,* 118–141.

Watkins, M. W., & Canivez, G. L. (2004). Temporal stability of the WISC-III subtest composite: Strengths and weaknesses. *Psychological Assessment, 16,* 133–138.

Webster, C. D., & Bailes, G. (2004). Assessing violence risk in mentally and personality disordered individuals. In C. R. Hollin (Ed.), *The essential handbook of offender assessment and treatment* (pp. 17–30). Chichester, UK: John Wiley & Sons.

Webster-Stratton, C. (in press). Quality training, supervision, ongoing monitoring, and agency support: Key ingredients to implementing *The Incredible Years* programs with fidelity. In T. K. Neill (Ed.), *Helping others help children: Clinical supervision of psychotherapy.* Washington, DC: American Psychological Association.

Webster-Stratton, C., & Reid, M. J. (2003). The Incredible Years parents, teachers, and children training series: A multifaceted treatment approach for young children with conduct problems. In A. E. Kazdin & J. R. Weisz (Eds), *Evidence-based psychotherapies for children and adolescents* (pp. 224–240). New York: Guilford.

Webster-Stratton, C., & Reid, M. J. (2004). Strengthening social and emotional competence in young children—the foundation for early school readiness and success. Incredible Years classroom social skills and problem-solving curriculum. *Infants and Young Children, 17,* 96–113.

Webster-Stratton, C., Reid, M. J., & Hammond, M. (2001). Preventing conduct problems, promoting social competence: A parent and teacher training partnership in Head Start. *Journal of Clinical Child Psychology, 30,* 283–302.

Wechsler, D. (1939). *The measurement of adult intelligence.* Baltimore, MD: Williams and Wilkins.

Wechsler, D. (1996). *Wechsler intelligence scale for children* (3rd ed.): *Canadian manual supplement.* Toronto: The Psychological Corporation.

Wechsler, D. (1997). *Manual for the Wechsler memory scale* (3rd ed.). San Antonio, TX: The Psychological Corporation.

Wechsler, D. (1997). *WAIS III Administration and scoring manual.* San Antonio, TX: Psychological Corporation.

Wechsler, D. (2001). *Wechsler adult intelligence scale* (3rd ed.): *Canadian technical manual.* Toronto: The Psychological Corporation.

Wechsler, D. (2003). *Wechsler intelligence scale for children* (4th ed.). San Antonio, TX: The Psychological Corporation.

Wechsler, D. (2004). *Wechsler preschool and primary scale of intelligence* (3rd ed.): *Canadian manual.* Toronto: The Psychological Corporation.

Weersing, V. R., & Weisz, J. R. (2002). Community clinical treatment of depressed youth: Benchmarking usual care against CBT clinical trials. *Journal of Consulting and Clinical Psychology, 70,* 299–310.

Wegner, D. M. (1994). Ironic process of mental control. *Psychological Review, 101,* 34–52.

Weinberger, J. (1995). Common factors aren't so common: The common factors dilemma. *Clinical Psychology: Science and Practice, 2,* 45–69.

Weiner, I. B. (1999). What the Rorschach can do for you: Incremental validity in clinical applications. *Assessment, 6,* 327–338.

Weiss, B., & Weisz, J. R. (1995). Relative effectiveness of behavioral versus nonbehavioral child psychotherapy. *Journal of Clinical and Consulting Psychology, 63,* 317–320.

Weiss, B., Catron, T., & Harris, V. (2000). A 2-year follow-up of the effectiveness of traditional psychotherapy. *Journal of Consulting and Clinical Psychology, 68,* 1094–1101.

Weiss, B., Catron, T., Harris, V., & Phung, T. M. (1999). The effectiveness of traditional psychotherapy. *Journal of Consulting and Clinical Psychology, 67,* 82–94.

Weiss, S. J., Ernst, A. A., Cham, E., & Nick, T. G. (2003). Development of a screen for ongoing intimate partner violence. *Violence & Victims, 18,* 131–141.

Weissberg, R. P., Kumpfer, K. L., & Seligman, M. E. P. (2003). Prevention that works for children and youth. *American Psychologist, 58,* 425–432.

Weissman, M. M., Markowitz, J. C., & Klerman, G. L. (2000). *Comprehensive guide to interpersonal psychotherapy.* New York: Basic Books.

Weisz, J. R., Donnenberg, G. R., Han, S. S., & Weiss, B. (1995). Bridging the gap between laboratory and clinical in child and adolescent psychotherapy. *Journal of Consulting and Clinical Psychology, 63,* 688–701.

Weisz, J. R., Doss, A. J., & Hawley, K. M. (2005). Youth psychotherapy outcome research: a review and critique of the evidence base. *Annual Review of Psychology, 56,* 337–363.

Weisz, J. R., Hawley, K. M., Pilkonis, P. A., Woody, S. R., & Follette, W. C. (2000). Stressing the (other) three Rs in the search for empirically supported treatments: Review procedures, research quality, relevance to practice and the public interest. *Clinical Psychology: Science and Practice, 7,* 243–258.

Weisz, J. R., Weiss, B., Alicke, M. D., & Klotz, M. L. (1987). Effectiveness of psychotherapy with children and adolescents: A meta-analysis for clinicians. *Journal of Consulting and Clinical Psychology, 55,* 542–549.

Weisz, J. R., Weiss, B., Han, S. S., Granger, D. A., & Morton, T. (1995). Effects of psychotherapy with children and adolescents revisited: a meta-analysis of treatment outcome studies. *Psychological Bulletin, 117,* 450–468.

Westen, D. (1991). Clinical assessment of object relations using the TAT. *Journal of Personality Assessment, 56,* 56–74.

Westen, D., & Morrison, K. (2001). A multidimensional meta-analysis of treatments for depression, panic, and Generalized Anxiety Disorder: An empirical examination of the status of empirically supported treatments. *Journal of Consulting and Clinical Psychology, 69,* 875–899.

Westen, D., & Weinberger, J. (2004). When clinical description becomes statistical prediction. *American Psychologist, 59,* 595–613.

Westen, D., Feit, A., & Zittel, C. (1999). Methodological issues in research using projective methods. In P.C. Kendall, J. N. Butcher, & G. N. Holmbeck (Eds.), *Handbook of research methods in clinical psychology* (2nd ed., pp. 224–240). New York: John Wiley & Sons.

Whitten, J., Slate, J. R., Jones, C. H., & Shine, A. E. (1994). Examiner errors in administering and scoring the WPPSI-R. *Journal of Psychoeducational Assessment, 12,* 49–54.

Widiger, T. A. (2004). Looking ahead to DSM-V. *The Clinical Psychologist, 57(1/2),* 18–24.

Widiger, T. A., & Clark, L. A. (2000). Toward DSM-V and the classification of psychopathology. *Psychological Bulletin, 126,* 946–963.

Widiger, T. A., & Sankis, L. M. (2000). Adult psychopathology: Issues and controversies. *Annual Review of Psychology, 51,* 377–404.

Wiggins, J. S., & Trapnell, P. D. (1997). Personality structure: The return of the big five. In R. Hogan, J. Johnson, & S. Briggs (Eds.), *Handbook of personality psychology* (pp. 737–766). San Diego, CA: Academic Press.

Wilkinson, L., & the Task Force on Statistical Inference. (1999). Statistical methods in psychology journals: Guidelines and explanations. *American Psychologist, 54,* 594–604.

Williams, C. (2001). You snooze, you lose? Sleep patterns in Canada. *Canadian Social Trends,* 10–14. Catalogue No. 11-008. Ottawa, ON: Minister of Industry.

Wilson, B. A. (2004). Theoretical approaches to cognitive rehabilitation. In L. H. Goldstein & J. E. McNeil (Eds.), *Clinical neuropsychology: A practical guide to assessment and management for clinicians* (pp. 345–366). Chichester, UK: John Wiley & Sons.

Wilson, D. B., Bouffard, L. A., & McKenzie, D. L. (2005). A quantitative review of structured, group-oriented, cognitive-behavioral programs for offenders. *Criminal Justice and Behavior, 32,* 172–204.

Wilson, G. T., & Rachman, S. J. (1983). Meta-analysis and the evaluation of psychotherapy outcomes: Limitations and liabilities. *Journal of Consulting and Clinical Psychology, 56,* 54–64.

Wilson, T. D. (2002). *Strangers to ourselves: Discovering the adaptive unconscious.* Cambridge, MA: Harvard University Press.

Wilson, T. D., & Dunn, E. W. (2004). Self-knowledge: Its limits, value, and potential for improvement. *Annual Review of Psychology, 55,* 493–518.

Wise, E. A. (2004). Methods for analyzing psychotherapy outcomes: A review of clinical significance, reliable change, and recommendations for future directions. *Journal of Personality Assessment, 82,* 50–59.

Wood, J. M., Garb, H. N., Lilienfeld, S. O., & Nezworski, M. T. (2002). Clinical assessment. *Annual Review of Psychology, 53,* 519–543.

Wood, J. M., Lilienfeld, S. O., Garb, H. N., & Nezworski, M. T. (2000). The Rorschach test in clinical diagnosis: A critical review, with a backward look at Garfield (1947). *Journal of Clinical Psychology, 56,* 395–430.

Wood, J. M., Nezworski, M. T., & Garb, H. N. (2003). What's right with the Rorschach? *The Scientific Review of Mental Health Practice, 2,* 142–146.

Wood, J. M., Nezworski, M. T., Garb, H. N., & Lilienfeld, S. O. (2001). The misperception of psychopathology: Problems with the norms of the Comprehensive System for the Rorschach. *Clinical Psychology: Science and Practice, 8,* 350–373. World Health Organization. (1992). *International Statistical Classification of Diseases and Related Health Problems* (10th ed.). Geneva, Switzerland: Author.

World Health Organization World Mental Health Survey Consortium. (2004). Prevalence, severity, and unmet need for treatment of mental disorders in the World Health Organization World Mental Health Surveys. *Journal of the American Medical Association, 291,* 2581–2590.

World Health Organization, Europe. (2004). *Young people's health in context: selected key findings from the Health behaviour in school-aged children study.* Factsheet EURO/04/04. Retrieved November 5, 2004, from http://www.euro.who.int/document/mediacentre/fs0404e.pdf

World Health Organization. (2002). *Towards a common language for functioning, disability, and health.* Retrieved February 4, 2005, from http://www.who.int/classification/icf

World Health Organization. (2003). *The history of vaccination.* Retrieved October 22, 2004, from http://www.who.int/vaccines-diseases/history/history.shtml

World Health Organization. (2004). *Prevention of mental disorders: Effective interventions and policy options.* Retrieved October 28, 2004, from

World Health Organization. (2004a). *Mental health: The bare facts.* Retrieved April 23, 2004, from http://www.who.int/mental_health/en/

World Health Organization. (2004b). *Project Atlas.* Retrieved April 23, 2004 from http://www.who.int

Wormith, J. S. (2002). Offender treatment attrition and its relationship with risk, responsivity, and recidivism. *Criminal Justice and Behavior, 29,* 447–471.

Yalom, I. D. (1995). *The theory and practice of group psychotherapy.* New York: Basic Books.

Young, A. S., Klap, R., Sherbourne, C. D., & Wells, K. B. (2001). The quality of care for depressive and anxiety disorders in the United States. *Archives of General Psychiatry, 58,* 55–60.

Zabinski, M. F., Wilfley, D. E., Winzelberg, A. J., Taylor, B., & Calfas, K. J. (2004). An interactive psychoeducational intervention for women at risk for developing an eating disorder. *Journal of Consulting and Clinical Psychology, 72,* 914–919.

Zucker, R. A. (2003). Causal structure of alcohol use and problems in early life. In A. Biglan, M. Wang, & H. J. Walberg (Eds.), *Preventing youth problems* (pp. 33–61). New York: Kluwer Academic.

Name Index

Subject Index

Photo Credits